POLITICS IN STATES AND COMMUNITIES

POLITICS IN STATES AND COMMUNITIES

Tenth Edition

Thomas R. Dye

Florida State University

Prentice Hall
Upper Saddle River, New Jersey 07458

Library of Congress Cataloging-in-Publication Data

Dye, Thomas R.
    Politics in states and communities / Thomas R. Dye.—10th ed.
        p.   cm.
    Includes bibliographical references and index.
    ISBN 0-13-020680-6
    1. States governments—United States.   2. Local government—United
States.   I. Title
JK2408.D82   2000
320.8'0973—dc21   99-29096
                                                                  CIP

Editorial Director: Charlyce Jones Owen
Editor-in-Chief: Nancy Roberts
Senior Acquisitions Editor: Beth Gillett Mejia
Associate Editor: Nicole Conforti
Editorial Assistant: Bryan Prybella
AVP, Director of Manufacturing
    and Production: Barbara Kittle
Exec. Managing Editor: Ann Marie McCarthy
Production Liaison: Fran Russello
Project Manager: Linda B. Pawelchak
Manfacturing Manager: Nick Sklitsis
Prepress and Manfacturing Buyer: Ben Smith

Creative Design Director: Leslie Osher
Interior Design: Nancy Camuso-Wells
Cover Design: Nancy Camuso-Wells
Cover Art: Stephen Simpson / FPG International LLC
Director, Image Resource Center: Melinda Reo
Manager, Rights and Permissions: Kay Dellosa
Photo Researcher: Melinda Anderson
Image Specialist: Beth Boyd
Electronic Art Creation: Gary Wells
Marketing Manager: Christopher DeJohn
Copy Editing: Stephen Hopkins
Proofreading: Nancy Menges

Photo acknowledgments appear on p. 527, which constitutes
a continuation of this copyright page.

This book was set in 9.75/12 Sabon by NK Graphics
and was printed and bound by Courier Companies, Inc.
The cover was printed by Phoenix Color Corp.

©2000, 1997, 1994, 1991, 1988, 1985, 1981, 1977,
1973, 1969 by Prentice-Hall, Inc.
Upper Saddle River, New Jersey 07458

Printed in the United States of America
10   9   8   7   6   5   4   3   2

ISBN 0-13-020680-6

Prentice-Hall International (UK) Limited, *London*
Prentice-Hall of Australia Pty. Limited, *Sydney*
Prentice-Hall Canada Inc., *Toronto*
Prentice-Hall Hispanoamericana, S.A., *Mexico*
Prentice-Hall of India Private Limited, *New Delhi*
Prentice-Hall of Japan, Inc., *Tokyo*
Pearson Education Asia Pte. Ltd., *Singapore*
Editora Prentice-Hall do Brasil, Ltda., *Rio de Janeiro*

To Joann

CONTENTS

PREFACE   XV

1   POLITICS IN STATES AND COMMUNITIES   1

A Political Approach to States and Communities   2
The Comparative Study to States and Communities   2
Race and Ethnicity   7
The Politics of Immigration   10
Liberalism and Conservatism in the States   12
Policy Responsibilities of States and Communities   15
"States," "Districts," and "Territories"   18

2   DEMOCRACY AND CONSTITUTIONALISM IN THE STATES   25

Constitutional Government in the States   26
State Constitutions: An Overview   29
Constitutional Change in the States   34
Democracy in the States   38
Direct versus Representative Democracy   40
The Politics of State Initiatives   43

3   STATES, COMMUNITIES, AND AMERICAN FEDERALISM   53

What Is Federalism?   54
Why Federalism?   54
Federalism's Faults   56
The Structure of American Federalism   58
Battles in the States over Constitutional Amendments   64
How Money Shifted Power to Washington   66
The Politics of Grants-in-Aid   73
Federalism: Variations on the Theme   75
Coercive Federalism: Preemptions and Mandates   79
Devolution: Can Federalism Be Revived?   81
Interstate Relations—Horizontal Federalism   83

4   PARTICIPATION IN STATE POLITICS   88

The Nature of Political Participation   89
Explaining Voter Turnout   89
Voting in the States   92
Securing the Right to Vote   97
Eighteen-Year-Old Voting   99

Minorities in State Politics   100
Women in State Politics   104
Young and Old in State Politics   105
Interest Groups in State Politics   106
Functions and Tactics of Interest Groups   110
Comparing Interest Group Power in the States   113
Protest as Political Participation   117

5   **PARTIES AND CAMPAIGNS IN THE STATES   124**
American Political Parties in Disarray   125
Parties and Primaries   127
State Party Organizations and Activists   132
Republican and Democratic Party Fortunes in the States   136
Party Competition in the States   138
The Policy Effects of Party Competition   141
Professional Media Campagins   143
Money in State Politics   147

6   **LEGISLATORS IN STATE POLITICS   156**
Functions of State Legislatures   157
The Making of a State Legislator   158
Minorities and Women in State Legislatures   161
Getting to the State Capitol   165
The Great Incumbency Machine   167
The Unpopularity of State Legislatures   168
Legislative Apportionment and Districting   170
Legislative Organization and Procedure   175
Legislative Committees   179
Legislative Institutionalization   182
Leadership and Role-Playing in Legislatures   186
Party Politics in State Legislatures   188
Are Legislators Responsible Policy Makers   191
Lobbying in State Legislatures   193

7   **GOVERNORS IN STATE POLITICS   199**
The Many Roles of a Governor   200
The Making of a Governor   202
Gubernatorial Politics   204
Executive Power in State Government   208
The Governor's Legislative Powers   214
Divided Government: Governor versus the Legislature   217
Impeachments and Investigations   219
The Governor as Political Leader   220
Other Executive Offices   223

8 BUREAUCRATIC POLITICS IN STATES AND COMMUNITIES 227

Government and Bureaucracy 228
Sources of Bureaucratic Power 228
The Growth of Bureaucratic Power 230
State Bureaucracies 230
Bureaucracy, Democracy and Responsiveness 234
The Power of Public Employee Unions 240
Reform, Privatization, and "Reinventing Government" 243
The Budgetary Process 248
The Politics of Budgeting 251

9 COURTS, CRIME, AND CORRECTIONAL POLICY 258

Politics and the Judicial Process 259
The Lawyering of America 260
The New Judicial Federalism 262
The Structure of Court Systems 264
The Making of a Judge 266
Judicial Decision Making 269
Crime in the States 271
The War on Drugs 274
Federalism and Law Enforcement 278
Police Protection in the States 279
Police and Law Enforcement 280
The Politics of Prosecution 283
State Prisons and Correctional Policies 285
The Death Penalty 289

10 COMMUNITY POLITICAL SYSTEMS 296

Communities as Settings for Politics 297
Eighty-Six Thousand Governments 299
County Governments: Rural and Urban 300
Cities as "Municipal Corporations" 308
Forms of City Government 311
Types of Cities and Forms of Government 315
Nonpartisan Elections 317
At-Large and District Elections 320

11 PARTICIPATION IN COMMUNITY POLITICS 325

Citizen Participation 326
Parties in Big-City Politics 329
Old-Style Machine Politics 330
Reformers and Do-Gooders 331
The Recruitment of City Council Members 338
Council Members: Responsible Policy Makers? 342
City Managers in Municipal Politics 344
Mayors in City Politics 347
Minorities and Women in Local Politics 349
Interest Groups in Community Politics 352

12 METROPOLITICS: CONFLICT IN THE METROPOLIS 360

The Metropolis: Setting for Conflict 361
Cities versus Suburbs 365
The Concentration of Social Problems in the Inner City 370
Suburban "Sprawl" 372
The Case for Metropolitan Consolidation 374
The Case for "Fragmented" Government 376
Metropolitan Government as Marketplace 377
Metropolitan Government "Solutions" 378
The Politics of Metropolitan Consolidation 381

13 COMMUNITY POWER AND LAND USE CONTROL 388

Models of Community Power 389
Elitism in America Communities 392
Economic Power in Communities 395
Political Power in Communities 397
Planning and Zoning: Instruments of Government Control 400
Planning Practices 405
No-Growth Politics 406
Housing and Community Development Policy 408
Transportation Policy 412

14 POLITICS AND CIVIL RIGHTS 423

From Protest to Power 424
The Struggle Against Segregation 425
State Resistance to Desegregation 427
Busing and Racial Balancing in Schools 429
The Civil Rights Act of 1964 431
Affirmative Action Battles 434
Hispanic Power 440
Native Americans and Tribal Government 443
Americans with Disabilities 446
Gender Equality 447
Battles over Abortion 449

15 THE POLITICS OF EDUCATION 456

Goals in Educational Policy 457
Educational Performance Measurement 458
Educational Reform 460
"Reinventing" Education 464
The Limited Federal Role in Education 467
Organizing Public Education in the States 469
Battles over School Finances 471
Governing Local Schools 473
The School District Superintendents 474
School Boards: Responsible Policy Makers? 475
The Politics of Higher Education 477
Reading, Writing, and Religion 481

16 The Politics of Poverty, Welfare, and Health   488

Poverty in America   489
Who Are the Poor?   490
Inequality in America   493
An Overview of Welfare Policy   494
Moving Toward Welfare Reform   496
Health Care Policy   498
Politics and Health Care Reform   501

17 The Politics of Financing and Taxation   506

An Overview of Government Finances   507
Types of Taxes and Tax Politics   507
Explaining State Tax Systems   512
Revolting Against Taxes   514
Explaining Tax Revolts   516
City Fiscal Stress and Cutback Management   517
When Ends Don't Meet: State and Local Debt   520
When a City Goes Bust   522

Photo Credits   527

Index   529

BOXES

PEOPLE IN POLITICS

Christie Whitman, Cutting State Taxes   16
Ward Connerly and the Citizens' Initiative to Ban Affirmative Action   42
Al Lawson, From Athlete to Legislator   103
Tom Loftus, The Art of State Legislative Politics   187
Jesse "The Body" Ventura   203
George W. Bush, Governing Texas   208
Rudolph Giuliani, Getting Tough on Crime   282
Mary McCarty, County Commissioner   307
The Daleys of Chicago   332
Alex Penelas, Metro Mayor   385
Martin Luther King, Jr.   432

RANKINGS OF THE STATES

Population Size and Growth Rates   6
Income and Education   8
African American and Hispanic Populations   9
Reliance on Federal Aid   72
Registration and Voting   93
African American and Hispanic Representation in Legislatures   162
Government Spending and Employment   236
Crime in the States   273
Local Governments   301
Metropolitanization in the States   366
Public Road and Street Mileage   413
Highway Conditions   415
Abortion Rates   451
Educational Performance   459
Elementary and Secondary Spending per Pupil   472
Poverty and Welfare   491
Health Care   503
Tax Burden   513

UP CLOSE

Can Washington, DC, Govern Itself?   21
State Constitutions and the Right to Bear Arms in Self-Defense   32
Are Terms Limits a Good Idea?   48
States Lead in the Fight Against Tobacco   57
Historical Landmarks in the Development of American Federalism   68
Federalism and the Drinking Age   71
Which Government Does the Best Job?   75
Getting into Politics   94
California Adopts the Blanket Primary   130
Texas Party Organizations   134
Organizing the Campaign   144
"Soft Money": How to Evade Campaign Finance Laws   151
Informal Rules of the Game   178
Governor Pataki Issues an Order   212
Arizona Impeaches Its Governor   220
Firing a Public Employee   238
How to Win at the Budget Game   250
Can Punishment Deter Crime?   290
Political Corruption   339
Power in "Regional City"   391
Sexual Harassment   448
The Texas High-Stakes Test   463
Florida's Experiment with Charter Schools   466
Is Welfare Reform a Success?   489
Orange County Goes Bankrupt   523

DID YOU KNOW?

How the American States Got Their Names   22
Nicknames of the States   51
What Are the "Most Livable" States   85
The States and Their Capitals   120
Songs, Flowers, Birds, and Trees   195
What Are the 100 Largest Governments in the United States   254
America's Most Crime-Ridden Cities   293
America's Big Cities, Gainers and Losers   322
Salaries of Public Officials   356
The Nation's Biggest Landowner   420
The "Best-Educated" State Populations   485
How Wall Street Rates Your City   524

PREFACE

Politics in States and Communities is distinguished by

Its focus on *politics*
Its *comparative* approach
Its concern with *explanation*
Its interest in *policy*

Its focus is on conflicts in states and communities and the structures and processes designed to manage conflict. This "conflict management" theme emphasizes the sources and nature of conflict in society, how conflict is carried on, how key decision makers in states and communities act in conflict situations, and how public "politicos" emerge and determine "who gets what." The political conflict management theme guides the discussion of formal governmental structures: federalism, state constitutions, parties and primaries, apportionment, legislative organizations, gubernatorial powers, court procedures, nonpartisanship, mayor and manager government, metropolitan government, community power, school boards and superintendents, tax systems, budget making, and so on.

An equally important theme is that states and communities in America play an important role in the political life of the nation. State and local governments do more than merely provide certain services such as education, road building, or fire protection. They also perform a vital political function by helping to resolve conflicts of interest in American society.

NEW TO THIS EDITION

This tenth edition is the most extensive revision of the text in its thirty-year history. Updates and new topics have been added throughout. Topics such as privatization, "reinventing government," devolution, women in state politics, immigration, divided government, judicial federalism, economic power in communities, affirmative action, Native Americans and tribal government, "reinventing" education, and inequality in America have been added or updated to reflect the recent, dynamic changes in state and local politics. Both the organization and pedagogy of the book have been refocused to make it easier for instructors to teach the material and easier for the students to learn, analyze, and review the information.

ORGANIZATION

In response to reviewers and changes in how the course is taught, we have reorganized and merged chapters on local government and community politics (now Chapters 10 and 11) and on community power, planning, and land use (now Chapter 13). Chapter 8, entitled "Bureaucratic Politics in States and Communities," is entirely new. This has resulted in reducing the total number of chapters to seventeen, making it easier to teach this material in a one-semester course.

INSTRUCTIONAL FEATURES

For the first time this book includes multiple instructional features designed to provide timeliness and relevance, to capture students' attention and interest, to involve students interactively with political questions, and to aid in the study of state and local politics. While the new instructional features should aid in teaching state and local politics, the text material was not "dumbed down." It still describes the most important research by students in the field, including updates of this research through 1999.

"Questions to Consider"   Each chapter now opens with a set of questions for students to think about as they read through the material. These questions include factual queries as well as opinion surveys, which are deliberately designed to inspire debate. For example, students are asked to consider whether states should deny welfare benefits to illegal aliens or whether they generally favor affirmative action. Many of these interactive questions are also found on our Web site (*www.prenhall.com/dye*). After students answer the questions on line, they can immediately see how their peers around the country answered the same questions.

"People in Politics"   These features are designed to personalize politics for students, to illustrate to them that the participants in the struggle for power are real people. They discuss where prominent people in politics went to school, how they got started in politics, how their careers developed, and how much power they came to possess. Examples include Governor Jesse "The Body" Ventura, County Commissioner Mary McCarty, Mayor Rudolph Giuliani, and the late Dr. Martin Luther King, Jr.

"Up Close"   These features illustrate the struggle over who gets what. They range over a wide variety of current political conflicts, such as federalism and the drinking age, state constitutions and the right to bear arms, power in "Regional City," Orange County's bankruptcy, and Florida's experiment with charter schools.

"Rankings of the States"   Comparative analysis is used throughout the text both to describe and to explain differences among states and communities in governmental structure, political processes, and public policy. Through the *Rankings of the States* boxes, students can observe their own state on such measures as population size and growth rate, income and education levels, liberalism and conservatism, crime rates, SAT scores, and educational spending.

"Did You Know?"   These features, designed to be both instructive and entertaining, inform students about various aspects of American states and communities—everything from state birds, songs, flowers, and nicknames to ratings for the "most livable" states and most crime-ridden cities.

Chapter Pedagogy   Each chapter contains a running glossary in the margin and Web information designed to help students better master the information as they read and review the chapters.

SUPPLEMENTS AVAILABLE FOR THE INSTRUCTOR

Companion Web Site   (*www.prenhall.com/dye*) Containing a wealth of additional resources, this free Web site offers interactive practice tests, writing instruction, career information, and the interactive survey for your students.

- Instructor's Manual. For each chapter, a summary, a review of concepts, lecture suggestions, topic outlines, and additional resource materials—including a guide to media resources—are provided.
- Test Item File. Thoroughly reviewed and revised to ensure the highest level of quality and accuracy, this file offers more than 1,800 questions in multiple choice, true/false, and essay format with page references to the text.
- Prentice Hall Custom Test. A computerized test bank contains the items from the Test Item File. The program allows full editing of questions and the addition of instructor-generated items. Available in Windows, DOS, and Macintosh versions.
- Telephone Test Preparation Service. With one call to our toll-free 800 number, you can have Prentice Hall prepare tests with up to 200 questions chosen from the Test Item File. Within 48 hours of your request, you will receive a personalized exam with answer key.

SUPPLEMENTS AVAILABLE FOR THE STUDENT

Companion Web site (*www.prenhall.com/dye*)   Students can now take full advantage of the World Wide Web to enrich the study of state and local politics through the *Politics in States and Communities* Web site. Created by Aubrey Jewett of the University of Central Florida, the site features interactive practice tests, chapter objectives and overviews, and additional Web links and exercises. Students can also access information on writing in political science, career opportunities, and internship information.

Political Science on the Internet, 1998–1999 Edition (ISBN 0-13-978768-2)   This brief guide introduces students to the origin and innovations behind the Internet and provides clear strategies for navigating the complexity of the Internet and World Wide Web. Exercises within and at the end of the chapters allow students to practice searching for the myriad of resources available to the student of political science. This 48-page supplementary book is free to students when purchased as a package with *Politics in States and Communities, 10th Edition.*

ACKNOWLEDGMENTS

The author of a textbook is deeply indebted to the research scholars whose labors produce the insight and understanding that a text tries to convey to its readers. This text contains more than 450 research citations relevant to state and local politics in America. Hundreds of scholars have contributed to this impressive body of literature. I have tried my best to accurately describe and interpret their work; I apologize for any errors in my descriptions or interpretations.

For many years I have depended heavily on the work of Harriet Crawford, who has labored diligently to turn my scriblings into manuscripts. And I am deeply indebted to Linda Pawelchak, who was especially burdened in the editorial preparation of this tenth edition.

The following reviewers provided helpful suggestions for this edition: J. Edwin Benton, University of South Florida; Richard Conboy, Lake Superior State University; James R. Forrester, West Liberty State College; and Doris E. McGonagle, Texas A&M University.

Thomas R. Dye

1

POLITICS IN STATES AND COMMUNITIES

QUESTIONS TO CONSIDER

★ ★ ★ ★ ★ ★ ★ ★ ★ ★

What is the most important responsibility of state and local government in the United States?

☐ Providing public services
☐ Managing social conflicts
☐ Both equally important

Do you think states should deny welfare benefits to illegal immigrants?

☐ Yes
☐ No

How would you describe your state politically?

☐ Conservative
☐ Liberal
☐ Moderate

What is the most costly state government function?

☐ Education
☐ Welfare
☐ Highways

A POLITICAL APPROACH TO STATES AND COMMUNITIES

Comparative political study.
Comparing political institutions and behaviors from state to state and community to community in order to identify and explain similarities or differences.

Politics is the management of conflict. An understanding of "politics" in American states and communities requires an understanding of the major conflicts confronting society and an understanding of political processes and governmental organizations designed to manage conflict. State and local governments do more than provide public services such as education, highways, police and fire protection, sewage disposal, and garbage collection. These are important functions of government to be sure; but it is even more important that government deal with racial tensions, school disputes, growth problems, economic stagnation, minority concerns, poverty, drugs, crime, and violence. These problems are primarily *political* in nature; that is, people have different ideas about what should be done, or whether government should do anything at all.

Moreover, many of the service functions of government also engender political conflict. Even if "there is only one way to pave a street," political questions remain. Whose street will get paved? Who will get the paving contract? Who will pay for it? Why not build a school gym instead of paving the street?

So it is appropriate that a book on *politics* in states and communities deals not only with the structure and organization of state and local government, but also with many of the central policy questions confronting American society. It is true that these problems are national in scope, but they occur in our communities and our states. And much of this book is devoted to describing how these questions arise in state and local settings, and how state and local governments confront them.

THE COMPARATIVE STUDY OF STATES AND COMMUNITIES

The task of political science is not only to *describe* politics and public policy in American states and communities, but also to *explain* differences encountered from state to state and community to community through comparative analysis. We want to know *what* is happening in American politics, and we want to know *why*. In the past, the phrase "comparative government" applied to the study of foreign governments, but American states and communities provide an excellent opportunity for genuine comparative study, which is comparing political institutions and behaviors from state to state and community to community in order to identify and explain similarities or differences.

Comparison is a vital part of explanation. Only by comparing politics and public policy in different states and communities with different socioeconomic and political environments can we arrive at any comprehensive explanations of political life. Comparative analysis helps us answer the question *why*.

American states and communities provide excellent "laboratories" for applying comparative analysis. States and communities are not alike in social and economic conditions, in politics and government, or in their public policies. These differences are important assets in comparative study because they enable us to search for relationships between different socioeconomic conditions, political system characteristics, and policy outcomes. For example, if differences among states and communities in educational policies are closely associated with differences in economic resources or in party politics, then we may assume that economic resources or party politics help "explain" educational policies.

State politics are often affected by unique historical circumstances. (See Figure 1–1, Table 1–1.) Louisiana is distinctive because of its French–Spanish colonial background, and the continuing influence of this background on its politics today. For nine years Texas was an independent republic (1836–1845) before it was annexed as a state by Congress. Eleven southern states were involved in a bloody war against the federal government from 1861 to 1865. Hawaii has a unique history and culture, combining the influence of Polynesian, Chinese, Japanese, and haole civilizations. Alaska's rugged climate and geography and physical isolation set it apart. Wisconsin and Minnesota reflect the Scandinavian influences of their settlers. Four states—Pennsylvania, Massachusetts, Kentucky, and Virginia—call themselves "commonwealths," but this title has no legal meaning. Life in Florida is more tourist oriented than anywhere else. Michigan is the home of the automobile industry. West Virginia is noted for its mountains and its coal mines. Utah was initially settled by members of the Church of Jesus Christ of Latter-day Saints, popularly known as the Mormons, and it retains much of its distinctly Mormon culture today.

These unique historical and cultural settings help to shape state political systems and public policies. However, the mere identification of unique traits or histories does not really "explain" why politics or public policy differs from state to state. Ad hoc explanations do not help very much in developing general theories of politics. For example, only Texas has the Alamo and only New York has the Statue of Liberty, but these characteristics do not explain why New York has a state income tax and Texas does not. Students of state politics must search for social and economic conditions that appear most influential in shaping state politics over time in all the states. Despite the uniqueness of history and culture in many of our states, we must *search for explanations* of why state governments do what they do.

Since it is impossible to consider all the conditions that might influence state politics, we must focus our attention on a limited number of variables. We can begin with economic development—one of the most influential variables affecting state politics and public policy. Economic development is defined broadly to include three closely related components: population growth, income, and education.

POPULATION GROWTH   The population of the United States currently grows about 1 percent per year. But population growth is spread unevenly among the fifty states; between 1990 and 1996, Nevada and Arizona grew by more than 20 percent, while Connecticut and Rhode Island actually lost population (see "*Rankings of the States: Population Size and Growth Rate*"). The largest numbers of new residents were recorded by California, Texas, Florida, Georgia, and Arizona, states that added nearly a million or more new residents since 1990. Current population projections indicate that western and southern "Sunbelt" states are expected to grow 25 percent or more by the year 2015, while Michigan, West Virginia, Pennsylvania, Ohio, and New York will grow by less than 5 percent.

■

State economic development. Broadly defined as population growth and the income and educational levels of a state's population.

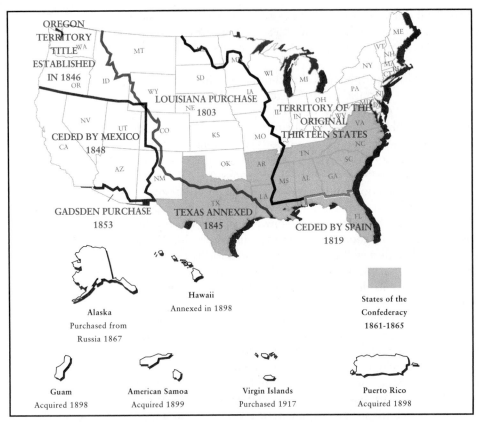

FIGURE 1–1 State Histories

By the Treaty of Paris, 1783, England gave up claim to the thirteen original Colonies, and to all land within an area extending along the present Canadian border to the Lake of the Woods, down the Mississippi River to the 31st parallel, east to the Chattahoochie, down that river to the mouth of the Flint, east to the source of the St. Mary's, down that river to the ocean. Territory west of the Alleghenies was claimed by various states but was eventually all ceded to the nation.

In 1803 President Thomas Jefferson engineered the Louisiana Purchase from France; it was the largest acquisition of territory in U.S. history, more than doubling the size of the nation.

American invasions of Canada were failures in both the Revolutionary War and the War of 1812. In the Rush-Bagot Treaty of 1817, the border between the United States and Canada was demilitarized and fixed at the forty-ninth parallel. Later, in 1846, the British relinquished their claims to the Oregon territory south of the forty-ninth parallel.

In 1819 Spain ceded Florida to the United States in the Adams-Onis Treaty, after General Andrew Jackson and his Tennessee volunteers invaded the territory in a war with the Seminole Indians.

Following battles at the Alamo in San Antonio and at the San Jacinto River, Texas declared its independence from Mexico in 1836, but the Mexican government refused to recognize the new Republic. In 1845 Congress annexed Texas at the Republic's request, ending nine years of independence. In 1846 Congress declared war on Mexico, and following the American army's capture of Veracruz and Mexico City, forced that nation to cede the territories that became California, Nevada, Utah, Arizona, and New Mexico. Later, in 1853, the Gadsden Purchase from Mexico extended the U.S. border further south.

Beginning with South Carolina on December 20, 1860, eleven southern states seceded from the United States of America, forming their own Confederate States of America. They were readmitted to the Union following their defeat in the Civil War, after they agreed to ratify the Thirteenth Amendment, abolishing slavery (1865), and later the Fourteenth Amendment, guaranteeing equal protection of the laws (1868), and the Fifteenth Amendment, preventing denial or abridgment of the right to vote on account of "race, color, or previous condition of servitude."

Twice the size of Texas, Alaska was purchased from Russia for $7.2 million in 1867. (At the time Secretary of State William Henry Seward was criticized for his extravagance, and Alaska was dubbed "Seward's folly" and "Seward's icebox.") Hawaii was annexed to the United States by congressional resolution in 1898 without consulting its residents.

Following victories in the Spanish American War in 1898, Spain ceded Puerto Rico, and Samoa and Guam, and the Philippines, which remained a U.S. territory until granted independence in 1946. The Virgin Islands were purchased from Denmark in 1917.

Table 1–1

State	Capital	Date Admitted to Union	Chronological Order of Admission to Union
Alabama	Montgomery	Dec. 14, 1819	22
Alaska	Juneau	Jan. 3, 1959	49
Arizona	Phoenix	Feb. 14, 1912	48
Arkansas	Little Rock	June 15, 1836	25
California	Sacramento	Sept. 9, 1850	31
Colorado	Denver	Aug. 1, 1876	38
Connecticut	Hartford	Jan. 9, 1788[a]	5
Delaware	Dover	Dec. 7, 1787[a]	1
Florida	Tallahassee	March 3, 1845	27
Georgia	Atlanta	Jan. 2, 1788[a]	4
Hawaii	Honolulu	Aug. 21, 1959	50
Idaho	Boise	July 3, 1890	43
Illinois	Springfield	Dec. 3, 1818	21
Indiana	Indianapolis	Dec. 11, 1816	19
Iowa	Des Moines	Dec. 28, 1846	29
Kansas	Topeka	Jan. 29, 1861	34
Kentucky	Frankfort	June 1, 1792	15
Louisiana	Baton Rouge	April 30, 1812	18
Maine	Augusta	March 15, 1820	23
Maryland	Annapolis	April 28, 1788[a]	7
Massachusetts	Boston	Feb. 6, 1788[a]	6
Michigan	Lansing	Jan. 26, 1837	26
Minnesota	St. Paul	May 11, 1858	32
Mississippi	Jackson	Dec. 10, 1817	20
Missouri	Jefferson City	Aug. 10, 1821	24
Montana	Helena	Nov. 8, 1889	41
Nebraska	Lincoln	March 1, 1867	37
Nevada	Carson City	Oct. 31, 1864	36
New Hampshire	Concord	June 21, 1788[a]	9
New Jersey	Trenton	Dec. 18, 1787[a]	3
New Mexico	Santa Fe	Jan. 6, 1912	47
New York	Albany	July 26, 1788[a]	11
North Carolina	Raleigh	Nov. 21, 1789[a]	12
North Dakota	Bismarck	Nov. 2, 1889	39
Ohio	Columbus	March 1, 1803	17
Oklahoma	Oklahoma City	Nov. 16, 1907	46
Oregon	Salem	Feb. 14, 1859	33
Pennsylvania	Harrisburg	Dec. 12, 1787[a]	2
Rhode Island	Providence	May 29, 1790[a]	13
South Carolina	Columbia	May 23, 1788[a]	8
South Dakota	Pierre	Nov. 2, 1889	40
Tennessee	Nashville	June 1, 1796	16
Texas	Austin	Dec. 29, 1845	28
Utah	Salt Lake City	Jan. 4, 1896	45
Vermont	Montpelier	March 4, 1791	14
Virginia	Richmond	June 25, 1788[a]	10
Washington	Olympia	Nov. 11, 1889	42
West Virginia	Charleston	June 20, 1863	35
Wisconsin	Madison	May 29, 1848	30
Wyoming	Cheyenne	July 10, 1890	44

[a] Date of ratification of U.S. Constitution.

POPULATION SIZE AND GROWTH RATE

Population Size

Growth Rate
Percentage Change 1990-1996

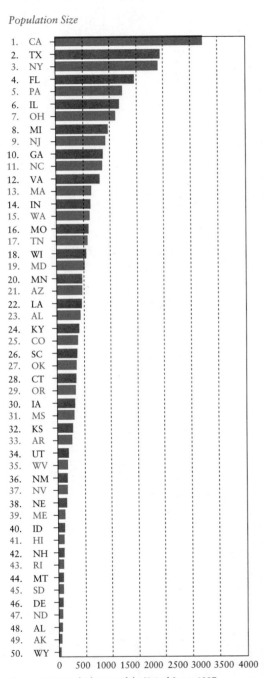

1.	CA
2.	TX
3.	NY
4.	FL
5.	PA
6.	IL
7.	OH
8.	MI
9.	NJ
10.	GA
11.	NC
12.	VA
13.	MA
14.	IN
15.	WA
16.	MO
17.	TN
18.	WI
19.	MD
20.	MN
21.	AZ
22.	LA
23.	AL
24.	KY
25.	CO
26.	SC
27.	OK
28.	CT
29.	OR
30.	IA
31.	MS
32.	KS
33.	AR
34.	UT
35.	WV
36.	NM
37.	NV
38.	NE
39.	ME
40.	ID
41.	HI
42.	NH
43.	RI
44.	MT
45.	SD
46.	DE
47.	ND
48.	AL
49.	AK
50.	WY

0   500 1000 1500 2000 2500 3000 3500 4000

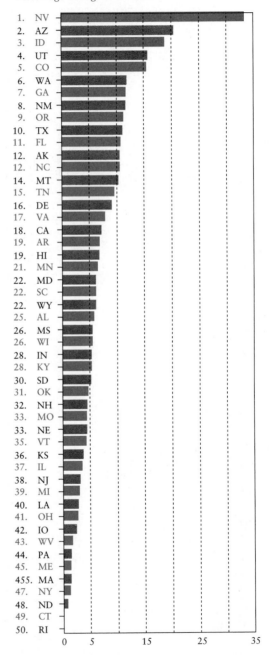

1.	NV
2.	AZ
3.	ID
4.	UT
5.	CO
6.	WA
7.	GA
8.	NM
9.	OR
10.	TX
11.	FL
12.	AK
12.	NC
14.	MT
15.	TN
16.	DE
17.	VA
18.	CA
19.	AR
19.	HI
21.	MN
22.	MD
22.	SC
22.	WY
25.	AL
26.	MS
26.	WI
28.	IN
28.	KY
30.	SD
31.	OK
32.	NH
33.	MO
33.	NE
35.	VT
36.	KS
37.	IL
38.	NJ
39.	MI
40.	LA
41.	OH
42.	IO
43.	WV
44.	PA
45.	ME
455.	MA
47.	NY
48.	ND
49.	CT
50.	RI

0   5   15   25   35

Source: Statistical Abstract of the United States 1997.

INCOME   Rising personal *income* is a key component of economic development. It indicates increased worker productivity and the creation of wealth. Per capita personal income in the United States grew from about $4,000 in 1970 to about $25,000 in 1997. This wealth was not evenly distributed throughout the states (see *"Rankings of the States:* Income and Education," p. 8). Per capita personal income in Connecticut is nearly $34,000, but it is less than $18,000 in Mississippi.

EDUCATION   An economically developed society requires educated workers. Many economists have asserted that economic growth involves an upgrading in the work force, the development of professional managerial skills, and an increase in the volume of research. These developments obviously involve a general increase in the *educational levels* of the adult population. In 1970 about 11 percent of the adult population of the United States had completed four years or more of college; by 1996 that figure had risen to over 25 percent. But high levels of educational attainment do not prevail uniformly throughout the states (see *"Rankings of the States:* Income and Education").

The extent to which economic development—population growth, income, and education—affects the politics of the states is an important question, which we will return to again in the chapters that follow.

RACE AND ETHNICITY

States differ in the racial and ethnic composition of their populations. These differences account for much of the variation in the politics of states and cities throughout the nation. Later we will be examining racial and ethnic cleavages in voting behavior and political participation (Chapter 4), state legislative politics (Chapter 6), community politics (Chapter 11), and civil rights policy (Chapter 14).

AFRICAN AMERICANS   In 1900, most African Americans (89.7 percent) were concentrated in the South. But World Wars I and II provided job opportunities in large cities of the Northeast and Midwest. Blacks could not cast ballots in most southern counties, but they could "vote with their feet." The migration of blacks from the rural South to the urban North was one of the largest internal migrations in our history. By 1990 only 53 percent of blacks lived in the South—still more than any other region but less of a concentration than earlier in American history. Today the nation's 33 million blacks comprise 12.6 percent of the total population of the United States. The distribution of blacks among the fifty states is shown in *"Rankings of the States:* African American and Hispanic Populations" (p. 9).

African American candidates have been increasingly successful in winning city and county offices and state legislative seats in the southern states and in big cities throughout the nation. (See Chapter 4 for a discussion of voting rights laws.) The largest number of black elected officials are found in the southern states. In 1989 the nation's first elected black governor, Douglas Wilder, moved into Virginia's statehouse, once the office of Jefferson Davis, president of the Confederacy. Black candidates have also been increasingly successful in winning election in large cities throughout the nation. Later in this book we will describe black representation in city councils (see Chapter 11) and in state legislatures (see Chapter 6), as well as civil rights policy (see Chapter 14).

INCOME AND EDUCATION

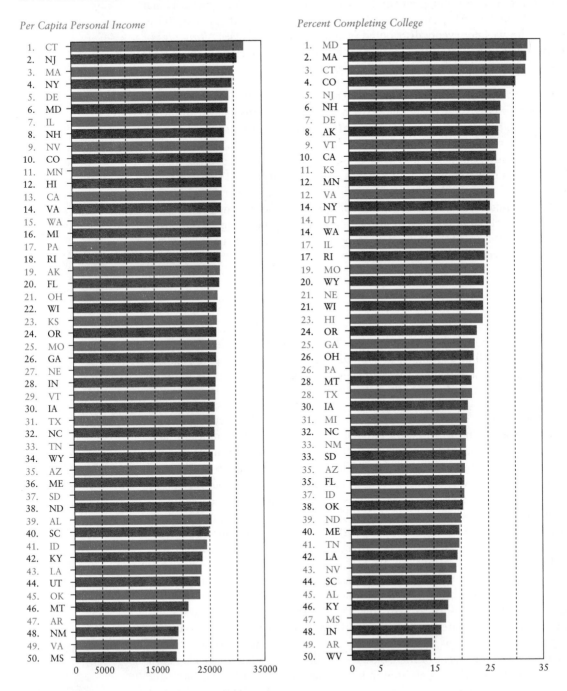

Per Capita Personal Income

1.	CT
2.	NJ
3.	MA
4.	NY
5.	DE
6.	MD
7.	IL
8.	NH
9.	NV
10.	CO
11.	MN
12.	HI
13.	CA
14.	VA
15.	WA
16.	MI
17.	PA
18.	RI
19.	AK
20.	FL
21.	OH
22.	WI
23.	KS
24.	OR
25.	MO
26.	GA
27.	NE
28.	IN
29.	VT
30.	IA
31.	TX
32.	NC
33.	TN
34.	WY
35.	AZ
36.	ME
37.	SD
38.	ND
39.	AL
40.	SC
41.	ID
42.	KY
43.	LA
44.	UT
45.	OK
46.	MT
47.	AR
48.	NM
49.	VA
50.	MS

0   5000   15000   25000   35000

Percent Completing College

1.	MD
2.	MA
3.	CT
4.	CO
5.	NJ
6.	NH
7.	DE
8.	AK
9.	VT
10.	CA
11.	KS
12.	MN
12.	VA
14.	NY
14.	UT
14.	WA
17.	IL
17.	RI
19.	MO
20.	WY
21.	NE
21.	WI
23.	HI
24.	OR
25.	GA
26.	OH
26.	PA
28.	MT
28.	TX
30.	IA
31.	MI
32.	NC
33.	NM
33.	SD
35.	AZ
35.	FL
37.	ID
38.	OK
39.	ND
40.	ME
41.	TN
42.	LA
43.	NV
44.	SC
45.	AL
46.	KY
47.	MS
48.	IN
49.	AR
50.	WV

0   5   15   25   35

Source: Statistical Abstract of the United States 1997. Figures for 1996.

AFRICAN AMERICAN AND HISPANIC POPULATIONS

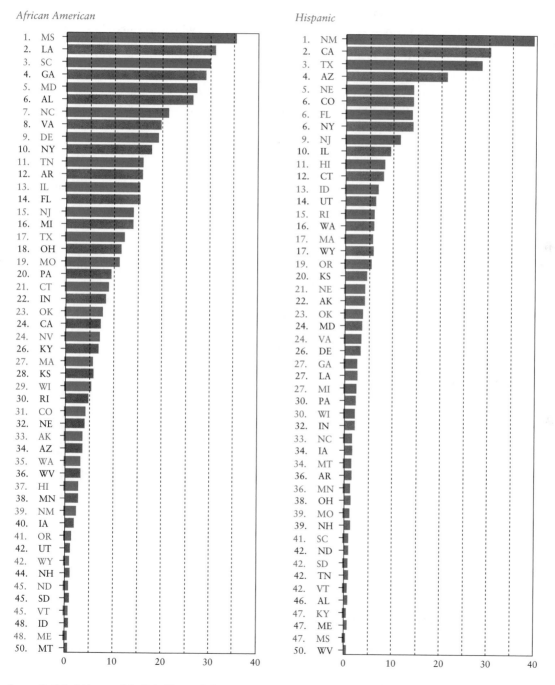

African American

1.	MS	
2.	LA	
3.	SC	
4.	GA	
5.	MD	
6.	AL	
7.	NC	
8.	VA	
9.	DE	
10.	NY	
11.	TN	
12.	AR	
13.	IL	
14.	FL	
15.	NJ	
16.	MI	
17.	TX	
18.	OH	
19.	MO	
20.	PA	
21.	CT	
22.	IN	
23.	OK	
24.	CA	
24.	NV	
26.	KY	
27.	MA	
28.	KS	
29.	WI	
30.	RI	
31.	CO	
32.	NE	
33.	AK	
34.	AZ	
35.	WA	
36.	WV	
37.	HI	
38.	MN	
39.	NM	
40.	IA	
41.	OR	
42.	UT	
42.	WY	
44.	NH	
45.	ND	
45.	SD	
45.	VT	
48.	ID	
48.	ME	
50.	MT	

Hispanic

1.	NM	
2.	CA	
3.	TX	
4.	AZ	
5.	NE	
6.	CO	
6.	FL	
6.	NY	
9.	NJ	
10.	IL	
11.	HI	
12.	CT	
13.	ID	
14.	UT	
15.	RI	
16.	WA	
17.	MA	
17.	WY	
19.	OR	
20.	KS	
21.	NE	
22.	AK	
23.	OK	
24.	MD	
24.	VA	
26.	DE	
27.	GA	
27.	LA	
27.	MI	
30.	PA	
30.	WI	
32.	IN	
33.	NC	
34.	IA	
34.	MT	
36.	AR	
36.	MN	
38.	OH	
39.	MO	
39.	NH	
41.	SC	
42.	ND	
42.	SD	
42.	TN	
42.	VT	
46.	AL	
47.	KY	
47.	ME	
47.	MS	
50.	WV	

Source: Statistical Abstract of the United States 1997.

■
Hispanic.
Referring to Spanish-
speaking ancestry and
culture.

HISPANICS   The term *Hispanic* refers to persons of Spanish-speaking ancestry and culture, regardless of race, and includes Mexican Americans, Cuban Americans, and Puerto Ricans. Today there are an estimated 28 million Hispanics or 10.7 percent of the U.S. population. The largest subgroup are Mexican Americans, some of whom are descendants of citizens living in Mexican territory that was annexed to the United States in 1848 (see Figure 1–1), but most of them have come to the United States in accelerating numbers in recent years. The largest Mexican American populations are found in Texas, Arizona, New Mexico, and California (see "*Rankings of the States:* African American and Hispanic Populations"). The second largest subgroup are the Puerto Ricans, many of whom retain ties to the Commonwealth and move back and forth from the island to the mainland, especially New York City. The third largest subgroup are Cubans, most of whom have fled from Castro's Cuba. They live mainly in the Miami metropolitan area. While these groups have different experiences, they share a common language and culture, and they have encountered similar difficulties in making government responsive to their needs (see Chapter 14).

NATIVE AMERICANS   It is estimated that 10 million Native Americans once inhabited the North American continent. By 1900 the Native American population had been reduced to barely a half million by wars, diseases, and forced privations inflicted upon them. Today Native Americans number about 2 million or slightly less than 1 percent of the U.S. population. Approximately half live on semiautonomous reservations in 280 federally recognized tribes, and in hundreds of native villages in Alaska. The largest concentrations of Native Americans are found in New Mexico, Oklahoma, South Dakota, Montana, and Arizona, as well as Alaska (see Chapter 14).

THE POLITICS OF IMMIGRATION

America is a nation of immigrants, from the first "boat people," the Pilgrims, to the latest Haitian and Cuban refugees. Americans are proud of their immigrant heritage and the freedom and opportunity the nation has extended to generations of "huddled masses yearning to be free"—words emblazoned upon the Statue of Liberty in New York's harbor.

Most immigrants come to the United States for economic opportunity. Most personify the traits we typically think of as American—opportunism, ambition, perseverance, initiative, and a willingness to work hard. As immigrants have always done, they frequently take dirty, low-paying, thankless jobs that other Americans shun. When they open their own businesses, they often do so in blighted, crime-ridden neighborhoods long since abandoned by other entrepreneurs.

NATIONAL IMMIGRATION POLICY   Immigration policy is a responsibility of the national government. Today, roughly a million people per year are admitted *legally* to the United States as "lawful permanent residents" (persons who have needed job skills or who have relatives who are U.S. citizens) or as "political refugees" (persons with "a well-founded fear of persecution" in their country of origin). In addition, each year more than 25 million people are awarded temporary visas to enter the United States for study, business, or pleasure. Finally, it is estimated that 2 to 3 million *illegal* immigrants come to America each year. Overall, more immigrants have come to the United States in the 1990s than in any other period of American history.

Immigration "reform" was the announced goal of Congress in the Immigration Reform and Control Act of 1986, also known as the Simpson-Mazzoli Act. It sought to control immigration by placing principal responsibility on employers; it set fines for knowingly hiring illegal aliens. However, it allowed employers to accept many different forms of easily forged documentation and at the same time subjected them to penalties for discrimination against legal foreign-born residents. To win political support, the act granted amnesty to illegal aliens who had lived in the United States since 1982. But the act failed to reduce the flow of either legal or illegal immigrants.

ILLEGAL IMMIGRATION   In theory, a sovereign nation should be able to maintain secure borders, but in practice the United States has been unwilling and unable to do so. Estimates of illegal immigration vary wildly, from the official U.S. Immigration and Naturalization Service (INS) estimate of 400,000 per year (about 45 percent of the legal immigration), to unofficial estimates ranging up to 3 million per year. The INS estimates that about 4 million illegal immigrants currently reside in the United States; unofficial estimates range up to 10 million or more. Many illegal immigrants slip across U.S. borders or enter ports with false documentation, while many more overstay tourist or student visas (and are not counted by the INS as illegal immigrants).[1]

Border control is an expensive and difficult, but not impossible, task. Localized experiments in border enforcement have indicated that illegal immigration can be reduced by half or more with significant increases in INS personnel and technology. However, political opposition to increased border enforcement and reduced immigration comes from a variety of sources. Large numbers of Americans identify with the aspirations of people striving to come to America, whether legally or illegally. Many Americans still have relatives living abroad who may wish to immigrate. Hispanic groups have been especially concerned about immigration enforcement efforts that may lead to discrimination against all Hispanic Americans. Powerful groups benefit from the availability of illegal immigrants, such as the agriculture, restaurant, clothing, and hospital industries; they regularly lobby in Washington to weaken enforcement efforts. Some employers prefer hiring illegal immigrants ("los indocumentados") because they are willing to work at hard jobs for low pay and few if any benefits. Even "high-tech" firms have found it profitable to bring in English-speaking immigrants as computer programmers.

IMMIGRATION AND FEDERALISM   Although the federal government has exclusive power over immigration policy, its decisions have very significant effects on states and communities—on their governmental budgets, on the use of their public services, and even on their social character. Immigration is by no means uniform across the states. On the contrary, legal and illegal immigration are concentrated in a relatively few states. California, Hawaii, New York, Florida, and Texas have the highest proportions of legal immigrants among their populations. And these states, together with Arizona, New Mexico, Colorado, Illinois, and New Jersey, probably have the highest numbers

Illegal immigration.
The unlawful entry of people from foreign nations into the United States.

■

Liberalism.
Referring to a state's tendency to expand welfare benefits, regulate business, adopt progressive state income taxes, and generally use the resources of government to achieve social change.

Conservatism.
Referring to a state's tendency to limit welfare benefits, deregulate business, keep taxes low, and generally place less reliance on government and more reliance on individuals and the marketplace to achieve social goals.

of illegal immigrants as well. Moreover, the populations of particular cities—such as Los Angeles, Miami, El Paso, and San Antonio—may be one-third to one-half foreign born.

Federal immigration policies impose expensive unfunded mandates on these states. (For a general discussion of unfunded mandates, see Chapter 3.) Although family "sponsors" may have pledged support of immigrants, and immigrants who become a "public charge" may be deported legally, these provisions of the law are almost never enforced. States and cities are obliged to provide educational, health, and social services to immigrants, both legal and illegal. (See *What Do You Think? Should States Deny Welfare Benefits to Illegal Immigrants?*) Thus, federal immigration policy heavily impacts state and local budgets, especially in California, Florida, Texas, and other states with disproportionate numbers of immigrants.

LIBERALISM AND CONSERVATISM IN THE STATES

State politics may differ in their prevailing ideological predispositions—that is, whether they are predominantly "liberal" or "conservative." There are various ways of defining and measuring ideological predispositions. Liberal and conservative states might be identified in terms of their policy enactments. For example, "policy liberalism" might be defined as the adoption of relaxed eligibility standards for receipts of welfare and medical benefits, decriminalization of marijuana possession and an absence of the death penalty, extensive regulation of business, state ratification of the Equal Rights Amendment, and the adoption of progressive state income taxes; "policy conservatism" would be defined as the opposite of these enactments. Or liberal and conservative states might be defined in terms of their voters' self-identification in opinion surveys as "liberal," "moderate," or "conservative." A common question on opinion polls is: "How would you describe your views on most political matters? Generally do you think of yourself as liberal, moderate, or conservative?" Political scientists have collected the results of national opinion polls and then observed the responses of voters in each state.[2] Nationwide during that period of study 32 percent of respondents identified themselves as "conservative," 40 percent, "moderate," and 21 percent, "liberal." Figure 1–2 shows the "conservative" responses in each state: The most conservative state in terms of voter self-identification was Utah, followed by Indiana. The most liberal states were Massachusetts, New York, and New Jersey. The researchers noted that ideological identification of the voters in the states correlated closely with measures of policy liberalism and conservatism.[3]

ETHNIC INFLUENCES   Patterns of immigration in the states have left their mark. It should come as no surprise that Canada is the leading country of origin for the states on our northern border, and Mexico is the leading country of origin for the states on our southern border. The Spanish heritage in Texas, New Mexico, Arizona, and southern California is important politically as well as culturally. Likewise the Cuban heritage in southern Florida creates the cultural background for politics in that state. Ethnicity-based political cultures throughout the nation show distinctive patterns

WHAT DO YOU THINK?

SHOULD STATES DENY WELFARE BENEFITS TO ILLEGAL IMMIGRANTS?

California's Proposition 187 in 1994 set off a national debate over immigration. Placed on the ballot by citizen initiative, Proposition 187 denies public education, nonemergency health care, and social service benefits to illegal aliens in that state. The initiative was supported by Republican Governor Pete Wilson and opposed by his Democratic opponent, Kathleen Brown. Wilson claimed that the state spent over $2 billion per year providing public support of over 2 million illegal aliens living in California. Hispanic groups in the state feared that the passage of Proposition 187 would lead to discrimination against legal immigrants and perhaps Hispanic American citizens generally. The denial of education and health care to children was branded as especially mean-spirited and cruel. Following a highly spirited and well-publicized contest over the initiative, California voters approved it by a solid 59 to 41 percent.[a]

The California vote seemed to send a message to Washington. In its comprehensive welfare reform act in 1996, Congress denied some federally funded welfare benefits to illegal aliens, as well as to legal aliens who had not yet become citizens. (One result of this act was a rush increase of more than a million new citizenship applications that year.)

But the constitutionality of these measures is questionable—the Fourteenth Amendment declares that no state shall "deny to any *person* within its jurisdiction the equal protection of the laws." The U.S. Supreme Court has mandated that state and local governments may not exclude either legal or *illegal* immigrants from public education, and by implication from any other benefits or services available to citizens.[b] A federal court declared that California's Proposition 187 was unconstitutional on the grounds that immigration is "unquestionably, exclusively a federal power" and that a state may not interfere with immigration in any way. California has appealed the decision to the U.S. Court of Appeals; the issue may ultimately be decided by the U.S. Supreme Court.

National surveys report that the denial of public services to illegal immigrants has widespread support. When asked, "Do you favor or oppose having a law in your state—similar to Proposition 187 in California—that requires state and local government agencies to stop providing health benefits and public education to illegal immigrants including children?" such a law was favored overall by 58 percent and was opposed by 36 percent.

Popular support for legal immigration appears to have declined over the years:[c]

Question: In your view should immigration be kept at its present level, increased, or decreased?

Year	Percent Saying Decreased
1965	33
1977	42
1994	63
1998	65

Yet most Americans agree that immigrants make valued contributions: that they "are productive citizens once they get their feet on the ground" (63 percent), "are hardworking" (58 percent), "are basically good honest people" (55 percent). However, majorities also believe that immigrants "are a burden on taxpayers" (66 percent), "take jobs from Americans" (58 percent), and "add to the crime problem" (56 percent).

[a]See Caroline J. Tolbert and Rodney E. Hero, "Race, Ethnicity and Direct Democracy," *Journal & Politics*, 58 (August 1996), 806–18.

[b]*Plyler v. Doe*, 457 U.S. 202 (1982).

[c]Gallup and Yankelovich polls, reported in *American Enterprise 6* (March/April 1995), 105; Hart-Teeter poll reported in the *Wall Street Journal*, March 5, 1998.

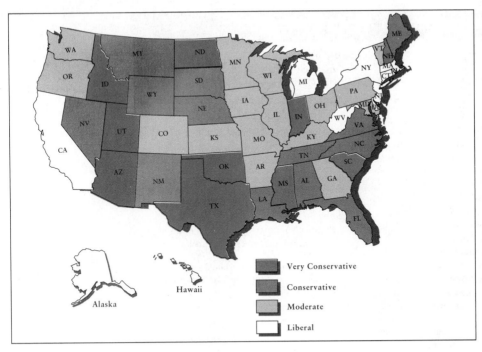

FIGURE 1–2
Liberalism and
Conservatism

Very Conservative

Conservative

Moderate

Liberal

■
Political culture.
Historical styles and traditions in states' politics that
cannot be directly attributed
to demographic factors.

based on the prevalence of "Nordic" (e.g., Wisconsin, Minnesota, North Dakota),
"Hispanic" (e.g., Texas, New Mexico, Arizona), "Mormon" (e.g., Utah), and other
cultural influences.[4]

STATE POLITICAL CULTURES   Do the states exhibit separate and identifiable political cultures? That is, are there political differences among the states that cannot be ac-
counted for by demographic characteristics, for example, race, ethnicity, income, or
education? It does appear that some states have developed historical traditions of Democratic and Republican party affiliation, as well as cultural patterns of liberal and
conservative politics, that are independent of any demographic features of their populations. For example, Minnesota has developed a liberal and Democratic tradition, Indiana a conservative and Republican tradition, and neither can be fully explained by
the socioeconomic composition of their populations. The liberal politics of Massachusetts, Rhode Island, and West Virginia, as well as the conservative politics of Idaho,
North Dakota, and Utah, are not fully explained by characteristics of these states' populations or by specific historical events. So we attribute to "political culture" the un-
explained variation in partisan affiliations and ideological predispositions that we
cannot explain by social or economic factors.

LEADERSHIP   Political leadership in a state also helps shape its politics and public
policy. While we can systematically examine the influence of population size and
growth, income, education, race, and ethnicity on state politics, we must also remind
ourselves that from time to time individual leaders have brought about political change

in their states—change that might not have occurred without their efforts. Electoral politics in states and communities as well as the nation encourage political entrepreneurship—that is, electoral politics provide incentives for candidates to propose policy innovations in order to publicize themselves and win votes. (See, for example, *"People in Politics:* Christie Whitman, Cutting State Taxes.")

Political entrepreneurship. The tendency of candidates in electoral campaigns to propose policy innovations in order to publicize themselves and win votes.

POLICY RESPONSIBILITIES OF STATES AND COMMUNITIES

Despite the glamour of national politics, states and communities carry on the greatest volume of public business, settle the greatest number of political conflicts, make the majority of policy decisions, and direct the bulk of public programs. They have the major responsibility for maintaining domestic law and order, for educating the children, for moving Americans from place to place, and for caring for the poor and the ill. They regulate the provision of water, gas, electric, and other public utilities; share in the regulation of insurance and banking enterprise; regulate the use of land; and supervise the sale of ownership of property. Their courts settle by far the greatest number of civil and criminal cases. In short, states and communities are by no means unimportant political systems.

EDUCATION   Education is the most important responsibility of state and local governments and the most costly of all state–local functions (see Figure 1–3). States and communities are responsible for decisions about what should be taught in the public schools, how much should be spent on the education of each child, how many children should be in each classroom, how much teachers should be paid, how responsibilities in education should be divided between state and local governments, what qualifications teachers must have, what types of rates and taxes shall be levied for education, and many other decisions that affect the life of every child in America. Support for higher education, including funds for state and community colleges and universities, is now a major expenditure of state governments. The federal government has never contributed more than 10 percent of the nation's total expenditures for education.

TRANSPORTATION   Transportation—more particularly, highways—is the second most costly function of state and local governments. There are over 3 million miles of surfaced roads in America, and over 180 million registered motor vehicles in the nation. States and communities must make decisions about the allocation of money for streets and highways, sources of funds for highway revenue, the extent of gasoline and motor vehicle taxation, the regulation of traffic on the highways, the location of highways, the determination of construction policies, the division of responsibility between state and local governments for highway financing administration, the division of highway funds between rural and urban areas, and other important issues in highway politics. While the federal government is deeply involved in highway construction, federal grants for highways amount to less than 30 percent of all expenditures for highways.

HEALTH AND WELFARE   States and communities continue to carry a heavy burden in the field of health and welfare—despite an extensive system of federal grants-in-aid for this purpose. States and communities must make decisions about participation in

PEOPLE IN POLITICS

CHRISTIE WHITMAN, CUTTING STATE TAXES

Christie Whitman is New Jersey's first woman governor, and the first person to defeat an incumbent governor in a general election in the modern history of the state. Her promise to cut state taxes was the key to her election. More important, she kept her pledge.

Christine Todd was raised in a political family; her father was Republican state chair in New Jersey. After earning a B.A. in political science from Wheaton College in Massachusetts in 1968, she worked on the staff of the Republican National Committee in Washington, where her job was to improve GOP contacts with students and minorities. Later she returned to New Jersey, married, and devoted much of her time to raising two daughters—"my greatest accomplishment."

In 1982 Christine Todd Whitman ran for and won her first elected office, to the Somerset County, New Jersey, Board of Chosen Freeholders (county commission). In 1988 the state's Republican governor appointed her president of the New Jersey Board of Public Utilities, where she developed a statewide reputation as a consumer advocate. In 1990 the state GOP needed a sacrificial lamb to fill the ballot space opposite the popular Democratic senator, Bill Bradley. But Whitman surprised both supporters and opponents by becoming a lion on the campaign trail and nearly upsetting the long-term incumbent. Indeed, Bill Bradley's close call in 1990 (Whitman won 49 percent of the vote) helped convince him to stay out of the presidential race in 1992 and allow Bill Clinton to win the Democratic nomination.

New Jersey's voters were upset by heavy tax increases imposed on them by Governor James Florio. Whitman pounded the tax-raising Democrat in newspaper columns and a radio talk show she hosted. When Florio came up for reelection in 1993, Whitman was well positioned to oust him with a hard-hitting campaign that featured an unlikely promise to reduce state income taxes by 30 percent.

Whitman's tax pledge was widely regarded as a political gimmick. But to the surprise of many observers, she delivered on her ambitious pledge, taking advantage of the state's economic recovery, privatizing several state functions, fighting the state's public employee unions, and making state government "smaller and smarter." Critics responded that many of her spending cuts were one-shot accounting ploys, that many state costs were shifted to local governments, that spending cuts hurt the poor, and that a state fiscal crisis would eventually develop. In the meantime, Whitman's success made her a national Republican star. In 1995 she gave the official Republican televised response to President Clinton's State of the Union Address.

But by 1997, New Jersey voters had shifted their attention from taxes to high auto insurance costs. Whitman was slow to respond to the new issue, and her support of abortion rights alienated some Republican voters.

The Libertarian Party candidate qualified for public campaign finance, participated in three-way television debates, and siphoned many Republican voters away from Whitman.

She was reelected by only a narrow margin, dimming her prospects of winning the vice presidential spot on the GOP ticket in 2000.

In addition to tax reduction, Whitman has focused on crime-fighting, welfare reform, and the creation of public-supported charter schools. She claims credit for helping to reduce New Jersey's crime rate, for Megan's law (which helps communities guard against sexual offenders), for a No Early Release Act requiring violent criminals to serve at least 85 percent of their term, and for a "Three Strikes and You're In" law mandating a life sentence for any violent criminal convicted of a third serious crime. She also claimed credit for reducing welfare case loads, limiting lifetime benefits to five years, and enforcing tougher work requirements, while increasing funding for child care.

federal programs and allocate responsibilities among themselves for health and welfare programs. While the federal government itself administers Social Security and Medicare, state governments administer the largest public assistance programs—Temporary Assistance for Needy Families (cash aid, formerly Aid to Families with Dependent Children), Medicaid, and food stamps, as well as unemployment compensation. Within the broad outlines of federal policy, states and communities decide the amount

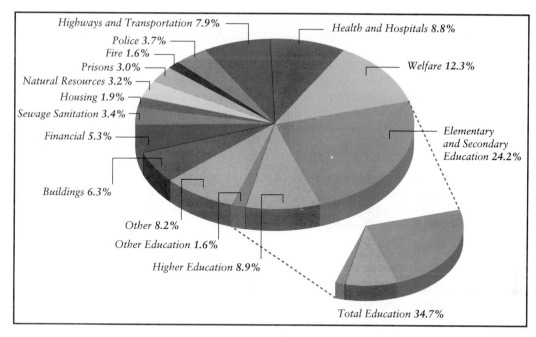

Highways and Transportation 7.9%

Police 3.7%

Fire 1.6%

Prisons 3.0%

Natural Resources 3.2%

Housing 1.9%

Sewage Sanitation 3.4%

Financial 5.3%

Buildings 6.3%

Other 8.2%

Other Education 1.6%

Higher Education 8.9%

Health and Hospitals 8.8%

Welfare 12.3%

Elementary and Secondary Education 24.2%

Total Education 34.7%

FIGURE 1–3 How State and Local Governments Spend Their Money

of money appropriated for health and welfare purposes, the benefits to be paid to recipients, the rules of eligibility, and the means by which the programs will be administered. States and communities may choose to grant assistance beyond the limits
supported by the national government.

CRIME   States and communities have the principal responsibility for public safety in
America. State police have important highway safety responsibilities and cooperate
with local authorities in the apprehension of criminals. However, community police
forces continue to be the principal instrument of law enforcement and public safety.
Local governments employ over a quarter of a million police in the United States today, and almost as many firefighters. Sheriffs and their deputies are still the principal
enforcement and arresting officers in rural counties. States and communities also have
the principal responsibility for maintaining prisons and correctional institutions. Each
year over 2 million Americans are prisoners in jails, police stations, juvenile homes, or
penitentiaries. More than 90 percent of these prisoners are in state and local rather
than federal institutions.

CIVIL RIGHTS   The national government has defined a national system of civil
rights, but these rights cannot become realities without the support of state and local
authorities. States and communities must deal directly with racial problems, such as

racial isolation in the public schools, job discrimination, and the existence of segregated housing patterns in the cities. They must also deal directly with the consequences of racial tension, including violence.

PHYSICAL ENVIRONMENT   Local governments have the principal responsibility for our physical environment. They must plan streets, parks, and commercial, residential, and industrial areas and provide essential public utilities for the community. The waste materials of human beings—rubbish, garbage, and sewage—exceed one ton every day per person. The task of disposal is an immense one; the problem is not only collecting it, but finding ways to dispose of it. If it is incinerated, it contributes to air pollution; and if it is carried off into streams, rivers, or lakes, it contributes to water pollution. Thus, communities are largely responsible for two of the nation's most pressing problems—air and water pollution.

TAXATION   To pay for these programs, states and communities must make important decisions about taxation: They must decide about levels of taxation and what tax burdens their citizens can carry. They must determine how much to rely upon income, sales, or property taxation. States and communities must raise over $600 billion per year and at the same time compete with one another to attract industry and commerce.

"STATES," "DISTRICTS," AND "TERRITORIES"

How did the states become states? The original thirteen states did so by ratifying the U.S. Constitution. The first new states to be admitted were Vermont in 1791 and Kentucky in 1792. States that sought admission began by petitioning Congress to allow them to elect delegates and draw up a state constitution. The Congress granted this permission in a series of enabling acts. Later, when the territorial voters approved the new constitution, the territory formally applied for admission and presented its constitution to Congress for approval. Congress accepted the application by a joint resolution of both houses, and a new star was added to the flag. The last admissions were Alaska and Hawaii in 1959.

Of course, from a political perspective, admission was not always an easy process. Long before the Civil War (or "The War Between the States" as it is still called in parts of the Old South), states were admitted roughly in pairs of free and slave states, so as not to upset the delicate balance in the U.S. Senate. Iowa and Wisconsin were admitted as free states in 1846 and 1848, while Florida and Texas were admitted in 1845 as slave states. When California was admitted as a free state in the famous Compromise of 1850, the balance was tilted toward the free states. The balance was further tipped when Minnesota was admitted in 1858 and Oregon in 1859. The Civil War followed in 1861.

Eleven states seceded from the Union that year—Alabama, Arkansas, Florida, Georgia, Louisiana, Mississippi, North Carolina, South Carolina (December 1860), Tennessee, Texas, and Virginia. Although the Supreme Court later voided the acts of secession as unconstitutional, Congress required all of these states to reapply for admission to the Union. These states were under military occupation by United States troops. The military governments drew up new state constitutions, registered black voters, and sent black representatives to Congress. Congress required these governments to ratify the Thirteenth, Fourteenth, and Fifteenth Amendments in order to be readmitted to the Union. The "reconstructed" southern state governments did so, and all were readmitted by 1870.

When Texas was admitted in 1845, Congress granted it a special privilege: The state might, if it wished, divide itself into four states. This provision recognized that Texas was a separate nation when it chose to become a state. A conservative Congress initially rejected Arizona's constitution because it included the progressive notion of popular recall of judges; the state obligingly changed its constitution, was admitted in 1912, and then promptly amended the constitution to put recall back in. Once admitted, there was nothing the Congress could do about Arizona's recalcitrance.

Hawaii and Alaska were the last states admitted to the Union (1959). Hawaii is the only state with an Asian majority population (62 percent). For many years following its annexation to the United States in 1898, Hawaii's economy depended primarily on sugar and pineapple exports. But today its economy depends heavily on tourists, not only from "the mainland" but also from Japan. Living costs in both Hawaii and Alaska are very high; these states frequently appear at or near the top of state rankings based upon dollar amounts.

THE DISTRICT OF COLUMBIA   The U.S. Constitution, Article I, Section 8, specified in 1787 that "the seat of the government of the United States" shall be in a "district not exceeding ten square miles" ceded to the federal government by the states (Maryland and Virginia). The District of Columbia was to be governed by the Congress. In defense of a separate district, Alexander Hamilton wrote:

> [Congressional control] of the seat of government . . . is an indispensable necessity. Without it not only the public authority may be insulted and its proceedings interrupted with impunity, but a dependence of the members of the general government of the state comprehending the seat of government . . . might bring the national councils an imputation of awe or influence . . . dishonorable to the government.[5]

Hamilton's language is stiff and formal, but his meaning is clear: Making Washington a state would generate undue local pressure on Congress.

Politically, Washington is heavily Democratic, liberal, and black. Its 607,000 residents are likely to support larger social welfare programs, an expanded bureaucracy, and increased federal spending. Opponents of these policies are not likely to be enthusiastic about DC representation in Congress.

The Twenty-third Amendment, ratified in 1961, gives Washington full participation in presidential elections. Congress has also granted by law full home rule to the city so it has its own elected mayor and city council. In 1978, Congress passed another constitutional amendment that would grant the District full congressional representation and the right to vote on ratification of future constitutional amendments. However, the necessary three-quarters of the states failed to ratify this amendment. So while DC res-

■

Commonwealth.
Although four states call
themselves Commonwealths
(Pennsylvania, Virginia,
Massachusetts, and Ken-
tucky), the term refers to any
self-governing community
and currently describes the
government of Puerto Rico,
a territory of the United
States.

idents can vote in presidential elections, they are not represented by voting members in
the U.S. Senate or House of Representatives.

Having failed to gain congressional representation by constitutional amendment,
District residents and their supporters in Congress turned to a new strategy—calling
on Congress to admit the District to the Union as a state. (While the Constitution specifies that Congress shall govern over "such District not exceeding ten miles square . . .
as the seat of the government," presumably Congress could satisfy this constitutional
mandate by reducing "the seat of the government" to a few blocks surrounding the
capitol, while admitting the bulk of the District as a state.) This strategy not only reduces the barrier in Congress from a two-thirds vote to a simple majority vote of both
houses, but, more importantly, eliminates the need to secure ratification by three-
quarters of the states. Nonetheless, so far Congress has refused to vote for District
statehood (presumably the state would be named "Columbia"). Troubles with District
self-government have convinced many Congress members that Washington is not
ready for statehood (see "*Up Close:* Can Washington, DC, Govern Itself?").

THE COMMONWEALTH OF PUERTO RICO   Over 3 million people live on the
Caribbean island of Puerto Rico. They are American citizens, and the government of
Puerto Rico resembles a state government, with a constitution and an elected governor
and legislature. However, Puerto Rico has no voting members of the Congress and no
electoral votes in presidential elections.

The population of Puerto Rico is greater than that of twenty states. Over 1 million
Puerto Ricans have migrated over the years to the U.S. mainland, particularly to New
York City. Median family income in Puerto Rico is the highest in the Caribbean, but it
is only half that of the poorest state in the United States. The population is largely
Spanish-speaking; as citizens they can move anywhere in the United States; and they
have been subject to the draft in wartime. The United States seized Puerto Rico in 1898
in the Spanish-American War. In 1950, its voters chose to become a "commonwealth,"
and self-governing commonwealth status was officially recognized in 1952. In a 1967
plebiscite, 60 percent of Puerto Ricans voted to remain a commonwealth, 39 percent
voted for statehood, and less than 1 percent voted for independence. In nonbinding
referenda in 1993 and 1998, Puerto Ricans continued to support commonwealth status, but opinion today appears to be almost equally divided between statehood and
commonwealth status, with independence as a distant third option.

Under "commonwealth" status Puerto Ricans pay no U.S. income tax, although local taxes are substantial. Yet, they receive all of the benefits that U.S. citizens are entitled to—Social Security, public assistance, food stamps, Medicaid, Medicare, and so
forth. If Puerto Rico was to become a state, its voters could participate in presidential
and congressional elections; but its taxpayers would not enjoy the same favorable cost-
benefit ratio they enjoy under commonwealth status. Some Puerto Ricans fear that
statehood would dilute the island's cultural identity and perhaps force English upon
them as the national language.

Statehood would grant two U.S. senators and perhaps six U.S. representatives to the
island. Most of these new members would be Democrats; the island's majority party,
the Popular Democratic party, is closely identified with the Democratic party. But the

UP CLOSE

CAN WASHINGTON, DC, GOVERN ITSELF?

"Welcome to Washington, DC—the nation's last colony!" For many years District residents have complained of their lack of representation in Congress. But political support for statehood in Congress and the nation has declined over the years with revelations of government corruption and mismanagement in the District.

The nation's capital is often a source of embarrassment to Americans. Its rates of overall crime, of violent crime, and of murder are regularly higher than those of any state. (Its murder rate is *ten times* higher than the national average.) Its schools have higher dropout rates than those of any other state, even though its school spending per pupil is higher than that of forty other states. Its infant death rate, as well as its death rate from AIDS, is higher than that of any state. And so is the percentage of the District's population receiving welfare assistance.[a]

Congress granted the nation's capital home rule in 1973. Marion Barry was first elected mayor in 1978, and the city's fortunes were closely linked to those of the controversial mayor for many years. Barry served three consecutive four-year terms. His bid for a fourth term was interrupted by his conviction on drug charges following an FBI sting operation in which he was videotaped smoking crack cocaine in a hotel room. (The incident produced a noteworthy political quote from the mayor, "Who are you going to believe, me or the videotape?") Following a six-month prison sentence, Barry

was elected to the city council in 1992 and then elected mayor again in 1994, soundly defeating reform mayor Sharon Pratt Kelly.

Congress, in response to reports of mismanagement and continuing financial deficits as well as to Barry's reelection, created a District of Columbia Financial Control Board in 1995 to oversee the city's government. The Board largely displaced District home rule: It took over operation of the school system and control of the city budget and appointed chief managing and chief financial officers for the city. It balanced the city's budget, but city services, from streets and water, fire and police protection, to schools and public housing remain very poor.

Over the years, the city's politics have been driven largely by racial issues. Its resident population is mostly (63 percent) African American, but tens of thousands of federal government workers live in surrounding white suburbs in Virginia and Maryland. The chairman of the Financial Control Board is a wealthy black investment banker, Andrew F. Brimmer, but oversight committees in the House and Senate are chaired by white Congress members. The Congress has never given the city the authority to tax suburban commuters. Congress determines its own payment in lieu of property taxes on federal buildings; residents believe these self-assessments are too low.

Even the retirement of Mayor Barry is not likely to move a Republican-controlled Congress to restore home rule to the city very soon. Congress is even less likely to admit "Columbia" as a state in the Union.

[a]*State Rankings 1998* (Lawrence, KS: Morgan Quito Press, 1998).

island's New Progressive party, identified with the Republican party, supports statehood, and many GOP leaders believe their party should appeal to Hispanic voters.

Puerto Rico will soon hold another referendum. Its choices will again be continued commonwealth status, statehood, or independence. If a majority chooses either statehood or independence, the president will submit legislation to Congress providing for a transition period of no more than ten years. Puerto Ricans will be asked to vote again to approve or disapprove the statehood plan passed by Congress.

U.S. TERRITORIES   The U.S. Virgin Islands were purchased from Denmark in 1917. Residents of the beautiful islands in the Caribbean are predominantly black, English-speaking, and poorer than most Americans on the mainland. The United States acquired Samoa and Guam from Spain in 1898; and after World War II, the United States held Wake, Midway, and the United Nations Trusteeships of the Caroline, Marianas, and Marshall Islands (the locations of some of the heaviest fighting in the Pacific). In

DID YOU KNOW?

HOW THE AMERICAN STATES GOT THEIR NAMES

Alabama—Indian for tribal town, later a tribe (Alabamas or Alibamons) of the Creek confederacy.

Alaska—Russian version of Aleutian (Eskimo) word, *alakshak,* for "peninsula," "great lands," or "land that is not an island."

Arizona—Spanish version of Pimo Indian word for "little spring place," or Aztec *arizuma,* meaning "silver-bearing."

Arkansas—French variant of Kansas, a Sioux Indian name for "south wind people."

California—bestowed by the Spanish conquistadors (possibly by Cortez). It was the name of an imaginary island, and earthly paradise, in "Las Serges de Esplandian," a Spanish romance written by Montalvo in 1510. Baja California (Lower California, in Mexico) was first visited by the Spanish in 1533. The present U.S. state was called Alta (Upper) California.

Colorado—Spanish, red, first applied to Colorado River.

Connecticut—From Mohican and other Algonquin words meaning "long river place."

Delaware—Named for Lord De La Warr, early governor of Virginia; first applied to river, then to Indian tribe (Lenni-Lenape), and the state.

District of Columbia—For Columbus, 1791.

Florida—Named by Ponce de Leon on Pascua Florida, "Flowery Easter," on Easter Sunday, 1513.

Georgia—For King George II of England by James Oglethorpe, colonial administrator, 1732.

Hawaii—Possibly derived from native word for homeland, Hawaiki or Owhyhee.

Idaho—A coined name from an invented Indian meaning: "gem of the mountains," originally suggested for the Pike's Peak mining territory (Colorado), then applied to the new mining territory of the Pacific Northwest. Another theory suggests Idaho may be a Kiowa Apache term for the Comanche.

Illinois—French for Illini or land of Illini, Algonquin word meaning men or warriors.

Indiana—Means "land of the Indians."

Iowa—Indian word variously translated as "one who puts to sleep" or "beautiful land."

Kansas—Sioux word for "south wind people."

Kentucky—Indian word variously translated as "dark and bloody ground," "meadow land," and "land of tomorrow."

Louisiana—Part of territory called Louisiana by Sieur de La Salle for French King Louis XIV.

Maine—From Maine, ancient French province. Also: descriptive, referring to the mainland in distinction to the many coastal islands.

Maryland—For Queen Henrietta Maria, wife of Charles I of England.

Massachusetts—From Indian tribe named after "large hill place" identified by Capt. John Smith as near Milton, MA.

Michigan—From Chippewa words *mici gama,* meaning "great water," after the lake of the same name.

Minnesota—From Dakota Sioux word meaning "cloudy water" or "sky-tinted water" of the Minnesota River.

Mississippi—Probably Chippewa; *mici zibi,* "great river" or "gathering-in of all the waters." Also: Algonquin word, *messipi.*

Missouri—Algonquin Indian tribe named after Missouri River, meaning "muddy water."

Montana—Latin or Spanish for "mountainous."

Nebraska—from Omaha or Otos Indian word meaning "broad water" or "flat river," describing the Platte River.

Nevada—Spanish, meaning snow-clad.

New Hampshire—Named in 1629 by Capt. John Mason of Plymouth Council for his home county in England.

New Jersey—The Duke of York, 1664, gave a patent to John Berkeley and Sir George Carteret to be called Nova Caesaria, or New Jersey, after England's Isle of Jersey.

New Mexico—Spaniards in Mexico applied term to land north and west of Rio Grande in the sixteenth century.

New York—For Duke of York and Albany who received patent to New Netherland from his brother Charles II and sent an expedition to capture it, 1664.

North Carolina—In 1619 Charles I gave a large patent to Sir Robert Heath to be called Province of Carolana, from Carolus, Latin name for Charles. A new patent was granted by Charles II to Earl of Clarendon and others. Divided into North and South Carolina, 1710.

North Dakota—Dakota is Sioux for "friend" or "ally."

Ohio—Iroquois word for "fine or good river."

Oklahoma—Choctaw coined word meaning red man, proposed by Rev. Allen Wright, Choctaw-speaking Indian.

Oregon—Origin unknown. One theory holds that the name may have been derived from that part of the Wisconsin River shown on a 1715 French map as "Ouaricon-sint."

Pennsylvania—William Penn, the Quaker, who was made full proprietor by King Charles II in 1681, suggested Sylvania, or woodland, for his tract. The king's government owed Penn's father, Admiral William Penn, £16,000, and the land being granted in part settlement, the king added the Penn to Sylvania, against the desires of the modest proprietor, in honor of the admiral.

Puerto Rico—Spanish for Rich Port.

Rhode Island—Exact origin is unknown. One theory notes that Giovanni de Verazano recorded an island about the size of Rhodes in the Mediterranean in 1524, but others believe the state was named Roode Eylandt by Adriaen Block, Dutch explorer, because of its red clay.

South Carolina—See North Carolina.

South Dakota—See North Dakota.

Tennessee—Tanasi was the name of Cherokee villages on the Little Tennessee River. From 1784 to 1788 this was the State of Franklin, or Frankland.

Texas—Variant of word used by Caddo and other Indians meaning friends or allies, and applied to them by the Spanish in eastern Texas. Also written *texias, tejas, teysas*.

Utah—From a Navajo word meaning upper, or higher up, as applied to a Shoshone tribe called Ute. Spanish form is Yutta, English Uta or Utah. Proposed name Deseret, "land of honeybees," from Book of Mormon, was rejected by Congress.

Vermont—From French words *vert*/green, and *mont*/mountain. The Green Mountains were said to have been named by Samuel de Champlain. The Green Mountain Boys were Gen. Stark's men in the Revolution. When the state was formed, 1777, Dr. Thomas Young suggested combining *vert* and *mont* into Vermont.

Virginia—Named by Sir Walter Raleigh, who fitted out the expedition of 1584, in honor of Queen Elizabeth, the Virgin Queen of England.

Washington—Named after George Washington. When the bill creating the Territory of Columbia was introduced in the 32d Congress, the name was changed to Washington because of the existence of the District of Columbia.

West Virginia—So named when western counties of Virginia refused to secede from the United States, 1863.

Wisconsin—An Indian name, spelled Quisconsin and Mesconsing by early chroniclers. Believed to mean "grassy place" in Chippewa. Congress made it Wisconsin.

Wyoming—The word was taken from Wyoming Valley, PA, which was the site of an Indian massacre and became widely known by Campbell's poem "Gertrude of Wyoming." In Algonquin "large prairie place."

Source: By permission of The Smithsonian Institution Press, Smithsonian Institution, Washington, DC.

1903 the United States encouraged a revolution and secession of Panama from Colombia, so that the new Panamanian nation would conclude an agreement with the United States to build a canal and govern a zone five miles wide on both sides of the canal. U.S. "Canal Zone" governance was ended by a new treaty with Panama in 1978.

ON THE WEB

A major source of information on state and local government in the United States is the annual publication of the Bureau of the Census, *Statistical Abstract of the United States,* the latest edition of which can be found in the reference section of most libraries. The Census Bureau also maintains one of the most interesting Web sites on the Internet at

www.census.gov

This home page of the Census Bureau directs visitors to a wide variety of information on "People," "Business," and "Geography" (including maps). The Census Bureau updates the estimated population of the United States on this page every five minutes!

Many of the "Rankings of the States" figures in this book are taken from Census Bureau data. For example, if you wish to observe the latest estimates of median family income for each state, click *people,* then *income,* then *median family income by state.* (The states are listed alphabetically with their median family income; you will have to rank them yourself.)

From the Census Bureau home page, you can also "select a state" and "get a state profile." Try it for your home state.

NOTES

1. American Security Council, *The Illegal Immigration Crisis* (Washington, DC: ASC, 1994).

2. Robert S. Erikson, John P. McIver, and Gerald C. Wright, "State Political Culture and Public Opinion," *American Political Science Review,* 81 (September 1987), 797–813.

3. Gerald C. Wright, Robert S. Erikson, and John P. McIver, "Public Opinion and Policy Liberalism in the American States," *American Journal of Political Science,* 31 (November 1987), 980–1001. See also William D. Berry et al., "Measuring Citizen and Government Ideology in the American States," *American Journal of Political Science,* 42 (January 1998), 327–48.

4. Daniel Elazar, *American Federalism: A View from the States* (New York: Thomas Y. Crowell, 1966). For a well-developed theory of America's political subcultures, ethnic migrations, and generational changes, see Daniel Elazar, *The American Mosaic* (Boulder, CO: Westview Press, 1994).

5. Alexander Hamilton, *The Federalist,* Number 43.

2

DEMOCRACY AND CONSTITUTIONALISM IN THE STATES

QUESTIONS TO CONSIDER

★ ★ ★ ★ ★ ★ ★ ★ ★

Are state constitutions necessary to limit the powers of state and local governments over their citizens?

❑ Yes ❑ No

Should voters decide key policy questions themselves in referenda elections, or should voters allow their elected representatives to make these decisions and then reward or punish them in the next election?

❑ Voters should decide policy

❑ Elected representatives should decide policy

Should state constitutions limit the types and amounts of taxes that a state can levy on its citizens?

❑ Yes ❑ No

Should state constitutions limit how many terms state legislators can serve?

❑ Yes ❑ No

Constitutionalism.
A government of laws, not people, operating on the principle that governmental power must be limited, that government officials should be restrained in their exercise of power over individuals.

Limited government.
The principle that government power over the individual is limited, that there are some personal liberties that even a majority cannot regulate, and that government itself is restrained by law.

Constitution.
The legal structure establishing governmental bodies, granting their powers, determining how their members are selected, and prescribing the rules by which they make their decisions. Considered basic or fundamental, a constitution cannot be changed by ordinary acts of governmental bodies.

Constitutional Government in the States

Constitutions govern governments. They set forth the structure and organization of government; they distribute powers among branches of government; they prescribe the rules by which decisions will be made. Most important, constitutions limit the powers of government and protect the rights of citizens. All fifty states have written constitutions.

Limited Government   The true meaning of constitutionalism is limited government. Today most of the world's governments, including even the most authoritarian regimes, have written constitutions that describe the formal structure of government. But the constitutions of authoritarian regimes rarely place any restrictions on the powers of government. In the English and American political heritage, constitutionalism means that the power of government over the individual is clearly limited, that there are some aspects of life that even majorities cannot regulate, and that government itself is restrained by a higher law. Constitutional government places individual liberty beyond the reach of governments, even democratic governments. Thus, if a majority of voters wanted to prohibit communists, or atheists, or racists, from writing or speaking or organizing themselves, they could not do so under a constitutional government that protected free speech and press and assembly.

All fifty state constitutions limit the powers of state government and protect individual liberty. While we have come to rely principally on the U.S. Constitution for the protection of individual liberty, every state constitution also contains a bill of rights that protects individuals in each state from deprivations of personal liberty by their state government. Most of these state constitutional guarantees merely reiterate rights guaranteed to all Americans in the U.S. Constitution, but some state documents extend rights *beyond* the federal guarantees.

Legal Status   State constitutions are the supreme law of the state. They take precedence over any state *law* in conflict with them. Since constitutions govern the activities of governments themselves, they are considered more fundamental than the ordinary laws passed by governments.

The U.S. Constitution is the *supreme law* of the nation. State constitutions take precedence over state law, but they are subordinate to the U.S. Constitution and the laws of the United States. The U.S. Constitution mentions state constitutions only once, and it does so to assert the supremacy of the U.S. Constitution and the laws and treaties of the United States. Article VI states:

> This constitution, and the laws of the United States which shall be made in pursuance thereof; and all treaties made, or which shall be made, under the authority of the United States, shall be the supreme law of the land; and the judges in every state shall be bound thereby, *anything in the constitution or laws of any state to the contrary notwithstanding.* (Italics added)

Origins of Written Constitutions   Probably no other people in the world are more devoted to the idea of written constitutions than are Americans. This devotion has deep roots in national traditions. In 1215 a group of English lords forced King John to sign a document, later known as the Magna Carta, that guaranteed them certain feudal rights and set a precedent for constitutional government. Although the British political tradition eventually rejected formal written constitutions, the idea of a written constitution was strongly reinforced by the experience in the American colonies. The colonies were legally established by charters given to companies establishing settlements in America. These charters became more elaborate as the colonial ventures succeeded, and depending upon a written code for the regulation of government organization and operation became strongly entrenched in the American colonies.

COLONIAL HISTORY   The charters, or "constitutions," were granted by royal action, either by recognizing proprietary rights, as in Maryland, Delaware, and Pennsylvania, or by granting royal commissions to companies to establish governments, as in Virginia, Massachusetts, New Hampshire, New York, New Jersey, Georgia, and North and South Carolina. Only in Connecticut and Rhode Island was there much popular participation in early constitution making. In these two colonies, royal charters were granted directly to the colonists themselves, who participated in drawing up the charter for submission to the Crown. The important point is that these charters, whatever their origin, were present in all the colonies, and many political traditions and expectations grew up around them.

All the colonies were subject to royal control. Yet colonists looked to their charters for protection against British interference in colonial affairs. This was particularly true in Connecticut and Rhode Island, which had elected governors and legislatures whose acts were not subjected to a royal governor's veto, nor sent to England for approval. The political importance of these early charters is illustrated by the conflict over the Fundamental Orders of Connecticut. In 1685 King James issued an order for the repeal of Connecticut's charter. In 1687 Sir Edmund Androse went to Hartford and in the name of the Crown declared the government dissolved. The charter was not surrendered, however, but hidden by Captain John Wadsworth in an oak tree, which is now displayed for sightseers. Immediately after the English revolution of 1688, the document was taken out of the "Charter Oak" and used again as the fundamental law of the colony. Succeeding British monarchs silently permitted this colonial defiance. After the Declaration of Independence, new constitutions were written in eleven states; Connecticut retained its charter as the fundamental law until 1818, and Rhode Island kept its charter until 1842. The colonial experience, together with the earlier English heritage, firmly implanted the tradition of written constitutions.

STATE CONSTITUTIONAL POLITICS   Theoretically, constitutional decision making is deciding *how to decide.* It is deciding on the rules for policy making; it is not policy making itself. Policies are to be decided later, according to the rules set forth in a constitution.

But realistically, all state constitutions not only specify organizations and processes of decision making, they also undertake to determine many substantive policy questions. Unlike the U.S. Constitution, state constitutions contain many policy mandates on topics as diverse as tax rates, utility regulation, labor–management relations, insurance regulation, debt limits, educational funding, gambling, and a host of other policy matters. In nearly every election, voters are asked to decide on proposed amendments to their state constitutions. Most of these amendments deal with policy questions about which the voters have little knowledge or information. The result, of course, is that most state constitutions have become ponderous tomes that look more like law books than constitutions. While the U.S. Constitution contains only about 8,700 words, the average state constitution contains 26,000, and some run to over 100,000 (see Table 2–1). Length itself is not the problem, but rather that these constitutions are laden with detailed policy decisions.

INTEREST GROUP INFLUENCE   Why have so many policy mandates crept into state constitutions? Inasmuch as constitutions govern the actions of governors, legislators, executive agencies, and courts, many special interest groups as well as citizen movements have sought to place their own policy preferences in constitutions. This places these preferences beyond the immediate reach of government officials, who are bound by constitutional mandates. If a policy preference is enacted into state law, it can be changed by ordinary actions of the legislature and governor. But if a policy preference is written into the state constitution, it can be changed only by extraordinary procedures—for most states a two-thirds vote in both houses of the legislature and majority approval of the voters in a statewide referendum. So interest groups frequently strive to "constitutionalize" their policy preferences.

CITIZENS' MOVEMENTS   Moreover, grass-roots citizen movements in the United States have frequently displayed a distrust of elected officials. Citizens have frequently sought to bind officials by constitutional mandates. Indeed, referenda on proposed state constitutional amendments confront voters in many states in almost every election. Over the years, specific constitutional amendments seeking to tell legislatures and governors what they can and cannot do have been accumulated in lengthy documents. The more detailed and specific a state's constitution, the more likely it is to require more amendments to meet changing circumstances over time, thus leading to an even longer document.

REFORMERS' INFLUENCE   Constitutional reformers and "good government" groups have sought for many years to take policy matters out of the state constitution. They argue that governors and legislators should not be bound by constitutional details, that they need flexibility in confronting new challenges, that state government should be strengthened, not weakened, in the modern era. These reform efforts have met with some success; newer state constitutions tend to be shorter than older ones.

GROWTH OF STATE CONSTITUTIONAL LAW   Along with interest groups and citizens' movements, lawyers and judges have also contributed to the growth of state constitutional law. In a significant number of cases, state court judges have interpreted their own constitutions independently of the U.S. Constitution regarding civil rights and other controversies (see "The New Judicial Federalism" in Chapter 9). An emerging body of state constitutional law is a reminder of the legal importance of state constitutions.[1]

STATE CONSTITUTIONS: AN OVERVIEW

BILL OF RIGHTS   All state constitutions have a bill of rights, which asserts the basic freedoms of speech, press, religion, and assembly. (See "*Up Close:* State Constitutions and the Right to Bear Arms in Self-Defense," p. 32.) There are frequent references to basic procedural rights, such as the writ of habeas corpus, trial by jury, protection against double jeopardy and self-incrimination, prohibitions against ex post facto laws, imprisonment for debt, unreasonable searches and seizures, and excessive bail. Most of these protections merely duplicate the guarantees of the U.S. Constitution. However, frequently one finds in the state constitutions interesting "rights," which are not found in the national Constitution. For example, the Florida Constitution guarantees "every natural person the right to be let alone and free from government intrusion into his private life"; Mississippi guarantees the right of victims of crime to speak in court and receive restitution; Indiana prohibits "unnecessary rigor" in punishment for crime. Some state constitutions have "little ERAs"—equal rights amendments, guaranteeing sexual equality under law. Moreover, a *state* supreme court may place a different interpretation on a state constitutional right than the *federal* courts place on the same guarantee in the U.S. Constitution. (See "The New Judicial Federalism" in Chapter 8.)

SEPARATION OF POWERS   All state constitutions reflect the American political tradition of separation of powers, with separate legislative, executive, and judicial articles establishing these separate branches of government, and ensuring a system of checks and balances. Generally, however, state constitutions emphasize legislative power over executive power. The historical explanation for this is that governors were appointed by the king in most colonies and the early constitutions reflected the colonists' distaste for executive authority. Yet the fact that constitutions are usually written by legislatures, legislative commissions, or constitutional conventions that resemble legislatures may also explain why legislative power is emphasized. Finally, the curtailment of executive power may reflect the desires of important interest groups in the states, who would prefer to deal with independent boards and commissions in the executive branch rather than with a strong governor. (See Chapter 7 for further discussion.)

WEAK GOVERNORS   Whether the reasons are historical or political, the executive branches of most state governments are weakened and divided by state constitutions. Executive powers are divided between the governor and many separately elected executive officers—attorney general, secretary of state, treasurer, auditor, lieutenant governor, state school superintendent, and others. State constitutions also curtail executive authority by establishing a multitude of boards or commissions to head executive departments. Membership on these boards and commissions is generally for long overlapping terms, which are not coextensive with the term of the governor.

LEGISLATIVE POWERS   Only the Nebraska Constitution provides for a unicameral legislature. All other state legislatures are divided into an upper and a lower chamber—making a total of ninety-nine state legislative bodies. In many states the basis for apportioning these bodies is set forth in the state constitution. However, since the guar-

■

Separation of powers.
The constitutional allocation of powers among the three branches of the national government: legislative, executive, and judicial.

Checks and balances.
Constitutional provisions giving each branch of the national government certain checks over the actions of other branches.

Table 2-1

General Information on State Constitutions

State or Other Jurisdiction	Number of Constitutions*	Dates of Adoption	Effective Date of Present Constitution	Estimated Length (Number of Words)	Number of Amendments	
					Submitted to Voters	Adopted
Alabama	6	1819, 1861, 1865, 1868, 1875, 1901	1901	220,000	860	618
Alaska	1	1956	1959	15,988	35	26
Arizona	1	1911	1912	28,876	221	121
Arkansas	5	1836, 1861, 1864, 1868, 1874	1874	40,720	176	84
California	2	1849, 1879	1879	54,645	826	493
Colorado	1	1876	1876	45,679	276	133
Connecticut[a]	4	1818, 1965	1965	9,564	30	29
Delaware	4	1776, 1792, 1831, 1897	1897	19,000	(b)	130
Florida	6	1839, 1861, 1865, 1868, 1886, 1968	1969	38,000	103	74
Georgia	10	1777, 1789, 1798, 1861, 1865, 1868, 1877, 1945, 1976, 1982	1983	25,000	63[c]	48
Hawaii	1	1950	1959	20,774	113	95
Idaho	1	1889	1890	23,239	195	115
Illinois	4	1818, 1848, 1870, 1970	1971	13,700	16	10
Indiana	2	1816, 1851	1851	10,230	72	40
Iowa	2	1846, 1857	1857	13,430	53	50
Kansas	1	1859	1861	11,900	119	91
Kentucky	4	1792, 1799, 1850, 1891	1891	27,199	68	35
Louisiana	11	1812, 1845, 1852, 1861, 1864, 1868, 1879, 1898, 1913, 1921, 1974	1975	54,112	117	79
Maine	1	1819	1820	13,500	196	166
Maryland	4	1776, 1851, 1864, 1867	1867	41,349	247	212
Massachusetts	1	1780	1780	36,700	145	117
Michigan	4	1835, 1850, 1908, 1963	1964	25,530	56	22
Minnesota	1	1857	1858	11,323	210	115
Mississippi	4	1817, 1832, 1869, 1890	1890	24,000	152	119

Table 2–1 (Continued)

State	Number of Constitutions	Dates of Constitutions	Date of Present Constitution	Estimated Length (number of words)	Number of Amendments Submitted	Number of Amendments Adopted
Missouri	4	1820, 1865, 1875, 1945	1945	42,000	147	90
Montana	2	1889, 1972	1973	13,218	41	21
Nebraska	2	1866, 1875	1875	20,048	305	199
Nevada	1	1864	1864	20,770	199	123
New Hampshire	2	1776, 1784	1784	9,200	280	143
New Jersey	3	1776, 1844, 1947	1948	17,800	61	48
New Mexico	1	1911	1912	27,200	259	134
New York	4	1777, 1822, 1846, 1894	1895	51,700	286	216
North Carolina	3	1776, 1868, 1970	1971	11,000	38	30
North Dakota	1	1889	1889	20,564	249	137
Ohio	2	1802, 1851	1851	36,900	261	158
Oklahoma	1	1907	1907	79,153	307	157
Oregon	1	1857	1859	26,090	417	210
Pennsylvania	5	1776, 1790, 1838, 1873, 1968	1968	21,675	30	24
Rhode Island[a]	2	1842	1843	10,233	105	59
South Carolina	7	1776, 1778, 1790, 1861, 1865, 1868, 1895	1896	22,500	659	474
South Dakota	1	1889	1889	25,000	198	103
Tennessee	3	1796, 1835, 1870	1870	15,300	55	32
Texas	5	1845, 1861, 1866, 1869, 1876	1876	80,806	547	377
Utah	1	1895	1896	11,000	140	90
Vermont	3	1777, 1786, 1793	1793	8,356	210	52
Virginia	6	1776, 1830, 1851, 1869, 1902, 1970	1971	18,500	37	31
Washington	1	1889	1889	29,400	161	91
West Virginia	2	1863, 1872	1872	26,000	114	67
Wisconsin	1	1848	1848	15,702	178	130
Wyoming	1	1889	1890	31,800	103	65

*The constitutions referred to in this table include those Civil War documents customarily listed by the individual states.

[a]Colonial charters with some alterations served as the first constitutions in Connecticut (1638, 1662) and in Rhode Island (1663).

[b]Proposed amendments are not submitted to the voters in Delaware.

[c]The new Georgia constitution eliminates the need for local amendments, which have been a long-term problem for state constitution makers.

Source: For more detailed information, see *Book of the States, 1998–99* (Lexington, KY: Council on State Governments, 1998). Data as of January 1, 1998.

STATE CONSTITUTIONS AND THE RIGHT TO BEAR ARMS IN SELF-DEFENSE

The Second Amendment to the U.S. Constitution states: "A well regulated Militia, being necessary to the security of a free State, the right of the people to keep and bear Arms, shall not be infringed." What is meant by the right of the people "to keep and bear arms"?

The Right of States to Maintain Militias

Many constitutional scholars argue that the Second Amendment protects only the *collective* right of the states to form militias—that is, their right to maintain National Guard units. They focus on the qualifying phrase "a well-regulated Militia, being necessary to the security of a free State." The Second Amendment merely prevents Congress from denying the states the right to organize their own military units. If the Founders had wished to create an individual right to bear arms, they would not have inserted the phrase about a "well-regulated militia." (Opponents of this view argue that the original definition of a militia included all free males over eighteen.) Interpreted in this fashion, the Second Amendment does *not* protect private groups who form themselves into militias, nor does it guarantee citizens the right to own guns.

The Right of Individuals to Bear Arms in Self-Defense

However, another view is that the Second Amendment confers on Americans an *individual* constitutional right, like the First Amendment freedom of speech or press; that is, the right to own and bear arms. The history surrounding the adoption of the Second Amendment reveals the concern of colonists with attempts by despotic governments to confiscate the arms of citizens and render them helpless to resist tyranny. James Madison wrote in the *Federalist Papers* No. 46 that "the advantage of being armed which the Americans possess over the people of almost every other nation, forms a barrier against the enterprise of [tyrannical] ambition."

Thomas Jefferson wrote "No free man shall ever be debarred the use of arms" in the Virginia Constitution; and he later argued that "Laws that forbid the carrying of arms . . . make things worse for the assaulted and better for the assailants . . . for an unarmed man may be attacked with greater confidence than an armed man."[a]

Gun Control

Federal gun control legislation frequently follows murders or assassination attempts on prominent figures. The Federal Gun Control Act of 1968 was a response to the assassinations of Senator Robert F. Kennedy and Martin Luther King, Jr., in that year. It banned mail-order sales of handguns and required that manufacturers place serial numbers on all firearms, that dealers record all sales, and that dealers be licensed by the Bureau of Alcohol, Tobacco and Firearms. In 1993, Congress passed the Brady Act, requiring a seven-day waiting period for the purchase of a handgun. The act is named for James S. Brady, former press secretary to President Ronald Reagan, who was severely wounded in the 1981 attempted assassination of the president. The Crime Control Act of 1994 banned the manufacture or sale of "assault weapons," generally defined to include both automatic and semiautomatic rifles and machine pistols.

Proponents of gun control cite the U.S. Supreme Court decision in *United States* v. *Miller* (1939). In this case, the Court considered the constitutionality of the federal National Firearms Act of 1934, which, among other things, prohibited the transportation of sawed-off shotguns in interstate commerce. The defendant claimed that Congress could not infringe upon his right to keep and bear arms. But the Court responded that a sawed-off shotgun had no "relationship to the preservation or efficiency of a well-regulated militia."[b] The clear implication of this decision is that the right to bear arms refers only to a state's right to maintain a militia. But even if an individual has a constitutional right to own a gun, the Supreme Court is likely to approve of reasonable restrictions on that right, including waiting periods for purchases, reporting, and registration. No constitutional right is viewed as absolute.

State Gun Laws

Many state constitutions include a provision guaranteeing the right to bear arms. Most of these state guarantees do not refer to a militia, but rather to the specific right of people to bear arms in self-defense. For example, Florida's constitution says: "The right of the people to keep and bear arms in defense of themselves and of the lawful authority of the state shall not be infringed." Changing state gun laws in states with such constitutional language usually requires voter approval of a constitutional amendment.

The Second Amendment does not necessarily include the right to carry a *hidden* gun. Currently about half of the states grant concealed carrying permits to applicants who have never been convicted of a felony. (Generally a "concealed weapon" refers to a handgun carried on a person or within immediate reach in an automobile.) Nine states and the District of Columbia prohibit the carrying of concealed weapons altogether. Other states require applicants for permits to prove that they have a specific need to carry a weapon.

[a]See Stephen P. Halbrook, *That Every Man Be Armed: The Evolution of a Constitutional Right* (Albuquerque: University of New Mexico Press, 1984).

[b]*United States* v. *Miller*, 307 U.S. 174 (1939).

antee of the U.S. Constitution that no state shall deny to any person the "equal protection of the laws" takes precedence over state constitutions, federal courts require state legislative apportionment in both houses to meet the constitutional standard of one person, one vote. (See Chapter 6.)

LOCAL GOVERNMENTS   All state constitutions have provisions regarding the organization and powers of local government. Local governments are really subdivisions of state governments; they are not independent governmental bodies. State constitutions generally describe the organization of counties, cities, towns, townships, boroughs, school districts, and special districts. They may delegate responsibilities to them for public safety, police, fire, sanitation, sewage and refuse disposal, hospitals, streets, and public health. State constitutions may establish tax and debt limits for local governments, describe the kinds of taxes they may levy, and prescribe the way in which their funds may be spent. In the absence of constitutional provisions governing local governments, these subordinate units must rely upon state legislatures for their organization and powers. In recent years there has been a movement toward greater home rule for communities. More than half the states have provided for some semblance of home rule, which removes some of the internal affairs of communities from the intervention of state legislatures. Of course, when a "home rule" charter is granted to a community by an act of the legislature, it can be readily withdrawn or revised by the legislature. Constitutional home rule is a more secure grant of power to communities than legislative home rule. (See Chapter 10 for further discussion.)

INTEREST GROUP REGULATION   Since state constitutions take precedence over state laws and are more difficult to amend, interest groups prefer to see special protections written into the state's fundamental document. This prevents legislatures from meddling in important business affairs each legislative session. Even reformers sometimes support the inclusion of regulatory language in the state's constitution, out of fear that later lobbying efforts by business could easily change state laws. So most state constitutions include long sections on regulation of insurance, utilities, corporations, alcoholic beverages, railroads, mining, medicine, real estate, the state bar association, and so forth.

TAXATION AND FINANCE   All state constitutions have articles on taxation and finance. Frequently these place severe restrictions on the taxing power of state and local governments. Taxpayer groups distrust state legislatures and wherever possible seek to restrict taxing powers by constitutional mandate. Many referenda votes are designed to amend the state's constitution to limit tax burdens. (See Chapter 17.) Local governments may also be limited in state constitutions to specific tax sources and upper limits or "caps" on local taxation. Certain classes of property may be protected, such as that devoted to religious, educational, or charitable uses; government property; some agricultural or forestry land; and even "homesteads," that is, low-priced, owner-occupied homes. Some constitutions may grant tax exemptions to new industries in order to attract industrial development. Constitutions may "earmark" certain tax revenues for specific purposes; for example, gasoline taxes may be earmarked for highway use only.

DEBT LIMITATION   Most state constitutions limit debt that can be incurred by the state only or by local governments. Many states *must* have a balanced operating budget. (Although such a constitutional command does not always succeed, on the whole, state governments are less burdened by debt than is the federal government.) Local governments are frequently limited to a debt that cannot exceed a fixed percentage of the value of property in the community. Moreover, state constitutions generally require a local referendum to approve any increase in local debt. Occasionally, however, state and local governments devise ways to get around constitutional debt limits; for example, they may pledge the revenues of a new project ("revenue bonds") to pay off the debt, rather than taxes ("full faith and credit bonds"). (See Chapter 17.)

CONSTITUTIONAL CHANGE IN THE STATES

The U.S. Constitution has been amended only twenty-six times in 200 years (and the first ten amendments, the Bill of Rights, were really part of the process of ratifying the original document). But state constitutions are so detailed and restrictive that they must be amended frequently. Nearly every year state voters must consider constitutional amendments on the ballot.

Throughout the fifty states, there are now four methods of constitutional change:

1. *Legislative proposal:* Amendments are passed by the state legislature and then submitted to the voters for approval in a referendum. This method is available in all states. (However, in Delaware amendments passed by the legislature need not be submitted to the voters.)

2. *Popular initiative:* A specific number of voters petition to get a constitutional amendment on the ballot for approval by the voters in a referendum. This method is available in seventeen states.

3. *Constitutional convention:* Legislatures submit to the voters a proposal for calling a constitutional convention, and if voters approve, a convention convenes, draws up constitutional revisions, and submits them again for approval by the voters in a referendum. This method is available in at least forty-one states.

4. *Constitutional commission:* Constitutional commissions may be created by legislatures to study the constitution and recommend changes to the state legislature, or in the case of Florida (only) to submit its recommendations directly to the voters in a referendum.

Over the years, the record of voters' response to state constitutional amendment (Table 2–2) shows that voters are more accepting of individual amendments submitted to them by *state legislatures* than any other method of constitutional change. In contrast, most popular initiatives are defeated at the polls, as are most amendments proposed by constitutional conventions. These figures suggest the key role that state

Table 2–2

THE SUCCESS OF STATE CONSTITUTIONAL AMENDMENTS BY METHOD OF INITIATION								
	Total Proposals				*Percent Adopted*			
	1990–91	1992–93	1994–95	1996–97	1990–91	1992–93	1994–95	1996–97
All Methods	226	239	233	233	63	66	70	76
Legislative Proposal	197	201	202	193	67	67	76	82
Popular Initiative	29	34	31	40	38	62	32	48
Constitutional Convention	—	1	—	—	—	0	—	—
Constitutional Commission	—	3	—	—	—	67	—	—

Source: Derived from *Book of the States, 1998–99.*

legislatures play in constitutional change. While it is true that many legislative proposals are merely "editorial," voters seem to prefer limited, step-by-step, constitutional change, rather than sweeping reform initiated by citizens.

LEGISLATIVE PROPOSAL   The most common method of amending state constitutions is by *legislative proposal*. Many states require that a constitutional amendment receive a two-thirds vote in both chambers of the legislature before submission to the voters; a few states require a three-fifths majority in both houses, while others require only simple legislative majorities. Some states require that a constitutional amendment be passed by two successive legislative sessions before being submitted to the voters. Every state except Delaware requires constitutional amendments proposed by the legislature to be submitted to the voters for approval in a referendum. (See Table 2–3.)

POPULAR INITIATIVE   Popular initiative for constitutional revision was introduced during the Progressive Era at the beginning of the twentieth century. These states usually require that an initiative petition be signed by 5, 10, or 15 percent of the number of voters in the last governor's election. The petition method allows citizens to get an amendment on the ballot *without the approval of the state legislature.* It is not surprising that measures designed to reduce the powers of legislators—for example, *tax limitation* measures and *term limits* for legislators—have come about as a result of citizen initiatives.

CONSTITUTIONAL CONVENTION   While there has been only one national Constitutional Convention, in 1787, there have been over 230 state constitutional conven-

Table 2–3

STATE CONSTITUTIONAL AMENDMENT BY LEGISLATURES			
	Legislative Vote Required for Proposal	*Consideration by Two Sessions Required*	*Referendum Vote Required for Ratification*
Alabama	3/5	No	Majority vote on amendment
Alaska	2/3	No	Majority vote on amendment
Arizona	Majority	No	Majority vote on amendment
Arkansas	Majority	No	Majority vote on amendment
California	2/3	No	Majority vote on amendment
Colorado	2/3	No	Majority vote on amendment
Connecticut	(a)	(a)	Majority vote on amendment
Delaware	2/3	Yes	Not required
Florida	3/5	No	Majority vote on amendment
Georgia	2/3	No	Majority vote on amendment
Hawaii	(b)	(b)	Majority vote on amendment
Idaho	2/3	No	Majority vote on amendment
Illinois	3/5	No	(c)
Indiana	Majority	Yes	Majority vote on amendment
Iowa	Majority	Yes	Majority vote on amendment
Kansas	2/3	No	Majority vote on amendment
Kentucky	3/5	No	Majority vote on amendment
Louisiana	2/3	No	Majority vote on amendment
Maine	2/3	No	Majority vote on amendment
Maryland	3/5	No	Majority vote on amendment
Massachusetts	Majority	Yes	Majority vote on amendment
Michigan	2/3	No	Majority vote on amendment
Minnesota	Majority	No	Majority vote in election
Mississippi	2/3	No	Majority vote on amendment
Missouri	Majority	No	Majority vote on amendment
Montana	2/3	No	Majority vote on amendment
Nebraska	3/5	No	Majority vote on amendment
Nevada	Majority	Yes	Majority vote on amendment
New Hampshire	3/5	No	2/3 vote on amendment
New Jersey	(d)	(d)	Majority vote on amendment
New Mexico	Majority	No	Majority vote on amendment
New York	Majority	Yes	Majority vote on amendment
North Carolina	3/5	No	Majority vote on amendment
North Dakota	Majority	No	Majority vote on amendment
Ohio	3/5	No	Majority vote on amendment
Oklahoma	Majority	No	Majority vote on amendment
Oregon	Majority	No	Majority vote on amendment
Pennsylvania	Majority	Yes	Majority vote on amendment
Rhode Island	Majority	No	Majority vote on amendment
South Carolina	2/3	Yes	Majority vote on amendment
South Dakota	Majority	No	Majority vote on amendment

Table 2–3 (Continued)

	Legislative Vote Required for Proposal	Consideration by Two Sessions Required	Referendum Vote Required for Ratification
Tennessee	2/3	Yes	Majority vote in election
Texas	2/3	No	Majority vote on amendment
Utah	2/3	No	Majority vote on amendment
Vermont	Majority	Yes	Majority vote on amendment
Virginia	Majority	Yes	Majority vote on amendment
Washington	2/3	No	Majority vote on amendment
West Virginia	2/3	No	Majority vote on amendment
Wisconsin	Majority	Yes	Majority vote on amendment
Wyoming	2/3	No	Majority vote in election

[a]3/4 vote at one session, or majority vote in two sessions between which an election has intervened.

[b]2/3 vote at one session or majority vote in two sessions.

[c]Majority voting in election or 3/5 voting on amendment.

[d]3/5 vote at one session or majority vote in two sessions.

Source: Derived from *Book of the States, 1998–99.*

tions. State constitutional conventions are generally proposed by state legislatures, and the question of whether or not to have a convention is generally submitted to the state's voters. (Some state constitutions require periodic submission to the voters of the question of calling a constitutional convention.) The legislature usually decides how convention delegates are to be elected and the convention organized. More important, the legislature usually decides whether the convention's work is to be *limited* to specific proposals or topics, or *unlimited* and free to write an entire new constitution.

In recent years, however, neither legislators nor voters have shown much enthusiasm for state constitutional conventions. No state conventions have been held in the 1990s. (The Louisiana legislature convened itself as the "Louisiana Convention of 1992," but the meeting was really only a special session of the legislature; moreover, its proposed constitutional revision failed by a wide margin at the polls. Hawaii voters came close to calling a convention in 1996; they cast more "Yes" than "No" votes but not the necessary majority of *all* votes after blank votes were counted.) Indeed, voters have regularly *rejected* convention calls in the states that require periodic votes on whether or not to hold a convention.

Political leaders and citizens alike appear wary of calling a constitutional convention. They are suspicious of "reform" and fearful about "runaway" conventions making unwanted changes in the political system. This is true of voters despite the fact that they always have the opportunity of later voting on the constitutional changes proposed by a convention. The current fear of conventions may also be a product of low levels of trust and confidence in government, as well as a lack of political consensus on many "hot button" issues such as abortion, affirmative action, gambling, gun control, tax limitations, and so forth. Advocates on both sides of these kinds of issues may be unsure of the outcome of a convention and therefore unite to oppose calling for one.

CONSTITUTIONAL REVISION COMMISSIONS   Constitutional revision commissions are supposed to "study and recommend" constitutional changes. These commissions are established by the legislatures and report their recommendations back to the legislature. (Only in Florida do the recommendations of the Constitutional Revision Commission go directly to the voters for ratification, and so far all of their proposals have been defeated.) Legislatures generally prefer constitutional commissions to a constitutional convention, because a commission can only study and report to the legislature. A commission can relieve the state legislature of a great deal of work. The typical commission is appointed by an act of the legislature, and its membership usually includes legislators, executive officials, and prominent citizens. Its recommendations are usually handled in the legislature like regular constitutional amendments, although they may be more sweeping than ordinary amendments.

Constitutional revision commissions have also been declining in number in recent years. (However, three of the nation's largest states—California, New York, and Florida—together with Arkansas and Utah created constitutional revision commissions in the 1990s.) The value of these commissions is in their supposed ability to review fundamental governmental processes, to inspire citizen participation in this review, and perhaps to provide an opportunity for legislatures to shift some especially controversial issues away from themselves and onto the shoulders of independent bodies.[2] And, of course, legislatures still retain control of the revision process, since commissions must usually make their recommendations to their legislatures, which then decide whether to place them on the ballot for voter approval. More often than not, legislators have ignored commission recommendations or watered them down before submitting them to the voters.

DEMOCRACY IN THE STATES

Representational democracy.
Popular participation in government through the selection of public officials by vote of the people in periodic, competitive elections in which candidates and voters can freely express themselves.

Democracy means popular participation in government. (The Greek root of the word means "rule by the many.") But popular participation can have different meanings. To our nation's Founders, who were quite ambivalent about the wisdom of democracy, it meant that the voice of the people would be *represented* in government. Representational democracy means the selection of government officials by vote of the people in periodic elections open to competition in which candidates and voters can freely express themselves. (Note that "elections" in which only one party is permitted to run candidates, or where candidates are not free to express their views, do not qualify as democratic.) The Founders believed that government rests ultimately on the consent of the governed. But their notion of "republicanism" envisioned decision making by representatives of the people, rather than direct decision making by the people themselves. The U.S. Constitution has no provision for direct voting by the people on national policy questions.

"Direct democracy" means that the people themselves can initiate and decide policy questions by popular vote. The Founders were profoundly skeptical of this form of democracy. They had read about direct democracy in the ancient Greek city-state of Athens, and they believed that "the follies" of direct democracy far outweighed any virtues it might possess. It was not until over one hundred years after the U.S. Constitution was written that widespread support developed in the American states for direct voter participation in policy making. Direct democracy developed in states and communities, and it is to be found today *only* in state and local government.

HISTORY OF DIRECT DEMOCRACY IN THE STATES   At the beginning of the twentieth century, a strong populist movement in the midwestern and western states attacked railroads, banks, corporations, and the political institutions that were said to be in their hands. The populists were later joined by progressive reformers who attacked "bosses," "machines," and parties as corrupt. The populists believed that their elected representatives were ignoring the needs of farmers, debtors, and laborers. They wished to bypass governors and legislatures and directly enact popular laws for railroad rate regulation, relief of farm debt, and monetary expansion. They believed that both the Democratic and Republican parties of their era were controlled by the trusts and monopolies. The progressives and reformers viewed politics as distasteful. They did not believe that government should be involved in resolving conflicts among competing interests or striving for compromises in public policy. Instead, government should serve "the public interest"; it should seek out the "right" answer to public questions; it should replace politicians with managers and administrators. The progressive reform movement was supported by many upper-middle-class, white, Anglo-Saxon, Protestant groups, who felt that political "machines" were catering to the votes of recent immigrants such as the Irish, Italians, eastern and southern Europeans, working-class people, Catholics, and Jews.[3] The progressive reform movement brought about many changes in the structure of municipal government. (See "Reformers and Do-Gooders" in Chapter 11.) The movement also brought about some interesting innovations in state government.

In order to reduce the influence of "politics," "parties," and "politicians," the populists and progressives advocated a wide range of devices designed to bypass political institutions and encourage direct participation by voters in public affairs. They were largely responsible for replacing party conventions with the primary elections we use today. They were also successful in bringing about the Seventeenth Amendment to the U.S. Constitution requiring that U.S. senators be directly elected by the voters, rather than chosen by state legislatures. They also supported women's suffrage, civil service, and restrictive immigration laws.

The populists and progressives were also responsible for the widespread adoption of three forms of direct democracy—the initiative, referendum, and recall. These reforms began in the farm states of the Midwest and the mining states of the West. The populists provided much of the early support for these devices, and the progressives and reformers carried them to fruition. President Woodrow Wilson endorsed the initiative, referendum, and recall, and most adoptions occurred prior to World War I.

■

Initiative.
A device by which a specific number or percentage of the voters may petition to have a constitutional amendment or law placed on the ballot for adoption or rejection by the electorate; found in some state constitutions but not in the U.S. Constitution.

Referenda.
Proposed laws or constitutional amendments submitted to the voters for their direct approval or rejection; found in some state constitutions but not in the U.S. Constitution.

Recall.
An election to allow voters to decide whether or not to remove an elected official before his or her term expires.

Direct democracy.
Popular participation in government through direct voter initiation of policy (usually by petition) and voter approval or rejection of policy decisions by popular vote.

INITIATIVE   The initiative is a device whereby a specific number or percent of voters, through the use of a petition, may have a proposed state constitutional amendment or a state law placed on the ballot for adoption or rejection by the electorate of a state. This process bypasses the legislature and allows citizens to both propose and adopt laws and constitutional amendments. Table 2–4 lists the states that allow popular initiatives for constitutional amendments, and those that allow popular initiatives for state law. Note that Alaska, Idaho, Maine, Utah, Washington, and Wyoming permit citizen initiatives for state *laws*, but not for constitutional *amendments*.

REFERENDUM   The referendum is a device by which the electorate must approve decisions of the legislature before these become law or become part of the state constitution. As we noted earlier, most states require a favorable referendum vote for a state constitutional amendment. Referenda on state laws may be submitted by the legislature (when legislators want to shift decision-making responsibility to the people), or referenda may be demanded by popular petition (when the people wish to change laws passed by the legislature).

RECALL   Recall elections allow voters to remove an elected official before his or her term expires. Usually a recall election is initiated by a petition. The number of signatures required is usually expressed as a percentage of votes cast in the last election for the official being recalled (frequently 25 percent). Currently sixteen states provide for recall election for some or all of their elected officials (see Table 2–4). Although officials are often publicly threatened with recall, rarely is anyone ever removed from office through this device. A recall of a state elected official requires an expensive petition drive as well as a campaign against the incumbent. Perhaps the mere existence of recall provisions in a state constitution makes public officials more responsive to popular moods.

DIRECT VERSUS REPRESENTATIVE DEMOCRACY

The U.S. Constitution has no provision for national referenda. Americans as a nation cannot vote on federal laws or amendments to the national constitution. But voters in the *states* can express their frustrations directly in popular initiatives and referenda voting.

ARGUMENTS FOR DIRECT DEMOCRACY   Proponents of direct democracy (see "*People in Politics:* Ward Connerly and the Citizens' Initiative to Ban Affirmative Action") make several strong arguments on behalf of the initiative and referendum devices:[4]

 * Direct democracy enhances government responsiveness and accountability. The threat of a successful initiative and referendum drive—indeed sometimes the mere circulation of a petition—encourages officials to take the popular actions.

Table 2–4

INITIATIVE AND RECALL IN THE STATES		
Initiative for Constitutional Amendments (Signatures Required to Get on Ballot)[a]	Initiative for State Laws	Recall (Signatures Required to Force a Recall Election)[b]
Arizona (15%)	Alaska	Alaska (25%)
Arkansas (10%)	Arizona	Arizona (25%)
California (8%)	Arkansas	California (12%)
Colorado (5%)	California	Colorado (25%)
Florida (8%)	Colorado	Georgia (15%)
Illinois (8%)	Idaho	Idaho (20%)
Massachusetts (3%)	Illinois	Kansas (40%)
Michigan (10%)	Missouri	Louisiana (33%)
Mississippi (12%)	Montana	Michigan (25%)
Missouri (8%)	Nebraska	Montana (10%)
Montana (10%)	Nevada	Nevada (25%)
Nebraska (10%)	North Dakota	North Dakota (25%)
Nevada (10%)	Ohio	Oregon (15%)
North Dakota (4% of state population)	Oklahoma	Rhode Island (15%)
Ohio (10%)	Oregon	Washington (25%)
Oklahoma (15%)	South Dakota	Wisconsin (25%)
Oregon (8%)	Utah	
South Dakota (10%)	Washington	

[a]Figures expressed as percentage of vote in last governor's election unless otherwise specified; some states also require distribution of votes across counties and districts.

[b]Figures are percentages of voters in last general elections of the official sought to be recalled.

Source: Derived from Council of State Governments, *The Book of the States, 1998–99.*

- Direct democracy allows citizen groups to bring their concerns directly to the public. Taxpayer groups, for example, who are not especially well represented in state capitols, have been able through initiative and referendum devices to place their concerns on the public agenda.

- Direct democracy stimulates debate about policy issues. In elections with important referendum issues on the ballot, campaigns tend to be more issue-oriented. Candidates, newspapers, interest groups, and television news are all forced to directly confront policy issues.

- Direct democracy stimulates voter interest and improves election-day turnout. Controversial issues on the ballot—the death penalty, abortion, gun control, taxes, gay rights, English only, and so on—bring out additional voters. There is some limited evidence that elections with initiatives on the ballot increase voter turnout by three to five percentage points over elections with no initiatives on the ballot.[5]

PEOPLE IN POLITICS

WARD CONNERLY AND THE CITIZENS' INITIATIVE TO BAN AFFIRMATIVE ACTION

Perhaps no other citizens' initiative has created more controversy than California's Proposition 209, which bans "granting preferential treatment to any individual or group" on the basis of "race, sex, color, ethnicity or national origin" in state employment, education, or contracting. The effect of the initiative, approved by 54 percent of California's voters in 1996, is to eliminate racial and gender preferences and quotas in the state's affirmative action programs.

Ward Connerly, a Sacramento housing and land use consultant, chaired the "California Civil Rights Initiative" campaign on behalf of Proposition 209. (For more information on affirmative action programs and the California Civil Rights Initiative itself, see Chapter 14.) Connerly is an African American who was born in Louisiana, orphaned at the age of four, and raised by his grandmother in California. He graduated from Sacramento State College in the 1960s and found a job in the California Depart-

ment of Housing and Community Development. He later worked for the Housing Committee of the state legislature where he met the rising Republican Pete Wilson. Following Wilson's election as governor, he appointed Connerly to the University of California Board of Regents.

Under Connerly's leadership, the Regents voted to end racial preferences in admissions to the state's universities in 1995. That same year, Connerly accepted the chairmanship of the Proposition 209 initiative campaign.

Connerly's prominence as a member of the University of California Board of Regents, as well as his friendship with Governor Pete Wilson, who actively supported the initiative, were central to its success at the polls. Connerly argued convincingly across the state on behalf of a "color-blind rather than a race conscious society." He was sharply attacked by the leaders of the National Association for the Advancement of Colored People (NAACP) and other defenders of affirmative action. But the combative Connerly chose to follow up his victory in California by chairing a new nationwide campaign to place a similarly worded ban on racial preferences on the ballot by citizen initiatives in other states. His efforts were successful in the state of Washington in 1998.

- Direct democracy increases trust in government and diminishes alienation. While it is difficult to substantiate such a claim, the opportunity to directly affect issues should give voters an increased sense of power.

ARGUMENTS FOR REPRESENTATIVE DEMOCRACY　Opponents of direct democracy, from our nation's Founders to the present, argue that representative democracy offers far better protection for individual liberty and the rights of minorities than direct democracy. The Founders constructed a system of checks and balances not so much to protect against the oppression of a ruler, but to protect against the tyranny of the majority. Opponents of direct democracy echo many of the Founders' arguments:

- Direct democracy encourages majorities to sacrifice the rights of individuals and minorities. This argument supposes that voters are generally less tolerant than elected officials, and there is some evidence to support this supposition. However, there is little evidence that public policy in states with the initiative and referendum is any more oppressive than public policy in states without these devices. Nonetheless, the potential of majoritarian sacrifice of the liberty of unpopular people is always a concern.

- Direct democracy facilitates the adoption of unwise and unsound policies. Although voters have rejected many bad ideas, frequently initiatives are less well drafted than legislation.

- Voters are not sufficiently informed to cast intelligent ballots on many issues. Many voters cast their vote in a referendum without ever having considered the issue before going into the polling booth.

- A referendum does not allow consideration of alternative policies or modifications or amendments to the proposition set forth on the ballot. In contrast, legislators devote a great deal of attention to writing, rewriting, and amending bills, and seeking out compromises among interests.

- Direct democracy enables special interests to mount expensive initiative and referendum campaigns. Although proponents of direct democracy argue that these devices allow citizens to bypass special-interest-group-dominated legislatures, in fact only a fairly well-financed group can mount a statewide campaign on behalf of a referendum issue. And the outcomes of the vote may be heavily influenced by paid television advertising. So money is important in both "representational" and "direct" democracy.

THE DECLINE OF REPRESENTATIVE GOVERNMENT   Direct, popular participation in government in the American states has been growing in strength at the expense of representative democracy. State legislatures, and indeed state governments generally, are perceived by the American public as largely unresponsive, frequently unethical, and dominated by special interests. Whether or not this popular image is accurate, it drives the political movement toward increasing numbers of popular initiatives and referenda votes. In American state and local government, "Participatory democracy is here to stay; there is no turning back."[6]

THE POLITICS OF STATE INITIATIVES

In theory the initiative device is ideologically neutral; both liberal and conservative groups can use this device to bypass state legislatures. During the progressive era at the beginning of the twentieth century, many *liberal* reforms were advanced by popular initiative. But in recent years, as the general public has moved in a *conservative* direction, many citizen initiative efforts have reflected conservative themes (see Table 2–5).

TAX LIMITATION INITIATIVES   The nation's "tax revolt" got its start with citizen initiatives in the states, beginning with California's Proposition 13 in 1978, and continuing in many tax limitation initiatives in other states in the years since then.

California has had a long history of citizen initiatives for constitutional change. So in 1978, in the wake of popular frustration over inflation and taxes, a Los Angeles real

Table 2–5

STATE VOTES ON SELECTED PROPOSITIONS		
TAX LIMITATIONS		*OUTCOME*
California (1986)	New local taxes require 2/3 vote	Pass
Nevada (1988)	Prohibits state income tax	Pass
Colorado (1992)	Require elections for tax increases	Pass
Nevada (1994)	Require 2/3 legislative vote and referendum for tax increase	Pass
Massachusetts (1994)	Enact graduated income tax	Fail
Montana (1994)	Require 2/3 legislative vote for tax increase	Fail
California (1998)	Raise cigarette tax	Pass
Nebraska (1998)	Limit future tax increases	Fail
CIVIL RIGHTS		
North Dakota (1984)	Guarantee right to bear arms	Pass
New Mexico (1986)	Guarantee right to bear arms	Pass
Vermont (1986)	Equal Rights Amendment	Fail
Arizona (1988)	Make English official language	Pass
Florida (1988)	Make English official language	Pass
Colorado (1992)	Deny homosexuals preferential protections against discrimination	Pass
Oregon (1992)	Require government to discourage homosexuality	Fail
Alaska (1994)	Guarantee right to bear arms	Pass
Florida (1998)	Equal rights for women	Pass
Alaska (1998)	Prohibit same sex marriages	Pass
Hawaii (1998)	Prohibit same sex marriages	Pass
CRIME		
Oregon (1984)	Reinstate death penalty	Pass
Massachusetts (1982)	Legalize death penalty	Pass
Oregon (1994)	Mandatory sentences for felonies	Pass
Colorado (1994)	No bail for violent offenders	Pass
GAMBLING		
Arkansas (1984)	Allow casino gambling	Fail
Colorado (1984)	Allow casino gambling	Fail
California (1984)	Authorize state lottery	Pass
Florida (1986)	Allow casino gambling	Fail
Florida (1986)	Authorize state lottery	Pass
California (1998)	Allow Indian tribes to operate casinos	Pass
EDUCATION		
California (1996)	End racial preferences (affirmative action)	Pass
California (1998)	End bilingual education in schools	Pass
Washington (1998)	End racial preferences (affirmative action)	Pass

Table 2–5 (Continued)

ABORTION

Colorado (1984)	Prohibit state funds for abortion	Pass
Washington (1984)	Prohibit state funds for abortion	Fail
Rhode Island (1986)	Prohibit state funds for abortion	Fail
Arkansas (1988)	Prohibit state funds for abortion	Pass
Colorado (1988)	Prohibit state funds for abortion	Fail
Wyoming (1994)	Prohibit abortion	Fail
Washington (1998)	Prohibit partial-birth abortions	Fail
Colorado (1998)	Prohibit partial-birth abortions	Fail

OTHER

California (1986)	Quarantine persons with AIDS	Fail
North Dakota (1994)	Repeal seat belt law	Fail
Oregon (1994)	Allow terminally ill to obtain lethal drugs	Pass
Michigan (1998)	Allow physician-assisted suicide	Fail
Arizona (1998)	Approve marijuana for medicinal purposes	Pass

Note: These are selected proposition votes from recent years.

estate developer, Howard Jarvis, found the state's voters more than willing to support a constitutional amendment initiative to reduce property taxes. His effort was funded by real estate developers, business, and agricultural interests, but he also succeeded in organizing statewide, grass-roots support for his initiative. Opposition to Proposition 13 was led by public officials who believed the amendment would cripple public services. The political establishment was joined by the League of Women Voters, the PTA, public employee unions, teachers, and environmental groups, in making dire predictions about the impact of the amendment. California voters went to the polls in record numbers to give approval to Proposition 13 by better than a two-to-one margin. The publicity surrounding the success of Proposition 13 gave the impression that this citizen initiative was the beginning of a national tax revolt. By 1980 Democrats and Republicans across the nation were campaigning as "tax cutters." Later President Ronald Reagan would interpret it as part of a general mandate for lower taxes and less government, and as a forerunner to his own federal income tax cuts. But not all states joined in the "tax revolt."

In the years since Proposition 13, however, almost as many states *defeated* tax limitation referenda as passed them. And California voters surprised antitax forces in 1998 by approving a citizens' initiative to raise cigarette taxes by 50 cents a pack. (In Chapter 17 we will devote more discussion to the politics of taxation.) In the years after Proposition 13, scholars tried to distinguish between states in which the tax revolt was successful and those where it was not. It turned out that the states *with constitutional provisions for citizen initiatives* were far more likely to join the "tax revolt"—that is, to pass tax limitation constitutional amendments—than states without provisions for citizen initiatives.[7]

SOCIAL ISSUES   Crime, gambling, abortion, and civil rights are issues frequently encountered in initiative politics (see Table 2–5). In recent years the initiative process has been used to "get tough on crime," including reinstatement of the death penalty. A number of states adopted their lotteries by citizen initiative, after legislatures chose not to offend church groups opposed to gambling. However, casino gambling has been much less popular with the voters. The abortion issue has been raised in a number of state initiative votes over whether to allow or prohibit state funding of abortions. Colorado voters approved a hotly contested initiative in 1992 that would deny homosexuals status as a protected class in civil rights laws; but the initiative later was declared to be invalid by the Colorado Supreme Court. The most publicized citizen initiative in 1994 was California's Proposition 187 prohibiting illegal aliens from receiving state-funded education, welfare, and health (except emergency) services. (See "*What Do You Think?* Should States Deny Welfare Benefits to Illegal Immigrants?" in Chapter 1.) And in recent years a number of states have approved citizens' initiatives to allow marijuana use for medicinal purposes, despite warnings by the U.S. Justice Department that such use continues to violate *federal* law.

TERM LIMITS FOR PUBLIC OFFICIALS   Citizen initiatives to limit the terms of public officials—Congress members, state legislators, and other state and local officials—have enjoyed great success whenever they have appeared on the ballot. The U.S. Supreme Court has held that a state can *not* impose term limits on *members of Congress* (see later). However, states, and citizens in states with the popular initiative and referenda, can limit the terms of their own *state legislators*. And indeed, term limits have usually won by landslide margins whenever they have appeared on referenda ballots (see Table 2–6).

Opponents of term limits, including state legislators themselves, have pursued the two-pronged strategy against the measure: first try to persuade the voters to reject it, and if that fails try to persuade a court to declare it unconstitutional. Supporters of term limits clearly have public opinion on their side. (See "*Up Close:* Are Term Limits a Good Idea?")

Constitutional arguments against term limits have led to prolonged litigation in the courts. Opponents argued that term limits placed an unconstitutional barrier on the right to be a candidate for public office, and that they violated the right of voters to cast their ballots for candidates of their choice. These arguments were rejected first by the California Supreme Court,[8] and later by the U.S. Court of Appeals (together with the argument that voters did not understand what they were voting for on term limits referenda).[9] The U.S. Supreme Court has declined to hear appeals of cases upholding the constitutionality of term limits.[10]

■
Term limits.
Constitutional limits on the number of terms or the number of years that a public official can serve in the same office.

SUPREME COURT REJECTION OF CONGRESSIONAL TERM LIMITS BY STATES

When the voters of Arkansas adopted a state constitutional amendment in 1992 set-

Table 2–6

VOTING ON TERM LIMITS FOR STATE LEGISLATORS		
State[a]	Year Adopted	Percent Support
Arizona	1992	74
Arkansas	1992	60
California[b]	1990	52
Colorado	1990	71
Florida	1992	77
Idaho	1994	59
Louisiana	1995	76
Maine	1993	68
Massachusetts[c]	1994	52
Michigan	1992	59
Missouri	1992	75
Montana	1992	67
Nebraska[d]	1994	68
Nevada	1994	70
Ohio	1992	66
Oklahoma	1990	67
Oregon	1992	70
South Dakota	1992	64
Utah	1994	65
Washington	1992	52
Wyoming	1992	77

[a]Twenty-two states enacted term limits for members of Congress between 1992 and 1994—twenty of those listed here, plus Alaska and North Dakota. (In addition, a federal as well as a state limitation was scheduled to be on the ballot in 1995 in Mississippi, and New Hampshire was about to enact term limits for members of Congress.) On May 23, 1995, the Supreme Court ruled 5–4 in *U.S. Term Limits* v. *Thornton* that these provisions were unconstitutional. In Florida, Michigan, Missouri, and Oregon, the term limits provision stated that, should any part of the law be declared unconstitutional, it is the wish of the voters that the expressed limits be respected voluntarily.

[b]In 1997, the U.S. Court of Appeals struck down the California term limits law on the grounds that voters had not been informed that individuals would be barred for their lifetimes from serving more than the stated limits. It is unknown whether the case will be heard by the Supreme Court.

[c]In 1997, the Massachusetts Supreme Court struck down the state term limit statute on constitutional grounds.

[d]Nebraska voters have twice approved state term limits. However, the law has been voided both times on technical grounds.

ting term limits for their U.S. Senators and Representatives, the U.S. Supreme Court ruled in 1995 that this action violated the U.S. Constitution by setting forth qualifications for Congress members beyond those found in Article I. Only three qualifications are specified in the U.S. Constitution: age, citizenship, and residence. (The Arkansas term limit amendment actually set qualifications for eligibility for name placement on the ballot; Arkansas argued that this was a permissible exercise of power to regulate

UP CLOSE

ARE TERM LIMITS A GOOD IDEA?

Distrust of politicians and declining confidence in the ability of government to confront national problems fueled grass-roots movements in many states to limit the terms of public officials—both Congress members and state legislators. National opinion polls have repeatedly shown widespread popular support for term limits:

How long should members of the House and Senate serve?

	1991	1992	1997	1998
A maximum of 12 years	61%	67%	72%	68%
As long as they get elected	37	31	25	27

But the enthusiasm of the general public for term limits was seldom matched by legislators—either in Washington or in state capitals—who are reluctant to limit their own legislative careers. Hence, citizens in states with the popular initiative and referenda turned to these instruments of direct democracy.

ARGUMENTS FOR TERM LIMITS   Proponents of term limits argue that "citizen-legislators" have largely been replaced by career "professional politicians." People who have held legislative office for many years become isolated from the lives and concerns of average citizens. Career politicians respond to the media, to polls, to interest groups, but they have no direct feeling for how their constituents live. Term limits, proponents argue, would force politicians to return home and live under the laws that they make.

Proponents also argue that term limits would increase competition in the electoral system. By creating "open seat" races on a regular basis, more people would be encouraged to seek public office. Incumbents do not win so often because they are the most qualified people in their districts, but rather because of the many electoral advantages granted by incumbency itself—name recognition, campaign contributions from special interests, pork barrel and casework, office staff, and so on (see "The Great Incumbency Machine" in Chapter 6). These incumbent advantages discourage good people from challenging officeholders.

ARGUMENTS AGAINST TERM LIMITS   Opponents of term limits argue that they infringe on the voters' freedom of choice. If voters are upset with the performance of their state legislators, they can always "throw the rascals out." If they want to limit a legislator's term, they can do so simply by not reelecting him or her. But if voters wish to keep popular, able, experienced, and hard-working legislators in office, they should be permitted to do so. Experience is a valuable asset in state capitals; voters may legitimately desire to be represented by senior legislators with knowledge and experience in public affairs.

Opponents also argue that inexperienced legislators would be forced to rely more on the policy information supplied to them by bureaucrats, lobbyists, and staff people. Term limits, they argue, would weaken the legislature, leaving it less capable of checking the power of the special interests. But proponents counter this argument by observing that the closest relationships in state capitals develop between lobbyists and senior legislators who have interacted professionally and socially over the years, and that most powerful lobbying groups strongly oppose term limits.

"times, places and manner of holding elections" granted to the states in Article I. But the Court dismissed this argument as an "indirect attempt to accomplish what the Constitution prohibits.") The Court held that a state cannot limit the terms of members of Congress:

> Allowing individual states to adopt their own qualifications for Congressional service would be inconsistent with the framers' vision of a uniform national legislature representing the people of the United States. If the qualifications set forth in the text of the Constitution are to be changed, that text must be amended.

Justice John Paul Stevens, writing for the majority in the controversial 5–4 decision, set forth two key arguments in opposition to state-imposed congressional term limits: first, that the power to do so is *not* among the powers reserved to the states by the

Tenth Amendment, and second, that the Founders intended age, citizenship, and residency be the *only* qualifications for members of Congress.

> [Arkansas argues] that the Constitution contains no express prohibition against state-added qualifications, and that Amendment 73 is therefore an appropriate exercise of a state's reserved power to place additional restrictions on the choices that its own voters may make. We disagree for two independent reasons. First, we conclude that the power to add qualifications is not within the "original powers" of the states, and thus is not reserved to the states by the 10th Amendment. Second, even if states possessed some original power in this area, we conclude that the framers intended the Constitution to be the exclusive source of qualifications for members of Congress, and that the framers thereby "divested" states of any power to add qualifications.

But Justice Clarence Thomas, in his dissenting opinion, set forth a compelling argument on behalf of the powers reserved to the people of the states by the Tenth Amendment:

> It is ironic that the Court bases today's decision on the right of the people to "choose whom they please to govern them." . . . The majority therefore defends the right of the people of Arkansas to "choose whom they please to govern them" by invalidating a provision that won nearly 60 percent of the votes cast in a direct election and that carried every Congressional district in the state.
>
> I dissent. Nothing in the Constitution deprives the people of each state of the power to prescribe eligibility requirements for the candidates who seek to represent them in Congress. The Constitution is simply silent on this question. And whether the Constitution is silent, it raises no bar to action by the states or the people.[11]

INITIATIVE CAMPAIGNS   Over time, initiative campaigns have become more sophisticated and costly. Supporters of an initiative must first of all circulate their petitions, often using paid as well as volunteer workers to obtain the necessary signatures.[12] Television, radio, and newspaper advertising usually accompany the drive for signatures. Once on the ballot, an initiative campaign can become very expensive, with television "infomercials," celebrity endorsements, and get-out-the-vote work on election day.

Some initiative campaigns are sponsored by "special interests"—specific businesses or industries; labor unions, including government employees; religious organizations; environmental groups; and public interest groups. The gambling industry, for example, often backs "citizens' initiatives" to legalize gambling. Many of the designated sponsoring groups for petitions—for example, "Citizens for Tax Justice" (tax limits) and "Eight is Enough" (term limits)—are organized and funded by established lobbying groups that have failed to accomplish their goals through the legislative process.

Opposition campaigns to initiatives may also be well funded by organized interests. Lobbying groups that are well entrenched in state capitals—public employee unions, teachers' unions, and utility, insurance, and liquor industries (see Chapter 6)—are usually leery of citizens' initiatives. Political officeholders are also generally skeptical of citizen initiatives, even though they may occasionally endorse particularly popular ones. After all, the initiative process is designed to *bypass* the state capital and its power holders. A proposal in New Jersey in 1992 to adopt the initiative process was successfully defeated by a strong coalition of well-established interest groups that mounted "an unprecedented joint lobbying effort."[13] Occasionally opposition groups have resorted to the "counter initiative"—deliberately adding an initiative to the ballot that is designed to undermine support for a popular citizen initiative. There is a tendency for voters to vote against initiatives when the issues are complex and confusing. Occasionally state supreme courts have denied an initiative a place on the ballot, not only for procedural reasons, but also because in the court's opinion it violated the U.S. Constitution.

THE THREAT OF INITIATIVES   Legislatures may be goaded at times into enacting legislation by the threat of a popular initiative. Recognizing that a popular initiative may gain a position on the ballot and win voter approval, legislatures may prefer to preempt an initiative movement by writing their own version of the policy. Indeed there is some evidence that legislatures in initiative states are more sensitive to majority preferences among voters than legislatures in states without the initiative device.[14]

REFORM PROPOSALS   Reformers have argued that initiative voting is becoming too common, that multiple initiatives on the ballot overload and confuse voters, that initiatives are often poorly drafted, and that voters are often poorly informed about the real purposes and intent of an initiative. They often urge that neutral voter guides be printed by the state, summarizing arguments for and against initiative questions; that the names and affiliations of major contributors to initiative campaigns be published; and that courts scrutinize titles on initiatives to ensure that they accurately reflect their purposes and intent.

Americans overwhelmingly support the initiative process. Indeed, 64 percent of Americans say that it is a good idea to let citizens place issues directly on the ballot by collecting petition signatures:

> Q. Many states have laws which allow citizens to place initiatives directly on the ballot by collecting petition signatures. If the initiative is approved by voters on election day, it becomes law. Is this a good idea?[15]
>
> Yes   64%
>
> No   17%
>
> Not sure 19%

Yet only eighteen states currently have a statewide constitutional initiative process (see Table 2–4). Despite the popularity of the initiative in referendum process, legislators in a majority of states are unlikely to grant initiative rights to their citizens in the near future.

DID YOU KNOW?

NICKNAMES OF THE STATES

One of the less important, yet sometimes very heated, issues that confront state legislatures is the selection of official nicknames for their state as well as official birds, flowers, trees, songs, and the like. If you think you know about the American states (or if you pass your driving time reading license plates), try to match the state with its official nickname without looking at the answers.

Easy Ones	*Answers*	*Hard Ones*	*Answers*
Heart of Dixie	Alabama	Land of Opportunity	Arkansas
Grand Canyon State	Arizona	Constitution State, Nutmeg State	Connecticut
Golden State	California	First State, Diamond State	Delaware
Centennial State	Colorado	Gem State	Idaho
Peach State, Empire State of the South	Georgia	Prairie State	Illinois
Sunshine State	Florida	Sunflower State	Kansas
Aloha State	Hawaii	Pelican State	Louisiana
Hawkeye State	Iowa	Pine Tree State	Maine
Hoosier State	Indiana	Old Line State, Free State	Maryland
Bluegrass State	Kentucky	North Star State, Gopher State	Minnesota
Bay State, Old Colony	Massachusetts	Magnolia State	Mississippi
Great Lake State, Wolverine State	Michigan	Treasurer State	Montana
Show Me State	Missouri	Silver Statte	Nevada
Cornhusker State	Nebraska	Granite State	New Hampshire
Empire State	New York	Garden State	New Jersey
Tar Heel State	North Carolina	Land of Enchantment	New Mexico
Buckeye State	Ohio	Sioux State, Flickertale State	North Dakota
Sooner State	Oklahoma	Keystone State	Pennsylvania
Beaver State	Oregon	Palmetto State	South Carolina
Little Rhody	Rhode Island	Coyote State	South Dakota
Volunteer State	Tennessee	Beehive State	Utah
Lone Star State	Texas	Green Mountain State	Vermont
Old Dominion	Virginia	Evergreen State	Washington
Mountain State	West Virginia	Equality State	Wyoming
Badger State	Wisconsin	None (only state with no official nickname)	Alaska

Source: Book of the States, 1988–89.

ON THE WEB

State constitutions were once condemned to the back shelves of law school libraries. Today, however, most state constitutions can be accessed through the Cornell University Law School Library Web site at

www.law.cornell.edu/statutes

by clicking a state's name under the heading "Constitutions, Statutes, and Legislative Information by State." State constitutions are lengthy and tedious; they are not intended for recreational reading. But students, especially prelaw students, should be able to access their own state's constitution and scroll through its various articles to answer specific questions, for example: Does your state's constitution limit the terms of legislators?

Several national organizations are promoting initiatives and referenda votes in multiple states. Among the more active organizations is US Term Limits, whose Web site is

www.termlimits.org

This organization provides arguments and information designed to promote term limits for all public officials. Another active organization is the American Civil Rights Institute:

www.acri.org

This group promotes state constitutional initiatives designed to end racial preferences in affirmative action programs.

NOTES

1. Advisory Commission on Intergovernmental Relations, *State Constitutional Law: Cases and Materials* (Washington, DC: ACIR, 1988).

2. See Bruce E. Cain and Roger G. Noll (eds.), *Constitutional Reform in California* (Berkeley, CA: Institute of Governmental Studies, 1995).

3. See Richard Hofstadter, *The Age of Reform* (New York: Knopf, 1955).

4. For a balanced summary and evaluation of direct democracy, see Thomas E. Cronin, *Direct Democracy: The Politics of Initiative, Referendum and Recall* (Cambridge, MA: Harvard University Press, 1989).

5. Ibid., p. 227.

6. Alan Rosenthal, *The Decline of Representative Democracy* (Washington, DC: Congressional Quarterly Press, 1998), p. 337.

7. Susan B. Hansen, *The Politics of Taxation* (New York: Praeger, 1983).

8. *Legislature* v. *EU,* California Supreme Court, 1991.

9. *Bates* v. *Jones,* U.S. Ninth Circuit Court of Appeals, December 1997.

10. *Bates* v. *Jones,* U.S. Supreme Court, March 23, 1998.

11. Quotation from *U.S. Term Limits* v. *Thornton* (1995).

12. The U.S. Supreme Court has held that a state may not prohibit financial payments for the circulation of petitions. *Meger* v. *Grant,* 486 U.S. 414 (1988).

13. Council of State Governments, *Book of the States, 1994–95,* p. 286.

14. Elizabeth A. Gerber, "Legislative Response to the Threat of Popular Initiatives," *American Journal of Political Science,* 40 (February 1996), 99–128. However, for evidence that public policy and public opinion are no closer in initiative states than noninitiative states (that is, for evidence that initiative states are no more "responsive" than noninitiative states), see Edward L. Lascher, Jr. et al., "Gun Behind the Door? Ballot Initiatives, State Politics and Public Opinion," *Journal of Politics,* 58 (August 1996), 760–75.

15. Rosmussen Research, March 3, 1998.

3
STATES, COMMUNITIES, AND AMERICAN FEDERALISM

QUESTIONS TO CONSIDER

★ ★ ★ ★ ★ ★ ★ ★ ★

Would the nation be better off with a single national government passing uniform laws and providing uniform services throughout the country, rather than 50 state governments with different laws and programs?

☐ Yes
☐ No

Should welfare benefits be the same in all states?

☐ Yes
☐ No

Which level of government does the best job of dealing with the problems it faces?

☐ Federal
☐ State
☐ Local

■

Federalism.
A constitutional arrange-
ment whereby power is di-
vided between national and
subnational governments,
each of which enforces its
own laws directly on its citizens and neither of which
can alter the arrangement
without the consent of the
other.

Unitary system.
Constitutional arrangement
whereby authority rests with
the national government;
subnational governments
have only those powers
given to them by the na-
tional government.

Confederation.
Constitutional arrangement
whereby the national gov-
ernment is created by and
relies on subnational governments for its authority.

WHAT IS FEDERALISM?

Virtually all nations of the world have some units of local government—states, re-
publics, provinces, regions, cities, counties, or villages. Decentralization of the administrative burdens of government is required almost everywhere. But not all nations
have federal systems of government.

Federalism is a system of government in which power is divided between national
and subnational governments with both exercising separate and autonomous authority, both electing their own officials, and both taxing their own citizens for the provision of public services. Moreover, federalism requires that the powers of the national
and subnational governments be guaranteed by a constitution that cannot be changed
without the consent of both national and subnational populations.[1]

The United States, Canada, Australia, India, the Federal Republic of Germany, and
Switzerland are generally regarded as federal systems. But Great Britain, France, Italy,
and Sweden are not. While these nations have local governments, they are dependent
on the national government for their powers. They are considered unitary systems
rather than federal systems, because their local governments can be altered or even
abolished by the national governments acting alone. In contrast, a system is said to be
a confederation if the power of the national government is dependent upon local units
of government. While these terms—unitary and confederation—can be defined theoretically, in the real world of politics it is not so easy to distinguish between governments that are truly federal and those that are not. Indeed, as we shall see in this
chapter, it is not clear whether the U.S. government today retains its federal character.

WHY FEDERALISM?

Why have state and local governments anyway? Why not have a centralized political
system with a single government accountable to national majorities in national elections—a government capable of implementing uniform policies throughout the country?

"AUXILIARY PRECAUTIONS" AGAINST TYRANNY   The nation's Founders understood that "republican principles," while they should be nurtured and cherished,
would not be sufficient in themselves to protect individual liberty. Periodic elections,
party competition, voter enfranchisement, and political equality may function to make
governing elites more responsive to popular concerns. According to the Founders, "A
dependence on the people is, no doubt, the primary control of government, but experience has taught mankind the necessity of auxiliary precautions."

Among the most important "auxiliary precautions" devised by the Founders to control government are *federalism*—dividing powers between the national and state governments—and *separation of powers*—the dispersal of power among the separate
executive, legislative, and judicial branches of government.

> In the compound republic of America, the power surrendered by the people is first di-
> vided between two distinct governments, and then the portion allotted to each subdi-

vided among distinct and separate departments. Hence a double security arises to the rights of the people. The different governments will control each other, at the same time that each will be controlled by itself.[2]

DISPERSING POWER   Decentralization distributes power more widely among different sets of leaders. Multiple leadership groups are generally believed to be more democratic than a single set of all-powerful leaders. Moreover, state and local governments provide a political base of offices for the opposition party when it has lost national elections. In this way state and local governments contribute to party competition in America by helping to tide over the losing party after electoral defeat so that it may remain strong enough to challenge incumbents at the next election. And finally, of course, state and local governments provide a channel of recruitment for national political leaders. National leaders can be drawn from a pool of leaders experienced in state and local politics.

INCREASING PARTICIPATION   Decentralization allows more people to participate in the political system. There are more than 86,000 governments in America—states, counties, townships, municipalities, towns, special districts, and school districts. Nearly a million people hold some kind of public office. The opportunity to participate doubtlessly contributes to popular support of the political system. Many people are given the opportunity to exercise political leadership; moreover, state and local governments are widely regarded as being "closer to the people." Thus, by providing more opportunities for direct citizen involvement in government, state and local governments contribute to the popular sense of political effectiveness and well-being.

IMPROVING EFFICIENCY   Decentralization makes government more manageable and efficient. Imagine the bureaucracy, red tape, and confusion if every government activity in every local community in the nation—police, schools, roads, fire fighting, garbage collection, sewage disposal, and so forth—were controlled by a centralized administration in Washington. If local governments did not exist, they would have to be invented. Government becomes arbitrary when a bureaucracy far from the scene directs a local administrator to proceed with the impossible—local conditions notwithstanding. Decentralization softens the rigidity of law.

ENSURING POLICY RESPONSIVENESS   Decentralized government encourages policy responsiveness. Multiple competing governments are more sensitive to citizen views than monopoly government. The existence of multiple governments offering different packages of benefits and costs allows a better match between citizen preferences and public policy. People and businesses can "vote with their feet" by relocating to those states and communities that most closely conform to their own policy preferences. Americans are very mobile. About four of every ten Americans move in any five-year period: One in five moves to a different county, and one in ten to a different state. Business and industry are also increasingly mobile. Mobility not only facilitates a better match between citizen preferences and public policy, it also encourages competition between states and communities to offer improved services at lower costs.

ENCOURAGING POLICY INNOVATION   Decentralization encourages policy experimentation and innovation. Federalism may be perceived today as a "conservative" idea, but it was once viewed as the instrument of "progressivism." A strong argument can be made that the groundwork for FDR's New Deal in the 1930s was built in state policy experimentation during the Progressive Era earlier in the century. Federal programs as diverse as the income tax, unemployment compensation, countercyclical public works, Social Security, wage and hour legislation, bank deposit insurance, and food stamps all had antecedents at the state level. Indeed, the compelling phrase "laboratories of democracy" is generally attributed to the great progressive jurist, Supreme Court Justice Louis D. Brandeis, who used it in defense of state experimentation with new solutions to social and economic problems.[3] But the states cannot serve as "laboratories," and the innovative potential of federalism cannot be realized, if the states are not free to pursue a wide range of policies. Competition among governments provides additional incentives for inventiveness and innovation in public policy.[4] (See "*Up Close:* States Lead in the Fight Against Tobacco.")

MANAGING CONFLICT   Political decentralization frequently reduces the severity of conflict in a society. Decentralization is a classic method by which different peoples can be brought together in a nation without engendering irresolvable conflict. Conflicts between geographically defined groups in America are resolved by allowing each to pursue its own policies within the separate states and communities; this avoids battling over a single national policy to be applied uniformly throughout the land.

FEDERALISM'S FAULTS

Federalism is not without its faults. Federalism can obstruct action on national issues. Although decentralization may reduce conflict at the national level, it may do so at the price of "sweeping under the rug" some serious, national injustices.

PROTECTING SLAVERY AND SEGREGATION   Federalism in America remains tainted by its historical association with slavery, segregation, and discrimination. An early doctrine of "nullification" was set forth by Thomas Jefferson in the Virginia and Kentucky Resolution of 1798, asserting states' right to nullify unconstitutional laws of Congress. Although the original use of this doctrine was to counter congressional attacks on a free press in the Alien and Sedition Acts, the doctrine was later revived to defend slavery. John C. Calhoun of South Carolina argued forcefully in the years before the Civil War that slavery was an issue for states to decide and that under the Constitution of 1787, Congress had no power to interfere with slavery in the southern states or in the new western territories.

In the years immediately following the Civil War the issues of slavery, racial inequality, and black voting rights were *nationalized*. The Thirteenth, Fourteenth, and Fifteenth Amendments to the Constitution were enforced with federal troops in the southern states during Reconstruction. But following the Compromise of 1876 federal troops were withdrawn from the southern states and legal and social segregation of

UP CLOSE

STATES LEAD IN THE FIGHT AGAINST TOBACCO

The American states have led the way in efforts to reduce smoking and the health hazards associated with it. The national government has trailed behind the states and thus far has obstructed a national solution.

It has long been recognized that cigarette smoking is the leading preventable cause of death in the United States. The federal government's efforts to reduce smoking have centered on educating the public to the health dangers involved. In 1964 the U.S. Surgeon General first reported (what most people suspected anyway) that smoking was related to cancer, heart disease, and emphysema. In 1965 Congress required health warnings on every pack of cigarettes sold. In 1970 Congress banned cigarette advertising from radio and television. Over time the percentage of the adult population that smoked fell from more than 50 percent in 1965 to about 25 percent by 1995.

The national government banned smoking on domestic airline travel, but states and cities led the way in banning smoking in public buildings, certain areas in restaurants, and so on. State taxes on cigarettes were gradually increased: Alaska added $1.00, Washington 82 cents, and Hawaii and New Jersey 80 cents to each pack of cigarettes. This was on top of the federal tax of 25 cents per pack. (Only the tobacco-producing states of Virginia, Kentucky, and North Carolina kept their per pack tax at 5 cents or less.) But Congress failed to act directly on the national health-care costs incurred by smoking. The states assumed the leadership in the tobacco fight.

But in 1994 Mississippi and Florida filed civil lawsuits against the major tobacco companies, demanding reimbursement for their states' share of Medicaid costs incurred through smoking-related diseases. Florida passed a new state law, a Medicaid Third Party Liability Act, allowing statistical evidence of illnesses among large numbers of people to be used as evidence of causation. This meant that Florida could recover damages without necessarily showing that a product (ciga-rettes) actually caused injury to particular defendants (smokers). More importantly, the law declared that product manufacturers (the tobacco companies) cannot escape liability by showing that users of their product knowingly assumed all or part of the risk of using it. In other words, the tobacco companies were denied the legal defense of showing that many individuals deliberately chose to smoke despite their awareness of the health risks.

In pretrial negotiations with the states, tobacco companies offered a nationwide settlement package. In exchange for dismissing the state cases and limiting the size of damages awards individuals could receive in smoking-related cases, the tobacco companies agreed to total payments of more than $368 billion to the states and to a national fund for children's health. The companies also agreed to end billboard and sports advertising and to other actions designed to reduce teen smoking over the years. The FDA would be given authority to reduce and eventually eliminate the nicotine content of cigarettes. Florida Attorney General Bob Butterworth boasted, "The Marlboro Man will be riding into the sunset on Joe Camel."

But clearly tobacco sales constitute "interstate commerce" and thus Congress has the final word on any settlement negotiated by the states. When the settlement reached Washington in 1998, Democrats and Republicans alike piled on amendments trying to make themselves look tough on "Big Tobacco" to the voters. They adopted punitive measures, stripping away a liability cap protecting tobacco companies from future lawsuits, raising the penalty to be paid by tobacco companies, and adding a federal tax of $1.10 per pack. The tobacco industry, which had earlier supported the state-negotiated settlement, began a grass-roots media blitz attacking the new tax. Public opinion appeared to shift against the congressional bill, and it went down to defeat.

The states went back into negotiations with the tobacco companies and produced a new agreement—one that did not require congressional approval. The tobacco companies agreed to limit smoking advertisements and to reimburse the states for more than $200 billion in Medicaid payments made over a twenty-five-year period. The tobacco companies were not given any protection from private lawsuits.

---

blacks became a "way of life" in the region. Segregation was *denationalized;* this reduced national conflict over race, but the price was paid by black Americans. Not until the 1950s and 1960s were questions of segregation and equality again made into national issues. The civil rights movement asserted the supremacy of national law, especially the U.S. Supreme Court's decision in *Brown* v. *Topeka,* 1954, that segregation violated the Fourteenth Amendment's guarantee of equal protection of the law, and later the national Civil Rights Act of 1964. Segregationists asserted the states' rights argument so often in defense of racial discrimination that it became a code word for racism.

Indeed, only now that *national* constitutional and legal guarantees of equal protection of the law are in place is it possible to reassess the true values of federalism. Having established that federalism will not be allowed to justify racial inequality, we are now free to explore the values of decentralized government.

OBSTRUCTING NATIONAL POLICIES   Federalism allows state and local officials to obstruct action on national problems. It allows local leaders and citizens to frustrate national policy, to sacrifice the national interest to local interests. Decentralized government provides an opportunity for local "NIMBYs" (not in my back yard) to obstruct airports, highways, waste disposal plants, public housing, and many other projects in the national interest.

ALLOWING INEQUALITIES   Finally, under federalism the benefits and costs of government are spread unevenly across the nation. For example, some states spend over twice as much on the education of each child in the public schools as other states (see Chapter 15). Welfare benefits in some states are over twice as high as in other states (see Chapter 16). Taxes in some states are over twice as high per capita as in other states (see Chapter 17). Competition among states may keep welfare benefits low in order not to encourage an in-migration of poor people. Federalism allows these differences in policy to develop. Federalism is the opposite of uniformity.

THE STRUCTURE OF AMERICAN FEDERALISM

In deciding in 1869 that a state had no constitutional right to secede from the union, Chief Justice Salmon P. Chase described the legal character of American federalism:

> The preservation of the states and the maintenance of their governments, are as much within the design and care of the constitution as the preservation of the union and the maintenance of the national government. The constitution, in all of its provisions, looks to an indestructible union, composed of indestructible states.[5]

What is meant by "an indestructible union, composed of indestructible states"? American federalism is an indissoluble partnership between the states and the national government. The Constitution of the United States allocated power between two separate authorities, the nation and the states, each of which was to be independent of the other. Both the nation and the states were allowed to enforce their laws directly on individuals through their own officials and courts. The Constitution itself was the only legal source of authority for the division of powers between the states and the nation. The American federal system was designed as a strong national government, coupled with a strong state government, in which authority and power are shared, constitutionally and practically.

The framework of American federalism is determined by (1) the powers delegated by the Constitution of the national government, and the declared supremacy of that government; (2) the constitutional guarantees reserved for the states; (3) the powers denied by the Constitution to both the national government and the states; (4) the constitutional provisions giving the states a role in the compositions of the national government; and (5) the subsequent constitutional and historical development of federalism.

DELEGATED POWERS AND NATIONAL SUPREMACY Article I, Section 8, of the U.S. Constitution lists eighteen grants of power to Congress. These "delegated" or "enumerated" powers include authority over matters of war and foreign affairs, the power to declare war, raise armies, equip navies, and establish rules for the military. Another series of delegated powers is related to control of the economy, including the power to coin money, to control its value, and to regulate foreign and interstate commerce. The national government has been given independent powers of taxation "to pay the debts and provide for the common defense and general welfare of the United States." It has the power to establish its own court system, to decide cases arising under the Constitution and the laws and treaties of the United States and cases involving certain kinds of parties. The national government was given the authority to grant copyright patents, establish post offices, enact bankruptcy laws, punish counterfeiting, punish crimes committed on the high seas, and govern the District of Columbia. (See Table 3–1.) Finally, after seventeen grants of express power, came the power "to make all laws which shall be necessary and proper for carrying into execution the foregoing powers, and all other powers vested by this constitution in the government of the United States or in any department or officer thereof." This is generally referred to as the Necessary and Proper Clause or the Implied Powers Clause.

These delegated powers, when coupled with the National Supremacy Clause of Article VI, ensured a powerful national government. The National Supremacy Clause was quite specific regarding the relationship between the national government and the states. In questions involving conflict between the state laws and the Constitution, laws, or treaties of the United States:

> This constitution, and the laws of the United States which shall be made in pursuance thereof; and all treaties made or which shall be made under the authority of the United States shall be the supreme law of the land; and the judges in every state shall be bound thereby, anything in the constitution or laws of any state to the contrary notwithstanding.

RESERVED POWERS Despite these broad grants of power to the national government, the states retained a great deal of authority over the lives of their citizens. The Tenth Amendment reaffirmed the idea that the national government had only certain delegated powers and that all powers not delegated to it were retained by the states:

> The powers not delegated to the United States by the constitution, nor prohibited by it to the states, are reserved to the states respectively, or to the people.

Delegated, or enumerated, powers. Powers specifically mentioned in the Constitution as belonging to the national government.

Necessary and Proper Clause. Clause in Article 1, Section 8, of the U.S. Constitution granting Congress the power to enact all laws that are "necessary and proper" for carrying out those responsibilities specifically delegated to it. Also referred to as the Implied Powers Clause.

Implied powers. Powers not mentioned specifically in the Constitution as belonging to Congress but inferred as necessary and proper for carrying out the enumerated powers.

National Supremacy Clause. Clause in Article VI of the U.S. Constitution declaring the constitution and laws of the national government "the supreme law of the land" superior to the constitutions and laws of the states.

Reserved powers. Powers not granted to the national government or specifically denied to the states in the Constitution that are recognized by the Tenth Amendment as belonging to the state governments. This guarantee, known as the Reserved Powers Clause, embodies the principle of American federalism.

Table 3–1

ORIGINAL CONSTITUTIONAL DISTRIBUTION OF POWERS

Under the Constitution of 1787, certain powers were delegated to the national government, other powers were shared by the national and state governments, and still other powers were reserved for state governments alone. Similarly, certain powers were denied by the Constitution to the national government, other powers were denied to both the national and state governments, and still other powers were denied only to state governments. Later amendments especially protected individual liberties. Article and section numbers of the U.S. Constitution are shown in parentheses.

Powers Granted by the Constitution

NATIONAL GOVERNMENT
DELEGATED POWERS

Military Affairs and Defense
- Provide for the common defense (I-8)
- Declare war (I-8)
- Raise and support armies (I-8)
- Provide and maintain a navy (I-8)
- Define and punish piracies (I-8)
- Define and punish offenses against the law of nations (I-8)
- Provide for calling forth the militia to execute laws, suppress insurrections, and repel invasions (I-8)
- Provide for organizing, arming, and disciplining militia (I-8)
- Declare the punishment of treason (III-3)

Economic Affairs
- Regulate commerce with foreign nations, among the several states, and with Indian tribes (I-8)
- Establish uniform laws on bankruptcy (I-8)
- Coin money and regulate its value (I-8)
- Fix standards of weights and measures (I-8)
- Provide for patents and copyrights (I-8)
- Establish post offices and post roads (I-8)

Governmental Organization
- Constitute tribunals inferior to the Supreme Court (I-8, III-1)
- Exercise exclusive legislative power over the seat of government and over certain military installations (I-8)
- Admit new states (IV-3)
- Dispose of and regulate territory or property of the United States (IV-3)

"Implied" Powers
- Make necessary and proper laws for carrying expressed powers into execution (I-8)

NATIONAL AND STATE GOVERNMENTS
CONCURRENT POWERS

- Levy taxes (I-8)
- Borrow money (I-8)
- Contract and pay debts (I-8)
- Charter banks and corporations (I-8)
- Make and enforce laws (I-8)
- Establish courts (I-8)
- Provide for the general welfare (I-8)

STATE GOVERNMENTS
RESERVED TO THE STATES

- Regulate intrastate commerce
- Conduct elections
- Provide for public health, safety, and morals
- Establish local government
- Maintain militia (National Guard)
- Ratify amendments to the federal Constitution (V)
- Determine voter qualifications (I-2)

"Reserved" Powers
- Powers not delegated to national government nor denied to the States by the Constitution (X)

Powers Denied by the Constitution

NATIONAL GOVERNMENT	NATIONAL AND STATE GOVERNMENTS	STATE GOVERNMENTS

NATIONAL GOVERNMENT

- Give preference to ports of any state (I-9)
- Impose tax or duty on articles exported from any state (I-9)
- Directly tax except by apportionment among states on population basis (I-9), now superseded as to income tax (Amendment XVI)
- Draw money from Treasury except by appropriation (I-9)

NATIONAL AND STATE GOVERNMENTS

- Grant titles of nobility (I-9)
- Limit suspension of habeas corpus (I-9)
- Issue bills of attainder (I-10)
- Make ex post facto laws (I-10)
- Establish a religion or prohibit free exercise of religion (Amendment I)
- Abridge freedom of speech, press, assembly, or rights of petition (Amendment I)
- Deny right to bear arms protected (Amendment II)
- Restrict quartering of soldiers in private homes (Amendment III)
- Conduct unreasonable searches or seizures (Amendment IV)
- Deny guarantees of fair trials (Amendment V, Amendment VI, and Amendment VII)
- Impose excessive bail or unusual punishments (Amendment VII)
- Take life, liberty, or property without due process (Amendment V)
- Permit slavery (Amendment XIII)
- Deny life, liberty, or property without due process of law (Amendment XIV)
- Deny voting because of race, color, previous servitude (Amendment XV), or sex (Amendment XIX), or age if 18 or over (Amendment XXVI)
- Deny voting because of nonpayment of any tax

STATE GOVERNMENTS

Economic Affairs
- Use legal tender other than gold or silver coins (I-10)
- Issue separate state coinage (I-10)
- Impair the obligation of contracts (I-10)
- Emit bills of credit (I-10)
- Levy import or export duties, except reasonable inspection fees, without consent of Congress (I-10)
- Abridge privileges and immunities of national citizenship (Amendment XIV)
- Make any law that violates federal law (VI)
- Pay for rebellion against United States or for emancipated slaves (Amendment XIV)

Foreign Affairs
- Enter into treaties, alliances, or confederations (I-10)
- Make compact with a foreign state, except by congressional consent (I-10)

Military Affairs
- Issue letters of marque and reprisal (I-10)
- Maintain standing military forces in peace without congressional consent (I-10)
- Engage in war, without congressional consent, except in imminent danger or when invaded (I-10)

The states retained control over the ownership and use of property; the regulation of offenses against persons and property (criminal law and civil law); the regulation of marriage and divorce; the control of business, labor, farming, trades, and professions; the provision of education, welfare, health, hospitals, and other social welfare activities; and provision of highways, roads, canals, and other public works. The states retained full authority over the organization and control of local government units. Finally, the states, like the federal government, possessed the power to tax and spend for the general welfare.

POWERS DENIED TO THE NATION AND STATES   The Constitution denies some powers to both national and state governments; these denials generally safeguard individual rights. Both nation and states are forbidden to pass ex post facto laws or bills of attainder. The first eight amendments to the Constitution, "the Bill of Rights," originally applied to the federal government, but the Fourteenth Amendment, passed by Congress in 1866, provided that the states must also adhere to fundamental guarantees of individual liberty. "No state shall make or enforce any law which shall abridge the privileges or immunities of the citizens of the United States; nor shall any state deprive any person of life, liberty or property without due process of law; nor deny to any person within its jurisdiction equal protection of the laws."

Some powers were denied only to the states, generally as a safeguard to national unity, including the powers to coin money, enter into treaties with foreign powers, interfere with the obligations of contracts, levy duties on imports or exports without congressional consent, maintain military forces in peacetime, engage in war, or enter into compacts with foreign nations or other states.

THE NATIONAL GOVERNMENT'S OBLIGATIONS TO THE STATES   The Constitution imposes several obligations on the national government in its relations with the states. First of all, the states are guaranteed *territorial integrity:* No new state can be created by Congress out of the territory of an existing state without its consent. (Nonetheless, Congress admitted West Virginia to the Union in 1863 when the western counties of Virginia separated from that state during the Civil War. Later a "reconstructed" Virginia legislature gave its approval.) The national government must also guarantee to every state *"a republican form of government."* A republican government is a government by democratically elected representatives. Presumably this clause in the Constitution means that the national government will ensure that no authoritarian or dictatorial regime will be permitted to rule in any state. Apparently this clause does *not* prohibit popular initiatives, referenda, town meetings, or other forms of direct democracy. The Supreme Court has never given any specific meaning to this guarantee. Each state is also guaranteed *equal representation in the U.S. Senate.* Indeed, the Constitution, Article V, prohibits any amendments that would deprive the states of equal representation in the Senate. Finally, the national government is required to *protect each state against foreign invasion and domestic violence.* The protection against foreign invasion is unequivocal, but the clause dealing with domestic violence includes the phrase "upon application of the legislature or the Executive (when the legislature cannot be convened)." Governors have called upon the national government to intervene in riots to maintain public order. But the national government has also intervened *without* "application" by state officials in cases where federal laws are being violated. Perhaps the most important direct intervention was President Dwight Eisenhower's decision to send federal troops to Little Rock High School in Arkansas in 1956 to enforce desegregation, and the Supreme Court's decision in *Brown* v. *Board of Education of Topeka, Kansas* (see Chapter 14).

STATE ROLE IN NATIONAL GOVERNMENT   The states also play an important role in the composition of the national government. U.S. representatives must be apportioned among the states according to their population every ten years. Governors have the authority to fill vacancies in Congress, and every state must have at least one representative regardless of population. The Senate of the United States is composed of two senators from each state regardless of the state's population. The times, places, and manner of holding elections for Congress are determined by the states. The president is chosen by electors, allotted to each state on the basis of its senators and representatives. Finally, amendments to the U.S. Constitution must be ratified by three-fourths of the states. (See Figure 3–1.)

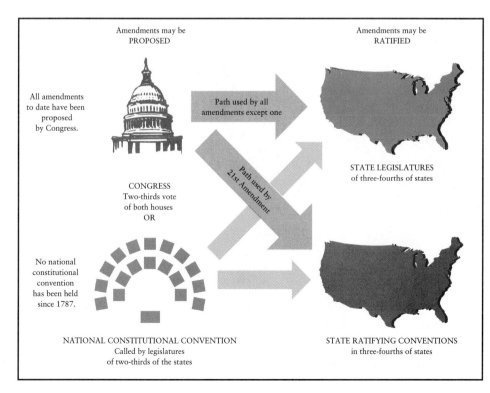

FIGURE 3–1 The States' Role in Constitutional Amendment

■

ERA (Equal Rights Amendment).
A constitutional amendment proposed by Congress but never ratified by the necessary two-thirds of the states. It would have guaranteed "equality of rights under law" for women and men.

BATTLES IN THE STATES OVER CONSTITUTIONAL AMENDMENTS

The power of the states in the American federal system has been demonstrated in several battles over constitutional amendments passed by Congress. According to Article V of the U.S. Constitution, *the Constitution cannot be amended without the approval of three-fourths of the states*, either by their state legislatures or by state constitutional ratifying conventions.

THE DEFEAT OF ERA   In 1972 when Congress sent the Equal Rights Amendment (ERA) to the states for ratification, it did so with overwhelming support of both Democrats and Republicans in the House and the Senate. National opinion polls and most national leaders, including Presidents Nixon, Ford, and Carter, strongly endorsed the simple language of the proposed amendment: "Equality of rights under law shall not be denied or abridged by the United States or by any State on account of sex."

ERA won quick ratification in about half of the states. By 1978, thirty-five state legislatures had ratified ERA. (See Figure 3–2.) (However, five states voted to rescind their earlier ratification. While there is some disagreement about the validity of these "rescissions," most constitutional scholars do not believe a state can rescind its earlier ratification of a constitutional amendment; there is no language in the Constitution referring to rescissions of constitutional amendments.) Leaders of the ERA movement

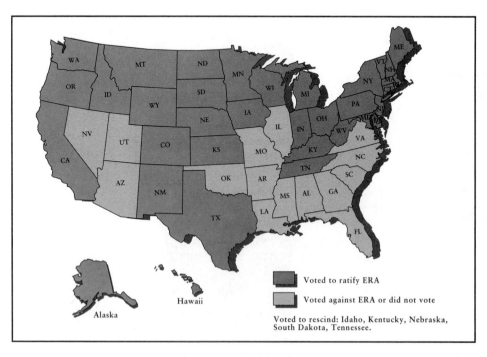

FIGURE 3–2 ERA in the States

Voted to ratify ERA

Voted against ERA or did not vote

Voted to rescind: Idaho, Kentucky, Nebraska, South Dakota, Tennessee.

called upon Congress to grant an unprecedented extension of time beyond the traditional seven years to continue the battle for ratification. (The Constitution, Article V, does not specify how long states can consider a constitutional amendment.) In 1978, Congress (by simple majority vote) granted ERA an unprecedented additional three years for state ratification; the new limit was 1982, a full ten years after Congress proposed the original ERA.

The "Stop ERA" movement gained strength in the states over time. Under the leadership of conservative spokeswoman Phyllis Schafly, an active group of women successfully lobbied *against* ERA in state legislatures. In spite of overwhelming support for ERA from Democratic and Republican presidents and congresses, leading celebrities from television and films, and even a majority of Americans surveyed by national polling organizations, these "ladies in pink" were influential in the defeat of ERA. (The phrase "ladies in pink" refers to a common practice of anti-ERA women lobbyists wearing pink, dressing well, baking apple pies for legislators, and otherwise adopting the traditional symbols of femininity.) Most of the lobbying against ERA in state legislatures was done by women's groups. While not as well organized as the leading feminist groups (NOW, the League of Women Voters, the Women's Political Caucus, and so on), the "ladies in pink" were very much in evidence when state legislatures considered ratification of ERA.[6]

Three-quarters of the states *must* concur in a constitutional amendment. This is a powerful tool of the states in our federal system. The wording of the Constitution cannot be altered without the approval of the states, regardless of how much support such a change in wording may have in Washington. Despite national support for ERA, the amendment fell *three states short* of ratification by the necessary thirty-eight states. Last-ditch attempts to pass ERA in states where the battle was close (Florida, Illinois, and North Carolina) failed in 1982.

THE DEFEAT OF THE DISTRICT OF COLUMBIA AMENDMENT   The Constitution grants Congress the power to govern the District of Columbia, but over time Congress has delegated considerable home rule to the District. Washington elects its own mayor and council, levies city taxes, and provides municipal services to its residents. The Twenty-third Amendment, ratified by the states in 1961, gives Washingtonians three *presidential* electors, but residents of the city have never had voting members of Congress. (The District's only congressional representation is its *nonvoting* delegates to the House and Senate, who may serve on committees and participate in debates on the floor.) In 1978 Congress passed and sent to the states a constitutional amendment to grant the District of Columbia two U.S. senators and as many representatives as their population would warrant if it were a state (currently one). Congress placed a seven-year time limit on ratification by the states in the amendment itself, thus preventing a time extension by simple majority vote of the House and Senate.

The DC amendment passed both houses of Congress with well over the necessary two-thirds majority and the support of both Democrats and Republicans. But opposition in the states arose quickly. Much of the opposition was political: The District was seen as predominantly black, liberal, and Democratic. Only about 8 percent of the District's voters are registered as Republicans. The District itself has a less-than-reassuring record of self-government. (See *"Up Close:* Can Washington, DC, Govern Itself?" in Chapter 1.) By the 1985 deadline only sixteen states, well short of the necessary thirty-eight, had ratified the amendment.

THE SURPRISE PASSAGE OF THE TWENTY-SEVENTH AMENDMENT   As part of the Bill of Rights, Congress in 1789 sent to the states an amendment that would prohibit a pay raise for members of Congress until after the intervention of an election for House members. The amendment had no time limit for ratification attached to it. But only six of the original thirteen states ratified Madison's pay raise amendment, and it was largely forgotten. However, as congressional scandals mounted in the 1980s and public confidence in Congress plummeted, the old amendment was rediscovered. (By one account, a University of Texas student ran across the amendment in 1982 and realized it had no time limit. Using his own money he undertook a national campaign that resulted in twenty-six states ratifying the amendment. But he received only a "C" on his research paper.)[7] As more and more states ratified the two-hundred-year-old amendment, Congress should have realized that their behavior was under scrutiny. But Congress proceeded in 1989 to vote itself a 50 percent pay raise, touching off a storm of protest. (Nationwide polls indicated that 82 percent of Americans opposed the pay increase.) Angry voters looked for ways to rein in an arrogant Congress. Fifteen additional states rushed to ratify Madison's amendment.

Some scholars, as well as leaders in Congress, argued that ratification of the amendment after 203 years did not meet "the standard of timeliness." They argued that even though the Constitution itself placed no time limits on ratification, Article V "implied" that ratification should occur within a "reasonable" time. But when the archivist of the United States, Don Wilson, officially certified the adoption of the Twenty-seventh Amendment in 1992 as he was authorized to do by law, congressional leaders were stymied. Although they were irate over the archivist's action, they were unable to reverse it. Individual members of Congress raced to join in the popular sentiment, fearing that any effort to undo the amendment would be dealt with severely by the voters in the next election. Both houses voted nearly unanimously to endorse the amendment. The states had succeeded in administering an unexpected reprimand to Congress.

HOW MONEY SHIFTED POWER TO WASHINGTON

Over the years the national government has acquired much greater power in the federal system than the Founders originally envisioned. (See *"Up Close:* Historic Landmarks in the Development of American Federalism," p. 68.) The "delegated" powers of the national government are now so broadly defined—particularly the power to tax and spend for the general welfare—that the government in Washington is involved in every aspect of American life. (The argument that constitutionally Congress can tax and spend only in support of its *enumerated* powers was rejected by the Supreme

Court.)[8] Today there are really no segments of public activity fully "reserved" to the states or the people.

THE EARLIEST FEDERAL AID   It is possible to argue that even in the earliest days of the Republic, the national government was involved in public activities that were not specifically delegated to it in the Constitution.[9] The first Congress of the United States in the famous Northwest Ordinance, providing for the government of the territories to the west of the Appalachian Mountains, authorized grants of federal land for the establishment of public schools, and by so doing, showed a concern for education, an area "reserved" to the states by the Constitution. Again in 1863, in the Morrill Land Grant Act, Congress provided grants of land to the states to promote higher education.

MONEY, POWER, AND THE INCOME TAX   The date 1913, when the Sixteenth Amendment gave the federal government the power to tax income directly, marked the beginning of a new era in American federalism. Congress had been given the power to tax and spend for the general welfare in Article I of the Constitution. However, the Sixteenth Amendment helped to shift the balance of financial power from the states to Washington, when it gave Congress the power to tax the incomes of corporations and individuals on a progressive basis. The income tax gave the federal government the power to raise large sums of money, which it proceeded to spend for the general welfare as well as for defense. It is no coincidence that the first major grant-in-aid programs (agricultural extension in 1914, highways in 1916, vocational education in 1917, and public health in 1918) all came shortly after the inauguration of the federal income tax.

FEDERAL GRANTS-IN-AID   The federal "grant-in-aid" has been the principal instrument in the expansion of national power. More than one-fifth of all state and local government revenues are currently derived from federal grants. This money is paid out through a staggering number and variety of programs. Federal grants may be obtained to assist in everything from the preservation of historic buildings, the development of minority-owned businesses, the education of the handicapped, the construction of airports, to the funding of disaster relief and tree preservation.

The largest portion of federal grant-in-aid money is devoted to health (especially Medicaid's health care for the poor) and welfare (especially Aid to Families with Dependent Children). In 1996, over 67 percent of total grant money was used for these purposes (see Table 3–2). Only 10 percent was used for highways and transit, and only about 16 percent for education, training, employment, and social services.

MONEY WITH STRINGS ATTACHED   Today, grant-in-aid programs are the single most important source of federal influence over state and local activity. A grand-in-aid is defined as payment of funds by one level of government (national or state) to be ex-

■
Grants-in-aid.
Payments of funds from the national government to state or local governments or from a state government to local governments for specific purposes.

UP CLOSE

HISTORIC LANDMARKS IN THE DEVELOPMENT OF AMERICAN FEDERALISM

The American federal system is a product of more than its formal constitutional provisions. It has also been shaped by interpretations by the courts of constitutional principles as well as the history of disputes that have occurred over state and national authority.

Marbury v. Madison (1803): Expanding Federal Court Authority

Chief Justice John Marshall, who presided over the Supreme Court from 1801 to 1835, became a major architect of American federalism. Under John Marshall, *the Supreme Court assumed the role of arbiter in disputes between state and national authority*. It was under John Marshall that the Supreme Court in *Marbury* v. *Madison* assumed the power to interpret the U.S. Constitution authoritatively. The fact that the referee of disputes between state and national authority has been the *national* Supreme Court has had a profound influence on the development of American federalism. Since the Supreme Court is a *national* institution, one might say that in disputes between nation and states, one of the members of the two contending teams is also serving as umpire. Constitutionally speaking then, there is really *no* limitation on national as against state authority *if* all three branches of the national government—the Congress, the president, and the Court—act together to override state authority.

McCulloch v. Maryland (1819): Expanding Implied Powers of the National Government

In the case of *McCulloch* v. *Maryland,* Chief Justice John Marshall provided a broad interpretation of the Necessary and Proper Clause:

> Let the end be legitimate, let it be within the scope of the Constitution, and all means which are appropriate, which are plainly adopted to the end, which are not prohibited but consistent with the letter and the spirit of the Constitution, are constitutional.[a]

The *McCulloch* case firmly established the principle that the Necessary and Proper Clause gives Congress the right to choose its means for carrying out the enumerated powers of the national government. Today, Congress can devise programs, create agencies, and establish national laws on the basis of long chains of reasoning from the most meager phrases of the constitutional text because of the broad interpretation of the Necessary and Proper Clause.

Secession and the Civil War (1861–1865): Maintaining the "Indestructable Union"

The Civil War was, of course, the greatest crisis of the American federal system. Did a state have the right to oppose national law to the point of secession? In the years preceding the Civil War, John C. Calhoun argued that the Constitution was a compact made by the *states* in a sovereign capacity rather than by the *people* in their national capacity. Calhoun contended that the federal government was an agent of the states, that the

pended by another level (state or local) for a specified purpose, usually on a matching-funds basis (the federal government puts up only as much as the state or locality) and "in accordance with prescribed standards of requirements." No state or local government is *required* to accept grants-in-aid. Participation in grant-in-aid programs is voluntary. So in theory, if conditions attached to the grant money are too oppressive, state and local governments can simply decline to participate and pass up these funds. Yet it is often asserted that states are "bribed" by the temptation of much-needed federal money and "blackmailed" by the thought that other states will get the money, which was raised in part by federal taxes on the state's own citizens. (See "*Up Close:* Federalism and the Drinking Age," p. 71.)

states retained their sovereignty in this compact, and that the federal government must not violate the compact, under the penalty of state nullification or even secession from the Union.

The issue was decided in the nation's bloodiest war. What was decided on the battlefield between 1861 and 1865 was confirmed by the Supreme Court in 1869: "Ours is an indestructible union, composed of indestructible states."[b] Yet the states' rights doctrines, and political disputes over the character of American federalism, did not disappear with Lee's surrender at Appomattox. The Thirteenth, Fourteenth, and Fifteenth Amendments, passed by the Reconstruction Congress, were clearly aimed at limiting state power in the interests of individual freedom. The Thirteenth Amendment eliminated slavery in the states; the Fifteenth Amendment prevented states from discriminating against blacks in the right to vote; and the Fourteenth Amendment declared that "No State shall make or enforce any law which shall abridge the privileges or immunities of citizens of the United States; nor shall any state deprive any person of life, liberty, or property without due process of law; nor deny to any person within its jurisdiction the equal protection of the laws." These amendments delegated to Congress the power to secure their enforcement. Yet for several generations these amendments were narrowly construed and added little, if anything, to national power.

National Labor Relations Board v. Jones and Laughlin Steel Corp. *(1937)*: *Expanding Interstate Commerce*

The Industrial Revolution in America created a *national* economy with a nationwide network of transportation and communication and the potential for national economic depressions. Yet for a time, the Supreme Court placed obstacles in the way of national authority over the economy, and by so doing the Court created a "crisis" in American federalism. For many years, the Court narrowly construed interstate commerce to mean only the movement of goods and services across state lines, insisting that agriculture, mining, manufacturing, and labor relations were outside the reach of the delegated powers of the national government. However, when confronted with the Great Depression of the 1930s and President Franklin D. Roosevelt's threat to "pack" the Court with additional members to secure approval of his New Deal measures, the Court yielded. In *National Labor Relations Board v. Jones and Laughlin Steel Corporation* in 1937, the Court recognized the principle that production and distribution of goods and services for a national market could be regulated by Congress under the Interstate Commerce Clause. The effect was to give the national government effective control over the national economy.

Brown *v.* Board of Education *(1954)*: *Guaranteeing Civil Rights*

After World War I, the Supreme Court began to build a national system of civil rights that was based upon the Fourteenth Amendment. In early cases, the Court held that the Fourteenth Amendment prevented states from interfering with free speech, free press, or religious practices. Not until 1954, in the Supreme Court's landmark desegregation decision in *Brown* v. *Board of Education* in Topeka, Kansas, did the Court begin to call for the full assertion of national authority on behalf of civil rights.[c] The Supreme Court's use of the Fourteenth Amendment to ensure a national system of civil rights supported by the power of the federal government was an important step in the evolution of the American federal system.

[a]*McCulloch* v. *Maryland,* 4 Wheaton 316.
[b]*Texas* v. *White,* 7 Wallace 700 (1869).
[c]*Brown* v. *Board of Education of Topeka, Kansas,* 347 U.S. 483 (1954).

Currently, federal grants-in-aid can be described as either "categorical grants" or "block grants," depending on the extent of federal oversight of how the money is spent.

Categorical Grants: Grants for specific, narrow projects. Each project must be approved by a federal administrative agency. Most federal aid money is distributed in the form of categorical grants. Categorical grants can be distributed on a project basis or a formula basis. Grants made on a project basis are distributed by federal administrative agencies to state or local governments that compete for project funds in their applications. Fed-

Table 3–2

FEDERAL GRANTS-IN-AID BY FUNCTION

	Millions of Dollars	Percent by Major Function
National defense	9	0.0
Energy	435	0.2
Natural resources and environmental protection	4,118	1.7
Agriculture	661	0.3
Transportation (airports, highways, transit)	25,877	11.0
Community and regional development	9,344	4.0
Education, employment, training, social services	35,926	15.2
Health (Medicaid)	103,407	43.9
Income security (family assistance, food stamps, housing)	59,888	25.4
Veterans benefits and services	279	0.1
Administration of justice	2,644	1.1
General government	2,191	0.9
Totals	235,435	100.0

Source: U.S. Office of Management and Budget, *Historical Tables, Budget of the State Government,* FY 98.

eral agencies have a great deal of discretion in selecting specific projects for support, and they can exercise direct control over the projects. Most categorical grants are distributed to state or local governments according to a fixed formula set by Congress. Federal administrative agencies may require reports and adherence to rules and guidelines, but they do not choose which specific projects to fund.

Block Grant: A grant for a general governmental function, such as health, social services, law enforcement, education, or community development. State and local governments have fairly wide discretion in deciding how to spend federal block grant money within a functional area. For example, cities receiving "community development" block grants can decide for themselves about specific neighborhood development projects, housing projects, community facilities, etc. All block grants are distributed on a formula basis set by Congress.

GRANTSMANSHIP   Federal money flows unevenly among the states (see "*Rankings of the States:* Reliance on Federal Aid," p. 72). The federal grant system is not neutral in its impact on the states, nor is it intended to be. Many grant programs are based upon formulas that incorporate various indications of need and financial ability. Federal aid is supposed to be "targeted" on national problems.[10] The effect of differential grant allocations among the states, combined with differences among state popula-

UP CLOSE

FEDERALISM AND THE DRINKING AGE

Nowhere among Congress's enumerated powers in the U.S. Constitution do we find the power to regulate the consumption of alcoholic beverages. Traditionally, the "reserved" powers of the states included the protection of the health, safety, and well-being of their own citizens. And every state set minimum drinking age laws of its own.

In the early 1970s most states lowered their drinking age to eighteen, influenced perhaps by the Twenty-sixth Amendment giving eighteen-year-olds the right to vote. But in the early 1980s, the states individually began to raise the drinking age, as part of a national movement against drunk driving. By 1984 about half of the states had changed the legal drinking age to twenty-one (such as California); other states chose nineteen (including New York, Florida, and Texas) or twenty (such as Massachusetts and Connecticut); and still other states allowed eighteen-year-olds to buy beer and wine but required a person to be twenty-one in order to buy "distilled spirits" (such as Colorado and Kansas). Only a few states (Vermont, Rhode Island, Louisiana, and Hawaii) retained a general eighteen-year-old drinking age.

The minimum drinking age became a national issue largely as a result of emotional appeals by groups such as Mothers Against Drunk Driving (MADD). Politically these appeals were more effective than any scientific studies of alcohol-related deaths. Nonetheless, statistical evidence presented to Congress by the National Transportation Safety Board showed that teenagers were more likely to be involved in alcohol-related traffic deaths than nonteenagers. Indeed, drunk driving was (and remains) the leading cause of death among teenagers.[a] The National Student Association, restaurant owners, and liquor industry countered that teenagers were no worse offenders than those in the twenty-one to twenty-five age group and that the selection of all teenagers for special restrictions was age discrimination. But the tragic stories told at televised committee hearings by grieving mothers of dead teenagers swept away the opposition.

Federalism arguments were also swept away. Several senators argued that a national drinking age infringed on the powers of the states in a matter traditionally under state control. However, the new law did not *directly* mandate a national drinking age. Instead, it ordered the withholding of 10 percent of all federal highway funds from any state that failed to raise its minimum drinking age to twenty-one. States retained the right to ignore the national drinking age and give up a significant portion of their highway funds. This was the same approach taken by Congress in 1974 in establishing a national 55-mile-per-hour speed limit. Opponents of this device labeled it "federal blackmail" and a federal intrusion into state responsibilities. For some state officials the issue was not teen drinking but rather the preemption of state authority.

Constitutionally, Congress was exercising its powers to spend money for the general welfare. Congress was not *directly* legislating in an area "reserved" to the states—protection of health, safety, and well-being. Instead, Congress was threatening to withhold some *federal* highway grant monies from states that did not meet a federal requirement.[b] Technically states remain free to set their own minimum drinking age. Despite heated arguments in many state legislatures, all adopted the twenty-one-year-old national drinking age by 1990. Money is power; this axiom holds true in the American federal system as in politics generally.

[a]*Congressional Quarterly Weekly Report,* June 30, 1984, p. 1557. National Highway Transportation Safety Administration, Federal Accident Report, July 1996. See also www.madd.org on the Internet.

[b]*South Dakota* v. *Debe,* 438 U.S. 203 (1987).

tions in federal tax collections, is to *redistribute* federal money throughout the nation. The big winners in the federal grant game are generally rural states; the losers are the urban states.

The rush to Washington to ensure that states and cities receive their "fair share" of federal grant money, together with concerns over federal interference in the conduct of state and local government, has produced a great deal of intergovernmental lobbying at the nation's capital. The most influential organizations seeking to influence intergovernmental affairs are listed in Table 3–3. In addition to these organizations, various professional associations represent specific state and local government officials. The most notable is the International City Managers Association; others include the National Association of State Budget Officers, National Association of Attorneys Gen-

RANKINGS OF THE STATES

RELIANCE ON FEDERAL AID

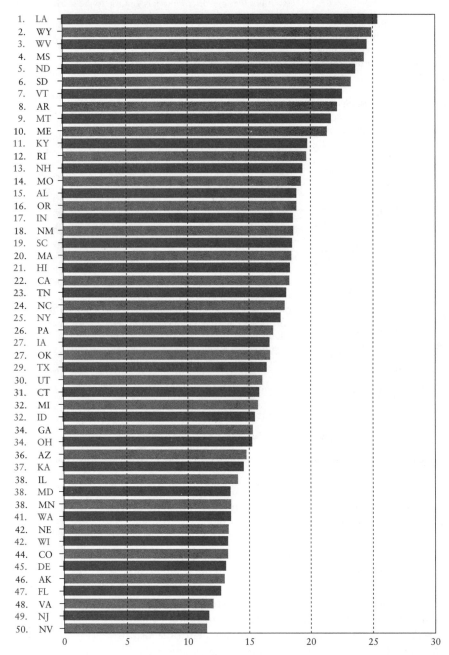

1. LA	
2. WY	
3. WV	
4. MS	
5. ND	
6. SD	
7. VT	
8. AR	
9. MT	
10. ME	
11. KY	
12. RI	
13. NH	
14. MO	
15. AL	
16. OR	
17. IN	
18. NM	
19. SC	
20. MA	
21. HI	
22. CA	
23. TN	
24. NC	
25. NY	
26. PA	
27. IA	
27. OK	
29. TX	
30. UT	
31. CT	
32. MI	
32. ID	
34. GA	
34. OH	
36. AZ	
37. KA	
38. IL	
38. MD	
38. MN	
41. WA	
42. NE	
42. WI	
44. CO	
45. DE	
46. AK	
47. FL	
48. VA	
49. NJ	
50. NV	

Percent of State and Local Government Revenue from Federal Government

Source: Data from U.S. Bureau of the Census, *Governmental Finances* (1997).

Table 3–3

INTERGOVERNMENTAL ORGANIZATIONS	
Council of State Governments 3560 Iron Works Pike Lexington, KY 40578	U.S. Conference of Mayors 1620 Eye St. N.W. Washington, DC 20006
National Governors Association 444 N. Capitol St. N.W. Washington, DC 20001	National Association of Counties 440 1st St. N.W. Washington, DC 20001
National Conference of State Legislatures 1560 Broadway Denver, CO 80202	National Association of Towns and Townships 1522 K St. N.W. Washington, DC 20005
National League of Cities 1301 Pennsylvania Ave. N.W. Washington, DC 20004	

eral, American Association of State Highway and Transportation Officials, and American Association of School Administrators. Most individual states now maintain offices in Washington with staff committed to looking after their interests.

THE POLITICS OF GRANTS-IN-AID

From the earliest days of the Republic, American statesmen have argued over federalism. In recent years, political conflict over federalism—over the decision between national versus state and local responsibilities and finances—has tended to follow traditional "liberal" and "conservative" political cleavages. Generally, liberals seek to enhance the power of the *national* government because they believe that people's lives can be changed—and bettered—by the exercise of national governmental power. The government in Washington has more power and resources than do state and local governments, which many liberals regard as too slow, cumbersome, weak, and unresponsive. Thus liberalism and centralization are closely related in American politics.

The liberal argument for national authority can be summarized as follows:

- There is insufficient awareness of social problems by state and local governments. The federal government must take the lead in civil rights, equal employment opportunities, care for the poor and aged, the provision of adequate medical care for all Americans, and the elimination of urban poverty and blight. Grants-in-aid permit the government to set national goals and priorities in all levels of government.

- Grants-in-aid provide the necessary impetus for social change. It is difficult to achieve change when reform-minded citizens must deal with fifty state governments and over 80,000 local governments. Change is more likely to be accomplished by a strong central government.

- Finally, grants-in-aid provide an opportunity for the national government to ensure a uniform level of public service throughout the nation—for example, federal grants-in-aid help ensure a minimum level of existence for the poverty-stricken regardless of where they live. This aspect of federal policy assumes that in some parts of the nation, state and local governments are unable, or perhaps unwilling, to devote their resources to raising public service levels to minimum national standards.

Conservatives, in contrast, are skeptical about the "good" that government can do and believe that adding to the power of the national government is not an effective way of resolving society's problems. On the contrary, they often argue that "government is the problem, not the solution." Excessive federal government regulation, burdensome taxation, and big spending combine to restrict individual freedom, penalize work and savings, and destroy incentives for economic growth. Government should be kept small, controllable, and close to the people.

Conservative objections to federal grant-in-aid programs can be summarized as follows:

- Grass-roots government promotes a sense of self-responsibility and self-reliance. State and local government can better adapt public programs to local needs and conditions. Federal grants-in-aid are invariably accompanied by federal standards or "guidelines," which must be adhered to if states and communities are to receive their federal money. While no state is required to accept a federal grant and its restrictions, it is very difficult for states and communities to resist the pressure to accept federal money.

- Federal grants cause state and local officials to overspend what looks to them like "free" money. Overspending on programs or services that local residents would not be willing to pay for out of their *own* tax revenues creates waste and inefficiency and contributes to the overall growth of government. Federal money is not "free": It comes from the *nation's* taxpayers. Local governments are sometimes pressured to apply for funds for projects they do not really need, simply because federal funds are available.

- Finally, the grant-in-aid system assumes that federal officials are better judges of goals and priorities at all levels of government than are state or local officials. In many grant programs federal officials must approve each funded project—a housing project in Des Moines, a sewage disposal system in Baton Rouge, an urban renewal project in Alabama. Block grants, which allocate federal funds on a formula basis to states and communities for general purposes like "community development" or "mental health" provide more flexibility than project grants. But Congress cannot resist attaching directions for the use of these grants.

UP CLOSE

WHICH GOVERNMENT DOES THE BEST JOB?

Americans appear to be ambivalent about federalism. On the one hand, most surveys show that Americans have greater confidence in their state and local governments than in the federal government. In general, they would prefer that power be concentrated at the state rather than the federal level. They believe that the federal government wastes more money than state or local governments.

Yet at the same time most Americans want the federal government, rather than state or local governments, to run programs in many specific policy areas.

Trust and Confidence

In which of the following people in government do you have the most trust and confidence?

Federal government	19
State government	22
Local government	37

Generally speaking, which do you trust to do a better job of running things—the federal government or your state government?

Federal government	27
State government	69

Power

Does the federal government have too much power, do the state governments have too much power, or is the balance about right?

Federal too much	48
States too much	6
About right	38

Best Job

Which level of government does the best job of dealing with the problems it faces?

Federal 14%
State 34%
Local 41%

Waste

From which level of government do you get the LEAST for your money?

Local government 19%
State government 21%
Federal government 46%

Involvement in Programs

Which level of government should run the following programs?

	Federal	State
Service to immigrants	60	15
Health care	36	28
Protection of civil rights	64	37

Note: All figures in percentages of U.S. public in national opinion surveys. No Opinions and Don't Knows not shown.

Sources: See Advisory Commission on Intergovernmental Relations, *Changing Public Attitudes on Governments and Taxes* (Washington, DC: ACIR, annual); and Rockefeller Institute, *Bulletin 1996: The Devolution Revolution* (Albany, NY: Rockefeller Institute, 1996), reporting surveys by ABC News/*Washington Post*, March 16–19, 1995; and *State Legislatures* (July/August 1995); responses on best job from Gallup/CNN/*USA Today* Poll reported in *The Polling Report* (February 10, 1997).

Americans are divided over the merits of these arguments. (See "*Up Close:* Which Government Does the Best Job?") Most national opinion surveys reveal greater trust and confidence in state and local government than in the federal government. But many Americans believe that the federal government can do a better job handling specific issues such as protecting civil rights. There is no way to settle these arguments about federalism; they have been heard for over 200 years in American politics.

FEDERALISM: VARIATIONS ON THE THEME

DUAL FEDERALISM (1787–1913)   For the nation's first hundred years, the pattern of federal–state relations has been described as dual federalism. Under this pattern, the

■
Dual federalism.
Early concept of federalism in which national and state powers were clearly distinguished and functionally separate.

Cooperative federalism.
Model of federalism in which national, state, and local governments work together exercising common policy responsibilities.

Centralized federalism.
Model of federalism in which the national government assumes primary responsibility for determining national goals in all major policy areas and directs state and local government activity through conditions attached to money grants.

states and the nation divided most governmental functions. The national government concentrated its attention on the "delegated" powers—national defense, foreign affairs, tariffs, commerce crossing state lines, coining money, establishing standard weights and measures, maintaining a post office and building post roads, and admitting new states. State governments decided the important domestic policy issues—slavery (until the Civil War), education, welfare, health, and criminal justice. This separation of policy responsibilities was once compared to a "layer cake,"[11] with local governments at the base, state governments in the middle, and the national government at the top.

COOPERATIVE FEDERALISM (1913–1964)   The Industrial Revolution and the development of a national economy, the income tax, which shifted financial resources to the national government, and the challenges of two world wars and the Great Depression, all combined to end the distinction between national and state concerns. The new pattern of federal–state relations was labeled cooperative federalism. Both the nation and the states exercised responsibilities for welfare, health, highways, education, and criminal justice. This merging of policy responsibilities was compared to a "marble cake." "As the colors are mixed in a marble cake, so functions are mixed in the American federal system."[12]

The Great Depression of the 1930s forced states to ask for federal financial assistance in dealing with poverty, unemployment, and old age. Governors welcomed massive federal public works projects. In addition, the federal government intervened directly in economic affairs, labor relations, business practices, and agriculture. Through the grant-in-aid device, the national government cooperated with the states in public assistance, employment services, child welfare, public housing, urban renewal, highway building, and vocational education.

Yet even in this period of shared national-state responsibility, the national government emphasized cooperation in achieving common national and state goals. Congress generally acknowledged that it had no direct constitutional authority to regulate public health, safety, or welfare.

CENTRALIZED FEDERALISM (1964–1980)   Over the years it became increasingly difficult to maintain the fiction that the national government was merely assisting the states in performing their domestic responsibility. By the time President Lyndon B. Johnson launched the "Great Society" in 1964, the federal government clearly set forth its own "national" goals. Virtually all problems confronting American society—from solid-waste disposal and water and air pollution to consumer safety, home insulation, noise abatement, and even metric conversion—were declared to be national problems. Congress legislated directly on any matter it chose, without regard to its "enumerated powers" and without pretense to financial assistance. The Supreme Court no longer concerned itself with the "reserved" powers of the states; the Tenth Amendment lost most of its meaning. The pattern of national–state relations became centralized. As for the cake analogies, one commentator observed: "The frosting had moved up to the top, something like a pineapple upside-down cake."[13]

NEW FEDERALISM (1980–1985)   From time to time efforts have been made to reverse the flow of power to Washington and return responsibilities to state and local government. The phrase "New Federalism" originated in the administration of President Richard M. Nixon, who used it to describe General Revenue Sharing—federal sharing of tax revenues with state and local governments with few strings attached. Later, "New Federalism" was used by President Ronald Reagan to describe a series of proposals designed to reduce federal involvement in domestic programs and encourage states and cities to undertake greater policy responsibilities themselves.

General Revenue Sharing (GRS) was begun in 1972 as a conservative alternative to categorical grants by federal agencies for specific projects. It was argued that unrestricted federal money grants to state and local government was preferable to centralized bureaucratic decision making in Washington. GRS promised to reverse the flow of power to federal bureaucrats, end excessive red tape, and revitalize state and local governments. GRS was strongly supported by state and local government officials, who were happy to have the federal government collect tax money and then turn it over to them to spend. But the Reagan administration, confronting high federal deficits and wanting to reduce Washington's role in domestic policy, undertook a long and eventually successful effort in 1986 to end General Revenue Sharing.

Another Reagan approach to cutting federal strings in grant-in-aid programs was greater reliance on the block grant. Congress endorsed many block grants in the early 1980s, but the struggle between categorical grant interest (liberals and Democrats) and the consolidationists (Reagan and the Republicans) was really a draw. Many categorical grant programs were merged (notably in health services; alcohol, drug abuse, and mental health; social services; maternal and child health; community services; community development; and education), but many others remained independent.

Another accomplishment of the Reagan administration's New Federalism was a temporary reversal of the historical trend of the greater dependence of state and local governments on federal money. In the years prior to 1980, state and local governments had become increasingly dependent on federal grants as sources of revenue. Federal grants rose to over one-quarter of all state–local expenditures in 1980 (see Table 3–4). Total federal aid dollars continued to rise during the Reagan years, but not at the same rate as in previous years.

However, it is not likely that presidents or Congress members or candidates for these national offices will ever be moved to restrain national power. People expect federal officials to "do something" about virtually every problem that confronts individuals, families, communities, or the nation. Politicians gain very little by telling their constituents that a particular problem is not a federal problem. Indeed, by the 1990s under Republican President George Bush as well as Democratic President Bill Clinton, the flow of federal aid dollars to the states accelerated. Reversing the trend of the 1980s, state and local government dependence on federal revenue began to rise again.

REPRESENTATIONAL FEDERALISM (1985–1994)   Despite centralizing tendencies, it was still widely assumed prior to 1985 that the Congress could not directly legislate how state and local governments should go about performing their traditional functions. However, in its 1985 *Garcia* decision,[14] the U.S. Supreme Court appeared to remove all barriers to direct congressional legislation in matters traditionally reserved to

Table 3–4

TRENDS IN FEDERAL GRANTS-IN-AID				

	Total Federal Grants	Federal Grants as a Percent of:		
	(BILLION DOLLARS)	TOTAL FEDERAL SPENDING	STATE AND LOCAL EXPENDITURES	GROSS NATIONAL PRODUCT
1950	2.3	5.3	10.4	0.8
1960	7.0	7.6	14.6	1.4
1970	24.1	12.3	19.2	2.4
1975	49.8	15.0	22.7	3.3
1980	91.5	15.5	25.8	3.4
1985	105.9	11.2	21.1	2.7
1990	136.9	11.0	18.0	3.0
1994	217.3	14.6	21.9	3.3
1996	227.8	14.8	22.2	3.1
1998 est.	244.7	15.0	23.5	3.0

Sources: Statistical Abstract of the United States 1997, p. 302; Budget of the United States Government 1999.

the states. The case arose after Congress directly ordered state and local governments to pay minimum wages to their employees. The Court dismissed arguments that the nature of American federalism and the Reserved Powers Clause of the Tenth Amendment prevented Congress from directly legislating in state affairs. The Court declared that there were *no* "a priori definitions of state sovereignty," *no* "discrete limitations on the objects of federal authority," and *no* protection of state powers in the U.S. Constitution. According to the Court: "State sovereign interests . . . are more properly protected by procedural safeguards inherent in the structure of the federal system than by judicially created limitations on federal power." It said that the only protection for state powers was to be found in the states' role in electing U.S. senators, members of the U.S. House of Representatives, and the president.

The Supreme Court's *Garcia* case ruling became known as "representational federalism"—a denial that there is any constitutional division of powers between states and nation and an assertion that federalism is defined by the role of the states in electing members of Congress and the president. The United States is said to retain a federal system because national officials are selected from subunits of government—the president through the allocation of electoral college votes to the states, and the Congress through the allocation of two Senate seats per state and the apportionment of representatives to states based on population. Whatever protection exists for state power and independence must be found in the national political process—in the influence of state and district voters on their senators and congress members. Representational federalism does not recognize any constitutionally protected powers of the states.

However, the Supreme Court may be unwilling to jettison altogether the notion of federalism as the division of power between nation and states. Justice Sandra Day O'Connor, a former Arizona legislator and appellate court judge, has been a staunch defender of federalism on the Supreme Court. Quoting from the *Federalist* and citing the Tenth Amendment, Justice O'Connor wrote the majority opinion in a case considering whether Congress's Age Discrimination Employment Act invalidated a provision of the Missouri Constitution requiring judges to retire at age 70.[15] She cited the "constitutional balance of federal and state powers" as a reason for upholding the Missouri Constitution. Only a "clear statement" by Congress of its intent to override a traditional state power would justify doing so. This "clear statement" rule presumably governs federal laws that may be in conflict with state laws or constitutions. The rule does not prevent Congress from directly regulating state government activity, but it requires Congress to say unambiguously that this is its intent.

COERCIVE FEDERALISM: PREEMPTIONS AND MANDATES

Can Congress *directly* regulate the traditional functions of state and local governments? We know that Congress can influence the actions of state and local governments by offering them grants of money and then threatening to withdraw them if they do not meet federal rules, regulations, or "guidelines." But can Congress, in the exercise of its broad constitutional powers, legislate directly about traditional functions of state and local governments—schools, streets, police and fire protection, water and sewers, refuse disposal? Can the national government by law treat the states as administrative units required to carry out the mandates of Congress?

Certainly the historical answer to this question was "No." A typical nineteenth-century description of federalism by the U.S. Supreme Court asserted that the federal government could not intrude or interfere with the independent powers of state governments and vice versa:

> There are within the territorial limits of each state two governments [state and national], restricted in their spheres of action, but independent of each other, and supreme within their respective spheres. Each has its separate departments, each has its distinct laws, and each has its own tribunes for their enforcement. Neither government can intrude within the jurisdiction of the other or authorize any interference therein by its judicial officers with the action of the other.[16]

Perhaps this separation and independence never really characterized relations between the national government and the state governments. But at least state governments were viewed as independent authorities that could not be directly coerced by the national government in their traditional functions.

CONGRESSIONAL REGULATION OF STATE TAXES   More than a century ago, the U.S. Supreme Court held that Congress could not levy taxes on the states or on their bonds or notes.[17] Intergovernmental tax immunity was believed to be an integral part of the Tenth Amendment's guarantee of the reserved powers of the states. The states could not tax federal bonds and the nation could not tax state bonds. But in 1987 the

U.S. Supreme Court shocked state and local officials and the municipal bond market by holding that Congress could if it wished levy taxes on the interest received from state and local bonds. In a dissent, Justice Sandra Day O'Connor observed that "the Court has failed to enforce the constitutional safeguards of state autonomy and self-sufficiency that may be found in the Tenth Amendment and the Guarantee Clause, as well as in the principles of federalism implicit in the Constitution."[18]

FEDERAL PREEMPTIONS   The supremacy of federal laws over those of the states, spelled out in the Supremacy Clause of the Constitution, permits Congress to decide whether or not state laws in a particular field are preempted by federal law. *Total preemption* refers to the federal government's assumption of all regulatory powers in a particular field—for example, copyrights, bankruptcy, railroads, and airlines. No state regulations in a totally preempted field are permitted. *Partial preemption* stipulates that a state law on the same subject is valid as long as it does not conflict with the federal law in the same area. For example, the Occupational Safety and Health Act of 1970 specifically permits state regulation of any occupational safety or health issue on which the federal Occupational Safety and Health Administration (OSHA) has *not* developed a standard; but once OSHA enacts a standard, all state standards are nullified. Yet another form of the partial preemption, the *standard partial preemption*, permits states to regulate activities in a field already regulated by the federal government, as long as state regulatory standards are at least as stringent as those of the federal government. Usually states must submit their regulations to the responsible federal agency for approval; the federal agency may revoke a state's regulating power if it fails to enforce the approved standards. For example, the federal Environmental Protection Agency (EPA) permits state environmental regulations that meet or exceed EPA standards. Occasionally Congress grants preemptive relief to states in response to protests that federal regulations are incompatible with state or local conditions. For example, Congress permits states to petition the U.S. Department of Transportation to limit the size of commercial tractor-trailers on interstate highways within a state.

FEDERAL MANDATES   Federal mandates are orders to state and local governments to comply with federal laws. Federal mandates occur in a wide variety of areas—from civil rights and voter rights laws to conditions of jails and juvenile detention centers, minimum wage and worker safety regulations, air and water pollution controls, and requirements for access for disabled people. (See Table 3–5.) State and local governments frequently complain that compliance with federal "unfunded mandates" imposes costs on them that are seldom reimbursed.

"UNFUNDED" MANDATES   Federal mandates often impose heavy costs on states and communities. When no federal monies are provided to cover these costs, the mandates are said to be unfunded mandates. Governors, mayors, and other state and local officials (including Bill Clinton, when he served as governor of Arkansas) have often urged Congress to stop imposing unfunded mandates on states and communities. Private industries have long voiced the same complaint. Regulations and mandates allow

■

Unfunded mandates.
Mandates that impose costs on state and local governments (and private industry) without reimbursement from the federal government.

Table 3–5

SELECTED FEDERAL MANDATES

EXAMPLES OF FEDERAL MANDATES TO STATE AND LOCAL GOVERNMENTS

- *Age Discrimination Act 1986*   Outlaws mandatory retirement ages for public as well as private employees, including police, firefighters, and state college and university faculty.
- *Asbestos Hazard Emergency Act 1986*   Orders school districts to inspect for asbestos hazards and remove asbestos from school buildings when necessary.
- *Safe Drinking Water Act 1986*   Establishes national requirements for municipal water supplies; regulates municipal waste treatment plants.
- *Clean Air Act 1990*   Bans municipal incinerators and requires auto emission inspections in certain urban areas.
- *Americans with Disabilities Act 1990*   Requires all state and local government buildings to promote handicapped access.
- *National Voter Registration Act 1993*   Requires states to register voters at driver's licensing, welfare, and unemployment offices.

Congress to address problems while pushing the costs of doing so onto others. In 1995 Congress finally responded to these complaints by requiring that any bill imposing unfunded costs of $50 million or more on state and local governments (as determined by the Congressional Budget Office) would be subject to an additional procedural vote; a majority must vote to waive a prohibition against unfunded mandates before such a bill can come to the House or Senate floor. But this modest restraint is not likely to be very effective.

DEVOLUTION: CAN FEDERALISM BE REVIVED?

Controversy over federalism—what level of government should do what and who should pay for it—is as old as the nation itself. Beginning in 1995, with a new Republican majority in both houses of Congress and Republicans holding a majority of state governorships, debates over federalism were renewed. The new phrase was devolution—the passing down of responsibilities from the national government to the states.

DEVOLUTION AND WELFARE REFORM   Welfare reform turned out to be the key to devolution. Bill Clinton once promised "to end welfare as we know it," but it was a Republican Congress in 1996 that did so. After President Clinton had twice vetoed welfare reform bills, he and Congress finally agreed to merge welfare reform with devolution by

- Ending a 60-year-old federal entitlement program for cash welfare aid (Aid to Families with Dependent Children), and substituting block

■
Devolution.
Passing down of responsibilities from the national government to the states.

grants with lump-sum allocations to the states for welfare payments (now known as Temporary Assistance to Needy Families).

- Granting the states broad flexibility in determining eligibility and benefit levels for persons receiving such aid.

- Allowing states to increase welfare spending if they choose to do so but penalizing states that reduce their spending for cash aid below 75 percent of their 1996 levels.

- Allowing states to deny additional cash payments for children born to women already receiving welfare assistance and allowing states to deny cash payments to parents under eighteen who do not live with an adult and attend school.

Early results indicate that the devolution of welfare reform to the states has been a success. Welfare caseloads have been reduced by an average of more than 25 percent throughout the states, although part of this reduction may be due to the healthy national economy. (For more information on welfare policy, see Chapter 16.) Welfare reform may represent the beginning of a reversal of the flow of power between the national government and the states.

SUPREME COURT REVIVAL OF FEDERALISM?   The U.S. Supreme Court reconsidered the nature of American federalism in several recent cases. For the first time in many years, the Court declared laws of Congress unconstitutional because they exceeded the enumerated powers of Congress in Article I and tread upon the powers reserved to the states in Article X of the Constitution.

When a student, Alfonso Lopez, was apprehended at his high school carrying a .38 handgun, federal agents charged him with violating the federal Gun-Free School Zones Act of 1990. He was convicted and sentenced to six months in prison. His attorney appealed on the ground that it was beyond the constitutionally delegated powers of Congress to police local school zones. In *U.S. v. Lopez* (1995) the U.S. Supreme Court issued its first opinion in more than sixty years that recognized a limit to Congress's power over interstate commerce and reaffirmed the Founders' notion that the federal government has only the powers enumerated in the U.S. Constitution. Attornies for the federal government argued that the Gun-Free School Zones Act was a constitutional exercise of its interstate commerce power because "possession of a firearm in a school zone may result in violent crime and that violent crime can be expected to affect the functioning of the national economy." But the Court rejected this argument, holding that such reasoning would remove virtually all limits to federal power. "To uphold the Government's contentions here, we would have to pile inference upon inference in a manner that would bid fair to convert congressional activity under the Commerce Clause to a general police power of the sort retained by the states."[19]

The U.S. Supreme Court again invalidated a provision of a law of Congress—the Brady Handgun Violence Prevention Act—by deciding that its command to local law enforcement officers to conduct background checks on gun purchasers violated "the very principle of separate state sovereignty." The Court affirmed that the "federal government may neither issue directives requiring the states to address particular problems, nor command the state's officers, or those of their political subdivisions, to administer or enforce a federal regulatory program."

It may be too early to judge the impact of these decisions on federalism—whether they represent the return to the traditional notions of enumerated powers of Congress and reserved powers of the states. Yet both decisions invalidated very popular laws of Congress—laws with broad political support across the country.

POLITICAL OBSTACLES TO FEDERALISM   It is not likely that presidents or members of Congress will ever be motivated to restrain their own power. Even when they recognize that they may be overstepping the enumerated powers of the national government, political pressures on them to "DO SOMETHING!" about virtually every problem that confronts individuals, families, or communities inspire them to propose federal interventions. Politicians gain very little by telling their constituents that a particular problem—violence in the schools, domestic abuse, physician-assisted suicide, and so forth—is not a federal responsibility and should be dealt with at the state or local level of government.

INTERSTATE RELATIONS—HORIZONTAL FEDERALISM

FULL FAITH AND CREDIT   The U.S. Constitution provides that "full faith and credit shall be given in each state to the public acts, records, and judicial proceedings of every other state." As more Americans move from state to state, it becomes increasingly important that the states recognize each other's legal instruments. This constitutional clause is intended to protect the rights of individuals who move from one state to another, and it is also intended to prevent individuals from evading their legal responsibilities by crossing state lines. Courts in Illinois must recognize decisions made by courts in Michigan. Contracts entered into in New York may be enforced in Florida. Corporations chartered in Delaware should be permitted to do business in North Dakota. One of the more serious problems in interstate relations today is the failure of the states to meet their obligations under the Full Faith and Credit Clause in the area of domestic relations, including divorce, alimony, child support, and custody of children. The result is now a complex and confused situation in domestic relations law.

PRIVILEGES AND IMMUNITIES   The Constitution also states: "The citizens of each state shall be entitled to all privileges and immunities of citizens in the several states." Apparently the Founding Fathers thought that no state should discriminate against citizens from another state in favor of its own citizens. To do so would seriously jeopardize national unity. This clause also implies that citizens of any state may move freely about the country and settle where they like, with the assurance that as newcomers they will not be subjected to unreasonable discrimination. The newcomer should not be subject to discriminatory taxation; nor barred from lawful occupations under the same conditions as other citizens of the state; nor prevented from acquiring and using property; nor denied equal protection of the laws; nor refused access to the courts.

However, states have managed to compromise this constitutional guarantee in several important ways. States establish residence requirements for voting and holding office, which prevent newcomers from exercising the same rights as older residents. States often require periods of residence as a prerequisite for holding a state job or for admission into professional practice such as law or medicine. States discriminate against out-of-state students in the tuition charged in public schools and colleges. Finally, some states are now seeking ways to keep "outsiders" from moving in and presumably altering the "natural" environment.

EXTRADITION   The Constitution also provides that "A person in any state with treason, felony, or other crime who shall flee from justice and be found in another state, shall on the demand of the executive authority from the state from which he fled, be delivered up, to be removed to the state having jurisdiction of the crime." In other words, the Constitution requires governors to extradite fugitives from another state's justice.

Governors have not always honored requests for extradition, but since no state wants to harbor criminals of another state, extradition is seldom refused. Among reasons advanced for the occasional refusals are (1) the individual has become a law-abiding citizen in his new state; (2) a northern governor did not approve of the conditions in Georgia chain gangs; (3) a black returned to a southern state would not receive a fair trial; and (4) the governor did not believe that there was sufficient evidence against the fugitive to warrant his conviction in the first place.

INTERSTATE COMPACTS   The Constitution provides that "No state shall without the consent of Congress . . . enter into any agreement or compact with another state." Over one hundred interstate compacts now serve a wide variety of interests, such as interstate water resources; conservation of natural resources, including oil, wildlife, and fisheries; the control of floods; the development of interstate toll highways; the coordination of civil defense measures; the reciprocal supervision of parolees; the coordination of welfare and institutional care programs; the administration of interstate metropolitan areas; and the resolution of interstate tax conflicts. In practice, Congress has little to do with these compacts; the Supreme Court has held that congressional consent is required only if the compact encroaches upon some federal power.

CONFLICTS BETWEEN STATES   States are not supposed to make war on each other, although they did so from 1861 to 1865. They are supposed to take their conflicts to the Supreme Court. The Constitution gives the Supreme Court the power to settle all cases involving two or more states. In recent years the Supreme Court has heard disputes between states over boundaries, the diversion of water, fishing rights, and the disposal of sewage and garbage.

DID YOU KNOW?

WHAT ARE THE "MOST LIVABLE" STATES?

Spirited debates are often engendered by rankings of states (or cities) by "livability." Each year the Morgan Quitno Press attracts both publicity and controversy with its livability ratings (shown below for the states). These ratings are calculated from each state's ranking on forty-three separate factors ranging from crime rates, infant mortality rates, deaths by suicide, and poverty rates (negative factors) to growth in personal income, home ownership rate, job growth, percent of population graduated from college, and percent of days that are sunny.

STATE	LIVABILITY RATING	STATE	LIVABILITY RATING
1 Minnesota	32.91	26 Maine	24.98
2 Nebraska	32.28	27 Ohio	24.98
3 Iowa	32.14	28 Michigan	24.98
4 Utah	31.84	29 Pennsylvania	24.74
5 Wisconsin	30.53	30 Hawaii	24.42
6 South Dakota	30.49	31 Rhode Island	24.30
7 Massachusetts	30.40	32 Montana	23.81
8 Colorado	29.90	33 Alaska	23.21
9 North Dakota	29.86	34 North Carolina	23.09
10 Kansas	29.49	35 New York	22.84
11 New Hampshire	29.09	36 California	22.67
12 Connecticut	28.65	37 Oklahoma	22.51
13 New Jersey	28.49	38 Georgia	22.40
14 Delaware	28.40	39 Florida	22.35
15 Virginia	28.19	40 Texas	22.14
16 Idaho	27.86	41 Arizona	21.95
17 Vermont	27.72	42 Kentucky	21.67
18 Oregon	27.28	43 South Carolina	20.72
19 Maryland	27.19	44 Arkansas	20.67
20 Wyoming	27.09	45 New Mexico	20.35
21 Missouri	26.91	46 Tennessee	19.91
22 Indiana	26.74	47 Alabama	19.70
23 Washington	26.28	48 West Virginia	18.86
24 Nevada	26.09	49 Mississippi	17.65
25 Illinois	25.60	50 Louisiana	14.79

Sources: State Rankings 1998 (Lawrence, KS: Morgan Quitno Press, 1998).

ON THE WEB

The National Association of State Information Resource Executives (NASIRE) maintains a very helpful Web site at

www.nasire.org

The site directs users to information on state government by category, for example, "criminal justice," "education," "finance," and so on, as well as governors' offices, state legislatures, and state home pages. You can click "State Home pages" to obtain a state index and click whichever state interests you.

Most states can also be accessed directly by inserting the state's postal abbreviation in the following address:

www.state.—us

for example,

www.state.ca.us for California

www.state.va.us for Virginia

Exceptions are Alabama (alaweb.asc.edu), Hawaii (www.hawaii.gov), Maryland (www.mec.state.md.us/mec), Massachusetts (www.magnet.state.ma.us), Michigan (www.migor.state.mi.us), Montana (www.mt.gov), North Carolina (www.sips.state.nc.us), Ohio (www.ohio.gov), Oklahoma (www.okla.sf.state.ok.us), Rhode Island (www.doa.ri.us/info), Texas (www.texas.gov), Vermont (www.cit.state.vt.us), and Washington (www.wa.gov).

Perhaps the most important single source of comparative information on the states is provided by the Council of State Governments in its annual publication *The Book of the States*. This publication is not online, but it can be found in most university library reference sections. The Council of State Governments Web site is found at

www.csg.org

The site provides a daily review of state government news to all viewers and access to state data archives for paid members as well as authorized state officials.

NOTES

1. Other definitions of federalism in American political science include: "Federalism refers to a political system in which there are local (territorial, regional, provincial, state, or municipal) units of government as well as a national government, that can make final decisions with respect to at least some governmental authorities and whose existence is especially protected." James Q. Wilson, *American Government*, 4th ed. (Lexington, MA: D.C. Heath, 1989), p. 47; "Federalism is the mode of political organization that unites smaller polities within an overarching political system by distributing power among general and constituent units in a manner designed to protect the existence and authority of both national and subnational systems enabling all to share in the overall system's decision-making and executing processes." Daniel J. Elazar, *American Federalism: A View from the States* (New York: Thomas Y. Crowell, 1966), p. 2.

2. James Madison, Alexander Hamilton, and John Jay, *The Federalist*, Number 51 (New York: Modern Library, 1958).

3. David Osborne, *Laboratories of Democracy* (Cambridge, MA: Harvard Business School, 1988).

4. The arguments for "competitive federalism" are developed at length in Thomas R. Dye, *American Federalism: Competition Among Governments* (Lexington, MA: Lexington Books, 1990). The book argues that competitive decentralized government has many advantages over centralized "monopoly" governments: greater overall responsiveness to citizen preferences; incentives for government to become efficient and provide quality services at lowest costs; restraints on the overall burdens of taxation and nonproportional taxes; encouragement of economic growth; and innovation in policies designed to improve the well-being of citizens.

5. *Texas* v. *White,* 7 Wallace 700 (1869).

6. See Val Burris, "Who Opposed the ERA? An Analysis of the Social Basis for Antifeminism," *Social Science Quarterly,* 64 (June 1983), 305–17.

7. See Ruth Ann Strikland, "The Twenty-seventh Amendment and Constitutional Change by Stealth," *P.S. Political Science and Politics,* 26 (December 1993), 716–22.

8. *Massachusetts* v. *Mellon,* 262 U.S. 447 (1923).

9. See Daniel J. Elazar, *The American Partnership: Inter-Governmental Cooperation in Nineteenth-Century United States* (Chicago: University of Chicago Press, 1962).

10. Robert M. Stein, "The Allocation of Federal Aid Monies: The Synthesis of Demand-Side and Supply-Side Explanations," *American Political Science Review,* 75 (June 1981), 334–43.

11. Morton Grodzins, *The American System* (Chicago: Rand McNally, 1966), pp. 8–9.

12. Ibid., p. 265.

13. Charles Press, *State and Community Governments in the Federal System* (New York: John Wiley, 1979), p. 78.

14. *Garcia* v. *San Antonio Metropolitan Transit Authority,* 469 U.S. 528 (1985).

15. *Gregory* v. *Ashcraft,* 11 S. Ct. 2395 (1991).

16. *Tarbels Case,* 13 Wall. 397 (1872). Also cited and discussed in Deil S. Wright, *Understanding Intergovernmental Relations* (Boston: Duxbury Press, 1978), p. 22.

17. *Pollock* v. *Farmers Loan and Trust Company,* 157 U.S. 429 (1895).

18. *South Carolina* v. *Barker,* 485 U.S. 505 (1988).

19. *United States* v. *Lopez,* 63 L.W. 4343 (1995).

4
PARTICIPATION IN STATE POLITICS

QUESTIONS TO CONSIDER
★ ★ ★ ★ ★ ★ ★ ★ ★

Are you registered to vote in your state?

☐ Yes
☐ No

What political activities have you undertaken in your state's most recent election?

☐ Worked in party or campaign
☐ Wore button or applied a bumper sticker to your car
☐ Made campaign contribution
☐ Voted
☐ Did not participate

Do you believe an interest group should be allowed to make campaign contributions to candidates who may later vote on bills affecting the group's interests?

☐ Yes
☐ No

Is it ever right to deliberately violate a law that you believe is unjust?

☐ Yes
☐ No

THE NATURE OF POLITICAL PARTICIPATION

Popular participation in politics is the very definition of democracy. Individuals can participate in politics in many ways. They may run for, and win, public office; participate in marches, demonstrations, and sit-ins; make financial contributions to political candidates or causes; attend political meetings, speeches, and rallies; write letters to public officials or to newspapers; wear a political button or place a bumper sticker on a car; belong to organizations that support or oppose particular candidates or take stands on public issues; attempt to influence friends while discussing candidates or issues; vote in elections; or merely follow an issue or a campaign in the media.

This listing probably constitutes a ranking of the forms of political participation in order of frequency. (See Figure 4–1.) Only about half of the voting age population vote in presidential elections. Far fewer vote in state and local elections. Over one-third of the population is politically apathetic: They do not vote at all, and they are largely unaware of the political life of the nation.

Sustained political participation—voting consistently in election after election for state and local offices as well as Congress and the president—is very rare. One study of voter participation over ten elections (including presidential, congressional, gubernatorial, and state and local legislative elections) showed that only 4 percent of the voting age population voted in nine or all ten of the elections; only 26 percent voted in half of the ten elections; and 38 percent did not vote in any election.[1] Age is the best predictor of sustained political activity; older citizens are more likely than young people to be regular voters.

EXPLAINING VOTER TURNOUT

A sign of the times: A bumper sticker reads, "DON'T VOTE. IT JUST ENCOURAGES THEM." Nearly half of America's eligible voters stay away from the polls, even in a presidential election. Voter turnout is even lower in congressional elections, where turnout falls to about 35 percent of the voting age population in the off years (when presidential candidates are not on the ballot). Turnouts in gubernatorial elections are roughly similar to turnouts for congressional races, rising and falling depending on whether the election is held simultaneously with a presidential election (see Figure 4–2). City and county elections, when they are held separately from national elections, usually produce turnouts of 25 to 35 percent.

IS VOTING RATIONAL?   Why is voter turnout so low? Actually, we could reverse the question and ask why people vote at all. A "rational" voter (one who seeks to maximize personal benefits and minimize costs) should vote only if the costs of voting (the time and energy spent first in registering, then in informing oneself about the candidates, and finally going to the polls on election day) are exceeded by the expected value of having the preferred candidate win (the personal benefits to be received from the winner) multiplied by the probability that one's own vote will be the deciding vote.[2] But under this "rational" notion, not many people would vote: Few Americans receive

■

Voter turnout.
The percentage of the voting age population that cast ballots in an election.

FIGURE 4–1
Political
Participation

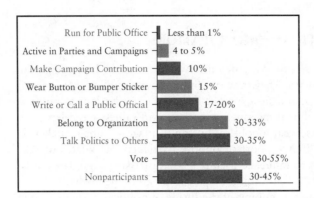

direct personal and tangible benefits from the election of one candidate versus another. And most Americans know that the likelihood of one vote determining the outcome of the election is very remote. Yet millions of Americans vote anyway.

In order to rescue the "rational" model, political theorists have added "the intrinsic rewards of voting" to the equation.[3] These rewards include the ethic of voting, patriotism, a sense of duty, and allegiance to democracy. In other words, people get psychic

FIGURE 4–2 The
Trend in Voter
Turnout

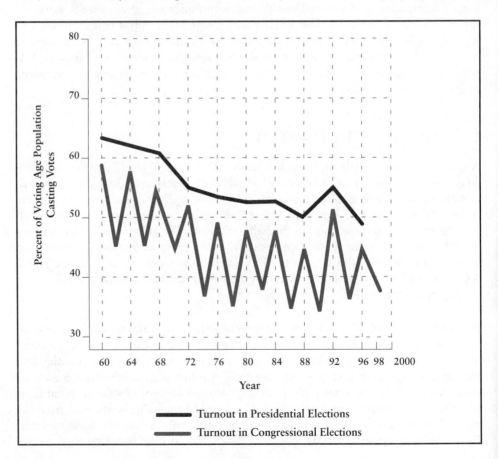

rewards from voting itself rather than tangible benefits, and these psychic rewards do not depend on who wins or whether a single vote determines the outcome. So more people vote out of a sense of civic duty and commitment to democracy than on a purely rational basis.

WHY PEOPLE STAY AT HOME   Nonetheless, millions of Americans stay at home on election day. We can apply some of the rational theorizing to understanding nonvoting in the states:

1. Registration requirements that are restrictive increase the costs of voting. By making it easier to register, states can increase voter turnout. Of the people who are registered in the nation, about three-quarters will vote in presidential elections.

2. Competition increases turnout. If a political contest appears close, more people believe that their vote might determine the outcome. Active campaigning by the candidates may not change people's minds, but it mobilizes supporters to get to the polls on election day.

3. Civic attachments and education increase voter turnout. People who believe they have a stake in the political system are more likely to vote than those who do not. Nonvoting may indicate a lack of faith in one's own power, a feeling of political impotency, or a lack of faith in the political system—a belief that it is too corrupt or too large for any single individual to make a difference.

WHO FAILS TO VOTE?   Political alienation involves a feeling that voting is useless, that nothing is really decided in an election, and that the individual cannot personally influence the outcome of political events. Political alienation explains the failure to vote by many people. Various socioeconomic factors also help to explain alienation and nonvoting (see Table 4–1). Blacks vote less frequently than whites. Hispanic Americans vote less frequently than either blacks or whites, suggesting that language differences may be a barrier to political participation. People who are working vote more frequently than the unemployed. Young people vote less often than older people. But the greatest differences in voter turnout are found among people with different educational backgrounds. Education apparently increases one's sense of civic responsibility and attachment to democratic norms.[4]

POLICY IMPLICATIONS OF NONVOTING   Do nonvoters differ significantly from voters on major policy questions? If so, then we might expect changes in government policy with a sustained increase in voter turnout. But the available evidence suggests that nonvoters generally hold policy views similar to those of voters.[5] Nonvoters are no more liberal or conservative than voters. In brief, despite a class bias in voter turnout, it is unlikely that nonvoting skews public policy in any particular direction.

■

OTHER FORMS OF PARTICIPATION   People who engage in other forms of participation besides voting—for example, making campaign contributions, writing or calling elected officials, joining and working in political organizations—are much better educated and enjoy much higher income than nonparticipants. (See *"Up Close: Getting into Politics,"* p. 94.) Moreover, people who receive government middle-class

Political alienation.
General feelings of estrangement from the political system; the belief that voting is useless and that individuals cannot influence political events.

Table 4–1

CHARACTERISTICS OF VOTERS	
	Percent Reporting They Voted[a]
Total	54.2
Sex	
Male	52.8
Female	55.5
Race	
White	56.0
Black	50.6
Hispanic	26.7
Age	
18–20	31.2
21–24	33.4
25–34	43.1
35–44	54.9
45–64	62.2
65 and over	67.9
Employment	
Employed	55.2
Unemployed	37.2
Education	
8 years	28.1
High school	49.1
College	73.0

[a]Figures are for the 1996 presidential election. Some people tell pollsters that they voted when they really did not. While 54.2 percent of the voting age population *reported* that they voted, the *actual* number of votes cast was only 49.0 percent of the voting age population.

Source: Statistical Abstract of the United States, 1997, p. 288.

benefits, such as Social Security, Medicare, and veterans' benefits, are much more active politically than those who receive poverty-tested welfare benefits such as cash assistance, Medicaid, and food stamps.[6] Some political scientists contend that lower-class political "mobilization"—organizations, activity, and voter turnout—where it does occur, produces higher levels of welfare benefits.[7]

VOTING IN THE STATES

There is a great deal of variation among the states in voter participation rates (see "*Rankings of the States:* Registration and Voting"). The turnout in presidential elections in the states ranges from less than 42 percent of the voting population to over 60 percent. The states with the lowest turnouts are the Deep South states; the next lowest are found in the border states. Midwestern, New England, and Mountain states rank

RANKINGS OF THE STATES

REGISTRATION AND VOTING[a]

Percent of Persons Eligible Registered

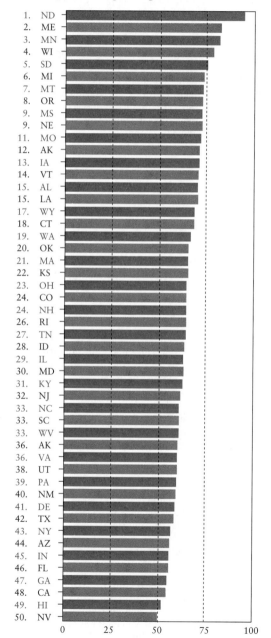

1.	ND
2.	ME
3.	MN
4.	WI
5.	SD
6.	MI
7.	MT
8.	OR
9.	MS
9.	NE
11.	MO
12.	AK
13.	IA
14.	VT
15.	AL
15.	LA
17.	WY
18.	CT
19.	WA
20.	OK
21.	MA
22.	KS
23.	OH
24.	CO
24.	NH
26.	RI
27.	TN
28.	ID
29.	IL
30.	MD
31.	KY
32.	NJ
33.	NC
33.	SC
33.	WV
36.	AK
36.	VA
38.	UT
39.	PA
40.	NM
41.	DE
42.	TX
43.	NY
44.	AZ
45.	IN
46.	FL
47.	GA
48.	CA
49.	HI
50.	NV

Percent of Persons Eligible Casting Votes

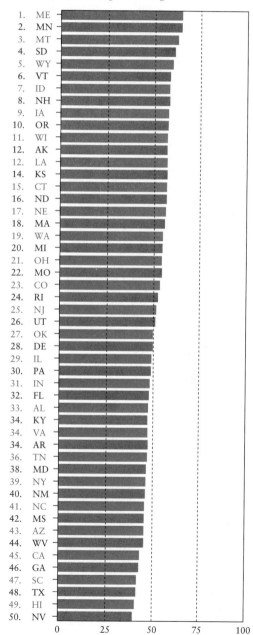

1.	ME
2.	MN
3.	MT
4.	SD
5.	WY
6.	VT
7.	ID
8.	NH
9.	IA
10.	OR
11.	WI
12.	AK
12.	LA
14.	KS
15.	CT
16.	ND
17.	NE
18.	MA
19.	WA
20.	MI
21.	OH
22.	MO
23.	CO
24.	RI
25.	NJ
26.	UT
27.	OK
28.	DE
29.	IL
30.	PA
31.	IN
32.	FL
33.	AL
34.	KY
34.	VA
34.	AR
36.	TN
38.	MD
39.	NY
40.	NM
41.	NC
42.	MS
43.	AZ
44.	WV
45.	CA
46.	GA
47.	SC
48.	TX
49.	HI
50.	NV

[a]1996 presidential election.

UP CLOSE

GETTING INTO POLITICS

Politics attracts both "amateurs" and "professionals." Amateurs may be defined as people who continue in a full-time job or occupation while engaging in politics part time, mainly for friendship and association or out of a sense of civic duty. Professionals are people who devote all their time and energy to politics, running for and occupying public office themselves, or working for candidates with the expectation of appointment to office upon the victory of their chosen candidate.

Get Involved

The most common way to get into politics is to get involved in the community. Look into various organizations in your community, including:
- Neighborhood associations.
- Chambers of commerce, business associations.
- Churches and synagogues (become an usher, if possible, for visibility).
- Political groups (Democratic or Republican clubs, League of Women Voters, and so on).
- Parent-Teacher Associations (PTAs).
- Service clubs (Rotary, Kiwanis, Civitan, Toastmasters).
- Recreation organizations (Little League, flag football, soccer leagues, running and walking clubs, for example, as participant, coach, or umpire).

You can find out when and where such groups meet by looking in the neighborhood section of your local newspaper, watching the community calendar on TV, or listening to it on radio. Become an active member and gain some visibility in your community.

Learn about Public Affairs

It is essential that you learn about the public issues confronting your community and state as well as the duties and responsibilities of various government offices. You should:
- Attend meetings of your council or commission or attend state legislative sessions and committee hearings.
- Become familiar with current issues and officeholders, and obtain a copy of and read the budget.
- Learn the demographics of your district (racial, ethnic, and age composition; occupational mix; average incomes; neighborhood differences, and so on).

Run for Public Office

Many rewards come with elected office—the opportunity to help shape public policy; public attention and name recognition; and many business, professional, and social contacts. But there are many drawbacks as well—the absence of privacy; a microscopic review of one's past; constant calls, meetings, interviews, and handshaking; and perhaps most onerous of all, the continual need to solicit campaign funds. Before deciding to run, potential candidates should seriously consider the tremendous amount of work required. If you decide to run, begin by contacting your county elections department and try to obtain the following:
- Qualifying forms and information.
- Campaign financing forms and regulations.
- District and street maps for your district.
- Recent election results in your district.
- Election-law book or pamphlet.
- Voter registration lists (usually sold as lists, labels, or tapes).

Also contact your party's county chairperson and ask for advice and assistance. Convince the party's leaders that you can win. Ask for a copy of their list of regular campaign contributors.

Raise Money

Perhaps the most difficult task in politics is that of raising campaign funds. The easiest way to finance a campaign is to be rich enough to provide your own funds. Failing that, you must:
- Establish a campaign fund, according to the laws of your state.
- Find a treasurer/campaign-finance chairperson who knows large numbers of wealthy, politically involved people.
- Identify, call, and meet personally with potential contributors and solicit pledges, or better yet, checks.
- Invite wealthy, politically involved people to small coffees, cocktail parties, dinners; give a brief campaign speech and then have your finance chairperson solicit contributions.
- Don't be shy in confronting potential contributors; use the direct approach (for example, "I know you want to help, Jim. How much can I put you down for?").
- Follow up fund-raising events and meetings with personal phone calls.
- Be prepared to continue fund-raising activities throughout your campaign; file accurate financial disclosure statements as required by law in your state.

Organize Your Campaign

Professional campaign managers and management firms almost always outperform volunteers. (Many firms advertise in the monthly magazine *Campaigns and Elections,* which can be accessed online at www.camelect.com). If you cannot afford professional management, you must rely on yourself or trusted friends to perform the following:

- Prepare and memorize a brief (preferably less than seven seconds) answer to the question, "Why are you running?"
- Ask trusted friends from various clubs, activities, neighborhoods, churches, and so on, to meet and serve as a campaign committee. If your district is racially or ethnically diverse, make sure all groups are represented on your committee.
- Decide on a campaign theme; research issues important to your community; develop brief, well-articulated positions on these issues.
- Open a campaign headquarters with desks and telephones. Buy a cell phone; use call forwarding; stay in contact. Use your garage if you can't afford an office.
- Arrange to meet with newspaper editors, editorial boards, TV station executives, and political reporters. Be prepared for tough questions.
- Hire a media consultant or advertising agency, or appoint a volunteer media director who knows television, radio, and newspaper advertising.
- Arrange a press conference to announce your candidacy. Notify all media well in advance. Arrange for overflow crowd of supporters to cheer and applaud.
- Produce eyecatching, inspirational fifteen- or thirty-second television and radio ads that present a favorable image of you and stress your campaign theme.
- Prepare and print attractive campaign brochures, signs, and bumper stickers.
- Prepare a schedule of community events, meetings, and other public happenings, and plan to make an appearance.
- If funds permit, hire a local survey-research firm or pollster to conduct continuous telephone surveys of voters in your district, asking what they think are the most important issues, how they stand on them, whether they recognize your name and your theme, and how they plan to vote. Be prepared to change your theme and your position on issues if survey results show strong opposition to your views.

Campaign Hard

Fund-raising, organizing, developing issues, writing speeches, and polling continue up to election day. Campaigns themselves may be primarily *media centered* or primarily *door-to-door* ("retail") or some combination of both.

- Attend every community gathering possible, just to be seen, even if you do not give a speech. Keep all speeches *short*. Focus on one or two issues that your polls show are important to voters.
- Recruit paid or unpaid volunteers to canvass neighborhoods door to door to hand out literature and whenever possible to engage potential voters in friendly favorable

conversations about you. Record names and addresses of voters who say they support you.
- Do door-to-door canvassing yourself with a brief (seven-second) self-introduction and statement of the reason you are running. Canvassing may also include offices, factories, coffee shops, shopping malls—anywhere you find a crowd—as well as neighborhoods. Use registration lists to identify members of your own party, and try to address them by name.
- Organize a phone bank, either professional or volunteer. Prepare *brief* introduction and phone statements. Your phone bank should become increasingly active as the election nears. Call only persons on election lists registered in your party. Record names of people who say they support you.
- Know your opponent: Research his or her past affiliations, indiscretions, if any, previous voting record, and public positions on issues.
- Be prepared to "define" your opponent in negative terms. Negative advertising works. But be fair: Base your comments about your opponent on supportable facts.

On Election Day

Turning out *your* voters is the key to success. Election day is the busiest day of the campaign for you and especially your staff.

- Use your phone bank to place as many calls as possible to your party members in your district (especially those who have indicated in previous calls and visits that they support you). Remind them to vote; make sure your phone workers can tell each voter where to go to cast their vote. Ask if they need a ride to the polls.
- Prepare volunteer drivers to take anyone to the polls who needs a ride. Send cars to condominiums, nursing homes, neighborhoods, and so on, clearly marked with your name but willing to assist anyone.
- Assign workers to as many polling places as possible. Most state laws require that they stay a specified distance from the voting booths. But they should be in evidence with your signs and literature to buttonhole voters before they go into the booth.
- Show up at city or county election office on election night with prepared victory statement thanking supporters and voters and pledging your service to the district, city, county, or state. (Also prepare a courteous concession statement pledging your support to the winner, in case you lose.)
- Attend victory party with your supporters; meet many "new" friends.

■

Registration.
The requirement that
prospective voters establish
their identity and place of
residence prior to an election
in order to be eligible to
vote.

very high in voter turnout. The urban industrial states, with large metropolitan populations, tend to cluster around the middle of the rankings.

SOCIOECONOMIC EXPLANATIONS   Much of the variation among the states in voter turnout can be explained by *socioeconomic characteristics* of their population. Indeed, most of the variation in voter turnout among the states can be attributed to differences in educational level, urbanization, median family income, and percentage black or Hispanic.

TURNOUT POLITICS   Partisan politics has always colored the debate over registration and voting requirements. Democrats generally favor easing these requirements. They believe that doing so will bring more current nonvoters to the polls and that nonvoters are heavily drawn from groups that characteristically support the Democratic party (e.g., African American, lower income, noncollege groups). Republican leaders are often less enthusiastic about easing voting requirements, but it is politically embarrassing to appear to oppose increased voter participation.

REGISTRATION   Voter registration is an obstacle to voting. Not only must citizens care enough to go to the polls on election day, they also must have previously registered their name and residence well before election day (usually thirty days before). Thus, registration must be accomplished at a time when interest in electoral campaigns is far from its peak. States must now allow registration by mail. Once registered, names remain on the list unless there is a change of residence. (Prior to 1993 states periodically dropped the names of individuals who failed to vote over a prolonged period of time, a practice now banned by federal law.) Registration is designed to prevent fraud. It originated as a reform to prevent corrupt political "machines" from marching supporters from one voting booth to another on election day. Only registered voters are permitted to cast ballots on election day. Persons must identify themselves and show that they have previously registered as residents of the voting district; once they have voted, their names are checked off and they cannot vote again. Maine, Minnesota, Wisconsin, and Wyoming allow same-day registration at the polls; only North Dakota does not require registration at all.

FEDERALLY MANDATED "MOTOR VOTER" LAW   Although Congress had previously passed voting rights laws designed to protect minorities, it had never directly intervened in the general process of state election administration prior to 1993. But with strong Democratic support, Congress passed the National Voter Registration Act of 1993, popularly known as the "motor voter" act. It mandates that the states offer people the opportunity to register when they apply for a driver's license or apply for welfare services. States must also offer registration by mail, and they must accept a simplified registration form prepared by the Federal Election Commission. Finally, the act bars states from removing the names of people from registration lists for failure to vote.

What is the impact of the motor voter law on voter turnout in the states? States that had enacted their own motor voter registration laws before the federal mandate appear to have increased their turnout rates by doing so.[8] However, although the law has increased voter *registration,* it is not yet clear whether the motor voter registrants add significantly to *turnout* on election day. Turnout in the 1996 presidential election was an all-time low (49 percent). Moreover, differences among the states in turnout attributable to socioeconomic characteristics of state populations have continued.

■

Interparty competition. The competitiveness of the two major parties, usually measured by the closeness of the vote for various offices.

REGION   Over time, differences among the states in voter turnout levels have diminished. Traditionally, turnout was low in the southern states, especially Arkansas, Florida, Georgia, Louisiana, Mississippi, South Carolina, Tennessee, Texas, and Virginia. While these states continue to rank low in turnout, they have moved closer to the other states. Federal civil rights laws, black voter mobilization, northern in-migration, and greater Republican competition may have all combined to help explain why voter participation has improved in these states.

COMPETITION   Voter participation rates can also be affected by the degree of interparty competition in a state. The more vigorous the competition between the parties, the greater the interest of citizens in elections, and the larger the voter turnout. When parties and candidates compete vigorously, they make news and are given a large play via the mass media. Thus, a setting of competitive politics tends to have a greater amount of political stimuli available in the environment than does a setting with weak competition. More money is spent in campaigning. People are also more likely to perceive that their votes count in a close, competitive contest, and thus they are more likely to cast them.[9]

SECURING THE RIGHT TO VOTE

The only mention of voting requirements in the Constitution of the United States as it was originally adopted is in Article I: "The electors in each state shall have the qualifications requisite for electors for the most numerous branch of the state legislature." Of course, "electors" (voters) for the most numerous branch of the state legislature are determined by *state* laws and constitutions. The effect of this constitutional provision was to leave to the states the power to determine who is eligible to vote in both state and federal elections. Over the years, however, a combination of constitutional amendments, congressional actions, and Supreme Court decisions has largely removed control over voting from the states and made it a responsibility of the national government.

ELIMINATION OF PROPERTY QUALIFICATIONS   Early in American history, voting was limited to males over twenty-one years of age, who resided in the voting district for a certain period and owned a considerable amount of land or received a large income from other investments. So great was the fear that "the common man" would use his vote to attack the rights of property that only 120,000 people out of 2 million were permitted to vote in the 1780s. Men of property felt that only other men of property had sufficient "stake in society" to exercise their vote in a "responsible" fashion. Gradually, however, Jeffersonian and Jacksonian principles of democracy, including confidence in the reason and integrity of the common man, spread rapidly in the new Republic. Most property qualifications were eliminated by the states themselves in the early nineteenth century.

FIFTEENTH AMENDMENT   The first constitutional limitation on state powers over voting came with the ratification of the Fifteenth Amendment: "The right of the citizens of the United States to vote shall not be denied or abridged by the United States or any state on account of race, color, or previous condition of servitude." The object of this amendment, passed by the Reconstruction Congress and adopted in 1870, was to extend the vote to former black slaves and prohibit voter discrimination on the basis of race. The Fifteenth Amendment also gives Congress the power to enforce black voting rights "by appropriate legislation." Thus, the states retained their right to determine voter qualifications, *as long as they do not practice racial discrimination,* and Congress was given the power to pass legislation ensuring black voting rights.

NINETEENTH AMENDMENT   Following the Civil War many of the women who had been active abolitionists, seeking to end slavery, turned their attention to the condition of women in America. They had learned to organize, conduct petition campaigns and parade and demonstrate, as abolitionists, and later they sought to improve the legal and political rights of women. In 1869 the Wyoming territory adopted women's suffrage; later several other western states followed suit. But it was not until the Nineteenth Amendment to the U.S. Constitution in 1920 that women's voting rights were constitutionally guaranteed.

THE "WHITE PRIMARY"   For almost 100 years after the adoption of the Fifteenth Amendment, white politicians in the southern states were able to defeat its purposes. Social and economic pressures and threats of violence were used to intimidate many thousands of would-be voters. There were also many "legal" methods of disenfranchisement.

For many years the most effective means of banning black voting was a technique known as the "white primary." So strong was the Democratic party throughout the South that the Democratic nomination for public office was tantamount to election. This meant that *primary* elections to choose the Democratic nominee were the only elections in which real choices were made. If blacks were prevented from voting in Democratic primaries, they could be effectively disenfranchised. Thus southern state legislatures resorted to the simple device of declaring the Democratic party in southern states a private club and ruling that only white people could participate in its elections, that is, in *primary* elections. Blacks would be free to vote in "official," general elections, but all whites tacitly agreed to support the Democratic, or "white man's," party, in general elections, regardless of their differences in the primary. Not until 1944, in *Smith* v. *Allright,* did the Supreme Court declare this practice unconstitutional.[10]

DISCRIMINATION   Black voting in the South increased substantially after World War II. (From an estimated 5 percent of voting age blacks registered in southern states in the 1940s, black registration rose to an estimated 20 percent in 1952, 25 percent in 1956, 28 percent in 1960, and 39 percent in 1964.) But as late as 1965 black voter turnout rate was little more than half of the white rate. In hundreds of rural counties throughout the South, blacks were prevented from registering and voting. Despite the Fifteenth Amendment, many local registrars in the South succeeded in barring black registration by means of an endless variety of obstacles, delays, and frustrations. Application forms for registration were lengthy and complicated; even a minor error would lead to rejection, such as underlining rather than circling in the "Mr.–Mrs.–Miss" set of choices as instructed. Literacy tests were the most common form of disenfranchisement. Many a black college graduate failed to interpret "properly" the complex legal documents that were part of the test. White applicants for voter registration were seldom asked to go through these lengthy procedures.

CIVIL RIGHTS ACT OF 1964   The Civil Rights Act of 1964 made it unlawful for registrars to apply unequal standards in registration procedures or to reject applications because of immaterial errors. It required that literacy tests be in writing and made a sixth-grade education a presumption of literacy.

TWENTY-FOURTH AMENDMENT   The Twenty-fourth Amendment to the Constitution was ratified in 1964, making poll taxes unconstitutional as a requirement for voting in national elections. In 1965 the Supreme Court declared poll taxes unconstitutional in state and local elections as well.[11]

VOTING RIGHTS ACT OF 1965   In Selma, Alabama, in early 1965, civil rights organizations effectively demonstrated that local registrars were still keeping large numbers of blacks off the voting rolls. Registrars closed their offices for all but a few hours every month, placed limits on the number of applications processed, went out to lunch when black applicants appeared; delayed months before processing applications from blacks, and discovered a variety of other methods to keep blacks disenfranchised. In response to the Selma march, Congress enacted a strong Voting Rights Act in 1965. The U.S. attorney general, upon evidence of voter discrimination, was empowered to replace local registrars with federal registrars, abolish literacy tests, and register voters under simplified federal procedures.[12] However, it turned out that federal registrars were sent to only a small number of southern counties. Many southern counties that had previously discriminated in voter registration hurried to sign up black voters just to avoid the imposition of federal registrars. The Voting Rights Act of 1965 proved to be very effective and Congress voted to extend it indefinitely. Direct discrimination in registration and voting was largely eliminated.

EIGHTEEN-YEAR-OLD VOTING

Before 1970 only three of the fifty states permitted residents eighteen to twenty-one years of age to vote—Georgia, Kentucky, and Alaska. All other states, in the exercise of their constitutional responsibility to determine the qualifications of "electors," had set the voting age at twenty-one. The movement for eighteen-year-old voting received its original impetus in Georgia in 1944 under the leadership of Governor Ellis Arnall, who argued successfully that eighteen-year-olds were then being called upon to fight and die for their country in World War II and, therefore, deserved to have a voice in the conduct of government. However, this argument failed to convince adult voters in other states; qualifications for military service were not regarded as the same as qualifications for rational decision making in elections. In state after state, voters rejected state constitutional amendments designed to extend the vote to eighteen-year-olds.

Congress intervened on behalf of eighteen-year-old voting with the passage of the Twenty-sixth Amendment to the Constitution in 1971.[13] The states quickly ratified this amendment, during a period of national turbulence over the Vietnam War. Many supporters of the amendment believed that protests on the campuses and streets could be reduced if youthful protesters were given the vote. Moreover, Democrats believed that their party would gain from the youth vote, and liberal candidates believed that idealistic young voters would spark their campaigns.

It turned out, however, that young people cast their votes for parties and candidates in the same proportions as older voters. The image of the idealistic, activist student is not an accurate image of the young voter in America. Less than one-third of people aged eighteen to twenty-four are in college. More than half of this age group are working and either living with their parents or are married and living in their own households. College students may achieve greater visibility in the news media than young working people, but the bulk of young voters are not on the campus.

MINORITIES IN STATE POLITICS

Racial conflict remains a central factor in the politics of nearly every state. In recent years, conflict over voting and representation has centered on the effects of various institutional arrangements on minority influence in government.

DILUTING MINORITY VOTES   Congress strengthened the Voting Rights Act in 1982 by outlawing any electoral arrangements that had the *effect* of weakening minority voting power. This "effects" test replaced the earlier "intent" test which required black plaintiffs to prove that a particular arrangement was adopted with the specific intent of reducing black voting power.[14] (An "intent" test invalidates laws or practices only if they are designed to discriminate; an "effects" test invalidates laws or practices that adversely affect racial minorities regardless of the original intent.) For example, at-large elections or multimember districts for city councils, county commissions, or state legislative seats may have the effect of weakening black voting power if a white majority in such districts consistently prevents blacks from winning office. Congress stopped short of directly outlawing such districts but established a "totality of circumstances" test to be used to determine if such districts had a discriminatory effect. The "circumstances" to be considered by the courts include whether or not there has been a history of racial polarization in voting and whether black candidates have ever won election to office in the district.[15]

AFFIRMATIVE RACIAL GERRYMANDERING   The U.S. Supreme Court requires states and cities to provide minorities with "a realistic opportunity to elect officials of their choice." In the key case of *Thornburg* v. *Gingles*,[16] the Court interpreted the Voting Rights Act Amendments of 1982 to require state legislatures to draw election dis-trict boundary lines in a way that guarantees that minorities can elect minority repre-sentatives to governing bodies. The burden of proof was shifted *from* minorities to show that district lines diluted their voting strength *to* state lawmakers to show that they have done everything possible to maximize minority representation. The effect of the Court's decision was to inspire affirmative racial gerrymandering—the creation of predominately black and minority districts wherever possible.

Racial gerrymandering dominated the redistricting process in all of the large states following the 1990 census. In many states Republican legislators allied themselves with black and Hispanic groups in efforts to create minority districts; Republicans un-derstood that "packing" minority (usually Democratic) voters into selected districts would reduce Democratic votes in many other districts.[17] The U.S. Justice Department also pressed state legislatures to maximize the number of "majority-minority" con-gressional and state legislative districts. With the assistance of sophisticated computer models, state legislatures and federal courts drew many odd-shaped minority congres-sional and state legislative districts.

CONTINUING CONSTITUTIONAL DOUBTS   Yet the Supreme Court has expressed constitutional doubts about bizarre-shaped districts based solely on racial composi-tion. In a controversial 5–4 decision, Justice Sandra Day O'Connor wrote: "Race ger-rymandering, even for remedial purposes, may balkanize us into competing racial factions. . . . A reapportionment plan that includes in one district individuals who have little in common with one another but the color of their skin bears an uncom-fortable resemblance to political apartheid."[18] (See Figure 4–3.) Later the Court held that the use of race as the "predominant factor" in dividing district lines is unconsti-tutional: "When the state assigns voters on the basis of race, it engages in the offensive and demeaning assumption that voters of a particular race, because of their race, think alike, share the same political interests and will prefer the same candidates at the polls."[19] But the Court stopped short of saying that all race-conscious districting is un-constitutional. Several states redrew the boundaries of majority-minority districts try-ing to conform to the Court's opinions. Incumbent African American Congress members managed to hold on to their seats in these states. But the constitutional sta-tus of affirmative racial gerrymandering remains unclear.

INCREASED BLACK REPRESENTATION   Black representation in state and local gov-ernment, as well as in the U.S. Congress, rose dramatically in the 1990s. The total number of blacks elected to state and local office rose rapidly after 1980 (see Table 4–2). New minority districts in many states boosted black representation in state leg-islatures. Today roughly 8 percent of all 7,424 state legislators in the nation are African Americans. We will return to the question of minority representation in state legislatures in Chapter 6 and on city councils in Chapter 11.

RACIAL POLARIZATION   Increases in the number of African American officeholders in state and local government are primarily the result of the creation of more black ma-jority districts in cities and states. Few blacks win office in majority white city council or state legislative districts. In legislative districts where the black population is 65 per-

■
Gerrymandering.
Drawing election district boundaries to give an advan-tage to a party, candidate, or racial or ethnic group.

Majority-minority districts.
Districts in which minority racial or ethnic group mem-bers constitute a majority of voters.

Affirmative racial gerrymandering.
Drawing election district boundaries to provide maxi-mum opportunities for the election of minorities.

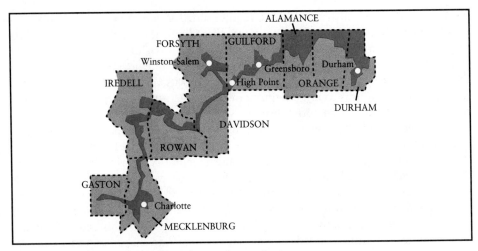

FIGURE 4–3 Affirmative Racial Gerrymandering

North Carolina's 12th congressional district was drawn up to be a "majority-minority" district by combining African American communities over a wide region of the state. The U.S. Supreme Court in *Shaw* v. *Reno* (1993) ordered a court review of this district to determine whether it incorporated any common interest other than race. The North Carolina legislature redrew the district in 1997, lowering its black population percentage from 57 to 46, yet keeping its lengthy connection of black voters from Charlotte to Greensboro.

Table 4–2

GROWTH IN NUMBER OF BLACK ELECTED OFFICIALS			
	1970	*1980*	*1996*
U.S. Congress	10	17	37[e]
State government[a]	169	309	533
City and county government[b]	719	2,871	4,816
Judicial and law enforcement[c]	213	534	922
Education[d]	368	1,232	1,682
Total	1,479	4,963	8,015

[a]Includes elected state administrators.

[b]County commissioners and council members, mayors, vice-mayors, city council members, regional officials, and other.

[c]Judges, magistrates, constables, marshals, sheriffs, justices of the peace, and other.

[d]Members of state education agencies, college boards, school boards, and other.

[e]Figure for 105th Congress, 1997–99.

Source: Joint Center for Political Studies, Washington, DC.

cent or more, black candidates win 98 percent of the legislative seats. Majority white districts elect black candidates to about 2 percent of their legislative seats. While a few notable black political leaders have won electoral support across racial lines (see "*People in Politics:* Al Lawson: From Athlete to Legislator"), racial polarization in voting remains a fact of life.[20]

HISPANIC POWER   The progress of Hispanics in state and local politics in recent years is reflected in the election of several governors and increasing numbers of state legislators, city and county commission members, and school board members (see Table 4–3).

However, Hispanic political influence in the states is still very limited. Hispanic voter turnout is much lower than that for other ethnic groups in America. Many Hispanics are resident aliens and therefore not eligible to vote. Language barriers may also present an obstacle to full participation. Finally, Hispanic voters divide their political loyalties. Cuban Americans tend to vote Republican. They are economically very successful; they are concentrated in the Miami area, and they are now a force in city and state politics in Florida. The largest Hispanic group, Mexican Americans, tends to vote Democratic; their power is concentrated in California, Texas, Arizona, and New Mexico.

PEOPLE IN POLITICS

AL LAWSON: FROM ATHLETE TO LEGISLATOR

Athletes who have combined studies with playing time in college often develop both the required knowledge and the popular following that can ease their way into politics. Florida state representative Al Lawson, Jr., a basketball star at Florida A.&M. University, graduated in 1970. After a brief career in the NBA, he enrolled at Florida State University in its Masters of Public Administration program. He received his MPA degree in 1973 and served briefly as assistant basketball coach at Florida State and director of the university's Black Student Center. In 1976, he opened an insurance agency and marketing firm in the state capital city, Tallahassee.

Becoming involved in community affairs is a necessary step to public office. Lawson continued to work with Florida A.&M. University (even serving as interim basketball coach when asked). He also became active in the powerhouse Tallahassee Area Chamber of Commerce, the Urban League, the Boy Scouts, and the alumni organizations of both Florida A.&M. and Florida State Universities.

Lawson ran for and won election to the state legislature from Leon County (Tallahassee) in 1982. At that time, his district had a white majority population, and Lawson was the only African American in the state legislature elected from a white majority district. He quickly became a recognized leader in the legislature. He organized and chaired the original Legislative Black Caucus.

At a towering six foot seven inches, the gregarious Lawson is an imposing figure on the statehouse floor. But his political independence may be an obstacle to his assuming leadership posts in the Democratic party. As a social conservative, he favors school prayer, charter schools, and a ban on late-term abortions. But he has turned down appeals from Republicans, including Governor Jeb Bush, to switch parties. And he has continued to champion issues of importance to rural, low-income, and minority voters. In 1992, his district was redrawn as a black majority district. Lawson has yet to confront any serious opposition for his legislative seat.

Table 4–3

GROWTH IN NUMBER OF HISPANIC ELECTED OFFICIALS		
	1984	*1995*
U.S. Congress	9	18[a]
State government	110	165
City and county government	1,276	2,023
Judicial and law enforcement	495	633
Education	1,173	2,332
Total	3,063	5,170

[a]Figure for 105th Congress, 1997–99.

Source: National Association of Latino Elected and Appointed Officials. Washington, DC: *National Roster of Hispanic Elected Officials.*

WOMEN IN STATE POLITICS

Traditionally women did not participate in politics as much as men. Women were less likely than men to contribute money, lobby elected officials, and run for or win public office.

Why was this so? Several explanations have been offered: (1) Women were socialized into more "passive" roles from childhood; (2) women with children and family responsibilities could not fully participate in politics; and (3) women did not have educations, occupations, and incomes equivalent to those of men. Perhaps all of these factors were at work in reducing female political participation.

WOMEN IN STATE OFFICES   Women have made impressive political gains in state politics in recent years. Today about 1,600 of the nation's 7,424 state legislators (more than 21 percent) are women. Over a dozen women have served as governors of their state[21] (including current Republican governors Christie Whitman of New Jersey and Jane Hull of Arizona, and Democratic governor Jeanne Shaheen of New Hampshire), and 91 of the 324 elective statewide executive offices across the country (over 28 percent) are held by women. (In the 106th Congress—1999–2001—56 women are serving in the House and 9 in the Senate.) While these figures are modest indeed, they represent significant advances over the recent past. In 1969 only 4 percent of the nation's state legislators were women. Until the election of Ella Grasso (D.–Connecticut) and Dixie Lee Ray (D.–Washington) in the late 1970s, no woman had won election to that office on her own; earlier women governors had succeeded their husbands to that office. Women are making even more rapid gains in city and county offices. The total number of women officeholders in local government has more than tripled over the last decade. This influx of women at the grass-roots level over the last decade is now contributing to the success of women in running for and winning higher state and national offices.

ELECTION CHALLENGES CONFRONTING WOMEN   Women continue to confront special challenges when running for office. In general, female candidates enjoy a slight advantage over male candidates in public perceptions of honesty, sincerity, and caring. However, women candidates are often perceived as "not tough enough" to deal with hard issues like drugs and crime. When women candidates seek to prove that they are "tough," they risk being branded with adjectives like "strident" or "abrasive."

> ■ **Gender gap.**
> In politics, a reference to differences between men and women in political views, party affiliations, and voting choices.

THE POLITICAL GENDER GAP   The gender gap in politics refers to differences between women and men in political views, party affiliation, and voting choices. This gap has widened in recent years, with women currently more likely to identify with the Democratic party (36 percent) than with the Republican party (26 percent), and men more likely to identify themselves as Republicans (31 percent) than Democrats (26 percent), with the remainder claiming to be independents or to have no party preference. Indeed, at the presidential level, national polls indicate that the majority of men voted for Republican Bob Dole in 1996 and Republican George Bush in 1992, and that Democrat Bill Clinton won both elections with the overwhelming support of women voters. This gender gap extends into state politics as well, with women frequently giving Democratic gubernatorial candidates 5 to 10 more percentage points than men.

> **Generation gap.**
> In politics, a reference to differences between young and old in political views and policy preferences.

WOMEN AND POLICY MAKING   Do greater numbers of women in state and local elected offices make any significant difference in public policy? Political scientists have attempted to learn whether or not increases in female elected officials actually bring about any significant policy changes. The evidence on this question is mixed. Male legislators support feminist positions on ERA, abortion, employment, education, and health just as often as female legislators. However, there is some evidence that women legislators give higher *priority* to these issues. Women are more likely than men to have as their "top legislative priority" bills focusing on women's and children's issues. However, state legislatures with larger percentages of women do *not* pass feminist legislation any more often than state legislatures with fewer women legislators.[22] (Women's priority issues are discussed in Chapter 14.)

There may also be gender-based attitudinal differences that affect a wide range of policy issues. For example, women state legislators may be more likely to view social problems such as crime in a larger societal context, leading them to focus on preventive and interventionist policies. Male legislators may view crime as an individual act that can be curtailed by certain swift and severe punishment. Over time as women increase their numbers in state legislatures and city councils, we might expect subtle changes in both the style and substance of policy making.[23]

YOUNG AND OLD IN STATE POLITICS

Generational conflict is intensifying in the nation and the states. The generation gap in politics—differences between young and old in political views and policy preferences—may not yet be as great as differences among races and ethnic groups or among educational and income classes, but serious studies of generational politics conclude that "age will take on an equal or greater weight [in politics] in the not too distant future."[24]

■

Interest groups.
People who come together
to exercise influence over
government policy.

Interest group influence.
The extent to which interest
groups as a whole influence
public policy as compared
with other components of
the political system.

SENIOR POWER   Senior citizens are the most politically powerful age group in the population. They constitute 28 percent of the voting-age population, but because of their high voter turnout rates, they constitute more than one-third of the voters on election day. Persons over sixty-five average a 68 percent turnout rate in presidential elections and a 61 percent rate in congressional elections. In contrast, the turnout rate for those aged eighteen to twenty-one is 36 percent in presidential elections and 19 percent in congressional elections. In short, the voting power of senior citizens is twice that of young people. No elected official can afford to offend the seniors.

SENIOR POLICY AGENDA   Senior policy preferences have been summarized as "resistance to government taxing and spending programs lacking immediate benefits for aging people, and increasing demands for services benefiting principally the elderly population at the expense of younger persons."[25] The most important policy programs for seniors—Social Security and Medicare—are governed by Congress and administered by the federal Social Security Administration. But seniors look to state and local governments to

- keep taxes low, especially property taxes, and prohibit state or local income taxation
- increase spending for crime fighting and prison building
- keep spending for education—elementary, secondary, and higher education—at a minimum.

INTEREST GROUPS IN STATE POLITICS

Both interest groups and political parties organize individuals to make claims upon government, but these two forms of political organizations differ in several respects. *An interest group seeks to influence specific policies of government—not to achieve control over government as a whole. A political party concentrates on winning public office in elections and is somewhat less concerned with policy questions.* An interest group does not ordinarily run candidates for public office under its own banner, although it may give influential support to party candidates. Finally, the basic function of a political party in a two-party system is to organize a *majority* of persons for the purpose of governing. In contrast, an interest group gives political expression to the interests of *minority* groups.

Interest groups arise when individuals with a common interest decide that by banding together and by consolidating their strength they can exercise more influence over public policy than they could as individuals acting alone. The impulse toward organization and collective action is particularly strong in a society of great size and complexity. Over time, individual action in politics gives way to collective action by giant organizations of businesspeople, professionals, and union members, as well as racial, religious, and ideological groups.

ORGANIZED INTERESTS   Groups may be highly organized into formal organizations with offices and professional staffs within the capitals of every state: The U.S.

Chamber of Commerce, the National Association of Manufacturers, the AFL-CIO, and the National Education Association are examples of highly organized interest groups that operate in every state. Other groups have little formal organization and appear at state capitals only when an issue arises of particular concern to them, for example, when motorcyclists assemble to protest mandatory helmets, or when commercial fishermen come to complain about banning of nets.

Interest groups may be organized around *occupational or economic interests* (for example, the Association of Real Estate Boards, the Association of Broadcasters, the Bankers Association, the Automobile Dealers Association, the Cattleman's Association, the Home Builders Association, the Insurance Council, the Association of Trial Lawyers), or on *racial or religious* bases (for example, the National Association for the Advancement of Colored People, the Christian Coalition, the National Council of Churches, the Anti-Defamation League of B'nai B'rith), or around *shared experiences* (for example, the American Legion, the Veterans of Foreign Wars, the League of Women Voters, the Automobile Association of America), or around *ideological positions* (for example, Americans for Democratic Action, Common Cause, Americans for Constitutional Action). *Labor unions,* especially those representing employees of governments and school districts (for example, the National Education Association; the American Federation of Teachers; and the American Federation of State, County, and Municipal Employees), as well as industrial unions and the state AFL-CIO federation, are well organized and well represented in virtually all state capitals.[26] *Government officials* and governments themselves organize and help exert pressure on higher levels of government (for example, the National Governors' Conference, the Council of State Governments, the National League of Cities, U.S. Conference of Mayors, the National Association of Chiefs of Police, and the National Association of Counties). Even the *recipients of government services* have organized themselves (for example, the American Association of Retired Persons).

Overall, economic interests are more frequently encountered in state politics than noneconomic interests. But certainly the proliferation of active noneconomic groups in America, from the environmentalists' Sierra Club to the senior citizens' AARP and the liberal-oriented Common Cause, testifies to the importance of organization in all phases of political life. *Particularly active at the state level are the businesses subject to extensive regulation by state governments.* The banks, truckers, doctors and lawyers, insurance companies, the gaming industry, utilities, hospitals, and liquor interests are consistently found to be among the most highly organized groups in state capitals. Chapters of the National Education Association are also highly active in state capitals, presenting the demands of educational administrators and teachers. And local governments and local government officials are well organized to present their demands at state capitals.

A national survey of interest group activity in all fifty state capitals identified groups that were rated "most effective" and "effective" in the states (see Table 4–4).

PROFESSIONAL LOBBYISTS

Often groups and corporations choose to be "represented" in state capitals by professional lobbyists. Many successful professional lobbyists are former legislators, or former executive officials, or former top gubernatorial or legislative aides, who have turned their state government experience into a career.

Lobbyists.
Individuals, groups, or organizations that actively seek to influence government policy.

Table 4–4

RANKING OF THE MOST INFLUENTIAL INTERESTS IN THE FIFTY STATES

	Number of States in Which Interest Ranked:	
Rank	MOST EFFECTIVE	MODERATELY EFFECTIVE
1 Schoolteachers' organizations (predominantly NEA)	43	5
2 General business organizations (chambers of commerce, etc.)	37	16
3 Utility companies and associations (electric, gas, water, telephones, cable TV)	23	24
4 Lawyers (predominantly trial lawyers and state bar associations)	26	14
5 Traditional labor associations (predominantly the AFL-CIO)	22	13
6 Doctors	22	12
7 Insurance: general and medical (companies and associations)	21	15
8 Manufacturers (companies and associations)	20	15
9 Health care organizations (mainly hospital associations)	15	24
10 Bankers' associations (includes savings & loan associations)	21	11
11 General local government organizations (municipal leagues, county organizations, etc.)	16	21
12 State and local government employee unions (other than teachers)	18	14
13 General farm organizations (mainly state farm bureaus)	14	20
14 Individual banks and financial institutions	14	8
15 Environmentalists	9	16
16 Universities and colleges (institutions and personnel)	7	16
17 Realtors' associations	8	12
18 Individual cities and towns	8	12
19 Gaming interests (race tracks, casinos, lotteries)	7	11
20 Contractors, builders, developers	7	10
21 Liquor, wine, and beer interests	7	10
22 Retailers (companies and trade associations)	6	11
23 Senior citizens (AARP chapters, etc.)	1	19
24 Mining companies and associations	6	7
25 Truckers and private transport interests (excluding railroads)	5	8
26 Taxpayers' interest groups	5	7
27 State agencies	5	7
28 Individual traditional labor unions (Teamsters, UAW, etc.)	6	4
29 Sportsmen/hunting and fishing (includes the NRA and antigun control groups)	3	10
30 Miscellaneous social issue groups (handicapped, crime victims, children and family [MADD, etc.])	2	11
31 Oil and gas (companies and associations)	3	7
32 Women and minorities (NOW, League of Women Voters, NAACP, etc.)	3	7
33 Religious interests (churches and religious groups)	2	9

Table 4-4 (Continued)

Rank		Number of States in Which Interest Ranked:	
		MOST EFFECTIVE	MODERATELY EFFECTIVE
34	Miscellaneous professional occupational groups	2	9
35	Public interest/good government groups (Common Cause, PIRGs, ACLU, etc.)	4	4
36	Agricultural commodity organizations (stock growers, grain growers, etc.)	1	12
37	Railroads	2	7
38	Forest product companies	3	4

Source: From Clive S. Thomas and Ronald J. Hrebenar, in Virginia Gray and Herbert Jacob, eds.,
Politics in the American States, 6th ed. Washington, DC: CQ Press, 1996.

They "know their way around" the capitol. They offer their services—access to legislative and executive officials, knowledge of the lawmaking process, ability to present information and testimony to key policy makers at the right time, political skills and knowledge, personal friendships, and "connections"—to their clients at rates that usually depend upon their reputation for influence. Occasionally their compensation is tied to their success in getting a bill passed; a six-figure fee may rest on the outcome of a single vote. Some professional lobbyists are attached to law firms or public relations firms and occasionally do other work; others are full-time lobbyists with multiple clients.

Most professional lobbyists publicly attribute their success to hard work, persistence, information, and ability to get along with others: "Being prepared, personal credibility"; "Legislators know I'm going to present the facts whether they're favorable to my client or not"; "I'm a forceful advocate—determined"; "Doing my homework on the issues"; "Knowledge of the issues I'm dealing with and knowledge of the system"; "I try to understand the political pressures on elected officials." Yet in more candid moments professional lobbyists will acknowledge that their success is largely attributable to personal friendships, political experience, and financial contributions: "Close friends I made in the legislature while I served as Speaker of the House"; "I raise a lot of money for people"; "My client has the largest political action committee in the state."[27]

LOBBY REGISTRATION   It is very difficult to get a comprehensive picture of interest group activity in state capitals. Many organizations, businesses, legal firms, and individuals engage in interest group activity of one kind or another, and it is difficult to keep track of their varied activities. Most states require the registration of "lobbyists" and the submission of reports about their membership and finances. These laws do not restrain lobbying (that would probably violate the First Amendment freedom to "petition" the government for "redress of grievances"). Rather, they are meant to spotlight the activities of lobbyists. However, many hundreds of lobbyists never register under the pretext that they are not *really lobbyists,* but, instead, businesses, public relations firms, lawyers, researchers, or educational people. Usually, only the larger, formal, organized interest groups and professional lobbyists are *officially* registered as lobbyists in their states.

FUNCTIONS AND TACTICS OF INTEREST GROUPS

Interest group techniques are as varied as the imaginations of their leaders. Groups are attempting to advance their interests when a liquor firm sends a case of bourbon to a state legislator; when the League of Women Voters distributes biographies of political candidates; when an insurance company argues before a state insurance commission that rates must be increased; when the National Education Association provides state legislators with information comparing teachers' salaries in the fifty states; when railroads ask state highway departments to place weight limitations upon trucks; or when the American Civil Liberties Union supplies lawyers for civil rights demonstrators.

TYPICAL TACTICS   Typical lists of lobbying activities as supplied by lobbyists themselves usually begin with testifying at legislative committee hearings, contacting legislators directly, and helping to draft legislation (see Table 4–5). These lists usually go on to include getting constituents to contact legislators, inspiring letter-writing campaigns, and entering coalitions with other groups to lobby about particular pieces of legislation. Somewhat fewer lobbyists admit to making monetary contributions to legislators and performing personal and political favors for them, but we know from campaign contribution records and anecdotal evidence that these practices are very common. Some lobbying organizations focus more on filing lawsuits or otherwise engaging in court litigation; indeed, some larger organizations have semiautonomous "legal defense" branches to carry on such activity. Relatively few interest groups resort to protests and demonstrations. None admit to direct bribery, but, as we shall see, reports of direct payments to legislators or their campaign funds in exchange for votes are not uncommon.

BILL MONITORING   More time is spent by lobbyists on monitoring the content and progress of bills affecting their clients and members than on any other activity. Just "keeping tabs" on what is going on each day in government is a time-consuming task. Lobbyists must be aware of any provisions of any bills affecting their clients, even provisions that are buried in a bill that does not mention them in its title or summary. Typically lobbyists may identify 100 or more bills that might affect their clients or members each legislative session, although they are likely to closely monitor the progress of only twenty or thirty bills that have a chance of becoming enacted.[28] (Only about 15 percent of bills introduced in a legislature are ever enacted in any form into law; see Chapter 6.) Lobbyists must be watchful: Nothing is more embarrassing to a lobbyist than to find that the legislature has passed a bill adversely affecting their client's interests without their ever knowing about it.

Table 4–5

TYPICAL LOBBYING ACTIVITIES

Ranked by frequency of mention by lobbyists and lobbying organizations themselves

1. Testifying at legislative hearings
2. Contacting government officials directly to present point of view
3. Helping to draft legislation
4. Alerting state legislators to the effects of a bill on their districts
5. Having influential constituents contact legislator's office
6. Consulting with government officials to plan legislative strategy
7. Attempting to shape implementation of policies
8. Mounting grass-roots lobbying efforts
9. Helping to draft regulations, rules, or guidelines
10. Shaping government's agenda by raising new issues and calling attention to previously ignored problems
11. Engaging in informal contacts with officials
12. Inspiring letter-writing or telegram campaigns
13. Entering into coalitions with other groups
14. Talking to media
15. Serving on advisory commissions and boards
16. Making monetary contributions to candidates
17. Attempting to influence appointment to public office
18. Doing favors for officials who need assistance
19. Filing suit or otherwise engaging in litigation
20. Working on election campaign
21. Endorsing candidates
22. Running advertisements in media about position
23. Engaging in protests or demonstrations

Sources: Anthony J. Nownes and Patricia Freeman, "Interest Group Activity in the States," *Journal of Politics,* 60 (February 1998), 92; Kay Lehman Schlozman and John T. Tierney, "More of the Same: Pressure Group Activity in a Decade of Change," *Journal of Politics,* 45 (May 1983), 357.

LOBBYING   *Lobbying* is defined as any communication, by someone acting on behalf of a group, directed at a government decision maker with the hope of influencing that person. Direct persuasion is usually more than just a matter of argument or emotional appeal to the lawmaker. Often it involves the communication of useful technical and political information. Many public officials are required to vote on, or decide about, hundreds of questions each year. It is impossible for them to be fully informed about the wide variety of bills and issues they face. Consequently, many decision makers depend upon skilled lobbyists to provide technical information about matters requiring action, and to inform them of the policy preferences of important segments of the population. (See "Lobbying in State Legislatures" in Chapter 6.)

The behavior of lobbyists depends on the interests they represent and the characteristics of the state political system in which they function. Some interests hire full-time

■

Lobbying.
Communications directed at government decision makers with the purpose of influencing policy.

■

"Schmoozing."
Informal contacts between
lobbyists and legislators.

Bribery.
Offering anything of value
to government officials with
the purpose of influencing
them in the performance of
their duties.

Grass-roots lobbying.
Influencing legislators by
contacting their constituents
and asking them to contact
their legislators.

lobbyists; others rely on attorneys or firms who lobby on behalf of more than one group. Still other interests rely on volunteers. Some maintain active contact with legislators or make campaign contributions. Some formulate a legislative agenda each session and trace the progress of bills in which they are interested. Indeed, one study of lobbying on behalf of the aging in four separate states revealed much variation in lobbying activity even on the same issues.[29]

"SCHMOOZING"   "Schmoozing" usually refers to informal contacts between lobbyists and legislators—at local bars, restaurants, country clubs, testimonial dinners, and occasionally during vacation travel. Typically lobbyists pick up the bill for these activities. This is not an illegal practice, although many states now require officially registered lobbyists to list such expenditures. Gifts are occasionally given by lobbyists to legislators, but states usually require legislators to report gifts over specified dollar values.

BRIBERY AND CORRUPTION   Lobbying in state capitals may be somewhat cruder—if not more corrupt—than lobbying in Washington. In interviewing lobbyists and legislators in Washington, Lester Milbrath found that they considered state lobbying much more corrupt than national lobbying. "'Lobbying is very different before state legislators; it is much more individualistic. Maybe this is the reason they have more bribery in state legislatures than in Congress.' 'In the state legislatures, lobbying is definitely on a lower plane. The lobbyists are loose and hand out money and favors quite freely.' 'Lobbying at the state level is cruder, more basic, and more obvious.'"[30] Needless to say, it is difficult to document such statements. However, it seems reasonable to believe that state legislators might be more subject to the appeals of organized interest groups than members of Congress.

State legislators, unlike most members of Congress, are only part-time lawmakers. They must manage their own business, professional, and investment interests in addition to their legislative duties. They may have personal business or professional or real estate or legal ties with the same interests that are seeking to influence their legislative behavior. Such "conflicts of interests"—legislators voting in committee or on the floor on issues in which they have a personal financial interest—are not uncommon. Indeed, some interests occasionally seek to establish business or professional ties with legislators just to win their support.

Bribery is the offering of anything of value to government officials to influence them in the performance of their duties. Vote buying is illegal, but not unheard of in state capitals. Instead of bribery, organized interests may contribute to a legislator's campaign chest without mentioning any specific quid pro quo.

GRASS-ROOTS LOBBYING, MEDIA CAMPAIGNS, AND PUBLIC RELATIONS
Most people think of interest group tactics as direct attempts to influence decision makers, but many groups spend more of their time, energy, and resources in general public relations activities than anything else. The purpose of a continuing public relations campaign is to create an environment favorable to the interest group and its program. It is hoped that a reservoir of public goodwill can be established, which can be relied on later when a critical issue arises.

Lobbyists know that legislators pay attention to their constituents. Grass-roots lobbying involves interest group efforts to get constituents to call or write their legislator on behalf of the group's position on pending legislation. Grass-roots campaigns are now highly professional. They "rely totally on mass marketing, high technology, and public relations ploys reminiscent of political campaigns."[31] Form letters supplied to constituents by interest groups to sign and send to their legislator may not be very effective. But direct calls and personal letters and faxes, especially from constituents who have previously contributed to a legislator's campaign, are seldom ignored.

Media campaigns are very effective, but also very expensive. These involve paid advertisements on radio or television designed to influence public opinion on pending legislation. Heavy media campaigns are more likely to be undertaken by lobbyists in Washington, DC, than in state capitals. Only about 20 to 30 percent of lobbyists in the states report having directly advertised in the media.[32]

PAC MONEY IN THE STATES   Political campaigns are very expensive, and it is always difficult for a candidate to find enough money to finance a campaign. This is true for officeholders seeking reelection as well as new contenders. It is perfectly legal for an interest group to make a contribution to a candidate's campaign fund. Ordinarily, a respectable lobbyist would not be so crude as to exact any specific pledges from a candidate in exchange for a campaign contribution. He or she simply makes a contribution and lets the candidate figure out what to do when in office to assure further contributions to the candidate's next campaign. (For further discussion, see "Money in State Politics" in this chapter.)

Interest groups, operating through political action committees or PACs, are becoming the major source of campaign funding for state office. As campaign costs increase, reliance on PAC money increases. In large urban states such as California and New York, where campaigns for state legislature may cost $100,000 or more, PAC contributions are the largest source of campaign funding (see Table 4–6).

PACs are politically sophisticated contributors. They do not like to back losers. Since incumbent members of state legislatures running for reelection seldom lose (see "The Great Incumbency Machine" in Chapter 6), PAC contributions are heavily weighted in favor of incumbents over challengers. Table 4–7 reveals the pattern of PAC contributions for state legislative races in eleven states. Note that PAC contributors in the larger states may account for as much as one-quarter to one-third of the total contributions to state legislative races.

COMPARING INTEREST GROUP POWER IN THE STATES

How do interest group systems in the states differ? Why do some states have strong, influential interest groups shaping public policy, while in other states the influence of interest groups is moderated by group competition, party rivalry, and electoral politics?

We might define overall interest group influence in a state as "the extent to which interest groups as a whole influence public policy when compared to other components of the political system, such as political parties, the legislature, the governor, etc."[33]

Table 4-6

INTEREST GROUP CAMPAIGN CONTRIBUTIONS: FUNDING THE FLORIDA SENATE PRESIDENT

As president of the Florida state senate, Democrat Pat Thomas was a favored recipient of PAC contributions in his 1992 reelection campaign. Florida law limits contributions to $500 for each election. The following is a partial list of Thomas's contributors.

Contributor	Business/Trade	Contributor	Business/Trade
Agents PAC	Insurance	Professional Fire Fighters of Fla.	Firefighters
Accredited Bond Agencies, Inc.	Bail Bonds	Funeral Directors	Funerals
American Cyanamid	Chemical	Florida Asphalt Contractors	Construction
American Family Corp.	Insurance	Florida Associated Services Inc.	Computer
American Family Life	Insurance	Florida Assn. of Surety Agents	Bail bonds
Anesthesiology PAC	Physicians	Florida Bankpac-State	Bank
Anheuser Bush Companies	Beer	Florida Beer Wholesalers	Beer
AFSCME	Public employees	Florida Business Forum Inc.	Business
American Publishers Assn.	Book publishers	Florida Chiropractic Association	Chiropractors
Associated Industries of Florida	Manufacturers	Florida CPA	CPAs
AT&T PAC–Florida	Telephone	Florida Dairy Farmers Association	Dairy farmers
Barnett People for Better Gov't	Bank	Florida Dental PAC	Dentists
Lewis Bear Co.	Wholesale	Florida Employers Insurance	Insurance
Ronnie Bergeron	Road construction	Florida Engineers	Engineers
Blue Cross/Blue Shield	Health insurance	Florida Farm Bureau	Agriculture
Calder Race Course, Inc.	Horse track	Florida Fruit and Vegetable Assn.	Agriculture
Cargill Poultry Products	Poultry	Florida Greyhound Track Owners	Dog tracks
Carson Farms	Farms	Florida Hearing Aid Society	Manufacturers
CAR PAC	Car dealers	Florida Hospital League	Hospital
Carlton, Fields PAC	Attorneys/lobbyists	Florida Medical PAC	Doctors
Centel Corp.	Telephone	Florida Osteopathic Medical Assn.	Osteopaths
Champion International Corp.	Paper	Florida Phosphate Committee	Phosphate industry
Citizens & Southern	Bank	Florida Podiatry PAC	Podiatrists
Clark, Roumelis and Associates	Engineering	Florida Premium Finance Assn.	Financial services
Coastal States Mgmt.	Energy	Florida Propane PAC	Propane gas
Coca-Cola Bottling Co.	Bottler	Florida Restaurant Assn.	Restaurants
CSX Transportation	Rail transportation	Florida RV Trade Assn.	Recreational vehicles
Eastern Airlines PAC	Airlines	Florida Shopping Center	Commercial
E. I. DuPont DeNemours & Co.	Chemical	Florida Transportation	Truckers
Everglades Agriculture PAC	Agricultural	Florida Trucking Assn.	Truckers
Exxon Corp. 500	Oil	GTE State PAC	Telephone

Source: Florida, Office of the Secretary of State.

Table 4–7

PAC CONTRIBUTIONS TO STATE LEGISLATIVE RACES				
	Percent of PAC Contributions Going to:			
State	INCUMBENTS	CHALLENGERS	OPEN SEAT CANDIDATES	TOTALS
California	39%	13%	23%	26%
Idaho	57%	12%	28%	31%
Minnesota	24%	8%	18%	16%
Missouri	21%	6%	9%	12%
Montana	28%	17%	9%	18%
North Carolina	49%	16%	16%	3%
New Jersey	28%	15%	15%	21%
Oregon	63%	21%	48%	43%
Pennsylvania	53%	19%	29%	35%
Washington	37%	31%	26%	33%
Wisconsin	22%	5%	14%	13%

Source: Derived from William E. Cassie, Joel A. Thompson, and Malcolm E. Jewell, "The Pattern of PAC Contributions in Legislative Elections: An Eleven-State Analysis." Paper delivered at the Annual Meeting of the American Political Science Association, Chicago, 1992.

Using this definition researchers have attempted to categorize the states as having a "dominant," "complementary," or "subordinate" interest group system, in terms of its policy impact relative to the parties and the branches of government (see Table 4–8).

Over time interest group influence appears to be increasing in all of the states. A major factor in this strengthening of interest groups is their increasing role in campaign finance. The more money coming from interest groups to political candidates, the greater is the influence of the interest group system.

Yet interest group influence in some states is greater than in other states, and our task is to search for explanations.

THE ECONOMIC DIVERSITY EXPLANATION   Wealthy urban industrial states (Connecticut, Massachusetts, Michigan, New Jersey, New York, Rhode Island) have weaker interest group systems because of the diversity and complexity of their economies. No single industry can dominate political life. Instead, multiple competing interest groups tend to balance each other, and this cancels the influence of interest groups generally. In contrast, in rural states with less economic diversity, a few dominant industries (oil and gas in Louisiana, coal in West Virginia) appear to have more influence. The reputation for influence for particular industries in these states causes them to be viewed as strong pressure group states.

Table 4–8

CLASSIFICATION OF THE FIFTY STATES ACCORDING TO THE OVERALL IMPACT OF INTEREST GROUPS

States Where the Overall Impact of Interest Groups Is:

DOMINANT (7)	DOMINANT/ COMPLEMENTARY (21)	COMPLEMENTARY (17)	COMPLEMENTARY/ SUBORDINATE (5)	SUBORDINATE (0)
Alabama	Alaska	Colorado	Delaware	
Florida	Arizona	Connecticut	Minnesota	
Louisiana	Arkansas	Indiana	Rhode Island	
Nevada	California	Maine	South Dakota	
New Mexico	Georgia	Maryland	Vermont	
South Carolina	Hawaii	Massachusetts		
West Virginia	Idaho	Michigan		
	Illinois	Missouri		
	Iowa	New Hampshire		
	Kansas	New Jersey		
	Kentucky	New York		
	Mississippi	North Carolina		
	Montana	North Dakota		
	Nebraska	Pennsylvania		
	Ohio	Utah		
	Oklahoma	Washington		
	Oregon	Wisconsin		
	Tennessee			
	Texas			
	Virginia			
	Wyoming			

Source: Clive Thomas and Ronald J. Hrebenar, "Interest Groups in the States," in Virginia Gray and Herbert Jacob, eds., *Politics in the American States,* 6th ed. Washington, DC: CQ Press, 1996.

THE PARTY EXPLANATION   According to political scientist Sarah McCally More-house, "Where parties are strong, pressure groups are weak or moderate; where parties are weak, pressure groups are strong enough to dominate the policy-making process."[34] Where competitive political parties are strong—where the parties actively recruit candidates, provide campaign support, and hold their members accountable after the election—interest groups are less powerful. Policy makers in these states look to the party for policy guidance rather than to interest groups. Interest group influence is channeled through the parties; the parties are coalitions of interest groups; no single interest group can dominate or circumvent the party. Strong party states (Connecticut, Illinois, New York, Minnesota, North Dakota, Rhode Island, Wisconsin, Massachusetts, Colorado) have weak interest group systems. Weak party states (primarily the one-party southern states) have strong interest group systems. Party competition is discussed earlier in this chapter.

Strong governors and strong legislative leadership, exercising their influence as party leaders, can provide a check on the lobbying efforts of interest groups. When the special interests lose, it is usually on issues on which the governor and the party leadership have taken a clear stand.[35]

Professionalism.
In legislatures, the extent to which members have the services of full-time, well-paid staff, as well as their access to research and sources of information.

THE PROFESSIONALISM EXPLANATION   State legislatures are becoming more professional over time. In Chapter 6 we define a *professional* legislature as a well-paid, full-time, well-staffed body, as opposed to an amateur legislature, which meets only a few weeks each year, pays its members very little, and has few research or information services available to it. Professional legislatures have less turnover in members and more experience in lawmaking. Clearly, these characteristics of legislatures affect the power of interest groups. Interest groups are more influential when legislatures are *less* professional. When members are less experienced, paid less, and have little time or resources to research issues themselves, they must depend more on interest groups, and interest groups gain influence.

THE GOVERNMENTAL FRAGMENTATION EXPLANATION   It is also likely that states with weak governors, multiple independently elected state officials, and numerous independent boards and commissions have strong interest group systems. In states with fragmented executive power (Florida, South Carolina), interest groups have additional points of access and control, and executive officials do not have counterbalancing power. Strong governors (as in New York, Massachusetts, New Jersey, Connecticut, Delaware, and Minnesota) are better able to confront the influence of interest groups when they choose to do so. (We will discuss governors' powers in Chapter 7.)

Fortunately, we do not have to choose one explanation to the exclusion of others. Economic diversity, party strength, professionalism, and governmental fragmentation all contribute to the explanation of interest group strength in the states.

PROTEST AS POLITICAL PARTICIPATION

Organized protests—marches, demonstrations, disruptions, civil disobedience—are important forms of political activity. Protest marches and demonstrations are now nearly as frequent at state capitols and city halls as in Washington.

It is important to distinguish between *protest, civil disobedience,* and *violence,* even though all may be forms of political activity. Most *protests* do *not* involve unlawful conduct and are protected by the constitutional guarantee of the First Amendment to "peaceably assemble and petition for redress of grievances." A march on city hall or the state capitol, followed by a mass assembly of people with speakers, sign-waving, songs, and perhaps the formal presentation of grievances to whichever brave official

■

Protest.
In politics, public activities designed to call attention to issues and influence decision makers.

Civil disobedience.
A form of protest that involves peaceful nonviolent breaking of laws considered to be unjust.

agrees to meet with the protesters is well within the constitutional guarantees of Americans.

PROTEST   Protest refers to direct, collective activity by persons who wish to obtain concessions from established power holders. Often the protest is a means of acquiring bargaining power by those who would otherwise be powerless. The protest may challenge established groups by threatening their reputations (in cases in which they might be harmed by unfavorable publicity), their economic position (in cases in which noise and disruption upset their daily activity), or their sense of security (when the threat exists that the protest may turn unruly or violent). The strategy of protest may appeal especially to powerless minorities who have little else to bargain with except the promise to stop protesting.

Protests may also aim at motivating uncommitted "third parties" to enter the political arena on behalf of the protesters. The object of the protest is to call attention to the existence of some issue and urge others to apply pressure on public officials. Of course, this strategy requires the support and assistance of the news media. If protests are ignored by television and newspapers, they can hardly be expected to activate support. However, the news media seldom ignore protests with audience interest; protest leaders and journalists share an interest in dramatizing "news" for the public.

CIVIL DISOBEDIENCE   Civil disobedience is a form of protest that involves breaking "unjust" laws. Civil disobedience is not new: It has played an important role in American history, from the Boston Tea Party to the abolitionists who illegally hid runaway slaves, to the suffragettes who demonstrated for women's voting rights, to the labor organizers who picketed to form the nation's major industrial unions, to the civil rights workers of the early 1960s who deliberately violated segregation laws. The purpose of civil disobedience is to call attention, or to "bear witness," to the existence of injustice. In the words of Martin Luther King, Jr., civil disobedience "seeks to dramatize the issue so that it can no longer be ignored."[36] There should be no violence in true civil disobedience, and only "unjust" laws are broken. Moreover, the law is broken "openly, lovingly" with a willingness to accept the penalty. Punishment is actively sought rather than avoided, since punishment will help to emphasize the injustice of the law. The object is to stir the conscience of an apathetic majority and win support for measures that will eliminate injustices. By willingly accepting punishment for the violation of an unjust law, people who practice civil disobedience demonstrate their sincerity. They hope to shame public officials and make them ask themselves how far they are willing to go to protect the status quo.

As in all protest activity, the participation of the news media, particularly television, is essential to the success of civil disobedience. The dramatization of injustice makes news; the public's sympathy is won when injustices are spotlighted; and the willingness of demonstrators to accept punishment is visible evidence of their sincerity. Cruelty or violence directed *against* the demonstrators by police or others plays into the hands of the protesters by further emphasizing injustices.[37]

VIOLENCE   *Violence* can also be a form of political participation. To be sure, it is criminal, and it is generally irrational and self-defeating. However, political assassination; bombing and terrorism; and rioting, burning, and looting have occurred with uncomfortable frequency in American politics.

It is important to distinguish violence from protest. Peaceful protest is constitutionally guaranteed. Most protests are free of violence. Occasionally there is an implicit *threat* of violence in a protest—a threat that can be manipulated by protesters to help gain their ends. However, most protests harness frustrations and hostilities and direct them into constitutionally acceptable activities. Civil disobedience should also be distinguished from violence. The civil disobedient breaks only "unjust" laws, openly and without violence, and willingly accepts punishment without attempting escape. Rioting, burning, and looting—as well as bombing and assassination—are clearly distinguishable from peaceful protest and even civil disobedience.

NEWS MEDIA   The real key to success in protest activity is found in the support or opposition of the news media to protest group demands. Virtually all of the studies of protest activity have asserted that it is the response of "third parties," primarily the news media, and not the immediate response of public officials, that is essential to success.[38] This is a plausible finding, because, after all, if protesters could persuade public officials directly there would be no need to protest. Indeed, one might even distinguish between "interest groups," which have a high degree of continuous interaction with public officials, and "protest groups," which do not regularly interact with public officials and must engage in protest to be heard. Furthermore, to be heard, reports of their protests must be carried in newspapers and on television.

THE EFFECTIVENESS OF PROTESTS   Several conditions must be present if protest is to be effective.[39] First of all, there must be a clear goal or objective of the protest. Protesters must aim at specific concessions or legislation they desire; generally, complex problems or complaints that cannot readily be solved by specific governmental action are not good targets for protest activity. Second, the protest must be directed at some public officials who are capable of granting the desired goal. It is difficult to secure concessions if no one is in a position to grant them. Third, the protest leaders must not only organize their masses for protest activity, but they must also simultaneously bargain with public officials for the desired concessions. This implies a division of labor between "organizers" and "negotiators."

OFFICIAL RESPONSES TO PROTESTS   Finally, we might note in this discussion the strategies available to public officials who are faced with protest activity. They may greet the protesters with smiles and reassurances that they agree with their objectives. They may dispense *symbolic* satisfaction without actually granting any tangible payoffs. Once the "crisis" is abated, the bargaining leverage of the protest leaders diminishes considerably. Public officials may dispense *token* satisfactions by responding, with much publicity, to one or more specific cases of injustice, while doing little of a broad-based nature to alleviate conditions. Or public officials may *appear to be constrained* in their ability to grant protest goals by claiming that they lack the financial resources or legal authority to do anything—the "I-would-help-you-if-I-could-but-I-can't" pose. Another tactic is to *postpone action* by calling for further study while of-

DID YOU KNOW?

THE STATES AND THEIR CAPITALS

For each state we have listed the capital city and the largest city. You might try to identify these cities *without* first looking at their names.

State	Capital	Largest City
Alabama	Montgomery	Birmingham
Alaska	Juneau	Anchorage
Arizona	Phoenix	Phoenix
Arkansas	Little Rock	Little Rock
California	Sacramento	Los Angeles
Colorado	Denver	Denver
Connecticut	Hartford	Bridgeport
Delaware	Dover	Wilmington
Florida	Tallahassee	Jacksonville
Georgia	Atlanta	Atlanta
Hawaii	Honolulu	Honolulu
Idaho	Boise	Boise
Illinois	Springfield	Chicago
Indiana	Indianapolis	Indianapolis
Iowa	Des Moines	Des Moines
Kansas	Topeka	Wichita
Kentucky	Frankfort	Louisville
Louisiana	Baton Rouge	New Orleans
Maine	Augusta	Portland
Maryland	Annapolis	Baltimore
Massachusetts	Boston	Boston
Michigan	Lansing	Detroit
Minnesota	St. Paul	Minneapolis
Mississippi	Jackson	Jackson
Missouri	Jefferson City	St. Louis
Montana	Helena	Billings
Nebraska	Lincoln	Omaha
Nevada	Carson City	Las Vegas
New Hampshire	Concord	Manchester
New Jersey	Trenton	Newark

fering assurances of sympathy and interest. Finally, public officials may try to *discredit* protesters by stating or implying that they are violence-prone or unrepresentative of the real aspirations of the people they seek to lead. This tactic is especially effective if the protest involves violence or disruption or if protest leaders have "leftist" or criminal backgrounds.

State	Capital	Largest City
New Mexico	Santa Fe	Albuquerque
New York	Albany	New York
North Carolina	Raleigh	Charlotte
North Dakota	Bismarck	Fargo
Ohio	Columbus	Cleveland
Oklahoma	Oklahoma City	Oklahoma City
Oregon	Salem	Portland
Pennsylvania	Harrisburg	Philadelphia
Rhode Island	Providence	Providence
South Carolina	Columbia	Columbia
South Dakota	Pierre	Sioux Falls
Tennessee	Nashville	Memphis
Texas	Austin	Houston
Utah	Salt Lake City	Salt Lake City
Vermont	Montpelier	Burlington
Virginia	Richmond	Norfolk
Washington	Olympia	Seattle
West Virginia	Charleston	Charleston
Wisconsin	Madison	Milwaukee
Wyoming	Cheyenne	Casper

ON THE WEB

The Internet offers yet another form of political participation. Virtually all serious candidates for national and statewide office—president, Congress, governor, and so on—open Web sites early in their campaigns. Typically campaign Web sites offer flattering profiles of the candidates together with their public records and policy statements (and, of course, addresses to send campaign contributions).

A good starting point for seeking out political information relevant to your state (or to particular issues or interest groups or election results) is

www.politicaljunkie.com

This is a comprehensive Web site with direct links to political news sources, columnists, candidates, parties, interest groups, lobbyists, PACs, think tanks, and much more (including political humor). It offers state-by-state links under "How to Register by State" and "Key Dates for Each State."

Among the many Web sites that encourage political participation is the League of Women Voters' site at

www.lwv.org

The Project Vote Smart site at

www.vote-smart.org

offers the opportunity to track the public records of candidates and elected officials, including the president, members of Congress, governors, and state legislators. If you do not know who represents you in Congress or your state legislature, you can simply enter your ZIP code where indicated and Project Vote Smart will provide that information.

Most major interest groups maintain national Web sites that include addresses and often direct links to state affiliates. And for most major interest groups, joining up is just a click away. See, for example:

American Association of Retired Persons (AARP) at

www.aarp.org

Common Cause at

www.commoncause.org

and Christian Coalition at

www.cc.org

NOTES:

1. Lee Sigelman et al., "Voting and Nonvoting: A Multi-Election Perspective," *American Journal of Political Science,* 29 (November 1985), 749–65.

2. William H. Riker and Peter C. Ordeshook, "A Theory of the Calculus of Voting," *American Political Science Review,* 62 (March 1968), 25–42.

3. J. A. Ferejohn and Morris Fiorina, "The Paradox of Voting," *American Political Science Review,* 18 (March 1974), 525–36.

4. See John R. Bauer, "Patterns of Voter Participation in the American States," *Social Science Quarterly,* 71 (December 1990), 824–34; education is even more important in determining voter turnout in states with restrictive registration laws and lower competition levels.

5. See Stephen Earl Bennett and David Resnick, "The Implications of Nonvoting for Democracy in the United States," *American Journal of Political Science,* 34 (August 1990), 771–802.

6. Sidney Verba, Kay Schlozman, Henry Brady, and Norman Nie, "Citizen Activity: Who Participates? What Do They Say?" *American Political Science Review,* 87 (June 1993), 303–18.

7. Kim Quaile Hill, Jan E. Laghley, and Angela Hinton-Anderson, "Lower-Class Mobilization and Policy Linkage in the States," *American Journal of Political Science,* 39 (February 1995), 75–86.

8. See Staci L. Rhine, "Registration Reform and Turnout Change in the American States," *American Politics Quarterly,* 23 (October 1995), 409–26; Stephen Knack, "Does Motor-Voter Work?

Evidence from State Level Data," *Journal of Politics,* 57 (August 1995), 796–811.

9. Samuel C. Patterson and Gregory A. Caldeira, "Getting Out the Vote: Participation in Gubernatorial Elections," *American Political Science Review,* 77 (September 1983), 675–89.

10. *Smith* v. *Allright,* 321 U.S. 649 (1941).

11. *Harper* v. *Virginia State Board of Elections,* 383 U.S. 663 (1966).

12. *South Carolina* v. *Katzenbach,* U.S. 301 (1966).

13. Congress had earlier passed the Voting Rights Act of 1970, which (1) extended the vote to eighteen-year-olds regardless of state law; (2) abolished residency requirements in excess of thirty days; and (3) prohibited literacy tests. However, there was some constitutional debate about the power of Congress to change state laws on voting age. While Congress can end *racial* discrimination, extending the vote to eighteen-year-olds was a different matter. All previous extensions of the vote had come by constitutional amendment. Hence, Congress quickly passed the Twenty-sixth Amendment.

14. *Mobile* v. *Bolden,* 446 U.S. 50 (1980).

15. See Susan A. MacManus, "Racial Representation Issues," *Political Science and Politics,* 18 (Fall 1985), 759–69.

16. *Thornburg* v. *Gingles,* 478 U.S. 30 (1986).

17. Kevin A. Hill, "Does the Creation of Majority Black Districts Aid Republicans?" *Journal of Politics,* 57 (May 1995), 384–401.

18. *Shaw* v. *Reno* (1993).

19. *Miller* v. *Johnson* (1995).

20. Bernard Grofman and Lisa Handley, "The Impact of the Voting Rights Act on Black Representation in Southern State Legislatures," *Legislative Studies Quarterly,* 16 (February 1991), 111–28; Benjamin Radcliff and Martin Saiz, "Race, Turnout, and Public Policy in the States," *Political Research Quarterly,* 48 (December 1995), 775–94.

21. Center for the American Woman and Politics, Eagleton Institute of Politics, Rutgers University. See also "Gender" in Chapter 6, Legislators in State Politics; "Gender" in Chapter 7, Governors in State Politics; and "Women in Local Politics" in Chapter 11, Participation in Community Politics.

22. Sue Thomas, "The Impact of Women on State Legislative Policies," *Journal of Politics,* 53 (November 1991), 958–76. See also Michelle A. Saint-Germain, "Does Their Difference Make a Difference?" *Social Science Quarterly,* 70 (December 1989), 956–68.

23. Lyn Kathlene, "Alternative Views of Crime: Legislative Policymaking in Gendered Terms," *Journal of Politics,* 57 (August 1995), 696–723.

24. Susan MacManus, *Young vs. Old: Generational Conflict in the 21st Century* (Boulder, CO: Westview Press, 1996), p. 23.

25. Walter A. Rosenbaum and James W. Batton, "Is There a Gray Peril? Retirement Politics in Florida," *Gerontologist,* vol. 29 (1995), 301.

26. See Benjamin Radcliff and Martin Saiz, "Labor Organization and Public Policy in the American States," *Journal of Politics,* 60 (February 1998), 113–25.

27. Quotations reported in *Tallahassee Democrat,* January 12, 1992.

28. Anthony J. Nownes and Patricia Freeman, "Interest Group Activity in the States," *Journal of Politics,* 60 (February 1998), 86–112.

29. See, for example, William P. Browne, "Variations in the Behavior and Style of State Lobbyists and Interest Groups," *Journal of Politics,* 47 (May 1985), 450–68.

30. Quotations from legislators in Lester Milbrath, *The Washington Lobbyists* (Chicago: Rand McNally, 1963), pp. 241–43.

31. Alan J. Cigler and Burdett A. Lomis, *Interest Group Politics,* 4th ed. (Washington, DC: Congressional Quarterly Press, 1995), p. 395.

32. Nownes and Freeman, "Interest Group Activity."

33. Clive S. Thomas and Robert J. Hrebenar, "Interest Groups in the States," in Virginia Gray et al., *Politics in the American States,* 5th ed. (New York: HarperCollins, 1990), p. 141.

34. Sarah McCally Morehouse, *State Politics, Parties and Policy* (New York: Holt, Rinehart and Winston, 1981), p. 118.

35. See Charles W. Wiggins, Keith E. Harmun, and Charles G. Bell, "Interest-Group and Party Influence Agents in the Legislative Process: A Comparative State Analysis," *Journal of Politics,* 54 (February 1992), 82–100.

36. For an inspiring essay on "nonviolent direct action" and civil disobedience in a modern context, read Martin Luther King, Jr., "Letter from Birmingham City Jail," April 16, 1963.

37. For a more detailed examination of the purposes, functions, and rationale of civil disobedience, see Paul F. Power, "Civil Disobedience as Functional Opposition," *Journal of Politics,* 34 (February 1972), 37–55; and "On Civil Disobedience in Recent American Thought," *American Political Science Review,* 64 (March 1970), 35–47.

38. Michael Lipsky, *Protest in City Politics* (Chicago: Rand McNally, 1970); Peter K. Eisinger, "The Conditions of Protest Behavior in American Cities," *American Political Science Review,* 67 (March 1973), 11–29; Paul D. Schumaker, "Policy Responsiveness to Protest Group Demands," *Journal of Politics,* 37 (May 1975), 488–521.

39. See Michael Lipsky, "Protest as a Political Resource," *American Political Science Review,* 62 (December 1968), 1144–58.

5

PARTIES AND CAMPAIGNS
IN THE STATES

QUESTIONS TO CONSIDER
★ ★ ★ ★ ★ ★ ★ ★ ★

Do you believe that the Democratic and Republican parties in your state offer clear policy alternatives to the voters?

❑ Yes
❑ No

In politics, do you generally identify yourself as a

❑ Democrat
❑ Republican
❑ Independent

Should candidates be limited in the amount of money they can spend in their campaigns?

❑ Yes
❑ No

Should public funds be used to pay for political campaigns?

❑ Yes
❑ No

AMERICAN POLITICAL PARTIES IN DISARRAY

Once upon a time, political parties were the central features on the American political landscape. Party loyalties were a way of life, passed on in families like religion. People identified themselves as Republicans or Democrats and usually voted for their party's nominees. Scholars wrote that parties were indispensable to democracy: "Political parties created modern democracy and modern democracy is unthinkable save in terms of parties."[1]

THE RESPONSIBLE PARTY MODEL   The parties were viewed as the principal instrument of majority control of public policy. "Responsible parties" were supposed to (1) develop and clarify alternative policy positions for the voters; (2) educate the people about the issues and simplify choices for them; (3) recruit candidates for public office who agreed with the parties' policy positions; (4) organize and direct their candidates' campaigns to win office; (5) hold their elected officials responsible for enacting the parties' policy positions after they were elected; and (6) organize legislatures to ensure party control of policy making. In carrying out these functions, responsible parties were supposed to modify the demands of special interests, build a consensus that could win majority support, and provide simple and identifiable, yet meaningful, choices for the voters on election day. In this way, disciplined, issue-oriented, competitive parties would be the principal means by which the people would direct public policy.

PROBLEMS WITH THE MODEL   Over the years, this "responsible party" model fell into disarray, if indeed it ever accurately described American political parties. There are fundamental problems with the responsible model itself:

- *The parties do not offer the voters clear policy alternatives.* Instead, each tries to capture the broad center of most policy dimensions, where it believes most Americans can be found. There is no incentive for parties to stand on the far right or far left when most Americans are found in the center. So the parties echo each other, and critics refer to them as Tweedledee and Tweedledum.

- *Voter decisions are not motivated primarily by policy considerations.* Most voters cast their votes on the basis of candidate "image," the "goodness" or "badness" of the times, and traditional voting habits. This means there is little incentive for either parties or candidates to concentrate on issues. Party platforms are seldom read by anyone. Modern campaign techniques focus on the image of the candidate—compassion, warmth, good humor, experience, physical appearance, ease in front of a camera, and so forth—rather than positions on the issues.

- *American political parties have no way to bind their elected officials to party positions or even their campaign pledges.* Parties cannot really discipline members of Congress or state legislatures for voting against the party position. Party cohesion, where it exists, is more a product of like-

Party.
An organization that seeks to achieve power by winning public office in elections.

Responsible party model.
A party system in which each party offers clear policy alternatives and holds their elected officials responsible for enacting these policies in office.

■

Party identification.
Self-described identification
with a political party, usually
in response to the question:
"Generally speaking, how
would you identify yourself:
as a Republican, Democrat,
independent, or something
else?"

mindedness among Democratic or Republican legislators than it is of party control.

WEAKENING OF THE PARTIES   In addition to these underlying problems, over time parties in America weakened by various political developments:

- *The rise of primary elections.* Party organizations cannot control who the party's nominee shall be. Nominations are won in primary elections. The progressive reformers who introduced primary elections at the beginning of the twentieth century wanted to undercut the power of party machines in determining who runs for office, and the reformers succeeded in doing so. Nominees now establish personal organizations in primary elections and campaign for popular votes; they do not have to negotiate with party leaders. Of course, the party organization may endorse a candidate in a primary election, but this is no guarantee of success with the party's voters.

- *The decline of party identification.* Democratic and Republican party loyalties have been declining over the years. Most people remain registered as Democrats or Republicans in order to vote in party primary elections, but increasing numbers of people identify themselves as "independent" and cast their vote in general elections without reference to party. Split-ticket voting (where a single voter casts his or her vote for a Democrat in one race and a Republican in another) has also increased.

- *The influence of the mass media, particularly television.* Candidates can come directly into the voter's living room via television. Campaigning is now largely a media activity. Candidates no longer need party workers to carry their message from block to block.

- *The decline of patronage.* Civil service reforms, at the national, state, and even city levels, have reduced the tangible rewards of electoral victory. Party "professionals"—who work in political campaigns to secure jobs and favors for themselves and their friends—are now being replaced by political "amateurs"—who work in political campaigns for the emotional satisfaction of supporting a "cause." Amateurs work intensely during campaigns, but professionals once worked year-round, off-years and election years, building party support with small personal favors for the voters. These party "regulars" are disappearing.

- *The rise of single-issue interest groups and PACs.* Parties have always coexisted with broad-based interest groups, many of whom contribute money to both Democratic and Republican candidates in order to ensure access regardless of who wins. But many of the more militant single-issue groups require a "litmus test" of individual candidates on single issues—abortion, gun control, and so forth. Their support and money hinge on the candidate's position on a single issue. Most PAC (political action committee) money goes directly to candidates, not to party organizations.

CONTINUING FUNCTIONS OF PARTIES   Despite these problems, the Democratic and Republican parties in America survive. They continue to perform important political functions:

- *Parties organize elections and narrow the choices of political office seekers confronting the voters.* In most state elections, the field of candidates in the November general election is narrowed to the Democratic and Republican party nominees. Very few independents are ever elected to high political office in the states. Only five governors in recent decades—Angus King and James Longley of Maine, Walter Hickel of Alaska, and Lowell Weicker of Connecticut—have been elected as independents. In 1998, Jesse Ventura, the Reform party candidate, won election as governor of Minnesota over his Democratic and Republican opponents. There are fewer than a dozen independent state legislators in the nation. Nebraska has the nation's only nonpartisan state legislature. Party nominees—for governor, attorney general, and other statewide executive offices, as well as state legislative seats—are selected in party primary elections in most states.

- *Parties continue to play an important role in voter choice.* It is true that political parties have lost much of their attractiveness to voters—a development described as dealignment. That is, fewer people identify themselves as "strong" Democrats or as "strong" Republicans; more people call themselves "Independents," and more people split their votes between candidates of different parties. However, despite dealignment, party labels remain an important influence on voter choice. People who identify themselves as Democrats tend to vote for Democratic candidates, just as people who identify themselves as Republicans vote for Republican candidates. Nationwide the Democratic and Republican parties have inspired popular images of themselves (see Table 5–1). Both parties maintain fairly stable coalitions of supporters. These national images and coalitions extend into the politics of most states.

- *Party organizations and activists in the states play an important role in guiding their party and in shaping its image with the voters.* Party activists are the people who serve on city, county, or state party committees, or who serve on the staffs of these committees. They regularly work in campaigns and serve on their state's delegation to the national party conventions. Democratic and Republican state party organizations are found in every state. In some states these organizations are more powerful than in other states, but in all fifty states, party organizations are becoming increasingly efficient in their operations.

- *Finally, the Democratic and Republican parties perform the central task of organizing state legislatures.* Only Nebraska has an official nonpartisan legislature. But in every other state, legislative leadership—for example, the house speaker and senate president—as well as committee chairs, are selected on a party basis. The majority party regularly votes for its own candidates for these posts. (See Chapter 6.)

PARTIES AND PRIMARIES

Party primary elections nominate most candidates for public office in America. For the nation's first century, candidates were nominated by party conventions, not primary elections, and as a result party organizations were far more influential than they are today. Primary elections were a key reform in the progressive movement of the early twentieth century. Primaries "democratized" the nomination process and reduced the power of party bosses.

Primary election.
An election held to decide a political party's nominee for public office.

Table 5–1

Images

"*In general, do you think the political views of the [see below] are too conservative, too liberal, or about right?*"

	Too Conservative %	Too Liberal %	About Right %	No Opinion %
Republican Party	39	15	41	5
Democratic Party	9	37	50	4

"*Thinking in general, do you think the [see below] generally favors the rich, favors the middle class, or favors the poor?*"

	Rich %	Middle Class %	Poor %	All/ None (vol.) %	No Opinion %
Republican Party	67	24	2	4	3
Democratic Party	20	43	28	4	5

Supporters

(SELF-IDENTIFIED; EXCLUDES "INDEPENDENT" RESPONSES)

	DEMOCRATIC	REPUBLICAN
All Voters	38	26
Family Income		
Under $10,000	41	19
$10,000–$30,000	42	20
$30,000–$50,000	35	30
Over $50,000	26	34
Religion		
Protestant	33	32
Catholic	41	21
Jewish	66	4
Race		
White	32	29
Black	65	5
Education		
Less than high school	44	16
High school graduate	38	22
Some college	32	29
College graduate	26	39

Sources: Data Images from Gallup/CNN/*USA Today* poll as reported in *The Polling Report,* November 30, 1998; supporters from National Election Studies (1996), University of Michigan.

FILING   Primary elections are governed by state law; anyone can *file* a petition with a minimum number of voter signatures, pay a small fee, and have his or her name placed on the primary ballot of either party for practically any public office. A candidate does *not* have to have experience in the party, or even the support of party officials, in order to file for elective office.

ENDORSEMENTS   Primaries, then, reduced the influence of party organizations in the political process. It is possible, of course, for party organizations at the city, county, or state levels to *endorse,* officially or unofficially, candidates in primary elections. The importance of endorsements varies with the strength and unity of party organizations. Where party organizations are strong at the city or county level, the word can be passed down to precinct committee members to turn out the party's faithful for the endorsed candidate. Party endorsement in a statewide race appears to have less value.

CLOSED AND OPEN PRIMARIES   Primary elections in most states are closed—that is, only voters who have *previously* registered as members of a party may vote in that party's primary. Only registered Democrats vote in the Democratic primary, and only registered Republicans vote in the Republican primary. Semiclosed primaries allow voters to change party registration on election day. Primaries in other states are *open*—voters can choose when they enter the polling place which party primary they wish to vote in. Alaska, California, and Washington have blanket primaries in which voters can vote in *both* party primaries simultaneously (see "*Up Close:* California Adopts the Blanket Primary"). Party leaders generally prefer the closed primary because they fear crossovers and raiding. *Crossovers* are voters who choose to vote in the primary of the party that they usually do not support in the general election. *Raiding* is an organized attempt to cross over and vote in order to defeat an attractive candidate running for the opposition party's nomination. However, there is no evidence that large numbers of voters connive in such a fashion. Louisiana is unique in its *nonpartisan* statewide elections: All candidates run in the same primary election. If a candidate gets over 50 percent of the vote, he or she wins the office; otherwise, the top two vote-getters run again in the general election. (See Table 5–2, p. 131.)

RUNOFF PRIMARIES   In most states, the *plurality* winner of the party's primary election—the candidate receiving the most votes, whether a majority or not—becomes the party's nominee. But in ten southern states, a candidate must win a *majority* of votes in a primary election to become the party's nominee. If no candidate succeeds in winning a majority in the first primary, a runoff primary is held between the top two vote-getters in the first primary.

First primary front-runners have a better-than-even chance of winning the runoff. Overall, front-runners win about two-thirds of runoff primaries for state legislative

Runoff primaries are linked to the traditional one-party politics of the southern states. Runoff primaries prevent a candidate with a minority of party voters from capturing the nomination in a race with three or more contenders. Presumably the runoff primary encourages candidates to seek majority support and prevents extremist candidates from winning nominations. No one can win a nomination by relying on splits among multiple opponents.

■

Closed primaries.
Primary elections in which voters must declare (or have previously declared) their party affiliation and can cast a ballot only in their own party's primary election.

Open primaries.
Primary elections in which a voter may cast a ballot in either party's primary election.

Crossover voting.
Voters affiliated with one party casting votes in the other party's primary election.

Blanket primary.
An open primary in which candidates from both parties appear on the same ballot.

Runoff primary.
An additional primary held between the top two vote-getters in a primary where no candidate has received a majority of the vote.

UP CLOSE

CALIFORNIA ADOPTS THE BLANKET PRIMARY

California has long been a political trendsetter for the nation. In 1996 California voters approved a constitutional amendment providing for the use of the "blanket primary" for the first time in its 1998 statewide elections. Now any registered voter in that state, regardless of party affiliation, may vote for any candidate, regardless of the candidate's party affiliation, in a primary election. This change was a marked departure from the state's historic reliance on closed primaries, in which only registered party members could vote for candidates seeking their party's nomination.

California's primary voters now receive a ballot that allows them to vote for any candidate for any elected office. (The only exception is that only persons registered with a political party are able to vote for that party's county and central committee members.) Candidates from each party who receive the most votes become the nominees of those parties and move on to face each other in the November general election. Even if the two highest vote-getters in the primary are from the same political party, only the one who received the most votes in that party becomes the nominee of that party in November. In other words, the top vote-getter among the candidates running as Democrats in the race becomes the Democratic nominee; the top vote-getter among the candidates running as Republicans will be the Republican nominee. It will not necessarily be the top two vote-getters in the primary who move on to the November general election (as in Louisiana), because the two top vote-getters may be from the same political party.

Each voter may cast a vote for only one candidate in each race, but voters are no longer restricted to voting for a candidate from their own party.

Supporters of the new California primary law argue that it will lure more voters to the polls by offering them more choices. Opponents of the law, including Democratic and Republican party officials in the state, argue that it weakens the parties and even infringes on the parties' rights of association. (This latter argument was rejected by a federal court.) They fear that crossover voting may lead to election shenanigans—Democrats voting for the weakest Republican candidate to ensure victory in the general election and Republicans doing the same. Opponents also claimed that voters in one party had no right to help select the candidates of the other party. However, other observers believe that the pattern of voting in primaries will remain much the same: Primary voters will continue to be largely committed Democrats and committed Republicans voting for candidates of their own party.

Despite this change, the 1998 California governor's primary election placed two seasoned party regulars in the November general election. Long-time Democratic officeholder Lieutenant Governor Gray Davis defeated two self-financed millionaires to become the Democratic nominee, and Attorney General Dan Lungren became the Republican nominee. Democrat Davis defeated Republican Lungren in the general election. In other words, party "outsiders" were unable to capture nominations in California's first blanket primary.

Officially, the California "*Open* Primary Initiative" amendment actually establishes a "*blanket* primary" because all candidates are listed on a single primary ballot.

---

seats, although they win only slightly more than half of the runoffs for governor and U.S. senator.[2]

Runoff primaries have been attacked as racially discriminatory. In districts where there is a large but less than majority black population and a history of racial block voting, black candidates who win a plurality of votes in the first primary may be defeated in the runoff if white voters unite behind the white runner-up. (It is possible, of course, for the reverse to occur in a majority black district.) A study of local runoff primaries in Georgia suggests that black plurality winners in the first primary are somewhat less likely to win a runoff against a white runner-up (50 percent black runoff victories) than white plurality winners against a black runner-up (84 percent white runoff victories).[3] But it is not likely that the elimination of runoff primaries would significantly increase the number of black officeholders.[4]

CONVENTIONS   State conventions continue in a handful of states. In New York and Connecticut, statewide party conventions nominate candidates; however, candidates

Table 5–2

Closed: Prior Party Registration Required	Semiclosed: Voters may register or change party on election day	Semiopen: Voters request party ballot	Open: Voter decides in which primary to vote in voting booth	Blanket	Nonpartisan	Runoff
Arizona	Colorado[a]	Alabama	Hawaii	Alaska	Louisiana	Alabama
Connecticut	Iowa[b]	Arkansas	Idaho	Washington		Arkansas
Delaware	Kansas[a]	Georgia	Michigan	California		Florida
Florida	Maine[a]	Illinois	Minnesota			Georgia
Kentucky	Massachusetts[c]	Indiana	Montana			Louisiana
Maryland	New Hampshire[c]	Mississippi	North Dakota			Mississippi
Nebraska	New Jersey[a]	Missouri	Utah			North Carolina
Nevada	Ohio[b]	South Carolina	Vermont			Oklahoma
New Mexico	Rhode Island[a]	Tennessee	Wisconsin			South Carolina
New York	Wyoming[b]	Texas				Texas
North Carolina		Virginia				
Oklahoma						
Oregon						
Pennsylvania						
South Dakota						
West Virginia						

[a]Persons not previously voting in a party primary may register with a party on election day.

[b]Party registration may be changed on election day.

[c]Independents are permitted to change registration on election day.

Source: Book of the States, 1998–99.

■

Party convention.
A meeting of party members, or delegates chosen by party members, held to choose the party's nominee and/or to write the party's platform and to rally party support.

Party organization.
National, state, county, and precinct party officials and workers, committee members, convention delegates, and others in party office.

Party activists.
People who serve in city, county, or state party organizations, or who regularly work in campaigns.

can "challenge" the convention nominee to a primary election if the challenger receives a specified share of the convention vote (25 percent in New York, 20 percent in Connecticut).

Statewide party organizations seldom have much influence over primary outcomes. First of all, party organizations are weak or nonexistent in many counties; many ward and precinct-levels positions are vacant. (Reasons for the decline of city and county party organizations are discussed in Chapter 10.) More important, traditional grassroots efforts—telephoning, canvassing, driving voters to the polls—which were once handled by party organizations, have largely given way to mass media campaigning. Television appearances, radio commercials, and mass mailings permit candidates to take their case directly to the voters.

STATE PARTY ORGANIZATIONS AND ACTIVISTS

State party organizations are "highly variable, elusive to find, difficult to define, and frustrating to study."[5] Indeed, both Democratic and Republican party organizations at the state and local levels are ill-defined, fluid, and very often "unoccupied." As many as half of the official party positions in the nation may be vacant. Moreover, many people who hold party positions do little or nothing to help their party or its candidates.

Nonetheless, a small core of Democratic and Republican party activists can be found in every state. They occupy positions on city, county, and state Democratic and Republican committees, and in the county and state conventions of their party. They represent their party on the national party committees and in the national party presidential nominating conventions. At the lowest level, they walk their neighborhood precinct, urging residents to register and vote, handing out party and candidate literature, and perhaps even trying to do small favors for their loyal voters.

ACTIVISTS AS IDEOLOGUES   While parties may be pushed toward the ideological center in order to win elections, the activists in the parties tend to be strong ideologues—people who take consistently "liberal" or "conservative" positions on the issues. Republican party activists in most states are more conservative than Democratic party activists. Indeed, Republican party activists tend to be more conservative than the general public, and Democratic party activists tend to be more liberal than the general public. This is true even though activists in both parties will tend to be more conservative in a conservative state and more liberal in a liberal state.

In the southern and border states, as the Republican party has grown in strength, Democratic and Republican party activists have clearly separated themselves along ideological lines. Today there are fewer conservatives among Democratic party activists in the South than in previous eras. As conservatives drift toward the Republican party, the liberal strength within the Democratic party increases. Blacks have assumed increasingly active and influential roles in southern Democratic party organizations, while fundamentalist white Protestants have become an increasingly active force in Republican circles.[6] The result is greater ideological cleavage between the parties.

ACTIVISTS AS POTENTIAL CANDIDATES   Party activists—people who serve on party posts as committee members or chairpersons at the city, county, or state level, or as delegates to party conventions—constitute a recruitment pool for candidates for public office. Often these people initially volunteered for party work with the expectation of eventually running for public office. Their party activity provides technical knowledge as well as personal contacts that become useful in their own future campaign. Party workers generally have voter registration lists available to them as well as information regarding ballot access, filing dates, campaign expenditure reporting, and other useful information. And, of course, party workers come into personal contact with campaign contributors. There is some evidence, however, that among party workers women are not as ambitious for public office as men, although gender differences in ambition for public office are diminishing.[7] Lawyers who volunteer as party workers are often seeking to make client contacts and enhance future opportunities to run for office.[8]

STATE PARTY ORGANIZATIONS   American political parties are decentralized in their organization. It is not really surprising in the American system of federalism—when only the president and vice-president have *national* constituencies, and senators, representatives, governors, state legislators, and county and city officials all have *state and local* constituencies—that the American parties are decentralized.

At the national level, the Democratic and Republican parties consist of a national committee; a House and Senate party conference; and various national clubs, such as Young Democrats and Young Republicans. There are also *fifty state parties*, which are composed of state committees and county and city organizations. This structure is tied together very loosely. State parties are not very responsive to national direction, and in most states, city and county organizations operate quite independently of the state committees. State committees are generally involved in important statewide elections—governors, U.S. senators, and representatives in the smaller states. City and county committees are generally responsible for county and municipal offices, state legislative seats, and congressional seats in the larger states. The Democratic and Republican National Committees exist primarily for the purpose of holding national conventions every four years to select the party's presidential candidate. Since each level of party organization has "its own fish to fry," each operates quite independently of the other levels (see *"Up Close:* Texas Party Organizations").

STATE LAWS GOVERN PARTIES   Party affairs are governed largely by the laws of the states. Each state sets forth the conditions that an organization must meet to qualify as a political party and to get its candidates' names printed on the official election ballots. Each state sets the qualifications for membership in a party and the right to vote in the party's primary election. State laws determine the number, method of selection, and duties of various party officials, committees, and conventions. The states, rather than the parties themselves, decide how the parties shall nominate candidates for public office. Most states require that party nominations be made by direct primaries, but several states still nominate by party caucuses or conventions. Most states also attempt to regulate party finances, although with little success.

STATE COMMITTEES   State party organizations officially consist of a "state committee," a "state chairman," or "chairwoman," and perhaps a small office staff

UP CLOSE

TEXAS PARTY ORGANIZATIONS

The Democratic and Republican party organizations in Texas are not unlike those of many states. Texas law provides for open primaries; voters can decide to cast their ballots in either the Democratic or Republican party primary without prior registration as party members. There are 254 counties in Texas and more than 8,700 local voting precincts. Many party committee posts are vacant or occupied by people who do little or nothing for their party. But some party activists devote a great deal of time and energy to their jobs. Some county committees meet only irregularly and have a difficult time getting a quorum of members to attend. Other counties (mostly in the state's larger cities) have active committees, office headquarters, and professional staff. The Democratic and Republican state committees have sixty-four members; these members are selected by party conventions held in each state senate district. The state Democratic and Republican party chairs and vice-chairs are selected at state party conventions held every two years. These conventions also adopt state party platforms, but party candidates are chosen by voters in primary elections.

TEMPORARY ORGANIZATION PERMANENT ORGANIZATION

State Chair and Vice Chair
State Executive Committee
The State Executive Committee and the chair and the vice chair are selected by the state convention, held in June of the even-numbered years.

State Convention
Delegates are selected from the district or senatorial conventions to attend the state convention, held in June.

County Chair
The county chair is elected by the voters countywide in the primary and, if required, the runoff primary.
County Executive Committee
The precinct chairs and the county chair comprise the party's County Executive Committee.

County or District Convention
Delegates from the precinct conventions are selected to attend the county convention or the senatorial district convention, held the second Saturday after the second Tuesday in March.

Precinct Convention
Any person who has participated in a party primary may attend the precinct convention, held the same day as the primary.

Precinct Chair
A precinct chair is selected by voters participating in the primary and, if required, the runoff primary.

Voters in the Party Primary
Any registered voter may participate in the primaries, held in even-numbered years on the second Tuesday in March.

Source: Thomas R. Dye, L. Tucker Gibson, Jr., and Clay Robinson, *Politics in America,* Texas Edition, 3rd ed. Upper Saddle River, N.J.: Prentice-Hall, 1999.

working at the state capitol. Democratic and Republican state committees vary from state to state in composition, organization, and function. Membership on the state committee may range from about a dozen up to several hundred. The members may be chosen through party primaries or by state party conventions. Generally, representation on state committees is allocated to counties, but occasionally other units of government are recognized in state party organization. A state party chairman or chairwoman generally serves at the head of the state committee; these people are generally selected by the state committee, but their selection is often dictated by the party's candidate for governor.

State committees are supposed to direct the campaigns for important statewide elections—governors and U.S. senators, and congressional representatives in the smaller states. They are supposed to serve as central coordinating agencies for these election campaigns and to serve as the party's principal fund-raising organization in the state. However, the role of the state committee very often depends upon the preferences of the party's statewide candidates regarding the handling of their campaigns. Today, most candidates have their own campaign organizations to plan and execute campaign strategy. State party organizations seldom play a major role in the candidate's campaign.

State committees are not very responsive to the direction of the national committee, and in most states, city and county party organizations operate quite independently of the state committees. In other words, there is no real hierarchy of authority in state party systems.

COUNTY COMMITTEES   Party organizations at the city and county levels are probably the most cohesive organizations within the parties. Yet these organizations are far from disciplined groups. City or county party organizations usually include:

- An active chairperson and executive committee, plus a few associated activists, who in effect make most of the decisions in the name of the party, who raise funds, who occasionally seek out candidates (or approve the candidates who select themselves), and who speak locally for the party
- A ward and precinct organization in which only a few local committee members are active and in which there is little door-to-door canvassing or other direct voter contact
- The active participation in organizational matters of some of the party's elected public officials, who may share effective control of the organization with the official leadership of the party organization
- Financial contributors to the party and its candidates, together with leaders of local interest groups that generally ally themselves with the party.[9]

Republican and Democratic county chairpersons probably constitute the most important building blocks in party organization in America. City and county party officers and committees are chosen locally and cannot be removed by any higher party authority. In short, authority is not concentrated in any single statewide organization but is divided among many city and county party organizations.

State committees.
Governing bodies of state party organizations.

County committees.
Governing bodies of county party organizations.

STATE PARTY CHAIRPERSONS   Although state party organizations are weakened by decentralization, state party chairpersons are by no means political hacks. Most state chairpersons have been successful business people, lawyers, or public officials who serve in their posts without salaries to satisfy their interest in politics and public affairs. Republican chairpersons are more likely to have held important positions in business and management, while Democratic chairpersons are more likely to be lawyers who have held political office previously.

State party chairpersons can play different roles from state to state. Some see themselves as mere "political agents" of their governor; others are independently powerful. In general, chairpersons of the party out of power have more independence and power than those of the party in power. The latter are overshadowed by their governor. Party chairpersons do not hold on to their jobs very long—the average is less than three years.[10]

PARTY ORGANIZATIONS   While party attachment among voters has weakened over the years, state party organizations have strengthened.[11] Today most state party organizations maintain a permanent party headquarters in the state capital. Most have full-time staffs, including an executive director; a budget official; and public relations, fund-raising, and research people. These state party organizations help to raise campaign funds for their candidates, conduct registration drives, provide advice and services to their nominees, and even recruit candidates to run in districts and for offices where the party would otherwise have no names on the ballot. Services to candidates may include advertising and media consulting, advice on election law compliance, polling, research (including research on opponents), registration and voter identification, mailing lists, and even seminars on campaign techniques.

Yet very few local organizations have a full-time staff, or a permanent headquarters, or even a telephone listing.[12] Most rely upon volunteers—precinct and county committee members—who seldom meet in nonelection years. Few local organizations have any budget. Yet most report election year efforts at distributing campaign literature, organizing campaign events, putting up posters and lawn signs, conducting registration drives, and even some door-to-door canvassing.

Strong city and county party organizations were traditionally found in the big cities of the Northeast. (City "machines" and "bosses" are discussed at length in Chapter 11, together with the reform movements that have severely reduced their power.) While these "machines" have lost most of their "clout," local party organizations are still more visible in New York, New Jersey, and Pennsylvania than in the southern or border states.

REPUBLICAN AND DEMOCRATIC PARTY FORTUNES IN THE STATES

Traditionally, the Democratic party held a decided edge in American politics. Nationwide, more people have identified themselves in opinion polls as Democrats than Republicans. But the ranks of self-identified "independents" has grown over time. The Democratic party appears to have lost more supporters to this dealignment than the

Table 5–3

PARTY IDENTIFICATION AMONG ALL AMERICANS								
	1937	1960	1972	1984	1988	1994	1996	1998
Democrats	50	47	43	40	42	40	38	30
Independents	16	23	29	29	28	34	33	36
Republicans	34	30	28	31	30	26	29	26

Source: Gallup Polls. Excludes mentions of other parties and "don't knows."

Republican party. The result in state politics has been a rise in party competitiveness across the states and a greater number of Republican victories in gubernatorial and legislative elections. (See Table 5–3.)

PARTY REGISTRATION   In states that register voters by party, the Democratic party does better in registration figures than it does in opinion polls.[13] The tendency for many independents and even some Republicans to register as Democrats is more pronounced in the southern states. Voters choose to register in the traditionally dominant party for several reasons: perhaps because the dominant party's primary is more interesting insofar as the winner is more likely to go on to win office; or perhaps because people seeking political favors (like jobs, contracts, zoning decisions) wish to be identified publicly with the dominant party; or perhaps because of social pressures and a desire to be seen as a member of the dominant party. Because the Democratic party was traditionally the dominant party in most states, registration figures remain skewed toward the Democrats.

CHANGING PARTY FORTUNES IN GUBERNATORIAL RACES   The Republican party enjoyed its greatest resurgence in nearly half a century in congressional and state politics in 1994. In that year Republicans captured control of the U.S. House of Representatives for the first time since 1954. At the state level, the GOP gained a majority of governorships for the first time in over three decades (see Figure 5–1). Following the 1998 elections, Republicans occupied governor's chairs in thirty-one states, including four of the nation's five largest states—New York, Texas, Florida, and Pennsylvania. (After sixteen years of Republican control, the California governor's office was recaptured by the Democrats in 1998.)

CHANGING PARTY SHARES OF STATE LEGISLATIVE SEATS   The Democratic party retains a slight edge in overall state legislative seats in the nation. However, the Democrats have experienced a long slide in legislative seats since their high-water mark in the 1970s. In historical context, the Republican achievement of capturing 48 percent of state legislative seats in 1994 is truly remarkable. Republican gains in the southern states account for the growing power of the GOP in state capitals. Democrats actually controlled more than 90 percent of all legislative seats in eleven southern states in the

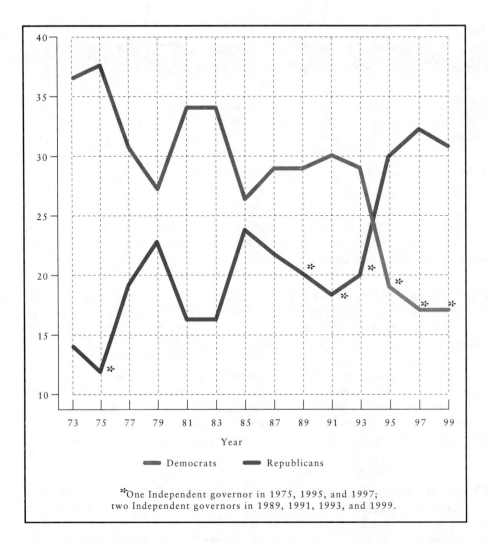

FIGURE 5–1 Party Control of Governorships

*One Independent governor in 1975, 1995, and 1997; two Independent governors in 1989, 1991, 1993, and 1999.

early 1960s. But Republicans have gained seats in the southern states in every election since 1982. Outside the South, Democratic and Republican legislative seats have been fairly well balanced. (See Figure 5–2.)

PARTY COMPETITION IN THE STATES

The ideal "responsible" party system is said to be one in which *competitive parties* present alternative programs in election campaigns, and the party winning the majority of votes captures all the power it needs to write its program into law. Moreover, in the responsible party system, the elected officials act cohesively so the voters can hold the

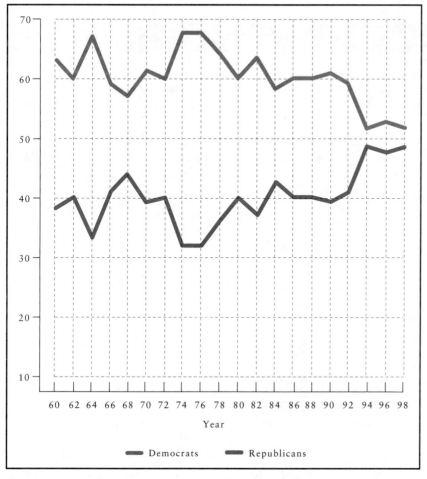

FIGURE 5–2 Party
Control of State
Legislative Seats

Source: National Conference
of State Legislatures, 1998.

party collectively responsible at the end of its term of office. The key to this ideal party system is the existence of competitive parties that are roughly balanced in strength.

HOW MUCH PARTY COMPETITION?   In reality, however, party competition throughout the fifty states is uneven. Traditionally, the dominance of the Democratic party precluded any real competition for control of upper or lower chambers of state legislatures in many states, especially in the South. Table 5–4 groups states according to the percentage of times between 1968 and 1996 that Democrats or Republicans captured control of the governorship and upper and lower houses of the state legislature.

GROWING REPUBLICAN STRENGTH IN THE SOUTH   The recent growth of Republican party strength in the eleven southern states has shifted several of these states

Table 5–4

PARTY COMPETITION IN STATE POLITICS				
Traditional Democratic Advantage	*Traditional Democratic but Growing Republican Strength*	*Competitive, Leaning Democratic*	*Competitive, Leaning Republican*	*Traditional Republican Advantage*
Arkansas	Alabama	Alaska	Arizona	Indiana
Hawaii	Florida	California	Colorado	New Hampshire
Kentucky	Georgia	Connecticut	Idaho	South Dakota
Louisiana	Mississippi	Delaware	Kansas	
Maryland	North Carolina	Illinois	North Dakota	
Massachusetts	Oklahoma	Iowa	Utah	
Missouri	South Carolina	Maine	Vermont	
New Mexico	Tennessee	Michigan	Wyoming	
Rhode Island	Texas	Minnesota		
West Virginia	Virginia	Montana		
		Nebraska		
		Nevada		
		New Jersey		
		New York		
		Ohio		
		Oregon		
		Pennsylvania		
		Washington		
		Wisconsin		

away from their traditional label as "one-party Democratic." For many years the southern states had been a partisan battleground in *presidential* elections, but remained solidly Democratic in *state and local* politics. Republican governors were occasionally elected, but very few Republicans served in southern state legislatures. However, Republican grass-roots strength in the South began to grow in the 1990s. During this decade, seven southern states (Alabama, Florida, Mississippi, South Carolina, Tennessee, Texas, and Virginia) elected Republican governors. In 1998 Florida became the first southern state in which the Republican party won full control of state government—the governorship and both houses of the state legislature. The growing GOP strength in the South has shifted more states into the "competitive" category. (These states are listed in Table 5–4 under "Traditional Democratic but Growing Republican Strength.") Party competition in the states is stronger today than at any time in recent history.

DIVIDED GOVERNMENT   The frequency of divided party government in the states— where one party controls one or both houses of the legislature and the other party controls the governorship—dilutes party responsibility. In recent years, over half of the states have experienced divided party control (see "Divided Government: Governor

Versus the Legislature" in Chapter 7). A unified party government—where the same party controls both houses of the legislature as well as the governorship—is presumed to be better able to enact its program into law. While many obstacles to program enactment may remain, at least party "gridlock" is avoided. More importantly, perhaps, voters are better able to attribute praise or blame for the direction of state government. Under unified party government, the dominant party cannot escape responsibility for poor performance by blaming it on the opponent party's control of one house or branch of state government.[14]

■

Divided government. In state government, when one party controls the governor's office while the other party controls one or both houses of the state legislature.

THE POLICY EFFECTS OF PARTY COMPETITION

What difference does it make in public policy whether a state has competitive or noncompetitive parties? Do states with a competitive party system differ in their approach to education, welfare, health, taxation, or highways from states with noncompetitive party systems? This is not an easy question to answer. Since historically competitive states tended to be wealthy, urban, and industrialized, and noncompetitive states poorer, rural, and agricultural, it was difficult to sort out the effects of party competition from those other socioeconomic variables. Some scholars asserted that a more competitive party system would lead to more liberal education, welfare, and taxation policies. However, available evidence indicates that education, welfare, taxation, and highway programs appear to be *more closely related* to socioeconomic factors in the states than to the degree of party competition itself.[15]

POLICY EFFECTS OF COMPETITION   The thesis that party competition produced liberal welfare programs was suggested many years ago by V. O. Key, Jr.:

> In the two-party states the anxiety over the next election pushes political leaders into serving the interests of the have-less elements of society, therefore putting the party into the countervailing power operation.
>
> . . . [I]n the one-party states it is easier for a few powerful interests to manage the government of the state without party interference since the parties are not representative of the particular elements that might pose opposition to the dominant group.
>
> . . . [O]ver the long run the have-nots lose in a disorganized politics.[16]

When these assertions were tested, however, it turned out that there were few significant *independent* relationships between party competition and levels of public taxing and spending in the American states. Once the effects of income, urbanization, and education are controlled, the initial relationships between competition and participation and public policy largely disappear. Competition and participation are dependent upon levels of economic development, and so are levels of public taxing and spending; the associations between competitive politics and public policies turned out to be largely spurious. Or, as Thomas R. Dye explains:

> Economic development shapes both political systems and policy outcomes, and most of the association that occurs between system characteristics and policy outcomes can be attributed to the influence of economic development. Differences in the policy choices of

■

Unimodal distribution of opinion.
This occurs when most voters prefer moderate or centrist policies, thereby causing the parties to move closer together in their policy positions.

Bimodal distribution of opinion.
This occurs when most voters are clearly divided in their policy preferences, thereby causing the parties to take divergent policy positions.

states with different types of political systems turn out to be largely a product of differing socioeconomic levels rather than a direct product of political variables.[17]

WHEN COMPETITION MAY NOT PRODUCE POLICY DIFFERENCES   Party competition itself does not necessarily cause more liberal welfare policies. If there is a unimodal distribution of voters' preferences in a state, and if the state parties are devoid of strong organizations and ideologically motivated activists, then the party system will have little meaning for public policy. This notion can be diagrammed as follows:

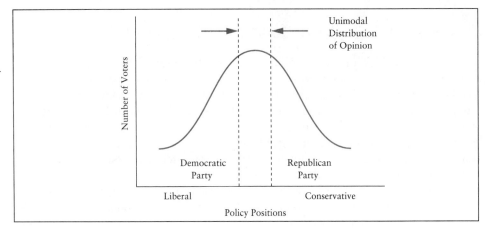

where there is unimodal distribution of opinion (most voters are found in the center) and the parties move toward the middle position to capture the greatest number of voters.

WHEN COMPETITION IS MORE LIKELY TO PRODUCE POLICY DIFFERENCES
However, the party system can be policy-relevant if there is a bimodal distribution of voters' preferences in a state; and if the parties have strong organization and ideologically motivated activists, then the parties in that state will offer clear policy alternatives. This notion can be diagrammed as follows:

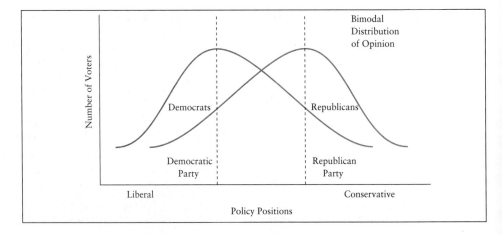

where there is a bimodal distribution of opinion (voters divide into liberals and conservatives) and the parties take the policy positions of their different groups of constituents.

POLICY RELEVANCE OF THE PARTIES Does this mean that there are no real differences between Republican and Democratic parties in the states? Certainly at the national level, it is not difficult to see the different coalitions that comprise the two parties. While the moderate viewpoints of American parties ensure that major social groups are seldom wholly within one party or another, differences between the Democratic and Republican parties at the national level are revealed by different proportions of votes given by major groups in the electorate to the two major political parties. The Democratic party receives a disproportionate amount of support from Catholics, Jews, blacks, less educated and lower-income groups; younger people; skilled, semiskilled, and unskilled laborers; union members; and big-city residents. The Republican party receives disproportionate support from Protestants, whites, better educated and higher-income groups; older people; professional, managerial, and other white-collar workers; nonunion members; and rural and small-town residents.

These differences between the Democratic and Republican parties at the national level can be observed in the politics of some states but not all. *State Republican and Democratic parties resemble the national Republican and Democratic parties only in those states where each party represents separate socioeconomic constituencies.*[18] Party conflict over policy questions is most frequent in those states in which the Democratic party represents central-city, low-income, ethnic, and racial constituencies, and the Republican party represents middle-class, suburban, small-town, and rural constituencies. In these states, the Democratic and Republican parties will tend to disagree over taxation and appropriations, welfare, education, and regulation of business and labor—that is, the major social and economic controversies that divide the national parties.[19]

PROFESSIONAL MEDIA CAMPAIGNS

Mass media campaigns, directed by professional public relations specialists, have replaced the party organizations' role in elections. Few candidates for governor or senator rely exclusively on the party organization to handle their campaigns. Most statewide candidates create their own campaign organizations, and increasingly these candidates are relying on professional public relations firms or consultants to manage their mass media campaigns. A whole new "image industry" has replaced the traditional role of party organizations in campaigns. (See "*Up Close:* Organizing the Campaign.")

"MARKETING" CANDIDATES If marketing, advertising, and public relations firms can sell toothpaste, why not political candidates? Indeed, today marketing and media specialists have largely taken over political campaigns for most important offices. Modern professional campaign management involves techniques that strongly resemble those employed in commercial product marketing, including the following:

Media campaign.
Contacting potential voters and soliciting their support primarily through television, radio, and newspaper advertising.

UP CLOSE

ORGANIZING THE CAMPAIGN

Candidates for statewide elected office—governor, attorney general, secretary of state, treasurer, and so on—are well advised to put together a professional campaign organization well in advance of the upcoming election. It is not uncommon for serious candidates for these offices to begin organizing their campaigns two years or more before the election.

Most statewide candidates begin organizing by selecting a campaign manager and a finance chair. A great deal of work must be done even before making a formal announcement of one's candidacy. It is very important to obtain pledges of campaign contributions as early as possible. Indeed, the decision to run or not may rest upon early success or failure in getting pledges of support from potential big donors. A full-time, experienced, professional campaign manager or campaign management firm should also be selected early. The campaign manager must coordinate a wide variety of activities—fundraising, the scheduling of candidate appearances, issue development, speech writing, the production and buying of media ads, opinion polling, advertising, compliance with election laws, and expenditures of campaign funds. (See organization chart.)

All states set forth filing dates for candidates—certain dates by which the candidates must get their names on the ballot. Although most statewide candidates make a formal announcement of their candidacy early in the election year and well before the filing date, a few "surprise" candidates may show up on the filing date. Candidates with good name recognition and heavy financial support often announce early hoping to "scare off" potential competitors.

Generally, the formal announcement is accompanied by the official establishment of the campaign fund. Early press releases describing a large amount of money in the candidate's campaign fund may signal to other contributors and interest groups (as well as to potential competitors) that the candidate is a "winner" and everyone should get aboard the train as it leaves the station. Early poll results showing a candidate's strength may have the same favorable effect.

When the campaign gets fully underway, campaign staff should try to relieve the candidate of as many burdensome chores as possible. Opinion polls must be completed and their meaning assessed; issues must be researched and developed; speeches must be written; advertising must be produced and disseminated; the candidates schedule of appearances (at both public events and fund-raisers) must be finely tuned; care must be taken to comply with all campaign finance and election laws; and trustworthy people must oversee campaign expenditures.

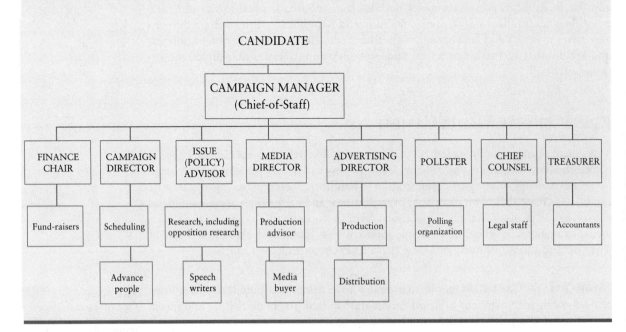

1. Computerized mailing lists for fund-raising and the preparation and mailing of slick brochures to the voters.

2. Computerized voter lists that include occupation, age, race, interests, memberships, and so on, of each voter, so that special statements by the candidate can be delivered to special groups of voters.

3. Public opinion polling on a regular basis throughout the campaign, which enables candidates to identify their opponents' weaknesses as well as their own and to assess the voters' moods and opinion shifts throughout the campaign.

4. The preparation of videotapes, radio broadcasts, signs, bumper stickers, and so on, which emphasize the candidate's "theme."

5. Developing "media events" that will attract the attention of television and newspapers, for example, walking across the state, working a day in the lettuce fields, and so forth.

PUBLIC RELATIONS FIRMS   Professional public relations firms come in different sizes and shapes. Some are all-purpose organizations that plan the whole campaign; select a theme; monitor the electorate with continuous polling; produce television tapes for commercials, newspaper advertisements, and radio spots; select clothing and hairstyles for their candidates; write speeches and schedule appearances (or avoid them if the candidates cannot speak well); and even plan the victory party. Other organizations limit themselves to particular functions, such as polling or television production. Some firms specialize by party, handling only Democratic or Republican candidates; a few firms specialize by ideology, handling liberal or conservative clients. Still other firms are strictly professional, providing services to any candidate who can afford them.

POLLING   Frequently, polling is at the center of strategic campaign decision making. At the beginning of the campaign, polls test the "recognition factor" of the candidate and assess what political issues are uppermost in the minds of voters. Special polling techniques can determine what a "winning candidate profile" looks like in a district. The results of these polls will be used to determine a general strategy—developing a favorable "image" for the candidate and focusing on a popular campaign "theme." Early polls can also detect weaknesses in the candidate, which can then be overcome in advertising (too rich—then show him in blue jeans digging ditches; too intellectual— then show him in a hog-calling contest; and so on). Polls can tell whether the party is stronger than the candidate (then identify the candidate as loyal to the party) or whether the candidate is stronger than the party (then stress the candidate's independent thinking). During the campaign the polls can chart the progress of the candidate and even assess the effectiveness of specific themes and "media events." A "media event" is an activity generated to attract news coverage, for example, walking the entire length of the state to show "closeness to the people," or carrying around a broom to symbolize "house cleaning," or spending occasional days doing manual work on a factory or farm. Finally, polls can identify the undecided vote toward the end of the campaign and help direct the time and resources of the candidate.

■
Polling.
Questioning a representative sample of the population (or of likely voters) to determine public opinion about candidates and issues.

■

Name recognition.
The likelihood that people recognize a candidate's name when questioned in opinion polls.

Grass-roots campaigning.
Directly soliciting voter support through telephone calls or face-to-face meetings.

NAME RECOGNITION   The first objective in a professional campaign is to increase the candidate's name recognition among the voters. Years ago, name recognition could only be achieved through years of service in minor public or party offices (or owning a well-known family name). Today, expert media advisors (and lots of money) can create instant celebrity. "Exposure" is the name of the game, and exposure requires attracting the attention of the news media. (As one commentator observed: "To a politician there is no such thing as indecent exposure. Obscurity is a dirty word and almost all exposure is decidedly decent.") A millionaire land developer (former Governor and now U.S. Senator Bob Graham of Florida) attracted attention by simply working a few days as ditch-digger, busboy, bulldozer operator, and so on, to identify with the "common people" and receive a great deal of news coverage.

CAMPAIGN THEMES   The emphasis of the professional public-relations campaign is on simplicity: a few themes, brief speeches, uncluttered ads, quick and catchy spot commercials. Finding the right theme or slogan is essential; this effort is not greatly different from that of launching an advertising campaign for a new detergent. A campaign theme should not be controversial. It might be as simple as "A leader you can trust"; the candidate would then be "packaged" as competent and trustworthy.

PERSONALITY, NOT POLICY   A professional media campaign generally focuses on the personal qualities of the candidate rather than his or her stand on policy issues. Professional campaigns are based on the assumption that a candidate's image is the most important factor affecting voter choice. This image is largely devoid of issues, except in very general terms, for example, "tough on crime," "stands up to the special interests," "fights for the taxpayer." Of course, there may be carefully chosen exceptions to this generalization: In 1994, Republican Governor Pete Wilson of California came from behind in the polls to defeat his challenger, Democrat Kathleen Brown, by strongly endorsing a popular policy position (limiting state services to illegal immigrants). And a favorite campaign tactic is to associate one's opponent with unpopular policy positions whenever possible.

GRASS-ROOTS CAMPAIGNING   Door-to-door campaigning by candidates or party workers has largely disappeared from American politics. Perhaps in small towns, candidates for local office still walk through neighborhoods handing out their brochures. But grass-roots campaigning has largely been replaced with media campaigning, especially for statewide offices.

MEDIA CAMPAIGNING   Media campaigning concentrates on obtaining the maximum "free" exposure on the evening news, as well as saturating television and newspapers with paid commercial advertising. To win favorable news coverage, candidates and their managers must devise attractive media events with visuals and sound bites too good for the television news to ignore. News coverage of a candidate is more credible than paid commercials. So candidates must do or say something interesting and "newsworthy" as often as possible during the campaign.

Television "spot" advertisements incur costs in both production and broadcast time. Indeed, television may consume up to three-quarters of all campaign costs; about one-third of TV costs go for production of ads and two-thirds to buying time from television stations. The Federal Communications Commission requires broadcasters to make available broadcast time to political candidates at the same rates charged to product advertisers. Broadcasters cannot raise rates during campaigns or charge some candidates more than others for the same broadcast time.

Negative campaigning. Soliciting voter support by attacking one's opponent.

NEGATIVE ADS   Professional media campaigns have increasingly turned to the airing of television commercials depicting the opponent in negative terms. The original negative TV ad is generally identified as the 1964 "daisy-picking" commercial, aired by the Lyndon B. Johnson presidential campaign, which portrayed Republican opponent Barry Goldwater as a nuclear warmonger. Over time the techniques of negative ads have been refined; weaknesses in opponents are identified and dramatized in emotionally forceful thirty-second spots.

While reformers bemoan "mudslinging," negative advertising can be very effective. Such advertising seeks to "define" an opponent in negative terms. Many voters cast their ballots *against* candidates they have come to dislike. Research into the opponent's public and personal background provides the data for negative campaigning. Previous speeches or writings can be mined for embarrassing statements, and previous voting records can be scrutinized for unpopular policy positions. Personal scandals can be exposed as evidence of "character." Victims of negative ads can be expected to counterattack with charges of "mudslinging" and "dirty" politics. If candidates fear that their personal attacks on opponents might backfire, they may "leak" negative information to reporters and hope that the media will do their dirty work for them.

FREE AIR TIME   Candidates also seek free air time on public service programs and televised debates. Underfunded candidates are more dependent upon these opportunities than their more affluent opponents. Thus, well-funded and poorly funded candidates may argue over the number and times of public debates.

MONEY IN STATE POLITICS

Running for public office costs money. Running for statewide offices in large states may cost millions; but even running for city council and school board seats can cost thousands. Candidates who do not have enough personal wealth to finance their own campaigns must find contributors. Fund-raising is one of the least pleasant aspects of politics.

WHAT MONEY CAN DO   Can money buy elections? Not always, but money can make a significant difference in the outcome. Let us summarize what research has shown about the effects of campaign spending:

- Campaign spending is generally more important in contested primary elections than general elections. In primary elections there are no party labels and the electorate is more easily influenced by the kinds of campaigning that money can buy.

- "Early money"—a sizable campaign treasury available at the beginning of the campaign—is usually more valuable than money coming in later and closer to election day.

- Campaign spending in primary elections is closely related to electoral outcome where the party organizations are weak; where they are strong and they endorse a primary candidate, money is less important.[20]

- Campaign spending is more important in larger jurisdictions, where face-to-face campaigning is not possible and mass media appeals are essential.

- After a certain level of campaign spending is reached, additional expenditures do not produce the same effect. A law of diminishing returns seems to operate to reduce the impact of very heavy campaign spending.[21]

- Incumbent officeholders have a very strong advantage over challengers in soliciting and receiving campaign contributions.[22]

- However, the advantage of incumbency itself is greater than the advantage of heavy campaign spending. While it is true that incumbents have an easier time obtaining campaign contributions than challengers, only part of the advantage of being an incumbent derives from easier access to money. Most of the incumbent's advantage is in name recognition and greater news media coverage.[23]

- Candidates who outspend their opponents win in two out of three elections. Of course, the higher-spending candidates are usually incumbents, and incumbents tend to win even when they are outspent. But in elections in which there is no incumbent seeking reelection, the candidate who spends the most money can be expected to win two of every three of these open-seat contests.[24]

FUND-RAISING   The need to raise millions of dollars for political campaigns, especially for costly television advertising, has stimulated the development of many new fund-raising techniques. Campaign financing has moved beyond the small, face-to-face, circle of contributing friends, supporters, and partisans. An important source of campaign money now are the political action committees, or PACs, which mobilize group financial support for candidates. PACs have been organized by corporations, unions, trade and professional associations, environmental groups, and liberal and conservative ideological groups. The wealthiest PACs are based in Washington, but PAC contributions are becoming increasingly important in state gubernatorial and legislative campaigns as well.[25]

Individual contributions are now sought through a variety of solicitation techniques, including direct mail to persons designated by computer programs to be likely contributors, direct telephone solicitation with recorded messages by the candidates, and live appeals by workers at telephone banks. These efforts have increased the *number* of political contributions in recent years as well as the *total amount* of political contributions.[26] About 10 percent of the population now claims to have contributed to candidates running for public office. However, contributors disproportionately represent high-income, well-educated, older, political partisans. There are, indeed, networks of contributors.[27] Some candidates have been able to tap into these networks through specialized mailing lists and telephone directories.

These specialized techniques supplement the more traditional fund-raising dinners, barbecues, fish frys, and cocktail parties. A successful fund-raising dinner usually includes an appearance by a national political figure, perhaps even the president, or an appearance by a show business celebrity. Tickets are sold in blocks to PACs and to well-heeled, individual contributors. Successful techniques may vary with the political culture of the state, for example, celebrity rock concerts in California versus barbecues in Texas.

CAMPAIGN SPENDING IN THE STATES   Campaign spending in state elections varies enormously from state to state. A gubernatorial campaign in a small state may cost only $2 to $5 million, but campaigns in California, New York, and Texas cost real money—$10 to $25 million or more.

State legislative campaigns may range in cost from $5,000 to over $500,000. Political scientist Frank Sorauf reports that California leads in campaign spending, not only because of its size, but also because of its sophisticated political culture.[28] Media consultants, pollsters, campaign strategists, and slick television advertising have become the political norm in the Golden State.

CAMPAIGN FINANCE LAWS   Many states, as well as the federal government, have laws designed to bring greater "ethics" into political campaigning and reduce the importance of large campaign contributions. Generally these laws attempt to do one or more of the following:

- Limit the size of campaign contributions and limit the overall spending of candidates and parties
- Require financial disclosure of a candidate's personal finances as well as campaign contributions and expenditures—"Who gave it? Who got it?"
- Establish public funding of campaign expenses
- Establish regulatory agencies, or "commissions," to oversee campaign practices

The model for state laws in this area was the Federal Election Campaign Act of 1974, which placed limits on the size of individual campaign contributions, required disclosure of campaign finances, provided for public funding of presidential elections through a tax checkoff on federal income tax returns, and established a Federal Elections Commission to supervise presidential elections and distribute public funds to candidates.

■
Soft money.
Largely *unregulated* monetary contributions to a party for activities such as party building or voter registration, but supposedly not for campaign expenses.

THE CONSTITUTIONAL RIGHT TO CAMPAIGN   However, reformers in the states and in Washington were surprised by the important U.S. Supreme Court decision in *Buckley* v. *Valeo* in 1976.[29] James L. Buckley, former U.S. Senator from New York and brother of William F. Buckley, the well-known conservative commentator, argued successfully in court that laws which limited an individual's right to participate in political campaigns, financially or otherwise, violated First Amendment freedoms. Specifically, the U.S. Supreme Court held that no government could limit an individual's right to spend money to publish or broadcast his or her own views on issues or elections. Candidates can spend as much of their own money as they wish on their own campaigns. Private individuals can spend as much as they wish to circulate their own views on elections (although their contributions to candidates and parties can still be limited). The Court, however, permitted government limitations on parties and campaign organizations and allowed the use of federal funds for financing campaigns.

Any candidate can spend unlimited personal wealth on his or her own election campaign, and individuals can spend any amount to advertise their own personal views, as long as they do not spend their money through a party or campaign organization. If anything, the personal wealth of the candidate has become an even more important qualification for successful campaigning.

SOFT MONEY   Unlimited amounts of money can be given to national and state political parties. The Federal Elections Campaign Act applies only to money given directly to candidates' campaigns. Direct contributions to parties, known as "soft money," are supposed to be used for general party building, not specific candidates' campaigns. But "soft money" is now a major source of campaign funding (see *"Up Close: 'Soft Money': How to Evade Campaign Finance Laws"*).

WHO GAVE IT? WHO GOT IT?   All states now have some form of campaign finance reporting. Almost everyone agrees that the public should know who is contributing to a candidate's campaign and how the candidate is spending the money. The press was largely responsible for pushing these laws through the legislatures of the states, and the success of these laws largely depends on the press's publishing these campaign reports. Half of the states have assigned collection of reports to an existing state official, usually the secretary of state. These officials ordinarily cannot bring enforcement actions against violators themselves but must instead turn over suspected cases to state law enforcement agencies such as the attorney general. Enforcement may be weakened if the attorney general's office does not wish to embarrass fellow state officials, or if elections law enforcement is assigned a low priority relative to more serious crimes.[30] Most of the states have created independent commissions resembling the Federal Elections Commission. Appointments to these commissions are usually made by the governor, or the governor and the legislature, and membership is usually divided between the parties. Staff members perform much of the filing, auditing, and investigating for these commissions, which are empowered to investigate election law violations and turn over evidence of wrongdoing to law enforcement officials. In addition, some commissions have the power to levy civil fines on their own authority.[31]

States with campaign finance laws requiring the disclosure of the names of contributors and their occupations give us only a small peek at the real sources of funding (see

UP CLOSE

"SOFT MONEY": HOW TO EVADE CAMPAIGN FINANCE LAWS

Campaign finance laws in the states, like federal law, apply to candidate campaign financing. Limits on the size of individual contributions apply *only* to money contributed directly to a candidate's campaign organization. In contrast, money given to political parties is unlimited. Technically this "soft money" is supposed to be used for party building, get-out-the-vote drives, issues education, and general party participation. In reality, both the Democratic and Republican parties use soft money to support their candidates in general elections.

Total soft money contributions are growing rapidly in both the nation and in the states. Most soft money is raised through large contributions. This is one reason that soft money is becoming so popular; that is, it allows big donors to give without having to abide by the limits imposed on direct contributions to candidates. Another political advantage of soft money contributions is that corporations, labor unions, and other groups can give directly from their organizations' treasuries, even though they are prohibited under law from giving directly to candidates from their treasuries.

Contributors who want to evade legal limits on campaign contributions to a particular candidate may reach an "understanding" with party officials to "earmark" party contributions for use in support of their favorite candidate. Legally, such contributions fall within a "gray" area; that is, contributors are well advised not to put in writing any specific directions to the party for the use of their money.

(Federal law limits the size of individual campaign contributions to $1,000 per candidate per election. State limits vary a great deal from lows of $500 in Florida and Kentucky to a high of $28,000 in New York for statewide candidates. States with no limits on the size of individual contributions include Alabama, Colorado, Idaho, Illinois, Indiana, Iowa, Mississippi, Nebraska, New Mexico, North Dakota, Ohio, Pennsylvania, Texas, Utah, and Virginia.)[a]

[a]*Book of the States*, 1998–99, pp. 186–195.

Figure 5–3). The heaviest campaign contributions in state races are usually garnered from lawyers and lobbyists, political consultants, physicians, hospital and health insurance representatives, real estate developers, bankers, contractors, and unions representing teachers and government employees. But it is not always clear from these reports who the contributing lawyers, lobbyists, and consultants represent. Moreover, big-money contributors often get around limitations on the size of individual contri-

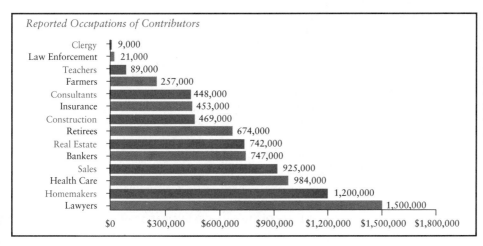

Reported Occupations of Contributors

Occupation	Amount
Clergy	9,000
Law Enforcement	21,000
Teachers	89,000
Farmers	257,000
Consultants	448,000
Insurance	453,000
Construction	469,000
Retirees	674,000
Real Estate	742,000
Bankers	747,000
Sales	925,000
Health Care	984,000
Homemakers	1,200,000
Lawyers	1,500,000

FIGURE 5–3
Reported Occupations of Campaign Contributors, Florida's Governor Race

Source: Florida Elections Commission. Figures from 1994.

butions by making multiple small contributions in the names of various representatives as well as their spouses (e.g., "homemakers" in Figure 5–3) and family members.

REGULATING PACs   The Federal Election Commission prohibits PACs from contributing more than $5,000 per election to any candidate *for federal office*. Federal law preempts state laws in regulating PACs in federal elections, but states can regulate PAC contributions in state elections. Indeed, most states currently do so, with limits varying from $1,000 to $5,000 per statewide candidate per election.

PERSONAL FINANCIAL DISCLOSURE   Most states now require candidates for public office to disclose their financial assets and sources of income. Financial disclosure laws have been upheld by the courts, although opponents of these laws have argued that such laws are an "invasion of privacy." These laws vary regarding the degree of detail required and whether or not the finances of the candidate's immediate family must also be disclosed. A glance at these required financial statements will convince anyone that candidates greatly understate their assets and income.

PUBLIC CAMPAIGN FINANCING   Some states provide some public funds for candidates or parties.[32] New Jersey was the first state to undertake major financial support for candidates for governor. The arguments for such public financing are that it (1) permits less affluent candidates to run for office, (2) removes some of the advantages of wealth in office seeking, and (3) reduces the dependency of candidates on large financial contributors.[33] But there is very little evidence to support or refute these arguments.

State public campaign finance laws differ from each other and from the federal model:

- *Check-offs* versus *add-ons:* Most state campaign finance laws allow taxpayers to check off one dollar of their state income tax payments with no additional tax liability, but some states have an add-on feature that increases liability. Experience indicates that about 20 percent of state taxpayers will contribute to campaign financing if there is no additional cost to them, but only 1 to 3 percent will do so if it adds to their taxes.[34]
- Party funds or general funds: Some state campaign finance laws allow contributors to designate which party should receive their dollar, while other state laws (like federal law) provide that all contributions go to a general fund for direct distribution to candidates.[35] Allowing party preference favors the Democratic party because of its majority status.
- General elections or general election plus primary elections: Most states with campaign finance laws limit funding to general elections, probably because of the added costs of funding primaries.
- Distribution of money to parties or directly to candidates: States that permit taxpayers to designate which party is to receive their contribution give these funds to party organizations. But states with general cam-

paign funds can distribute them either to the parties or directly to the candidates.

- Gubernatorial elections only or elections for all constitutional officers and legislators: Some states subsidize only the gubernatorial election, while others subsidize all statewide elections and even state legislative campaigns.

The real stimulus to public campaign funding schemes arises from the distaste with which most politicians approach the task of soliciting contributions. Many complain that fund-raising takes more time and effort than campaigning itself. Moreover, limits on campaign spending help protect incumbents by denying their opponents the funds to overcome the advantages of incumbency.

FEDERAL TAX LAWS   Finally, the U.S. Internal Revenue Service plays an overseer role in political finance. It is a violation of federal tax laws for a candidate to use campaign contributions for personal expenses without declaring this money as personal income. Indeed, serious legal consequences for office seekers can occur when campaign funds are directed to personal use. Surplus funds may be retained in a campaign account for a future campaign, or they may be given back to contributors, or to charity, or to other candidates in the party, without incurring federal tax liability.

ON THE WEB

Both the Democratic and Republican parties maintain national Web sites. The Democratic National Committee (DNC) site can be found at

www.democrats.org

The DNC site offers many direct links—"The Democratic Web"—to party committees, events, candidates, office holders, and others. It also provides links to *state* party Web sites, for example, the California Democratic Party's site at

www.ca-dem.org

The Republican National Committee (RNC) also maintains a comprehensive Web site at

www.rnc.org

This site includes a "Locate My State Party" index with direct links to Republican *state* party Web sites, for example:

California Republican party at

www.cagop.org

Texas Republican party at

www.texasgop.org

New York Republican party at

www.nygop.org

These party sites offer encouragement to participate in party affairs, campaigns and elections, and, of course, campaign fund-raising.

NOTES

1. E. E. Schattschneider, *Party Government* (New York: Rinehart, 1942), p. 1.

2. See Charles S. Bullock and Lock K. Johnson, "Sex and the Second Primary," *Social Science Quarterly,* 66 (December 1985), 933–42.

3. Charles S. Bullock and A. Brock Smith, "Black Success in Local Run-off Elections," *Journal of Politics,* 52 (November 1990), 1205–20.

4. Joseph Stewart, James F. Sheffield, and Margaret E. Ellis, "The Mechanisms of Runoff Primary Disadvantage," *Social Science Quarterly,* 76 (December 1995), 807–22.

5. Robert J. Huckshorn, *Party Leadership in the States* (Amherst: University of Massachusetts Press, 1976), p. 1.

6. See Harold Clarke, Frank B. Feigert, and Marianne C. Stewart, "Different Contents, Similar Packages: The Domestic Political Beliefs of Southern Local Party Activists," *Political Research Quarterly,* 48 (March 1995), 151–67.

7. Janet Clark, Charles D. Hadley, and R. Darcy, "Political Ambition Among Men and Women State Party Leaders," *American Politics Quarterly,* 17 (April 1989), 194–207.

8. Stephen S. Meinhold and Charles D. Hadley, "Lawyers as Political Party Activists," *Social Science Quarterly,* 76 (June 1995) 364–80.

9. See Paul Allen Beck and Frank J. Sorauf, *Party Politics in America,* 7th ed. (New York: Harper-Collins, 1992), Chapter 2.

10. Huckshorn, *Party Leadership,* p. 46.

11. See James L. Gibson et al., "Assembling Party Organization Strength," *American Journal of Political Science,* 27 (May 1983), 193–222.

12. James L. Gibson et al., "Whither the Local Parties?" *American Journal of Political Science,* 29 (February 1985), 139–60.

13. See Steven E. Finkel and Howard A. Scarrow, "Party Identification and Party Enrollment," *Journal of Politics,* 47 (May 1985), 624–42.

14. See Kerin M. Leyden and Stephen A. Borrelli, "The Effect of State Economic Conditions on Gubernatorial Elections: Does Unified Government Make a Difference?" *Political Research Quarterly,* 48 (June 1995), 275–90.

15. The traditional assumption that party competition had an important liberalizing effect on public policy is found in V. O. Key, Jr., *American State Politics: An Introduction* (New York: Knopf, 1956). The effect of party competition on public policy was shown in statistical analysis to be *less* influential than economic conditions in Thomas R. Dye, *Politics, Economics, and the Public* (Chicago: Rand McNally, 1966).

16. V. O. Key, Jr., *Southern Politics in State and Nation* (New York: Knopf, 1949), p. 307.

17. Dye, *Politics, Economics, and the Public,* p. 293.

18. See Thomas R. Dye, "Party and Policy in the States," *Journal of Politics,* 46 (November 1984), 1097–1116.

19. See also Robert D. Brown, "Party Cleavages and Welfare Effort in the American States," *American Political Science Review,* 89 (March 1995), 23–33.

20. See Sarah M. Morehouse, "Money versus Party Effect: Nominating for Governor," *American Journal of Political Science,* 34 (August 1990), 706–24.

21. W. P. Welch, "The Effectiveness of Expenditures in State Legislative Races," *American Politics Quarterly,* 4 (July 1976), 333–56.

22. Frank J. Sorauf, *Money in American Elections* (Boston: Scott, Foresman, 1988).

23. Welch, "The Effectiveness of Expenditures."

24. Larry Sabato, *Goodbye to Good-time Charlie,* 2nd ed. (Washington, DC: Congressional Quarterly Press, 1983), p. 152.

25. Michael J. Malbin, *Money and Politics in the United States* (Washington, DC: American Enterprise Institute, 1984).

26. Ruth S. Jones and Warren E. Miller, "Financing Campaigns," *Western Political Quarterly,* 38 (June 1985), 187–210.

27. Ruth S. Jones and Ann H. Hopkings, "State Campaign Fund Raising," *Journal of Politics,* 47 (May 1985), 427–49.

28. Sorauf, *Money in American Elections,* pp. 262–64.

29. *Buckley* v. *Valeo,* 424 U.S. 1 (1976).

30. See Robert J. Huckshorn, "Who Gave It? Who Got It?," *Journal of Politics,* 47 (August 1985), 773–89.

31. See *Book of the States, 1994–95,* pp. 236–37.

32. Including Hawaii, Idaho, Iowa, Kentucky, Michigan, Minnesota, New Jersey, North Carolina, Rhode Island, Utah, and Wisconsin.

33. See James M. Penning and Corwin Smith, "Public Funding of Gubernatorial Elections," *American Politics Quarterly,* 10 (July 1982), 315–32.

34. Jack L. Noragon, "Political Finance and Political Reform: The Experience with State Income Tax Checkoffs," *American Political Science Review,* 75 (September 1981), 667–87.

35. See Ruth S. Jones, "State Campaign Finance: Implications for Partisan Politics," *American Journal of Political Science,* 25 (May 1981), 342–61.

6
LEGISLATORS IN STATE POLITICS

QUESTIONS TO CONSIDER

★ ★ ★ ★ ★ ★ ★ ★ ★ ★ ★

How would you rate the job your own state legislature is doing?

☐ Excellent ☐ Good

☐ Average ☐ Poor

Can you follow the path of a bill through the legislative process in your state?

☐ Yes ☐ No

Do full-time, well-paid professional legislatures with large staffs generally make better policies than those with part-time, lower-paid, citizen members who do most of the work?

☐ Yes ☐ No

Would you prefer legislators who act as "trustees" and use their own best judgment in voting or "delegates" who will vote the way a majority of their constituents wish?

☐ Prefer "trustee" representation

☐ Prefer "delegate" representation

FUNCTIONS OF STATE LEGISLATURES

If you were to ask state legislators what the job of the legislature is, they might say: "Our job is to pass laws," or "We have to represent the people," or "We have to make policy." All the answers are correct, but none by itself tells the whole story.

ENACTING LAWS   It is true that, from a *legal viewpoint,* the function of state legislatures is to "pass laws," that is, the enactment of statutory law. Legislatures may enact more than a thousand laws in a single legislative session. The average legislator introduces ten to twelve bills each year. Many are never expected to pass. They are introduced merely as a favor to a constituent or an interest group, or to get a headline in a newspaper back home.

The range of subject matter of bills considered by a legislature is enormous. A legislature may consider the authorization of $50 billion of state spending, or it may debate the expansion of the hunting season on raccoons, or it may increase teachers' salaries, or it may argue whether or not inscribing license plates with "The Poultry State" would cause the state to be called "chicken." Obviously, these considerations range from the trivial to the vital.

CONSIDERING CONSTITUTIONAL AMENDMENTS AND GUBERNATORIAL APPOINTMENTS   In addition to the enactment of statutory law, legislatures share in the process of state constitutional revision (see "Constitutional Change in the States" in Chapter 2) and consider amendments to the U.S. Constitution. (See "Battles in the States over Constitutional Amendments" in Chapter 3.) Many governors' appointments to high state offices require legislative approval (see "The Governor's Managerial Powers" in Chapter 7).

APPROVING BUDGETS   Perhaps their single most important function is the passage of the appropriation and tax measures in the state budget. No state monies may be spent without a legislative appropriation, and it is difficult to think of any governmental action that does not involve some financial expenditure. Potentially, a legislature can control any activity of the state government through its power over appropriations.

SERVING CONSTITUENTS   Legislators spend a great deal of time answering requests from constituents—"servicing the district." Many letters and phone calls will come from interest groups in their districts—business, labor, agriculture, school teachers, municipal employees, and so on. These communications may deal with specific bills or with items in the state budget. Other communications may come from citizens who want specific assistance or favors—help with getting a state job, help with permits or licenses, voicing an opinion about whom the state university should hire as a new football coach, and so forth.[1]

OVERSEEING STATE AGENCIES   Legislative "oversight" of state agencies and programs is another important function. Legislators frequently challenge state adminis-

Constituents.
Residents of a legislator's district; the people who are represented by a legislator.

■
Legislative oversight.
The monitoring of the activities of the executive branch of government by the legislature and its committees.

Sunset laws.
Laws that fix termination dates for programs and agencies in order to force the legislature to renew them if the legislators wish the programs to continue.

trators to explain why they are doing what they do. Frequently, committee hearings and budget hearings, in particular, provide opportunities for legislators to put administrators "through the wringer" about programs and expenditures. Often embarrassed administrators feel harassed at these meetings, but the true purpose is to remind state administrators that elected representatives of the people are the final legal authority.

Most states now have "sunset" laws that call for their legislatures to reenact programs every few years or else see them go out of existence (sunset). Few programs or agencies are ever sunseted, but such laws force periodic legislative reexamination and evaluation of the performance of state bureaucracies.

THE MAKING OF A STATE LEGISLATOR

State legislators are not "representative" of the population of their states in the sense of being typical cross sections of them. On the contrary, the nation's 7424 state legislators are generally selected from the better-educated, more prestigiously employed, middle-class segments of the population.

STATUS   Social background information on state legislators also indicates that legislators tend to come from the "upwardly mobile" sectors of the population. This places many of them among the "second-rung" elites in the status system rather than the established wealth. Although the sons and grandsons of distinguished old families of great wealth frequently enter presidential and gubernatorial politics in the states, they seldom run for the state legislature. Legislators are frequently among the middle status groups for whom politics is an avenue of upward mobility.

OCCUPATION   Legislators must come from occupational groups with flexible work responsibility. The lawyer, the farmer, or the business owner can adjust his or her work to the legislative schedule, but the office manager cannot. The overrepresented occupations are those involving extensive public contact. The lawyer, real estate agent, insurance agent, tavern owner, and merchant establish in their business the wide circle of friends necessary for political success. In short, the legislator's occupation should provide free time, public contacts, and social respectability. (See Figure 6–1.)

EDUCATION   State legislators are generally well educated. More than three-quarters of them are college educated, compared to only one-quarter of the general population.

PERSONAL WEALTH   Legislators frequently claim that public service is a financial burden. While this may be true, legislators are generally recruited from among the more affluent members of society, and they become even more affluent during their tenure. Indeed, there is evidence that (1) the average net worth of new legislators is increasing over time, and (2) the average legislator increases his or her net worth while serving in the legislature. (Net worth is the total value of all assets—houses, autos, stocks, bonds, property, etc.—after subtracting the total value of all outstanding debts—mortgages, loans, etc.) For example, in Florida, the average legislator more than *tripled* his or her net worth in ten years of legislative service. Asked to explain

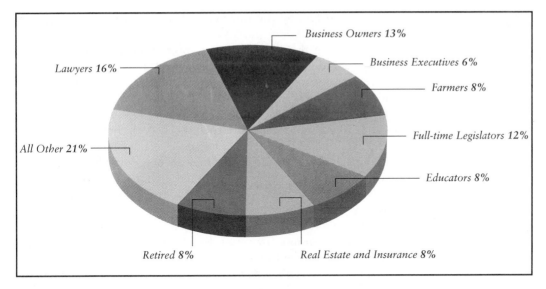

FIGURE 6–1 Legislators' Careers
Source: National Conference of State Legislatures, 1995.

these increases in personal wealth, one legislator said, "Maybe they do well because they're achievers. That's why they win when they run for office and that's why they make money."[2] But it's more likely that legislative service, and the public name recognition that comes with it, enhances one's legal practice, real estate or insurance business, as well as investment opportunities.

LAWYERS   Lawyers are overrepresented in legislative bodies at all levels of government. It is sometimes argued that the lawyer brings a special kind of skill to politics. The lawyer's occupation is the representation of clients, so he or she makes no great change in occupation when going from representing clients in private practice to representing constituents in the legislature. Lawyers are trained to deal with public policy as it is reflected in the statute books, so they may be reasonably familiar with public policy before entering the legislature. Moreover, service in the legislature can help a lawyer's private practice through free public advertising and opportunities to make contacts with potential clients.

There are also important institutional advantages for lawyers to enter state politics—specifically, the availability of a large number of highly valued "lawyers-only" posts in state government, such as judge and prosecuting attorney. Lawyers are eligible for many elective and appointive public jobs from which nonlawyers are excluded. State legislative seats are viewed by lawyers as stepping stones to these posts—appellate court judge, Supreme Court justice, attorney general, regulatory commissioner, and so on. The postlegislative careers of lawyers shows that over half go on to other public offices, compared to less than one-third of the nonlawyer legislators.[3]

Do lawyers behave any differently from nonlawyers in the legislature? Lawyers do *not* vote any differently from nonlawyers on most issues; lawyers are neutral "contractors" for parties, interest groups, constituents, and others. Generally, they do not vote together as a bloc.

However, lawyers do act together in legislatures to protect the legal profession. The opposition of trial lawyers to insurance reform, including "no-fault" insurance, and their opposition to reform of liability laws, has become a national scandal. In recent years "tort reform" (a tort is a civil wrong that results in damages) has been a major item on the agenda of state legislatures. Reform proposals include capping "pain and suffering" awards at $250,000 or $500,000; restricting the fees a trial lawyer can take from a victim's award; and ending the rule of "joint and several liability," which forces wealthy defendants to pay the total award even if they are only partially at fault. Businesses, doctors, hospitals, municipalities, and insurance companies have all lobbied heavily at state capitals for these liability law reforms. But they have generally been defeated in state legislatures. The reason: Lawyers are disproportionately represented in these bodies. And it is certainly not in the financial interest of lawyers themselves to limit jury awards or restrict their fees or prevent them from suing the deepest pockets. (See "The Lawyering of America" in Chapter 8.)

Finally, it is argued that lawyers bring distinctive values and ways of thinking to the political process. Legal education—learning "to think like a lawyer"—develops habits that focus the mind on the precise wording of laws, rules, and regulations. Lawyer-legislators are often resented by their nonlawyer colleagues and accused of having tunnel vision, a superiority complex, and a tendency to miss the "human side" of politics. Lawyer-legislators are more likely to see themselves as "trustees" of their constituents, as occupying leadership positions in the legislature, and as harboring ambitions for higher office.[4]

AMATEURS   Most state legislatures are still part-time bodies. There are constitutional limits to the length of legislative sessions in most states; the most common limit is sixty days per year. Most state legislatures put in fewer than 100 working days a year. It is true that interim committee meetings and other legislative responsibilities may add to the duties of legislators, and over the years sessions have grown longer. But most state legislators have other occupations, and few rely on their legislative compensation alone.[5]

In recent years, however, an increasing number of state legislators are full-time representatives. The "citizen legislator" who spends two months in the state capitol and then returns home to his or her own business or profession still predominates in the states, but the proportion of full-time legislators is now 12 percent (see Figure 6–1). Full-time legislators are even more frequent in large states with better-paid legislatures, such as California, New York, and Michigan.

PSYCHOLOGY   We know, then, that legislators differ from their constituents in certain *socioeconomic* background characteristics—social class, education, occupation. But are there *psychological* differences between legislators and their constituents that are independent of these socioeconomic differences? Years ago, a political scientist succeeded in getting South Carolina state legislators to submit to extensive psychological testing.[6] The results suggested that legislators were more self-sufficient, more self-confident, more extroverted, slightly more dominant, and less neurotic than the average American. A later study of Iowa state legislators found that legislators are generally more tolerant toward others, less authoritarian, and more favorably disposed toward minority groups than a cross section of Iowa voters, even when the effects of socioeconomic backgrounds are controlled.[7] In short, there is some evidence that psychological predispositions—self-confidence, gregariousness, tolerance toward others—operate as self-selective factors in determining who will choose to make a career in political life.

MINORITIES AND WOMEN IN STATE LEGISLATURES

Minorities and women have made impressive gains in American state legislatures in the last decade. Today, African Americans occupy about 7.5 percent of all state legislative seats in the nation; Hispanics occupy about 2.4 percent of these seats; and women occupy about 21 percent.

AFRICAN AMERICAN REPRESENTATION IN STATE LEGISLATURES   Black voter mobilization, stemming initially from the Voting Rights Act of 1965 and later from federal court enforcement of amendments to that act following the 1990 census (see "Minorities in State Politics" in Chapter 4), has resulted in the election of substantial numbers of African American state legislators. Most are elected from majority black districts. Southern states, with larger black populations, have the largest percentages of African American state legislators (see "*Rankings of the States:* African American and Hispanic Representation in Legislatures").

Nonetheless, nationwide the percentage of African American state legislators (7.5 percent) is somewhat less than the percentage of African Americans in the voting-age population (11.2 percent). Therefore, it can be argued that African Americans remain underrepresented in the nation's state legislatures. The ratio, achieved by calculating the African American percentage of state legislators divided by the African American percentage of the voting-age population, is 0.66 for the nation as a whole. This ratio varies a great deal from state to state. It is 1.0 or higher (suggesting racial equality in representation) in only thirteen states.

Black legislators in the states have had a significant impact on legislative voting. Their voting on civil rights and welfare issues is clearly distinguishable in southern states.[8] White legislators, even those with substantial numbers of black constituents, are not as strong in support of these issue as black legislators.

HISPANIC REPRESENTATION IN STATE LEGISLATURES   Hispanic membership in state legislatures is significant in a number of states. The largest Hispanic delegations are found in those states with the largest Hispanic populations—New Mexico, Texas, Arizona, Colorado, and California. However, Hispanic representation in state legislatures remains well below what we would expect given the growing Hispanic percentage of the nation's population. Indeed, the ratio, achieved by calculating the Hispanic percentage of state legislators divided by the percentage of the voting-age Hispanic population, is only 0.25. This underrepresentation of Hispanics may be a product of the same forces that appear to reduce Hispanic political participation generally. (See "Minorities in State Politics" in Chapter 4.)

RANKINGS OF THE STATES

AFRICAN AMERICAN REPRESENTATION IN LEGISLATURES

Percentage of African Americans in Legislature

Ratio of African Americans in Legislature to Percent of Voting-Age Population

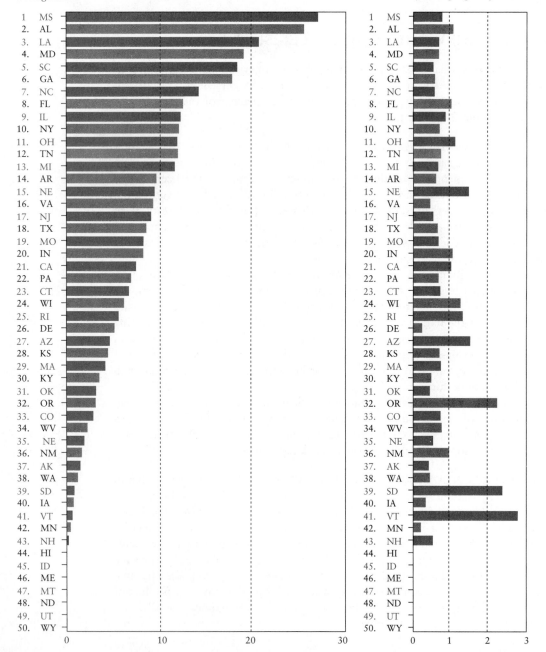

HISPANIC REPRESENTATION IN LEGISLATURES

*Percentage of Hispanics
in Legislature*

*Ratio of Hispanics in Legislature
to Percent of Voting-Age Population*

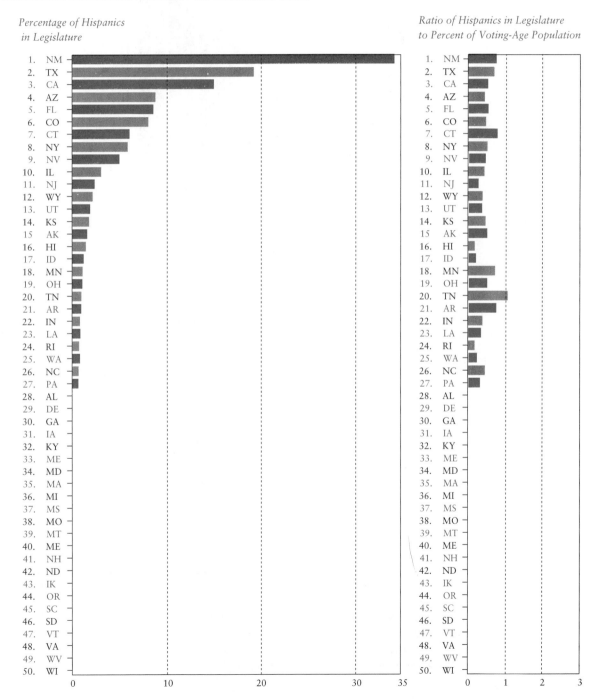

Source: *Book of the States*, 1998–99.

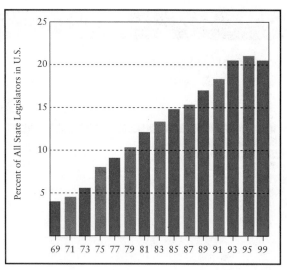

FIGURE 6–2
Women in State
Legislatures

The ten states with the highest percentages of women state legislators are

STATE	% WOMEN	STATE	% WOMEN
Washington	40.8	New Hampshire	31.6
Nevada	36.5	Vermont	31.1
Arizona	35.5	Oregon	30.0
Colorado	33.0	Connecticut	29.4
Kansas	32.7	Maryland	29.3

The ten states with the lowest percentages of women state legislators are

STATE	% WOMEN	STATE	% WOMEN
Alabama	7.9	Louisiana	12.5
Oklahoma	10.1	Pennsylvania	12.6
Kentucky	11.6	South Dakota	14.3
South Carolina	11.8	Arkansas	14.8
Mississippi	12.1	Virginia	15.7

Source: Data supplied by Center for the American Woman in Politics, Eagleton Institute of Politics, Rutgers University, 1999.

WOMEN IN STATE LEGISLATURES   While women today occupy only about 22 percent of all state legislative seats in the nation, this is a significant increase over the scant 4 percent female state legislators in 1969 (see Figure 6–2). Like their male counterparts, female legislators tend to come from politically active families, to have lived in their communities for a long time, to be representative of their district in race and ethnicity, and to enjoy somewhat higher social status than most of their constituents. Women are somewhat better represented in the New England and western states with less "professional" legislatures; the large urban industrial states with more "professional" legislatures have fewer female representatives.[9] Southern states also tend to have fewer female legislators. Among the factors associated with increased representation of women are the female percentage of the labor force and the proliferation of active women's organizations in the states.[10] Certain cultural forces in the states, notably Christian fundamentalism, may also be an obstacle to women gaining political office.[11]

Women candidates are just as successful in primary and general elections as men.[12] Voters are *not* predisposed to cast ballots either for or against female candidates.[13] Incumbency gives all officeholders an electoral advantage; since more males held office in the past, women challengers have faced the obstacle of incumbency. But women and men fare equally in races for open seats. So why are women underrepresented in state legislatures?

Fewer women than men run for state legislative seats. Scholars frequently cite women's traditional family roles of wife and mother as obstacles to a political career. Female legislative candidates with young children are very rare; newly elected women legislators are four years older on the average than newly elected male legislators—a fact generally attributed to women waiting until their children are older.[14] Many women who confront conflicts between family life and political activity choose in favor of their families. One study found that more women serve in the legislatures of states whose capitals are located close to the major population centers than in the legislatures of states whose capitals are isolated and require long commutes from home.[15]

WOMEN IN LEGISLATIVE LEADERSHIP POSITIONS   Traditionally, state legislative chambers were regarded as "male clubs." Women were considered to have "crashed the gates" when they won legislative seats. Although men continue to outnumber women by four to one in overall state legislative membership, more and more women are gaining power within state legislative bodies.

Although there continue to be a lot of "firsts" in the various states—first woman speaker of the house, first woman president of the senate, first woman majority or minority leader, and so on—over time women have gained a fair share of leadership posts. Those who have done so, however, believe that they had to work harder, study the issues more closely, and overcome more stereotyping than their male counterparts in order to win respect in their chambers.[16]

Women have also won their fair share of committee chairs; that is, in most states they occupy as many or more committee chairs than the percentage of women in the legislative body would indicate.[17] Indeed, they chair a disproportionate number of education, health, and human service committees, while at the same time, they chair a fair share of the key budget and taxation committees. To the extent that committee chairs represent successful access to power and authority within legislatures, then women have gained a share equal to their legislative representation.

GETTING TO THE STATE CAPITOL

The state legislature is a convenient starting place for a political career. About one-half of the state legislators in the nation never served in public office before their election to the legislature, and a greater percentage of new members are in the lower rather than upper chambers. The other half had only limited experience on city councils, county commissions, and school boards.

GETTING INTO POLITICS   Why does a legislator decide to run for office in the first place? It is next to impossible to determine the real motivations of political office seekers—they seldom know themselves. Legislators will usually describe their motivations in highly idealistic terms: "I felt that I could do the community a service"; "I considered it a civic duty." Only seldom are reasons for candidacy expressed in personal terms: "Oh, I just think it's lots of fun." Gregariousness and the desire to socialize no doubt contribute to the reasons for some office seekers. Politics can have a special lure of its own: "It gets into your blood and you like it." Particular issues may mobilize a political career, but ideological involvement occupies a relatively unimportant place in a candidate's motives. Activity in organizations that are deeply involved in politics is more likely to lead to candidacy.[18]

POLITICAL EXPERIENCE   States with stronger parties are more likely to nominate people who have worked for the party in some previous appointed or elective office.[19] States with weaker parties are more likely to elect "amateurs" with no previous political experience. The stronger the party organization, the more likely a legislative candidate will have to serve a political apprenticeship in some local or party offices. However, as party organizations weaken, the easier it becomes for individuals with little or no prior governmental experience to win legislative seats.

RAISING CAMPAIGN MONEY   The first challenge that an aspiring legislator faces is raising money to finance the campaign. In some states with small legislative districts, nonprofessional legislatures, and largely rural constituencies, a state legislative race may cost only $10,000 to $25,000. But large urban state legislative races may cost $50,000 to $100,000 or more. On the average, senate contests cost more than house contests, and winners spend more than losers. Money allows a candidate to produce commercials, buy television and radio time, buy newspaper ads, travel around the district, and distribute bumper stickers and campaign buttons. Some state legislative candidates employ professional campaign management firms. Most state legislative campaigns are relatively amateurish, but they still cost money. When campaigns are relatively inexpensive, the candidate and his or her friends contribute most of the money. But in more expensive races, candidates may turn to PACs. Corporate, labor, environmental, and ideological PACs are becoming increasingly active in state capitals, particularly in the larger states. (See "Money in State Politics" in Chapter 5.) Perhaps as much as one-quarter to one-third of money for state legislative campaigns now comes from PAC contributions, most of which goes to incumbents.

FACING THE PRIMARIES   Candidates face two important obstacles when they decide to run for the state legislature: the primary and the general election. A seat in the legislature depends on how much competition a candidate encounters in these elections. First, let us consider competition in the primary elections. Available evidence indicates that more than half of the nation's state legislators are *unopposed* for their party's nomination in primary elections. Many legislators who do face primary competition have only token opposition. Most primary competition occurs in a party's "sure" districts, some competition occurs in "close" districts, and there is a distinct shortage of candidates in districts where the party's chances are poor. In other words, primary competition is greater where the likelihood of victory in the general election is greater.

Some states require runoff elections when no candidate wins a majority in the first primary. Thus, some candidates face three elections on their way to the legislature—a first primary, a runoff primary, and the general election.

THE GENERAL ELECTION   The culmination of the recruitment process is in the general election, yet in many legislative constituencies one party is so entrenched that the voters have little real choice at the general election. In some districts, the minority party is so weak that it fails to run candidates for legislative seats.

"Competition" implies more than a name filed under the opposition party label. Generally a competitive election is one in which the winning candidate wins by something less than two to one. In light of this more realistic definition of competition, the absence of truly competitive politics in state legislative elections is striking. Overall, more than half of the nation's legislators are elected in *noncompetitive* general elections, where their opponents are either nonexistent or receive less than one-third of the vote. Even in competitive states, such as California, Michigan, Minnesota, New York, Pennsylvania, and Wisconsin, over half the state legislators face only token opposition in the general election.[20] Moreover, competition is *declining* over time, as more legislators are winning by lopsided margins.[21]

THE GREAT INCUMBENCY MACHINE

Legislators who choose to run for reelection are seldom defeated. Indeed, they are usually unopposed in the primary election, and sometimes unopposed in the general election. Potential challengers are discouraged by the record of success of incumbents.[22] *Nearly 90 percent of incumbent state legislators who seek reelection are successful.* (The reelection rate of incumbents in New York is over 98 percent, the highest in the nation.) Aspiring newcomers in politics are advised to wait for incumbents to leave office voluntarily. Redistricting also opens up legislative seats and occasionally forces incumbents to run against each other. Although there is some evidence that "quality challengers"—people who have won previous state or local elections and can raise campaign funds—have a better chance than newcomers to defeat incumbents, nonetheless, the likelihood of defeating an incumbent in either the primary or general election is very low.[23]

VISIBILITY   Why do incumbents win? First of all, they enjoy greater visibility and name recognition in their districts: "The reason I get 93 percent victories is what I do back home. I stay highly visible. No grass grows under my feet. I show I haven't forgot from whence I came."[24] Incumbents spend a major portion of their time throughout their term of office campaigning for reelection: "I have the feeling that the most

Competition.
In electoral politics, confronting an opponent or party that has a reasonable chance to win the election.

Incumbents.
Persons currently serving in elective or appointed positions in government.

effective campaigning is done when no election is near. During the interval between elections you have to establish every personal contact you can." Legislators regularly appear at civic clubs, social and charitable events, churches, and many other gatherings: "Personally, I will speak on any subject. I talk on everything whether it deals with politics or not." Indeed, many legislators spend more time campaigning for reelection than lawmaking. Few challengers can afford to spend two or four years campaigning.

PROFESSIONALISM   As legislatures become more professional over time—employing large professional staffs; providing offices, expense accounts, and travel budgets to legislators; and increasing their pay—incumbents acquire greater resources to assist them in servicing constituents. Constituents' services or "casework" is growing in state legislatures; legislators are increasingly involved in assisting constituents in dealing with state bureaucracies, providing information, and doing small favors at the capital. Over time this form of "retail" politics gradually builds a network of grateful voters.

Legislators in professionalized legislatures are given large sums to subsidize what are really campaign activities—printing and mailing of newsletters; press rooms and video studios; travel reimbursement; and aides, assistants, and secretaries who spend much of their time on constituent services.

MONEY   Finally, and perhaps most importantly, incumbents attract much more in the way of campaign contributions than challengers. Interest group contributions go overwhelmingly to incumbents. (See "Money in State Politics" in Chapter 5.) These groups are seeking access and influence with decision makers, so they direct their contributions to people in office. Moreover, group leaders know that incumbents are rarely defeated and they do not want to antagonize incumbents by contributing to challengers. Incumbents can build a "war chest" over time; often the size of the war chest itself is enough to discourage potential challengers from entering races against them.

THE UNPOPULARITY OF STATE LEGISLATURES

The public's disdain of politicians has fueled a movement to limit the terms of both Congress members and state legislators throughout the country. While the U.S. Supreme Court has declared state attempts to limit the terms of *Congress members* unconstitutional,[25] term limits have recently been imposed upon *state legislators* in twenty-one states. (In three of these states, state supreme courts have invalidated term limit provisions; see Table 6–1.)

Most of these term limit amendments have come about through citizens' initiatives and have won overwhelming support in referenda votes (see *"What Do You Think?: Are Term Limits a Good Idea?"* in Chapter 2). The most common limit for state senate members is eight years (two 4-year terms); state house members are often limited to six years (three 2-year terms). Most of these limits have been incorporated into state constitutions; a few have been enacted only by statute and could more easily be repealed.

■
Term limits.
Provisions in constitutions or laws that limit elected officials to a specific number of terms in office.

Table 6–1

TERM LIMITS ON STATE LEGISLATORS				
State*	*Year Enacted*	*Constitutional (C) (% voting yes) Statutory (S)*	*Limits in Years* SENATE	HOUSE
Arizona	1992	C (74)	4 2-yrs.	4 2-yrs.
Arkansas	1992	C (60)	2 4-yrs.	3 2-yrs.
California	1990	C (52)	2 4-yrs.	3 2-yrs.
Colorado	1990	C (71)	2 4-yrs.	4 2-yrs.
Florida	1992	C (77)	8-yrs.	8-yrs.
Idaho	1994	S	8-yrs.	8-yrs.
Louisiana	1995	C (76)	3 4-yrs.	3 4-yrs.
Maine	1993	S	4 2-yrs.	4 2-yrs.
Michigan	1992	C (59)	2 4-yrs.	3 2-yrs.
Missouri	1992	C (75)	8-yrs.	8-yrs.
Montana	1992	C (67)	8-yrs.	8-yrs.
Nevada	1994	C (70)	3 4-yrs.	6 2-yrs.
Ohio	1992	C (68)	2 4-yrs.	4 2-yrs.
Oklahoma	1990	C (67)	12-yrs.	12-yrs.
Oregon	1992	C (70)	8-yrs.	6-yrs.
South Dakota	1992	C (64)	4 2-yrs.	4 2-yrs.
Utah	1994	S	12-yrs.	12-yrs.
Wyoming	1992	S	3 4-yrs.	3 2-yrs.

Note: Unlisted states do not limit the terms of their state legislators.

*State supreme courts have voided term limit provisions in Massachusetts, Nebraska, and Washington.

Source: National Conference of State Legislatures.

UNPOPULAR LEGISLATURES   State legislatures, like other governmental institutions in America, have suffered a decline in popular approval in recent years. Public evaluations of legislature performance appear to be sagging everywhere. When citizens are asked in statewide polls to "rate the job [their state legislature] is doing," ratings of "fair" and "poor" regularly outnumber ratings of "excellent" and "good."

The unpopularity of state legislatures is doubtless related to the national disdain for government and politics. But economic recessions, well-publicized scandals, stalemates over policy, tax increases, an inability to deal effectively with crime or other state problems, all appear to contribute to legislative unpopularity from time to time.

Yet despite the unpopularity of state legislatures, the powers of incumbency are so great that individual members are regularly reelected. This apparent paradox—regular reelection of members of an unpopular legislature—helped inspire the term limit movement in the states.

■

Turnover.
In legislatures, the percentage of members replaced in each legislative session.

Turnover   In states *without* term limits, the overall turnover rate is roughly 25 percent. This means that about one-quarter of all state legislators are newcomers at any legislative session. They have taken the seats of members who do not return to the state house because of a career change, a run for higher office, retirement, illness or death, or, in relatively rare instances, defeat in their bid for reelection. Turnover rates vary by state, ranging from below 5 percent to above 40 percent. Interestingly, it is *not* party competition that increases turnover; far more legislators voluntarily quit than are defeated for reelection. There is *less* turnover in the larger states, which have longer legislative sessions and pay their legislators more money. In other words, more "professional" legislatures have lower turnover rates than the "amateur" legislatures.[26]

In states that have imposed term limits on their legislators (see Table 6–1), the turnover rate is projected to jump to 40 to 50 percent. These high rates will be a product of combining normal membership turnover with the impact of term limits. These projections suggest that state legislatures with term limits will confront considerable legislative inexperience, with up to half of their members at any session being newcomers.

Facing Up to Term Limits   Term limits are now beginning to force incumbent lawmakers to leave office. Overall 2,615 of the nation's 7,424 state legislators (35 percent) are currently subject to term limits. The term limit casualty list began to grow in 1998 when terms ran out for more than 200 members in half a dozen states. The Michigan House was hit hardest when 67 of 110 members came up against term limits in 1998.[27] We will soon be able to assess the impact of term limits on legislature performance, that is, to evaluate some of the arguments for and against term limits. Inasmuch as some states have adopted term limits and some have not, we will soon be able to compare results from our "laboratories of democracy." For example, proponents of term limits argue that they will inspire greater competition for legislative seats and encourage more qualified people to run for office. They argue that term limits will reduce the influence of well-entrenched interest groups in state capitals and make legislatures more responsive to public opinion. Opponents of term limits believe they will weaken the power of legislatures in relation to executive branch bureaucracies. They believe that term limits will lead to less experienced legislative leadership and less professional legislatures. Within a few years, we may be able to test the validity of these arguments.

Legislative Apportionment and Districting

Legislative apportionment refers to the allocation of seats to specific populations. Prior to 1962, malapportionment was common in American state legislatures. Malapportionment occurs when there are differing numbers of people in legislative districts that receive the same number of seats. Malapportionment creates inequality of representation: If one single-member district has twice the population of another, the value of a vote in the larger district is only half the value of a vote in the smaller district. Small minorities of the population could elect a majority of the house or senate or both in most of the states. Generally, it was the rural voters in a state who controlled a majority of legislative seats, and it was the urban voters who were discriminated against in the value of their vote.

SUPREME COURT INTERVENTION   After years of avoiding the issue of malapportionment, the U.S. Supreme Court acted in 1962 in the landmark case of *Baker* v. *Carr*.[28] This case involved the complaint of urban residents in Tennessee where the largest district in the lower house was twenty-three times larger than the smallest district. The Supreme Court decided that such inequalities in state apportionment laws denied voters "equal protection of the laws" guaranteed by the Fourteenth Amendment and that the federal courts should grant relief from these inequalities. The Supreme Court did not decide on any firm mathematical standard of correct apportionment, holding only that "as nearly as practicable, one man's vote should be equal to another's."[29] The Supreme Court required that *both* houses of the state legislature be apportioned on the basis of population; the Court rejected the federal analogy of a senate based upon geographic units: "Legislators represent people, not trees or acres. Legislators are elected by voters, not farms or cities or economic interests."[30] State after state was forced to reapportion its legislature under the threat of judicial intervention. In addition to requiring population equality in legislative districting, the Supreme Court also required population equality in congressional districting by state legislatures. The philosophy underlying these decisions was expressed by the Court: "The conception of political equality from the Declaration of Independence to Lincoln's Gettysburg Address, to the Fourteenth, Fifteenth, Seventeenth, and Nineteenth Amendments, can mean only one thing—one person, one vote."[31]

THE IMPACT OF REAPPORTIONMENT   The reapportionment revolution of the 1960s significantly increased the representation afforded urban interests in state legislatures. Reapportionment also seemed to bring younger, better-educated, more prestigiously employed people into state legislatures. It also brought many "new" people into legislative politics—people who had little or no previous experience in public office. Some political scientists maintain that the long-term effect of reapportionment was to: (1) increase party competition in state legislatures; (2) distribute more educational and highway funds to urban areas; and (3) produce more environmental regulation.[32]

STANDARDS OF EQUALITY AMONG DISTRICTS   Today there is very little inequality among legislative districts in any state, and "one person, one vote" is the prevailing form of representation. But federal courts have not always been consistent or precise in determining exactly *how equal* congressional and state legislative districts must be. In several early cases, federal courts calculated an "ideal" district by dividing the total population of the state by the number of legislative seats and then comparing all district populations to this ideal district. Variations of more than 2 percent in any district from the ideal often led to federal court invalidation of a state's redistricting plan. Later the federal courts began calculating an "overall range" by adding the deviations of the largest district and the smallest district from the ideal, disregarding the plus and

■

Apportionment.
The allocation of legislative seats to a population; the determination of how many residents should live in a representative's district.

■

Districting.
Drawing geographical boundaries of representatives' districts.

Gerrymandering.
The drawing of electoral district boundary lines to grant political advantage to a particular party, candidate, or group.

Splintering.
In districting, dividing and diluting a strong minority to deny it the ability to elect a number of representatives comparable to its percentage of the population.

Packing.
Concentrating partisan voters in a single district in order to maximize the number of representatives that can be elected by the opposition in other districts.

minus signs. (Thus if the largest district was 2 percent larger than the ideal, and the smallest district 1 percent smaller than the ideal, the "overall range" would be 3 percent.)

With regard to *congressional* districts, the U.S. Supreme Court has required strict standards of equality. Indeed, no population inequality that "could practically be avoided" is permitted in congressional districts; a New Jersey plan with an overall range of 0.70 percent was struck down upon presentation of evidence that the legislature could have reduced the range to 0.45.[33]

However, the U.S. Supreme Court has been somewhat more lenient in considering *state legislative* districting plans. The Court has refused to set any specific mathematical standards of equality for legislative districts. Nonetheless, districting plans with an overall range of more than 10 percent "create a prima facie case of discrimination and therefore must be justified by the state."[34] Federal courts will allow some deviations from absolute equality in order to recognize political subdivision (e.g., city, county) boundaries.

DISTRICTING   Districting refers to the drawing of boundary lines for legislative districts. While malapportionment refers to inequality in representation, gerrymandering refers to the drawing of district lines for political advantage. The population of districts can be equal, yet the districts drawn in such a fashion as to give advantage to one party or group over another. Consider a very simple example:

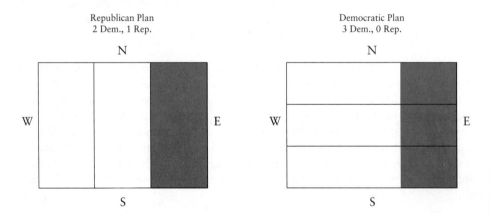

Republican Plan
2 Dem., 1 Rep.

Democratic Plan
3 Dem., 0 Rep.

For a city that is entitled to three representatives, the eastern third of the city is Republican while the western two-thirds is Democratic. If the Republicans draw the district lines, they will draw them along a north-south direction to allow them to win in one of the three districts; if Democrats draw the district lines, they will draw them along an east-west direction to allow them to win all three districts by diluting the Republican vote. Often, gerrymandering is not as neat as our example; district lines may twist and turn and create grotesque geographic patterns.

Gerrymandering can be accomplished by the combined methods of splintering and packing. Splintering involves dividing up and diluting a strong minority to deny it the power to elect a representative (see accompanying diagram). Packing involves the con-

THE ORIGINAL GERRYMANDER

The term *gerrymander* immortalizes Governor Elbridge Gerry (1744–1814) of Massachusetts, who in 1812 redistricted the state legislature to favor Democrats over Federalists. A district north of Boston was designed to concentrate and thus waste Federalist votes. The district was portrayed in a political cartoon in the *Boston Gazette* on March 26, 1812, as a "gerrymander."

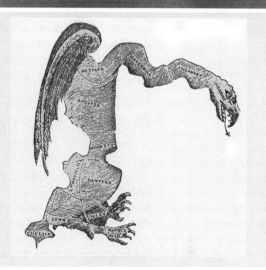

centration of partisan voters in a single district in order to "waste" their votes in large majorities for a single representative and thereby protect modest majorities in other districts (see box, "The Original Gerrymander").

As long as districts are equal in population, partisan gerrymandering does *not* violate federal court standards for "equal protection" under the Fourteenth Amendment of the U.S. Constitution. There is no constitutional obligation to allocate seats "to the contending parties in proportion to what their anticipated statewide vote will be."[35] However, the federal courts may intervene in political gerrymandering if it "consistently degrades a voter's or a group of voters' influence on the political process as a whole." This vague standard set forth by the U.S. Supreme Court opens the door to judicial intervention in particularly grievous cases of political gerrymandering.

Incumbent gerrymandering sometimes supplements traditional partisan gerrymandering. The object of incumbent gerrymandering is to protect the seats of incumbents. Often if party control of state government is divided, thus preventing the passage of a partisan gerrymander, legislators will agree to protect themselves.

THE SEATS–VOTES RELATIONSHIP   One way to determine whether partisan gerrymandering has short-changed a party is to compare the total statewide vote compiled by all of the party's candidates with the proportion of legislative seats it won.[36] For example, if a party's candidates won 55 percent of the total votes cast in all legislative elections, but won only 45 percent of the seats, we might conclude that partisan gerrymandering was to blame. This comparison is not always valid, however, especially when it is understood that a party that wins a slight majority of votes would normally be expected to win a much larger proportion of seats. For example, a party that wins 52 percent of total votes cast in all legislative elections might win 65 percent of the seats; theoretically it could win 100 percent of the seats in the unlikely event that

■

Affirmative racial gerrymandering. Drawing legislative district lines in order to maximize opportunities for minority candidates to win elections.

its 52 percent of the votes was spread evenly in every legislative district. The U.S. Supreme Court has held that "a mere lack of proportionality in results in one election" cannot prove an unconstitutional gerrymander; however, the Court said that it might intervene when there is "a history of disproportionate result."[37] It is important to remember that the United States does not employ proportional representation as do many European democracies. Hence we cannot expect proportionality in the seats–votes relationship. However, extreme and persistent differences in this relationship may signal the existence of partisan gerrymandering.

AFFIRMATIVE RACIAL GERRYMANDERING   Gerrymandering designed to *disad-vantage* blacks is a violation of the Equal Protection Clause of the Fourteenth Amendment of the U.S. Constitution, and it is a violation of the federal Voting Rights Act of 1965.[38] In 1982 Congress strengthened the Voting Rights Act by outlawing any electoral arrangements that had the *effect* of weakening minority voting power (see "Securing the Right to Vote" in Chapter 4). The U.S. Supreme Court obliged the states whenever possible to maximize opportunities for blacks and minority candidates to win election.[39] This apparent mandate for affirmative racial gerrymandering governed redistricting following the 1990 census and resulted in a significant increase in black and minority representation in many state legislatures. However, the creation of some bizarre-shaped "majority-minority" congressional districts (see Figure 4–4 in Chapter 4) led the U.S. Supreme Court to express constitutional doubts about districts that appear designed exclusively to separate the races.

MULTIMEMBER DISTRICTS   Multimember legislative districts were once very common (seventeen states had multimember districts in at least one of their legislative chambers before 1990). But court challenges and complaints by minority parties and racial minorities have restricted their use. The U.S. Supreme Court has never held multimember districts to be unconstitutional per se, as long as the population representation is equal.[40] (A two-member district, for example, should have twice the ideal district population.) However, multimember district plans that discriminate against racial minorities are unconstitutional.[41] Single-member districts are strongly preferred by minorities—minority parties as well as racial minorities.

DISTRICT SIZE   State legislative districts, in both upper and lower chambers, are much smaller than congressional districts. Each of the 435 members of the U.S. House of Representatives serves about 610,000 constituents. (The only state legislative chamber in which members serve so many constituents is the Texas Senate, where 31 senators each serve 617,000 constituents.) Some house districts in rural states have fewer than 10,000 constituents, while house districts in large urban states (California, Florida, Illinois, New York, Ohio, and Texas) have more than 100,000 constituents. (New Hampshire with 400 house members serving a total population of only 1.2 million has the nation's smallest legislative constituencies—2,900 persons.) Senate districts across the nation regularly exceed 100,000 constituents.

WHO DRAWS THE LINES?   Traditionally, legislatures drew up their own district lines. In most states this continues to be the case. Many legislatures employ private consultants to assist in the task, and computer mapping is now common. Legislatures generally try to protect incumbents, and the majority party frequently tries to maximize its advantages over the minority party. But in recent years, because of court challenges over apportionment (equality of population in districts) and racial gerrymandering, most legislative districting plans must be approved by courts. Reformers (Common Cause, National Municipal League, League of Women Voters) have urged state legislatures to turn over redistricting to independent nonpartisan commissions, and some states have done so. Reformers argue that partisan gerrymandering devalues voter participation, reduces competition for legislative seats, and reduces the responsiveness of legislators by creating "sure" seats. There is some evidence that independent commissions go about their task of redistricting without much regard for incumbent protection or party advantage.[42]

LEGISLATIVE ORGANIZATION AND PROCEDURE

The formal rules and procedures by which state legislatures operate are primarily designed to make the legislative process fair and orderly. Without established customs, rules, and procedures, it would be impossible for 50, 100, or 200 people to arrive at a collective decision about the thousands of items submitted to them at a legislative session. State legislatures follow a fairly standard pattern in the formal process of making laws. Figure 6–3 provides a brief description of some of the more important procedural steps in lawmaking.

PROCEDURES HAVE CONSEQUENCES   What are the political consequences of the legislative procedures described in Figure 6–3? Obviously, it is a very difficult process for a bill to become a law—legislative procedures offer many opportunities to defeat legislation. Formal rules and procedures of state legislatures lend themselves easily to those who would delay or obstruct legislation. Figure 6–3 illustrates the deliberative function of legislatures and the consequent procedural advantages given to those who would defend the status quo. Moreover, these procedures imply that the legislature is structured for deliberation and delay in decision making, rather than speed and innovation. This suggests that the legislature functions as an arbiter, rather than an initiator, of public policy, since its procedures are designed to maximize deliberation, even at the expense of granting advantage to those who oppose change.

DISORDERLINESS   As experienced legislators are fond of saying: "There are two things in the world you do not want to watch being made—sausages and laws." Lawmaking is a disorderly process, in spite of the formal procedures listed in Figure 6–3. Students often express shock and dismay when they spend some time watching or working in their legislature. After studying the formal rules, they may be unprepared for the "actual" haste, disorganization, logrolling, informality, infighting, petty jealousies, vote trading, ignorance, and ineptitude that they encounter. (See "*Up Close:* Informal Rules of the Game," p. 178.)

WORKLOAD   Fewer than one in four bills introduced in a legislative session actually makes its way through the whole process and becomes law. In large states such as Cal-

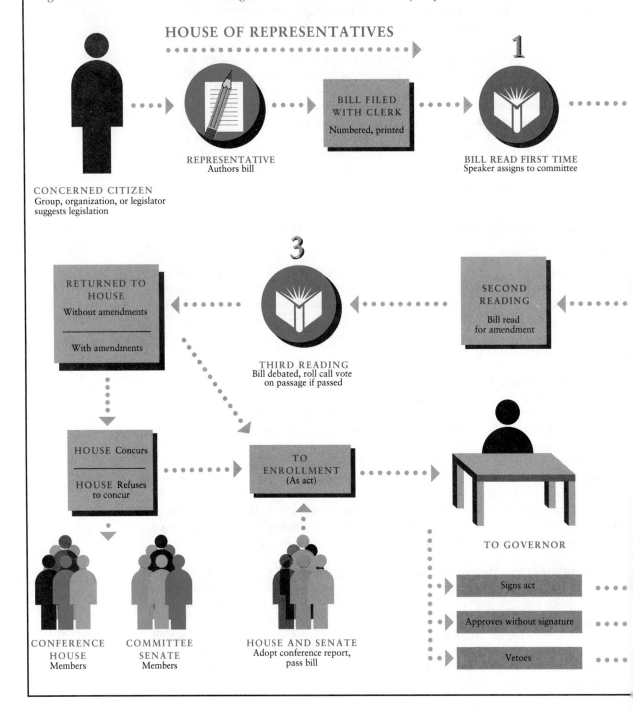

A simplified chart showing the route a bill takes through the Florida Legislature. Bills may originate in either house. This bill originated in the Florida House of Representatives.

HOUSE OF REPRESENTATIVES

REPRESENTATIVE
Authors bill

BILL FILED
WITH CLERK
Numbered, printed

1

BILL READ FIRST TIME
Speaker assigns to committee

CONCERNED CITIZEN
Group, organization, or legislator
suggests legislation

RETURNED TO
HOUSE
Without amendments
_____
With amendments

3

THIRD READING
Bill debated, roll call vote
on passage if passed

SECOND
READING
Bill read
for amendment

HOUSE Concurs
_____
HOUSE Refuses
to concur

TO
ENROLLMENT
(As act)

TO GOVERNOR

CONFERENCE
HOUSE
Members

COMMITTEE
SENATE
Members

HOUSE AND SENATE
Adopt conference report,
pass bill

Signs act

Approves without signature

Vetoes

FIGURE 6–3 How an Idea Becomes Law

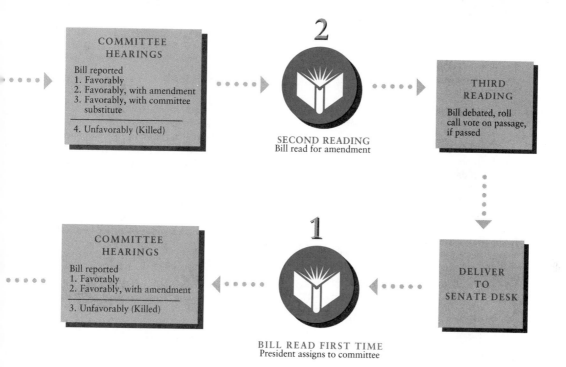

COMMITTEE HEARINGS

Bill reported
1. Favorably
2. Favorably, with amendment
3. Favorably, with committee substitute

4. Unfavorably (Killed)

2

SECOND READING
Bill read for amendment

THIRD READING

Bill debated, roll call vote on passage, if passed

COMMITTEE HEARINGS

Bill reported
1. Favorably
2. Favorably, with amendment

3. Unfavorably (Killed)

1

BILL READ FIRST TIME
President assigns to committee

DELIVER TO SENATE DESK

SENATE

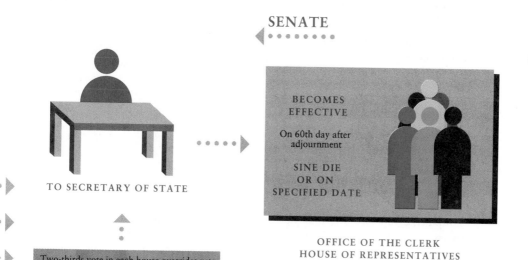

TO SECRETARY OF STATE

BECOMES EFFECTIVE

On 60th day after adjournment

SINE DIE OR ON SPECIFIED DATE

Two-thirds vote in each house overrides veto

OFFICE OF THE CLERK HOUSE OF REPRESENTATIVES

UP CLOSE

INFORMAL RULES OF THE GAME

Partly to counteract the impact of formal rules and procedures, legislatures have developed a number of informal "rules of the game." These unwritten rules are not merely quaint and curious folkways. They support the purposes and functions of the legislature by helping to maintain the working consensus among legislators so essential to legislative output. Some rules contribute to the legislative task by promoting group cohesion and solidarity. In the words of legislators themselves: "Support another member's local bill if it doesn't affect you or your district"; "Don't steal another's bill"; "Accept the author's amendments to a bill"; "Don't make personal attacks on other members." Other informal rules promote predictability of behavior: "Keep your word"; "Don't conceal the real purpose of bills or amendments"; "Notify in advance if you cannot keep a commitment." Other rules try to put limits on interpersonal conflict: "Be willing to compromise"; "Accept half a loaf"; "Respect the seniority system"; "Respect committee jurisdiction." Finally, other rules are designed to expedite legislative business: "Don't talk too much"; "Don't fight unnecessarily"; "Don't introduce too many bills and amendments"; "Don't point out the absence of a quorum"; "Don't be too political."[*]

"Highly Undesirable" Legislative Behaviors[a]

1. Concealing the real purpose(s) of a bill or purposely overlooking some portion of it in order to assure its passage.
2. Dealing in personalities in debate or in other remarks made on the floor of the chamber.
3. Being a thorn to the majority by refusing unanimous consent, etc.

[a]Items which at least 40 percent of Iowa House and Senate members checked as "highly undesirable." See F. Ted Hebert and Lelan E. McLemore, "Character and Structure of Legislative Norms," *American Journal of Political Science*, 17 (August 1973), 506–27.

4. Talking about decisions that have been reached in private to the press or anyone else.
5. Seeking as much publicity as possible from the press back home.
6. Being generally known as a spokesperson for some special-interest group.
7. Introducing as many bills and amendments as possible during any legislative session.
8. Talking on a subject coming before the legislature about which you are not completely informed.
9. Giving first priority to your reelection in all of your actions as a legislator.

A very important informal device is unanimous consent for the suspension of formal rules; this permits a legislature to consider bills not on the calendar, pass bills immediately without the necessary three readings, dispense with time-consuming formalities, permit nonmembers to speak, and otherwise alter procedure. Another informal rule is the practice in many states of passing "local bills" that would affect only one area of a state without debate or opposition when the delegation in that area unanimously supports the bill.

Most of these rules are enforced by informal sanctions. The most frequently mentioned sanction involves obstructing the bills of errant legislators by abstaining or voting against them, keeping their bills in committee, and amending their bills; more personal sanctions are using the "silent treatment," not trusting the legislator, and removing patronage and good committee assignments. Other sanctions include denial of legislative courtesies and occasionally even overt demonstrations of displeasure, such as ridicule, hissing, or laughing. The observance of rules, however, is not obtained primarily through fear of sanction so much as the positive recognition by legislators of the usefulness of rules in helping the legislature perform its chores.

[*]Quotations from state legislators interviewed by John C. Wahlke et al., *The Legislative System* (New York: John Wiley, 1962), pp. 146–61.

---

ifornia and New York, nearly 10,000 bills may be introduced in a single legislative session, and 2,000 to 3,000 may be enacted into law. In smaller states, a typical legislative session may produce 300 to 500 laws. Most bills die in committee. Many bills are introduced with no real expectation they will pass; legislators simply seek to "go on record" as working for a particular goal.

Logjams.
In legislative affairs, the rush to pass a large number of bills at the end of the session.

LOGJAMS   The end-of-session logjam is typically the most disorderly phase of lawmaking. In the closing days of a legislative session, hasty efforts are made to win approval for many bills and amendments that are still languishing somewhere in the legislative process. Legislative chambers sometimes become scenes of noisy confusion, with legislators voting blindly on bills described only by number. Most reformers condemn the end-of-session logjam as a source of inferior quality legislation. Other observers consider it an inevitable product of workload. For still others, the logjam is a strategy to enhance the power of legislative leaders. These leaders control the daily agenda and grant recognition to members seeking the floor; these decisions in a confused end-of-session logjam can determine whose bills get passed and whose do not. In some states in some sessions, over half of all the bills passed will be pushed through in the last few days of the session.[43]

SESSIONS   Traditionally, state constitutions limited legislative sessions to thirty or sixty days once every two years. These limits reflected the "citizen" nature of state legislatures, in contrast to the "professional" full-time congressional model of a legislature. Many observers still argue that the predominant occupation of members should *not* be "legislator," and that legislative sessions should be kept short so that citizens with other occupations can serve in the legislature. But the growing demands of legislative business have led to longer sessions.

Most states now hold annual legislative sessions; only a few are limited to biennial sessions (see Table 6–2). Twelve states place no limit on the length of sessions while thirty-two states have constitutional limits, and six states have statutory limits. The most common limit is sixty days; most legislatures convene in January and adjourn in March.

Frequently legislatures convene in "special sessions" in addition to those regularly scheduled. Special sessions may be called by the governor, or in some states by the legislative leadership, to consider special topics, for example, projected budget deficits or reapportionment. Usually these sessions are limited to the topic for which they were called.

We should remember that legislators have many duties between sessions; their work does not end when the session adjourns. Often legislative committees meet between sessions, and constituents continue to contact legislators for services.

LEGISLATIVE COMMITTEES

While it is most convenient to study legislative decision making by observing floor actions, particularly the division of ayes and nays, the floor is not the only locus of important legislative decisions. Committee work is essential to the legislative process. It is here that public hearings are held, lobbyists plead their case, policies are debated, legislation amended and compromised, bills rushed to the floor or pigeonholed. The function of the committee system is to reduce legislative work to manageable proportions by providing for a division of labor among legislators. However, by so doing the committees themselves often come to exercise considerable influence over the outcome of legislation. Another opportunity is provided for delay and obstruction by less than the majority of legislators, sometimes by a single committee chairperson.

FUNCTIONS   A typical legislative chamber will have between twenty and thirty standing committees that consider all bills in a particular area, such as revenue,

■
Sessions.
The meetings of elected legislative bodies from their initial convening to their official adjournment.

Table 6–2

THE STATE LEGISLATURES

State	Official Name	Senate		House		Salaries	Regular Sessions
		NUMBER	TERM	NUMBER	TERM	(+ INDICATES ADDED PER DIEM)	
Alabama	Legislature	35	4	105	4	Per diem	Annual
Alaska	Legislature	20	4	40	2	$24,112+	Annual
Arizona	Legislature	30	2	60	2	$15,000+	Annual
Arkansas	General Assembly	35	4	100	2	$12,500+	Biennial
California	Legislature	40	4	80	2	75,600+	Annual
Colorado	General Assembly	35	4	65	2	17,500+	Annual
Connecticut	General Assembly	36	2	151	2	16,760	Annual[a]
Delaware	General Assembly	21	4	41	2	27,500+	Annual
Florida	Legislature	40	4	120	2	24,912+	Annual
Georgia	General Assembly	56	2	180	2	11,347+	Annual
Hawaii	Legislature	25	4	51	2	32,000+	Annual
Idaho	Legislature	42	2	84	2	12,360+	Annual
Illinois	General Assembly	59	4	118	2	47,039+	Annual
Indiana	General Assembly	50	4	100	2	11,600+	Annual
Iowa	General Assembly	50	4	100	2	20,120+	Annual
Kansas	Legislature	40	4	125	2	Per diem	Annual
Kentucky	General Assembly	38	4	100	2	Per diem	Biennial
Louisiana	Legislature	39	4	105	4	16,800+	Annual[a]
Maine	Legislature	35	2	151	2	7,500+	Annual[a]
Maryland	General Assembly	47	4	141	4	29,700+	Annual
Massachusetts	General Court	40	2	160	2	46,410+	Annual
Michigan	Legislature	38	4	110	2	51,895	Annual
Minnesota	Legislature	67	4	134	2	29,675+	Biennial[b]

Table 6-2 (Continued)

Mississippi	Legislature	52	4	122	4	10,000+	Annual
Missouri	General Assembly	34	4	163	2	26,802+	Annual
Montana	Legislature	50	4	100	2	Per diem	Biennial
Nebraska	Legislature	49	4	Unicameral		12,000+	Annual
Nevada	Legislature	21	4	42	2	Per diem	Biennial
New Hampshire	General Court	24	2	400	2	100	Annual
New Jersey	Legislature	40	4	80	2	35,000	Annual
New Mexico	Legislature	42	4	70	2	Per diem	Annual[a]
New York	Legislature	61	2	150	2	57,500+	Annual
North Carolina	General Assembly	50	2	120	2	13,951+	Biennial[b]
North Dakota	Legislative Assembly	53	4	106	2	Per diem	Biennial
Ohio	General Assembly	33	4	99	2	42,426	Annual
Oklahoma	Legislature	48	4	101	2	32,000+	Annual
Oregon	Legislative Assembly	30	4	60	2	13,104+	Biennial
Pennsylvania	General Assembly	50	4	203	2	57,367+	Annual
Rhode Island	General Assembly	50	2	100	2	10,250	Annual
South Carolina	General Assembly	46	4	124	2	10,400+	Annual
South Dakota	Legislature	35	2	70	2	4,267+	Annual
Tennessee	General Assembly	33	4	99	2	16,500+	Annual
Texas	Legislature	31	4	150	2	7,200+	Biennial
Utah	Legislature	29	4	75	2	Per diem	Annual
Vermont	General Assembly	30	2	150	2	510/week+	Biennial[b]
Virginia	General Assembly	40	4	100	2	18,000+	Annual
Washington	Legislature	49	4	98	2	28,800+	Annual
West Virginia	Legislature	34	4	100	2	15,000+	Annual
Wisconsin	Legislature	33	4	99	2	39,211+	Annual
Wyoming	Legislature	30	4	64	2	Per diem	Annual[a]

Source: Book of the States, 1998–99, various tables.

[a]Meets annually but second session limited to specific types of legislation, usually fiscal and budgetary.

[b]Officially biennial, but in practice annual.

■

Standing committees.
Regular committees of a legislature that deal with bills within specified subject areas.

Institutionalization.
The development of rules and procedures, organizational structures, and standard patterns of behavior in political bodies.

Professionalism.
In legislatures, the extent to which members are devoted full-time to their legislative jobs and have the assistance of staffs and other legislative support services.

appropriations, highways, welfare, education, labor, judiciary, or local government. Typically, a legislator will serve on three, or four, or five committees. In most state legislatures, committee assignments, including the assignment of chairpersons, are made by the speaker of the house and the president of the senate in their respective bodies. This power of appointment gives these leaders some control over the actions of committees.

Committees may decide to hold early hearings on a bill, send it to the floor with little or no revision, and recommend it favorably. Or committees may simply ignore a bill ("pigeonholing"), fail to schedule hearings on it, allow hostile witnesses to testify against it, write extensive revisions and amendments into it, and so forth. Some states reduce the power of committees by allowing bills to be considered on the floor even though they have not been reported out of committee, or by requiring that all bills be reported out either favorably or unfavorably.

PERSONNEL   Committee assignments in most legislatures are made by the leadership. Occupational background frequently determines a legislator's committee assignments. Thus, lawyers are frequently assigned to committees on the judiciary and civil and criminal law, educators to education committees, farmers to agricultural committees, bankers to banking committees, and so on.[44] The effect of these assignments is to further strengthen the power of special interests in the legislative process. Legislators with occupational ties to various interests dominate the committees that consider legislation dealing with those same interests.

LEGISLATIVE INSTITUTIONALIZATION

Over time political bodies develop their own rules, organizational structures, and patterns of behavior. Social scientists refer to this process as "institutionalization." In legislative bodies, institutionalization is said to occur when (1) membership stabilizes and legislators come to look upon their service as a career, (2) staffs are added, salaries increased, and internal operations expanded, and (3) rules of procedure become more complex.[45]

State legislatures have gradually become more institutionalized. We have already observed that membership turnover has diminished over time. Legislative salaries and perks are increasing over time, and incumbents enjoy a heavy advantage in seeking reelection. And we have observed that more legislators are coming to see their jobs as full-time occupations. Now we shall observe increasing institutionalization in the internal functioning of state legislatures.

PROFESSIONALISM   Some state legislatures are highly professional, while others are not. By *professional* we mean that in some legislatures the members are well paid and tend to think of their jobs as full-times ones; members and committees are well staffed and have good informational services available to them; and a variety of legislative services, such as bill drafting and statutory revision, are well supported and maintained. In other legislatures, members are poorly paid and regard their legislative work as part-time; there is little in the way of staff for legislators or committees; and little is provided in the way of legislative assistance and services. Table 6–3 groups the states by the professionalism of their legislatures.

Table 6–3

PROFESSIONALISM IN STATE LEGISLATURES		
Professional—Full-time, large staff, high pay		
California	Michigan	Ohio
Illinois	New York	Pennsylvania
Massachusetts	New Jersey	Wisconsin
Professional–Citizen—Moderate pay, staff, and time		
Alabama	Indiana	North Carolina
Alaska	Iowa	Oklahoma
Arizona	Kansas	Oregon
Colorado	Kentucky	South Carolina
Connecticut	Maryland	Tennessee
Delaware	Minnesota	Texas
Florida	Mississippi	Virginia
Georgia	Missouri	Washington
Hawaii	Nebraska	
Citizen—Part-time, low pay, small staff		
Arkansas	Nevada	South Dakota
Idaho	New Hampshire	Utah
Louisiana	New Mexico	Vermont
Maine	North Dakota	West Virginia
Montana	Rhode Island	Wyoming

Source: National Conference on State Legislatures, *State Legislatures,* 20 (November 1994), 5.

REFORM   Reform organizations (for example, the Advisory Commission on Intergovernmental Relations, the Council on State Governments, the Eagleton Institute, and the Citizens Conference on State Legislatures) generally argue that state legislatures should be

> *Small in size.*   This is supposed to enhance the prestige of legislative service, improve public accountability, and recruit more qualified people. The recommended size is no more than 100 members total in both upper and lower chambers. However, currently only eight state legislatures (Alabama, Arizona, Delaware, Hawaii, Nebraska, Nevada, Oregon, and Wyoming) have fewer than 100 total members. New Hampshire has 400 house members and 24 senators. Most states have between 150 and 200 legislators. (See Table 6–2.)

> *Well paid.*   Annual salaries vary a great deal from state to state. The large urban industrial states generally pay their legislators more than small, rural states. (See Table 6–2.) Reformers argue that better pay would make legislators full-time pro-

fessional representatives, rather than part-time amateurs who must spend time on their private business interests in order to make a living.

Well staffed.   Reformers argue that experienced, knowledgeable staffs are required to provide information, draft bills, analyze the potential impact of proposed legislation, study the governor's budget proposals, and evaluate the impact of existing programs. Less professional legislatures have only a single small "reference service" for the entire legislature; this service is mainly concerned with drafting bills with only minimal research. However, most legislatures provide professional staff for their major committees and for leadership. Some states also provide each house and senate member with year-round personal staff.

Flexible.   Reformers generally argue that legislatures should be free from constitutional restrictions, for example, restrictions on the maximum number of days they can meet annually or biennially, and restrictions on budget powers through constitutional earmarking of revenues for special purposes.

Functional.   Reformers argue that legislatures should have clear and simple procedures, well-defined committee responsibilities, published schedules for testimony, committee consideration, and floor debate, and a smooth flow of bills through the legislative process. Yet most legislatures suffer the traditional "end-of-session logjam" when many bills are passed in haste without careful consideration of their merits and other important pieces of legislation are lost in the shuffle. Most abuses of the legislative process occur in this last-minute frenzied period of lawmaking.

Well policed.   Reformers have put forward a variety of proposals to ensure the integrity of the legislative process:

1.   Public financing of all state elections
2.   Limitations on campaign contributions
3.   Reporting of all campaign contributions
4.   Registration of lobbyists and regulation of lobbying activity
5.   Creation of ethics commissions
6.   Sunshine laws that open all legislative activity to the media

PROFESSIONALISM AND CAREERISM   Professionalism in state legislatures encourages careerism. It encourages people who view politics as a career to seek and win a seat in the state legislature. Higher pay makes the job more attractive and allows legislators to devote all their time to politics and policy making. Year-round sessions discourage people who cannot take leave from their business or profession. Greater resources available to legislators allow them to perform more casework for constituents and to build a personal organization devoted to keeping themselves in office. Additional resources make life at the state capital more comfortable. There is less voluntary turnover in professional legislatures, and less likelihood that an incumbent will be defeated. Political scientist Alan Rosenthal writes, "One quality that distinguishes the new breed of full-time, professional politicians from the old breed of part-time, citizen legislators is ambition. The latter were content to spend a few years in legislative office and then return to private careers. The former, by contrast, would like to spend most of their careers in government and politics. They find public office appealing and the game of politics exhilarating."[46]

■
Careerism.
In politics, the tendency of people to view running for and occupying elected public office as a full-time career.

Careerism fosters individualism among legislators. With their own careers paramount in their calculations, professional legislators are less likely to follow the lead of the governor or party leaders. They have their own agendas to pursue. Professionalism grants some advantage to liberals and Democrats in state politics. Liberals are more likely to view government as a career; conservatives view government service as a sacrifice of business or professional time. Republicans have more difficulty finding business people willing to meet the demands of running for office and serving full time.

PROFESSIONALISM AND PUBLIC POLICY   Does it make any difference in public policy whether a legislature is "professional" or not? Reformers often *assume* that "professionalism" will result in legislatures that are "generally innovative in many different areas of public policy, generous in welfare and educational spending and services, and 'interventionist' in the sense of having powers and responsibilities of broad scope."[47] Does legislative reform, however, *really* have any policy consequences?

Unfortunately there is little systematic evidence that legislative professionalism has any direct effect on public policy. While it is true that professional legislatures spend more per person on welfare and more per pupil on education than nonprofessional legislatures, professional legislatures are found in the wealthier, urban states with well-educated populations, and these states spend more on welfare and education anyway. (See Chapter 15, "The Politics of Education," and Chapter 16, "The Politics of Poverty, Welfare, and Health.") In other words, there is little evidence that legislative professionalism *causes* increased spending for welfare and education. Instead, both legislative professionalism *and* spending for welfare and education are caused by income, urbanization, and education.

LEGISLATIVE STAFFING   Years ago, state legislatures employed only a few clerks and secretaries to handle the clerical chores and a few lawyers in a small "legislative reference service" to draft bills at the request of lawmakers. Today, the movement toward professionalism in state legislatures has created large professional staffs to serve the needs of the leadership and the standing committees. Some more "professional" legislatures have full-time professional staffs—lawyers, researchers, and speechwriters, as well as secretaries—for the house speaker, senate president, majority and minority leaders, and all standing committees; and many states now even provide full-time, year-round staff for each house and senate member. Only the less "professional" rural, small-state legislatures still depend on a small legislative reference service to serve all legislators in drafting bills and doing research.

Legislative staffs have grown rapidly over the last decade, so that today this new "legislative bureaucracy" is itself becoming an important political force. Staff members are political appointees, and they are supposed to reflect the political views of their legislator-bosses in their work. However, some "staffers" become so knowledgeable about state government, or about the state budget, or about their aspects of legislative work, that they are kept on in their jobs even when their original sponsor leaves the capital.

The staffs are expected to research issues, find out what other states are doing, assist in analyzing the budget, schedule legislative hearings, line up experts and interest groups to testify, keep abreast of the status of bills and appropriation items as they

Staff.
In legislatures, aides employed to assist individual members or committees in their work.

move through the legislature, maintain contact with state agencies and the governor's staff, make coffee and fetch doughnuts, write and rewrite bills, and perform other assorted chores and errands. As legislators come to rely on trusted "staffers," the "staffers" themselves become more powerful. Their advice may kill a bill or an appropriation item, or their work may amend a bill or alter an appropriation, without the legislator becoming directly involved. Often "staffers" are young, and they exercise a great deal of influence in policy making.

LEADERSHIP AND ROLE-PLAYING IN LEGISLATURES

Roles are expectations about the kind of behavior people ought to exhibit. Expectations are placed upon a legislator by fellow legislators, the legislator's party, the opposition party, the governor, constituents, interest groups, and by friends, as well as by the legislators themselves.

LEADERSHIP ROLES   Perhaps the most distinctive roles in the legislative process are those of the leadership.[48] A typical legislative chamber has a presiding officer (usually a house "speaker" and a senate "president"), a majority and a minority floor leader, a number of committee chairpersons, and a steering committee. These leaders perform functions similar to the functions of rules. First of all, leaders are expected to help make the legislative system stable and manageable. They are expected to maintain order, to know the rules and procedures, to follow the rules, and to show fairness and impartiality. Leaders are also expected to help focus the issues and resolve conflict by presenting issues clearly, narrowing the alternatives, organizing public hearings, and promoting the party or administrative point of view on bills. The majority leader is supposed to "get the administrative program through," while the minority leader develops a "constructive opposition."

Leaders are also expected to administer the legislature and expedite business. This includes "promoting teamwork," "being accessible," starting the sessions on time, keeping them on schedule, and distributing the workload. It involves communication, coordination, and liaison with the governor, the administrative departments, and the other chambers.

MEMBERS' EXPECTATIONS OF LEADERS   From the members' perspective, successful leaders are those who assist them in achieving their personal political goals. Most legislators possess a desire for reelection, as well as power and policy influence within the legislature. The relative importance of these goals will vary for each individual member. A freshman lawmaker who feels electorally insecure will have different priorities than a senior legislator from a safe district. The key to effective leadership is to understand the particular needs and goals of individual members and to respond as necessary.[49] (See "*People in Politics:* Tom Loftus, The Art of State Legislative Politics.")

LEADERS' LEGISLATIVE PRIORITIES   Leaders face a difficult challenge in balancing competing priorities with limited resources. In recent years the top priorities identified by state legislative leaders across the country have been in the areas of crime and

PEOPLE IN POLITICS

TOM LOFTUS, THE ART OF STATE LEGISLATIVE POLITICS

Tom Loftus served a record four terms as speaker of the Wisconsin Assembly and wrote about his experiences in an entertaining book, *The Art of Legislative Politics*. His stories, anecdotes, and insights about legislative life make for fun reading as well as generate serious thinking about problems confronting state legislatures today.

Like many Wisconsinites, Loftus descended from Norwegian immigrants. His father was a successful farm machinery dealer in a small town near the state capital of Madison. He graduated from the University of Wisconsin and landed a job as a speech writer for the Democratic caucus in the state legislature. Later he became a staff aide to the Assembly speaker. He waited for an open Assembly seat and entered his first electoral race in 1976. Among his observations about campaigning, he says:

> Some think campaigns are to educate the voters. They are wrong . . . the actual outcome of a campaign is to educate the candidate about his or her constituency. . . . If you talk to people at their doors . . . you will begin to understand your prospective constituents.

Regarding the issue content of state legislative campaigns, he writes:

> There are important issues in a race for the state legislature, but they do not determine the outcome. . . . In most campaigns the real issue is the comfort level the voter has with the candidate.

Loftus acknowledges that he came into office with considerable experience as a legislative staffer. He warns less well prepared legislators:

> In most state legislatures, unlike Congress, there is no apprenticeship. . . . Your productive years start when you arrive, regardless of your age.

A strong liberal Democrat, Loftus rose to his party's leadership in just four years. As speaker, he often battled with both Republicans and conservative Democrats, as well as with Wisconsin's popular Republican governor, Tommy Thompson. He fought giving the governor line-item veto power, believing that it weakens the legislative branch of government. But he lost that battle. He acknowledges the difficult ethics problems that confront legislators when they are offered money and perks by lobbyists. A two-year investigation of legislative ethics in Wisconsin, begun in 1988, did little to help Loftus or his party. Loftus admits that:

> The asking for and giving of campaign money has its own language and is accompanied by a lot of winking, blinking and nodding. Rarely is any quid pro quo discussed. . . . Some legislators and lobbyists, however, go close to the line of illegality in order to try to gain an accomplice and an edge.

After fourteen years in the legislature, Loftus ran for governor in 1990 but lost in a popular landslide to the incumbent Republican, Tommy Thompson. Loftus went off to the Kennedy School of Government at Harvard to write his book, later chaired Clinton's 1992 presidential campaign in Wisconsin, and was rewarded by appointment as ambassador to Norway.

Source: Quotations from Tom Loftus, *The Art of Legislative Politics* (Washington, DC: Congressional Quarterly Press, 1995).

law enforcement, tax reform, education, and health care.[50] Dealing with crime has been the top priority; surveys reveal that more people name crime as the "most important problem confronting the nation" than any other concern. State legislatures have focused on keeping convicted criminals behind bars for longer periods of time, eliminating early releases due to prison overcrowding, building more prison cells, and reorganizing the juvenile justice system to handle juveniles who commit increasingly more violent crimes (see Chapter 9). Much of the recent fiscal talk in state capitals has been about tax cutting (see Chapter 17). In education, the issues include equitable distribution of school funds to achieve equality of educational opportunity across school districts (often ordered by state courts), the imposition of statewide testing of students

■

Trustee.
A role that representatives adopt when they decide to vote their conscience and use their best personal judgment, rather than catering to the narrow interests of their constituents.

Delegate.
A role that representatives adopt when they set aside their own best judgment and vote according to the wishes of their constituents.

and teachers, and experimenting with school vouchers and privately operated public schools (see Chapter 15). Health care reform is also a common topic of discussion in state legislatures. States themselves continue to worry about improving access to care while containing costs, especially the costs of Medicaid, the fastest-growing expenditure of state government (see Chapter 16). Finally, state legislative leaders across the country echo a familiar theme: They want fewer unfunded federal mandates to the states and greater control over federal programs in their state (see Chapter 3).

EXPERT ROLES   Another set of legislative roles that are commonly encountered and make important contributions to the legislative process are the "subject-matter experts." Unlike leadership roles, the roles of subject-matter experts are not embodied in formal offices. The committee system introduces specialization into the legislature, and the seniority system places at the head of the committee those persons longest exposed to the information about the committee's subject matter. Thus, subject-matter experts emerge among legislators in the fields of law, finance, education, agriculture, natural resources, local government, labor, transportation, and so on.

TRUSTEES AND DELEGATES   Another way of describing roles in a legislature is to discover the legislators' orientations toward the expectations of constituents. Legislators can be classified as trustees (those who are guided in legislative affairs solely by their personal conscience) and delegates (those who are guided by instructions or wishes of their constituents). Should legislators represent their constituency or their own conscience? Actually, few legislators exhibit in their behavior a firm commitment to either one of these roles. Most legislators when facing specific issues do not see any conflict between the wishes of their constituents, their party, and their own judgment. Even when such conflict is perceived, most legislators attempt to find a compromise between conflicting demands rather than choose one role or the other exclusively. Of course, if legislators are asked how they make their decisions, they *claim* to be guided solely by their own conscience. However, this is little more than a verbalism; it reflects a heroic image of the courageous defender of the public interest, who acts out of personal virtue and conviction regardless of the consequences.

The more politically experienced legislator is more likely to assume the role of a trustee. There is some evidence that legislators who come to the office with little prior experience as public officials, and those with less service in the legislature, are more likely to respond in the manner of a "delegate," while their more experienced colleagues give "trustee" responses to interviewers.[51]

PARTY POLITICS IN STATE LEGISLATURES

While the influence of parties varies from state to state, overall, parties are perhaps the single most important influence over legislative behavior.

ONE-PARTY STATES   Traditionally the party in one-party (Democratic) states did not exercise tight party discipline over the voting of legislators. Being a Democrat in the legislature of a one-party southern Democratic state did not influence roll-call voting behavior very much. Democratic governors in these states could not depend upon party loyalty to win legislative support for their programs. However, the *minority* Republicans in these states tended to stick together.

EMERGING LEGISLATIVE PARTY CONFLICT   As Republicans won more seats in the southern and border state legislatures, party organizations and party voting within the legislatures increased. Republican legislators became more likely to organize themselves into a party caucus, to develop a party legislative program, and to vote cohesively. The emerging "threat" of a Republican opposition usually spurred the Democrats to do the same.[52]

INCREASING PARTY COMPETITION   Traditionally the Democrats have controlled more state legislatures than the Republicans (see Figure 6–4). But Republican victories in the 1994 elections extended from Congress (where Republicans won control of the U.S. House of Representatives for the first time in forty years) to the nation's state leg-

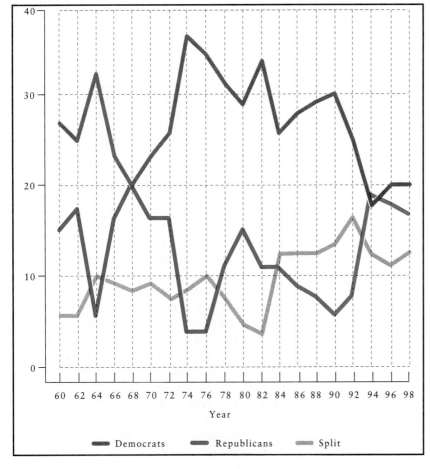

FIGURE 6–4
Democratic and Republican Control of State Legislatures

■

Party voting.
In legislatures, voting in
which a majority of one
party's members vote in opposition to a majority of the
other party's members.

islatures. For the first time in more than thirty years, the GOP won control of more state legislatures than the Democrats. Over time, the Republicans have gained near parity in the total number of legislative seats they occupy throughout the nation (see Figure 5–2 in Chapter 5).

TWO-PARTY STATES   As the parties have become more competitive in the states, party divisions on legislative roll-call votes have become more frequent than any other divisions, including rural–urban divisions. One common measure of party influence on voting is the percentage of nonunanimous roll-call votes on which a majority of Democrats voted against the majority of Republicans. Compilations by the *Congressional Quarterly* show that the proportion of roll calls in Congress in which the two parties have been in opposition has ranged from 35 to 50 percent over the years. Party voting in competitive state legislatures such as New York, Pennsylvania, Ohio, Delaware, Rhode Island, Massachusetts, and Michigan may be even higher than it is in Congress.

LEADERSHIP VOTES   Voting along strict party lines is the norm for legislative leadership posts, notably for speaker of the house and president of the senate. Leaders are initially selected in the majority party's caucus; all party members are then expected to support their party's choice in the official house vote that follows. Indeed, real difficulties have emerged where parties have evenly divided legislative seats in a state house. (The Indiana house once resolved the issue by agreeing to "co-speakers" who would preside on alternate days; the Florida senate once resolved the issue by agreeing to switch presidents each year of the session.) Rarely do legislators break party lines in voting on leadership posts, although considerable pressure may be placed upon some to do so where the parties are evenly or almost evenly divided. Long-term Democratic Speaker of the California House, Willie Brown, managed to swing some Republican votes his way in 1995, and to retain the speakership even though more Republicans than Democrats sat in the legislature. But this political feat is unlikely to be replicated anywhere else.

PARTY ISSUES   On what types of issues do the parties exercise their greatest influence? Parties usually display the greatest cohesion on issues involving taxation and appropriations, welfare, and regulation of business and labor—in short, the major social and economic controversies that divide the national parties. Minor bills involving the licensing of water well drillers, beauticians, or barbers do not usually become the subject matter of party votes, and only infrequently will the parties divide over such matters as the designation of an official state bird. Party influence in budgetary matters is particularly apparent, since the budget often involves issues of social welfare and class interest on which parties in many states are split. In addition, the budget is clearly identified as the product of the governor and carries the label of the party of the governor. Another type of bill that is often the subject of party voting is one involving the party as an interest group. Parties often exhibit an interest in bills proposing to transfer powers from an office controlled by one party to an office controlled by the other, or bills proposing to create or abolish non–civil service jobs. Parties display considerable interest in bills affecting the organization of local government, state administration, the civil service, registration and election laws, and legislative procedure.

SOURCES OF PARTY VOTING   What factors distinguish those states in which the party substantially influences legislative decision making from those states in which it does not?

Party cohesion is strongest in those urban industrial states in which the parties represent separate socioeconomic constituencies. Party voting occurs in those competitive states in which Democratic legislators represent central-city, low-income, ethnic, and racial constituencies, and Republican legislators represent middle-class, suburban, small-town, and rural constituencies. Party cohesion is weak in states where party alignments do not coincide with socioeconomic divisions of constituencies.

It is this division of constituencies that is the basis of party cohesion and influence in the legislature. Even within each party, members from districts typical of their party in socioeconomic attributes support the party position more often than members from districts atypical of the party. Constituency characteristics, then, help to explain not only the outcome of elections but also the behavior of the elected.

PARTY DISCIPLINE   In a few states the party leadership sets the legislative agenda, determines committee assignments, and tries to bind legislators to vote for the position taken by the party caucus. But because of the weaknesses of the parties in the electoral process (see Chapter 5), party discipline in most state legislatures is very weak. Reformers in Colorado passed a constitutional referendum specifically designed to weaken the powers of party leaders and committees in the legislative process. It requires consideration "on its merits" of every bill referred to a committee, specifies that the full house can always bring a bill out of committee, and outlaws binding party caucuses, saying that legislators cannot "commit themselves or any other member or members, through a vote in a party caucus or any similar procedure, to vote in favor of or against any bill."[53]

ARE LEGISLATORS RESPONSIBLE POLICY MAKERS?

A classic dilemma of representative government is whether the legislator should vote his or her own conscience—"the trustee"—or vote the constituency's wishes—"the delegate." Good philosophical arguments can be found to support either of these guiding principles. Nearly 200 years ago the English political philosopher Edmund Burke confronted this question directly and urged representatives to vote their own conscience about what is right for society. Burke believed that the voters should elect wise and virtuous representatives to govern *for* them—to use their own judgment in deciding issues regardless of popular demands. Even today the term *Burkean representation* refers to the willingness of a representative to ignore public opinion and decide public issues on the basis of one's own best judgment about what is right for society.

Other political philosophers stress responsiveness of representatives to the views of their constituents. Consider, for example, philosopher Hanna Pitkin's definition of representation: "Representation means acting in the interest of the represented, in a manner responsive to them."[54] Responsiveness connotes a deliberate effort by legislators to match their votes on public policy issues to their constituency's preferences. However, to be "responsive" to one's constituents, two conditions must be met: (1) the legislator

Burkian representation.
The belief that legislators should use their own best judgment about what is good for their state or nation, rather than conforming to their constituents' narrow interests.

Responsiveness.
The extent to which legislators appear to reflect the views of their constituents in their lawmaking.

FIGURE 6–5
A Model of
Constituency
Influence

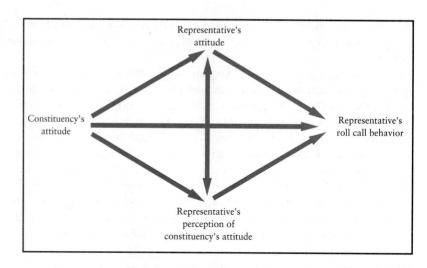

must correctly perceive the constituents' views on the issues, and (2) the legislator must act in accord with these views. (See Figure 6–5.)

LEGISLATORS' KNOWLEDGE OF CONSTITUENTS' VIEWS   Let us consider the first condition: Do legislators know the views of their constituents on public issues? Unfortunately, the evidence is mixed. When Iowa legislators were asked to predict whether their own district would vote for or against some proposed constitutional amendments, the resulting predictions were good on some issues but poor on others.[55] Interestingly, the poorest predictions came from legislators from poor districts, suggesting that legislators have less understanding of the views of poor constituents than affluent ones. In contrast, when Florida legislators were asked to predict how both their state and district would vote on referenda on school busing and school prayer, nearly all of them made accurate predictions for both their district and the state.[56] Perhaps one explanation for these apparently conflicting findings is that legislators know their constituents' views on well-publicized, controversial, emotionally charged issues, but that legislators are poor predictors of constituent opinion on other kinds of issues.

LEGISLATORS' PERSONAL VIEWS   State legislators may indeed vote their own attitude on *most* issues coming before the legislature. A careful study of voting on welfare, tax, and consumer issues in the Texas legislature revealed that "In both houses, in every issue-area examined, the path connecting the representative's attitude with his roll-call vote is far more important than the path linking his perceptions of his constituency's attitude with his voting."[57] The explanation offered was that activities of the governor and his or her staff, other legislators and legislative leaders, and outside interest groups, create "the din of the immediate legislative struggle," which "muffles" the voices from the home district. Even legislators from competitive districts were seemingly unaffected by their views of their constituents' attitudes. As expected, legislators who opted for the role of "delegate" voted what they believed to be their constituents' attitudes more than legislators who opted for the role of trustee.

In summary, the absence of direct evidence that (1) legislators know their constituents' views and (2) vote their constituents' views rather than their own views creates difficulties for the "responsiveness" theory of democracy. There is a great deal of "noise" along the lines from constituents' views to their legislator's roll-call vote.

Personal ideology rather than lobbying pressures or constituents' views is a major factor in deciding legislative votes.

> None of this denies that legislators endeavor in some decisions to please interest groups or other actors. Cowed by threats, lured by enticements, legislators often make decisions they do not believe in. In most sessions, too, they confront a few highly publicized, controversial issues; their private policy views may matter little then. Nonetheless . . . representatives have the freedom on a range of issues to weigh priorities and evaluate policy options on their merits: to decide in accord with their own private conceptions of good public policy.[58]

LOBBYING IN STATE LEGISLATURES

The influence of organized interest groups in the legislative process varies from state to state. Earlier (Chapter 5) we discussed interest groups in the fifty states and their involvement in public relations, campaign financing, and lobbying. We defined lobbying as any communication by someone acting on behalf of a group directed at a government decision maker with the hope of influencing decisions.

NARROW ISSUES   On what kinds of decisions are interest groups more likely to exercise influence? Party and constituency interests are most apparent on broad social and economic issues. On narrower issues voters are less likely to have either an interest or an opinion. The legislator is, therefore, freer to respond to the pleas of organized groups on highly specialized topics than on major issues of public interest. Economic interests seeking to use the law to improve their competitive position are a major source of group pressure on these specialized topics. Particularly active in lobbying are the businesses subject to extensive government regulation. The truckers, railroads, insurance companies, and race track and liquor interests are consistently found to be among the most highly organized and active lobbyists in state capitals. Organized pressure comes from associations of governments and associations of government employees. State chapters of the National Education Association are persistent in presenting the demands of educational administrators and occasionally the demands of the dues-paying teachers as well.

INFORMATION EXCHANGE   Legislators depend on lobbyists for much of their information on public issues. Legislators are aware of the potential bias in information given them by lobbyists. But the constant proximity of lobbyists to legislators facilitates information exchange.[59] Legislators *use* lobbyists, just as lobbyists use legislators:

> Typically, legislators utilize lobbyists as sources of influence in three ways: by calling upon lobbyists to influence other legislators, by calling upon lobbyists to help amass

public opinion in favor of the legislator's position, and by including lobbyists in planning strategy in an effort to negotiate a bill through the legislature.[60]

THREATS   It is unwise for lobbyists to threaten legislators, for example, by vowing to defeat them in the next election. This is the tactic of an amateur lobbyist, not a professional. It usually produces a defensive response by the legislator. As one lobbyist put it: "Once you have closed the door you have no further access to the individual. Once you've threatened an individual, there is no possibility of winning in the future."[61]

GETTING THE MESSAGE   Testimony at legislative committee hearings is a common form of information exchange between lobbyists and legislators. Often this testimony is the legislators' primary source of information about legislation. Direct meetings in legislators' offices are also frequent and effective. Social gatherings (where the liquor is usually furnished by the lobbyist) are more important in establishing friendships; professional lobbyists seldom bring up "business" on such occasions. Legislators are wined and dined so much during legislative sessions that attendance at social functions is sometimes viewed as a chore. The least effective method of lobbying is the submission of long letters or reports.

LOBBYING THE STAFF   One form of lobbying that is growing rapidly in importance is communication with legislative *staff* personnel. As state legislatures acquire more full-time staff for their standing committees, house and senate leaders, and majority and minority party caucuses, professional lobbyists are coming to recognize that these staff people can have as much or more to do with the specific content of bills as legislators themselves. Many of the more "modernized," "professional" state legislatures rely heavily on the advice of professional staffs. The wise lobbyist in these states cultivates friendships among staff personnel.

REGULATION OF LOBBYING   The U.S. Constitution guarantees the right "to petition the government for redress of grievances." This First Amendment right protects individuals and groups in their attempts to communicate with and influence their lawmakers. Nonetheless, lobbying is regulated in some fashion in all of the states. Most state laws require lobbyists ("anyone receiving compensation to influence legislative action") to (1) register with the clerk or secretary of the house or senate, and (2) file periodic reports of direct expenditures for lobbying activity. These regulations have relatively little impact on lobbying activity; many organizations claim that they are educational or religious in nature and not really lobbies, and they do not register. Many lobbies do not report all of their educational and public relations expenditures, but only a small portion, which they attribute directly to lobbying. Campaign contributions usually must be reported under state election laws. Of course, bribery and conspiracy may be prosecuted under criminal laws.

State legislatures and agencies charged with enforcement of lobbying regulations have traditionally been notorious for their neglect of their responsibilities. However, increasing professionalization of state legislatures appears to increase both their capacity and willingness to regulate lobbying.[62]

DID YOU KNOW?

SONGS, FLOWERS, BIRDS, AND TREES

State	State Song	State Flower	State Tree	State Bird
Alabama	Alabama	Camellia	Southern Pine	Yellowhammer
Alaska	Alaska's Flag	Forget-Me-Not	Sitka Spruce	Willow Ptarmigan
Arizona	Arizona	Saguaro Cactus Blossom	Paloverde	Cactus Wren
Arkansas	Arkansas	Apple Blossom	Pine	Mockingbird
California	I Love You, California	Golden Poppy	California Redwood	California Valley Quail
Colorado	Where the Columbines Grow	Rocky Mountain Columbine	Colorado Blue Spruce	Lark Bunting
Connecticut	Yankee Doodle Dandy	Mountain Laurel	White Oak	American Robin
Delaware	Our Delaware	Peach Blossom	American Holly	Blue Hen Chicken
Florida	Swanee River	Orange Blossom	Sabal Palmetto Palm	Mockingbird
Georgia	Georgia on My Mind	Cherokee Rose	Live Oak	Brown Thrasher
Hawaii	Hawaii Ponoi	Yellow Hibiscus	Candlenut	Hawaiian Goose
Idaho	Here We Have Idaho	Syringa	White Pine	Mountain Bluebird
Illinois	Illinois	Native Violet	White Oak	Cardinal
Indiana	On the Banks of the Wabash, Far Away	Peony	Tulip Poplar	Cardinal
Iowa	The Song of Iowa	Wild Rose	Oak	Eastern Goldfinch
Kansas	Home on the Range	Sunflower	Cottonwood	Western Meadowlark
Kentucky	My Old Kentucky Home	Goldenrod	Kentucky Coffee Tree	Cardinal
Louisiana	Give Me Louisiana	Magnolia	Cypress	Eastern Brown Pelican
Maine	State of Maine Song	White Pine Cone and Tassel	Eastern White Pine	Chickadee
Maryland	Maryland, My Maryland	Black-eyed Susan	White Oak	Baltimore Oriole
Massachusetts	All Hail to Massachusetts	Mayflower	American Elm	Chickadee
Michigan	Michigan, My Michigan	Apple Blossom	White Pine	Robin
Minnesota	Hail! Minnesota	Pink and White Lady's Slipper	Red Pine	Common Loon
Mississippi	Go, Mississippi!	Magnolia	Magnolia	Mockingbird
Missouri	Missouri Waltz	Hawthorn	Dogwood	Bluebird
Montana	Montana	Bitterroot	Ponderosa Pine	Western Meadowlark
Nebraska	Beautiful Nebraska	Goldenrod	Cottonwood	Western Meadowlark
Nevada	Home Means Nevada	Sagebrush	Single-Leaf Pinon	Mountain Bluebird
New Hampshire	Old New Hampshire	Purple Lilac	White Birch	Purple Finch
New Jersey	Ode to New Jersey	Purple Violet	Red Oak	Eastern Goldfinch
New Mexico	O Fair New Mexico	Yucca	Pinon	Roadrunner
New York	I Love New York	Rose	Sugar Maple	Bluebird

North Carolina	The Old North State	Dogwood	Pine	Cardinal
North Dakota	North Dakota Hymn	Wild Prairie Rose	American Elm	Western Meadowlark
Ohio	Beautiful Ohio	Scarlet Carnation	Buckeye	Cardinal
Oklahoma	Oklahoma!	Mistletoe	Redbud	Scissortailed Flycatcher
Oregon	Oregon, My Oregon	Oregon Grape	Douglas Fir	Western Meadowlark
Pennsylvania	Hail! Pennsylvania	Mountain Laurel	Hemlock	Ruffed Grouse
Rhode Island	Rhode Island	Violet	Red Maple	Rhode Island Red
South Carolina	Carolina	Yellow Jessamine	Palmetto	Carolina Wren
South Dakota	Hail, South Dakota	Pasque Flower	Black Hills Spruce	Ringnecked Pheasant
Tennessee	The Tennessee Waltz	Iris	Tulip Poplar	Mockingbird
Texas	Texas, Our Texas	Bluebonnet	Pecan	Mockingbird
Utah	Utah, We Love Thee	Sego Lily	Blue Spruce	Seagull
Vermont	Hail, Vermont	Red Clover	Sugar Maple	Hermit Thrush
Virginia	Carry Me Back to Old Virginia	Dogwood	Dogwood	Cardinal
Washington	Washington, My Home	Western Rhododendron	Western Hemlock	Willow Goldfinch
West Virginia	The West Virginia Hills; This Is My West Virginia; and West Virginia, My Home, Sweet Home	Big Rhododendron	Sugar Maple	Cardinal
Wisconsin	On Wisconsin!	Wood Violet	Sugar Maple	Robin
Wyoming	Wyoming	Indian Paintbrush	Cottonwood	Meadowlark

ON THE WEB

Each state's governmental home page provides a direct link to the state legislature (See "On the Web," Chapter 3). These state legislative pages usually include information on the current legislative session, access to bill monitoring, and biographical information on each member of the legislature.

The best source of comparative information on state legislatures is the National Conference of State Legislatures:

www.ncsl.org

This site includes schedules of all state legislative sessions in the nation, the partisan composition of each state's House and Senate, and a brief overview of key issues currently confronting state legislatures.

The Center for the Study of Women in Politics at Rutgers University is an important source of information on women in both legislative and executive offices in the states. Its site can be found at

www.rci.rutgers.edu/cswp

Included in the information found at this site is a count of women in the state legislature of every state.

NOTES

1. See Patricia K. Freeman and Lilliard E. Richardson, "Casework in State Legislatures" (Knoxville: Department of Political Science, University of Tennessee, 1993).

2. *Tampa Tribune,* July 27, 1987.

3. See Paul J. Hain and James E. Pierson, "Lawyers and Politics Revisited: Structural Advantages of Lawyer-Politicians," *American Journal of Political Science,* 19 (February 1975), 41–51.

4. Mark C. Miller, *The High Priests of American Politics* (Knoxville: University of Tennessee, 1995).

5. Wayne L. Francis, "Costs and Benefits of Legislative Service in the American States," *American Journal of Political Science,* 29 (August 1985), 626–42.

6. John B. McConaughy, "Some Personality Factors of State Legislators," in *Legislative Behavior: A Reader in Theory and Research,* eds. John C. Wahlke and Heinz Eulau (Glencoe, IL: Free Press, 1959).

7. Ronald W. Hedlund, "Psychological Predispositions: Political Representatives and the Public," *American Journal of Political Science,* 19 (August 1973), 489–505.

8. Mary Herring, "Legislative Responsiveness to Black Constituents in Three Southern States," *Journal of Politics,* 52 (August 1990), 740–58; for a report on the differing experiences of black legislators, see David Hedge, James Button, and Mary Spear, "Accounting for the Quality of Black Legislative Life," *American Journal of Political Science,* 40 (February 1996), 82–98.

9. See Emmy F. Werner, "Women in State Legislatures," *Western Political Quarterly,* 21 (March 1968), 40–50; Paula J. Dubeck, "Women and Access to Political Office," *Sociological Quarterly,* 17 (March 1976), 42–52; Susan Welch, "The Recruitment of Women to Public Office," *Western Political Quarterly* (June 1978), 372–80.

10. Wilma Rule, "Why More Women Are State Legislators," *Western Political Quarterly,* 43 (June 1990), 437–48.

11. Sue Vandenbosch, "A Negative Relationship Between Religion and the Percentage of Women State Legislators in the United States," *Journal of Legislative Studies,* 2 (Winter 1996), 322–38.

12. Susan Welch et al., "The Effect of Gender on Electoral Outcomes in State Legislative Races," *Western Political Quarterly,* 38 (September 1985), 464–75.

13. Susan Welch and Lee Sigelman, "Changes in Public Attitudes Toward Women in Politics," *Social Science Quarterly,* 63 (June 1982), 321–22.

14. Virginia Shapiro, "Private Costs of Public Commitments: Family Roles versus Political Ambition," *American Journal of Political Science,* 26 (May 1982), 265–79.

15. Carol Nechemias, "Geographic Mobility and Women's Access to State Legislatures," *Western Political Quarterly,* 38 (March 1985), 119–31.

16. Lesley Dahlkemper, "Growing Accustomed to Her Face," *State Legislatures* (July/August 1996), 37–45.

17. R. Darcy, "Women in the State Legislative Power Structure," *Social Science Quarterly,* 77 (December 1996), 888–98.

18. Quotations from state legislators interviewed by Wahlke et al., *Legislative Behavior,* pp. 95–134.

19. Richard J. Tobin, "The Influence of Nominating Systems on the Political Experience of State Legislators," *Western Political Quarterly,* 28 (September 1975), 553–66.

20. David Ray and John Havick, "A Longitudinal Analysis of Party Competition in State Legislative Elections," *American Journal of Political Science,* 25 (February 1981), 119–28.

21. Ronald Weber, Harvey Tucker, and Paul Brace, "Vanishing Marginals in State Legislative Elections," *Legislative Studies Quarterly,* 16 (February 1991), 29–47.

22. Malcolm E. Jewell, "State Legislative Elections," *American Politics Quarterly,* 22 (October 1994), 483–509.

23. Emily Van Dunk, "Challenger Quality in State Legislative Elections," *Political Research Quarterly,* 50 (December 1997), 793–807.

24. Quotations of legislators from William J. Keefe and Morris S. Ogul, *The American Legislative Process: Congress and the States,* 8th ed. (Englewood Cliffs, NJ: Prentice Hall, 1993).

25. *U.S. Term Limits v. Thornton* (1995).

26. Wayne L. Francis and Lawrence W. Kenny, "Consequences of Term Limits Upon Expected Tenure, Institutional Turnover, and Membership Experience," *Journal of Politics,* 59 (February 1997), 240–52.

27. National Conference of State Legislators.

28. *Baker v. Carr,* 369 U.S. 186 (1962).

29. *Reynold v. Sims,* 84 S. Ct. 1362 (1964).

30. *Wesberry v. Sanders,* 84 S. Ct. 526 (1964).

31. *Gray v. Sanders,* 83 S. Ct. 801 (1963), p. 809.

32. See Michael A. Maggiotto et al., "The Im-

pact of Reapportionment in Public Policy," *American Politics Quarterly,* 13 (January 1985), 101–21.

33. *Karchev* v. *Daggett,* 462 U.S. 725 (1983).

34. *Brown* v. *Thompson,* 462 U.S. 835 (1983).

35. *Davis* v. *Bandemer,* 106 S. Ct. 2797 (1986).

36. See Harry Basehart, "The Seats/Vote Relationship and the Identification of Partisan Gerrymandering in State Legislature," *American Politics Quarterly,* 15 (October 1987), 484–98. See also Gerard S. Gryski, Bruce Reed, and Euel Elliot, "The Seats–Vote Relationship in State Legislative Elections," *American Politics Quarterly,* 18 (April 1990), 141–57, for an estimate of bias for each state prior to 1990 redistricting.

37. *Davis* v. *Bandemer,* 106 S. Ct. 2797 (1986).

38. *Fortson* v. *Dorsey,* 179 U.S. 433 (1965).

39. *Thornbury* v. *Gingles,* 478 U.S. 30 (1986).

40. *Connor* v. *Johnson,* 407 U.S. 640 (1971).

41. *White* v. *Regester,* 412 U.S. 755 (1973).

42. See Harry Basehart and John Comer, "Redistricting and Incumbent Reelection in State Legislatures," *American Politics Quarterly,* 23 (April 1995), 241–53.

43. Harvey J. Tucker, "Legislative Logjams: A Comparative State Analysis," *Western Political Quarterly,* 38 (September 1985), 432–46.

44. Keith E. Hamm and Ronald D. Hedlund, "Occupational Interests and State Legislative Committees." Paper delivered at the Midwest Political Science Association, Chicago, 1989.

45. The "institutionalization" theme was first developed to understand changes in the U.S. House of Representatives by Nelson Polsby, "The Institutionalization of the U.S. House of Representatives," *American Political Science Review,* 62 (March 1968), 144–68.

46. Alan Rosenthal, *Governors and Legislatures: Contending Powers* (Washington, DC: CQ Press, 1990), 63.

47. Citizens Conference on State Legislatures, *The Sometimes Governments* (New York: Bantam Books, 1971), p. 77.

48. See Malcolm E. Jewell and Marcia Lynn Whicker, *Legislative Leadership in the United States* (Ann Arbor: University of Michigan Press, 1994).

49. Thomas H. Little, "A Systematic Analysis of Members' Environments and Their Expectations of Elected Leaders," *Political Research Quarterly,* 47 (September 1994), 733–47.

50. National Conference of State Legislatures, *State Legislative Priorities* (Denver: NCSL, 1995).

51. Charles G. Bell and Charles E. Price, "Pre-Legislative Sources of Representational Roles," *Midwest Journal of Political Science,* 13 (May 1969), 254–70. See also Corey M. Rosen, "Legislative Influence and Policy Orientation in American State Legislatures," *American Journal of Political Science,* 18 (November 1974), 681–91.

52. See Robert Harmel and Keith E. Hamm, "Development of a Party Role in a No-Party Legislature," *Western Political Quarterly,* 39 (March 1986), 79–92. See also Cole Blease Graham and Kenny J. Whitby, "Party-Based Voting in a Southern State Legislature," *American Politics Quarterly,* 17 (April 1989), 181–93.

53. *State Legislation,* August 1989, p. 16.

54. Hanna Pitkin, *The Concept of Representation* (Berkeley: University of California Press, 1967), p. 154.

55. Ronald D. Hedlund and H. Paul Friesma, "Representatives' Perceptions of Constituency Opinion," *Journal of Politics,* 34 (August 1971), 730–52.

56. Robert S. Erikson, Norman R. Luttbeg, and William V. Holloway, "Knowing One's District: How Legislators Predict Referendum Voting," *American Journal of Political Science,* 19 (May 1975), 231–41.

57. Bryan D. Jones, "Competitiveness, Role Orientations, and Legislative Responsiveness," *Journal of Politics,* 35 (November 1973), 924–47.

58. Robert M. Entman, "The Impact of Ideology on Legislative Behavior," *Journal of Politics,* 45 (February 1983), 165.

59. Christopher A. Mooney, "Peddling Information in the State Legislature: Closeness Counts," *Western Political Quarterly,* 44 (June 1991), 433–44.

60. Harmon Zeigler and Michael A. Baer, *Lobbying: Interaction and Influence in American State Legislatures* (Belmont, CA: Wadsworth, 1969), p. 107.

61. Ibid., p. 121.

62. Cynthia Opheim, "Explaining the Differences in State Lobbying Regulation," *Western Political Quarterly,* 44 (June 1991), 405–21.

7
GOVERNORS IN STATE POLITICS

THE MANY ROLES OF A GOVERNOR

Governors are central figures in American state politics. People are more likely to be able to recall their governor's name than the name of any public official other than the president and vice-president of the United States. In the eyes of many citizens, governors are responsible for everything that happens in their states during their terms of office, whether or not they have the authority or the capacity to do anything about it. Governors are expected to bring industry into their states, prevent prison riots, raise teachers' salaries, keep taxes low, see that the state gets its fair share of grant money from Washington, provide disaster relief, and bring tourists into the state. Governors offer reassurance to citizens during crises and disasters—everything from floods, hurricanes, fires, and droughts, to toxic waste spills and nuclear plant accidents. These public expectations far exceed the formal powers of governors. In many ways the expectations placed upon the governor resemble those placed upon the president. Like the president, governors are expected to be their state's chief administrator, chief legislator, leader of their party, ceremonial head of their government, chief ambassador to other governments, leader of public opinion, and chief crisis manager.

CHIEF ADMINISTRATOR   As *chief administrator,* the governor must try to coordinate the state's bureaucracy, oversee the preparation of the state's budget, and supervise major state programs. Governors must resolve conflicts within their administrations and troubleshoot where difficulties arise. They must be concerned with scandal and endeavor to prevent it from becoming public, or act decisively to eliminate it if it does. The public will hold them responsible for any scandal in their administration, whether they were a party to it or not. The public will hold them responsible for the financial structure of the state, whether it was they or their predecessors who were responsible for the state's fiscal troubles.

Yet, as we shall see in this chapter, the formal administrative powers of a governor are severely restricted. Many of the governor's administrative agencies are headed by elected officials or independent boards or commissions, over which the governor has little or no control. Governors' powers of appointment and removal are severely restricted by state constitutions. Governors do not have control over their administration that is commensurate with their responsibility for it.

CHIEF LEGISLATOR   As *chief legislator,* the governor is responsible for initiating major statewide legislative programs. There is a general public expectation that every governor will put forward some sort of legislative program. By sending bills to the legislature, governors are cast in the role of the "initiator" of public policy decisions. If they want to see their legislative proposals enacted into law, they must also persuade legislators to support them. In other words, they must involve themselves directly in legislative decisions.

Veto.
Rejection of proposed legislation by the chief executive (governor), usually subject to legislative override by a two-thirds vote of both houses.

The veto power gives the governor bargaining power with the legislature. Few vetoes are overridden; in most states a two-thirds majority vote in both houses is required to override a veto. This means a governor needs only one-third plus one in either house to sustain his or her veto. So even the *threat* of a veto can force changes in a bill under consideration in the legislature. Moreover, in most states, the governor possesses the line-item veto, allowing the governor to veto specific items in an appropriations bill, including legislators' home district "pork" or "turkeys." The threat of vetoing these vote-winning projects gives the governor additional bargaining power with legislators. A governor can also call special sessions of the legislature, allowing the governor to spotlight specific issues and pressure the legislature to do something about them.

PARTY LEADER   Traditionally governors were regarded as the head of their party in the state. But governors do not have the power to deny party nominations to recalcitrant legislators of their own party. Party nominations are won independently by legislators in their own districts. Governors have no formal disciplinary powers over members of their own party. And governors may choose to emphasize their own independence from their national party to further their own electoral ambitions.

However, within the legislature, parties still count. The governor usually receives greater support for his or her program from members of his or her own party. Legislators who run for office under the same party label as the governor have a stake in his or her success. Since all who run under the party's label share its common fortunes, and since its fortunes are often governed by the strength of its gubernatorial candidate, there will always be a tendency for loyal party members to support their governor. The organization of the legislature along party lines reinforces the party role of the governor. Legislative leaders of the governor's party—whether in the majority or minority—are expected to support the governor's program.

CEREMONIAL HEAD   *Ceremonial* duties occupy a great deal of a governor's time. A governor may not be able to mobilize the symbolic and ceremonial power of the office on behalf of state goals in the same way that the president can mobilize the power of that office on behalf of national goals. Nonetheless, the skillful use of symbols and ceremonies can add to a governor's prestige and popularity. These assets can in turn contribute to political power.

CHIEF NEGOTIATOR   The governor is the *chief negotiator* with other governments in the American federal system, a variation of the diplomatic role of the president. Governors must negotiate with their local governments on the division of state and local responsibilities for public programs, and with other state governments over coordinating highway development, water pollution, resource conservation, and reciprocity in state laws. Governors must undertake responsibility for negotiation with the national government as well. The governor shares responsibility with the state's United States senators in seeing to it that the state receives a "fair share" of federal contracts, highway monies, educational monies, poverty funds, and so on.

OPINION LEADER   Governors are *leaders of public opinion* in their states. They are the most visible of state officials. Their comments on public affairs make news, and they are sought after for television, radio, and public appearances. They are able to focus public opinion on issues they deem important. They may not always be able to win public opinion to their side, but at least they will be heard.

CRISIS MANAGER   Finally, governors may be called upon to *manage crises* in their states—hurricanes, floods, droughts, and other disasters. Indeed, a governor's performance in a crisis may determine his or her standing with the public.

THE MAKING OF A GOVERNOR

As the central position in American state politics, the governorship is a much sought-after office. The prestige of being called "governor" for the rest of one's life, and the opportunity to use the office as a steppingstone to the United States Senate, or even the presidency or vice-presidency of the United States, is extremely attractive to people of ambition in American politics.

VARIETIES OF BACKGROUND   Many governors have been the sons of families of great wealth, who have chosen public service as an outlet for their energies—the Roosevelts, the Harrimans, the duPonts, the Rockefellers, the Scrantons, and, more recently, the Bushes. Others have been men who emphasized, or exaggerated, their humble beginnings—Huey Long of Louisiana, "Big Jim" Folsom of Alabama, "Pitchfork Ben" Tillman of South Carolina, "Old Gene" Talmadge of Georgia. The southern "populist" governors, however, were gradually replaced by more moderate and better educated men—Bob Graham of Florida, Bill Clinton of Arkansas, and Jimmy Carter of Georgia. George C. Wallace of Alabama may have been the last governor in the true populist tradition.

Governors have been movie actors (Ronald Reagan of California), restaurant owners (Lester Maddox of Georgia), truck drivers (Harold Hughes of Iowa), and country music singers (Jimmie Davis of Louisiana wrote "You Are My Sunshine"). Now even professional wrestling has produced a governor—Jesse "The Body" Ventura of Minnesota (see "*People in Politics:* Jesse 'The Body' Ventura"). However, the majority of governors have been *lawyers* by profession. (The predominance of lawyers in public office was explained in Chapter 6.)

Governors George W. Bush of Texas and Jeb Bush of Florida are not the first brothers to hold governorships of separate states. A generation earlier, Nelson Rockefeller, four-term governor of New York, served in Albany while his brother, Winthrop Rockefeller, was governor of Arkansas, and his nephew, John D. Rockefeller IV, was governor of West Virginia. Pat Brown defeated Richard Nixon in 1962 to win the governorship of California; his son, Jerry Brown, won the same office in 1974; but Kathleen Brown failed in her bid in 1994 to follow in the footsteps of her father and brother. James B. Longley of Maine was the first independent candidate to win a governorship in modern history; he was followed by independent mavericks Walter Hickel of Alaska and Lowell Weicker of Connecticut.

AGE   Television has accented youth and good looks among state governors. It helps "image-wise" to be tall, slim, handsome, fashionable, and smiling. The median beginning age of governors has declined over the last few decades to a youngish forty-seven. Bill Clinton became the nation's youngest governor when he won that post in Arkansas in 1978 at age thirty-two.

PEOPLE IN POLITICS

JESSE "THE BODY" VENTURA

"Retaliate in '98" was his campaign slogan. Retaliate for what? Apparently Minnesotians were asked to retaliate against two-party politics-as-usual in their state. They did so in a colorful three-way race in which the Reform Party candidate Jesse "The Body" Ventura, former Navy Seal, pro wrestler, and talk show host, upended the more politically experienced Republican and Democratic candidates, St. Paul Mayor Norm Coleman and state attorney general Hubert Humphrey III. Ventura's victory stunned the nation's political establishment; even Ross Perot was notably silent about his party's first statewide win.

Although the six foot four inch, 250 pound, shaved-headed, former wrestler is a frequent target of late-night TV comedians, Ventura argues "I'm not some big dumb wrestler." He served a four-year term as mayor of Brooklyn Park, a medium-size city in Minnesota, and as a popular radio talk show host in the Twin Cities.

Born James Janos in blue-collar Minneapolis, he joined the Navy after high school and was trained as a Navy Seal. After six years of Navy service, which included a tour in Viet-

nam, he rode with a motorcycle club in California, worked as a bodyguard, and then took up professional wrestling under a new name, Jesse "The Body" Ventura. He was very successful in his new profession, becoming a regular opponent of top wrestling star Hulk Hogan.

Ventura was forced to retire from wrestling in 1984 with a pulmonary embolism. But he maintained his charismatic tough-guy image by playing roles in action movies, including Arnold Schwarzenegger's popular film *Predator*. Later his deep booming voice and straight talk served him well as a talk show host in his hometown of Minneapolis. He expressed generally populist political views on his show—opposing taxes and big government as well as corporate welfare, and favoring gay rights laws and the legalization of marijuana. He became especially popular with young people who turned out in surprising numbers to support him on election day.

Ventura himself acknowledges he must now learn on the job, get along with Democratic and Republican legislators, and perhaps hold in check his free-wheeling nature. But with characteristic bravado, he says "I can do the job. It's not like it's transplanting kidneys."

RACE Until Douglas Wilder's successful run for the Virginia statehouse in 1989, no state had ever elected a black governor. California came close to doing so in 1982, when Democratic Mayor Thomas Bradley of Los Angeles lost to Republican George Deukmejian by less than 1 percent of the vote. Several Hispanics have been elected governor: Jerry Abodaca of New Mexico, Raul Castro of Arizona, Toney Anaya of New Mexico, and Bob Martinez of Florida.

GENDER Women have become increasingly successful in winning statewide executive office. Currently about 25 percent of all elected statewide executive officials—governors, lieutenant governors, attorneys general, treasurers, comptrollers, secretaries of state, and commissioners of education, labor, public service, and so forth—are women.[1] However, there have never been more than four women governors serving at any one time in the fifty states.

Prior to 1974, only three women had *ever* served as governor of a U.S. state, and all three succeeded their husbands in office—Nellie Ross of Wyoming and Miriam "Ma" Ferguson of Texas in the 1920s, and Lurleen Wallace of Alabama in the 1960s. In 1974, Ella T. Grasso of Connecticut became the first woman governor whose husband had not previously held the office. Later that same year, Dixey Lee Ray of Washington accomplished the same feat. Martha Collins was elected governor of Kentucky in

1983; Kay Orr won the governorship of Nebraska in 1986; and Madeleine Kunin won the office in Vermont that same year. Democrat Ann Richards's hard-fought victory in the Texas governor's race in 1990 demonstrated that women can triumph in rough, bitter personal campaigns. Richards lost to George W. Bush, the former president's son, in 1994. Other women governors in the 1990s included Joan Finney (D.–Kansas), Barbara Roberts (D.–Oregon), Christine Whitman (R.–New Jersey), Jane Hull (R.–Arizona), and Jeanne Shaheen (D.–New Hampshire).

POLITICAL EXPERIENCE   Governors usually come to their office with considerable experience in public affairs. Only about 8 percent come into the governor's chair without prior officeholding. "Promotion" from a statewide elective office—lieutenant governor and attorney general, especially—is the most well-worn path to the governorship. Many governors have experience in state legislatures: Nearly half of all governors have previously served in the legislature and about one-fifth run directly from their legislative seats. Some members of Congress and some federal cabinet officers give up their seats to run for governor—an indication of the power and prestige of the office of governor. Pete Wilson of California was the first U.S. senator in modern times to leave that body to run for governor; Lawton Chiles of Florida left the U.S. Senate and later decided to run for governor.

GUBERNATORIAL POLITICS

COMPETITION   Competition is usually strong, both in primary and general elections, for the governorship. Indeed, competition for the job has been increasing over time, especially in the southern states where Republican candidates now have an equal chance of winning governorships. Yet traditionally the Democratic party has dominated state gubernatorial politics. In 1994, for the first time in thirty years Republican governors (30) outnumbered Democratic governors (19), and Republican governors have continued to outnumber Democratic governors since then. (See Figure 5–1 in Chapter 5.)

GETTING ELECTED   What forces influence the outcome of gubernatorial elections? Are gubernatorial elections affected by national voting trends—"coattails"? Or are they more affected by conditions within the states, especially the performance of the state's economy? Or are gubernatorial elections primarily "candidate centered"—influenced mostly by the personal qualities of the candidates, their handling of state issues, the strength of their own political organizations, and their success in fund-raising and campaigning?

GUBERNATORIAL VOTE CHOICE   If voters are asked "What mattered most in voting for governor?," they cite personal leadership qualities of the candidate more often than anything else (see Table 7–1). Party affiliation and agreement on issues follow in importance. Negative voting—dislike of the opponent—also plays a significant role in gubernatorial voting.

Governors are better known to the voters than any other state officials or even U.S. senators and House members. Governors receive more media attention than any other

Table 7–1

GUBERNATORIAL VOTE CHOICE			
Q. "What mattered most in voting for governor?"	%	Q: "Who is to blame for the state's economic problems?"	%
Strong leadership	21.1	President	25.4
Management ability	19.7	Both president and governor	18.4
Political party	19.0	Governor	15.4
Agreement on issues	18.2	Neither	34.5
Dislike opponent	12.0		
Don't know/No answer	10.0		

Source: Gubernatorial vote choice information derived from "Economic Voting for Governor and U.S. Senator" by Robert M. Stein, in *Journal of Politics*, 52:1 (February 1990), 29–53, by permission of the author and the University of Texas Press. Based on *New York Times*/CBS News Election Day surveys in 27 states in 1982, during a national economic recession.

state official. This does not make governors better liked than other elected officeholders. On the contrary, governors are usually rated less favorably on job performance than U.S. senators and House members.[2]

Voters do not usually hold a governor solely responsible for economic problems confronting the state. Most voters recognize that state economic conditions depend more on market factors, or on the actions of the national government, including the president, than on the governor. State (or local) officials may be held responsible for actions that make an already weak economy worse; voters may expect a governor to do all that he or she can to ameliorate hard times. But few voters hold governors directly responsible for the state's economic well-being.[3]

While presidential and congressional elections are influenced by national economic conditions (recessions adversely affect the vote for candidates of the party in power, while prosperity generally helps), no similar influences can be seen in state legislative or gubernatorial elections. Political scientist John E. Chubb concludes: "Voters in state elections appear to hold politicians outside of the state, specifically the president and the president's party, responsible for economic conditions, and if conditions in a state should differ from those in neighboring states, to hold the governor only minimally responsible."[4]

COATTAIL EFFECTS   There are some coattail effects in state gubernatorial and legislative elections. Gubernatorial candidates running on the same party ticket as popular presidential candidates enjoy a significant advantage. But most gubernatorial elections are held in "off years"—years in which the nation is not electing a president. Off-year elections are deliberately designed to minimize the effects of presidential voting trends on state governors' elections. Nonetheless, there is some evidence that the electoral fate of gubernatorial candidates is affected by the popularity of the president. Gubernatorial candidates of the president's party attract more votes when the presi-

■
Coattails.
In politics, a reference to the effect that a party's leader may have on voting for that party's candidates for other offices.

dent's popularity in opinion polls is high. This is true whether the candidates are incumbents or aspirants.[5] Conversely, gubernatorial candidates of the president's party suffer when the president's popularity is low. Insofar as a president's popularity is affected by national economic trends, gubernatorial candidates of the president's party can suffer from national recessions and benefit from national prosperity.

CANDIDATE EFFECTS   Despite these coattail effects, gubernatorial elections are mostly candidate centered. Governors are less closely tied to national policy issues than Congress members; governors are not called upon by the media to explain their votes in support or opposition to the president's policy positions. The outcome of gubernatorial elections depends mostly on the personal qualities of the candidates, their ability to associate themselves with popular issues, the strength of their personal political organizations, their ability to raise campaign funds, and their skills in campaigning.

REELECTION   Incumbent governors who seek reelection are usually successful. In primary elections, incumbent governors usually face *little* serious opposition.[6] In recent years the overall success rate for incumbent governors seeking reelection has averaged about 75 percent. However, governors are somewhat more vulnerable to defeat than U.S. senators (whose reelection rate is 85 percent) or House members (whose reelection rate is over 90 percent).[7] Occasionally governors are defeated, and it is interesting to try to understand these failures.

Political folklore includes the belief that any governor who raises taxes during his or her term will be defeated for reelection. But a careful study of this notion shows only a weak connection between tax increase and electoral defeat for governors.[8] Most governors who raise taxes and then seek reelection are successful! Frequently, however, those who are defeated *blame* their loss on raising taxes.

Economic conditions occasionally hurt an incumbent governor seeking reelection. Although the national economy is an important factor in presidential elections, adverse economic conditions do less harm to incumbent governors.[9] Many voters see the economy as a national issue and governors are not blamed for recessions.

CAMPAIGNING   Modern gubernatorial campaigns are quite professional: They usually involve professional public relations organizations, experienced mass media and television advertising firms, professional polling and political consultants, and sophisticated direct mail and fund-raising techniques. (See "Professional Media Campaigns" in Chapter 5.) Party organizations and amateur volunteers play a very limited role in most modern campaigns in the states. The traditional barnstorming, stump-speaking, hand-shaking, and door-to-door canvassing campaigns have largely disappeared. Candidates still do these things, but the focus of the campaign is on media advertising.

Of course, campaign themes and candidate "images" must be tailored to a state's political culture and tradition. Campaign "gimmicks" are increasingly popular, particularly in state elections. Gimmicks can be as varied as the minds of advertising specialists. An example of an especially successful gimmick was the "working days" of Governor Bob Graham of Florida. Graham is a Harvard-educated, millionaire lawyer and real estate developer from Miami, whose brief career in the Florida legislature was generally perceived as unproductive. But Graham was ambitious for higher office, and he and his professional consultants realized that he must develop an image with which working people could identify. So they selected as the campaign theme for his gubernatorial race: "Bob Graham—Working for Governor," and Graham undertook during the campaign to work a full day at each of 100 different jobs. Graham's television ads showed him collecting garbage, picking oranges, herding dairy cows, and so forth, and he garnered a great deal of local television time with these colorful media events. Critics argued that Graham's "working days campaign" were the only days of his life that he had ever worked. But this campaign gimmick was so successful that he continued his well-publicized working days even after he won the governorship. After two terms in the state capital, Graham easily won a seat in the U.S. Senate.

MONEY Modern mass media campaigns—with professional media advertising, opinion polls, direct mail persuasion, political consultants—are very costly. In the 1950s a typical gubernatorial campaign cost between $100,000 and $200,000; today a typical gubernatorial campaign costs $2 million to $5 million in small states and $10 million to $20 million or more in the larger states. Television advertising is the major reason for increased costs. Candidates for governor should expect to spend between $2 and $10 *per vote*.

Although money cannot buy a governorship, it is important to realize that (1) no one can mount a serious gubernatorial campaign without either personal wealth or strong financial backing by others, and (2) the heavier-spending candidate wins in two out of three elections. Most states require public reporting of campaign contributions and expenditures, and most states place limits on contributions by individuals and groups. Nonetheless, individuals can spend what they wish in order to express their personal political preferences separate from official campaigns; fund-raising political action committees (PACs) can multiply in number; and wealthy candidates can spend as much of their own money as they wish on their own campaigns. (See Chapter 5.)

POLITICAL AMBITIONS Historically, presidents were chosen from among the ranks of America's state governors, particularly the governors of the larger states. During the Cold War, the importance of international affairs in American politics detracted somewhat from the popular image of the governorship as the steppingstone to the presidency. Governors tend to be associated with domestic rather than foreign policy questions. Men such as Truman, Nixon, McGovern, Humphrey, Kennedy, Goldwater, and Johnson found the United States Senate a good place to promote their campaigns for vice-presidential and presidential nominations. For a while, scholars attributed the decline in the number of governors selected as presidential candidates to a general decline in the popularity of governors.

But in recent years, distrust of "the government in Washington" and the low esteem of Congress in the eyes of the general public have improved the presidential fortunes of governors. Georgia Governor Jimmy Carter skillfully exploited his image as an "outsider" in his successful 1976 presidential campaign. And Ronald Reagan, whose only political experience was his two terms as governor of California, reaffirmed the importance of governors in presidential politics. Massachusetts Governor Michael Dukakis lost to George Bush in 1988. (Bush had no experience in state government; he won election to Congress for two terms and then served in appointed federal posts—

ambassador to China, UN ambassador, CIA director, vice-president.) But the end of the Cold War brought domestic issues to the forefront of the nation's political agenda. The focus on the economy in 1992, and continuing popular distrust of Congress, paved the way for the presidential election of Arkansas Governor Bill Clinton.

EXECUTIVE POWER IN STATE GOVERNMENT

Frequently we speak of "strong" and "weak" governors. Yet it is difficult to compare the power of one governor with that of another. To do so, one must examine the constitutional position of governors, their powers of appointment and removal over state officials, their ability or inability to succeed themselves, their powers over the state

PEOPLE IN POLITICS

GEORGE W. BUSH, GOVERNING TEXAS

George W. Bush had never held public office before being elected governor of Texas. But the son of former president George Bush not only enjoyed widespread name recognition in the Lone Star State (perhaps even name confusion), but also served as the managing general partner of the homestate Texas Rangers American League baseball team. His victory over popular incumbent governor Ann Richards in 1994 and his landslide reelection in 1998 propelled him to the top of the Republican presidential opinion polls.

Born in 1946 into the Bush family's tradition of wealth, privilege, and public service (Bush's grandfather was a U.S. senator from Connecticut and chairman of Yale University's governing board), George W. followed his father to Yale University and later received an M.B.A. from Harvard. And like his father, he founded a Texas oil and gas exploration company. He remained in the energy business until 1986 when he went to Washington to run his father's presidential campaign.

George W. reflects his father's moderate Republicanism. Yet his political style fits comfortably with Texas "good old boys." Early in his administration he supported legislation that gave law-abiding adult Texans the right to carry concealed handguns. Yet at the same time he did little to restrict abortion in his state despite cries from his Christian conservative supporters to do so. A strong economy has allowed him to improve public services in the state while lowering school

property taxes. Texas remains one of the few states that has no state income tax. Bush failed, however, to broaden the state's sales tax to include tax on services. He has supported educational reform by opposing the practice of "social promotion" and urging the public schools in Texas to require every third-, fifth-, and eighth-grade pupil to pass statewide tests before advancing to the next grade.

Bush has helped lead the gradual realignment of Texas away from its traditional Democratic roots and toward its current Republican coloration. (In 1998 Republicans not only occupied the governorship and both of the state's U.S. Senate seats but also all other statewide elected offices.) Yet George W. has proven that he can work with Democrats in the Texas legislature. His style is to meet privately and frequently with his Democratic opponents and to remain on friendly personal terms with them. He is willing to accept legislative compromises and he tries to avoid controversy wherever possible. But, perhaps as a result of this style, Bush is unable to point to any landmark achievement in his administration (comparable, for example, to Christine Whitman's slashing of income taxes in New Jersey). (See Chapter 1, "*People in Politics:* Christine Whitman, Cutting State Taxes.")

George W. currently leads all other potential Republican 2000 presidential candidates in opinion polls.

Only one other son (John Quincy Adams) ever followed his father (John Adams) to the White House. But George W. Bush is in a strong position to lead the Republican Party into the next century.

budget, their legislative influence, their position in their own party and its position in state politics, and their influence over public opinion in the state.

GOVERNORS, WEAK AND STRONG   In many ways the organization of American state government resembles political thinking of earlier historical eras. Jacksonian "popular democracy" brought with it the idea that the way to ensure popular control of state government was to elect separately as many state officials as possible. The Reform movement of the late nineteenth and early twentieth centuries led to merit systems and civil service boards, which further curtailed the governor's power of appointment. Many important state offices are governed by boards or commissions whose members may be appointed by the governor with the consent of the state senate but for long overlapping terms, which reduces the governor's influence over members of these boards and commissions. Not all of these trends were experienced uniformly by all fifty states, and there are considerable variations from state to state in the powers that governors have over the state executive branch. Today there are over 300 separately elected executive branch officials in the fifty states (see Table 7–2). Only Maine, New Hampshire, New Jersey, and Tennessee have a single statewide elected official, the governor.

EXECUTIVE REORGANIZATION   Modern public administration generally recommends a stronger governor and more centralized state executive branch. Reform and reorganization proposals usually recommend (1) four-year terms for governors with the ability to succeed themselves; (2) the elimination of many separately elected state executive officials and limiting the statewide ballot to governor, lieutenant governor, and attorney general; (3) elimination of boards and commissions as heads of agencies and their replacement by single, removable gubernatorial appointees; and (4) the consolidation of many state agencies into larger departments reporting directly to the governor. However, states have been slow to adopt these reforms.

POLITICAL OPPOSITION TO REORGANIZATION   Separately elected officials and independent boards and officials will be around for a long time. Political parties and public officials develop a stake in the continued existence of these elected offices. Moreover, many interest groups prefer to be governed by boards and commissions or separately elected officials. They feel they have more influence over these independent offices than those that come directly under a governor's authority. Interest groups, from educational administrators and teachers' unions, to the agriculture, insurance, real estate, and public utility industries, prefer to have direct access to executive officials. Incumbent officeholders are usually able to rally their client groups to defeat reorganization proposals that threaten their office.

TENURE POWER   Another component of a governor's influence is the ability or inability to succeed him- or herself in office. Governors with the highest "tenure power" are those who are elected for a four-year term and are permitted to succeed themselves indefinitely (see Table 7–3). Governors with the lowest "tenure power" are those who have only two-year terms. The Twenty-Second Amendment to the U.S. Constitution restricts executive tenure at the presidential level to two terms, and most states now have similar restrictions on their governors.

Tenure.
The length of time an elected official can serve in office.

Table 7–2

STATES AND ELECTED EXECUTIVE OFFICIALS

Seven or More

Alabama	North Carolina
California	North Dakota
Florida	Oklahoma
Georgia	South Carolina
Idaho	South Dakota
Louisiana	Texas
Nebraska	

Five to Seven

Arizona	Mississippi
Arkansas	Missouri
Colorado	Montana
Connecticut	Nevada
Delaware	New Mexico
Illinois	Ohio
Indiana	Pennsylvania
Iowa	Rhode Island
Massachusetts	Utah
Minnesota	Vermont

Two to Four

Alaska	Michigan
Hawaii	New York
Kansas	Oregon
Maryland	

One (Governor/Lt. Governor only)

Maine
New Hampshire
New Jersey
Tennessee

Source: Book of the States, 1998–99, p. 33.

Table 7–3

| TENURE PROVISIONS FOR GOVERNORS |

Four-Year Term, No Restrictions on Reelection

Connecticut	Montana	Texas
Idaho	New York	Utah
Illinois	North Carolina	Washington
Iowa	North Dakota	Wisconsin
Massachusetts	Rhode Island	Wyoming
Minnesota		

Four-Year Term, Restricted to Two Terms

Alabama	Kansas	New Jersey
Alaska	Kentucky	New Mexico
Arizona	Louisiana	Ohio
Arkansas	Maine	Oklahoma
California	Maryland	Oregon
Colorado	Michigan	Pennsylvania
Delaware	Mississippi	South Carolina
Florida	Missouri	South Dakota
Georgia	Nebraska	Tennessee
Hawaii	Nevada	West Virginia
Indiana		

Four-Year Term, Consecutive Reelection Prohibited

Virginia

Two-Year Term, No Restrictions on Reelection

New Hampshire	Vermont

Source: Book of the States, 1998–99.

MANAGERIAL POWERS   Governors are chief executives; they are supposed to manage state governmental bureaucracies. But aside from interviewing occasionally in response to a crisis, governors generally turn over their management chores to others. According to political scientist Alan Rosenthal, governors downplay their managerial role and avoid expending energy and power on management because "greater rewards derive from the pursuit of other functions—formulating policy, building popularity and support among the public, helping develop the state economy."[10]

EXECUTIVE ORDERS   Managing in the state bureaucracy is generally left to the governor's staff and department heads (see Chapter 8). But from time to time governors

■

Executive order.
A directive issued by a chief
executive to administrative
agencies.

directly intervene in well-publicized, politically sensitive executive decisions. Governors may do so by executive order—a special directive issued by the governor to one or more executive agencies. Executive orders must be based on state constitutional powers given governors or on powers delegated to them by state laws. Executive orders are often issued to deal with public emergencies or disasters. (See "*Up Close:* Governor Pataki Issues an Order.")

APPOINTMENT POWERS   Perhaps the most important managerial power is the power to appoint subordinate officials. Appointment of subordinates does not guarantee their responsibility, but there is a greater likelihood that an official appointed by a governor will be someone whose values coincide with those of the governor. If an agency head is separately elected by the people (as are most attorneys general, treasurers, and secretaries of state), then the governor has little direct control over them. If the governor can appoint an agency head *without* the need for legislative approval, we can say that the governor has stronger appointive powers than if legislative confirmation of appointment is required. Indeed, agency heads themselves tend to evaluate the governor's influence largely in terms of his or her ability to appoint them to office.[11]

We have classified the states according to the number of functions over which the governors have direct control (see Table 7–4). States that have had major constitutional revisions in recent decades, such as New York and Illinois, tend to give their governor strong appointive powers. This is a reflection of the extent of management reform in these states.[12] At the other extreme, Florida's governor has weak appointive powers, not only because the secretary of state, attorney general, secretary of agriculture, superintendent of public instruction, treasurer and insurance commissioner, and controller are popularly elected, but also because major departments are headed by

UP CLOSE

GOVERNOR PATAKI ISSUES AN ORDER

Following a number of incidents in which women were chased or stopped by unmarked state police cars as well as by criminals impersonating police officers, Governor George Pataki of New York issued an executive order in 1996 that barred unmarked state police cars from stopping motorists for routine traffic violations. In a well-publicized press conference, the governor read parts of his executive order:

WHEREAS, motorists have been victimized after being stopped by criminals falsely impersonating police officers on patrol;

WHEREAS, the use of unmarked patrol vehicles in traffic stops on the highways and roads of the state may, and not

uncommonly does, engender confusion and anxiety in the minds of motorists uncertain whether the vehicles attempting to stop them are in fact authorized police vehicles....

NOW, THEREFORE, I, GEORGE E. PATAKI, Governor of the State of New York, by virtue of the authority vested to me by the Constitution in Laws of the State of New York, do hereby order ... that unmarked or concealed identity police vehicles of the State of New York are not [to be] used for routine stopping or apprehension of motorists for offenses relating to the Vehicle and Traffic Law....

Governor Pataki issued his order after seeing a graphic videotape on television showing a woman being abused by a police officer for failing to stop after he signaled her to do so from an unmarked car.

Table 7–4

APPOINTIVE POWERS OF GOVERNORS				
Very Strong	*Strong*	*Moderate*	*Weak*	*Very Weak*
Connecticut	Arkansas	Georgia	Alaska	Florida
Delaware	California	Kansas	Arizona	Mississippi
Hawaii	Colorado	Louisiana	Alabama	South Carolina
Kentucky	Illinois	Maine	Idaho	Texas
Massachusetts	Indiana	Michigan	Missouri	
Minnesota	Iowa	Montana	Nevada	
New Jersey	Maryland	Nebraska	New Mexico	
New York	Ohio	New Hampshire	North Dakota	
North Carolina	South Dakota	Rhode Island	Oklahoma	
Pennsylvania		Utah	Oregon	
Tennessee			Washington	
Vermont			Wisconsin	
Virginia			Wyoming	
West Virginia				

Source: Calculated from information provided in *Book of the States, 1998–99.*

boards on which the governor has only one vote. Florida calls this its "cabinet system."

STATE CABINETS   State cabinets, composed of the heads of the major executive departments, advise the governors in most of the states. Indeed, in a few states the cabinet is recognized in the state constitution and given more than just advisory powers. Cabinets range in size from less than ten members to more than twenty-five. Most cabinets meet at the governor's discretion and function more or less in the fashion of the president's cabinet in the national government.

REMOVAL POWERS   Restrictions on governors' powers of appointment are further complicated by restrictions on their powers of removal. A common statutory or constitutional provision dealing with governors' removal powers states that removal must be "for cause only"; that is, governors must provide a clear-cut statement of charges and an opportunity for an open hearing to the employee they are trying to oust. This process is often unpleasant, and governors seek to avoid it unless they have strong evidence of incompetence, fraud, or mismanagement. When a governor's removal powers are limited "for cause only," it is next to impossible to remove a subordinate for policy differences. A governor may request an officeholder to resign, even when the governor's removal power is limited, and such a request may be honored by the officeholder in preference to continued unhappy relationships with the governor's office or in fear of the governor's ability to mobilize public opinion against him or her. As a final resort, a determined governor with influence in the legislature can always oust an official by a legislative act, which abolishes the office or agency the official heads and replaces it with another; this device is sometimes called a "ripper bill."

Cabinet.
The heads of executive departments of a government.

FISCAL POWER   Governors are generally responsible for preparing the state budget for consideration by the legislature. The state budget is the single most important policy document in state government. Although the legislature must enact the state budget into law, and no state monies may be spent without the passage of an appropriations act by the legislature, in practice the governor exercises considerable influence over state spending in the preparation of the state budget. Governors are aided by their budget offices in preparation of each fiscal year's "Budget Recommendations" to the legislatures (see Chapter 8).

THE GOVERNOR'S LEGISLATIVE POWERS

The responsibility for initiating major statewide legislative programs falls upon the governor. The governor's programs are presented to the legislature in various governor's messages and in the budget. While these instruments are only recommendations, the governor can set the agenda for policy debate with them. "Agenda setting" is an important power. Much of the governor's power over the legislature stems from his or her power to set the policy agenda.

SETTING PRIORITIES   Governors are well advised to limit their policy agenda to a few priority issues each year, rather than sending the legislature a smorgasbord of items without any unifying goal or theme. A governor wants to develop a strong "batting average"—a reputation for getting a high percentage of his or her recommendations enacted by the legislature. Submitting multiple proposals increases the chances for defeat. Submitting only a few high-visibility proposals, and concentrating energy and power on securing their passage, usually increases the ratio of bills passed to bills submitted. But it is often difficult for governors to select their priority issues from the host of recommendations that come to them from interest groups and executive agencies. Governors can expand their policy agenda in good economic times when there are more revenues to pay for new initiatives. But in recessionary times, governors are constrained to few if any new initiatives.

PROVIDING LEADERSHIP   "What does the governor want?" is a frequent question heard in legislative debate. Leadership requires the governor to do more than simply propose legislation. The governor must also "make it happen." Governors must rally public support, packaging their proposals in a way that people will understand and support. They must make speeches and public appearances and prepare news releases highlighting their proposals. This "outside" strategy must be integrated with an "inside" strategy to persuade legislators to support the program. Governors must carefully steer their proposals through the legislative process—the committee system, floor proceedings, votes on amendments, conference committees, and final passage. They must develop good working relationships with the legislative leadership and with as many rank-and-file members as possible. They must mobilize the support of interest groups behind their proposals. Finally, governors must be willing to compromise—to take "half a loaf" and declare victory. Governors must be flexible, accepting legislative amendments when necessary to preserve the major thrust of their program.

SPECIAL SESSIONS   Governors can increase pressure on legislatures to act on particular recommendations by calling special sessions. The governor can specify the topics that should be considered in the special session. This device can be particularly effective if the legislature has buried one of the governor's favorite programs in the regular session. Legislators do not like to be called back from their businesses to the state capital for a special session, so even the threat of one may force them to pass the governor's program in the regular session. Of course, legislatures can defeat a governor's program even in special session, but their actions will be spotlighted.

VETOES   The governor's veto power is a major source of power within the legislature. Only in North Carolina does the governor have no veto power at all. In some states, the veto power is restricted by giving the governor only a short time to consider a bill after it has passed the legislature, by permitting a simple majority of legislative members to override the veto, or by requiring vetoed bills to reappear at the next legislative session. In other states, governors are given longer periods of time to consider a bill, and a two-thirds vote of both houses of the legislature is required to override a veto, rather than a simple majority. (See Table 7–5.)

The veto is often the governor's principal source of bargaining power in the legislature. Veto overrides by legislatures are rare. While the possibility of override gives the legislature "the last word" in theory, in practice few governors are so weak that they cannot garner at least one-third plus one of either house to sustain a veto. Only about 5 percent of bills passed by state legislatures are vetoed by governors, and governors are overridden on less than 10 percent of their vetoes. Of course vetoes are more common when a governor faces a legislature controlled by the opposition party.[13]

The *threat* of a veto may be a more important bargaining tool than the actual exercise of the veto. A governor can threaten to veto a bill with objectionable provisions before it reaches a floor vote. Governors can negotiate from a position of strength throughout the legislative process, shaping the bill to their preferences.

Occasionally legislatures may challenge governors to veto bills. This is more likely to occur with divided party control of state government—one party controls the legislature with a governor from the opposition party. The legislature can pass a popular bill opposed by the governor and then dare the governor to veto it. Even if the governor's veto is sustained, the majority party leaders in the legislature may feel they have created an issue for the next gubernatorial election. But this strategy usually guarantees a failure to get the bill enacted into law. Legislative leaders must decide whether they want the bill passed (for which they must bargain with the governor for his or her signature) or whether they want an issue for the next election.

ITEM VETO   Most governors also have the power to veto particular items in larger appropriations bills. This allows them to pick out particular legislative spending proposals (frequently labeled "turkeys" by unsympathetic governors) and veto those proposals without jeopardizing the entire budget. In states *without* the item veto, governors may be forced to accept many legislative spending proposals in order to get a budget passed.

The line-item veto can be a powerful weapon in the governor's arsenal. The line-item veto allows the governor to take legislators' pet budget items as hostage for their

■

Item veto.
The power of a governor to reject certain portions of a legislative appropriations bill without killing the entire bill.

Table 7–5

GOVERNORS' VETO POWERS

Votes Required to Override Veto			Line-Item Veto on Appropriations Bills	
2/3	3/5	MAJORITY	LINE-ITEM VETO	NO LINE-ITEM VETO
Alaska	Illinois	Alabama	Alabama	Indiana
Arizona	Maryland	Arkansas	Alaska	Iowa
California	Nebraska	Indiana	Arkansas	Maine
Colorado	Ohio	Kentucky	Arizona	Nevada
Connecticut	Rhode Island	Tennessee	California	New Hampshire
Delaware		West Virginia	Colorado	North Carolina
Florida			Connecticut	Rhode Island
Georgia			Delaware	Vermont
Hawaii			Florida	
Idaho			Georgia	
Iowa			Hawaii	
Kansas			Idaho	
Louisiana			Illinois	
Maine			Kansas	
Massachusetts			Kentucky	
Michigan			Louisiana	
Minnesota			Maryland	
Mississippi			Massachusetts	
Missouri			Michigan	
Montana			Minnesota	
Nevada			Mississippi	
New Hampshire			Missouri	
New Jersey			Montana	
New Mexico			Nebraska	
New York			New Jersey	
North Dakota			New Mexico	
Oklahoma			New York	
Oregon			North Dakota	
Pennsylvania			Ohio	
South Carolina			Oklahoma	
South Dakota			Oregon	
Texas			Pennsylvania	
Utah			South Carolina	
Vermont			South Dakota	
Virginia			Tennessee	
Washington			Texas	
Wisconsin			Utah	
Wyoming			Virginia	
			Washington	
			West Virginia	
			Wisconsin	
			Wyoming	

Source: Book of the States, 1998–99.

support on other unrelated legislation favored by the governor. Legislators who fail to support the governor risk losing their "turkeys." Trade-offs need not be explicit. Legislators who consistently oppose the governor's programs throughout the legislative session risk losing pork for their district when the governor goes through the appropriations acts line by line.

GOVERNOR–LEGISLATURE RELATIONS   For most governors, working with the legislature is considered the most difficult and demanding part of their job.[14] "Practically all governors regard their legislature as a problem and are happy when the legislature leaves town."[15] About half of all governors have had some legislative experience before becoming governor. They may have some friends and acquaintances left over from their legislature days. And they may have greater respect for the legislative branch and greater empathy with the concerns of legislators. But many governors have little sympathy or patience with the slow and complicated legislative process.

Frequently legislators resent the exalted role of the governor. As a New York legislator remarked about Governor Cuomo: "Relating to the governor is like relating to the Pope, except that the only thing you have to kiss on the Pope is his ring."[16] Legislatures do not want to appear to be pushed around by governors. Many legislators develop a loyalty to the institution itself; they wish to preserve the independence of the legislature.

What works with the legislature? Political scientist Alan Rosenthal provides some pointers. Governors should

Stand tall.   This entails not only the appearance of strength and decisiveness but a willingness to punish one's enemies.

Consult members.   Inform legislators of plans and programs and listen to their concerns.

Talk turkey.   Communicate in legislators' language of patronage and deals, give and take, reciprocity.

Rub elbows.   Stay in personal contact with legislators on a regular basis.

Massage egos.   Legislators like to share center stage with the governor, to be seen at bill signings, to be invited to dinner at the governor's mansion, to have the governor praise them in public.

DIVIDED GOVERNMENT: GOVERNOR VERSUS THE LEGISLATURE

Divided government, where one party controls one or both houses of the legislature and the other party controls the governorship, is increasingly frequent in American state politics. In recent years over half of the states have experienced divided party control (see Figure 7–1). The election of Republican governors in southern states with heavily Democratic legislatures helps to explain the increased occurrence of divided government in the states, as well as an increased tendency of voters everywhere to split their tickets. Republican governors are more likely to face Democratic-controlled leg-

■

Divided government.
A government in which one party controls the governor's office while another party controls one or both houses of the legislature.

FIGURE 7–1
Divided
Government in
the States

Source: National Conference
of State Legislatures.

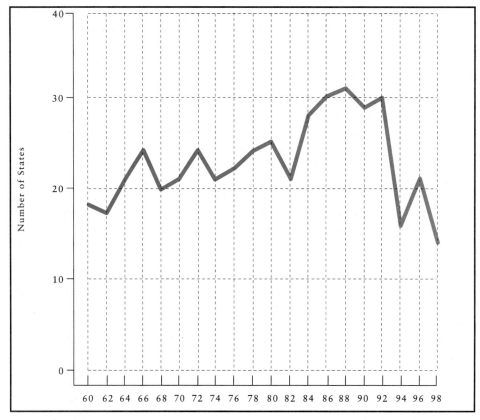

islatures than the reverse. But divided government itself has a major impact on executive-legislature relations.

PARTISANSHIP CUTS BOTH WAYS   Party works to the advantage of governors when their party has a majority in the legislature. The governor and a legislature controlled by the same party have an incentive to produce results. There is still institutional rivalry, wherein governors contend with legislatures for policy leadership. But both have an interest in compiling a record of success that the voters can attribute to everyone running under the party label in the next election.[17] But when partisan differences are added to institutional rivalry, conflict rather than cooperation is more likely to characterize relations between governor and legislature.

CONFRONTING GRIDLOCK   A governor confronting opposition party control of the legislature must spend a great deal of time bargaining and compromising with legislative leaders of the opposition party. Governors must ensure that they keep their own party's legislators behind their proposals and then either work out accommodations with the opposition leadership or try to chip off enough votes from less loyal opposition members to win passage of their proposals. Neither is an easy task. Party activists, including legislators, differ on ideological grounds and policy issues. Moreover, the opposing party looks forward to defeating the governor in the next election. Often one or more opposition party aspirants for the governorship are sitting in the legislature. They seek to discredit the governor, not only during the election campaign, but during his or her entire term of office. Often the opposition party in the legislature will prefer that a needed bill go down to defeat just to hurt the governor's reputation. Only a very able governor can avoid gridlock with divided party control of state government.

Impeachment.
The power of legislatures to remove executive and judicial officers from office for good cause; generally the lower house must first vote for impeachment, then the upper house must hold a trial and vote for removal.

IMPEACHMENTS AND INVESTIGATIONS

Impeachment is a *political* process, not a legal process. While state constitutions, like the U.S. Constitution, usually define an impeachable offense as "treason, bribery, or other high crimes and misdemeanors," the political errors of impeached officials are usually more important than their legal offenses.

IMPEACHMENT, TRIAL, AND REMOVAL   All state constitutions, except Oregon's, provide for the impeachment of elected state officials by the legislature. Impeachment proceedings are initiated in the lower houses of forty-seven states, in the unicameral legislature of Nebraska, and the upper house in Alaska. Impeachment trials are held in the upper houses in forty-five states, in a special court of impeachment in Nebraska, in the lower house in Alaska, in a special commission in Missouri, and in the senate and court of appeals in New York. Most states require a two-thirds vote to convict and remove an official.

These impeachment provisions are rarely used. There appear to have been only eighteen gubernatorial impeachments since the nation's birth and eight trial convictions. When Arizona Governor Evan Mecham was impeached and convicted by the state legislature in 1988, it was the first such event in nearly sixty years. (See "*Up Close: Arizona Impeaches Its Governor.*") Several other governors have resigned when threatened with impeachment.[18]

CRIMINAL INVESTIGATIONS   Criminal investigations have led to the demise of several governors. Former Tennessee Governor Ray Blanton was convicted in 1981 for crimes committed while in office; former Maryland Governor Marvin Mandel was convicted and later pardoned for crimes committed while in office. Governor Edwin Edwards of Louisiana was acquitted in 1986 in a criminal trial; the racketeering charges temporarily undermined his support with voters and he lost a close vote in the next gubernatorial election. However, in 1991 Edwards was again elected governor in a runoff against former Ku Klux Klan member David Duke. In 1993 Republican Governor Guy Hunt of Alabama was convicted of misusing inauguration funds by the state's Democratic attorney general. The state's constitution required removal from office of anyone convicted of a felony; Hunt was replaced by Jim Folsom, Jr., the son of former Alabama Governor "Big Jim" Folsom for whom the state's prison is named.

The lengthy "Whitewater" investigation, headed by special prosecutor Kenneth Starr and aimed principally at Bill and Hillary Clinton, swept Arkansas governor Jim Guy Tucker out of office in 1996. As lieutenant governor Tucker had succeeded

UP CLOSE

ARIZONA IMPEACHES ITS GOVERNOR

Arizona's flamboyant Governor Evan Mecham managed to offend virtually every important political interest group in his state in his first few months in office. Mecham was a staunchly conservative Mormon, a successful Phoenix automobile dealer, and a political maverick who had perennially entered his name in governors' races with little chance of success. But in 1986 he surprised everyone by defeating an established Republican opponent in the primary and then squeaking out a victory with only 39 percent of the vote in a three-way race in the general election. His political troubles began with his inauguration day announcement that he was cancelling the state's Martin Luther King, Jr. Day holiday.

Mecham's short-lived governorship was one long publicized "gaffe" after another. He publicly blamed working women for the high divorce rate; he told a Jewish audience that the United States was a Christian nation; and he ridiculed a petition by homosexuals to oust him. His appointments stirred additional controversy; they included a tax commissioner who had not filed his own state income tax and an education commissioner who testified that teachers should never contradict parents even if parents tell their children the world is flat. He embarrassed Republicans and enraged Democrats.

Less than a year after his election, a recall petition succeeded in getting the necessary 400,000 signatures, and a recall election was scheduled for 1988. In the meantime the state's attorney general indicted the governor on a series of campaign law violations. Before these charges came to trial, the state house of representatives initiated impeachment proceedings for "high crimes, misdemeanors, and maleficence in office." The state's senior Republican, former U.S. Senator Barry Goldwater, announced that "Mecham has got to go."

Mecham did not choose to go quietly, even after the house voted for impeachment. He defended himself at a bitter senate trial, during which he argued that he had committed no illegal acts and that the charges represented a vendetta against him by the press and his political enemies. Mecham was convicted by bipartisan votes (21–9 on one charge and 26–4 on another) in the senate and removed from office. The secretary of state, Rose Mofford, a Democrat, immediately succeeded him. The recall election was cancelled.

Later in criminal court, Mecham was acquitted of all of the charges of campaign law violations. The jury returned the verdict in less than three hours; several jurors reportedly hugged the ex-governor. There is little doubt that his impeachment and removal from office were political acts. Or, as the speaker of the Arizona house was later quoted as saying, "if Ed Mecham had just kept his damn mouth shut and used his brain and not been so stubborn, he would still be governor today."

Governor Bill Clinton in 1993 when Clinton had moved on to the White House. Earlier Tucker had been legal counsel to the failed Madison Guaranty Bank, which had lent money to the Whitewater development company, owned in part by Bill and Hillary Clinton. Tucker was convicted of fraud, sentenced to four years probation, and forced to resign his office. In 1988, he also pleaded guilty to income tax evasion.

THE GOVERNOR AS POLITICAL LEADER

The formal powers of governors are not the equivalent of political influence. Formal powers can only be translated into control over public policy, legislative output, and bureaucratic performance through a governor's use of his or her own political "clout." A landslide election that carries the governor's party into control of both houses of the legislature can overcome many formal weaknesses in a governor's powers. A politically resourceful governor enjoying widespread public popularity who can skillfully employ the media to his or her advantage can overcome many constitutional weaknesses in the office.

Governors spend more time meeting the general public, attending ceremonial functions, and working with the press and television than they do managing state government and working with the legislature. They focus on these public relations tasks not only to improve their chances for reelection, but also to give themselves the political clout to achieve their goals for state government. All fifty governors have press secretaries or public information offices, some with large staffs. Press conferences, policy announcements, and other media events are carefully orchestrated for maximum coverage in the nightly news and morning papers. Increasingly, state legislatures are creating their own media offices, but media coverage of state legislatures has traditionally been very sparse.

MEDIA ACCESS   Governors are the most visible figures in state politics. An attractive governor who is skillful in public relations can command support from administrators, legislators, local officials, and party leaders through public appeals to their constituents. Politicians must respect the governor's greater access to the communications media and hence to the minds of their constituents. Effective governors not only understand the broad range of issues facing their states but also are able to speak clearly and persuasively about them.

STATE MEDIA COVERAGE   However, press and television coverage of state government suffers a great deal of neglect.[19] Governors are far more visible in the media than state legislators, but the focus of the media—even local television news broadcasts—is on national events. In many states a majority of even *daily* newspapers do not have full-time reporters assigned to the state capital.

Overall, state media, like the national media, are biased in their partisan affiliation toward the Democratic party. Democratic governors generally get more positive coverage than Republican governors. But "media savvy"—skill in working with the media—is more important than partisan affiliation in winning good media coverage. A governor who "knows what's newsworthy," puts ideas across in brief "sound bites," makes timely use of widely reported events to get into the news, "hangs around the press area in the state capitol building," and cultivates good relationships with reporters is far more likely to garner favorable media stories than a governor who is "media shy," "tongue-tied," "standoffish," self-conscious, or who "hates the press," "blames the media," and thereby encourages an adversarial relationship with them.[20]

POPULARITY   Media access and the visibility it produces provide governors with the opportunity to promote their personal popularity with the citizens of the state. The legislature is seldom as popular as the governor. Even if individual legislators are popular in their districts, the legislature as an institution is rarely very popular. (See Figure 7–2.) Statewide opinion polls do not track governors' popularity as closely as national polls track the president of the United States. But opinion in most large states is regularly surveyed by private, university, and newspaper polls. All governors have press secretaries whose responsibility it is to develop and maintain a favorable media image for the governor. Many governors devote a great deal of their personal attention to this task—massaging the capital press, organizing media events, holding town meetings, traveling about the state, and so on. There may be some tendency for legislators and interest groups to avoid direct confrontations with a popular governor. Certainly a popular governor is in a better position to advance his or her program than an *un*popular governor. But the real problem is turning personal popularity into political power.

FIGURE 7-2
Governor and
Legislatures:
Popularity
Ratings in Florida
Q: "How would you
rate the job [governor]
[the Florida legisla-
ture] is doing?"
Percent saying excel-
lent or good, versus
fair or poor or don't
know.

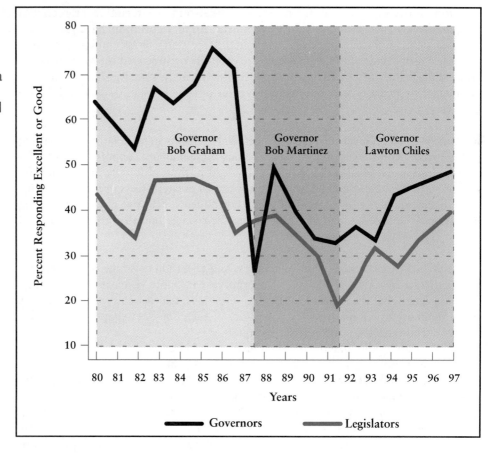

LEADERSHIP   Governors' reputations as leaders stem not only from what they say
but also from what they do. Their reputations must include a capacity to decide issues
and to persist in the decision once it is made. A reputation for backing down, for
avoiding situations that involve them in public conflict, or for wavering in the face of
momentary pressures invites the governors' adversaries to ignore or oppose them. A
sense of insecurity or weakness can damage a governor's power more than any constitutional limitation. Governors can also increase their influence by developing a reputation for punishing their adversaries and rewarding their supporters. Once the
reputation as an effective leader is established, cooperation is often forthcoming in an-
ticipation of the governor's reaction.

PARTY   Governors are also the recognized leaders of their state parties. In a majority
of states, it is the governor who picks the state party chairperson and who is consulted
on questions of party platform, campaign tactics, nominations for party office, and
party finances. The amount of power that a governor derives from the position of
party leader varies from state to state according to the strength, cohesion, and discipline of the state parties.

But there are limitations to the power that governors derive from their role as party leader. First of all, a governor cannot deny party renomination to disloyal members. Nominations are acquired in primary elections. Legislators must first consider the demands of their own constituents, not the voice of the governor. Second, the frequency of divided control, where governors face legislatures dominated by the opposition party, requires them to bargain with individuals and groups in the opposition party. If they have acquired a reputation for being too "partisan" in their approach to state programs, they will find it difficult to win over the necessary support of opposition party members. Finally, the use of patronage may make as many enemies as friends. There is an old political saying: "For every one patronage appointment, you make nine enemies and one ingrate."

EXPECTATIONS   It is difficult to generalize about the power of fifty state governors, especially when changes over time affect every state. Powerful governors (judged in terms of their accomplishments in office) may be followed by weak governors, even in the same state. Nevertheless, it is possible to offer a few generalizations from our studies.

First of all, governors, unlike legislators, are expected to *initiate* public policies. These policy initiatives are developed in messages, speeches, news releases, press conferences, public appearances, bills drafted by the governor's office or other executive agencies, and, most of all, in the state budget. The public *expects* governors to take the lead in solving state problems, whether they are really able to do anything about them or not.

Indeed, our second generalization is that governors do not really have sufficient powers in state government to deal effectively with the demands and expectations placed upon them. State constitutions not only divide power between the governor and legislature, but also divide the executive itself, with many separately elected officials.

OTHER EXECUTIVE OFFICES

LIEUTENANT GOVERNOR   The lieutenant governor's office in many states is looked upon as a campaign platform for the governorship. Lieutenant governors are said to have a four-year head start for the top job. The lieutenant governor's formal duties are comparable to those of the vice-president of the United States; in other words, lieutenant governors have relatively little to do. The two basic functions of the office are to serve in direct line of succession to the governor and replace him or her in the event of a vacancy in that office, and to be the presiding officer of the state senate. Since lieutenant governors generally have political ambitions of their own, they seldom make good "assistant governors" who will submerge their own interests for the success of the governor's administration. Unlike the vice-president, lieutenant governors are separately elected in most states and are sometimes members of the governor's opposition party. Some efforts have been made to reduce the boredom of the lieutenant governor's office by assigning them membership on various boards and commissions.[21]

ATTORNEY GENERAL   The office of attorney general has more real powers and responsibilities than that of the lieutenant governor. Attorneys general are elected in forty-three states, and appointed in the other states, usually by the governor. Attorneys general are the chief legal counsel for their states. They represent the state in any suits to which it is a party. They act as legal counsel for the governor and for other state officials. The legal business of state agencies is subject to their supervision. The source of the attorney general's power comes from the quasi-judicial duty of rendering formal written opinions in response to requests from the governor, state agencies, or other public officials regarding the legality and constitutionality of their acts. These opinions have the power of law in state affairs unless they are successfully challenged in court. The governor and other officials are generally obliged to conform to the attorney general's legal opinion until a court specifies otherwise. Attorneys general render authoritative interpretations of state constitutions, laws, city ordinances, and administrative rulings.

The attorney general also has substantial law enforcement powers. Most states allow attorneys general to initiate criminal proceedings on their own motion, and nearly all states assign them responsibility for handling criminal cases on appeal to higher state courts or to federal courts. In some states the attorney general has supervisory powers over law enforcement throughout the state.

TREASURERS, AUDITORS, AND COMPTROLLERS   Most states have elected *treasurers,* and treasurers in other states are appointed by either the governor or the legislature. Treasurers are custodians of state funds: collecting taxes, acting as paymaster for the state, and administering the investment of state funds. The principal job of the treasurer is to make payments on departmental requisitions for payrolls and for checks to be issued to those who have furnished the state with goods and services. Generally, the department's requests for checks must be accompanied by a voucher showing the proper legislative authority for such payment. Requests for payment usually are accompanied by a statement from the auditor's or the comptroller's office that legislative appropriations are available for such payment. Thus, the treasurer's office works in close relation to another executive office of importance: that of auditor or comptroller.

The principal duty of the office of state *auditor* is that of assuring the legislature that expenditures and investment of state funds have been made in accordance with the law. This function is known as a "postaudit" and occurs after state expenditures have been made.

The primary duty of the office of the state *comptroller* is to ensure that a prospective departmental expenditure is in accordance with the law and does not exceed the appropriations made by the legislature. This "preaudit" occurs before any expenditure is made by the treasurer. Public administration experts consider the comptroller's job of preaudit to be an executive function, and they urge that the comptroller be appointed by the governor. On the other hand, the job of postaudit is essentially a legislative check on the executive, and students of public administration generally feel that the auditor should be elected or appointed by the legislature. However, there is still some confusion in state organizations about the separate functions of auditors and comptrollers—some auditors do "preauditing" and some comptrollers do "postauditing."

SECRETARY OF STATE   Another interesting state office is that of secretary of state. Thirty-six states elect secretaries of state. Secretaries of state are the chief custodians of state records and, in the case of several states, "keepers of the great seal of the commonwealth." They keep many state documents filed in their office, including corporation papers. They also supervise the preparation of ballots and certify election results for the state. The keeping of documents and the supervision of elections does not involve much discretionary power, since these activities are closely regulated by law.

PERSONAL STAFF   All governors are permitted to maintain a small group of loyal, dedicated personal aides—the governor's staff. Many staff members previously worked in the governor's political campaign. Most work long hours in small offices for relatively low pay. Most are young. Most envision some sort of political career for themselves in the future; they believe the experience they are acquiring in the governor's office, and the contacts they are making, will help in their careers. The governor may have a chief of staff, an appointments secretary, a press secretary, a legal counsel, several speechwriters, one or more legislative aides, and perhaps some advisors in key policy areas—education, welfare, highways. These people are *not* civil service employees; their jobs depend directly on their value to the governor.

ON THE WEB

The Office of the Governor in each state maintains its own Web site. These sites can be accessed through each state's governmental home page (see "On the Web" in Chapter 3). Usually the governor's Web site includes a flattering biography of the governor, statements and policy positions of the governor, and links to state executive departments and agencies.

The best source of comparative information on governors in all fifty states is the National Governors Association Web site:

www.nga.org

This site includes the latest news releases and policy positions of the National Governors Association. Perhaps more important, it provides biographical information on each governor in a comparative format, and it also offers complete texts of the latest inaugural addresses and/or state-of-the-state addresses of each governor.

NOTES

1. Center for the American Woman and Politics, Rutgers University, 1998.

2. Peverill Squire and Christina Fastnow, "Comparing Gubernatorial and Senatorial Elections," *Political Research Quarterly,* 47 (September 1994), 703–20.

3. See Robert M. Stein, "Economic Voting for Governor and U.S. Senator," *Journal of Politics,* 52 (February 1990), 29–53.

4. John E. Chubb, "Institutions, the Economy and the Dynamics of State Elections," *American Political Science Review,* 82 (March 1988), 151. However, for contrary evidence showing that retrospective evaluations of a state's economy affects voter choice, see Craig J. Svoboda,

"Retrospective Voting in Gubernatorial Elections," *Political Research Quarterly,* 48 (March 1995), 117–34; Richard G. Niemi, Harold W. Stanley, and Ronald J. Vogel, "State Economies and State Taxes: Do Voters Hold Governors Accountable," *American Journal of Political Science,* 39 (November 1995), 936–57.

5. Dennis M. Simon, "Presidents, Governors and Electoral Accountability," *Journal of Politics,* 51 (May 1989), 286–304; Thomas M. Holbrook-Provow, "National Factors in Gubernatorial Elections," *American Politics Quarterly,* 15 (October 1987), 471–83.

6. Andrew D. McNitt and Jim Seroka, "Intraparty Challenges of Incumbent Governors and

Senators," *American Politics Quarterly,* 9 (July 1981), 321–40.

7. Peverill Squire and Christina Fastnow, "Comparing Gubernatorial and Senatorial Elections," *Political Research Quarterly,* 47 (September 1994), 703–20.

8. Susan L. Kane and Richard F. Winters, "Taxes and Voting: Electoral Retribution in the American States," *Journal of Politics,* 55 (February 1993), 22–40.

9. Patrick J. Kenney, "The Effect of State Economic Conditions on the Vote for Governor," *Social Science Quarterly,* 64 (March 1983), 154–62.

10. Alan Rosenthal, *Governors and Legislatures: Contending Powers* (Washington, DC: Congressional Quarterly Press, 1990), p. 170.

11. F. Ted Hebert, Jeffrey L. Brudney, and Deil S. Wright, "Gubernatorial Influence and State Bureaucracy," *American Politics Quarterly,* 11 (April 1983), 243–44.

12. See Keith J. Muller, "Explaining Variation and Change in Gubernatorial Power," *Western Political Quarterly,* 85 (September 1985), 424–31.

13. Charles Wiggins, "Executive Vetoes and Legislative Overrides in the American States," *Journal of Politics,* 42 (November 1980), 1110–17.

14. Thad Beyle and Robert Dalton, *Being Governor: The View from the Office* (Durham, NC: Duke University Press, 1983), p. 135.

15. Rosenthal, *Governors and Legislatures,* p. 69.

16. Ibid., pp. 47, 294, 296–98.

17. See Kevin M. Leyden and Stephen A. Borrelli, "The Effect of State Economic Conditions on Gubernatorial Elections: Does Unified Government Make a Difference?" *Political Research Quarterly,* 48 (June 1995), 275–90.

18. *Book of the States, 1988–89,* p. 27. Other twentieth-century impeachments and removals include New York Governor William Sulzer in 1913; Oklahoma Governor John Walton in 1923; and Oklahoma Governor Henry S. Johnson in 1929.

19. William T. Gormley, "Coverage of State Government in the Mass Media," *State Government,* 52 (December 1979), 46–51.

20. Thad Beyle, G. Patrick Lynch, and Donald Ostdiek, "Perceptions of the State Media." Paper presented at the Annual Meeting of the Southern Political Science Association, Atlanta, Georgia, 1994.

21. For a review of a lieutenant governor's functions, see Daniel G. Cox, "The Subterranean Influence of Lieutenant Governors." Paper presented at the Midwest Political Science Association Meeting, Chicago, 1993.

8

BUREAUCRATIC POLITICS IN STATES AND COMMUNITIES

CHAPTER 8

GOVERNMENT AND BUREAUCRACY

Bureaucracy.
Departments, agencies, bureaus, and offices that perform the functions of government.

Implementation.
The development by executive bureaucracies of procedures and activities to carry out policies enacted by the legislature.

Political conflict does not necessarily end after the state legislature passes a law or the city council enacts an ordinance. Dedicated opponents of a law not only regroup to fight for repeal by the legislative body, but they also turn their attention to the bureaucracy, hoping to delay, modify, or even cripple the implementation of the law. Dedicated supporters of the law must also turn to the bureaucracy to ensure the law's prompt implementation and strict enforcement. Over time, bureaucrats themselves come to exercise considerable power in state and local politics.

In popular conversation, "bureaucracy" has come to mean red tape, needless paperwork, waste and inefficiency, senseless regulations, impersonality, and unresponsiveness to the needs of people. And indeed bureaucracy is all of that. But its true meaning is simply a "rational" way for an organization to go about carrying out its tasks. Bureaucracies may be governmental or corporate or military. All that is required for an organization to be a bureaucracy is

- A chain of command in which authority flows downward;
- A division of labor in which workers specialize in their tasks;
- Clear lines of responsibility;
- Specific organizational goals; and
- Impersonal treatment of all persons equally and according to rules.

There are more than 16 million state and local government employees in the nation. (There are also 2.8 million federal employees.) About 5 million of these employees work directly for state governments; about 11 million work for counties, cities, school districts, townships, and special districts (see Chapter 10, "Community Political Systems"). Bureaucracies organize these people to perform the many tasks of governments.

SOURCES OF BUREAUCRATIC POWER

In theory, government bureaucracies, whether at the federal, state, or local level, do *not* make policy. Rather, they are created to implement policies passed by legislative bodies. But in practice, government bureaucracies do engage in policy making as they go about their tasks. How do bureaucrats exercise power and why has their power grown over the years?

IMPLEMENTATION Implementation is the development of procedures and activities to carry out policies enacted by the legislative body. It may involve creating new agencies or bureaus or assigning new responsibilities to old agencies. It often requires bureaucracies to translate laws into operational rules and regulations and usually to allocate resources—money, personnel, offices, supplies—to the new function. All of these tasks involve decisions by bureaucrats—decisions that drive how the law will actually affect society.

Implementation is the continuation of policy making. For example, bureaucrats may delay the development of regulations based on a new law, assign enforcement responsibility to existing offices with other higher-priority tasks, and allocate few people with limited resources to the task. Or alternatively, bureaucrats may act promptly in making new regulations, insist on strict enforcement, assign responsibilities to newly created aggressive offices with no other assignments, and allocate a great deal of staff time and agency resources to the task. Interested groups have a strong stake in these decisions, and they actively seek to influence the bureaucracy.

REGULATION   Regulation is the development of formal rules for implementing legislation. State agencies charged with the task of regulating various activities—for example, environmental protection, business and professional codes, banking and insurance regulations, consumer affairs, public utilities, and so forth—must develop and publish very specific (and sometimes very lengthy) sets of rules. Most states require that proposed new regulations be published in advance of any action, that hearings be held to allow individuals and groups to comment on the proposed new regulations, and that new regulations be formally published prior to implementation. This process is designed to allow all interested parties the chance to help shape the actual rules that set policy.

ADJUDICATION   Adjudication is bureaucratic decision making about individual cases. While regulation resembles the legislative process, adjudication resembles the judicial process. In adjudication, bureaucrats must decide whether an individual or firm is failing to comply with laws or regulations and, if so, what penalties or corrective actions are to be applied. Bureaucrats can decide to hold individuals strictly accountable to rules, to impose heavy penalties, or to mandate expensive corrective actions. Alternatively, they can interpret the rules loosely and allow individuals or firms that violate rules to get off lightly.

DISCRETION   Bureaucrats almost always have some discretion in performing even the most routine tasks. Discretion is greatest in cases that do not exactly fit established rules, or when more than one rule might be applied to the same case, resulting in different outcomes. Bureaucrats may be courteous, helpful, and accommodating to citizens; or alternatively, impersonal, unhelpful, and even downright frustrating.

BUREAUCRATIC GOALS   Bureaucrats generally believe strongly in the value of their programs and the importance of their tasks. But beyond these public-spirited motives, bureaucrats, like everyone else, seek added power and prestige for themselves. These public and private motives converge to inspire them to seek to expand their authority, functions, and budgets. (Rarely do bureaucrats request a reduction in their authority, the elimination of the program under their direction, or a decrease in their agency's budget.) Rather, over time, bureaucrats help to expand governmental functions and increase governmental spending.

Regulation.
The development by the bureaucracy of formal rules for implementing legislation.

Adjudication.
Decision making by bureaucracies as to whether or not an individual or organization has complied with or violated government laws and/or regulations.

THE GROWTH OF BUREAUCRATIC POWER

Bureaucracies at all levels of government—federal, state, and local—have grown over time. Several explanations have been offered for this growth.

SOCIETAL COMPLEXITY   One standard explanation for the growth of bureaucratic power cites advances in technology and increases in the size and complexity of society. Governors and legislators must delegate more and more authority to experts who have the time, energy, and knowledge to handle the details of policy making. Elected officials cannot be expected to deal with the myriad details of environmental protection, insurance and banking regulations, law enforcement, highway planning and construction, university governance, school curriculum, and so forth. They must, therefore, create bureaucracies, appropriate money to run them, and authorize them to draw the rules and regulations that actually govern us.

POLITICAL ADVANTAGE   It is not uncommon for elected officials to deliberately pass vague and ambiguous laws, allowing them to demonstrate their concern for problems confronting their states or communities, but without actually deciding how to solve the problems. Legislators can express lofty goals in legislation yet avoid controversies surrounding the actual attainment of these goals. Bureaucrats must give practical meaning to the symbolic measures passed by politicians. If bureaucratic implementation to enforce laws proves unpopular, elected politicians can blame the bureaucrats and avoid direct responsibility themselves for the failure of legislation.

BUREAUCRATIC EXPANSIONISM   As noted earlier, bureaucrats themselves have both public and personal motives to expand their own authority, increase the amount of money they can spend, and augment the number of employees under their supervision.

INCREMENTALISM   Bureaucracies expand because governmental decision making is incremental. By that we mean that each year bureaucrats and elected officials focus on proposed *new* programs and policies and *increases* in budgets and personnel. Existing policies, programs, agencies, or expenditures are seldom reviewed as a whole each year. Doing so would require far too much time and energy, simply to confirm decisions that had been made in previous years. But over time the effect of incremental decision making is to expand the size of bureaucracies, as new programs and new spending are authorized while old programs and previous spending levels are seldom reconsidered.

■
Incrementalism.
In government budget making, the tendency of bureaucrats and elected officials to focus on new programs and increases in spending, while seldom reviewing existing programs or previous levels of spending.

STATE BUREAUCRACIES

State governments in America spend most of their money on (1) education, (2) welfare, (3) health, (4) highways, and (5) corrections, in that order. (See Figure 8–1.) State departments and agencies responsible for these functions are usually the largest bureau-

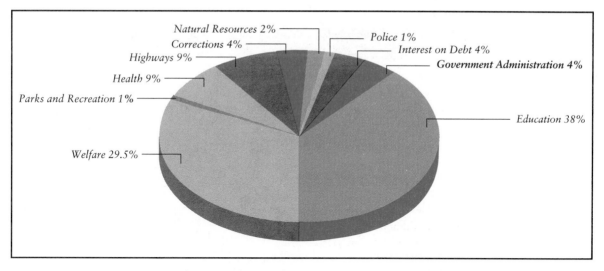

FIGURE 8–1 State Government Expenditures by Function

cracies at the state capital. However, the authoritative *Book of the States* lists forty-six separate bureaucratic functions in state governments:

Adjutant general	Emergency management	Parks and recreation
Administration	Energy	Personnel
Agriculture	Environment	Planning
Banking	Finance	Postaudit
Budget	Fish and game	Preaudit
Civil rights	General services	Public library
Commerce	Health	Public utility regulation
Community affairs	Highways	Purchasing
Comptroller	Historic preservation	Revenue
Consumer affairs	Information systems	Social services
Corrections	Insurance	Solid waste
Economic development	Labor relations	State police
Education, higher	Licensing	Tourism
Education, public schools	Mental health	Transportation
Elections administration	Natural resources	Welfare
Employment services		

Not all states have separate agencies for each of these functions; on the contrary, many functions are combined in larger departments.

ORGANIZATIONAL DISARRAY   The executive branches of virtually all state governments in the United States are fragmented, complex, and unwieldy. These organizational problems arise, first of all, as a result of the separate election of many statewide officials—for example, attorney general, secretary of state, treasurer, comptroller, su-

Table 8–1

ELECTED EXECUTIVE OFFICIALS IN THE STATES	
Governor	50
Lieutenant Governor	42
Attorney General	43
State Treasurer	38
Secretary of State	36
State Auditor	25
Superintendent of Education	16
Agriculture Commissioner	8
Public Service Commission	9
Controller	10
Insurance Commissioner	8
Land Commissioner	5
Labor Commissioner	5
University Regents	5
Education Board	11
Railroad Commission	2
Others	
Corporation Commissioner	Arizona
Mine Inspector	Arizona
Elections Commissioner	Louisiana
Highway Commissioner	Mississippi
Tax Commissioner	North Dakota
Adjutant	South Carolina

Source: Book of the States, 1998–99.

perintendent of education, and others (see Table 8–1). There are more than 300 separately elected executive-branch officials in all the states. Only four states—Maine, New Hampshire, New Jersey, and Tennessee—have a single statewide elected executive, the governor, who heads the executive branch of government.

Organizational problems also arise as a result of the extensive use of boards and commissions throughout the states to head executive departments. Appointments to these boards and commissions are often for long terms and members cannot be removed except for "cause"—proven misconduct in office. Governors can rarely remove the members of these independent entities for their policy decisions, no matter how at odds these decisions may be with the governors' preferences.

The proliferation of separately elected executive officers in the states as well as independent boards and commissions creates very messy organizational charts for state governments. Florida presents an especially complex and fragmented executive branch structure (see Figure 8–2), but many other states also suffer organizational disarray.

EXECUTIVE REORGANIZATION   Modern public administration generally recommends a stronger governor and a more centralized state executive branch. Reform and

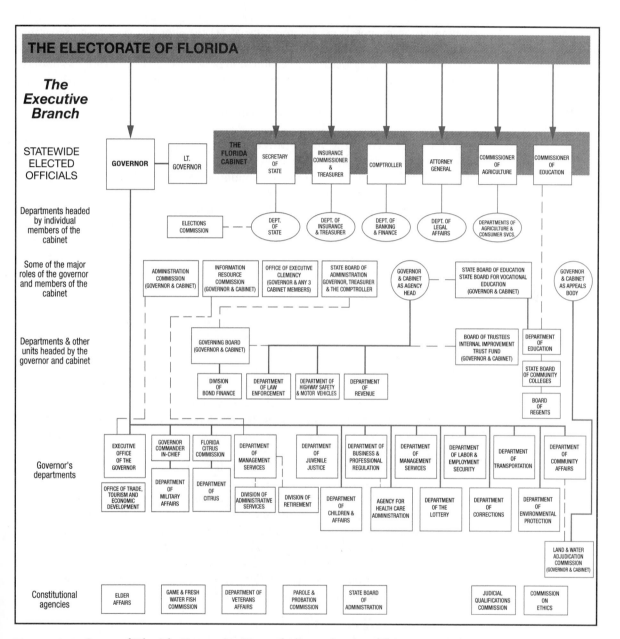

FIGURE 8–2 State of Florida Executive Branch Organization Chart

■
Bureaucratization.
A general reference to the size of government, often measured by spending per capita and public employment per 10,000 population.

reorganization proposals usually recommend (1) the elimination of many separately elected state executive officials and limiting the statewide ballot to governor, lieutenant governor, and attorney general; (2) elimination of boards and commissions as heads of agencies and their replacement by single, removable gubernatorial appointees; and (3) the consolidation of many state agencies into larger departments reporting directly to the governor. However, states have been slow to adopt these reforms.

POLITICAL OPPOSITION TO REORGANIZATION   Separately elected officials and independent boards and officials will be around for a long time. Political parties and public officials develop a stake in the continued existence of these elected offices. Moreover, many interest groups prefer to be governed by boards and commissions or separately elected officials. They feel they have more influence over these independent offices than those that come directly under a governor's authority. Interest groups, from educational administrators and teachers' unions, to the agriculture, insurance, real estate, and public utility industries, prefer to have direct access to executive officials. Incumbent officeholders are usually able to rally their client groups to defeat reorganization proposals that threaten their office.

VARIATIONS IN BUREAUCRACY AMONG THE STATES   Bureaucracies are frequently measured by how much money they spend and how many people they employ. As we would expect, states with larger populations spend more money and employ more people than states with smaller populations. Perhaps "bureaucratization" might be better measured by state and local spending per capita and state and local employment per 10,000 population. These measures control for population size and tell us how large a part state and local government spending and employment play relative to the population of each state (see "*Rankings of the States:* Government Spending and Employment," pp. 236–37).

Populous states require big bureaucracies. It is no surprise that California, New York, Texas, Florida, and Pennsylvania, the nation's five largest states in terms of population, spend more money and employ more people than other states. However, when population size is controlled, it turns out that the largest states are not necessarily the biggest spenders. In terms of spending, New York ranks second, California ranks ninth, while Pennsylvania is twentieth, Florida thirty-eighth, and Texas forty-second.

Nor are these states necessarily the most "bureaucratized" in terms of government employment in relation to their populations. California and Pennsylvania rank as the least bureaucratized states according to this measure.

BUREAUCRACY, DEMOCRACY, AND RESPONSIVENESS

How can we overcome the "bankruptcy of bureaucracy"—the waste, inefficiency, impersonality, and unresponsiveness of large government organizations? How can democratic governments overcome the "routine tendency to protect turf, to resist change, to build empires, to enlarge one's spheres of control, to protect programs regardless of whether or not they are any longer needed?"[1] Should governments be staffed by people politically loyal and responsive to elected officials? Or should governments be staffed by nonpartisan people selected on the basis of merit and protected from political influence?

THE PATRONAGE SYSTEM   Historically, government employment in states, counties, and cities was allocated by the patronage system. Jobs were handed out on the basis of party loyalty, electoral support, political influence, personal friendships, family ties, and financial contributions, rather than on the basis of job-related qualifications.

Although widely condemned by reformers, the traditional patronage system helped to strengthen political parties. It helped organize voters and motivated them to go to the polls. It maintained discipline within a party's ranks. Patronage was a central component of political "machines" and a source of power for political "bosses" (see "Old Style Machine Politics" in Chapter 11).

Patronage was also a major source of power for state governors. As late as the 1960s almost half of all state jobs were filled by the governor or the governor's patronage advisors from the ranks of "deserving" party workers. Party organizations were sustained with jobs in tax collection, licensing, parks, commerce, agriculture, welfare, and especially highways. The governor's office would "clear" appointments with party county chairpersons throughout the state, and patronage appointees were expected to work for the party organization at election time. Often state patronage employees held party posts themselves. Patronage was especially widespread in the older, two-party states of the East and Midwest.

THE MERIT SYSTEM   The merit system—government employment based on competence, neutrality, and protection from partisanship—was introduced at the federal level in the Pendleton Act of 1883. This act created the federal Civil Service Commission (now called the Office of Personnel Management) for selecting government personnel based on merit. That same year New York became the first state to enact a merit system. Yet for many years only a few states adopted merit systems, and even in those states only a small proportion of government employees came under civil service protection.

But over time the merit system came to replace patronage as the principal means of staffing state and local government. In 1939 Congress amended the Social Security Act of 1935 to require states to set up merit systems in welfare and unemployment compensation agencies that received federal grants-in-aid. Gradually the states expanded their merit systems to encompass most of their employees.

In some states nearly all state workers are covered by civil service, and patronage is limited to boards, commissioners, policy-making offices, university trusteeships, and judicial posts. The patronage system was always awkward to administer; many lower-paid menial jobs were unattractive to party workers. As the influence of parties declined in electoral politics (see "American Political Parties in Disarray" in Chapter 5), governors themselves came to view patronage systems as more of a burden than a benefit to their administrations. Reform governors capitalized on the public's image of patronage as corrupt, and they gradually expanded civil service coverage. Finally, the federal courts began to strike at patronage systems with decisions preventing governments from firing their employees for partisan political reasons.[2]

■
Patronage system.
Selection of employees for government agencies on the basis of political loyalty and electoral support.

Merit system.
Selection of employees for government agencies on the basis of competence, with no consideration of an individual's political loyalties or support.

GOVERNMENT SPENDING AND EMPLOYMENT

Total State and Local Expenditures
(in millions of dollars)

Total State and Local Expenditures
per Capita (in dollars)

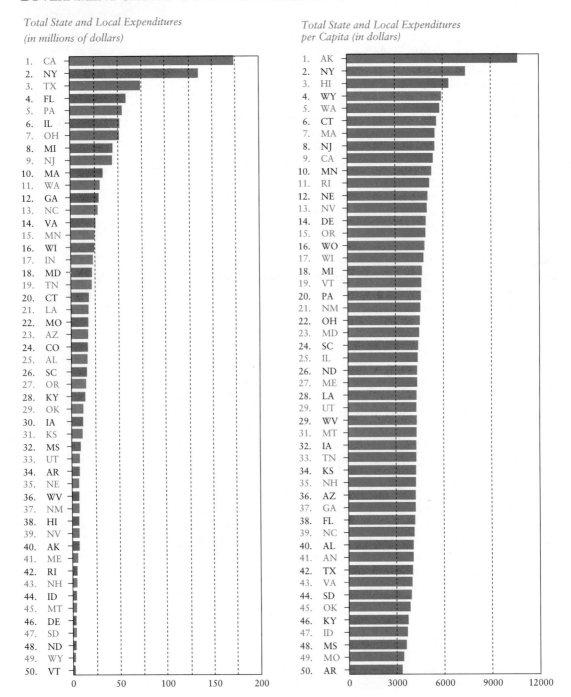

Source: Derived from U.S. Bureau of the Census, Government Finances, 1993–94 (1997).

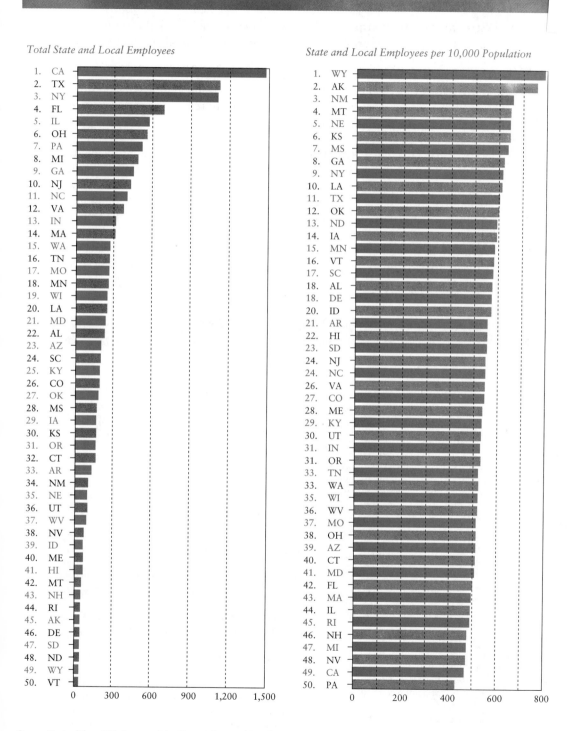

Total State and Local Employees

1.	CA
2.	TX
3.	NY
4.	FL
5.	IL
6.	OH
7.	PA
8.	MI
9.	GA
10.	NJ
11.	NC
12.	VA
13.	IN
14.	MA
15.	WA
16.	TN
17.	MO
18.	MN
19.	WI
20.	LA
21.	MD
22.	AL
23.	AZ
24.	SC
25.	KY
26.	CO
27.	OK
28.	MS
29.	IA
30.	KS
31.	OR
32.	CT
33.	AR
34.	NM
35.	NE
36.	UT
37.	WV
38.	NV
39.	ID
40.	ME
41.	HI
42.	MT
43.	NH
44.	RI
45.	AK
46.	DE
47.	SD
48.	ND
49.	WY
50.	VT

0   300   600   900   1,200   1,500

State and Local Employees per 10,000 Population

1.	WY
2.	AK
3.	NM
4.	MT
5.	NE
6.	KS
7.	MS
8.	GA
9.	NY
10.	LA
11.	TX
12.	OK
13.	ND
14.	IA
15.	MN
16.	VT
17.	SC
18.	AL
18.	DE
20.	ID
21.	AR
22.	HI
23.	SD
24.	NJ
24.	NC
26.	VA
27.	CO
28.	ME
29.	KY
30.	UT
31.	IN
31.	OR
33.	TN
33.	WA
35.	WI
36.	WV
37.	MO
38.	OH
39.	AZ
40.	CT
41.	MD
42.	FL
43.	MA
44.	IL
45.	RI
46.	NH
47.	MI
48.	NV
49.	CA
50.	PA

0   200   400   600   800

Source: Derived from U.S. Bureau of the Census, *State and Local Government Employment, 1995.*

■

Bureaucratic "culture."
Support within an agency
for its own function and for
its clients and the pay, perks,
and security of its employees.

Productivity.
In government, performing
functions and producing desired results at the least possible cost to taxpayers.

BUREAUCRATIC "CULTURES"   Bureaucracies often develop their own "cultures," usually in strong support of the function they serve, their client interest group, and of course, their own pay, perks, and job security.

Government agencies become dominated by people who have worked there for most of their lives. They believe that their work is important, and they resist efforts by governors, legislators, mayors, and council members to reduce the authority, size, or budget of their agency.

THE PROBLEM OF PRODUCTIVITY   Another troublesome problem in federal, state, and local bureaucracies is that of insuring productivity—producing desired results at the least possible cost to taxpayers. Civil service employees suffer a popular reputation for inefficiency. Government executives often find it difficult to improve job performance because of the obstacles to rewarding or punishing public employees. Seldom can good performance be rewarded with raises or bonuses as in private employment. And, at the same time, poor performance often goes unpunished. It is very difficult to fire a public employee (see *"Up Close:* Firing a Public Employee"). Often a state executive confronting a poorly performing employee must spend more than a

UP CLOSE

FIRING A PUBLIC EMPLOYEE

It is not impossible to fire the poorly performing state employee. But it takes a lot of managerial skill and tenacity.

It is a common perception that public employees cannot be fired for incompetence, that civil service protections, union contracts, court decisions, and smart lawyers can keep even the worst state and city employee on the public payroll. And, indeed, it is true that the involuntary discharge rate for public employees is estimated to be well below 1 percent, compared to 10 percent for privately employed service workers. But if government executives follow specific processes for firing a truly poor-performing employee, they can do so. This means successfully negotiating a myriad of legal constraints, contract provisions, published regulations, appeals, and other assorted hoops and hurdles. For example, typically the following steps are required to fire a state or city employee:

1. The employee is given a notice of disciplinary termination.
2. The employee has 15 to 30 days to respond.
3. If the employee responds, the agency must schedule a hearing before an uninterested officer.
4. The decision of the hearing officer following the hearing may be appealed by the employee to the personnel or civil service board.
5. The employee is entitled to legal counsel during all phases of the process. Unionized em-

ployees are often provided free counsel by their union.
6. Personnel boards frequently have lengthy backlogs. They review written appeals, hold hearings, listen to testimony, and often delay their final decisions for many months. Normally the employee remains on the public payroll during this time.
7. The decisions of the personnel board may be appealed to state or federal courts, which may under some circumstances issue an injunction against firing the employee until after the case is fully resolved.

A common problem in firing a public employee is the manager's failure to maintain a written record of poor performance. Or worse yet, the manager may have previously provided regular satisfactory job evaluations. Having checked "satisfactory" on previous standardized forms, perhaps in haste or to avoid conflict, the manager is in a poor position to later fire an employee for unsatisfactory performance. Government managers must carefully document poor job performance over time, logging in absences, tardiness, insubordination, incompetence, and so forth each time these offenses occur. Managers must communicate with errant employees after each and every offense and give them some opportunity to improve their performance. Most important, managers must carefully follow all procedural rules and regulations set forth in state laws, city ordinances, personnel manuals, and union contracts.

year in extended proceedings to secure a dismissal. As a result, sometimes costly substitute strategies are devised, for example, transferring nonperforming employees to other agencies or taking away their responsibilities while letting them keep their jobs.

CENTRALIZED PERSONNEL MANAGEMENT   Today virtually all states (Texas is a notable exception) have centralized personnel management systems that purport to function under the merit principle. State personnel offices are generally responsible for recruitment and testing of prospective employees. The personnel offices classify jobs in state government and determine the qualifications needed to perform them. They establish uniform pay and compensation systems, oversee performance evaluations, assist and counsel employees, and hear complaints and appeals from employees who have been disciplined.

But the merit system is frequently circumvented in states and cities across the nation. Very few people ever get hired by taking a state or city civil service examination and then waiting to be called for an interview by an agency. Most bureaucratic hiring actually comes about through "networks" of personal friends and professional associates. Agency insiders contact their friends and associates when they know a position will become vacant. Thus, some candidates know about openings well before they appear on any list of vacant positions published by the central personnel office. They can apply early and tailor their applications to the official job description. Personnel offices usually send three or more names of qualified people to an agency with a vacancy; the agency itself usually makes the final employment decision. Network recruiting generally insures that new people entering a bureaucracy will share the same values and attitudes of people already there.

Moreover, civil service systems, particularly those administered by independent civil service commissions, significantly reduce executive control over program administration. There is a persistent tendency for civil service systems to be routine, mechanical, and unimaginative. Job classification schemes, to which recruitment, qualifications, and pay scales are closely tied, become so rigid with time that executives have little flexibility in recruiting really talented people to state government. Executives whose authority to promote, hire, and fire their employees is severely curtailed can hardly be expected to obtain maximum effort and cooperation from their employees.

THE PROBLEM OF REPRESENTATIVENESS   Democratic governments generally seek to insure a representative bureaucracy. This means the recruitment and employment of a work force that generally reflects the social composition of the population being served. It is believed that a representative work force will reflect the values and interests of the people it serves and will be responsive to their problems and concerns. Moreover, a representative work force provides symbolic evidence of a government "of the people, by the people, and for the people."

Protection against discrimination based on race, gender, age, physical handicap, and other factors unrelated to job performance is embodied in the Civil Rights Act of 1964, the Age Discrimination Act of 1973, and the Americans with Disabilities Act of 1990, as well as the Fourteenth Amendment to the U.S. Constitution.

But how can state and local governments go about insuring representativeness of their work forces without compromising the merit principle? Should state and local

■
Networking.
The use of personal friendships and professional associations to advance one's career.

Representativeness.
As applied to public bureaucracies, the extent to which their work forces generally reflect the social characteristics of the citizens they serve.

■
Affirmative action programs.
In government agencies, efforts to achieve minority and gender representativeness in the work force through preferential hiring and promotion.

Collective bargaining.
The determination of wages, benefits, and working conditions through bargaining with unions that represent employees.

governments extend preferential treatment to minority job applicants in order to achieve a representative work force?

Affirmative action programs were initially developed in the federal bureaucracy. Affirmative action programs seek to achieve minority and gender representativeness in the work force through preferential hiring and promotion schemes designed to redress perceived imbalances. Virtually all state and local governments in the United States today have affirmative action programs.

The constitutional question posed by affirmative action programs is whether or not they discriminate against nonminorities in violation of the Equal Protection Clause of the Fourteenth Amendment. (We shall explore this topic in more detail in Chapter 14, "Politics and Civil Rights.") The Supreme Court has generally approved of affirmative action programs when there is evidence of past discriminatory employment practices. However, the Court has also held that race-based actions by government—any differences in treatment of the races by public agencies—must be found necessary to remedy past proven discrimination, or to further clearly identified, compelling, and legitimate government objectives. Moreover, race-based actions must be "narrowly tailored" so as not to adversely affect the rights of nonminority individuals.

Overall, state and local government employment in the United States is fairly representative of the general population. About 44 percent of the public work force is female (compared to 51 percent of the population), 19 percent of the work force is African American (compared to 12 percent of the population), and 7 percent is Hispanic (compared to 9 percent of the population). But these figures vary widely by occupational category (see Table 8–2). Today, African Americans and Hispanics are fairly well represented nationwide among firefighters, police officers, correctional guards, and technicians and among the support, service, and maintenance jobs. But they are still somewhat underrepresented among higher officials and administrators.

Women and minority employment at all levels of state and local government exceeds that in the private sector work force.

THE POWER OF PUBLIC EMPLOYEE UNIONS

Unions among public employees further complicate executive control of the bureaucracy. Today, over one-third of all state and local government employees are unionized. The largest public employee union in the states is the American Federation of State, County, and Municipal Employees (AFSCME). Collective bargaining agreements between state and local governments and public employee unions usually stipulate salaries and wages, pensions and benefits, grievance procedures, and seniority. These restrict executive authority over dismissals, layoffs, reorganization, elimination of positions, merit and incentive pay plans, and other actions affecting public employees.

Indeed, unionization of public employees continues to grow, while unions in the private sector have shrunk (see Figure 8–3).

COLLECTIVE BARGAINING   Most state laws today recognize the right of public employees to organize unions and bargain collectively with state and local governments

Table 8–2

WOMEN AND MINORITIES IN STATE AND LOCAL GOVERNMENT EMPLOYMENT			
	Percent of Total Employed		
	WOMEN	AFRICAN AMERICANS	HISPANICS
Total	44.3	18.7	7.1
Categories			
Officials/Administrators	32.8	10.3	4.0
Professionals	52.5	13.9	5.2
Technicians	42.0	14.7	7.1
Protective services	15.2	17.2	7.4
Support services	86.7	20.2	8.8
Service/Maintenance	22.1	32.2	10.2
Occupations			
Social workers	68.5	22.6	7.7
Firefighters	2.1	13.5	5.6
Police officers	15.8	16.0	8.2
Correctional guards	17.3	24.1	9.2

Source: Statistical Abstract of the United States, 1993, p. 322.

over wages, hours, and conditions of work. However, only a handful of states continue to resist collective bargaining with public employees (including Arizona, Colorado, Utah, Arkansas, Louisiana, Mississippi, North Carolina, South Carolina, and Virginia). Public employees everywhere have a constitutional right to *join* a union, but governments are not required by federal laws or the U.S. Constitution to *bargain* with them. Nevertheless, nearly 50 percent of all state and local government employees are covered by collective bargaining agreements.

STRIKES   In contrast to *private* employees, *public* employees are generally prohibited by law from striking. Instead, most state laws stipulate that public employee labor disputes are to go to arbitration—that is, be submitted to neutral third parties for decision. Decisions of arbitrators (or arbitration boards consisting of equal representation from employees and employers, together with neutral members) may or may not be binding on both the city and union, depending on specific provisions of each state's laws. However, many public employee unions throughout the country have rendered "no-strike" laws practically useless in a heated labor dispute. Police, firefighters, teachers, sanitation workers, and others have struck in many large cities, and there have been statewide strikes as well. Unions can nullify no-strike laws by simply adding another demand—no legal prosecution of strikers or union leaders—as a condition of going back to work.

FIGURE **8–3**
Unionization of
Public versus
Private Employees

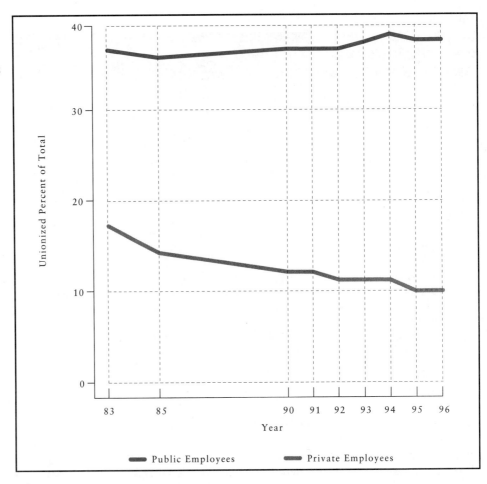

WAGES AND BENEFITS   State and local employees, who for generations were paid wages below those for comparable jobs in private enterprise, now at least match private employees in salaries, benefits, pensions, and so on. Theoretically, public employee unions should be very effective in raising wages. It might be reasoned that: (1) Elected government officials are less constrained than private employers by profit and loss considerations, and more likely to grant union demands; and (2) unlike employees in the private sector, public employees participate in electing their own bosses, placing additional pressure on them to succumb to union demands. Empirical research does suggest that unionized municipal workers earn more than nonunionized municipal workers.[3] But unions may have even greater impact on raising fringe benefits (retirement, health benefits, vacations, etc.) and ensuring job security of government employees.

POLITICAL CLOUT   Unions in the *private* sector of the American economy have been in steep decline in recent decades; today only about 10 percent of the private work force is unionized. But unions in the *public* sector have grown dramatically. The American Federation of State, County, and Municipal Employees (AFSCME) is the nation's second largest union, after the Teamsters, and it adds members each year. Most of its membership is concentrated in ten states—New York, Ohio, Pennsylvania, Michigan, Illinois, Wisconsin, Massachusetts, Minnesota, Connecticut, and Hawaii.

Government employee unions can usually be counted on to lend strong support for tax increases at all levels of government. They are also vigorous opponents of privatization (see later discussion). The AFSCME objects strongly to the idea that private contractors can provide services more efficiently than municipal bureaucracies. Moreover, the union claims that privatization "diminishes government accountability to citizens."

Public sector unions, notably the AFSCME and state chapters of the National Education Association (NEA) and the American Federation of Teachers (AFT), are regularly ranked among the most effective lobbying groups in state capitals (see Table 4–4 in Chapter 4). And public employee union PACs regularly rank among the largest campaign contributors in state gubernatorial and legislative elections. Public employees and their families turn out on election day far more frequently than the average voter.

REFORM, PRIVATIZATION, AND "REINVENTING GOVERNMENT"

People are angry at government at all levels. People believe governments are spending more but delivering less; they are frustrated with bureaucracies over which they have little control and tired of politicians who raise taxes and cut services. They believe that government bureaucracies have become "too powerful."

Today, bureaucratic regulations of all kinds—environmental controls, workplace safety rules, municipal building codes, government contracting guidelines—have become so numerous, detailed, and complex that they are stifling initiative, curtailing economic growth, wasting billions of dollars, and breeding popular contempt for law and government. One critic summarizes the problem as follows:

> Our regulatory system has become an instructional manual. It tells us and the bureaucrats exactly what to do and how to do it. Detailed rule after detailed rule addresses every eventuality or at least every situation that lawmakers and bureaucrats can think of. Is it a coincidence that almost every encounter with government is an exercise in frustration? . . . We have constructed a system of regulatory law that basically outlaws common sense.[4]

The result is that we direct our energy and wealth into defensive measures, designed not to improve our lives but to avoid tripping over senseless rules. People come to see government as their adversary and government regulations as obstacles in their lives.

Bureaucrats become more concerned with following rules than with promoting sensible outcomes. They seek to protect themselves by following detailed rules and by focusing on time-consuming and costly procedures (paperwork, forms, hearings, appeals, and delays) rather than the actual effect of their decisions. Following procedures substitutes for personal responsibility.

■

Privatization.
Shifting the production of
government services from
public bureaucracies to private firms.

PRIVATIZATION AS REFORM   Political conservatives have mounted a reform movement in state and local government, centering on the notion of the "privatization" of
public services. Traditionally, conservatives have sought to restrain the growth of government:

> The bigger the government the greater the force for even bigger government. Budgets
> will expand, resulting in the appointment of more officials and the hiring of more work-
> ers. These will go to work at once to enlarge their budgets, do less work, hire still more
> workers, obtain better-than-average raises, and vote for more spending programs, while
> encouraging their constituents and beneficiaries to do the same. The forecast seems omi-
> nous: Sooner or later everyone will be working for government.[5]

Occasionally citizens revolt against the trend toward ever larger governments by voting for tax limitation proposals or threatening to move to lower tax jurisdictions. But
according to the proponents of privatization, "a more educated, critical, and sophisticated" approach to controlling the growth of government is needed, namely the privatization of government services wherever and whenever possible.

PRIVATIZATION   In the broadest sense, privatization includes the shifting of many
responsibilities *from* government *to* the private marketplace. "Load shedding" implies
that government should sell off many of its enterprises—for example, housing projects,
airports, stadiums—to private individuals or firms who would operate them more efficiently and effectively. But privatization has also generally come to mean greater reliance on private providers of governmental services functioning in a competitive
marketplace and giving individuals greater choice in services.

   Privatization recognizes a distinction between government *provision* of a service and
government *production* of a service. Governments may decide to *provide* citizens with
certain goods and services—for example, schools, police and fire protection, garbage
collection, bus transportation, street maintenance, and so on—but not necessarily *produce* these services directly through government bureaucracies—public schools, municipal police and fire departments, municipal garbage collection, city-owned buses,
city street maintenance departments, and so on. Rather, a variety of other methods of
"service delivery" are available that rely more on private, competitive producers and
individual choice.

HOW TO PRIVATIZE   The following are among the most common methods of privatizing the provision of government services:

- *Contracting:* Governments contract with private organizations to provide a publicly funded service. Private firms compete to win and keep the
  contracts by providing quality services at low costs.
- *Franchising:* Governments grant exclusive contracts for a certain period
  of time to a private firm to provide a monopoly service—for example,
  cable television or garbage collection. The private firm collects fees directly from citizens under contractual terms agreed to by the govern-

ment. The franchise firm may pay a fee to the government for the privilege. Government may terminate the franchise for poor performance or excessive fees charged to citizens.

• *Grants:* Governments provide direct grants of money to private firms or nonprofit organizations conditioned on their providing low-cost services to citizens. Grants are typically made to hospitals and health facilities, libraries and cultural centers, and low-cost housing projects, among others.

• *Vouchers:* Vouchers are given directly to citizens who qualify for them, allowing these citizens to exercise free choice in selecting the producers of the service. Unlike grants, in which the government chooses the producers of the service, vouchers give citizens the power to choose the producer. Producers compete to attract citizens who have vouchers; the vouchers are later turned in to the government by producers for cash. For example, rent vouchers to the poor or homeless allow them to select housing of their choice; grants to public housing organizations oblige the poor and homeless to seek shelter in specific projects. Education vouchers (see Chapter 15) would allow parents to choose any school, public or private, for their children. Schools would compete to attract pupils, cashing in their accumulated vouchers.

Surveys of the extent of privatization in city government services suggest that many cities have succeeded in contracting out services for

Vehicle towing and storage
Commercial solid waste disposal
Residential solid waste disposal
Day care facilities
Street light operation
Traffic signal installation/maintenance
Street repairs
Bus system operation
Ambulance service
Airport operation
Hospital operations/management

roughly in that order of frequency.[6] A few cities and counties have even experimented with privatization of jail operations, building and grounds maintenance, data processing, tax billing, delinquency tax collection, and other functions traditionally performed by government employees.

THE POLITICS OF PRIVATIZATION Privatization is usually defended as a cost-saving measure—a way of reducing the waste, inefficiency, and unresponsiveness of

■
"Reinventing government."
A reform movement that encourages government bureaucracies to be more entrepreneurial, mission-driven, results-oriented, decentralized, and responsive to citizens' needs.

"bloated municipal bureaucracies." It is argued that private contractors, operating in a competitive marketplace, can provide the same services at much lower costs than government bureaucracies. At the same time, privatization strengthens private enterprise.

But privatization is usually opposed by powerful political groups—especially municipal employees and their unions and teachers' unions and public school administrators. They argue that the cost savings of privatization are often exaggerated and that the savings come at the price of reduced quality and/or a failure to serve all of the people. There is also concern about the loss of public control of services through privatization and a belief that government contractors and franchises can become at least as arrogant and unresponsive as government bureaucracies.

Some reformers acknowledge that privatization is not a cure-all. Reformer David Osborne writes that "privatization is one answer, but not *the* answer."[7] Government's job, according to Osborne, is to determine whether a particular function can best be produced by government employees; private contractors; or nonprofit, voluntary organizations. Governments cannot hand over the responsibility of *governance* to others; governments still make the policy decisions and provide the financing.

"REINVENTING GOVERNMENT"   Reformers have also argued that "Our fundamental problem today is not too much government or too little government . . . [but] the wrong kind of government." Rather than rely exclusively on either bureaucratization or privatization, they call for an "entrepreneurial" government that "searches for efficient and effective ways of managing."

How is the "entrepreneurial spirit" to be encouraged in government? A widely read and cited book, *Reinventing Government*, sets out ten principles of government entrepreneurialship:

- *Steer rather than row.* Separate policy decisions (steering) from service delivery (rowing). Government should focus on steering while relying more on private firms to deliver services. Government should be a catalyst.

- *Empower people rather than simply deliver services.* Governments should encourage communities and neighborhoods to undertake ownership and control of public services. Government should be community-owned.

- *Inject competition into service delivery.* Competition between public and private agencies, among private contractors, or between different governments encourages efficiency, innovation, and responsiveness. Government should be competitive.

- *Make government organizations mission-driven rather than rule-driven.* Do not prescribe how government organizations should go about doing things by prescribing rules, procedures, and regulations; but rather set goals and encourage government organizations to find the best ways to achieve them. Government should be mission-driven.

- *Encourage governments to be results oriented.* Government bureaucracies should be measured in terms of their results, not their size, numbers, or services. Government should fund outcomes, not inputs.

- *Focus on the needs of customers, not the bureaucracy.* Governments should treat citizens as if they were customers, responding to their needs, "putting them in the driver's seat." Government should be customer-driven.

- *Encourage governments to earn money through user charges.* Charging the users of government services, whenever possible, is fair; it raises revenues and balances demands for services. Governments should be enterprising.

- *Practice prevention rather than cure.* Problems from fires to ill-health are cheaper to address through prevention than services. Government should be anticipatory.

- *Decentralize government organizations.* Decentralization increases flexibility, effectiveness, innovation, morale, and commitment. Government should be decentralized.

- *Use market incentives to bring about change rather than command and control.* Market mechanisms are preferred over regulations. Government should be market oriented.[8]

Note that these are guiding principles, rather than recommendations for changes in the structure of state or local government. Unlike earlier reformers who focused on structural changes, today's reformers are more concerned about *how* governments go about their tasks.

POLITICS OF REINVENTION   The principles of "reinvention" are identified with the "neoliberal" ("new" liberals) and Democrats who acquired influence in state and local politics in the 1980s. A recognized leader of the movement was Arkansas Governor Bill Clinton, who was widely praised for his innovative efforts in education and economic development in that state.[9] Clinton served for several years as chair of the Democratic Leadership Conference (DLC), designed to move the national Democratic party toward a more moderate, centrist position that could win back the support of white middle-class voters in presidential elections. Upon entering the Oval Office, Clinton commissioned Vice President Al Gore to head a National Performance Review specifically committed to "reinventing" the federal government.[10]

But political opposition to the new reform arises from many of the core constituency groups of the Democratic party—government employees, teachers' unions, environmental groups, and black leaders and organizations. Jesse Jackson once described the DLC derisively as "Democrats for the Leisure Class." Government employees and their unions are concerned about the antibureaucratic thrust of many of the new reforms; they fear a loss of the government sector jobs to private contractors. Likewise, ,teachers' unions have been concerned with the reformers' focus on government performance, fearing that it means competence testing of students and teachers (see Chapter 15). Blacks and other minority groups fear that the focus on efficiency and productivity will overshadow concerns about equity. User fees and charges often place heavy burdens on the poor.

Support for "reinvention" is strong in the business community. Business interests have long bemoaned bloated government bureaucracies and senseless rules and regulations. High-tech companies have an added interest in selling governments computer hardware and software designed to make governmental operations more efficient. Major management consulting firms, like Peat Marvick and Price Waterhouse, are anxious to win contracts from state and local governments to proceed with reinvention. And many elected state and local officials understand the political appeal to taxpayers of efforts to reinvent government. Various "cookbooks" are now available to assist them in these efforts.[11]

THE BUDGETARY PROCESS

Too often we think of budgeting as the dull province of clerks and statisticians. Nothing could be more wrong. Budgets are political documents that record the struggles over "who gets what." The budget is the single most important policy statement of any government. It is prepared by the executive branch but must be approved by the legislative body. There are very few government activities or programs that do not require an expenditure of funds, and no public funds may be spent without budgetary authorization. The budget sets forth government programs, with price tags attached. The size and shape of the budget is a matter of serious contention in the political life of any state or community. Governors, mayors, administrators, legislators, interest groups, and citizens all compete to have their policy preferences recorded in the budget. The budget lies at the heart of the political process. (See Figure 8–4.)

THE EXECUTIVE BUDGET   The budgetary process begins with the governor or mayor's budget office sending to each governmental agency and department a budget request form, accompanied by broad policy directives to agency and department heads about the size and shape of their requests. Very often these budget requests must be made six to twelve months prior to the beginning of the fiscal year for which the requests are made; state and local governmental fiscal years usually run from July 1 to June 30.[12] After all requests have been submitted to the budget office, the serious task of consolidating these many requests begins. Individual department requests are reviewed, revised, and generally scaled down; often departments are given more or less formal hearings on their budget request by the budget director. The budget agency must also make revenue estimates based upon information it obtains from the tax department.

Governors or mayors must decide whether their budget is to be balanced or not; whether particular departmental requests should be increased or reduced, in view of the programs and promises important to their administrations; whether economies should involve overall "belt tightening" by every agency or merely the elimination of

GOVERNOR/ BUDGET OFFICE	DEPARTMENTS/ AGENCIES	GOVERNOR/ BUDGET OFFICE	LEGISLATURE	GOVERNOR
■ Provide Budget Instruction to Departments ■ Estimate Revenue	■ Prepare Strategic Plans ■ Prepare Legislative Budget Request ■ Prepare Capital Improvement Plan	■ Review/Analyze Agency Legislative Request, Strategic Plan, Capital Improvement Plan, Information Resource Plan ■ Hold Public Hearings ■ Develop Recommendations Based on Governor's Priorities and Available Revenues	■ Prepare Appropriations Act Review Governor's Recommendations Review/Analyze/ Revise Budget ■ Appropriations Act Passed by Both Houses	■ Review/Analyze Changes Governor May Line-Item Veto Specific Appropriations ■ Governor Signs into Law

FIGURE 8–4 The Budgetary Process

particular programs; or finally, whether they should recommend the raising of new taxes or the incurring of additional debt. These decisions may be the most important that mayors or governors make in their terms of office, and they generally consult both political and financial advisors—budget and tax experts, party officials, interest group representatives, and legislative leaders. Ordinarily, these difficult decisions must be made before governors or mayors present their budget message to the legislature. This budget message explains and defends the final budget presented by the chief executive to his legislative branch.

BUDGET MAKING   Budget making involves bringing together the requests of all existing state agencies, calculating the costs of new state programs, estimating the probable income of the state, and evaluating these costs and income estimates in light of program and policy objectives. The final budget document is submitted to the legislature for its adoption as an appropriations bill. No state monies can be spent without a legislative appropriation, and the legislature can make any alterations in the state budget that it sees fit. Potentially, then, a legislature can control any activity of the state government through its power over appropriations, but as a practical matter, the legislature seldom reviews every item of the governor's budget. In practice, budgets tend to reflect the views of those responsible for their preparation, namely the governor.

The most common budgetary behaviors in the states are

Agency heads consistently request higher funds.

Governors' budget staffers consistently reduce agency requests.

■

Appropriation.
An act of the legislature that authorizes executive agencies to spend a specific amount of money.

The governor consistently pursues a balanced budget at higher expenditure levels than the previous year.

Legislatures approve higher appropriations but try to blame the governor if higher taxes are required.

AGENCY PRESSURE   The pressure for budget increases comes from the requests of agency officials. Most agency officials feel compelled to ask for more money each year. Requesting an increase in funds affirms the significance and protects the status of agency employees, and it assures clientele groups that new and higher standards of service are being pursued aggressively. Requested increases also give the governor's office and the legislature something to cut that will not affect existing programs. The governor's budget staff generally recognizes the built-in pressure to expand budgets. The budget staff see themselves as "cutters." Agencies press for budgetary expansion with better programs in mind, while the governor's budget staff tries to reduce expenditures with cost cutting in mind (see *"Up Close:* How to Win at the Budget Game").

THE LEGISLATIVE APPROPRIATION   The governor's budget generally appears in the legislature as an appropriations bill, and it follows the normal path of any bill. It is assigned to an appropriations committee, which often holds hearings on the bill and occasionally reshapes and revises the executive budget. The fate of the governor's budget in the legislature generally depends upon his or her general political power, public reactions to recommendations, the degree of support he or she receives from depart-

UP CLOSE

HOW TO WIN AT THE BUDGET GAME

Experienced bureaucrats have learned a number of strategies that help them "maximize" their budgets.

Spend it all. Spend all of your current year's appropriation. A failure to use up an appropriation indicates that the full amount was unnecessary in the first place, which in turn implies that your budget should be cut next year.

Ask for more, not less. Never request a sum less than your current appropriation. It is easier to find ways to spend up to current appropriation levels than it is to explain why you want a reduction. Besides, a reduction indicates your program is not growing and this is an embarrassing admission to most government administrators.

Hide new programs in the base. Put top priority programs into the base, that is, that part of the budget that is within current appropriations levels. Budget offices, governors and mayors, and legislative bodies will seldom challenge programs that appear to be part of existing operations.

Make changes appear incremental. Increases that are desired should be made to appear small and should appear to grow out of existing operations. The appearance of a fundamental change in a budget should be avoided.

Give them something to cut. Give the budget office, chief executive, and the legislature something to cut. Normally it is desirable to submit requests for substantial increases in existing programs and many requests for new programs, in order to give higher political authorities something to cut. This enables them to "save" the public untold millions of dollars and justify their claim to promoting "economy" in government. Giving them something to cut also diverts attention away from the basic budget with its vital programs.

Make cuts hurt. If confronted with a real budget cut—that is, a reduction from last year's appropriation—announce reductions in, or elimination of, your agency's most popular program. Never acknowledge that cuts might be accommodated without reducing needed services.

ment heads, who are often called to testify at legislative budget hearings, his or her relationships with key legislative leaders, and the effectiveness of interest groups that favor or oppose particular expenditures.

After it is passed in identical form by both houses, the final appropriations measure is sent to the governor for signature. If the governor has an item veto, he or she can still make significant changes in the budget at that time.

THE POLITICS OF BUDGETING

Budgeting is very *political*. Being a good politician involves (1) the cultivation of a good base of support for one's requests among the public at large and among people served by the agency, (2) the development of interest, enthusiasm, and support for one's program among top political figures and legislative leaders, and (3) skill in following strategies that exploit one's opportunities to the maximum. Informing the public and one's clientele of the full benefit of the services they receive from the agency may increase the intensity with which they will support the agency's request. If possible, the agency should inspire its clientele to contact governors, mayors, legislators, and council members and help work for the agency's request. This is much more effective than the agency's trying to promote for its own requests.

"INCREMENTALISM" IN BUDGETING   What forces are actually involved in the budget-making process? Invariably, the forms provided by the budget office require departments to prepare budget requests alongside the previous year's expenditures. Decision makers generally consider the last year's expenditures as a base. Consequently, active consideration of budget proposals is generally narrowed to new items or requested increases over the last year's base. The attention of governors and legislators, and mayors and councils, is focused on a narrow range of increases or decreases in a budget. A budget is almost never reviewed as a whole every year, in the sense of reconsidering the value of existing programs. Departments are seldom required to defend or explain budget requests that do *not* exceed current appropriations; but requested increases in appropriations require extensive explanation, and they are most subject to downward revision by higher political officials.

NONPROGRAMMATIC BUDGETING   Finally, budgeting is *nonprogrammatic*. For reasons that accountants have so far kept to themselves, an agency budget typically lists expenditures under ambiguous phrases: "personnel services," "contractual services," "travel," "supplies," "equipment." Needless to say, it is impossible to tell from such a listing exactly what programs the agency is spending its money on. Obviously, such a budget obscures policy decisions by hiding programs behind meaningless phrases. Even if these categories are broken down into line items (for example, under "personnel services," the line-item budget might say, "John Doaks, Assistant Administrator $35,000"), it is still next to impossible to identify the costs of various programs. Reform-oriented administrators have called for budgeting by programs for many years; this would present budgetary requests in terms of end products or program packages, like aid to dependent children, vocational rehabilitation, administration of

■

Zero-based budgeting.
A method of budgeting that
demands justification for the
entire budget request of an
agency, not just its requested
increase in funding.

Earmarking.
In government budgeting,
the practice of allocating
specific revenue sources to
specific programs, such as
gasoline taxes to highways.

fair employment practices laws, highway patrolling, and so on. Many chief executives favor program budgeting because it will give them greater control over the policy. However, very often administrative agencies are hostile toward program budgeting; it certainly adds to the cost of bookkeeping, and many agencies feel insecure in describing precisely what it is they do. Moreover, there are some *political* functions served by nonprogram budgeting. Compromise comes much more readily when the items in dispute can be treated in dollars instead of differences in policy. Political bargaining and logrolling are made easier when discussions focus on increases and decreases in budgets rather than the desirability of whole programs.

The result of incremental budgeting is that many programs, services, and expenditures continue long after there is any real justification for them. When new needs, services, and functions arise, they do not displace older ones but rather are *added* to the budget. Budget decisions are made incrementally because policy makers do not have the time, energy, or information to review every dollar of every budget request every year. Nor do policy makers wish to refight every political battle over existing programs every year. So they generally accept last year's base spending level as legitimate and focus attention on proposed increases for each program.

FAILURE OF BUDGET REFORM   Reformers often propose "sunset" laws requiring bureaucrats to justify their programs every five to seven years or else the programs go out of existence, as well as zero-based budgeting that would force agencies to justify every penny requested—not just requested increases. In theory, sunset laws and zero-based budgeting would regularly prune unnecessary government programs, agencies, and expenditures and thus limit the growth of government and waste in government. But in reality, sunset laws and zero-based budgeting require so much effort in justifying already accepted programs that executive agencies and legislative committees grow tired of the effort and return to incrementalism.

Thus, the "incremental" nature of budgetary politics helps reduce political conflict and maintains stability in governmental programs. As bruising as budgetary battles may be in state capitols and city halls, they would be much worse if governments tried to review the value of *all* existing expenditures and programs each year. Comprehensive budgetary review would "overload the system" with political conflict by refighting every policy battle every year.

"EARMARKING"   Chief executives have little influence over many items of state and local government spending. Over 50 percent of state finances come from specially earmarked funds. It is quite common to earmark in state constitutions and laws certain funds for particular purposes, such as gasoline taxes for highways. The earmarking device provides certain agencies with an independent source of income, thus reducing the chief executive's control over operations. What is left, "general fund expenditures," is also largely committed to existing state programs, particularly welfare and education.

"UNCONTROLLABLES"   Politicians typically campaign on platforms stressing both increased service and lower taxes. Once in office, however, they typically find it impossible to accomplish both and very difficult to accomplish either one. Often new programs planned by a governor must be put aside, because of "uncontrollable" growth in existing programs. For example, additional money may be required to educate more students who are entitled to an education under existing programs; or money must be found to pay the welfare benefits of additional clients or the Medicaid costs of additional patients "entitled" to care under existing laws. These entitlement programs constitute over three-quarters of state general fund appropriations.

BALANCING THE BUDGET   Unlike the federal government, most state budgets must be balanced. The same is true for most cities, counties, and school districts. This means that chief executives must submit to the legislature a budget in which projected revenues are equal to recommended expenditures. And the legislature must not appropriate funds in excess of projected revenues. There are, of course, many accounting devices that allow governors and mayors and legislatures and councils to get around the balanced budget limitation—devices known as "blue smoke and mirrors." These include "off-budget" special funds, separate state authorities, capital budgets, and so on (see Chapter 17).

Nonetheless, balanced budget requirements are a major restraint on state and local government spending. Indeed, often revenue "shortfalls"—revenues that fall below those estimated for the year in the budget—force painful midyear spending cuts. Only a few states allow deficits to be carried over into the next fiscal year. And these carryover deficits force governors and legislatures to be more conservative in their spending plans for the following year.[13]

■
"Uncontrollables."
In government spending, increases that cannot be easily limited because of prior commitments to existing programs.

Shortfalls.
Revenues that fall below those estimated in the budget and force spending cuts during a fiscal year.

DID YOU KNOW?

WHAT ARE THE 100 LARGEST GOVERNMENTS IN THE UNITED STATES

GOVERNMENTS RANKED BY TOTAL REVENUES

(States in capital letters; city and county governments in lowercase. Eighteen local governments are larger than the smallest state government, #68 South Dakota.)

Rank	Jurisdiction	Revenue ($ billions)	Population
1	CALIFORNIA	$100	30,380,000
2	NEW YORK	$75	18,058,000
3	New York City, NY	$45	7,322,564
4	TEXAS	$37	17,349,000
5	PENNSYLVANIA	$36	11,961,000
6	OHIO	$35	10,939,000
7	NEW JERSEY	$29	7,760,000
8	FLORIDA	$28	13,277,000
9	ILLINOIS	$28	11,543,000
10	MICHIGAN	$26	9,368,000
11	MASSACHUSETTS	$20	5,996,000
12	NORTH CAROLINA	$18	6,737,000
13	WISCONSIN	$18	4,955,000
14	WASHINGTON	$17	5,018,000
15	VIRGINIA	$15	6,286,000
16	MINNESOTA	$15	4,432,000
17	GEORGIA	$15	6,623,000
18	INDIANA	$14	5,610,000
19	MARYLAND	$14	4,860,000
20	Los Angeles County, CA	$13	8,863,164
21	LOUISIANA	$12	4,252,000
22	CONNECTICUT	$12	3,291,000
23	MISSOURI	$12	5,158,000
24	TENNESSEE	$11	4,953,000
25	KENTUCKY	$11	3,713,000
26	ALABAMA	$11	4,089,000
27	OREGON	$10	2,922,000
28	SOUTH CAROLINA	$10	3,560,000
29	ARIZONA	$10	3,750,000
30	COLORADO	$9	3,377,000
31	OKLAHOMA	$8	3,175,000
32	IOWA	$8	2,795,000
33	Los Angeles, CA	$7	3,485,398
34	ALASKA	$6	570,000
35	MISSISSIPPI	$6	2,592,000
36	ARKANSAS	$6	2,372,000
37	KANSAS	$6	2,495,000
38	NEW MEXICO	$6	1,548,000
39	WEST VIRGINIA	$5	1,801,000
40	HAWAII	$5	1,135,000
41	UTAH	$5	1,770,000
42	Washington, DC	$5	606,900
43	Chicago, IL	$5	2,783,726
44	NEVADA	$4	1,284,000
45	MAINE	$4	1,235,000

46	NEBRASKA	$4	1,593,000
47	RHODE ISLAND	$4	1,004,000
48	Philadelphia, PA	$3	1,585,577
49	San Francisco City/County, CA	$3	723,959
50	Metropolitan Dade County, FL	$3	1,937,094
51	IDAHO	$3	1,039,000
52	NEW HAMPSHIRE	$3	1,105,000
53	DELAWARE	$3	680,000
54	MONTANA	$3	808,000
55	Fairfax County, VA	$2	818,584
56	Orange County, CA	$2	2,410,556
57	San Diego County, CA	$2	2,498,016
58	Detroit, MI	$2	1,027,974
59	NORTH DAKOTA	$2	635,000
60	WYOMING	$2	460,000
61	Baltimore, MD	$2	736,014
62	VERMONT	$2	567,000
63	Memphis, TN	$2	610,337
64	Nassau County, NY	$2	1,287,348
65	Boston, MA	$2	574,283
66	Houston, TX	$2	1,630,553
67	Montgomery County, MD	$2	757,027
68	SOUTH DAKOTA	$2	703,000
69	San Bernardino County, CA	$2	1,418,380
70	Santa Clara County, CA	$2	1,497,577
71	Metro Nashville/Davidson, TN	$2	488,374
72	Cook County, IL	$2	5,105,067
73	Jacksonville, FL	$2	635,230
74	Sacramento County, CA	$1	1,041,219
75	Alameda County, CA	$1	1,279,182
76	San Diego, CA	$1	1,110,549
77	San Antonio, TX	$1	935,933
78	Suffolk County, NY	$1	1,321,864
79	Dallas, TX	$1	1,006,877
80	Prince George's County, MD	$1	729,268
81	Westchester County, NY	$1	874,866
82	Harris County, TX	$1	2,818,199
83	Baltimore County, MD	$1	692,134
84	Riverside County, CA	$1	1,170,413
85	Denver City/County, CO	$1	467,610
86	Phoenix, AZ	$1	983,403
87	Erie County, NY	$1	968,532
88	Austin, TX	$1	465,622
89	Clark County, NV	$1	741,459
90	Seattle, WA	$1	516,259
91	Maricopa County, AZ	$1	2,122,101
92	Cuyahoga County, OH	$1	1,412,140
93	Hillsborough County, FL	$1	834,054
94	Wayne County, MI	$1	2,111,687
95	Hennepin County, MN	$1	1,032,431
96	Indianapolis, IN	$1	731,327
97	Milwaukee County, WI	$1	959,275
98	Honolulu City/County, HI	$1	836,231
99	Contra Costa County, CA	$1	803,732
100	Monroe County, NY	$1	713,968

ON THE WEB

The American Society for Public Administration is the largest association in the field of public administration. It includes both "practitioners" and faculty who teach public administration in colleges and universities; it also welcomes student members. It maintains a Web site at

www.aspanet.org

This site contains general information on governmental administration, links to the association's publications, including the monthly *PA Times* and the quarterly *Public Administration Review,* and it even offers a listing of current job openings in public administration across the nation.

Major state executive departments and agencies often form national associations to exchange information, assist in bureaucratic networking, and lobby in Washington to expand federal aid to their particular function. The following associations all maintain interesting Web sites:

National Association of State Budget Officers

www.nasbo.org

National Association of State Purchasing Officials

www.naspo.org

National Association of Medicaid Directors

www.medicaid.apwa.org

Council of Chief State School Officials

www.ccsso.org

American Association of State Highway and Transportation Officials

www.autometric.com

Most of these sites cover topics of interest to professionals in the field, report on Washington lobbying activities, and describe meetings and publications of the organization.

NOTES

1. David Osbourne and Ted Gaebler, *Reinventing Government* (New York: Addison-Wesley, 1992), p. 24.

2. *Elrod v. Burns,* 96 S. Ct. 2673 (1976); *Branti v. Finkel,* 445 U.S. 507 (1980).

3. For a summary of research on this topic, see Gregory B. Lewis and Lana Stein, "Unions and Municipal Decline," *American Politics Quarterly,* 17 (April 1989), 202–22.

4. Philip K. Howard, *The Death of Common Sense* (New York: Random House, 1995), p. 10.

5. E. S. Savas, *Privatizing the Public Sector* (Chatham, NJ: Chatham House, 1982), p. 25.

6. *Municipal Yearbook, 1987* (Washington, DC: ICMA, 1988), pp. 44–53.

7. David Osbourne, "Privatization: One Answer, Not *the* Answer," *Governing* (April 1992), 83.

8. Osbourne and Gaebler, *Reinventing Government.*

9. See Thomas Osborne, *Laboratories of Democracy* (Boston: Harvard Business School, 1988), chap. 3, "Arkansas: The Education Model."

10. See National Performance Review, *Creating a Government That Works Better and Costs Less* (Washington, DC: Government Printing Office, 1994).

11. In addition to Osborne and Gaeber, *Reinventing Government,* see National Commission on State and Local Government Public Service, *Hard Truths/Tough Choices: An Agenda for State and Local Government Reform* (Washington, DC: Government Printing Office, 1993).

12. The federal government's fiscal year is October 1 to September 30.

13. James E. Alt and Robert C. Lowry, "Divided Government, Fiscal Institution, and Budget Deficits," *American Political Science Review,* 88 (December 1994), 811–28.

9
COURTS, CRIME, AND CORRECTIONAL POLICY

POLITICS AND THE JUDICIAL PROCESS

Courts are "political" institutions because they attempt to resolve conflicts in society. Like legislative and executive institutions, courts make public policy in the process of resolving conflict. Some of the nation's most important policy decisions have been made by courts rather than legislative or executive bodies. Federal courts have taken the lead in eliminating racial segregation, ensuring the separation of church and state, defining the rights of criminal defendants, guaranteeing individual voters an equal voice in government, and establishing the right of women to obtain abortions. These are just a few of the important policy decisions made by courts—policy decisions that are just as significant to all Americans as those made by Congress or the president. Courts, then, are deeply involved in policy making, and they are an important part of the political system in America. Sooner or later in American politics, most important policy questions reach the courts.

THE JUDICIAL STYLE OF DECISION MAKING   In resolving conflict and deciding about public policy, courts function very much like other government agencies. However, the *style* of judicial decision making differs significantly from legislative or executive decision making. Let us try to distinguish between courts as policy-making institutions and other legislative and executive agencies.

- *A "Passive" Appearance:* First of all, courts rarely initiate policy decisions. Rather, they wait until a case involving a policy question they must decide is brought to them. The vast majority of cases brought before courts do not involve important policy issues. Much court activity involves the enforcement of existing public policy. Courts punish criminals, enforce contracts, and award damages to the victims of injuries. Most of these decisions are based upon established law. Only occasionally are important policy questions brought to the court.
- *Special Rules of Access:* Access to courts is through "cases." (Only rarely do state courts render advisory opinions to governors or legislatures.) A "case" requires two disputing parties, one of which must have suffered some damages or face some penalties as a result of the action or inaction of the other.
- *Legal Procedures:* The procedures under which judges and other participants in the judicial process operate are also quite different from procedures in legislative or executive branches of government. Facts and arguments must be presented to the courts in specified forms—writs, motions, written briefs, and oral arguments that meet the technical specifications of the courts. While an interest group may hire lobbyists to pressure a legislature, they must hire a law firm to put their arguments into a legal context.
- *Decisions in Specific Cases:* Courts must limit their decisions to specific cases. Rarely do the courts announce a comprehensive policy in the way

■

Common law.
Legal traditions developed through court cases going back to England.

Statutory law.
Laws passed by legislatures.

Tort.
A legal harm caused by civil wrongdoing.

Liability.
Legal responsibility for damages caused by a civil wrongdoing.

the legislature does when it enacts a law. Of course, the implication of a court's decision in a particular case is that future cases of the same nature will be decided the same way. This implication amounts to a policy statement; however, it is not as comprehensive as a legislative policy pronouncement, because future cases with only slightly different circumstances might be decided differently.

- *Appearance of Objectivity:* Perhaps the most important distinction between judicial decision making and decision making in other branches of government is that judges must not appear to permit political consideration to affect their decisions. Judges must not appear to base their decisions on partisan considerations, to bargain, or to compromise in decision making. The *appearance of objectivity* in judicial decision making gives courts a measure of prestige that other governmental institutions lack. Court decisions appear more legitimate to the public if they believe that the courts have dispensed unbiased justice.

FOUNDATION OF COMMON LAW   Legal traditions are influential in court decisions. English common law has affected the law of all of our states except Louisiana, which was influenced by the Napoleonic Code. English common law developed in the thirteenth century through the decisions of judges who applied their notions of justice to specific cases. This body of judge-made law grew over the centuries and is still the foundation of our legal system today. However, statutory law—laws passed by legislatures—take precedence over common law. The common law is only applied by the courts when no statutory provisions are relevant or when statutory law must be interpreted. The degree to which statutory law has replaced common law varies among the states according to the comprehensiveness of state statutes and codes. Common law covers both criminal and civil law, although the common law of crimes has been replaced by comprehensive criminal codes in the states.

THE LAWYERING OF AMERICA

The United States is the most litigious society in the world. We are threatening to drown ourselves in a sea of lawsuits. The rise in the number of lawsuits in the United States corresponds to a rise in the number of lawyers. There were 285,000 practicing lawyers in the nation in 1960; by 1995 this figure had grown to over 850,000 (compared to 650,000 practicing physicians). The continuing search for legal fees by these bright professional people has brought an avalanche of civil liability suits in federal and state courts—about 15 million per year.

Lawyers are in business, and their business is conflict. Generating business means generating conflict. Just as businesses search for new products, lawyers search for new legal principles upon which to bring lawsuits. Lawyers have been successful over the years in expanding tort liability, that is, liability for damages incurred in a civil wrongdoing. Negligence is the most common civil wrongdoing or tort.

EXPANDED LIABILITY   Virtually any accident involving a commercial product can inspire a product liability suit. An individual who gets cut opening a can of peas can sue the canning company. Manufacturers must pay large insurance premiums to insure themselves against such suits and pass on the costs of the insurance in the price of the product. Municipal and state governments, once generally protected from lawsuits by citizens, have now lost most of their "immunity" and must purchase liability insurance for activities as diverse as recreation, street maintenance, waste collection, and police and fire protection. Real estate brokers may be sued by unhappy buyers and sellers. Homeowners and bar owners may be sued by persons injured by their guests. Hotels have paid damages to persons raped in their rooms. Coastal cities with beaches have been successfully sued by relatives of persons who drowned themselves in the ocean.

CONTINGENCY FEES   Many of these lawsuits are initiated by lawyers who charge fees on a contingency basis; the plaintiff pays nothing unless the attorney wins an award. Up to half of that award may go to the attorney in expenses and fees. Trial attorneys argue that many people could not afford to bring civil cases to court without a contingency fee contract.

THIRD-PARTY SUITS   Defendants in civil cases are not necessarily the parties directly responsible for damages to the plaintiff. Instead, wealthier third parties, who may indirectly contribute to an accident, are favorite targets of lawsuits. For example, if a drunk driver injures a pedestrian, but the driver has only limited insurance and small personal wealth, a shrewd attorney will sue the bar that sold the driver the drinks, instead of the driver. Insurance premiums have risen sharply for physicians seeking malpractice insurance, as have premiums for recreation facilities, nurseries and day care centers, motels, and restaurants.

"PAIN AND SUFFERING" AND "PUNITIVE" AWARDS   Awards in liability cases, sometimes running into tens of millions of dollars, cover much more than the doctor bills, lost wages, and cost of future care for injured parties. Most large damage awards are for *pain and suffering*. Pain and suffering awards are *added* compensation for the victim, beyond actual costs for medical care and lost wages. So also are punitive damage awards, multiples of the actual damages designed to deter and punish persons or firms found to be at fault.

"JOINT AND SEVERAL" LIABILITY   Moreover, a legal rule known as joint and several liability allows a plaintiff to collect the entire award from any party that contributed in any way to the accident, if other defendants cannot pay. So if a drunk driver crosses a median strip and crashes into another car leaving its driver a cripple, the victim may sue the city for not placing a guard railing in the median strip. The rule encourages trial lawyers to sue the party "with the deepest pockets," that is, the wealthiest party rather than the party most responsible for the accident. Unsophisticated juries can be emotionally manipulated into granting huge damage awards, especially against businesses, municipalities, and insurance companies.

■
Joint and several liability.
Legal responsibility for full damages regardless of the degree of contribution to harm.

TORT REFORM   Reforming the nation's liability laws is a major challenge confronting the nation's state governments. The most common reform proposals are capping the award for "pain and suffering" at $250,000 or $500,000; eliminating punitive damage awards; restricting the fees that lawyers can subtract from a victim's award; and ending the rule of "joint and several" liability. Perhaps the simplest reform is a "loser pays" law—a requirement that the losing party in a civil suit pay the legal fees of the winner. This would discourage frivolous suits that are often designed to force innocent parties to pay damages rather than incur even higher costs of defending themselves.

Many of these reforms are currently being considered by state legislatures across the country. The reform movement can count on support from some normally powerful groups—the insurance companies, product manufacturers, physicians and hospitals, and even municipal governments. But a major obstacle remains the trial lawyers, who are disproportionately represented in state legislatures (see Chapter 6). The American Trial Lawyers Association is bitterly opposed to reform, and they are active in every state legislature as well as Congress.

THE NEW JUDICIAL FEDERALISM

The Supremacy Clause of the U.S. Constitution (Article VI) ensures that the federal constitution supercedes state constitutions and binds the judges in every state. State constitutions cannot deny rights granted by the U.S. Constitution, and state courts may not limit federal constitutional guarantees. But state constitutions cover many topics that are not addressed in the U.S. Constitution. More importantly, state constitutions may *add* individual rights that are not found in the U.S. Constitution, and state courts may interpret state constitutional language to *expand* individual rights beyond federal constitutional guarantees. We might think of the U.S. Constitution as a floor, providing minimum protection of individual rights for all persons in the nation. But state constitutions can build upon that floor, adding individual protections for persons within their state.

JUDICIAL FEDERALISM   Judicial federalism refers to state courts' exercise of their authority to interpret their own state constitutions to guarantee protections to individual rights beyond those protected by the U.S. Constitution. While this authority has always existed under the American federal system, it was seldom exercised. Historically, the remedy to civil rights violations was to be found in federal court if it was to be found at all. Civil rights attorneys almost always turned to federal courts and the U.S. Constitution to seek protection for their clients. But the new activism of state courts in interpreting their own states' constitutional guarantees has begun to change this pattern. "Forum shopping" is a common strategy of lawyers; it involves the search for a court that will be most favorably disposed to one's argument. In the past, federal courts were almost always the forum of choice for civil rights claims. But recently state courts have become the forums of choice for some claims.

Many state constitutions contain rights not explicitly found in the U.S. Constitution. For example, various state constitutions guarantee rights to privacy, rights of political participation, rights of victims of crime, rights to public information, rights to work, rights to free public education, and equal gender rights (state ERAs).

■
Judicial federalism.
State courts' authority to interpret their own constitutional guarantees to expand upon those in the U.S. Constitution.

EXTENDING PERSONAL LIBERTIES   Several state supreme courts have taken the lead in extending personal liberties under their own *state constitutions*, even when the U.S. Supreme Court has declined to incorporate these same liberties within the U.S. Constitution. Some examples include:

- The Florida Supreme Court decided that the state constitutional guarantee of the right of privacy struck down laws restricting abortion, although the U.S. Supreme Court had earlier upheld similar restrictions as permissible under the U.S. Constitution (*Webster* v. *Reproduction Health Services*, 1989).

- The Texas Supreme Court (and several other states' high courts) held that the state's constitutional guarantee of equality in public education required the system of local school finance to be replaced with statewide financing that equalized educational spending throughout the state. Years earlier, the U.S. Supreme Court had decided that the U.S. Constitution did *not* include a right to equal educational funding across school districts (*San Antonio Independent School District* v. *Rodriguez*, 1973).

- New York and Pennsylvania Supreme Courts were the first to strike down state sodomy laws (anal sexual penetration) under privacy provisions of their state constitution, although the U.S. Supreme Court had upheld a Georgia sodomy statute ruling that "there is no constitutional right to commit sodomy" (*Bowers* v. *Hardwick*, 1986).

- California's Supreme Court ruled that the state's constitution compelled the state to pay for abortions for poor women, although the U.S. Supreme Court ruled that there was no requirement in the U.S. Constitution that states fund abortions (*Harris* v. *McRae*, 1980).

- The Massachusetts Supreme Court ruled that nude go-go dancing is a protected form of free expression under the state's constitution, even though the U.S. Supreme Court had ruled that it is *not* protected by the First Amendment (*Barnes* v. *Glen Theatre Inc.*, 1991).

Judicial activism by state supreme courts encourages interest groups to bring cases and amici curiae briefs (written arguments submitted by "friends of the court") to state "forums." Of course, the state strategy has significant drawbacks compared to winning at the U.S. Supreme Court level; interest groups must proceed from state to state instead of dealing with the issue once and for all in the nation's highest court.[1]

JUDICIAL POLICY DIVERGENCE   While civil rights organizations generally applaud the new judicial federalism, others have expressed concern over increased divergence between U.S. Supreme Court policy and the policies of state courts. A stable and predictable system of law is essential for democracy. Judicial federalism seems to open the law to diversity between federal and state law as well as to the "Balkanization" of law from state to state. Judicial policy diversity opens the nation's court system to intensified interest group activity and perhaps greater partisan political influence.[2]

■

Amicus curie.
"Friends of the court"—persons or groups not directly involved in a case who submit written arguments to the court.

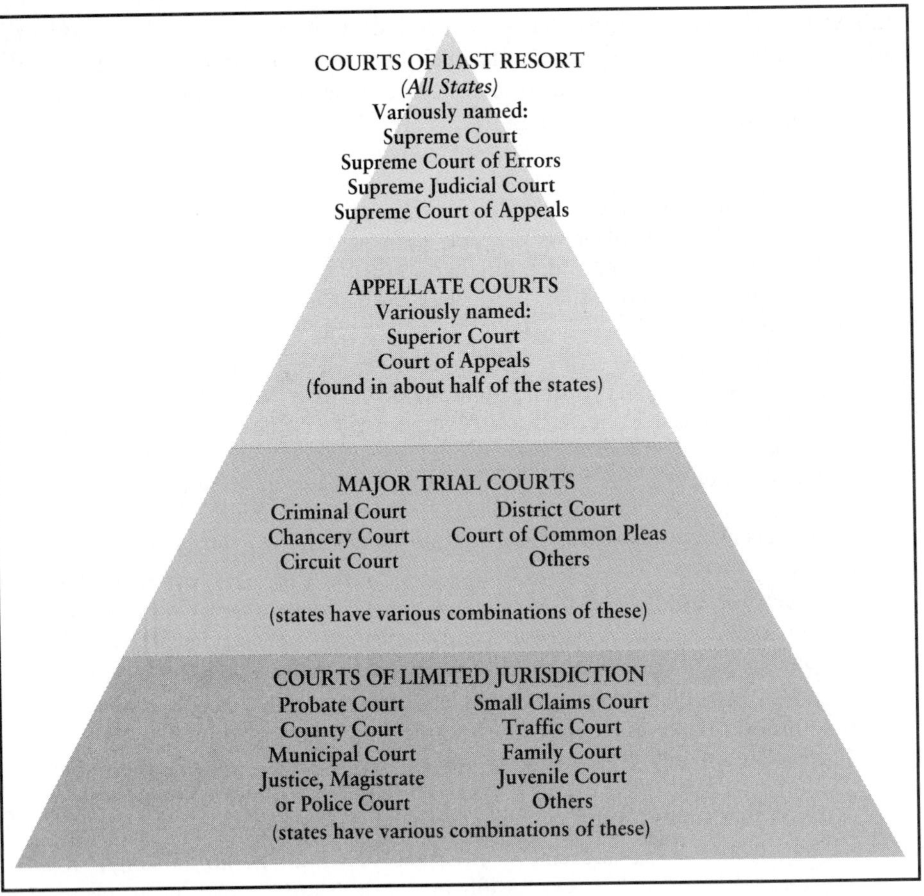

FIGURE **9–1** The
Structure of State
and Local Courts

COURTS OF LAST RESORT
(All States)
Variously named:
Supreme Court
Supreme Court of Errors
Supreme Judicial Court
Supreme Court of Appeals

APPELLATE COURTS
Variously named:
Superior Court
Court of Appeals
(found in about half of the states)

MAJOR TRIAL COURTS

Criminal Court   District Court
Chancery Court   Court of Common Pleas
Circuit Court   Others

(states have various combinations of these)

COURTS OF LIMITED JURISDICTION

Probate Court   Small Claims Court
County Court   Traffic Court
Municipal Court   Family Court
Justice, Magistrate   Juvenile Court
or Police Court   Others
(states have various combinations of these)

THE STRUCTURE OF COURT SYSTEMS

State courts are generally organized into a hierarchy similar to that shown in Figure 9-1. The courts of a state constitute a single, integrated judicial system; even city courts, traffic courts, and justices of the peace are part of the state judicial system.

MINOR COURTS   At the lowest level are minor courts. These may be municipal courts, magistrate courts, police courts, traffic courts, family courts, and small claims courts. They are presided over by justices of the peace, magistrates, or police judges, not all of whom are trained in the law. These courts are concerned principally with traffic cases, small claims, divorces and child custody, juvenile offenses, and misdemeanors, although they may hold preliminary hearings to determine whether a person accused of a felony shall be held in jail or placed under bond.

In many cities, municipal courts dispense justice in a "production line" style. Courtrooms are old, crowded, noisy, and confusing; witnesses, defendants, friends, relatives, all wait for hours for their cases to be called. Most cases are handled informally at the bench in discussions with the judge. Leniency is the rule with most judges, unless the face of the defendant is very familiar to the judge; then thirty-, sixty-, or ninety-day sentences may be imposed very quickly.

The growth of small claims courts throughout the country has helped millions of people who could not afford an attorney to bring a civil claim into the court with simplicity and low cost. Proceedings in these courts are very informal: Both sides simply "tell it to the judge." Buyers and sellers, landlords and tenants, creditors and debtors, can get a resolution to their case quickly and easily. The television show *The People's Court* has popularized the functioning of small claims courts.

TRIAL COURTS

Major trial courts of general jurisdiction—sometimes called district courts, circuit courts, superior courts, chancery courts, county courts, criminal courts, or common pleas courts—handle major civil and criminal cases arising out of statutes, common law, and state constitutions. The geographic jurisdiction of these courts is usually the county or city; there are about 1,500 major trial courts in the United States. Juries are used in these courts, and judges are generally qualified in the law. These courts handle criminal cases involving felonies and important civil suits. Almost all cases decided by state courts originate in these major trial courts; trial courts make the initial decisions in cases carried to appellate and supreme courts and may also handle some appeals from minor courts.

SUPREME COURTS

Every state has a court of last resort, which is generally called the supreme court. These courts consist of three to nine judges, and most of their work is devoted to cases on appeal from major trial courts, although some states grant original jurisdiction to supreme courts in special types of cases. Since they consider questions of law rather than questions of fact, they sit without jury. State supreme courts are the most important and visible judicial bodies in the states. Their decisions are written, published, and distributed like the decisions of the U.S. Supreme Court. Judges can express their views in majority opinions, dissenting opinions, or concurring opinions. These courts get the most controversial cases and those with the most at stake, since these cases are most likely to be appealed all the way to the state's highest court. To relieve supreme courts of heavy case burdens, many of the more populous states maintain intermediate courts of appeal between trial courts and courts of last resort.

All state supreme courts stand atop their own state's judicial system. But some state supreme courts enjoy national reputations. Their decisions on points of law are often cited by other state supreme courts as well as by federal courts. Indeed, it is possible to identify judicial leadership among state courts by examining the number of times they are cited by other courts.[3] Supreme courts in California, New York, New Jersey, Massachusetts, and Pennsylvania enjoy superior reputations, followed by those in Illinois, Wisconsin, Washington, Michigan, Iowa, Colorado, and Minnesota.

APPEALS TO THE U.S. SUPREME COURT

Appeals from the state supreme courts may go directly to the U.S. Supreme Court on federal constitutional grounds. State supreme courts have the final word in the interpretation of *state* constitutions and laws. But many cases also raise federal constitutional questions, especially under the

■

State trial courts.
State courts that initially hear and decide civil and criminal cases.

State supreme courts.
The highest courts of appeal in the states.

broad meaning of the "due process" clause and "equal protection" clause of the Fourteenth Amendment. So while most judicial appeals will end in state courts, the U.S. Supreme Court exercises general oversight through its power to accept appeals based on federal questions.

THE MAKING OF A JUDGE

Political debate over methods of selecting judges in the states has been going on for many years. In writing the federal Constitution, the Founding Fathers reflected conservative views in establishing an independent federal judiciary, whose members were appointed by the president for life terms and were not subject to direct popular control. Jacksonian views of popular election were strong in the states, however, and today a majority of state judges are directly elected by the people on partisan or nonpartisan ballots.

Five different methods of selecting judges are found in the fifty states: *partisan election, nonpartisan election, appointment by the governor, legislative selection,* and the *appointment–retention-election plan* (see Table 9-1). Many states use more than one method.

Table 9–1

METHODS OF JUDICIAL SELECTION IN THE STATES[a]				
Partisan Election	*Selection by Legislature*	*Nonpartisan Election*	*Governor Appointment*	*Appointment– Retention- Election*
Alabama	Connecticut	Georgia	Delaware	Alaska
Arkansas	Rhode Island	Idaho	Hawaii	Arizona
Illinois	South Carolina	Kentucky	Maine	California
Mississippi	Virginia	Louisiana	Massachusetts	Colorado
New Mexico		Michigan	New Hampshire	Florida
New York		Minnesota	New Jersey	Indiana
North Carolina		Montana	Vermont	Iowa
Pennsylvania		Nevada		Kansas
Tennessee		North Dakota		Maryland
Texas		Ohio		Missouri
West Virginia		Oregon		Nebraska
		Washington		Oklahoma
		Wisconsin		South Dakota
				Utah
				Wyoming

[a]States are listed by method of selection used for supreme court. In some states different methods of selection are used for different courts.

Source: Book of the States, 1997–98.

Most states elect their judges, some in partisan elections and some in nonpartisan elections in which candidates for the bench do not carry party labels. In four states, judges are chosen by their legislatures, and in eight states, they are appointed by the governor. Other states have adopted the appointment–retention-election plan (initially called the Missouri plan), in which governors appoint judges on the recommendation of a select committee, and after the judge has been in office for a year or more, the voters are given the opportunity to retain or oust the appointed judge.

APPOINTMENT   The argument for selecting judges by appointment rests upon the value of judicial independence and isolation from direct political involvement. Critics of the elective method feel that it forces judges into political relationships and compromises their independence on the bench. This is particularly true if judicial elections are held on a partisan rather than a nonpartisan ballot, where judges must secure nomination with the support of party leaders. Moreover, it is argued that voters are not able to evaluate "legal" qualifications—knowledge of the law, judicial temperament, skill in the courtroom, and so on. Hence, judges should be appointed, rather than elected by voters. Attorneys, bar associations, and judges themselves prefer an appointive method in which they are given the opportunity to screen candidates and evaluate legal qualifications prior to appointment.

Actually it is not possible to "take judges out of politics." Selection by appointment removes the selection of judges from *party* politics but simply places the selection in different political hands. Instead of party leaders, the governor or the bar association become the principal actors in judicial selection. It is not clear which system leads to "better" judges, or whether "better" judges are those more sensitive to community values or more trained in legal procedures.

INTERIM APPOINTMENT   In practice many judges come to the bench in elective states through the appointment procedure. The apparent paradox comes about because even in elective states, governors generally have the power to make interim appointments when a judgeship is vacant because of the retirement or death of a judge between elections. Interim-appointed judges must seek election at the next regular election, but by that time they have acquired the prestige and status of a judge, and they are unlikely to be defeated by an outsider. Many members of the judiciary in elective states deliberately resign before the end of their term, if they are not seeking reelection, in order to give the governor the opportunity to fill the post by appointment. It is interesting to note that over half of the supreme court judges in states that elect their judiciary come to the bench initially by means of appointment. In practice, then, the elective system of judicial selection is greatly compromised by the appointment of judges to fill unexpired terms.

ELECTION   Few incumbent judges are ever defeated in running for reelection. The majority of judges seeking reelection are unopposed by anyone on the ballot, and very few judges seeking reelection are ever defeated. Voter interest in judicial elections is quite low.[4] Given a lack of information and interest in these elections, incumbent judges have an enormous advantage. They have the prestigious title "Judge" in front of their names and some name recognition. In states with partisan elections, judges are

Interim appointment.
In government, appointment to a vacancy created by death or resignation prior to the expiration of an elected term.

■

Missouri plan.
A method of judicial selection in which a nominating committee sends names to the governor, who then makes the appointment; appointees must win a retention vote in the next election.

Retention election.
A judicial election in which voters choose between keeping or ousting an incumbent judge.

occasionally defeated if their party loses badly.[5] But even in these partisan elections judges enjoy more stability and independence from popular control than do legislators or governors.

Very few voters know anything about judicial candidates. Indeed, one study suggests that fewer than 15 percent of voters *coming from the polls* remembered the name of one candidate for the state supreme court, and fewer than 5 percent could remember the name of one candidate for county court.[6]

APPOINTMENT–RETENTION-ELECTION PLAN Appointment by the governor followed by a retention-election combines the elective and appointive systems of selection. Under this Missouri plan, a select committee of judges, attorneys, and laypeople make nominations for judicial vacancies. (In various states these nominating committees are called the Judicial Nominating Commission, or the Judicial Council, or the Commission on Court Appointments, etc.) The governor appoints one of the committee's nominees to office. After the judge has served a specified time period (usually one year), the judge's name is placed on a nonpartisan ballot without any other name in opposition. "Shall judge (the name of the judge is inserted) of the (the name of the court is inserted) be retained in office? Yes____ No____." If voters vote yes, the judge is then entitled to a full term of office. If the voters vote no, the governor must select another name from those submitted by his nominating committee and repeat the whole process. In practice, a judge is hardly ever defeated in a retention election, in part for the same reasons that make it difficult to defeat an incumbent judge (see preceding discussion). Moreover, since "you can't beat somebody with nobody," running in a judicial retention election is the equivalent of being unopposed. Less than 1 percent of judges are voted out of office in retention elections.[7] The effect is to place judicial selection in the hands of the judges or attorneys who compose the nominating committee and the governor, with only a semblance of voter participation. Reformers argue that the plan removes judges from politics and spares the electorate the problem of voting on judicial candidates when they know little about their professional qualifications.

WHETHER THE SELECTION METHOD MATTERS There seems to be very little difference in the kinds of people (educational qualifications, experience, or social background) who are elevated to judgeships by different judicial selection methods (except that judges selected by state legislatures are more likely to have been state legislators).[8] However, there is some conflicting evidence on the question of whether state supreme courts selected by different methods show significant differences in judicial decision making. An early study found that courts selected by partisan or nonpartisan elections, appointed by governors or legislators, or selected under appointment–retention-election plans, showed no clear and consistent trends in deciding for the state when it is a party to the case, or for criminal defendants, or for corporations, or for superior or inferior economic interests.[9] However, a more recent study found that in states with partisan competitive judicial elections, judges were more likely to support the death penalty.[10] And another recent study indicates that judges selected by election, especially by partisan election, are "more willing to consider political as opposed to legal factors in the decision-making process."[11]

STATUS   Judges are rarely recruited from among the most prestigious high-paying law firms. Judges at the trial level may earn $85,000 to $120,000 per year, and appellate and supreme court judges up to $125,000 or more. These incomes exceed those of the average attorney, but they are lower than salaries of senior partners at elite law firms. Moreover, judges are restricted in investments and opportunities for outside income by judicial ethics codes. While a judge enjoys status in his or her courtroom, much of the work at the trial court level is tedious and repetitious. Finally, many elite lawyers do not relish the political tasks required to secure a judgeship—garnering the support of the bar association's judicial selection panel, or attracting the nod of the governor, or worse, campaigning for the office in an election.

PARTY AFFILIATION   Traditionally, Republicans fared better in capturing judgeships than in winning legislative seats or governors' chairs. Republicans did proportionately better in winning judgeships than in winning legislative seats or governorships. Most of the judges selected in nonpartisan elections refuse to identify themselves with a political party, as do nearly all the judges selected under the appointment–retention-election plans. Judges selected in partisan elections, of course, usually do not hesitate to identify themselves as Republicans or Democrats.

THE PSYCHOLOGY OF JUDGES   While most judges share a common background before coming to the bench—law school, practicing attorney, prosecutor—they are not always well prepared to assume judicial robes. The high esteem and prestige of the judiciary tend to obscure the negative aspects of the job: the requirement to remain aloof from courtroom battles, to isolate oneself, and to deal with the routines of judging. Apparently it takes several years for attorneys to adjust fully to their new roles as judges. Coping with the social and political *isolation* appears to be the most difficult problem. As one judge complained, "The longer you stay on the bench, the fewer close friendships you have with lawyers. . . . As you go on it becomes more and more restrictive."[12]

JUDICIAL DECISION MAKING

Social scientists know more about the behavior of U.S. Supreme Court justices and federal court judges than they know about the thousands of state and local judges throughout the nation. This is largely because the decisions of federal courts are very visible and closely watched by lawyers and scholars.

TRIAL COURTS   The actions of trial judges do not appear, at first glance, to have broad political impact. Nevertheless, trial court judges have enormous discretion in both civil and criminal cases. Perhaps the most dramatic and visible area of trial judge discretion is *sentencing*. Trial court judges display great disparities in the sentences they give out in identical cases. As most good attorneys know, as well as many defendants with long criminal records, it matters a great deal who sits as the judge in your case. The outcome of *most* criminal cases is decided in "plea bargaining" between prosecuting attorneys and defense attorneys, where defendants agree to plead guilty to a lesser offense and the prosecution agrees not to press more serious charges or ask for stiffer penalties. However, the bargain must be approved by the judge. Wise attorneys know in advance what kinds of bargains different judges are likely to accept. It is *not* the determination of guilt or innocence that concerns judges, so much as the processing of cases, the acceptance of pleas, and sentencing. One study presented forty-eight trial judges in Wisconsin with the same hypothetical case: breaking and entering, one count, in which the defendant was a twenty-five-year-old, employed, white male without any previous record. The sentences ranged from eleven months in jail to thirty days of unsupervised probation.[13]

The trial court judges have a difficult yet vital job to perform. They must oversee the record of a case to prevent "reversible" error—that is, to see that no legal errors have been made that would result in a conviction being reversed or appealed. At the same time they must deal with human problems at an individual level. As one judge put it: "A trial judge is a pioneer; he approaches each case without any help. He is the first to deal with problems. . . . Sometimes I don't think that appellate judges understand that."

SUPREME COURTS   Criminal appeals account for less than one-third of the workload of state supreme courts. The largest proportion of state supreme court decision making involves economic interests. A large number of cases involving economic interests result from the important role of the states in the allocation of economic resources. All states regulate public utilities, including water, electrical companies, gas companies, and public transportation companies. The insurance industry is state regulated. Labor relations and worker's compensation cases are frequently found in state courts. Litigation over natural resources, real estate, small-business regulations, gas, oil, lumber and mining, alcoholic beverage control, racing, and gambling reflects the importance of state regulation in these fields. There is a correlation between the kinds of economic litigation decided by state supreme courts and the socioeconomic environment of the state. Supreme courts in poorer, rural states spend more time on private economic litigation (wills, trusts, estates, contracts, titles, and so on), while courts in urban industrial states wrestle with corporate law and governmental regulation of large economic interests. Judges are also called upon to make decisions in political controversies—disputes over elections, appointments to government positions, and jurisdictional squabbles between governments.

PARTISANSHIP IN STATE COURTS   What is the impact of the party affiliation of the judges in court decision making? Party affiliation probably has little impact in decisions in lower trial courts, where much of the litigation has little to do with policy making. However, several early studies showed that party affiliation tended to correlate with state supreme court decision making.[14] Democratic judges tended to decide more frequently (1) for the administrative agency in business regulation cases; (2) for the claimant in unemployment compensation; (3) for the government in tax cases; (4) for the tenant in landlord–tenant cases; (5) for the consumer in sale-of-goods cases; and (6) for the employee in employee injury cases. And a more recent study showed that Democratic judges, especially those appointed rather than elected and those serving for long terms, were more likely to oppose the death penalty than Republican judges.[15]

JUDICIAL ACTIVISM VERSUS RESTRAINT   Great legal scholars have argued the merits of activism versus self-restraint in judicial decision making for more than a century.[16] The traditional restraint of state courts has been increasingly challenged in recent years by activism on the part of some state courts. As noted earlier, some state supreme courts have decided to go beyond the U.S. Supreme Court in finding new constitutional rights for citizens. And several state supreme courts have insisted on protections for criminal defendants that go beyond those provided by the U.S. Supreme Court.[17]

LIBERALS, CONSERVATIVES, AND JUDICIAL ACTIVISM   Theoretically, activist and restraintist views of the judicial role are independent of liberal or conservative ideology. That is, judicial activism could be used in support of either liberal or conservative goals; or alternatively, judicial restraint could limit the lawmaking of judges disposed to either liberal or conservative ideas. However, there appears to be a tendency for liberal judges to be more activist than conservative judges. But the major impact of ideology is *through* the role orientation of judges. Self-restraint reduces the impact of ideology on judges' decisions. Activism greatly increases the impact of judges' ideologies. Activist judges are overtly ideological in reactions to criminal appeals—activist liberal judges vote for the defendant far more frequently than activist conservative judges who tend to support the prosecution.[18]

CRIME IN THE STATES

Crime rates are the subject of a great deal of popular discussion. Crime rates are based upon the Federal Bureau of Investigation's *Uniform Crime Reports*, but the FBI reports are compiled from figures supplied by state and local police agencies. (See Table 9-2.) The FBI has established a uniform classification of the number of serious crimes per 100,000 people that are known to the police: violent crimes (crimes committed against persons)—murder and nonnegligent manslaughter, forcible rape, robbery, and aggravated assault; property crimes (crimes committed against property)—burglary, larceny, arson, and theft, including auto theft. However, one should be cautious in interpreting official crime rates. They are really a function of several factors: the tendencies of victims to report crimes to police, the adequacy of police departments in tabulating crime, and the amount of crime itself.

TRENDS IN CRIME RATES   From 1960 to 1980 the national crime rate rose dramatically, and "law and order" became an important political issue. But in the early 1980s crime rates leveled off and even declined slightly from their record years. It was widely believed that the early rapid increase and later moderation was a product of age group changes in the population: The early baby boom had expanded the size of the

---

Judicial activism.
The making of new laws through judicial interpretation of laws and constitutions.

Judicial restraint.
Self-imposed limits on courts to defer to legislative intent or to previous court decisions.

Crime rate.
The number of serious offenses reported to police per 100,000 population, as tabulated by the FBI.

Violent crime.
Crimes against persons, including murder and nonnegligent manslaughter, forcible rape, robbery, and aggravated assault.

Property crime.
Crimes against property, including burglary, larceny, arson, and theft.

Table 9–2

CRIME RATES IN THE UNITED STATES							
Offenses Reported to Police per 100,000 Population							
	1960	1970	1980	1985	1990	1995	1997
Violent Crimes	160	360	581	557	732	685	612
Murder	5	8	10	8	9	8	7
Forcible Rape	9	18	36	37	41	37	35
Robbery	60	172	244	209	257	221	187
Assault	85	162	291	303	424	418	385
Property Crimes	1,716	3,599	5,319	4,651	4,903	4,593	4,321

Sources: F.B.I., *Uniform Crime Reports,* 1997, Preliminary Annual Release, 1998.

"crime-prone" age group in the population, people fifteen to twenty-four; later, crime rates leveled off when this age group was no longer increasing as a percentage of the population. In the early 1980s many analysts were looking forward to gradual decreases in crime rates based on smaller crime-prone age groups. But by 1990 crime rates had soared upward again. The new factor in the crime rate equation appeared to be the introduction of relatively cheap "crack" cocaine. Perhaps as many as one-half of all crimes today are drug-related.

Since peaking in the early 1990s, crime rates have actually declined. Law enforcement officials attribute recent successes in crime-fighting to police "crackdowns," more aggressive "community policing," and longer prison sentences for repeat offenders, including "three strikes you're out" laws. (All are discussed later in this chapter.) In support of this claim, they observe that the greatest reductions in crime have occurred in the nation's largest cities, especially those such as New York that have adopted tougher law enforcement practices.

VARIATIONS AMONG THE STATES   Crime rates in some states (e.g., Florida, Arizona) are over three times greater than in other states (e.g., North Dakota, West Virginia). (See "*Rankings of the States:* Crime and Law Enforcement.") Crime rates in the states appear related to population growth, urbanization, and economic development. Generally the urban states with more mobile populations have higher crime rates than rural states with more stable populations. Variations in crime rates among cities are even greater. Each year Miami, Atlanta, St. Louis, New Orleans, Ft. Lauderdale, Detroit, Newark, Chicago, and Washington, DC struggle to avoid the designation "crime capital of America." All rank high nearly every year in crime rates.

JUVENILE CRIME   The juvenile system is not designed for deterrence. Children are not held personally responsible for their actions, in the belief that they do not possess the ability to understand the nature or consequences of their behavior or its rightness

RANKINGS OF THE STATES

CRIME AND LAW ENFORCEMENT

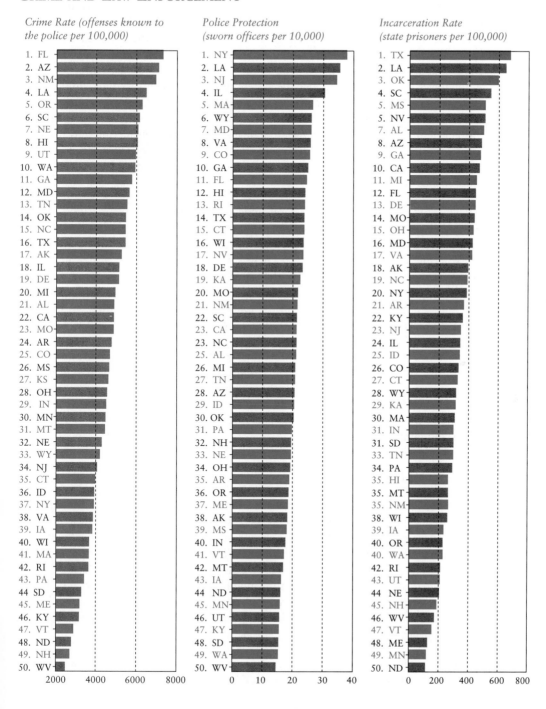

Crime Rate (offenses known to the police per 100,000)

1. FL
2. AZ
3. NM
4. LA
5. OR
6. SC
7. NE
8. HI
9. UT
10. WA
11. GA
12. MD
13. TN
14. OK
15. NC
16. TX
17. AK
18. IL
19. DE
20. MI
21. AL
22. CA
23. MO
24. AR
25. CO
26. MS
27. KS
28. OH
29. IN
30. MN
31. MT
32. NE
33. WY
34. NJ
35. CT
36. ID
37. NY
38. VA
39. IA
40. WI
41. MA
42. RI
43. PA
44. SD
45. ME
46. KY
47. VT
48. ND
49. NH
50. WV

2000   4000   6000   8000

Police Protection (sworn officers per 10,000)

1. NY
2. LA
3. NJ
4. IL
5. MA
6. WY
7. MD
8. VA
9. CO
10. GA
11. FL
12. HI
13. RI
14. TX
15. CT
16. WI
17. NV
18. DE
19. KA
20. MO
21. NM
22. SC
23. CA
23. NC
25. AL
26. MI
27. TN
28. AZ
29. ID
30. OK
31. PA
32. NH
33. NE
34. OH
35. AR
36. OR
37. ME
38. AK
39. MS
40. IN
41. VT
42. MT
43. IA
44. ND
45. MN
46. UT
47. KY
48. SD
49. WA
50. WV

0   10   20   30   40

Incarceration Rate (state prisoners per 100,000)

1. TX
2. LA
3. OK
4. SC
5. MS
5. NV
7. AL
8. AZ
9. GA
10. CA
11. MI
12. FL
13. DE
14. MO
15. OH
16. MD
17. VA
18. AK
19. NC
20. NY
21. AR
22. KY
23. NJ
24. IL
25. ID
26. CO
27. CT
28. WY
29. KA
30. MA
31. IN
31. SD
33. TN
34. PA
35. HI
35. MT
35. NM
38. WI
39. IA
40. OR
40. WA
42. RI
43. UT
44. NE
45. NH
46. WV
47. VT
48. ME
49. MN
50. ND

0   200   400   600   800

■

Victimization rate.
In law enforcement, the
number of people who in
surveys say that they were
victims of crime, in comparison to the population as a
whole.

or wrongness. Yet juvenile crime, most of which is committed by fifteen- to seventeen-year-olds, accounts for about 20 percent of the nation's overall crime rate. Offenders under eighteen years of age are usually processed in a separate juvenile court system, regardless of the seriousness of their crime. Only about 5 percent of all young violent offenders are tried as adults. Very few juveniles are sentenced to detention facilities for very long. Their names are withheld from publication, eliminating the social stigma associated with their crimes. Their juvenile criminal records are expunged when they become adults, so that they can begin adulthood with "clean" records.

Whatever the merits of the juvenile system in the treatment of young children, it is clear that the absence of deterrence contributes to criminal behavior among older youths—fifteen-, sixteen-, and seventeen-year-olds. Indeed these years are among the most crime-prone ages. Currently some state legislatures are considering reforms of the juvenile system, including more detention facilities, "boot camps" with intensive disciplinary training, and the transfer of older youths who commit violent crimes to the adult justice system.

VICTIMIZATION   Official crime rates understate the real amount of crime. Citizens do not report many crimes to police. "Victimization" surveys regularly ask a national sample of individuals whether they or any member of their household has been a victim of crime during the past year.[19] These surveys reveal that the actual amount of crime is greater than that reported to the FBI. The number of forcible rapes is twice the number reported, burglaries and aggravated assaults and larcenies more than double, and robbery 50 percent greater than the reported rate. Only auto theft statistics are reasonably accurate, indicating that most people call the police when their cars are stolen.

Interviewees give a variety of reasons for their failure to report crime to the police. The most common reason is the feeling that police could not be effective in dealing with the crime. Other reasons include the feeling that the crime was "a private matter," that the offender was a member of the family, or that the victim did not want to harm the offender. Fear of reprisal is mentioned much less frequently, usually in cases of assaults and family crimes.

THE WAR ON DRUGS

Public policy in the United States toward drug use is inconsistent. Alcohol and cigarettes are legal products, but Congress has banned their advertising on radio and television. Marijuana has been "decriminalized" in several states, making its possession a misdemeanor comparable to a traffic offense. Yet the production and sale of marijuana remain criminal offenses in every state. The use and possession of heroin and cocaine is a criminal offense everywhere in the United States. Drug trafficking can be prosecuted in either state or federal courts. Federal drug laws are generally harsher than those of the states; the minimum federal sentence for possession of specified amounts of illegal drugs is five years.

ALCOHOL   The United States government attempted to prohibit the manufacture and sale of alcohol for only thirteen years, during Prohibition, 1920–1933. Today, the alcoholic beverage industry is a major component of our national economy, and nearly two-thirds of the adult population drink occasionally. But according to the U.S. National Center for Health Statistics, about 5 percent of the population over eighteen averages two or more drinks each day.[20] Almost half of all highway accident deaths are alcohol-related. About 1.1 million people are arrested for driving while intoxicated (DWI) each year.[21]

Alcohol is controlled in the states primarily by laws dealing with the age of the purchaser. Immediately following the passage of the Twenty-Sixth Amendment lowering the voting age to eighteen, most states dropped the legal drinking age to eighteen. But later the states reversed themselves, and today most states have returned the legal drinking age to twenty-one. In 1984 Congress required the U.S. Department of Transportation to withhold 10 percent of federal highway funds from any state that did not raise its drinking age to twenty-one (see "*Up Close:* Federalism and the Drinking Age" in Chapter 3). The argument for raising the legal drinking age generally centers on the higher automobile accident rate for young people. The states have also tried to deal directly with drunk driving by all age groups by setting specific blood alcohol concentration (BAC) standards for intoxication, usually 0.10; increasing the penalties for driving while intoxicated (DWI); and even holding bars legally accountable if their patrons are found DWI.

MARIJUANA   The medical evidence on the health effects of marijuana is mixed; conflicting reports have been issued about whether or not it is more dangerous than alcohol.[22] Estimates of the number of "regular" marijuana users is slightly higher than estimates of the number of heavy drinkers—about 6 percent of the population age twelve and over. Marijuana users are younger than the general population. Decriminalizing marijuana use does not make its production or sale legal, but makes its possession (generally an ounce or less) a civil offense, much like a traffic offense.

COCAINE   The burgeoning market for cocaine currently challenges law enforcement efforts. Cocaine is not regarded as physically addictive, although the psychological urge to continue use of the drug is strong. It is made from coca leaves and imported into the United States. At one time, its high cost and use by celebrities made it the drug of choice in middle- and upper-class circles. In the 1980s a cheap yet potent version, "crack," spread rapidly in the nation's cities. The health problems associated with cocaine are fairly serious, as reported by the National Institute on Drug Abuse.[23] Death, although rare, can occur from a single ingestion.

DRUG POLICY   Antidrug efforts can be divided into three categories: interdiction, enforcement, and education.

Interdiction: Efforts to seal U.S. borders against the importation of drugs have been frustrated by the sheer volume of smuggling. Each year increasingly large drug shipments are intercepted by the U.S. Drug Enforcement Administration, the U.S. Customs Service, the Coast Guard, and state and local agencies. Yet each year the volume of drugs entering the country seems to increase. Drug "busts" are considered just another cost of business to the traffickers. It is not likely that the use of U.S. military forces to augment other federal agencies can succeed in sealing our borders. American pressure against Latin American governments to destroy coca crops and assist in interdiction has already resulted in strained relationships. Our neighboring countries wonder why the U.S. government directs its efforts at the suppliers, when the demand for drugs arises within the United States itself.

Enforcement: The FBI and state and local law enforcement agencies already devote great effort to combating drugs; an estimated 40 percent of all arrests in the United States are drug-related. Federal and state prisons now hold a larger percentage of the nation's population than ever before. Sentences have lengthened for drug trafficking, and prisons are overcrowded as a direct result of drug-related convictions. Drug testing in government and private employment is increasing, but unless it is random it is not very useful, and some courts have prevented random testing of individuals without their consent.

Education: Efforts at educating the public about the dangers of drugs have inspired many public and private campaigns, from former First Lady Nancy Reagan's "Just say no" to Jesse Jackson's "Up with hope, down with dope" to D.A.R.E. (drug abuse resistance education) programs in local communities. But it is difficult to evaluate the effects of these efforts. The number of people arrested for drug offenses in the United States remains at over one million per year.[24] Reported drug use is down, yet there appears to be no significant reduction in the availability of drugs on the street.

FEDERAL POLICY   Congress created a cabinet-level "drug czar," a National Drug Control Policy Director, in 1988 to develop and coordinate antidrug policy in the United States. The national "war on drugs" has included funds for federal prison construction and more courts and prosecutors; grants for state and local drug law enforcement; increased money for border control for the Coast Guard, Customs Service, and Immigration and Naturalization Service; authorization for use of U.S. military in drug enforcement; and additional funds for the Drug Enforcement Administration. Congress added funds for treatment programs in states and cities.

DRUGS AND CRIME   Police officials are convinced that drugs cause crime—not just violation of drug laws, but robbery, burglary, assault, and murder. Indeed, drug use among persons arrested for nondrug crimes is very high; reports from various cities indicate that half to two-thirds of all persons arrested for nondrug crimes test positive for drug use.[25] But this does not necessarily mean that drugs cause crime. A majority of criminals may use drugs, but the vast majority of drug users do not commit other crimes.

WHO'S WINNING THE WAR ON DRUGS?   The U.S. government's National Household Survey on Drug Abuse regularly asks Americans whether they have ever used particular drugs and whether they have used them in the past year or month. These surveys suggest that about 6 percent of the U.S. population have used an illicit drug in the previous thirty days (see Figure 9-2). Marijuana is the most commonly used illicit drug (4.7 percent of the population); followed by cocaine (0.8 percent of the population).

According to the survey evidence, the number of people using illicit drugs has declined in recent years. However, the U.S. Drug Enforcement Administration (DEA) re-

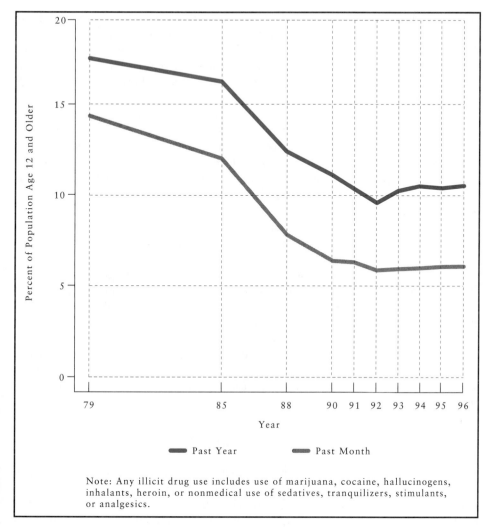

FIGURE 9–2
**Reported Illicit
Drug Use**
(All ages 12 and older)
Source: National Household
Survey on Drug Abuse.

Note: Any illicit drug use includes use of marijuana, cocaine, hallucinogens, inhalants, heroin, or nonmedical use of sedatives, tranquilizers, stimulants, or analgesics.

ports increased numbers of drug seizures each year. There appear to be no significant reductions in the volume of drugs entering the country or reaching the streets.

Educational campaigns against drugs may actually reduce the number of casual users, or these campaigns may signal that drug use is socially unacceptable and inhibit respondents from admitting use even in anonymous interviews. Perhaps the reported reduction in drug use over the years reflects both effects.

The most common interpretation of the poll results showing reduced drug use, and the law enforcement data showing continued volume of drug availability, is that *casual* use is down but daily use by *hard-core* addicted persons remains high.

LEGALIZATION?   The failure of antidrug policies to produce any significant reductions in drug supply or demand, coupled with the high costs of enforcement and the loss of civil liberties, has caused some observers to propose the legalization of drugs and government control of their production and sales. "Prohibition" failed earlier in the century to end alcohol consumption, and the crime, official corruption, and enormous cost of futile efforts to stop drinking eventually forced the nation to end Prohibition. Similarly, it is argued that the legalization of drugs would end organized crime's profit monopoly over the drug trade, raise billions of dollars by legally taxing drugs, end the strain on relations with Latin American nations caused by efforts to eradicate drugs, and save additional billions in enforcement costs, which could be used for education and treatment.[26] If drugs were legally obtainable under government supervision, it is argued that many of society's current problems would be alleviated: the crime and violence associated with the drug trade, the corruption of public officials, the spread of diseases associated with drug use, and the many infringements of personal liberty associated with antidrug wars.

But even the suggestion of drug legalization offends Americans who believe that legalization would greatly expand drug use in the country. Cheap, available drugs would greatly increase the numbers of addicted persons, creating a "society of zombies" that would destroy the social fabric of the nation. Cocaine and heroin are far more habit-forming than alcohol, and legalization would encourage the development of newer and even more potent and addictive synthetic drugs. Whatever the health costs of drug abuse today, it is argued that legalization would produce public health problems of enormous magnitude.[27] Cocaine is very cheap to produce; the current $5 to $10 cost of a "hit" is mostly drug dealer profit; legalization even with taxation might produce a 50 cent "hit." Whatever the damages to society from drug-related crime and efforts to prohibit drugs, the damages to society from cheap, available drug usage would be far greater.

FEDERALISM AND LAW ENFORCEMENT

The public demand to DO SOMETHING! about crime inspires political officeholders in Washington as well as those in state capitols and city halls. Neither Democrats nor Republicans in Washington are willing to risk their political futures by restricting the federal government's role and telling their constituents that crime control is principally a state and local responsibility.

TRADITIONAL DIVISION OF POWERS   Traditionally the federal government's responsibilities were limited to the enforcement of a relatively narrow range of federal criminal laws, including laws dealing with counterfeiting and currency violations; tax evasion, including alcohol, tobacco, and firearm taxes; fraud and embezzlement; robbery or theft of federally insured funds, including banks; interstate criminal activity; murder or assault of a federal official; and federal drug laws. While some federal criminal laws overlapped state laws, most criminal activity—murder, rape, robbery, assault, burglary, theft, auto theft, gambling, sex offenses, and so on—fell under state jurisdiction.

FEDERALIZING CRIME FIGHTING   But pressure mounted over the years for greater federal involvement in crime fighting. Congress made more and more offenses *federal* crimes. Today federal offenses range from drive-by shootings to obstructing sidewalks in front of abortion clinics. (In 1995 the U.S. Supreme Court struck down a *federal* law prohibiting the carrying of a gun near a school, declaring the law to be beyond the powers delegated to Congress in Article I of the Constitution.[28]) The greatest impact of federal legislation is found in drug-related crime. Federal as well as state laws prohibit drug trafficking; offenders may be tried in either federal or state courts.

The U.S. Department of Justice, headed by the Attorney General, handles all criminal prosecutions for violation of federal laws. The federal government's principle investigative agencies are the Federal Bureau of Investigation (FBI) and the Drug Enforcement Administration (DEA), both units of the Department of Justice, and the Bureau of Alcohol, Tobacco and Firearms (ATF) in the Treasury Department. Efforts to combine these federal law enforcement agencies have consistently floundered in bureaucratic turf battles.

CONTINUED DOMINANCE OF STATES IN LAW ENFORCEMENT   Yet despite growing federal activity in law enforcement, state and local governments continue to bear the major burden of fighting crime in America. (See Table 9-3.) About 11 million people are arrested and charged with a crime in the United States each year. But only about 50,000 people are prosecuted for crimes by federal authorities in federal courts.

POLICE PROTECTION IN THE STATES

State, county, and municipal governments are all directly involved in law enforcement. Every state has a central law enforcement agency, sometimes called the state police, state troopers, state highway patrol, or even Texas Rangers. At one time, state governors had only the National Guard at their disposal to back up local law enforcement efforts, but the coming of the automobile and intercity highway traffic led to the establishment in every state of a centralized police system. In addition to patrolling the state's highways, these centralized agencies now provide expert aid and service for lo-

Table 9–3

CRIMINAL JUSTICE ACTIVITY BY LEVEL OF GOVERNMENT		
	Federal	*State and Local*
Full-time Personnel (1,000)		
Law Enforcement	65	735
Judicial	22	203
Corrections	22	534
Prisoners		
Number (1,000) sentenced to more than one year (excludes local jails and juvenile detention centers)	83.7	1,001.7

Source: Statistical Abstract of the United States, 1995, p. 210, and 1997, p. 220.

cal police officers and strengthen law enforcement in sparsely populated regions. Most of the states have given their central police agencies full law enforcement authority in addition to highway duties: They may cooperate with local authorities in the apprehension of criminals, or even intervene when local authorities are unable or unwilling to enforce the law. The size and influence of these agencies vary from state to state. On the whole, however, state police forces constitute a very small proportion of the total law enforcement effort in America. About 15 percent of all law enforcement officers are state police, 5 percent are federal officers, and the remaining 80 percent are city and county officers. Law enforcement in the nation is principally a *local* responsibility.

THE COUNTY SHERIFF   Historically, the county sheriff has been the keystone of law enforcement in the United States. Sheriffs and their deputies are still the principal enforcement and arresting officers in the rural counties and in the unincorporated fringe areas of many urban counties. In addition, the sheriff serves as an executive agent for county and state courts in both civil and criminal matters, and maintains the county jail for the retention of persons whose trials or sentences are pending or who are serving short sentences. The sheriff's office is a political one; in every state except Rhode Island the sheriff is an elected official. Reliance upon the sheriff's office for law enforcement is a characteristic of rural states. Since city police forces usually assume the sheriff's law enforcement duties within the boundaries of cities, the sheriff's office has seriously atrophied in most urban states; often the sheriff is reduced to a process server for the courts.

CITY POLICE   Urban police departments are the most important instruments of law enforcement and public safety in the nation today. City police officers vastly outnumber all other state and county law enforcement officers combined. The urban police department does more than merely enforce the law; it engages in a wide range of activities for social control.

POLICE AND CRIME   The total number of police officers nationwide has grown to about 1.3 million—about 25 full-time police officers per 10,000 population. This figure includes all city, county, state, federal, and specialized law enforcement agencies. But police protection varies considerably among the fifty states, with some states providing over 35 police officers per 10,000 population, and other states providing fewer than 20 (see "Police Protection" in "*Rankings of the States:* Crime and Law Enforcement," p. 273). But the number of officers has *not* kept abreast of crime. On the contrary, the number of police officers relative to the number of reported crimes has declined steadily. This decline is unique to police personnel, as growth in the number of other state and local employees has generally exceeded the growth of their workload.

POLICE AND LAW ENFORCEMENT

Police perform at least three important functions in urban society—law enforcement, keeping the peace, and furnishing services. Actually, law enforcement may take up only a small portion of a police officer's daily activity, perhaps only 10 percent. The service function is far more common—attending accidents, directing traffic, escorting crowds, assisting stranded motorists, and so on. The function of peace keeping is also very common—breaking up fights, quieting noisy parties, handling domestic or neighborhood quarrels, and the like. It is in this function that police exercise the greatest discretion in the application of the law. In most of these incidents blame is difficult to determine, participants are reluctant to file charges, and police must use personal discretion in handling each case.

Police are on the front line of society's efforts to resolve conflict. Indeed, instead of a legal or law enforcement role, the police are more likely to adopt a peace-keeping role. Police are usually lenient in their arrest practices; that is, they use their arrest power less often than the law allows. Rather than arresting people, the police prefer first to reestablish order. Of course, the decision to be more or less lenient in enforcing the law gives the police a great deal of discretion.

POLICE "CULTURE"   What factors influence police decision making? Probably the first factor to influence police behavior is the attitude of the other people involved in police encounters. If people adopt a cooperative attitude, display deference and respect for the officers, and conform to police expectations, they are much less likely to be arrested than those who show disrespect or use abusive language toward police.[29] Formal police training emphasizes self-control and caution in dealing with the public, but on-the-job experiences probably reinforce predispositions toward distrust of others. The element of danger in police work makes police officers naturally suspicious of others. They see many of the "worst kind" of people, and they see even the "best kind" at their worst.

POLICE AND CRIME REDUCTION   Does increased police protection significantly reduce crime? The common assumption is that increased numbers of police officers and increased police expenditures can significantly reduce crime in cities. However, unfortunately, it is very difficult to produce firm evidence to support this assumption. So many other factors may affect crime rates in cities—size, density, youth, unemployment, race, poverty, and so on—that police activity appears insignificant.

COMMUNITY POLICING   Most police activity is "reactive": typically two officers in a patrol car responding to a radio dispatcher who is forwarding reports of incidents. Police agencies frequently evaluate themselves in terms of the number and frequency of patrols, the number of calls responded to, and the elapsed time between the call and the arrival of officers on the scene. But there is little evidence that any of these measures affect crime rates or even citizens' fear of crime or satisfaction with the police.

An alternative strategy is for police to become more "proactive": typically becoming more visible in the community by walking or bicycling the sidewalks of high crime areas; learning to recognize individuals on the streets and winning their confidence and respect; deterring or scaring away drug dealers, prostitutes, and their customers by a police presence. But this "community policing" is often expensive and potentially more dangerous for police officers.

Community policing.
More active involvement of police with individuals and groups on streets and sidewalks.

POLICE CRACKDOWNS   Police crackdowns—beefed up police actions against juvenile gangs, prostitutes, and drug traffickers; the frisking of likely suspects on the street for guns and drugs; and arrests for (often ignored) public drinking, graffiti, and vandalism—can reduce crime only if supported by the community as well as prosecutors and judges. Crime rates, even murder rates, have been significantly reduced during periods of police crackdowns in major cities.[30] But these efforts are often sporadic; enthusiasm ebbs as jails fill up and the workload of prosecutors and courts multiplies.

CITIZEN ACTION Anticrime efforts by private citizens have risen dramatically over the last decade. Today there are over one million private security guards, overseeing businesses, banks, airports, stores, hotels, and residential communities. (In effect, this

PEOPLE IN POLITICS

RUDOLPH GIULIANI, GETTING TOUGH ON CRIME

New York City, "The Big Apple," has the largest city government in the nation. Its annual expenditures exceed those of forty-eight of the states (only the states of New York and California have larger budgets) as well as every other city in the nation. The mayoralty of New York may be the toughest executive job in the nation after the presidency itself.

Rudolph W. Giuliani, the grandson of Italian immigrants, was educated in Catholic schools in New York and graduated from Manhattan College in 1965 and New York University Law School in 1968. He built a career as a hard-nosed federal prosecuting attorney. He boasted of a record of more than 4,000 criminal convictions with only twenty-five reversals by higher courts. He successfully prosecuted top mafia crime family heads, exposed massive fraud and bribery in New York's parking-violations bureau, and won indictments against prominent Wall Street investors for insider trading. Although frequently accused of grandstanding, his tough-guy approach won him widespread support in a city obsessed with crime.

Republican Giuliani's first race in 1989 for "Gracie Mansion," New York City's mayor's residence, ended in a narrow loss to Democrat David Dinkins. But the closeness of the race, in a city in which Democrats outnumber Republicans by five to one, inspired a second try by Giuliani in 1993. In both races Giuliani campaigned largely on his anticrime reputation. But in a city with a history of racial conflict, crime is often a code word for race. In both 1989 and 1993, New York City voters divided largely along racial lines.

Giuliani's crime-fighting strategies appear to have brought about an unprecedented 50 percent reduction in overall crime and a 69 percent reduction in murder in New York City between 1993 and 1998. How did he do it?

Giuliani began by implementing the "Broken Windows" strategy, which holds that one neglected broken window in a building will soon lead to many other broken windows. In crime-fighting, this theory translates into arrests for petty offenses (for example, subway fare evasion, graffiti, vandalism, aggressive panhandling) in order to not only improve the quality of life in the city but also to lead to the capture of suspects wanted for more serious crimes. Yet another strategy of the mayor was to use the latest computer mapping technology to track crime statistics and pinpoint unusual activity in specific neighborhoods. All seventy-six police precincts in New York are now regularly evaluated on the number and types of crimes occurring in each one. It is reported that if Giuliani sees the numbers begin to climb in any precinct, he quickly gets on the phone with the precinct commander.

Giuliani's hard-line tactics have created more than a little controversy. Civil libertarians, as well as some minority-group leaders, complain that these police tactics fall disproportionately on minorities and the poor. And it is alleged that Giuliani's hard-nosed attitude toward crime creates an atmosphere that leads to increased police brutality.

These strategies appear to have made New York City, once among the highest crime-rate cities in the nation, now the safest large city in America. After three decades of social and economic malaise, New York City is no longer seen as "ungovernable," but rather as one of the nation's leading tourist destinations and the self-proclaimed "Capital of the World." In 1997 Giuliani was re-elected to a second term.

force doubles the size of the nation's police force.) Improved security devices are now found in virtually all commercial establishments—from gas stations and neighborhood convenience stores to banks and schools. Millions of Americans live in communities with security gates and guards and millions more have installed security systems in their houses. Citizen patrol groups and "town watch" associations have multiplied.

Prosecutor.
The attorney acting on behalf of the government in a criminal case.

POLICE EFFICIENCY Most crimes are never solved. This is particularly true of property crimes like burglary; these crimes seldom produce eyewitnesses or other useful information. On average across the nation police claim to solve about 14 percent of burglaries; this is their official "clearance rate." Police "clear" only about 50 percent of all violent crimes, and 70 percent of murders. (See Table 9-4.) Most clearances occur in cases in which the victim and perpetrators know each other.

About 11 million people are arrested each year, and many more millions of traffic citations are issued. But even this huge number is less than the 14 million crimes reported to police and the 20 to 30 million crimes estimated from victimization surveys.

THE POLITICS OF PROSECUTION

Prosecution is also part of the political process. Legislatures and governors enact policy, but its enforcement depends upon the decisions of prosecutors as well as judges. Political pressures are most obvious in the enforcement of controversial policies—gambling laws, Sunday closing laws, liquor rules, laws against prostitution, and other laws that are contrary to the interests of significant segments of the population. Prosecution also involves decision making about the allocation of law enforcement resources to different types of offenses—traffic violations, juvenile delinquency, auto theft, assault, burglary, larceny, and robbery. Decisions must be made about what sections of the city should be most vigorously protected and what segments of the population will be most closely watched. The public prosecutor, sometimes called the district attorney (D.A.) or state's attorney, is at the center of diverse pressures concerning law enforcement.

Table 9–4

CRIME AND ARREST	
	Percent of Crimes Cleared by Arrest
Murder	70.0
Rape	52.1
Robbery	25.6
Aggravated Assault	56.8
Burglary	13.5
Larceny/Theft	19.7

Source: National Center for Policy Analysis, "Crime Pays, But So Does Imprisonment," Dallas: National Center for Policy Analysis, 1992. Calculated from Federal Bureau of Investigation, *Crime in the United States, Uniform Crime Reports,* annual issues (Washington, DC: Government Printing Office).

■

Grand jury.
A jury that decides whether sufficient evidence exists to indict and try a defendant.

Trial (petit) jury.
A jury that determines the guilt or innocence of criminal defendants.

Plea bargain.
An agreement by a criminal defendant to plead guilty to lesser charges with lighter penalties in order to avoid a jury trial.

The political nature of the prosecutor's job is suggested by the frequency with which this job leads to higher political office. Prosecuting attorney is often a steppingstone to state and federal judgeships, congressional seats, and even the governorship. Ambitious D.A.s, concerned with their political future, may seek to build a reputation as a crusader against crime and vice, while at the same time maintaining the support and friendship of important interests in the community.

PROSECUTOR'S DISCRETION   The political power of prosecutors stems from their discretion in deciding (1) whether or not to prosecute in criminal cases, and (2) whether prosecution will be on more serious or less serious charges. Prosecutors may decide simply to drop charges ("nol-pros") when they feel adequate proof is lacking, or when they feel that police have committed a procedural error that infringed on the defendant's rights, or when they feel that the resources of their office would be better allocated by pursuing other cases. About half of all felony arrests result in dismissal of charges against the defendant. Prosecutors may also engage in "plea bargaining"—reducing the charges from more serious to less serious crimes in exchange for defendants' promises to plead guilty. Or prosecutors may reduce charges because they believe it will be easier in court to obtain a guilty verdict on the lesser charge.

GRAND JURIES   Are there any checks on the power of prosecutors? In principle, the grand jury is supposed to determine whether evidence presented to it by the prosecutor is sufficient to warrant the placing of a person on trial in a felony case. Ideally, the grand jury serves as a check against the overzealous district attorney, and as a protection for the citizen against unwarranted harassment. However, in practice, grand juries spend very little time deliberating on the vast majority of the cases.[31] A typical grand jury spends only five to ten minutes per case, primarily listening to the prosecutor's recommendation as to how the case should be decided. Over 80 percent of the cases may be decided on an immediate vote, without discussion among jurors, and almost always with unanimous votes. Finally, and most importantly, grand juries follow the recommendations of prosecutors in over 98 percent of the cases presented to them. The prosecutor controls the information submitted to grand juries, instructs them in their duties, and is usually perceived by jurors as an expert and relied on for guidance. In short, there is no evidence that grand juries provide much of a check on the power of prosecutors.

PLEA BARGAINING   Most convictions are obtained by guilty pleas. Indeed, about 90 percent of the criminal cases brought to trial are disposed of by guilty pleas before a judge, not trial by jury. The Constitution guarantees defendants a trial by jury (Sixth Amendment), but guilty pleas outnumber jury trials by ten to one.

Plea bargaining, in which the prosecution either reduces the seriousness of the charges, drops some but not all charges, or agrees to recommend lighter penalties in exchange for a guilty plea by the defendant, is very common. Some critics of plea bargaining view it as another form of leniency in the criminal justice system that reduces its deterrent effects. Other critics view plea bargaining as a violation of the Constitution's protection against self-incrimination and guarantee of a fair jury trial. Prosecutors, they say, threaten defendants with serious charges and stiff penalties to force a guilty plea. Still other critics see plea bargaining as an under-the-table process that undermines respect for the criminal justice system.

It is very fortunate for the nation's court system that most defendants plead guilty. The court system would quickly break down from overload if any substantial proportion of defendants insisted on jury trials.

STATE PRISONS AND CORRECTIONAL POLICIES

The United States has experienced an explosive growth in its prison population in recent years. Millions of Americans each year are brought to a jail, police station, or juvenile home or prison. The vast majority are released within hours or days. There are, however, over 1.2 million inmates in state and federal prisons in the United States. These prisoners are serving time for serious offenses. Ninety percent had a record of crime before they committed the act that led to their current imprisonment. An additional 500,000 persons are temporarily residing in city or county jails at any one time across the country. The rate of incarceration (prisoners per 100,000 population) in the United States is one of the highest in the world. (See Figure 9-3.)

Why are so many people behind bars? Because they have committed so many crimes. The crime rate in the United States is also one of the highest in the world. Indeed, the number of prisoners in the United States *relative to the numbers of crimes* is no higher than in other industrialized nations.

PRISONERS IN THE STATES   States differ a great deal in the number of prisoners and the proportion of their populations behind bars. (See "Incarceration Rate" in "*Rankings of the States:* Crime and Law Enforcement," p. 273.) As might be expected, prisoner populations generally reflect the crime rate in the states; higher crime rate states have larger proportions of their population in prison. (See also Figure 9-3.)

Another cause of increased prison populations in the states is an increase in the length of criminal sentences. In recent years many states have attempted to "get tough on crime" by legislating longer sentences for particular crimes, specifying mandatory minimum sentences for crimes, eliminating judicial variation in sentences, adding years to the sentences given repeat or "habitual" criminals, and abolishing parole.

THE FAILURE OF REHABILITATION   For many years the prevailing philosophy in corrections was that of rehabilitation. In deciding sentences judges were free to consider not only the crime, but personal characteristics of the defendant. State criminal codes stated broad ranges of sentences for various crimes, for example, two to ten years. Moreover, judges in many states had the option of imposing "indeterminant" sentences (e.g., not less than one nor more than five years) and leaving the decision concerning how long a prisoner would serve to parole boards. While in prison, individuals were expected to "rehabilitate" themselves through education, job training, counseling, and other programs. Prisons were called "correctional institutions" to reflect their therapeutic value.

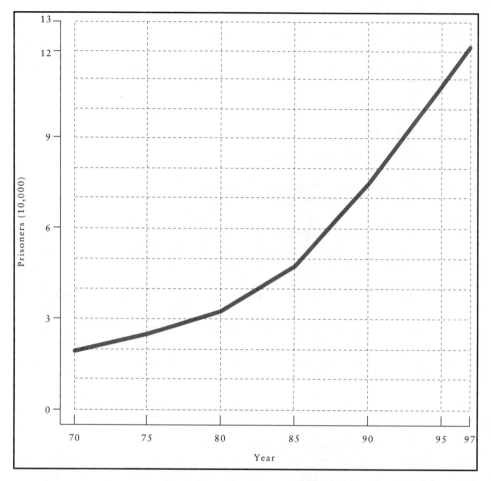

Over time it became increasingly difficult to maintain the fiction that prisons were designed to rehabilitate people. Over 80 percent of all felonies are committed by repeaters—individuals who have had prior contact with the criminal justice system and were not corrected by it. Over two-thirds of all prison admissions are "recidivists"—people returned to prison for new crimes. Almost half have had three or more prior prison sentences.[32] Reformers generally recommend more education and job training, more and better facilities, smaller prisons, halfway houses where offenders can adjust to civilian life before parole, more parole officers, and greater contact between prisoners and their families and friends. But there has never been any convincing evidence that these investments reduce what criminologists call "recidivism," the offenders' return to crime. There is no evidence that people *can* be "rehabilitated," no matter what is done. Even the maintenance of order *within* prisons and the protection of the lives of guards and inmates have become serious national problems.

Prison life does little to encourage good behavior. For the most part, inmates spend their days in idleness—watching television, weight lifting, walking and talking in the yard. "Meaningful educational, vocational, and counseling programs are rare. Strong inmates are permitted to pressure weaker prisoners for sex, drugs, and money. Gangs organized along racial and ethnic lines are often the real 'sovereign of the cellblocks.'"[33] About 55 percent of the nation's overall prison population is black; about 94 percent are male. Most of the nation's 1,300 state prisons and 70 federal prisons have more inmates than their rated capacity. Most state prison systems, like the Federal Bureau of Prisons, operate maximum security institutions for high-risk inmates who have proven too violent to mix with the general prison population.

SENTENCING   Clearly, indeterminant sentencing and discretion given parole boards do *not* serve the goal of deterrence. Rather deterrence is served by making prison sentences predictable (certain) and long (severe). Potential lawbreakers are supposed to say to themselves, "If you can't serve the time, don't do the crime." Throughout the 1980s states enacted amendments to their criminal codes specifying determinant sentences for various crimes. The discretion of judges was restricted. Variation in sentencing was reduced (although not eliminated); judges were obliged by law to mete out sentences based on the crime and the number of previous convictions amassed by the defendant. Greater uniformity of sentencing also served the goal of reducing arbitrary, unfair, and discriminatory sentencing. For many crimes, deterrence was also strengthened by long mandatory minimum sentences. For example, many states enacted mandatory one-, two-, or three-year prison terms for the use of a gun in the commission of a felony.

But many mandatory minimum sentence laws focused on drug offenses. And the "war on drugs" in the state and federal law enforcement agencies directed resources away from investigation and prosecution of property crimes, and even violent crimes, toward drug offenses.[34] The result was that prisons soon filled with drug offenders; today over half of the nation's prisoners are incarcerated for drug offenses.

PRISON OVERCROWDING   The effect of longer sentences, combined with higher crime rates and more prisoners, has been to create mammoth prison overcrowding. Overcrowding contributes directly to unsanitary and dangerous prison living conditions; overcrowding is associated with assaults, rapes, homicides, suicides, and riots. Prison staff are also placed at risk by overcrowding and the violence it produces.

Federal courts have determined that prison overcrowding is a violation of the U.S. Constitution's Eighth Amendment prohibition against "cruel and unusual punishments." (Simple crowding per se is not unconstitutional; federal courts must also find evidence of adverse effects of overcrowding.) Virtually all of the states confront federal court orders to reduce prison overcrowding at one or more of their prisons or their entire prison system. Most state prison systems are near, at, or over their capacity to house prisoners.

EARLY RELEASES   As a result of overcrowding, most states have had to resort to *early release* programs. Sentences of prisoners are automatically reduced and those near the end of their terms are let go first. Some states deny early release to certain violent offenders. Nonetheless, violent criminals on the average serve less than half of their sentences, and nonviolent offenders less than one-third of their sentences. In some states, due to prison overcrowding, inmates serve only one-quarter of their sentences.[35]

Recidivism.
The likelihood of a former convict returning to prison for new crimes.

Determinant sentences.
Sentences for various crimes enacted into law and limiting the discretion of judges.

Mandatory minimum sentences.
Minimum sentences for various crimes enacted into law by state legislatures.

FIGURE 9–4 Violent Crime Sentences versus Time Served

Source: U.S. Bureau of Justice Statistics.

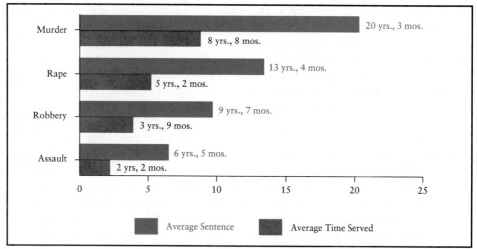

In many states, early release programs have become institutionalized. The national average prison time actually served by convicted murderers is eight years, eight months (see Figure 9-4).

THE 85 PERCENT SOLUTION   Media reports of "avertible crimes"—crimes committed by persons who would still have been imprisoned based on earlier convictions if they had served their full sentence—has placed heavy pressure on state legislatures to end early releases. (It is estimated that 20 percent of all violent crimes and 30 percent of property crimes are committed by persons who would still be in prison if they had been forced to serve their full sentence.[36]) In order to stem the tide of early releases, state legislatures are increasingly turning to the "85 percent solution"—mandating that all convicted felons serve at least 85 percent of the length of their sentences. This means that the average time served by prisoners is gradually lengthening. (Courts have held that prisoners convicted prior to the passage of such laws cannot be held to the new standard.) In recent years, prosecutors have been pressing for longer sentences and judges have been imposing them. This trend, together with a mandated serving of 85 percent of sentences, has added to the need for more prison space.

BUILDING MORE PRISONS   States have been compelled to build more prisons in recent years. But taxpayers are understandably upset with the prospects of spending $50,000 to $75,000 for each new prison bed, and $15,000 to $25,000 per year to keep a prisoner behind bars. But if the costs of incarceration are weighed against its benefits, taxpayers may feel better about prison construction and maintenance. A prisoner's "rap sheet" may list only three or four convictions and a dozen arrests. But interviews with offenders suggest the typical convict has committed hundreds of crimes. Various studies have attempted to estimate the dollars lost to society in the crimes committed by the typical convict in a year.[37] Estimates run from $200,000 to $400,000. This means that a year of crime may be ten to twenty times more costly to society than a year of incarceration.

"THREE STRIKES YOU'RE OUT"   The "revolving door" syndrome, with its heavy toll in crimes committed by persons previously convicted of crimes, has led to a nationwide movement to impose minimum 25-years-to-life sentences on criminals convicted of a third felony or third violent felony crime. A California citizens' initiative in 1994, Three Strikes You're Out, illustrates the popularity of this crackdown with voters; it passed 72 to 28 percent. The initiative was begun by a father whose eighteen-year-old daughter had been murdered by a parolee. Some of these initiatives are broadly written to include *all* felony convictions and therefore often encompass drug offenders, bad-check writers, and other nonviolent criminals. Other initiatives specify three *violent* felony convictions and thus target a smaller population of repeat criminals. In 1995, Congress mandated life sentences for federal defendants convicted of their third violent felony.

THE FAILURE OF PROBATION AND PAROLE   In addition to the over 1 million people behind bars, an additional 2.8 million are currently on probation and 600,000 on parole for serious crimes. But parole and probation have been just as ineffective as prison in reducing crime. Even though persons placed on probation are considered less dangerous to society than persons imprisoned, studies indicate that nearly two-thirds of probationers will be arrested and over one-half will be convicted for a serious crime committed *while on probation.*

The function of parole and postrelease supervision is (1) to procure information on the parolee's postprison conduct and (2) to facilitate and graduate the transition between prison and complete freedom. These functions are presumably oriented toward protecting the public and rehabilitating the offender. However, studies of recidivism indicate that up to three-quarters of persons paroled from prison will be rearrested for serious crimes. There is no difference in this high rate of recidivism between persons released under supervised parole and those released unconditionally. Thus, it does not appear that parole succeeds in its objectives. (See also "*Up Close:* Can Punishment Deter Crime?")

THE DEATH PENALTY

Perhaps the most heated debate in criminal justice today concerns capital punishment. Opponents of the death penalty argue that it is "cruel and unusual punishment" in violation of the Eighth Amendment of the U.S. Constitution. They also argue that the death penalty is applied unequally. A large proportion of those executed have been poor, uneducated, and nonwhite.

In contrast, there is a strong sense of justice among many Americans that demands retribution for heinous crimes—a life for a life. The death penalty dramatically signifies that society does not excuse or condone the taking of innocent lives. It symbolizes the value that society places on innocent lives. A mere jail sentence for murder devalues the life of the innocent victim. In most cases, a life sentence means less than ten years in prison under the current parole and probation policies of most states. Convicted murderers have been set free, and some have killed again. Moreover, prison guards and other inmates are exposed to convicted murderers who have "a license to kill," because they are already serving life sentences and have nothing to lose by killing again.

UP CLOSE

CAN PUNISHMENT DETER CRIME?

Can punishment deter crime? This is a difficult question to answer. First of all, we must distinguish between *deterrence* and *incapacity*. Incapacity can be imposed by long terms of imprisonment, particularly for habitual offenders; the policy of "keeping criminals off the streets" does indeed protect the public for a period of time, although it is done at a considerable cost. The object of *deterrence* is to make the certainty and severity of punishment so great as to inhibit potential criminals from committing crimes.

In theory, deterrence is enhanced by:

1. The *certainty* that a crime will be followed by costly punishment. Justice must be sure.

2. The *swiftness* of the punishment following the crime. Long delays between crime and punishment break the link in the mind of the criminal between the criminal act and its consequences. And a potential wrong-doer must believe that the costs of a crime will occur within a meaningful time frame, not in a distant, unknowable future. Justice must be swift.

3. The *severity* of the punishment. Punishment that is perceived as no more costly than the ordinary hazards of life on the streets which the potential criminal faces anyhow will not deter. Punishment must clearly outweigh whatever benefits might be derived from a life of crime in the minds of potential criminals. Punishment must be severe.

FIGURE 9–A Crime and Punishment

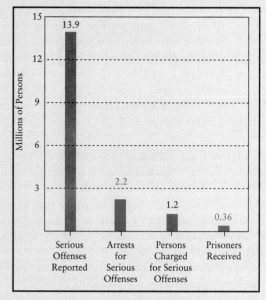

Source: Statistical Abstract of the United States, 1997.

These criteria for an effective deterrent policy are ranked in the order of their probable importance. That is, it is most important that punishment for crime be certain. The severity of punishment is probably less important than its swiftness or certainty. However, the best available estimates of the *certainty* of

---

Capital punishment. The death penalty. (The word *capital* is derived from the Latin word for "head"— *caput*. The Latin word for "punish" is *punire*. Combined, they mean "head punishment," that is, a cutting off of one's head.)

FURMAN V. GEORGIA AND UNFAIR APPLICATION Prior to 1972, the death penalty was officially sanctioned by about one half of the states. Federal law also retained the death penalty. However, no one had actually suffered the death penalty since 1967, because of numerous legal tangles and direct challenges to the constitutionality of capital punishment. In 1972, the Supreme Court ruled that capital punishment as it was then imposed violated the Eighth and Fourteenth Amendment prohibitions against cruel and unusual punishment and due process of law. The decision was made by a narrow 5–4 vote of the justices, and the reasoning in the case is very complex. Only two justices—Brennan and Marshall—declared that capital punishment itself is cruel and unusual. The other three justices in the majority—Douglas, White, and Stewart—felt that death sentences had been applied unfairly: A few individuals were receiving the death penalty for crimes for which many others were receiving much lighter sentences. These justices left open the possibility that capital punishment would be constitutional if it was specific for certain kinds of crime and applied uniformly.

punishment for serious crime suggest that very few crimes actually result in jail sentences for the perpetrators. About 14 million serious crimes were reported to police in 1995, but only 2.2 million persons were arrested for these crimes (see Figure 9–A). Some of those arrested were charged with committing more than one crime, but it is estimated that police clear less than 20 percent of reported crimes by arresting the offender. Prosecutors do not charge about half of the persons arrested for serious offenses. Some offenders are handled as juveniles; some are permitted to plead guilty to minor offenses; others are released because witnesses fail to appear or evidence is weak or inadmissible in court. Of the persons charged with serious offenses by prosecutors, only about 25 percent receive jail sentences for their crimes. Convicted felons are three times more likely to receive probation instead of a prison sentence. Thus, even if punishment could deter crime, our current criminal justice system does *not* ensure punishment for crime.

Of course, there are many other conflicting theories of crime in America. For example, it is sometimes argued that this nation's high crime rate is a product of its social heterogeneity—the multiethnic, multiracial character of the American population. Low levels of crime in European countries, Japan, and China are often attributed to their homogeneous populations and shared cultures. Blacks in the United States are both victims and perpetrators of crime far more frequently than whites. While blacks constitute only about 12 percent of the population, they account for over 30 percent of all persons arrested for serious crimes (see Table 9–A). A larger segment of the black population is in the young crime-prone age (fifteen to twenty-four years), and these youths are more likely to live outside husband–wife families. It is argued that "the streets" of the nation's black inner cities produce a subculture that encourages crime.

It is also argued that crime is irrational, that is, the criminal does not weigh benefits against potential costs before committing the act. Many "crimes of passion" are committed by persons acting in blind rage—murders and aggravated assaults among family members, for example. Many rapes are acts of violence, inspired by hatred of women, rather than efforts to obtain sexual pleasure. More murders occur in the heat of arguments than in the commission of other felonies. These are crimes of passion rather than calculated acts. Thus, it is argued, no rational policies can be devised to deter these irrational acts.

Table 9–A

ARRESTS BY AGE, SEX, AND RACE

	Percent of Total Arrests
Male	79.6
Female	20.4
White	66.8
Black	30.9
Native American, Asian, other	2.2
Under 18	18.3
18–24	26.1
25–44	47.4
45–54	5.9
55 and over	2.3

Source: Statistical Abstract of the United States, 1997, pp. 210–11.

THE DEATH PENALTY REINSTATED   After *Furman* v. *Georgia*, most states rewrote their death-penalty laws to try to ensure fairness and uniformity of application. As of 1998, the states *with* the death penalty were Alabama, Arizona, Arkansas, California, Colorado, Connecticut, Delaware, Florida, Georgia, Idaho, Illinois, Indiana, Kansas, Kentucky, Louisiana, Maryland, Mississippi, Missouri, Montana, Nebraska, Nevada, New Hampshire, New Jersey, New Mexico, North Carolina, Ohio, Oregon, Oklahoma, Pennsylvania, South Carolina, South Dakota, Tennessee, Texas, Utah, Virginia, Washington, and Wyoming. The states with *no* death penalty were: Alaska, Hawaii, Iowa, Maine, Massachusetts, Michigan, Minnesota, New York, North Dakota, Rhode Island, Vermont, West Virginia, Wisconsin, and the District of Columbia. Generally, these laws mandate the death penalty for murders committed during rape or robbery, hijacking or kidnapping; murders of prison guards; murder with torture; multiple murders; and so on. Two trials are held: one to determine guilt or innocence and another to determine the penalty. At the second trial, evidence of "aggravating" and "mitigating" factors are presented; if there are aggravating factors but no mitigating factors, the death penalty is mandatory. In 1976, in *Gregs* v. *Georgia, Profit* v. *Florida,* and *Jurek* v. *Texas,* the Supreme Court upheld state laws that were carefully written to ensure fairness and due process in the application of the death penalty. The Court declared that capital punishment itself was not "cruel or unusual" within the meaning of the Eighth Amendment; that the authors of the Constitution did not consider it cruel or unusual; and that the reenactment of the death penalty by so many state legislators was evidence that the death penalty was not considered cruel or unusual by contemporary state lawmakers.

FEW EXECUTIONS   Despite these new laws, very few executions have been carried out. Over 3,000 prisoners are awaiting execution on "death row," but only 313 persons were executed in twenty-four states from 1976 through 1995. Texas, Florida, Virginia, Louisiana, and Georgia led the states in the number of executions. California has had the highest number of prisoners on death row (nearly 400), but it carried out only two executions prior to 1995.

With less than 1 percent of death sentences actually carried out over the past decade, the death penalty cannot possibly be a deterrent to murder. Respect for the court system is eroded when the decisions of juries and judges are frustrated by convicted murderers. As trial judges and juries continue to impose the death penalty, and appellate courts continue to grant stays of execution, the number of prisoners on death row grows. The few who have been executed have averaged ten years' delay between trial and execution.

RACIAL BIAS?   The U.S. Supreme Court is especially sensitive to arguments based on racial discrimination. Defense lawyers have challenged the death penalty in several states by attempting to prove that racial bias infects the application of capital punishment. While white murderers are just as likely to receive the death penalty as black murderers, there are statistical disparities in sentencing between killers of whites and killers of blacks. If the *victim* is white, there is a greater chance that the killer will be sentenced to death than if the victim is black. But in 1987 the U.S. Supreme Court ruled (in a 5–4 decision) that statistical disparities in the race of the victim do not by themselves bar the death penalty; there must be evidence of racial bias against a particular defendant in order for the Court to reverse a death sentence.[38]

DOES THE DEATH PENALTY DETER?   The death penalty as it is employed today—inflicted on so few and so many years after the crime—has little deterrent effect. However, it gives prosecutors some leverage in plea bargaining with murder defendants. They may choose to plead guilty in exchange for a life sentence, when confronted with the possibility that the prosecutor may win a conviction and the death penalty in a jury trial.

PUBLIC OPINION AND CAPITAL PUNISHMENT   Much of the debate in the states over the death penalty, however, has *not* centered on the question of deterrence. Opponents of the death penalty call it "murder" and contend that it is morally indefensible for the state to take away life. Proponents of the death penalty say that the unwillingness of the state to impose capital punishment implies that little value is placed upon the lives of innocent victims. Public opinion now favors the death penalty by over

3 to 1. Only for a few years during the mid-1960s did public opinion oppose the death penalty, and then only by a small margin. With increases in the crime rate in the 1970s, heavy majorities swung back in favor of capital punishment. Public support for capital punishment remains high today.

DID YOU KNOW?

AMERICA'S MOST CRIME-RIDDEN CITIES

Crime rates in large cities are generally higher than those in suburbs, small towns, and rural areas. Indeed, overall crime rates in some of America's big cities are three times the national rate (5,278 per 100,000 population in 1995). The murder rate in Washington, DC, is nearly ten times higher than the national rate (8.2 per 100,000 population in 1995). The ten most crime-ridden cities and the ten cities with the highest murder rates are listed below. Some big cities remain near or below national crime, rates. Note, for example, that New York, once regularly listed among America's most crime-ridden cities, is now one of the safest.

CITIES WITH HIGHEST CRIME RATES

Total Crime Rates	*Murder Rates*
Atlanta	New Orleans
St. Louis	Washington, DC
Miami	St. Louis
Newark	Detroit
Tampa	Baltimore
Baton Rouge	Oklahoma City
Baltimore	Atlanta
Birmingham	Birmingham
Washington, DC	Newark
Tucson	Chicago

CITIES WITH LOWEST CRIME RATES

Total Crime Rates	*Murder Rates*
Denver	Raleigh
Colorado Springs	Anchorage
Lexington	El Paso
Aurora	Lexington
Anaheim	Colorado Springs
Pittsburgh	Mesa, AZ
New York	San Jose
San Diego	Honolulu
Santa Ana	Virginia Beach
Virginia Beach	Arlington

Source: Statistical Abstract of the United States, 1997, p. 203.

ON THE WEB

Courts, crime, and correctional issues are well documented on the Internet. The Cornell University Law School maintains a free Web site with access to *all* U. S. Supreme Court decisions from 1990 to the present, together with 610 most important historical decisions of the Court:

www.supct.law.cornell.edu/supct

These are indexed by topic as well as name.

State court decisions usually must be researched in law school libraries. But the National Center for State Courts maintains a site at

www.ncsc.dnc.us

This organization is primarily concerned with court administration, the processing of cases, case loads, and related issues. Its Web site contains links to the Conference of Chief Justices (of state courts) and the Conference of State Court Administrators.

The U.S. Bureau of Justice Statistics provides a goldmine of information on crime rates (total and by type of crime), victimization rates, arrests, prosecutions, and federal and state prison, parole, and probation populations. Both nationwide and state-by-state figures are provided. Moreover, most of the data are presented in trend lines for the past twenty to thirty years in both table and graphic form. This site can be accessed at

www.ojp.usdoj.gov/bjs

The Federal Bureau of Investigation maintains its own Web site at

www.fbi.gov

This is a frequently accessed site; it includes the FBI's Ten Most Wanted list. It also includes the semiannually updated *Uniform Crime Reports*. These UCRs are provided for all types of crime both nationwide and by city. (However, the latest figures are given as percentage increases or decreases from the previous year, requiring viewers to access the previous year and do the math themselves to obtain the latest actual crime rates.)

NOTES

1. See Donald R. Souger and Ashlyn Kuersten, "The Success of Amici in State Supreme Courts," *Political Research Quarterly*, 48 (March 1995), 31–42.

2. John C. Kilwein and Richard A. Brisbin, Jr., "Policy Convergence in a Federal Judicial System," *American Journal of Political Science,* vol. 41 (January 1997), 122–48.

3. See Gregory A. Caldereira, "On the Reputations of State Supreme Courts," *Political Behavior,* 5 (1983), 89.

4. Philip L. Dubois, "Voter Turnout in State Judicial Elections," *Journal of Politics,* 41 (1979), 865–87.

5. Philip L. Dubois, "The Significance of Voting Cues in State Supreme Court Elections," *Law and Society Review,* 13 (Spring 1979), 759–79.

6. Charles A. Johnson, Roger C. Schaefer, and R. Neal McKnight, "The Salience of Judicial Candidates and Elections," *Social Science Quarterly,* 59 (September 1978), 371–78.

7. William Jenkins, "Retention Elections: Who Wins When No One Loses," *Judicature,* 61 (August 1977), 79–86.

8. Bradley Cannon, "The Impact of Formal Selection Processes on Characteristics of Judges—Reconsidered," *Law and Society Review,* 13 (May 1972), 570–93. An updated analysis showing that "no method of recruitment selects judges with substantially different credentials" is found in Craig F. Emmert and Henry R. Glick, "The Selection of State Supreme Court Judges," *American Politics Quarterly,* 16 (October 1988), 445–65.

9. Burton M. Atkins and Henry R. Glick, "Formal Judicial Recruitment and State Supreme Court Decisions," *American Politics Quarterly,* 2 (October 1974), 427–49.

10. Paul Brace and Melinda Gann Hall, "Studying Courts Comparatively," *Political Research Quarterly,* 48 (March 1995), 5–29.

11. James T. Wenzel, Shaun Bowler, and David J. Lanoue, "Legislating from the State Bench," *American Politics Quarterly,* vol. 25 (July 1997), 363–79.

12. Quotations from Lenore Alpert, Burton M. Atkins, and Robert C. Ziller, "Becoming a Judge: The Transition from Advocate to Arbiter," *Judicature,* 62 (February 1979), 325–35.

13. Austin Sarat, "Judging Trial Courts," *Journal of Politics,* 39 (May 1977), 368–98.

14. Stuart Nagel, "Political Party Affiliation and Judges' Decisions," *American Political Science Association,* 55 (1961), 843-51; and Sidney Ulmer, "The Political Party Variable on the Michigan Supreme Court," *Journal of Public Law,* 11 (1962), 352–62.

15. Brace and Hall, "Studying Courts Comparatively."

16. Jerome Frank, *Law and the Modern Mind* (New York: Coward-McCann, 1930); Benjamin N. Cardozo, *The Nature of the Judicial Process* (New Haven: Yale University Press, 1921); and Roscoe Pound, *Justice According to Law* (New Haven: Yale University Press, 1951).

17. See John Patrick Hagan, "Patterns of Activism on State Supreme Courts," *Publius,* 18 (Winter 1988), 97–115.

18. John M. Scheb, Terry Bowen, and Gary Anderson, "Ideology, Role Orientations and Behav-

ior in State Courts of Last Resort," *American Politics Quarterly,* 19 (July 1991), 324–35.

19. U.S. Bureau of Justice Statistics, *Criminal Victimization in the United States,* annual.

20. *Statistical Abstract of the United States, 1995,* p. 145.

21. *Statistical Abstract of the United States, 1997,* p. 210.

22. For a summary of this evidence and references to the relevant health literature, see Richard C. Schroeder, *Politics of Drugs* (Washington, DC: Congressional Quarterly Press, 1980).

23. Ibid., p. 148.

24. Office of National Drug Control Policy, *National Drug Control Strategy* (Washington, DC: Government Printing Office, 1994), p. 104.

25. *Statistical Abstract of the United States, 1997,* p. 210.

26. Ethan A. Nadelmann, "The Case for Legalization," *The Public Interest* (Summer 1988), 3–31.

27. John Kaplan, "Taking Drugs Seriously," *The Public Interest* (Summer 1988), 32–50.

28. *United States* v. *Lopez* (1995).

29. Stuart A. Scheingold, "Cultural Cleavage and Criminal Justice," *Journal of Politics,* 40, 865–97.

30. For a summary, see John J. DiIulio, Jr., "Arresting Ideas: Tougher Law Enforcement Is Driving Down Crime," *Policy Review* (Fall 1995), 12–16.

31. The following discussion relies on evidence presented by Robert A. Carp, "The Behavior of Grand Juries: Acquiescence or Justice," *Social Science Quarterly,* 55 (March 1975), 853–70.

32. Bureau of Justice Statistics, *Survey of State Prison Inmates* (1994).

33. John J. DiIulio, Jr., "Punishing Smarter," *Brookings Review* (Summer 1989), 8.

34. See David W. Rasmussen and Bruce L. Benson, *The Economic Anatomy of the Drug War* (Latham, MD: Rowan and Littlefield, 1994).

35. Richard B. Abell, "Beyond Willie Horton: The Battle of the Prison Bulge," *Policy Review,* 47 (Winter 1989), 32–35.

36. DiIulio, "Punishing Smarter," pp. 3–12.

37. See Abell, "Beyond Willie Horton," pp. 32–35.

38. *McCluskey* v. *Kemp,* 481 U.S. 279 (1987).

10

COMMUNITY POLITICAL SYSTEMS

COMMUNITIES AS SETTINGS FOR POLITICS

American communities come in different shapes and sizes, and community politics come in a variety of styles. Generalizing about community politics is perhaps even more difficult than generalizing about American state politics. There are more than 86,000 local governments in the United States. These include cities, municipalities, townships, counties, and a host of other school districts and special districts. (See Table 10–1.) Two-thirds of the American people live in urban units of local government known as "municipalities," including "cities," "boroughs," "villages," or "towns." Other Americans are served by county or township governments. Moreover, there are over 250 metropolitan areas in the United States; these are clusterings of people and governments around a core city of 50,000 or more residents. These metropolitan areas range in size up to the New York area, which has 600 local governments and 18 million people. In short, one may conceive of community political systems as rural counties, towns, and villages, cities of all sizes, or even sprawling metropolitan areas.

MANAGING CONFLICT   Community political systems serve two principal functions. One is that of supplying goods and services—for example, police protection or sewage disposal—that are not supplied by private enterprise. This is the "service" function. The other function is the "political" one, that of *managing conflict* over public policy. Of course, the "political" and the "service" functions of local governments are often indistinguishable in practice. A mayor who intervenes in a dispute about the location of a park is managing a local government service, namely recreation, at the same time that he or she is managing political conflict about whose neighborhood should get the most benefit from the new park.

Occasionally, students are led to believe that local governments should be less "political" than state or national governments. Many people feel that it would be best to eliminate "politics" from local government. However, politicians who respond to political considerations, in contrast to service considerations, are not necessarily sacrificing the welfare of the community. It is not always true that the community is best served by treating the service function of government as if it were more important or more worthy of government attention than the political one. A politician who undertakes to arrange political compromises and balance competing interests in a community is performing a very important function. Helping people with different incomes, occupations, skin colors, religious beliefs, and styles of living to live together in a reasonably peaceful fashion is a vital task.

SOURCES OF COMMUNITY CONFLICT   What are the sources of community conflicts? Human diversity is the source of all political conflict—differences among people in wealth, occupation, education, ethnicity, race, religion, and style of living. In the United States, there are many rural communities, small towns and cities, and compact suburbs with relatively homogeneous populations. In these communities, there are few differences among citizens that create permanent lines of cleavage or that run very deep. Some conflicts occur in these communities, of course, but groupings of forces are usually temporary. In contrast, in most large cities and metropolitan areas there are

Table 10–1

LOCAL GOVERNMENTS IN THE UNITED STATES	
Counties	3,043
Municipalities	19,296
Townships	16,666
School Districts	14,586
Special Districts	33,131
Total (including States and National Government)	86,743

Source: U.S. Bureau of the Census, *Census of Governments, 1992.* Latest figures available.

many different kinds of people living closely together, and there are more lasting cleavages, or "fault lines," which tend to open when controversial issues arise. These cleavages are readily recognized in disputes among upper-, middle-, and lower-income groups; ethnic groups; property owners and nonproperty owners; families with children and those without; suburbanites and city dwellers; and traditional political party divisions.[1] Increasingly in America's large cities, *race* is becoming the major source of conflict.

COPING WITH DISSATISFACTION   How do individuals cope with community problems? If you are dissatisfied with the way things are going in your community, you have three choices: (1) resign yourself to the situation, do nothing, and just tolerate it; (2) move away and find a community that provides more satisfactions; (3) stay and make an attempt to change things. Political scientists tend to focus their attention on the people who try to change things, implying that this is the only way to respond rationally to community problems. However, economists have developed theories of residential mobility that focus on the individual's choice of community based on a rational calculation of personal costs and benefits.[2] (The theory is most applicable to metropolitan areas where many different kinds of communities are available.) There are recognized negative "push" factors—crime, congestion, noise, overcrowding, racial conflict—and positive "pull" factors—more space, larger houses, better schools, "nice" playmates for the children—both of which affect decisions to move. One might move to the suburbs "for the kids," or move to the city to be close to good restaurants, fine entertainment, cultural events, and specialty shops, or to reduce the trip to work. In short, economists emphasize rational calculations and freedom of choice, which they assume most citizens possess.

How do people actually respond to community dissatisfactions? There is some evidence to suggest that, in the face of community problems:[3]

- Higher-status whites tend either to become politically active or to move out, with political activity somewhat more common.
- Lower-status whites tend to move out rather than become politically active.

- Blacks are more likely to become politically active than to move out, probably because of the increased difficulties most blacks face in residential relocation.
- City residents are more likely to move out, whereas suburbanites are more likely to become politically active.
- People who have been generally satisfied with the past performance of their local government, as well as people who have invested in home ownership or local businesses, are more likely to become politically active to solve a current problem, rather than to move out or do nothing.
- Dissatisfied affluent residents may choose to "privatize" the community services that distress them. The most common example is the choice of private schools over the public school system, but occasionally residents and businesses also turn to private police protection, security services, garbage collection, and so on.

Overall, the tendency to "move away" from urban problems has greatly accentuated the difficulties of the nation's largest central cities. Many of these cities are actually declining in population—losing middle-class residents to their surrounding suburbs. We will return to this problem in Chapter 12, but it is important to know how individual citizens as well as governments cope with community problems.

EIGHTY-SIX THOUSAND GOVERNMENTS

Local government is not mentioned in the U.S. Constitution. Although we regard the American federal system as a mixture of federal, state, and *local* governments, from a constitutional point of view, local governments are really parts of state governments. Communities have no right to self-government in the U.S. Constitution. All of their governmental powers legally flow from state laws and constitutions. Local governments—cities, townships, counties, special districts, and school districts—are creatures of the state, subject to the obligations, privileges, powers, and restrictions that state governments impose upon them. The state may create or destroy any or all units of local government. To the extent that local governments can collect taxes, regulate their citizens, and provide services, they are actually exercising *state* powers delegated to them by the state in either its constitution or its laws.

Different units of government are assigned different responsibilities by each of the states, so it is difficult to generalize about what each of these types of local governments is supposed to do. Indeed, even in the same state, there may be overlapping functions and responsibilities assigned to cities, counties, school districts, and special districts. Nevertheless, let us try to make some generalizations about what each of these types of government does, realizing of course that in any specific location the pattern of governmental activity may be slightly different:

COUNTIES
—Rural: keep records of deeds, mortgages, births, marriages; assess and levy property taxes; maintain local roads; administer elections and certify election results to

state; provide law enforcement through sheriff; maintain criminal court; maintain a local jail; administer state welfare programs.

—Urban: most of same functions as rural counties (except police and court systems, which often become city functions), together with planning and control of new subdivisions; mental health; public health maintenance and public hospitals; care of the aged; recreation, including parks, stadiums, and convention centers; and perhaps some city functions.

CITIES

—provide the "common functions" of police, fire, streets, sewage, sanitation, and parks; over half of the nation's large cities also provide welfare services and public education. (In other cities welfare is handled by county governments or directly by state agencies, and education is handled by separate school districts.)

SCHOOL DISTRICTS

—organized specifically to provide public elementary and secondary education; community colleges may be operated by county governments or by special districts with or without state support.

TOWNSHIPS

—generally subdivisions of counties with the same responsibilities as their county.

SPECIAL DISTRICTS

—may be as large as the Port Authority of New York and New Jersey with billions in diversified assets. However, special districts are usually established for mass transit, soil conservation, libraries, water and irrigation, mosquito control, sewage disposal, airports, and so on.

The fifty states vary a great deal in the numbers of local governments they authorize. (See "*Rankings of the States:* Local Governments.") Hawaii is the nation's most centralized state: There are only eighteen local governments in the Aloha State; fourteen of these are special districts without taxing power; three are counties; and one is the city of Honolulu. In contrast, there are 6,627 local governments in Illinois, including 1,279 cities, 102 counties, 1,434 townships, 1,029 school districts, and 2,783 special districts.

COUNTY GOVERNMENTS: RURAL AND URBAN

All states, with the exception of Connecticut and Rhode Island, have organized *county* governments. In Louisiana, counties are called "parishes," and in Alaska they are called "boroughs." It is difficult to generalize about the powers of the nation's 3,402 counties. The legal powers, organization, and officers of counties vary a great deal. Perhaps it would be best to begin a description of county government by distinguishing between *rural* and *urban* counties. Obviously there is a great deal of difference between Los Angeles County, with 8.5 million people; Cook County, Chicago, with 5.2 million; and Harris County, Houston, with 2.8 million; and the 725 rural counties in the nation with populations of 10,000 or less.

Local Governments

All Local Governmental Units

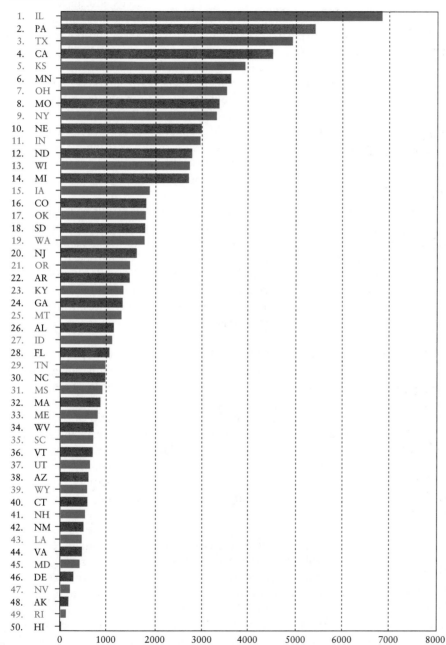

Source: *Statistical Abstract of the United States*, 1997, p. 297.

■

Rural county.
The traditional administrative subdivision of state government. It is responsible for law enforcement, courts, roads, elections, and the recording of legal documents.

Urban county.
County governments that perform all of the services of traditional rural counties together with many contemporary urban services.

Sheriff.
The chief law enforcement officer in a county.

Coroner.
The county official responsible for determining causes of death occurring under violent, unusual, or suspicious circumstances.

County commission structure.
The traditional organization of county government in which elected commissioners directly supervise county functions.

RURAL COUNTIES   Traditionally, the rural county was the most important unit of local government: It handled such essential matters as law enforcement, courts, roads, elections, poor relief, and the legal recording of property deeds, mortgages, wills, and marriages. Rural communities competed with each other for the location of the county seat, because the community named as county seat won social and political prestige, county jobs, a county fair, and preferential treatment in county roads and public buildings. Moreover, many rural dwellers identify themselves as "coming from" a particular county. The county seat attracted retail business: Farm markets were generally located in county seats, where a farmer could transact both public and private business. Rural county government provided an arena for a folksy, provincial, individualistic, "friends and neighbors" type of politics. Rural county government was the province of amateurs rather than experts or professionals. Decision making was personalized and informal. Often rural counties resemble urban counties about as much as the old-fashioned country store resembles a modern supermarket.

URBAN COUNTIES   County government in urban areas is acquiring many of the responsibilities of city governments. Urban counties may provide traditional "city services" to the unincorporated areas of the county, that is, to the areas not within the boundaries of cities, and occasionally to cities as well. This is particularly true of the county governments located in large metropolitan areas (see Table 10–2). Urban county governments generally provide all of the services of traditional rural counties together with a host of additional contemporary government services, from mass transit facilities and airports to sports stadiums and convention centers (see Table 10–3).

THE STRUCTURE OF COUNTY GOVERNMENT   Although county governments may differ markedly in their organization, they generally have (1) a governing body variously called the "county commissioners," "county board," "board of supervisors," or even "judges," which is composed of anywhere from three to fifty elected members; (2) a number of separately elected officials with countywide jurisdictions, such as sheriff, county attorney, auditor, recorder, coroner, assessor, judge, treasurer, and so on; (3) a large number of special boards or commissions which have authority over various functions, whose members may be elected or appointed by the county commissioners or may even include the county commissioners in an ex officio capacity; and (4) an appointed county bureaucracy in planning, transportation, health, welfare, libraries, parks, and so on.

TRADITIONAL COUNTY COMMISSION STRUCTURE   Traditionally, county governments have been organized around the commission structure (see top of Figure 10–1). Over half of the nation's counties still operate under this structure. Typically there are three or five county commissioners, elected for overlapping four-year terms, and a large number of separately elected county officials. There is no single person responsible for administration of county functions. The commissioners may supervise some functions themselves and share supervision of other functions with other elected officials. Thus, for example, both the elected sheriff and the county commissioners share responsibility for the county jail, with the sheriff supervising day-to-day operations, but the commissioners deciding on its construction, repair, and financing. The

Table 10–2

URBAN COUNTIES OF ONE MILLION OR MORE PERSONS	
County	*Population (millions)*
Arizona	
Maricopa (Phoenix)	2.0
California	
Alameda (Oakland and Berkeley)	1.2
Los Angeles	8.6
Orange (South of Los Angeles)	2.3
San Diego	2.4
Santa Clara (San Jose)	1.4
Florida	
Broward (Ft. Lauderdale)	1.2
Dade (Miami)	1.8
Illinois	
Cook (Chicago)	5.3
Michigan	
Oakland (North of Detroit)	1.1
Wayne (Detroit)	2.1
Minnesota	
Hennepin (Minneapolis)	1.0
Missouri	
St. Louis	1.0
New York	
Bronx (part of New York City)	1.2
Kings (part of New York City)	2.3
Nassau (part of New York City)	1.3
New York (part of New York City)	1.5
Queens (part of New York City)	1.9
Suffolk (part of New York city)	1.3
Ohio	
Cuyahoga (Cleveland)	1.4
Pennsylvania	
Allegheny (Pittsburgh)	1.4
Philadelphia	1.6
Texas	
Bexar (San Antonio)	1.2
Dallas	1.9
Harris (Houston)	2.8
Tarrant (Fort Worth)	1.1
Washington	
King (Seattle)	1.4

Source: U.S. Bureau of the Census.

Table 10–3

COUNTY FUNCTIONS	
Traditional, Rural	*Contemporary, Urban*
Property tax assessment and collection	Mass transit
Election administration	Airports
Judicial administration, including civil	Libraries
and criminal courts, probate, etc.	Water supply and sewage disposal
Recording of deeds, mortgages, and other	Water and air pollution control
legal instruments	Building and housing code enforcement
Recording of vital statistics, including	Natural resource preservation
births, deaths, and marriages	Planning and land use control
Local roads and bridges, construction and	Community development and housing
maintenance	Parks and recreation
Law enforcement (sheriff and coroner)	Stadiums, convention and cultural centers
County jail maintenance	Public health, including clinics
Administer state welfare and social	Public hospitals
service programs	Disaster preparedness together with
Other: county fairs, agricultural extension	traditional functions
service	

commissioners usually decide on the property tax *rate* (or "millage," with one mill equal to one-tenth of a percent) to be imposed on property owners (subject to maximums usually set by the state legislature). But the tax *assessor* determines the value of each parcel of property in the county against which the rate is to be applied. And in some counties a separate tax *collector* actually sends out the tax bills and undertakes to collect the revenue. A separate *treasurer* may maintain the county's financial accounts and write the checks. Thus, responsibility for county government is fragmented and dispersed.

Reformers view this traditional structure of county government as lacking in efficiency and accountability. Governmental functions are usually in the hands of untrained nonprofessional county officeholders. County jobs are awarded to "friends and neighbors and relatives." Few voters, even in small rural counties, know enough about what goes on in various offices in the "county courthouse" to hold individual officers responsible for their administration. Typically, independently elected county officials are returned to office term after term with little or no opposition. Only the sheriff's race in rural counties stirs up much interest.

COUNTY ADMINISTRATOR STRUCTURE   Urbanization and the proliferation of county functions usually result in demands for more professional administration of county government. When county commissioners find that they cannot cope with the volume and complexity of county business, they often seek professional assistance. The county administrator or county-manager structure of government offers a solution. It is based on the council-manager form of city government (see "Forms of City

■

County commissioner.
An elected member of the governing body of a county.

County administrator structure.
The organization of county government in which the elected commission appoints an administrator/manager who supervises county functions.

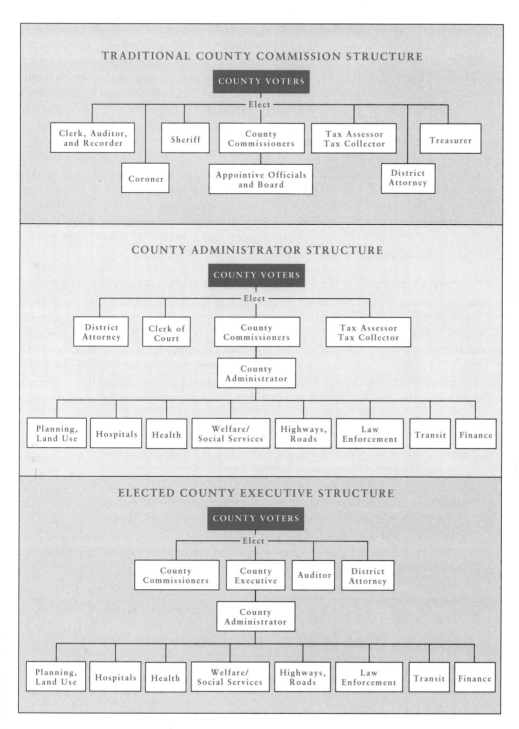

FIGURE 10-1 Structures of County Government

■

Elected county executive.
The organization of county government in which a chief executive officer is elected separately from the county commission.

Government" later in this chapter). An appointed county administrator, responsible to the commission, is placed in charge of the various county departments and agencies. The commission makes policy and appoints the administrator to *implement* policy. The administrator prepares the budget for the commission's approval and then implements it; the administrator hires and fires department heads and reports back regularly to the commission on county business. It seldom works out as neatly as it appears on the organization chart, but the use of the county administrator plan has grown rapidly throughout the United States in recent years.

Voters lose some direct control over county functions with the adoption of the county administrator structure. And county commissioners themselves are usually obliged to go through the county administrator to influence activities in a county department. But the advantage is the professional leadership, administrative efficiency, and functional accountability that the structure brings to county government. The role of the administrator is similar to that of a city manager (see "City Managers in Municipal Politics" in Chapter 11).

ELECTED COUNTY EXECUTIVE STRUCTURE   A few counties in the United States have adopted a governmental structure that features an elected "county executive." Voters elect both a county commission and a separate county executive officer, who exercises formal responsibility over county departments. The elected county executive usually appoints the county administrator subject to approval of the commission. This structure envisions the separation of legislative and executive powers, much like American state and national governments. The elected county executive, like the county administrator, has won approval in many urban counties over recent years.

COUNTY OFFICIALS   Typically, county officials have the following duties:

Commissioners: elected governing body with general responsibility for all county functions; most commissions have three to seven members with election by the county's voters at large.

Sheriff: maintains jail; furnishes law enforcement in unincorporated areas; carries out orders of the county court.

Auditor: maintains financial records; authorizes payment of county obligations.

County or district attorney: serves as chief prosecuting attorney; conducts criminal investigations and prosecutes law violators.

Coroner: conducts medical investigations to determine cause of death; maintains county morgue.

Tax collector: collects taxes.

Treasurer: maintains and disperses county funds; makes county fiscal reports.

Clerk: registers and records legal documents including deeds, mortgages, subdivision plots, marriages, divorces, births; certifies election returns.

Tax assessor: determines value of all taxable property in the county.

The many separately elected county officials are generally considered an obstacle to the emergence of strong executive leadership at the county level. The ability of county governments to assume more important functions and responsibilities, particularly in

PEOPLE IN POLITICS

MARY MCCARTY, COUNTY COMMISSIONER

Mary McCarty learned that "all politics are local" while serving as an intern for the author of that truism, long-time Speaker of the House of Representatives Thomas P. "Tip" O'Neill. O'Neill was the acknowledged master of Boston politics, as well as the U.S. House of Representatives. McCarty is frequently described as a tough-talking, no-nonsense politician who has built a formidable political base in one of the fastest growing urban counties in the nation.

A graduate of the University of Florida with a degree in journalism, McCarty and her husband Kevin became active in Palm Beach County Republican politics soon after moving to the seaside community of Delray Beach, Florida. Kevin worked for a municipal bond underwriting firm (a firm that arranges bond sales for local governments), a job that requires close relationships with local officials. (Critics have attacked the McCartys for having *too* close financial relationships with local governments in the county.) Mary ran successfully for the Delray Beach City Commission in 1987, and Kevin became vice-chairman of the Delray Beach Community Redevelopment Agency. Both were active in the dramatic renaissance of the once-seedy downtown area of the city.

As a Republican, McCarty won a hotly contested election (by 52 percent) to the Palm Beach County Commission in 1990. She immediately focused her attention on economic development, including the replacement of high-tech jobs lost to the county when IBM moved its headquarters to upstate New York. She claims success for an early initiative, the Palm Beach County Economic Summit, a private-public partnership designed to attract high-tech firms from around the country. Her pro-business image might have offended more environmentalists had she not also worked closely with planning and growth management organizations in the county. She boasts of sitting on the governing board of the Teddy Roosevelt Society, a Republican foundation dedicated to environmental issues.

An advocate of welfare reform, McCarty appears to practice what she preaches—welfare to work transition. She offers internships to single mothers on welfare in her own office. She responds to opponents' charges that her internships are a cheap publicity stunt: "I get tired of politicians talking mumbo-jumbo. The only way we can help people get off welfare is if each one of us finds them a job."

McCarty faced no challengers at all in her 1994 reelection campaign, and only token opposition in 1998. Yet her campaign contributions, mostly from builders, bond brokers, and attorneys, exceeded $100,000 in 1998. She pledged to donate unused campaign funds to help other single mothers get off welfare.

---

urban areas, probably hinges upon a reorganization of county government to provide for stronger executive leadership (see "*People in Politics:* Mary McCarty, County Commissioner").

TOWNSHIPS   Another interesting unit of local government is the "township," which is found in about half of the states—the northern states from New England to the Midwest. Southern and western states have made little use of this unit of government. Townships are subdivisions of counties and perform many of the functions of county governments at a grass-roots level—elections, road repair, tax administration, fire protection, and even law enforcement through local justices of the peace. Townships are unincorporated, which means they do not have charters from state governments guaranteeing their political independence or authorizing them to provide many municipal services. The jurisdiction of townships may extend over many square miles of sparsely populated rural territory. About 40 million people, or one-fifth of the U.S. population, live under township governments today.

Township.
The traditional administrative subdivision of county government.

■

Town meeting government.
A form of local government in which the entire citizenry meets periodically to govern the community.

City charter.
The document that grants powers to, and determines the structure of, a city government.

Municipal corporation.
A city government chartered by the state government.

Township governments vary considerably in their powers and organization. Perhaps it would be best to classify them as "rural townships," and "urban townships." Rural townships outside of New England have lost much of their vitality in recent years. The school district consolidation movement (see Chapter 15) has centralized the control of public schools at the county level or in school districts that span villages and townships.

Some urban townships appear to have a brighter future as units of government than do rural townships. This is particularly true in certain suburban areas of larger cities where metropolitan growth has enveloped township governments. Some states, Pennsylvania for example, have authorized urban townships to exercise many of the powers and provide many of the services previously reserved to city governments.

THE NEW ENGLAND TOWN   In the New England states, the "town" is a significant unit of local government, with long traditions and deep roots in the political philosophy of the people of the region. In fact, the New England "town meeting" is often cited by political philosophers as the ideal form of *direct* democracy as distinguished from *representative* democracy. For the town meeting was, and to some extent still is, the central institution of "town" government. The New England town included a village and all of its surrounding farms. The town meeting was open to all eligible voters; it was generally an important social as well as political event. The town meeting would levy taxes, make appropriations, determine policy, and elect officers for the year. Between town meetings, a board of selected officials would supervise the activities of the town—schools, health, roads, care of the poor, and so on. Other officers include town clerk, tax assessors and collectors, justices of the peace, constables, road commissioners, and school board members. Although the ideal of direct democracy is still alive in many smaller New England towns, in the large towns, the pure democracy of the town meeting has given way to a representative system (representative town meeting government), in which town meeting members are elected prior to the town meeting. Moreover, much of the determination of the towns' financial affairs, previously decided at town meetings, has now been given over to elected officials, and many towns have appointed town managers to supervise the day-to-day administration of town services.

CITIES AS "MUNICIPAL CORPORATIONS"

Legally speaking, cities are "municipal corporations" that have received charters from state governments setting forth their boundaries, governmental powers and functions, structure and organization, methods of finance, and powers to elect and appoint officers and employees. The city charter is intended to grant the powers of local self-government to a community. Of course, the powers of self-government granted by a municipal charter are not unlimited. A state can change its charter or take it away altogether, as it sees fit. Cities, like other local governments, have only the powers that state laws and constitutions grant them. They are still subdivisions of the state. And, of course, state laws operate within the boundaries of cities. In fact, municipal corporations are generally responsible for the enforcement of state law within their boundaries. However, they also have the additional power to make local laws, "ordinances," which operate only within their boundaries.

DILLON'S RULE   Perhaps the most serious limitation on the powers of cities is the fact that American courts have insisted upon interpreting the powers granted in charters very narrowly. The classic statement of this principle of restrictive interpretation of municipal powers was made by John F. Dillon many years ago and is now well known as "Dillon's rule":

> It is a general and undisputed proposition of law that a municipal corporation possesses and can exercise the following powers, and no others: first, those granted in express words; second, those necessarily or fairly implied in or incident to the powers expressly granted; third, those essential to the accomplishment of the declared objects and purposes of the corporation—not simply convenient, but indispensable. Any fair, reasonable, substantial doubt concerning the existence of power is resolved by the courts against a corporation, and the power is denied.[4]

STATE LEGISLATORS RETAIN LOCAL POWERS   The restrictive interpretation of the powers of cities leads to rather lengthy city charters, since nearly everything a city does must have specific legal authorization in the charter. The city charter of New York, for example, is several hundred pages long. City charters must cover in detail such matters as boundaries, structure of government, ordinance-making powers, finances, contracts, purchasing, bonds, courts, municipal elections, property assessments, zoning laws and building codes, licenses, franchises, law enforcement, education, health, streets, parks, public utilities, and on and on. Since any proposed change in the powers, organization, or responsibilities of cities requires an act of a state legislature amending the city's charter, state legislatures are intimately involved in local legislation. This practice of narrowly interpreting city charters may appear awkward, but its effect is to increase the power of state legislators in city affairs. State legislators from cities acquire power because legislatures usually grant a local legislator the courtesy of accepting his or her views on local legislation that affects only that legislator's constituency.

SPECIAL ACT CHARTERS   State legislative control over cities is most firmly entrenched in special act charters. These charters are specially drawn for the cities named in them. Cities under special act charters remain directly under legislative control, and specific legislative approval for that city and that city alone must be obtained for any change in its government or service activities. Such charters give rise to local acts dealing with small details of city government in a specially named city, for example, "that West Fall River be authorized to appropriate money for the purchase of uniforms for the park police." Under special act charters, laws that apply to one city do not necessarily apply to others.

GENERAL ACT CHARTERS   In contrast, general act charters usually classify cities according to their size and then apply municipal laws to all cities in each size classification. Thus, a state's municipal law may apply to all cities of less than 10,000 people, another law to all cities with populations of 10,000–25,000, another to cities with

---

■

Dillon's rule.
The legal doctrine that cities possess only those powers expressly granted in their charter.

Special act charter.
A charter granted by the state to a particular city.

General act charter.
A charter granted by the state to all cities in a specified size classification.

■

Home rule charter.
A charter that authorizes a city to exercise all powers not specifically prohibited by law or by charter.

25,000–50,000 people, and so on. These general act charters make it difficult to interfere in the activities of a particular city without affecting the activities of all cities of a similar size category. Yet in practice there are often exceptions and modifications to general act legislation. For example, since legislators know the populations of their cities, they can select size categories for municipal law that apply to only one city.

OPTIONAL CHARTERS   Optional charter laws provide cities with some choice in the structure and organization of their governments. Such laws generally offer a choice of governmental forms: strong mayor and weak council, weak mayor and strong council, commission, city manager, or some modification of these.

HOME RULE   Home rule charters are designed to give cities the power to adopt governmental forms and provide municipal services, as they see fit, without state legislative interference. Home rule charters may be given to cities by state constitutions or by legislative enactments; legislative home rule is considered less secure, since a legislature could retract the grant if it wished to do so. Beginning with Missouri in 1875, more than half the states have included in their constitutions provisions for the issuance of home rule charters. About two-thirds of the nation's cities with populations over 200,000 have some form of home rule.

The intended effect of home rule is to reverse "Dillon's rule" and enable cities to "exercise all legislative powers not prohibited by law or by charter." In other words, instead of preventing a city from doing anything not specifically authorized, home rule permits the city to do anything not specifically prohibited. The theory of home rule grants sweeping powers to cities; however, in practice, home rule has not brought self-government to cities.

Home rule provisions in state constitutions range from those that grant considerable power and discretion over local affairs, to provisions that are so useless that no city has ever made use of them. First of all, these constitutional provisions may be too cumbersome or vague for effective implementation. In some states, cities feel that it is easier to use the general law charters, particularly if they provide for optional forms of government, than to use the cumbersome procedures for obtaining home rule.

Another important limitation on home rule is the distinction between "self-enforcing" and "non–self-enforcing," or "permissive," home rule provisions in state constitutions. Non–self-enforcing home rule provisions merely permit the state legislature to grant home rule to its cities; cities cannot acquire home rule without legislative action. Only about a dozen states have "self-enforcing" home rule provisions, which enable cities to bypass the state legislature and adopt home rule for themselves.

Finally, home rule may be limited by court interpretations of the language of the constitutional provisions granting power to home rule in cities. Constitutional provisions may grant to home rule cities the power to make "all laws and ordinances relating to municipal concerns," or the "powers of local self-government," or all powers "in respect to municipal affairs." Of course, ordinances passed under home rule authority cannot be in conflict with state law. Courts must distinguish between municipal and statewide concerns. In cases where doubt exists, legal traditions of municipal law require that courts resolve the doubt in favor of the state and against local powers of home rule. State legislatures can intervene in local affairs in home rule cities by simply deciding that a particular matter is of statewide concern.

POLITICS OF HOME RULE   The politics of home rule often pits reform groups, city mayors, and administrators against state legislators and large municipal taxpayers. State legislators are generally wary of giving up their authority over cities. Rural legislators have little reason to support city home rule, and even city legislators seldom welcome proposals to give up their authority over local bills. Sometimes city employees with good access to the legislature will oppose giving a mayor or a city manager too much control over their employment. Taxpayer groups may fear that home rule will give the city the ability to increase taxes. Local bills may be pictured as a distraction to legislators by reformers, but many legislators enjoy the power that it brings them in local affairs and welcome the opportunity to perform legislative services for their constituents. And so, even with reapportionment adding to the number of urban legislators, the League of Women Voters, good-government groups, and mayors may still be frustrated in their attempts to achieve genuine home rule for American cities.

COURTS RETAIN LOCAL POWERS   Courts figure prominently in municipal politics. This is because of the subordinate position of the municipal corporation in the hierarchy of governments, and legal traditions, such as Dillon's rule, which narrowly interpret the power of local governments. The power of courts over municipal affairs grants leverage to defenders of the status quo in any political battle at the local level. Proponents of a new municipal law or municipal service not only must win the battle over whether a city *ought* to pass the new law or provide the new service but also must win the legal battle over whether the city *can* pass the law or provide the service. Limitations and uncertainties abound about the validity of local enactments. Legal challenges to the authority of the city to pass new regulations or provide new services are frequent. The city attorney becomes a key official because he or she must advise the city about what it can or cannot do. Not only must the city obey the federal constitution, but it is also subject to the restraints of the state constitution, state laws, its municipal charter, and of course, Dillon's rule. The result is to greatly strengthen courts, attorneys, and defenders of the status quo.

FORMS OF CITY GOVERNMENT

American city government comes in various structural packages (see Figures 10–2 and 10–3). There are some adaptations and variations from city to city, but generally one can classify the form of city government as mayor-council, commission, council-manager, town meeting, or representative town meeting. Over half of American cities now operate under council-manager governments (see Table 10–4, p. 314).

COMMISSION   The traditional commission form of city government gives both legislative and executive powers to a small body, usually consisting of five members. The commission form originated at the beginning of the century as a reform movement designed to end a system of divided responsibility between mayor and council. One of the

■

Commission government. The traditional form of city government in which legislative and executive powers are combined in an elected commission that directly supervises city departments.

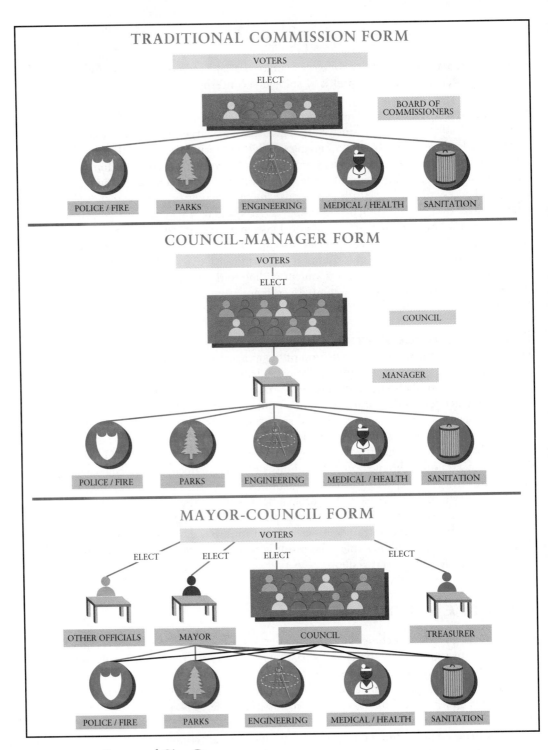

FIGURE 10–2 Forms of City Government

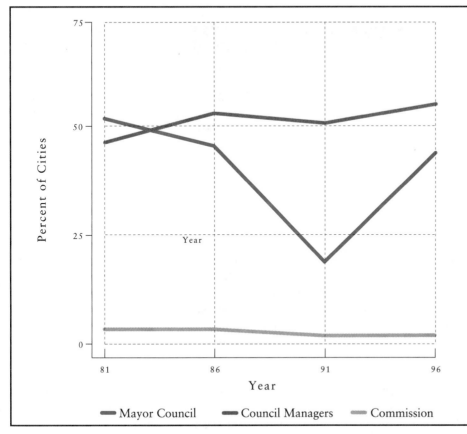

FIGURE 10–3
**Forms of City
Government:
Changes Over
Time**

Source: International City
Managers' Association, *Municipal Yearbook, 1998.*
Table 5–3. Excludes town
meeting government.

commission members is nominally the mayor, but he or she has no more formal powers than the other commissioners. The board of commissioners is directly responsible
for the operation of city departments and agencies. In practice, one commission member may take on responsibility for the management of a specific department, such as finance, public works, or public safety. As long as the council members are in agreement
over policy, there are few problems; but when commissioners differ among themselves
and develop separate spheres of influence in city government, city government becomes a multiheaded monster, totally lacking in coordination. The results of a commission form of government were generally so disastrous that the reform movement
abandoned its early support of this form of government in favor of the council-
manager plan.

COUNCIL-MANAGER   The council-manager form of government revived the distinction between legislative "policy making" and executive "administration" in city
government. Policy-making responsibility is vested in an elected council, and administration is assigned to an appointed professional administrator known as a manager.
The council chooses the manager who is responsible to it. All departments of the city
government operate under the direction of the manager, who has the power to hire and

■

**Council-manager
government.**
The form of city government
in which the elected council
or commission appoints a
manager to supervise city
departments.

Table 10–4

AMERICAN CITIES: FORMS OF GOVERNMENT		
	Number	*Percent*
Mayor-council	1,604	39
Council-manager	2,206	53
Commission	66	2
Town meeting	214	5
Representative town meeting	24	1

Source: International City Managers' Association, *Municipal Yearbook, 1998.* Washington, DC: ICMA, 1998, Table 5–2.

fire personnel within the limits set by the merit system. The council's role in administration is limited to selecting and dismissing the city manager. The plan is based on the idea that policy making and administration are separate functions, and that the principal task of city government is to provide the highest level of services at the lowest possible costs—utilities, streets, fire and police protection, health, welfare, recreation, and so on. Hence, a professionally trained, career-oriented administrator is given direct control over city departments.

MAYOR-COUNCIL   The nation's largest cities tend to function under the mayor-council plan. This form of government is designed in the American tradition of separation of powers between legislature and executive. One may also establish subcategories of "strong" or "weak" mayor forms of mayor-council government. A strong mayor is one who is the undisputed master of the executive agencies of city government and who has substantial legislative powers in the form of budget making, vetoes, and opportunity to propose legislation. Only a few cities make the mayor the sole elected official among city executive officers; it is common for the mayor to share powers with other elected officials—city attorney, treasurer, tax assessor, auditor, clerk, and so on. Yet many mayors, by virtue of their prestige, persuasive abilities, or role as party leader, have been able to overcome most of the weaknesses of their formal office.

In recent years, large cities have been adding to the formal powers of their chief executives. Cities have augmented the mayors' role by providing them with direction over budgeting, purchasing, and personnel controls; and independent boards and commissions and individual councilmen have relinquished administrative control over city departments in many cities. Moreover, many cities have strengthened their mayors' position by providing them with a chief administrative officer, "CAO," to handle important staff and administrative duties of supervising city departments and providing central management services.

TOWN MEETING AND REPRESENTATIVE TOWN MEETING   Town-meeting and representative town-meeting governments are currently found in Connecticut, Maine,

■
Mayor-council government.
The form of city government in which legislative power is exercised by an elected council, and city departments are supervised by a separately elected mayor.

Massachusetts, New Hampshire, and Vermont. Most town meetings are held in response to the issuance of a warrant (agenda) by an elected town clerk and/or by the elected town council. The town meeting is open to all residents and it possesses full legislative authority. A town meeting may be called once or twice a year. In most town meetings, the passage of the annual budget is the most important item of business.

Town meetings usually choose a board to oversee business between meetings. Voters separately elect a town clerk, treasurer, assessor, constable, school board, and other officers. The town meeting may also elect a finance committee to prepare the budget.

While the town meeting has been celebrated by many political philosophers as "pure democracy," the reality is much less than full participatory democracy. Attendance at town meetings is usually less than 10 percent of the town's voters. In larger towns, the participation rate may be only 1 or 2 percent of the voters. The idealized town meeting democracy is really governance by a very small group of political activists. Special interest groups can easily pack a town meeting. Senior citizens attend these meetings in disproportionate numbers. And employees, members of the volunteer fire company, school teachers, and business and civic association members are also overrepresented. Of course, attendance increases when controversial items are on the agenda. And in many town-meeting governments, a decision can be overturned by citizen initiative and referendum.[5]

Representative town-meeting government (RTM) is a hybrid political institution that seeks to combine features of the open town meeting with representative government. In RTM the voters elect a relatively large number of persons to vote at meetings, yet voters retain the right to attend and speak at town meetings themselves. However, in practice the number of candidates for town-meeting members is frequently equal to or even smaller than the number of town-meeting members to be elected. Town clerks often must recruit people to become town-meeting members. In theory, representative town-meeting members should be more attentive than townspeople because they accepted the responsibility of public office. But attendance is also a problem in RTM government.

TYPES OF CITIES AND FORMS OF GOVERNMENT

Let us examine the social, economic, and political forces shaping the structure of city government—that is, the conditions associated with the selection of one of the principal forms of government.

SIZE OF CITY   First of all, council-manager government is closely associated with the *size* of cities. Large cities show a preference for the more "political" form of mayor-council government in contrast to the more "efficient" form of council-manager government. All cities over 1 million population have the mayor-council form of government. Only a few large cities have council-manager government. The council-manager form of government is most popular in the middle-sized cities—those with populations of 25,000 to 250,000 people. Probably, cities with fewer than 10,000 residents do not have sufficient resources to justify hiring a trained professional city manager nor, in all probability, do they have the administrative problems requiring the expertise of such an individual. Thus, small cities, like large cities, tend to rely upon mayor-council government, although probably for different reasons.

POLITICAL CONFLICT What explains the absence of council-manager government in large cities? A common explanation is that the political environment of large cities is so complex, with many competing interests, that these cities require strong *political* leadership that can arbitrate struggles for power, arrange compromises, and be directly responsible to the people for policy decisions. A large city requires a political form of government that can resolve the conflicting claims of diverse interests. This implies that in smaller cities there are fewer competing interests. A professional city manager would have less difficulty in accepting cues about correct behavior in a small city than in a large city with its complex political structure. There is a greater degree of consensus on policy direction in a smaller city; therefore, such a city requires a professional administrator rather than a political negotiator. The question is whether or not political skill or administrative expertise is more important in a city, and there is reason to believe that larger cities require political skills more than professional administration.

GROWTH RATE Growing cities face more administrative and technical problems than cities whose population is stable. There is a strong relationship between population *growth* and council-manager government. A rapidly growing city faces many administrative problems in providing streets, sewers, and the many other services required by an expanding population. This creates a demand for a professional administrator.

In contrast, the mayor-council form of government is associated with cities having relatively stable populations, in which administrative and technical problems are not quite so pressing, and political conflict is more likely to be well-defined and persistent. Council-manager government is more popular in the rapidly growing cities of the West and the South; mayor-council government is preferred in cities in the East and Midwest. Indeed, council-manager government has become more popular among all cities than mayor-council government (see Table 10–4, p. 314).

SOCIAL CLASS Council-manager cities tend to be *middle-class* cities. Cities with large proportions of working-class residents, low-income families, and ethnic minorities prefer mayor-council government.[6]

Why is it that middle-class communities prefer the manager form of government while working-class communities prefer a mayor-council government? Middle-class citizens, those in white-collar jobs with good educations and reasonably high incomes, are more likely to want government conducted in a businesslike fashion, with a council serving as a board of directors and a city manager as the president of a "municipal corporation." These goals are not necessarily shared by labor, low-income, ethnic, and minority groups, which may prefer a government that grants small favors, dispenses patronage jobs, awards representation and "recognition" to minority groups, and can be held directly responsible by the voters at election time. In a campaign for city-manager government, one usually finds business leaders, newspapers, and civic associations supporting the plan, and labor unions and minority group organizations far less enthusiastic. Party organizations and professional politicians often oppose this plan. Its support generally comes from white-collar, high-income, well-educated, white neighborhoods, and its opposition from low-income, blue-collar, black, and ethnic neighborhoods.

PARTY COMPETITION   Communities with well-organized *competitive party systems* are less likely to have manager government than one-party communities or communities in which the formal party organization is weak. It is sometimes argued that the introduction of the manager plan decreases party activity in communities, but it is also true that the presence of strong party organizations may be a significant factor in the defeat of manager plans. Thus, manager government may depress party activity, or strong parties may kill off manager government, or both; but whatever the case, manager government appears incompatible with strong partisan politics in a community.

REGION   Cities in the Northeast and Upper Midwest are more likely to have the mayor-council form of government as well as partisan elections. Cities in the South and West are more likely to have council-manager governments and nonpartisan elections. This regional pattern emerges as the strongest single correlate of local government structure.[7] This strong correlation between *region* and governmental structure is explained in part by the fact that southern and western cities are younger, growing cities without any history of strong party organizations; whereas northeastern and upper midwestern cities are older, stable cities with histories of strong party "machines." However, geographic region itself, apart from these other social and political factors, may also explain governmental form. In other words, there may be some "imitation" effect within regions that is separate from the effects of other causal factors.

NONPARTISAN ELECTIONS

Most of America's cities use the nonpartisan ballot to elect local officials. Reformers believed that nonpartisanship would take the "politics" out of local government and raise the caliber of candidates for elected offices (see Chapter 11). They believed that nonpartisanship would restrict local campaigning to local issues and thereby rule out extraneous state or national issues from local elections. They also believed that by eliminating party labels, local campaigns would emphasize the qualifications of the individual candidates rather than their party affiliations.

Nonpartisanship is found in both large and small cities. Nonpartisanship is even more widespread than council-manager government. However, there is a tendency for these two forms to be related: 83 percent of all council-manager cities have nonpartisan ballots, while only 65 percent of all mayor-council cities are nonpartisan (see Table 10–5). Party politics is still the prevailing style of local elections in eastern cities, except for New England. Elsewhere in the nation nonpartisanship prevails. The nonpartisan ballot is more likely to be adopted in homogeneous middle-class cities, where there is less social cleavage and smaller proportions of working-class and ethnic group members.

Do nonpartisan elections remove politics? To what extent has nonpartisanship succeeded in removing "politics" from local government? Of course, if "politics" is defined

Nonpartisan elections. Elections in which candidates' names appear on a ballot without indication of their party affiliation.

Table 10–5

FORMS OF GOVERNMENT AND TYPE OF ELECTIONS		
	Percent	
CLASSIFICATION	PARTISAN	NONPARTISAN
All Cities	24.0	76.0
METROPOLITAN STATUS		
Central city	21.0	79.0
Suburb	28.8	71.2
Independent city	18.1	81.9
FORMS OF GOVERNMENT		
Mayor-council	35.2	64.8
Council-manager	16.7	83.3
Commission	27.2	72.8
Town meeting	23.5	76.5
Rep. town meeting	34.1	65.9

Source: Municipal Yearbook, 1998.

as conflict over public policy, then "politics" has certainly not disappeared with the elimination of party labels. There is no evidence that eliminating party ballots can reduce the level of community conflict. If we define "politics" to mean "partisanship," that is, *party* politics, then nonpartisanship can remove party influences from local government.

Apparently several types of political systems can be found in nonpartisan cities. First of all, in some nonpartisan cities, parties continue to operate effectively behind the scenes in local affairs. *Disguised party politics* is most likely to be found in big cities of the Northeast and Midwest, in states where political parties are strong and competitive. In these cities, persons who are known Democratic and Republican candidates run in officially "nonpartisan" elections.

Another type of nonpartisan political system is one in which the major parties are inactive, but clear *coalitions* of socioeconomic groups emerge that resemble the national Democratic and Republican parties. These opposing coalitions may involve liberal, labor, Catholic, and black groups on one side; and conservative, business, Protestant, middle-class groups on the other.

Nonpartisan systems may feature the activities of independent community *groups* and organizations. Frequently, these groups are civic associations led by newspapers, chambers of commerce, or neighborhood associations. These organizations may "slate" candidates, manage their campaigns, and even exercise some influence over them while they are in office. These organizations are not usually as permanent as parties, but they may operate as clearly identifiable political entities over the years.

In still another type of nonpartisan political system, neither parties, nor coalitions, nor groups play any significant role, and there are no local slate-making associations. Individual candidates select themselves, collect their own money, and create their own temporary campaign organizations. Voting does not correlate with issues, or party identification, or socioeconomic groups, but instead tends to follow a *friends and neighbors* pattern. Indeed, voting in local nonpartisan elections often depends on factors such as incumbency, name recognition, position on the ballot (the first name on the list gets more votes), and very brief personal contacts (a handshake at the office or factory, or a door-to-door canvass, or even a telephone call).

POSSIBLE REPUBLICAN ADVANTAGE   Does nonpartisanship increase Republican influence in city government? It is sometimes arued that the removal of party designations from local elections hurts Democrats by disengaging their traditional support from urban voters—the low-income, labor, ethnic, and black groups that traditionally vote the Democratic ticket. Moreover, the well-educated, high-income groups and interests that are normally Republican have a natural edge in organization, communication, and prestige in the absence of parties. Republicans also have better turnout records in nonpartisan elections. Surveys of local officials elected under partisan and nonpartisan systems tend to confirm that nonpartisanship results in the election of more Republicans. However, this Republican advantage in nonpartisan elections is very modest; it appears to be limited to smaller cities and cities that are dominated by Democrats.[8]

NONPARTISAN CANDIDATES   Does nonpartisanship result in "better-qualified" candidates winning public office? Of course, the answer to this question depends upon one's definition of better qualified. Nonpartisanship does result in more high-income, "respectable," older, white Anglo-Saxon Protestants with prestige jobs running for public office.[9] Working-class candidates are disadvantaged by nonpartisanship for several reasons. First, nonpartisanship reduces the turnout of labor, low-income, ethnic, Democratic voters and, consequently, increases the influence of well-educated, high-income, white, Anglo-Saxon, Protestant Republican voters who continue to come to the polls in nonpartisan elections. In addition, nonpartisanship means that recruitment of candidates will be left to civic associations, or ad hoc groups of one kind or another, rather than to Democratic or Republican party organizations. This difference in recruitment and endorsement practices tends to give an advantage to middle-class candidates. Working-class candidates seldom have the organizational ties or memberships that would bring them to the attention of civic associations that recruit in nonpartisan elections.

INCUMBENT ADVANTAGE   Nonpartisanship appears to contribute to the reelection of incumbent council members, particularly when nonpartisanship is combined with at-large elections. Incumbent council members are reelected on the average about 80 percent of the time. When incumbents *are* defeated, they tend to suffer defeat in a group as a result of intensive community conflict.[10] Incumbents are more likely to have a name that is known to the voters. Incumbent council members in partisan cities are not reelected as often as incumbents in nonpartisan cities. This suggests that it is difficult to hold public officials accountable in nonpartisan elections. The voter does

■

At-large elections.
Elections in which candidates are chosen by all of the voters in a community.

District elections.
Elections in which candidates are chosen by voters in separate geographically defined districts.

not have the opportunity to hear organized criticisms of incumbent officeholders from an opposition party. When the only challenge to an incumbent officeholder is an unknown name on the ballot, he or she is more likely to be reelected than if he or she is challenged by a candidate backed by an opposition party. The higher rates of reelection in nonpartisan systems suggest that accountability is harder to achieve where party labels are absent.

AT-LARGE AND DISTRICT ELECTIONS

At-large elections are designed to promote a citywide approach to municipal problems among council members. Roughly 60 percent of American cities elect their council members at-large, about 17 percent by districts, and 22 percent by a combination of at-large and district constituencies.[11] (There is always some confusion in counting cities as having at-large or ward elections, not only because some cities have "combination" elections with some council members elected by district and others at-large, but also because some cities *elect* council members at-large yet require that they *reside* in the districts they are supposed to represent.)

THE CASE FOR AT-LARGE ELECTIONS   Traditionally, reformers believed that district elections encourage parochial views, neighborhood interests, "logrolling," and other characteristics of "ward politics." These "undesirable" characteristics occur because council members are responsible to local majorities in the particular sections or wards from which they are elected. In contrast, council members elected at-large are responsible to citywide majorities; this should encourage impartial, communitywide attitudes. Moreover, in council-manager cities, it is argued that the manager can be more effective in serving the "general good" of the whole community if the manager is responsible to council members elected at-large rather than by districts. (Of manager cities, 70 percent elect council members at-large, compared to only 50 percent of mayor-council cities.)

MINORITY OPPOSITION   Minorities, who might be able to capture some council seats if these seats are elected by district, may oppose at-large elections if they feel unable to influence council members elected by communitywide majorities. Blacks especially have raised objections to at-large elections in predominantly white cities and counties. Council members and commissioners elected at-large by white majorities are perceived by many black voters as unresponsive to minority concerns.

CIVIL RIGHTS TESTS   The use of at-large elections to discriminate against racial minorities in their ability to participate in the political process and elect candidates of their own choice clearly violates the Equal Protection Clause of the Fourteenth Amendment and the federal Voting Rights Act. The U.S. Supreme Court in *Mobile* v. *Bolden* (1980) held that at-large elections are *not* unconstitutional in the absence of any evidence of discriminatory intent.[12] However, Congress amended the Voting Rights Act in 1982 to substitute a *results test* for the more difficult to prove *intent test* in assessing discrimination. But Congress stopped short of declaring all at-large elections discriminatory and illegal. Instead Congress established a "totality of circumstances" test to be used in deciding whether the at-large elections resulted in racial discrimination. The elements to be considered by the federal courts are:[13]

- A history of official discrimination. (This test applies primarily to southern states.)
- A record of racial polarization in voting.
- Unusually large election districts.
- The existence of candidate slating by parties or groups, and whether minority members have been slated.
- The extent to which minorities have been adversely affected by local government decisions.
- Whether political campaigns have been characterized by racial appeals.
- The extent to which minority group members have been elected to office.

The federal courts are prepared to evaluate the use of at-large elections in each community by these tests.[14]

FEDERAL COURT INTERVENTION   Federal court cases in recent years involving at-large elections suggest that it is becoming increasingly difficult for cities, counties, and even school districts to defend exclusive reliance on at-large elections. Civil rights groups have effectively utilized the "totality of circumstances" test to invalidate at-large elections across the country and especially in southern states. In some cases federal courts have ordered district elections for all officials, and in other cases federal courts have accepted combination plans—some council members elected by district and some at-large. The U.S. Supreme Court does *not* require proportional representation for minorities, that is, a council that is 20 percent black if the city's population is 20 percent black. However, lower federal courts have tended to compare the black proportion of the council with the black proportion of residents in determining whether the "totality of circumstances" suggests discrimination.

MINORITY REPRESENTATION   Until recently, blacks were significantly *underrepresented* on city councils that elected their members at-large. In the 1970s several studies reported that blacks won fewer than 50 percent of the seats they deserved (based on their percentage of a city's population) in *at-large* cities, compared to 85 to 100 percent of the seats they deserved in cities that elected council members *by districts*.[15] However, by the late 1980s, black representation on city councils throughout the nation had increased dramatically, and it no longer made much difference in black representation whether councils were elected at-large or by district.[16] For cities with more than 10 percent and less than 50 percent black population, black representation on city councils is only slightly below black population percentages, and the difference between at-large and district elections is minuscule. For cities with black populations over 50 percent, "then it is whites who need district representation to obtain their proportion share of council seats."[17]

DID YOU KNOW?

AMERICA'S BIG CITIES, GAINERS AND LOSERS

America's big cities differ significantly in their rates of population change. Some cities are losing population at a fairly rapid rate, notably Washington, DC; St. Louis, Missouri; Philadelphia, Pennsylvania; and Milwaukee, Wisconsin. Many of their residents are exiting the central cities for their surrounding suburbs. A majority of big cities have failed to match the nation's overall population growth rate of recent years (from 249 million to 265 million between 1990 and 1996, a 6.4 percent increase). The populations of the nation's three largest cities—New York, Los Angeles, and Chicago—are fairly stagnant. In contrast, some big cities are growing very rapidly, including Las Vegas, Colorado Springs, Phoenix, El Paso, and Austin. Note that these rapidly growing cities are in America's southern and western "Sunbelt."

1996 rank	1990 rank	City/state	1996 estimate	1990 population	1990–96 change	Pct. change
1	1	New York, NY	7,380,906	7,322,564	58,342	0.8%
2	2	Los Angeles, CA	3,553,638	3,485,557	68,081	2.0%
3	3	Chicago, IL	2,721,547	2,783,726	-62,179	-2.2%
4	4	Houston, TX	1,744,058	1,637,859	106,199	6.5%
5	5	Philadelphia, PA	1,478,002	1,585,577	-107,575	-6.8%
6	6	San Diego, CA	1,171,121	1,110,623	60,498	5.4%
7	9	Phoenix, AZ	1,159,014	984,310	174,704	17.7%
8	10	San Antonio, TX	1,067,816	959,295	108,521	11.3%
9	8	Dallas, TX	1,053,292	1,007,618	45,674	4.5%
10	7	Detroit, MI	1,000,272	1,027,974	-27,702	-2.7%
11	11	San Jose, CA	838,744	782,224	56,520	7.2%
12	13	Indianapolis, IN	746,737	731,278	15,459	2.1%
13	14	San Francisco, CA	735,315	723,959	11,356	1.6%
14	15	Jacksonville, FL	679,792	635,230	44,562	7.0%
15	12	Baltimore, MD	675,401	736,014	-60,613	-8.2%
16	16	Columbus, OH	657,053	632,945	24,108	3.8%
17	22	El Paso, TX	599,865	515,342	84,523	16.4%
18	18	Memphis, TN	596,725	618,652	-21,927	-3.5%
19	17	Milwaukee, WI	590,503	628,088	-37,585	-6.0%
20	20	Boston, MA	558,394	574,283	-15,889	-2.8%
21	19	Washington, DC	543,213	606,900	-63,687	-10.5%
22	26	Austin, TX	541,278	472,020	69,258	14.7%
23	21	Seattle, WA	524,704	516,259	8,445	1.6%
24	25	Nashville, TN	511,263	488,366	22,897	4.7%
25	23	Cleveland, OH	498,246	505,616	-7,370	-1.5%
26	27	Denver, CO	497,840	467,610	30,230	6.5%
27	28	Portland, OR	480,824	463,634	17,190	3.7%
28	29	Fort Worth, TX	479,716	447,619	32,097	7.2%
29	24	New Orleans, LA	476,625	496,938	-20,313	-4.1%
30	30	Oklahoma City, OK	469,852	444,724	25,128	5.7%
31	34	Tucson, AZ	449,002	411,480	37,522	9.1%
32	33	Charlotte, NC	441,297	419,539	21,758	5.2%
33	31	Kansas City, MO	441,259	434,829	6,430	1.5%
34	37	Virginia Beach, VA	430,385	393,089	37,296	9.5%
35	39	Honolulu, HI	423,475	377,059	46,416	12.3%
36	32	Long Beach, CA	421,904	429,321	-7,417	-1.7%
37	38	Albuquerque, NM	419,681	384,915	34,766	9.0%
38	36	Atlanta, GA	401,907	393,929	7,978	2.0%

39	47	Fresno, CA	396,011	354,091	41,920	11.8%
40	44	Tulsa, OK	378,491	367,302	11,189	3.0%
41	63	Las Vegas, NV	376,906	258,204	118,702	46.0%
42	42	Sacramento, CA	376,243	369,365	6,878	1.9%
43	40	Oakland, CA	367,230	372,242	-5,012	-1.3%
44	46	Miami, FL	365,127	358,648	6,479	1.8%
45	48	Omaha, NE	364,253	342,862	21,391	6.2%
46	43	Minneapolis, MN	358,785	368,383	-9,598	-2.6%
47	35	St. Louis, MO	351,565	396,685	-45,120	-11.4%
48	41	Pittsburgh, PA	350,363	369,879	-19,516	-5.3%
49	45	Cincinnati, OH	345,818	364,114	-18,296	-5.0%
50	54	Colorado Springs, CO	345,127	280,430	64,697	23.1%

ON THE WEB

The National Association of Counties (NACO) maintains an interesting Web site at

www.naco.org

This association provides extensive information on the nation's 3,000 plus counties, from the smallest (Loving County, Texas, with 140 people) to the largest (Los Angeles County, with its population of 9.1 million). NACO is the principal lobbying organization for counties in Washington. Its online database includes county policies, ordinances, codes, and model programs.

The National League of Cities claims a membership of 18,000 municipalities across the nation. Its Web site is found at

www.nlc.org

The league lobbies in Washington on behalf of city governments, "influencing national policy and building understanding and support for cities and towns." Its Web site includes policy positions on unfunded federal mandates, federal housing and community development programs, federal transportation programs, and other matters directly affecting cities.

Increasingly, large cities and counties in the nation are constructing and maintaining their own Web pages. Many city homepage addresses on the Internet resemble those of the following:

Boston	www.ci.boston.ma.us
New York	www.ci.nyc.ny.us
Los Angeles	www.ci.la.ca.us
Dallas	www.ci.dallas.tx.us

Many, but not all, county homepage addresses resemble the following:

Fairfax County, VA	www.co.fairfax.va.us
Harris County, TX	www.co.harris.tx.us
Los Angeles County	www.co.la.ca.us
St. Louis County	www.co.st-louis.mo.us

NOTES

1. For some empirical support for these speculations, see Gordon S. Black, "Conflict in the Community: A Theory of the Effect of Community Size," *American Political Science Review,* 68 (September 1974), 1245–61; see also Timothy A. Almy, "Residential Locations and Electoral Cohesion," *American Political Science Review,* 67 (September 1973), 914–23, who argues that conflict is greater in communities where different social groups are residentially segregated.

2. The widely cited classic essay is Charles M. Tiebout, "The Pure Theory of Local Expenditure," *Journal of Political Economy,* 64 (October 1956), 416–24.

3. John M. Orbell and Toru Uno, "A Theory of Neighborhood Problem Solving: Political Action versus Residential Mobility," *American Political Science Review,* 66 (June 1972), 471–89; William E. Lyons and David Lowery, "Citizen Response to Dissatisfaction in Urban Communities," *Journal of Politics,* 51 (November 1989), 841–68.

4. John F. Dillon, *Commentaries on the Laws of Municipal Corporations,* 5th ed. (Boston: Little, Brown, 1911), p. 448.

5. See Joseph F. Zimmerman, "The New England Town Meeting: Pure Democracy in Action?" *Municipal Yearbook, 1984* (Washington, DC: International City Managers' Association, 1984), pp. 102–6.

6. Thomas R. Dye and Susan MacManus, "Predicting City Government Structure," *American Journal of Political Science,* 20 (May 1976), 257–72.

7. See Paul G. Farnhorn and Stephen N. Bryant, "Form of Local Government," *Social Science Quarterly,* 66 (June 1985), 386–400.

8. Susan Welch and Timothy Bledsoe, "The Partisan Consequences of Nonpartisan Elections," *American Journal of Political Science,* 30 (February 1986), 128–39.

9. Carol A. Cassel, "Social Background Characteristics of Nonpartisan City Council Members," *Western Political Quarterly,* 38 (September 1985), 495–501.

10. John J. Kirlen, "Electoral Conflict and Democracy in Cities," *Journal of Politics,* 37 (February 1975), 262–69.

11. International City Managers' Association, *Municipal Yearbook, 1998.*

12. *Mobile v. Bolden,* 446 U.S. 55 (1980).

13. For a discussion of federal court applications of these tests, see Susan A. MacManus and Charles S. Bullock, "Racial Representation Issues," *PS,* 18 (Fall 1985), 759–69.

14. *Thornburgh v. Gingles,* 106 S. Ct. 2752 (1986).

15. Albert K. Karnig, "Black Representation on City Councils," *Urban Affairs Quarterly,* 12 (December 1976), 223–43; Thomas R. Dye and Theodore P. Robinson, "Reformism and Black Representation on City Councils," *Social Science Quarterly,* 59 (June 1978).

16. Susan Welch, "The Impact of At-Large Districts on the Representation of Blacks and Hispanics," *Journal of Politics,* 52 (November 1990), 1050–76. See also Charles S. Bullock and Susan M. MacManus, "Municipal Electoral Structure and the Election of Councilwomen," *Journal of Politics,* 53 (February 1991), 75–89.

17. Ibid, p. 1072.

11
PARTICIPATION IN COMMUNITY POLITICS

QUESTIONS TO CONSIDER
★ ★ ★ ★ ★ ★ ★ ★ ★ ★

Do nonpartisan elections make city governments more or less responsive to citizens' demands?

❑ More responsive
❑ Less responsive
❑ No difference

How much corruption do you think takes place in your city government?

❑ A great deal
❑ Some
❑ Hardly any

Should mayors have veto powers over the actions of city councils?

❑ Yes
❑ No

What are the most influential interest groups in your community?

❑ Business groups
❑ Neighborhood associations
❑ Environmentalists
❑ Real estate developers
❑ Other

CITIZEN PARTICIPATION

Ideally, democracy inspires widespread citizen participation in government—as voters, community activists, neighborhood association and interest group members, party workers, and candidates for public office. But in fact, rarely do many citizens participate actively in community politics.

A "communitarian" view praises the many values of direct citizen participation in community affairs, not just by voting, but perhaps more importantly, by participating in groups and forums, working with neighbors to solve the problems of the community. This view asserts that where neighbors talk about community affairs in face-to-face meetings, they learn from one another, become more tolerant of different people with different views, create bonds of friendship, and look to common solutions to their problems.

But in reality relatively few people are interested in community affairs. They are busy at their jobs and professions, concerned with raising their children, and more interested in watching sports on television than broadcasts of city council meetings. And it may be naive to believe that community political activism always engenders tolerance, respect, and common efforts to resolve problems. Often, increased participation inspires rancorous conflict, intolerant popular policy initiatives, and even violence. Indeed, a surge of participation, with resulting conflicting claims upon a government that cannot satisfy everyone, may simply engender cynicism and disrespect toward government. Citizen activists are not always well informed even on the issue on which they are most vociferous. Activism—particularly neighborhood NIMBY activity ("not in my backyard" opposition to community projects)—may paralyze local government, preventing it from effectively addressing communitywide problems.[1]

VOTERS IN LOCAL ELECTIONS   Voter turnout in local elections is substantially lower than in state or national elections. While 55 percent of the nation's eligible voters may cast ballots in a presidential election, voter turnouts of 25 to 35 percent are typical in local elections.

Nonpartisanship in local elections depresses voter turnout substantially. Voter turnout for municipal elections in nonpartisan cities averages closer to 25 percent, compared to over 35 percent for cities with partisan elections. Partisan campaigns heighten voter turnout, in part because of the greater interest they generate and in part because of the role of party workers in getting out to vote.

Voter participation in local government can be further reduced by holding municipal elections at odd times of the year when no other state or national elections are being held. Approximately 60 percent of the nation's cities hold municipal elections that are completely independent of state or national elections. A common rationale for holding municipal elections at times other than state or national elections is to separate local issues from state or national questions, but the real effect of scheduling local elections independently is to reduce voter turnout and to increase the influence of groups who vote more regularly.

Voter turnout in cities with a mayor-council form of government is higher than in cities with a council-manager plan. In summary, nonpartisanship, council-manager government, and separate municipal elections—all part of the municipal "reform" movement—operate to reduce voter turnout and probably strengthen the influence of middle-class voters at the polls.

Voter turnout in municipal elections is also affected by the social character of cities. Social cleavages, especially race, increase voter turnout. Mayoral elections in which the racial or ethnic backgrounds of the candidates are well publicized inspire heavy voter turnout. Social homogeneity, on the other hand, is associated with lower voter interest.

In summary, voter turnout in municipal elections can be described as follows:

Lower voter turnout is expected with

- Nonpartisan electoral systems
- Council-manager form of government
- City elections held separately from state and national elections
- Small or middle-sized cities
- Middle-class, homogeneous cities

Higher voter turnout is expected with

- Partisan elections with competitive parties
- Strong mayor form of government
- City elections held concurrently with state and national elections
- Large cities
- Ethnic, heterogeneous cities

■

Referenda voting.
In local government, usually voters deciding whether or not to approve a bond issue and increased taxation for a specific project.

LOCAL REFERENDA VOTERS   Referenda voting is an important aspect of local politics—an aspect not found at the national level. City charters frequently require that referenda be held on all proposals to increase indebtedness or to increase property taxation. Over three-quarters of American cities have referenda provisions in their charters. (See Table 11–1.) Recall elections are permitted in over half of all American cities. (See Chapter 2 for definitions of initiative, referenda, and recall elections.) Many voters in local referenda will weigh the benefits that will come to them from a bond issue against the amount of the tax that will fall on them as a result of the expenditure. Non–property owners, having nothing to lose by the expenditure and something to gain, however small, can be expected to favor the passage of bond and expenditure referenda. (Renters seldom realize that landlords will pass the tax increase on to them in higher rent.) Homeowners are more likely to oppose public expenditures that are financed from property taxes than nonhomeowners. Among homeowners, support for local public expenditures often *increases* with education, wealth, and income. This ten-

Table 11–1

CITIES WITH INITIATIVE, REFERENDUM, AND RECALL			
Form of Government	*Initiative*	*Referendum*	*Recall*
Mayor-council	36.8%	71.4%	52.9%
Council-manager	58.8	82.9	70.4
Commission	36.5	76.1	59.4

Source: International City Managers' Association, *Municipal Yearbook*, 1994, p. 12.

dency of upper-class, liberal voters to support recreational, cultural, environmental projects (e.g., parks, museums, stadiums, libraries, art centers) was once labeled "public-regardingness."[2]

CAMPAIGN CONTRIBUTORS Money is playing an increasingly influential role in politics at all levels of government.[3] The costs of campaigning, especially the costs of television advertising, are rising rapidly. Earlier we observed that it is not uncommon for candidates for governor in large states to raise and spend $5 to $10 million or more in an election, and campaigns for state legislative seats often require $50,000 to $100,000 (see "Money in State Politics" in Chapter 5).

In local politics it is still possible to run a low-budget, door-to-door "shoe leather" campaign, especially in suburbs and small towns. It is still possible for many candidates for city council and county commission to rely on small contributions from friends, neighbors, and relatives, or on their own pocketbooks, to pay for signs, brochures, and newspaper ads.[4]

But in big cities, candidates for mayor, as well as city council and county commission, must raise substantial campaign money. Mayoral campaigns in America's big cities may cost $1 million or more, and even city council campaigns may cost $50,000 or more. These costs increase the influence of wealthy contributors in big-city politics.

Who contributes to candidates for local office? The largest sources of campaign contributions for city and county offices usually come from business interests with direct contacts with these governments—real estate developers, builders, and contractors. They seek to "invest" in winners, in order to establish access and goodwill among the officials who will be deciding on zoning and land-use questions, building and construction codes, environmental regulations, and various "growth management" policies (see Chapter 13, "Community Power and Land Use Control"). Their campaign contributions usually go to incumbents running for reelection on the (correct) assumption that they are likely to remain in office. A local officeholder must be particularly antigrowth in order to lose the contributions of developers and builders. Neighborhood associations that oppose development, environmental groups, and affluent residents occasionally combine their contributions to challenge the monetary advantage of prodevelopment candidates. Municipal employee unions, including police, firefighters, and sanitation workers, are another common source of campaign contributions in big cities. Law and accounting firms, printing and construction companies, and other businesses that have contracts with the city and county are also likely to be contributors, again usually to incumbents.

It is difficult to say whether money "buys" local elections. Incumbents raise and spend much more money than challengers, and incumbents almost always win reelection. But name recognition, friendships, contacts, and gratitude for services and favors, accumulated by incumbents during their terms of office, may be more important than the money they spend on their reelection campaigns. In open-seat elections the best-financed candidate usually wins, but this may be because contributors correctly judged that he or she would be the winner.

PARTIES IN BIG-CITY POLITICS

Traditionally, Democrats have dominated politics in the nation's large central cities, even while their surrounding suburbs have usually been governed by Republicans. Social groups that normally vote Democratic—white ethnic groups, Catholics and Jews, African Americans, union members, low-income families—tend to be concentrated in big cities. Since the formation of the modern "New Deal" Democratic party coalition under President Franklin D. Roosevelt in the 1930s, most big cities in the United States have been governed by Democrats. This has been true whether or not the city's electoral system has officially been partisan (e.g., New York, Chicago, Philadelphia, Boston) or nonpartisan (e.g., Los Angeles, Detroit, Miami).

SPLITS AMONG URBAN DEMOCRATS   Political cleavages *within* the Democratic party have been a driving force in big-city politics over the years. Political conflict in many of America's largest cities has centered on differences between working-class, Catholic, white ethnic (especially Irish, Italian, Polish) Democrats *versus* upper-class, white, liberal Protestants and Jews, allied with black Democratic voters. These factions within the Democratic party have frequently battled over such issues as affirmative action hiring in city government, busing in schools to achieve racial balance, and the behavior of police and prosecutors in crime control. And they have often differed over the burdens of public spending for welfare, health, and public housing—with working-class white ethnics, who are often homeowners and property tax payers, opposed to higher taxes and spending for these services; and upper-class liberals and blacks, many of whom are renters whose property taxes are hidden in rent payments, supporting these expenditures (see "Minorities and Women in Local Politics" later in this chapter).

Occasionally Democratic party organizations have been strong enough to hold these diverse Democratic groups together. Traditional party "machines" would slate candidates for city office with an eye to racial and ethnic group balance. But as these party machines lost influence over time, intraparty factional conflict—especially between working-class white ethnics and blacks—intensified in many cities.

The growing Hispanic vote in many of America's largest cities adds another potentially unstable element to the Democratic party coalition. Both African Americans and Hispanics have suffered discrimination in a predominantly white, "Anglo" society, and both have higher-than-average rates of poverty and unemployment and lower median family incomes. But a number of studies have shown this coalition to be unstable, occasionally engaging in competition over city jobs, language issues, and representation (e.g., as in Chicago, Denver, and Miami).[5]

REPUBLICAN BIG-CITY RESURGENCE?   Splits among urban Democrats, combined with continuing big-city ills—huge deficits, violent crime, racial conflict—have opened up new opportunities for Republican candidates. Despite overwhelming Democratic registration, big-city voters have recently elected a number of Republican mayors to cope with urban problems. Republican prosecuting attorney Rudolph Giuliani was elected mayor of New York in 1994, the first Republican to govern that city in

■

Machine.
In politics, a tightly disciplined political organization, historically centered in big cities, which traded patronage jobs, public contracts, services, and favors for votes.

Boss.
The acknowledged leader of a political machine, who may or may not occupy a public office.

over twenty years (see *"People in Politics:* Rudolph Giuliani, Getting Tough on Crime" in Chapter 9). Richard Riordan, a multimillionaire lawyer-businessman, was elected mayor of Los Angeles in 1994, the first Republican to hold that office in twenty years. Other Republicans and some conservative Democrats (e.g., Edward Rendell in Philadelphia) have won unexpected victories in heavily Democratic cities in recent elections. Certain common themes have driven their campaigns: a crackdown on crime, cutting the size of the city bureaucracy, reducing city deficits, easing tax burdens, and stimulating the city's economy. But it is not clear yet whether these Republican inroads in big-city politics are temporary responses to voter frustration or a more permanent resurgence of Republican strength.

OLD-STYLE MACHINE POLITICS

Machine politics has gone out of style. Machines—tightly disciplined party organizations, held together and motivated by a desire for tangible benefits rather than by principle or ideology and run by professional politicians—emerged in the nation's large cities early in the nineteenth century. This style of city politics has historical importance. Between the Civil War and the New Deal, every big city had a machine at one time or another, and it is sometimes easier to understand the character of city politics today by knowing what went on in years past. A more important reason for examining the machine style of politics is to understand the style of political organization that employs personal and material rewards to achieve power. These kinds of rewards will always be important in politics, and the big-city machine serves as a prototype of a style of politics in which ideologies and issues are secondary and personal friendships, favors, and jobs are primary.

   The political machine was essentially a large brokerage organization. Its business was to get votes and control elections by trading off social services, patronage, and petty favors to the urban masses, particularly the poor and the recent immigrants. To get the money to pay for these social services and favors, it traded off city contracts, protection, and privileges to business interests, which paid off in cash. Like other brokerage organizations, a great many middlemen came between the cash paid for a franchise for a trolly line or a construction contract and a Christmas turkey sent by the ward chairman to the Widow O'Leary. However, the machine worked. It performed many important social functions for the city.

   PERSONAL ATTENTION   First of all, it personalized government. With keen social intuition, the machine recognized the voter as a person, generally living in a neighborhood, who had specific problems and wants. The machine provided individual attention and recognition. As Tammany Hall boss George Washington Plunkitt, the philosopher king of old-style machine politics, explained: "I don't trouble them with political arguments. I just study human nature and act accordin'."[6] The machine also performed the functions of a welfare agency. According to Plunkitt, "What tells in holdin' your grip on your district is to go right down among the poor families and help them in the different ways they need help."[7] In the absence of government unemployment insurance or a federal employment service, patronage was an effective political tool, particularly in hard times. Not only were city jobs at the disposal of the machine, but the machine also had its many business contacts. Yet it was not so much the petty favors and patronage that won votes among urban dwellers, as it was the sense of friendship and humanity that characterized the "machine" and its "boss."[8]

ASSIMILATION   The machine also played an important role in educating recent immigrants and assimilating them into American life.[9] Machine politics provided a means of upward social mobility for ethnic group members, which was not open to them in businesses or professions. City machines sometimes met immigrants at dockside and led them in groups through naturalization and voter registration procedures. Machines did not keep out people with "funny" sounding names but instead went out of the way to put these names on ballots. Politics became a way "up" for the bright sons of Irish and Italian immigrants.

"GETTING THINGS DONE"   Finally, for businesses, and particularly for public utilities and construction companies with government contracts, the machine provided the necessary franchises, rights of way, contracts, and privileges. As Lincoln Steffens wrote: "You cannot build or operate a railroad, or a street railway, gas, water, or power company, develop and operate a mine, or cut forests or timber on a large scale, or run any privileged business, without corrupting or joining in the corruption of government."[10] The machine also provided the essential protection from police interference, which is required by illicit businesses, particularly gambling. In short, the machine helped to centralize power in large cities. It could "get things done at city hall" (see "*People in Politics:* The Daleys of Chicago").

REFORMERS AND DO-GOODERS

A reform style of politics appeared in the United States shortly after the Civil War to battle the "bosses." Beginning in 1869, scathing editorials in the *New York Times* and cartoons by Thomas Nast in *Harper's Weekly* attacked the "Tammany Society" in New York City, a political organization that controlled the local Democratic party. William M. Tweed was president of the board of supervisors of New York County and undisputed boss of "Tammany Hall," as the New York County Democratic committee was called, after its old meeting place on Fourteenth Street. This early reform movement achieved temporary success under the brilliant leadership of Samuel J. Tilden, who succeeded in driving the "Tweed Ring" out of office and went on in 1876 to be the only presidential candidate ever to win a majority of popular votes and then be denied the presidency through the operation of electoral college.

Early municipal reform is closely linked to the Progressive movement in American politics. Leaders such as Robert M. La Follette of Wisconsin, Hiram Johnson of California, Gifford Pinchot of Pennsylvania, and Charles Evans Hughes of New York backed municipal reform at the local level as well as the direct primary and direct election of senators and women's suffrage at the national level.[11] In 1912 social worker Jane Addams, who labored in slums and settlement houses, sang "Onward Christian Soldiers" at the Progressive party convention that nominated Teddy Roosevelt for

■

Reform.
In local government, a general reference to efforts to eliminate political machines, patronage, and party influence, and to install professional city management, nonpartisan elections, at-large districts, and the merit system.

THE DALEYS OF CHICAGO

For over two decades Mayor Richard J. Daley governed Chicago in the style of traditional machine politics. (When Mayor Daley himself was asked about his "machine," he replied, "Organization, not machine. Get that. Organization, not machine.") In Chicago, few others understood so well the labyrinths of formal and informal power. Daley won election to six four-year terms as mayor of Chicago, beginning in 1955. He remained the captain of his old Eleventh Ward Democratic committee, and he was chairman of the Cook County Democratic committee. He picked candidates' slates, ran the patronage machinery, and worked his will on nearly all of Chicago's city council. Illinois Democratic governors were usually responsive to his wishes, and Chicago's nine-member delegation to the U.S. House of Representatives also acted promptly on Daley's recommendations. The Cook County Democratic delegation to the Illinois legislature was firmly in his hands. No presidential candidate could ignore Daley's political "clout," either in the Democratic National Convention or in the general election. Daley may have been the most successful mayor in America, not only for his political acumen, but also for his ability to manage a great metropolis.[a]

The late Richard J. Daley, generally regarded as the last of the big-city bosses, won six four-year terms as Mayor of Chicago. When he died in office in 1976, the Chicago "machine" began to lose its clout.

Conflict Management

As a political broker, Daley was seldom the initiator of public policy. His approach to policy questions was more like that of an arbitrator between competing interests. When political controversies developed, Daley waited on the sidelines without committing himself, in the hope that public opinion would soon "crystallize" behind a particular course of action. Once the community was behind a project—and this determination Daley made himself after lengthy consultations with his political advisors—he then awarded his stamp of approval. This suggests that in policy matters many political "bosses" were not so much bosses as referees among interested individuals and groups. The boss was really "apolitical" when it came to policy matters. He was really more concerned with resolving conflict and maintaining his position and organization than he was with the outcome of public policy decisions. Boss Daley's politics: "Don't make no waves; don't back no losers."

The Machine Loses Clout

When Mayor Daley died in office in 1976, a lackluster machine replacement, Michael Bilandic, tried unsuccessfully to fill the shoes of the nation's most successful "boss." However, the once powerful Cook County Democratic committee gradually lost its direction, leadership, and "clout." Mayor Bilandic failed to hold together the coalition of white ethnic groups, blacks, Catholics, labor unions, and city employees, which were the backbone of the machine. In 1979 Jane Byrne defeated Bilandic and because Chicago's first female mayor. As the machine stumbled, the city's black voters became increasingly restless. In the 1983 Democratic mayoral primary the black community, under the leadership of Congressman Harold Washington, split from the Democratic machine. The machine went into the 1983 election hopelessly fractured. Mayor Byrne sought reelection and claimed control over city job holders; state attorney Richard M. Daley, son of the late mayor, challenged Byrne's control of the machine and called upon old loyalties to the family name; and Harold Washington worked hard to register and mobilize the city's black residents, 40 percent of Chicago's total population. The resulting split in the Democratic primary was: Washington, 37 percent; Byrne, 33 percent; Daley, 30 percent.

In the general election, several prominent white Democratic machine politicians deserted the Democratic candidate. Race dominated the campaign. Voter turnout in Chicago's 1983 mayoral election was a record 82 percent of registration. Washington won with 51.4 percent. He had the near-unanimous support of black voters combined with just enough "Lakefront liberal" white voters to provide a thin margin of victory. But most white voters, including the white ethnic voters who provided the machine with its traditional base of support, cast their ballots against the black Democratic nominee.[b]

Racial Politics

The demise of the old Daley political machine allowed racial divisions to surface as the major force in the city's political life. Harold Washington faced formidable opposition among many white city workers, police officers and firefighters, and a majority of white council members elected from wards. As council meetings deteriorated from parliamentary pandemonium to near fistfights, the courts were called upon to resolve many city issues.

Harold Washington's personal popularity among blacks and Hispanics and a significant portion of affluent, liberal whites was a major factor in his success as mayor. The city itself was almost evenly divided between white and black residents, with Hispanics comprising a smaller but important constituency. Washington's popularity, together with the gradual decline of the white percentage of the city's population, led many observers to believe that Chicago had seen its last white mayor. But Wahsington's untimely death in 1988 brought a new administration to the city.

Old Name, New Style

Richard M. Daley is the eldest son of the former mayor and long-time boss of Chicago's politics, Richard J. Daley. His father found him a job in the city attorney's office and later persuaded an incumbent state senator to give up his seat so that young "Richie" could start a political career. At the state capital, young Daley was unswervingly loyal to his father's machine. But after the mayor's death, and the personal tragedy of the death of a severely handicapped child, Richard M. Daley began to emerge as his own man.

In 1989 Daley won the Democratic primary against a black candidate with 56 percent of the vote. He held on to white ethnic voters who had so long supported his father, won the Hispanic vote, and won back many white liberals who were convinced the younger Daley stood for reform.

As mayor, Daley presented himself not as a "politician" but rather as a "manager" trying to reform a costly, unresponsive city bureaucracy. While critics claim that Daley's image as a reformer is only a cover for his political ambition, Daley's growing popularity in the job indicates that governmental reform is good politics. Chicago's voters seem to agree. Daley won the Democratic primary in 1991 with 63 percent of the vote (surpassing the best primary showing ever posted by his father), and then won an overwhelming 71 percent of the vote in the general election.

Daley's efforts to reform the city bureaucracy present an ironic twist to the long history of machine and reform politics in Chicago. Daley's father had overstaffed city hall with patronage appointees who worked his precincts at election time. But over time, the courts had given most city workers civil service protection as a "reform" of patronage practices. The result was a bloated bureaucracy unresponsive to either the mayor or the council. "You get elected mayor to make decisions, and then you find out the bureaucracy is against you," complained Daley. "Their attitude is 'we're going to be here when you leave!'"[c] Daley pushed to contract out to private firms—to "privatize"—many city functions, from janitorial services and parking fine collections to towing of abandoned cars.

Richard M. Daley, son of the late "Boss" Daley, won election to the Chicago Mayor's office once occupied by his father, but he did so by projecting the image of a "reform" rather than a "machine" candidate.

Privatization efforts are bitterly opposed by Chicago's public employee unions, especially the American Federation of State, County and Municipal Employees (AFSCME). By pursuing privatization, Daley cut the political ties between the city's employee unions and the mayor's office, a strategy his father would never have considered. But the "Son of Boss" put together a new political coalition, consisting of the city's white ethnic groups and its rapidly growing Hispanic population. Black leaders charge that Daley's privatization schemes have disproportionately impacted black employees, who were concentrated in service and maintenance jobs, those easiest to privatize. But Daley's style is to appeal to *taxpayers:* "Minorities are taxpayers. You go out to a homeowner—who is black, Hispanic, female, or Asian—and they pay taxes!"[d]

Perhaps Mayor Daley's boldest move was his 1995 decision to intervene in Chicago's failing school system. Decades of poor classroom performance and administrative chaos made the move look hopeless. But Daley installed his own school board members, who promptly dismissed dozens of poorly performing teachers and administrators. Both discipline and test scores began to improve.[e]

[a] For an excellent description of the functions of Mayor Daley's political organization in Chicago, see Edward C. Banfield, *Political Influence* (Glencoe, IL: The Free Press, 1961). For a hostile account of Mayor Daley, see Mike Royko, *Boss: Richard J. Daley of Chicago* (New York: E. P. Dutton, 1971).

[b] Michael B. Preston, "The Election of Harold Washington," *P.S. Political Science* (Summer 1983), 486.

[c] Quoted in *U.S. News and World Report*, March 23, 1992, p. 41.

[d] Quoted in Charles Mahtesian, "Taking Chicago Private," *Governing* (April 1994), 26–31.

[e] See *Governing* (December 1997), 22.

president. Lincoln Steffens wrote in *The Shame of the Cities* ". . . St. Louis exemplified boodle; Minneapolis, police graft; Pittsburgh, a political industrial machine; and Philadelphia (the worst city in the country), general civic corruption."[12]

SOCIAL BASES OF REFORM   From its beginning, reform politics was strongly supported by the upper-class, Anglo-Saxon, Protestant, longtime residents of cities whose political ethos was very different from that which the new immigrants brought with them. The immigrant, the machine that relied upon his vote, and the businessman who relied upon the machine for street railway and other utility franchises, had formed an alliance in the nineteenth century that had displaced the native, old family, Yankee elite that had traditionally dominated northern cities. This upper-class elite fought to recapture control of local government through the municipal reform movement.

Machine politicians catered to ethnic groups, organized labor, blue-collar workers, and other white working-class elements of the city. The reform politician appealed to the upper- and middle-class affluent Americans who were well educated and public-service minded. Reform was popular among liberals, newspaper reporters, college professors, and others who considered themselves "intellectuals."

REFORM GOALS   Reform politics included a belief that there was a "public interest" that should prevail over competing, partial interests in a city. The idea of balancing competing interests or compromising public policy was not part of the reformers' view of political life. Rather, the reform ethos included a belief that "politics" was distasteful. Enlightened people should agree on the public interest; municipal government is a technical and administrative problem rather than a political one. City government should be placed in the hands of those who are best qualified, by training, ability, and devotion to public service, to manage public business. These best-qualified people can decide on policy and then leave administration to professional experts. Any interference by special interests in the politics or administration of the best-qualified people should be viewed as corruption.

The objectives of early reform movements were:

- *Eliminate corruption.* The elimination of corruption in public office, and the recruitment of "good people" (educated, upper-income individuals who were successful in private business or professions) to replace "politicians" (who were no more successful than their constituents in private life and who were dependent upon public office for their principal source of income).
- *Nonpartisanship.* The elimination of parties from local politics by nonpartisan elections.
- *Manager government.* The establishment of the council-manager form of government, and the separation of "politics" from the "business" of municipal government.
- *At-large districts.* The establishment of at-large citywide constituencies in municipal elections in lieu of "district" constituencies in order to ensure that an elected official would consider the welfare of the entire city in public decision making and not merely his or her own neighborhood or "ward."

■

Corruption.
In politics, the use of public office for private gain, including bribery, conflict of interest, and the misuse and abuse of power.

- *Short ballot.* The reorganization of local government to eliminate many separately elected offices (the "short-ballot" movement) in order to simplify the voters' task and focus responsibility for the conduct of public affairs on a small number of top elected officials.

- *Strong executive.* The strengthening of executive leadership in city government—longer terms for mayors, subordination of departments and commissions to a chief executive, and an executive budget combined with modern financial practices.

- *Merit system.* The replacement of patronage appointments with the merit system of civil service.

- *Home rule.* The separation of local politics from state and national politics by home-rule charters and the holding of local elections at times when there were no state and national elections.

All these objectives were interrelated. Ideally, a "reformed city" would be one with the manager form of government, nonpartisan election for mayor and council, a home-rule charter, a short ballot, at-large constituencies, a strong executive, a merit service personnel system, and honest people at the helm. Later, the reform movement added comprehensive city planning to its list of objectives—official planning agencies with professional planners authorized to prepare a master plan of future development for the city. The National Municipal League (now the National League of Cities) incorporated its program of reform into a *Model City Charter,* which continues today to be the standard manual of municipal reform.[13]

REASONS FOR THE MACHINE'S DECLINE   Parties in general are losing their appeal to many Americans. Increasing proportions of voters are identifying themselves as "independents," rather than as Democrats or Republicans. (See Chapter 5.) Party offices (precinct committee, ward chairperson, county committee, and so on) are vacant in many cities and counties. The general decline in parties has contributed to the decline of machine politics. Several additional factors might be cited as contributing to the decline of machine politics:

- *The decline in European immigration* and the gradual assimilation of white ethnic groups—Irish, Italians, Germans, Poles, Slavs.

- *Federal social welfare programs,* which undercut the machine's role in welfare work—unemployment insurance, workers' compensation, social security, and public assistance.

- *Rising levels of prosperity* and higher educational levels, which make the traditional rewards of the machine less attractive.

- *The spread of middle-class values* about honesty, efficiency, and good government, which inhibit party organizations in purchases, contracts, and vote buying, and other cruder forms of municipal corruption.

- *New avenues of upward social mobility* that have opened up the sons and daughters of working-class families, and higher education, which has allowed many to join the ranks of professionals, corporate executives, educators, and so on so that the party machine is no longer the only way "up" for persons at the bottom of the social ladder.

- *Structural reforms* such as nonpartisanship, better voting procedures, city-manager government, and—most important of all—civil service, which have weakened the party's role in municipal elections and administration.

REFORMISM AND PUBLIC POLICY   What are the policy consequences of reform government? Traditionally, political scientists assumed that the reform of city government would bring about changes in public policy. Reform was expected to result in better public services, lower tax rates, and more professional administration. However, it is not easy to distinguish *independent* effects of reform on public policy from the effects of other urban characteristics associated with reform—smaller size, southern and western regions, less ethnicity, more middle-class residents.

It is true that reformed cities tend to tax and spend *less* than unreformed cities.[14] But socioeconomic conditions associated with reformism have an even more important impact than reform on tax and spending policies. For example,

- The more middle class the city, measured by income, education, and occupation, the lower the general tax and spending levels.
- The greater the home ownership in a city, the lower the tax and spending levels.
- The larger the percentage of racial and ethnic minorities in the population, the lower the city's taxes and expenditures.

But perhaps an even more important difference between the two kinds of city governments—reformed and unreformed—is their *responsiveness* to the socioeconomic composition of their populations. *Reformed* cities (cities with manager governments, at-large constituencies, and nonpartisan elections) appeared to be *un*responsive in their tax and spending policies to differences in income and educational, occupational, religious, and ethnic characteristics of their populations. In contrast, unreformed cities (cities with mayor-council governments, ward constituencies, and partisan elections) reflected class, racial, and religious composition in their taxing and spending decisions.

RACE AND REFORMISM   Reformism appears to reduce the importance of race, class, home ownership, ethnicity, and religion in city politics. It tends to minimize the role that social conflicts play in public decision making. In contrast, mayor-council governments, ward constituencies, and partisan elections permit social cleavages to be reflected in city politics and public policy to be responsive to socioeconomic factors. These findings suggest that reformed cities have gone a long way toward accomplishing the reformist goal—that is, "to immunize city governments from 'artificial' social cleavages—race, religion, ethnicity, and so on."[15]

The assertion that reformism lessens the responsiveness of city governments is reinforced by observing the responses of cities to civil rights group activity. In community politics, civil rights groups—the National Association for the Advancement of Colored People (NAACP), the National Urban League, the Southern Leadership Conference (SCLC)—are generally associated with the needs of poor and black people—low-rent housing, community-action programs, and neighborhood youth-corp programs. The strength of civil rights organizations is usually related to increased community efforts in these areas. However, *reformed governments appear less responsive* to these civil rights groups than unreformed governments. The associations between civil rights group activity and policies favoring the poor and blacks are *lower* in cities with non-partisan elections, manager governments, and at-large elections. This evidence suggests that blacks and other urban minorities have little to gain through reformism.[16]

Indeed, to many African American leaders it seems that the triumph of reform politics came just when blacks were finally beginning to gain control of municipal government in many big cities. Civil service is perceived as an obstacle to blacks finally receiving their "fair share" of municipal patronage. Relatively few city managers are African Americans. These structural reforms, together with the reform emphasis on economy and efficiency in government and its deemphasis on "politics," all combine to frustrate black communities in many cities.

THE NEW PERSONALIZED MACHINES   Some big-city mayors have been successful in building personal political organizations centered on the mayor's office. They have expanded their supply of patronage jobs by enlarging the mayoral office staff and creating public authorities and agencies that are directly responsible to the mayor's office. Appointees to these fairly high-paying staff and administrative positions form the nucleus of the mayor's personal campaign organization. A resourceful mayor can augment his or her immediate staff people ("the palace guard") with appointments to city economic development authorities, community rehabilitation agencies, housing authorities, and other quasi-governmental bureaucracies. Many of these bureaucracies are federally funded and their top posts can be filled by an astute mayor using "creative" personnel practices.[17] In many large cities, elements of the old ward politics survive in particular neighborhoods. The neighborhood politician, perhaps a state senator or city council member, still strolls the sidewalks, glad-handing constituents, and promising to find a job for someone, fix a street light, and see about uncollected trash. Indeed, the modern neighborhood politician may enter each constituent's name in the office computer system and keep track of individual requests and favors rendered.[18] It still matters to many voters that their representative grew up in the neighborhood, still lives there, can be contacted day or night, knows their names, and gives personal attention to their problems.

If we define patronage to include a wide range of tangible benefits—construction contracts, insurance policies, printing and office supplies, architectural services, and other government contracts for goods or services—then patronage may still be important in many communities. Competitive bidding by potential government contractors is required in most states and cities, but it is not difficult to "rig" the process. The fact that the firms that do much of their business with government are also the largest contributors to political campaigns cannot be coincidence. Another source of patronage is the power of courts to appoint referees, appraisers, receivers in bankruptcies, and trustees and executors of estates; these plums require little work and produce high fees for attorneys who are "well connected." Few cities have ever been able to remove zoning from politics: Rezoning property from lower-value classifications (single-family residential) to higher-value classifications (apartments, commercial, industrial) is one of the most important "goodies" available to municipal governments. In addition, mu-

■

Patronage.
Rewards granted by government officeholders to political supporters in the form of government jobs.

nicipal construction permits, inspection, and licensing can be slow and cumbersome, or fast and painless, depending on the political resources of the builder-developer.[19] (See "*Up Close:* Political Corruption.")

THE RECRUITMENT OF CITY COUNCIL MEMBERS

Political ambition is the most distinguishing characteristic of elected officeholders at all levels of government. The people who run for and win public office are not necessarily the most intelligent, best-informed, wealthiest, or most successful business or professional people. At all levels of the political system, from presidential candidates, members of Congress, governors, and state legislators, to city council and school board members, it is the most politically ambitious people who are willing to sacrifice time, family and private life, and energy and effort for the power and celebrity that comes with public office.

Most politicians publicly deny that personal ambition is their real motivation for seeking public office. Rather they describe their motives in highly idealistic terms— "civic duty," "service to community," "reform the government," "protect the environment." These responses reflect the norms of our political culture: People are not supposed to enter politics to satisfy *personal* ambitions, but rather to achieve *public* purposes. Many politicians do not really recognize their own drive for power—the drive to shape their community according to their own beliefs and values. But if there were no personal rewards in politics, no one would run for office.

PROFESSIONALIZATION   Politics is becoming increasingly professionalized. "Citizen-politicians"—people with business or professional careers who get into politics part time or for short periods of time—are being driven out of political life by career politicians—people who enter politics early in life as a full-time occupation and expect to make it their career.[20] Politics is increasingly demanding of time and energy. At all levels of governments, from city council to state legislatures to the U.S. Congress, political work is becoming full time and year-round. It is not only more demanding to *hold* office than it was a generation ago, but also far more demanding to *run* for office. Campaigning has become more time-consuming, more technically sophisticated, and much more costly over time.

Traditionally, city council members and county commissioners were local business people who were respected in the community and active in civic organizations. They were likely to own small businesses and to have many contacts among constituents— retail merchants, real estate brokers, insurance agents, and so on. (Seldom do executives of large corporations concern themselves with local affairs, although they may encourage lower-management personnel to do so.) The part-time nature of traditional community governance, combined with only nominal pay and few perks of office, made local office holding a "community service." It attracted people whose business brought them into close contact with the life of the community and allowed them spare time to attend to community affairs.

These civic-minded small business people are still politically dominant in many small towns and rural counties throughout the nation. But they are gradually being

■

Professionalization.
In politics, a reference to running for and holding public office as a full-time career.

POLITICAL CORRUPTION

Corruption is an ever-present theme in American political life. We all know that "politics is corrupt," but with the exception of some well-publicized cases we really do not know *how* much corruption takes place. Corruption may be more widespread in state and local politics than in national politics, because state and local officials avoid the spotlight of the national news media. One major problem in studying corruption is defining the term. What is "corrupt" to one observer may be "just politics" to another or merely "an embarrassment" to someone else.

For example, here is a list of hypothetical acts that state senators in twenty-four states were asked to rate as more or less corrupt, together with the percentage of senators who viewed each act as corrupt.[a]

- The driveway of the mayor's home being paved by the city crew—95.9 percent.
- A public official using public funds for personal travel—95.2 percent.
- A state assembly member, while chairman of the public roads committee, authorizing the purchase of land he or she had recently acquired—95.1 percent.
- A legislator accepting a large campaign contribution in return for voting "the right way" on a legislative bill—91.9 percent.
- A judge with $50,000 worth of stock in a corporation hearing a case concerning that firm—78.8 percent.
- A presidential candidate promising an ambassadorship in exchange for campaign contributions—71.1 percent.
- A secretary of defense owning $50,000 in stock in a company with which the Defense Department has a million-dollar contract—58.3 percent.
- A member of Congress who holds a large amount of stock (about $50,000 worth) in Exxon working to maintain the oil depletion allowance—54.9 percent.
- A member of Congress using seniority to obtain a weapons contract for a firm in his or her district—31.6 percent.
- A public official using influence to get a friend or relative admitted to law school—23.7 percent.

The line between unethical behavior and criminal activity is a fuzzy one. Unethical behavior includes lying and misrepresentation; favoritism toward relatives, friends, and constituents; conflicts of interest, in which public officials decide issues in which they have a personal financial interest. Not all unethical behavior is criminal conduct. But bribery is a criminal offense—soliciting or receiving anything of value in exchange for the performance of a governmental duty.

How Much Corruption?

It is difficult to estimate the extent of corruption in American politics, in part because public officials do not usually volunteer information on their own corrupt behavior! The U.S. Justice Department reports on *federal* prosecutions of public officials for violations of criminal statutes (see Figure). These figures do not include state prosecutions, so they do not cover all of the criminal indictments brought against public officials each year. (And, of course, they do not tell us how much corruption went undetected.) Nonetheless, these figures indicate that now over one thousand public officials are indicted and convicted of criminal activity each year.

Federal Prosecutions of Public Corruption

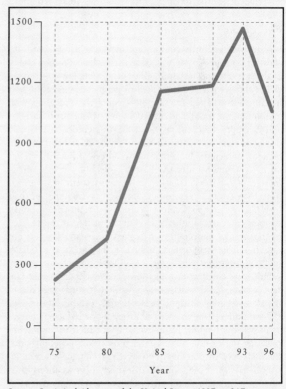

Year

Source: Statistical Abstract of the United States, 1997, p. 217.

Explaining Corruption

Why do some government officials engage in corruption? We can think of at least three reasons: (1) for personal gain, that is, simply to enrich themselves; (2) to benefit friends, constituents, or ethnic groups with contracts, jobs, and aid; and (3) to bring coordination to fragmented government by exchanging favors simply "to get things done." Often we think of activities under these last two categories as less corrupt than efforts to achieve personal gain. Corruption for personal gain is less acceptable. Yet such corruption is almost an American tradition. Politicians over the years could echo Tammany Hall's George Washington Plunkitt, "I seen my opportunities and I took 'em."[b]

Political corruption is more common in some cities and states than in others. Generally corruption is measured by federal prosecutions because it is more common in large cities and larger states. Competitive parties tend to dampen corruption somewhat, suggesting that strong opposition parties perform a watchdog function. Gambling is closely associated with official corruption. But the size of government bureaucracies appears to be the strongest determinant of corruption: As government grows, so do the opportunities for corruption.[c]

Prosecuting Corruption

Investigating and prosecuting state and local government officials for corrupt activity was once the exclusive responsibility of the state attorney general's office using state laws. But today U.S. attorneys have largely taken over this responsibility. Acting under broad federal statutes—federal laws dealing with mail fraud, tax fraud, and the RICO Act (Racketeer Influenced and Corrupt Organizations)—federal prosecutors have largely displaced state prosecutors in dealing with official corruption.[d] Federal prosecutors have the vast resources of the FBI, the Internal Revenue Service, the Postal Inspection Service, and a myriad of other federal agencies to assist them in investigations. Moreover, U.S. attorneys have great discretion in their investigatory and prosecutory decisions. U.S. attorneys, unlike regional directors of other federal departments, are nominated by the president and confirmed by the U.S. Senate. They are not only free from state or local influence, they are also free from interference from federal elected officials. They can initiate lengthy and complex investigations, convene federal grand juries, obtain indictments, arrange plea bargains with defendants, and build "pyramid" cases against prominent officials. ("Pyramid building" consists of dropping or reducing charges against lower-level figures in exchange for their testimony implicating higher officials.) Federal prosecutors generally pride themselves on their ability to prosecute prominent state and local officials. And well-publicized successful prosecutions often provide a springboard for their own political ambitions.

The great discretion given U.S. attorneys, combined with partisan politics and their own personal ambitions, can lead to selective use of federal laws against prominent officials. Indeed, the possibility of "targeting" by a federal prosecutor should inspire caution in even the most honest state and local officials. Cleaning up political corruption in state and local government is *not* an enumerated or implied power of the federal government. This is one more activity that has shifted from the state to the national level and undermined earlier

ideas of the American federalism (see Chapter 3). The states have a special interest in policing their own political processes. The principal responsibility for attacking corruption should rest with the states themselves and the people who elect state and local officials.

Voter Reaction

Do voters punish officials for corrupt activities? Not always. Voters sometimes reelect officials who have been convicted of criminal offenses. There are various reasons for the continued voter support of corrupt politicians. First of all, *charges* of corruption are so frequent in election campaigns that voters disregard information about improprieties in office. Or voters may perceive both candidates as more or less corrupt and simply make their voting choices on other factors. Second, if voters believe that officials' corrupt acts were designed to benefit their district or their race or their ethnic group, they may support them despite (or even because of) their corrupt acts. Third, corrupt politicians may be popular with their constituents, whether personally or because of their stand on issues; constituents may knowingly ignore corruption because they value the representation more. There are many other issues besides "honesty in government."[e]

A strategy of some disgraced officeholders today is to publicly acknowledge one's past errors, claim personal redemption, go on television talk shows, and ask voters to accept a restored and chastised candidate. Mayor Marion Barry of Washington, DC, was tried and convicted on cocaine charges arising out of a sting operation that videotaped him at a DC hotel in 1991. His initial response: "Who are you going to believe—me or the videotape?" But after serving a jail term and enduring nationwide ridicule, he made a strong political comeback and recaptured the mayor's chair in 1994. He campaigned on his own redemption: "God has made it possible for me to overcome many obstacles. I stand here with you stronger and wiser and better than ever before."[f]

[a] John G. Peters and Susan Welch, "Political Corruption in America: A Search for Definitions and a Theory," *American Political Science Review*, 72 (September 1978), 974–84, 978.

[b] Riordan, *Plunkitt of Tammany Hall*, p. 3.

[c] These findings are set forth in Kenneth J. Meier and Thomas M. Holbrook, "I Seen My Opportunities and I Took 'Em: Political Corruption in the American States," *Journal of Politics*, 54 (February 1992), 135–55.

[d] See Arthur Maass, "Public Policy by Prosecution," *The Public Interest* (Fall 1987), 107–27.

[e] For some tests about voter reaction to corruption, see Barry S. Rundquist, Gerald S. Strom, and John G. Peters, "Corrupt Politicians and Their Electoral Support," *American Political Science Review*, 71 (September 1977), 954–63.

[f] Quoted in *Governing* (February 1995), 7.

replaced by lawyers, government employees, teachers, and professional officeholders in medium to large cities. In these cities, council pay is higher, the work more time-consuming, greater celebrity attaches to council membership (television interviews, newspaper stories, deference, and respect), and greater opportunities exist for political advancement.

> Full-timers drive part-timers out of circulation. The city councilman who spends his days building political coalitions, meeting with constituents, and cultivating financial support sets a standard of political sophistication that colleagues pretty much have to meet if they are going to stay effective or even stay in office. Once a city council attracts its full-time members, it is on the way to becoming a de facto full-time institution, even if it does not think of itself as one.[21]

As a result of the increasing professionalization of local politics, liberals and Democrats are more likely to win office. Increasing demands of time and energy attract people for whom politics is more important and more rewarding than business or professional success. Older business and professional leaders, who once managed city affairs on a part-time basis while still tending to their businesses and professions, tended to be conservatives and Republicans. But these part-time, civic-minded business leaders are gradually being replaced by younger people for whom politics is a career.

CITY COUNCILS: TERMS AND ELECTIONS   In most American cities, especially those with nonpartisan at-large elections, getting elected to city council is a do-it-yourself project. Most party organizations and civic associations are unreliable as sources of money and workers. Candidates must mobilize their own resources and create their own organizations. It is generally unwise to challenge an incumbent; over 80 percent of all incumbent council members seeking reelection are returned to office.[22] When vacancies occur, there are likely to be many candidates in the race. Since local races lack the visibility of national or statewide races, most focus on the personality, style, or image of the candidate. Even when local issues divide the candidates, most voters in local elections will be unaware of the candidates' stands on these issues.

In this fluid setting, electoral success depends on (1) the social acceptability of candidates relative to the community (especially their race and ethnic background); (2) their personal recognition in the community (name recognition, contacts from business, church, civic activity, etc.); and (3) their political resources (endorsements by newspapers and civic associations, access to political contributors, people willing to serve as volunteer workers, etc.). These factors are especially important for first-time candidates.[23] In subsequent campaigns, candidates develop more stable political followings.

Most city councils have five or seven members, but large city councils with up to twenty-two members are found in the larger, older cities of the Northeast and Midwest (see Table 11–2). Four-year terms for council members are most frequent, but some council members are elected for two- or three-year terms. In most cities, council member terms overlap, so that some council seats are filled at every municipal election. Presumably overlapping terms ensure continuity in the deliberations of the council. Although term limits for council members are growing in popularity, as yet fewer than 10 percent of cities have adopted them.

The mayor's role relative to the city council varies according to the form of govern-

Incumbent.
The person currently serving in a public office.

Table 11–2

CITY COUNCILS	
Average size	6.5 members
Terms	
two years	30%
three years	10%
four years	60%
Term limits	9%
Mayor sits on council	
mayor-council cities	22%
council-manager cities	75%
commission cities	91%
Mayor can veto council ordinances	
mayor-council cities	56%
council-manager cities	11%
commission cities	2%

Source: International City Managers' Association, *Municipal Yearbook, 1998.*

ment. In mayor-council cities, the mayor does not usually sit on the council. However, in over half of these cities the mayor can veto council-passed ordinances; the mayor's veto can usually be overridden by a vote of two-thirds of the council. In council-manager and commission cities, the mayor is usually a council member, often selected by the council itself or on the basis of seniority on the council. These mayors may perform symbolic functions (for example, presenting the "keys to the city" to visiting celebrities), but they seldom can veto council ordinances.

FRIENDS AT CITY HALL A surprising number of council members are initially *appointed* to their office to fill the unexpired terms of resigning members. Those appointees are likely to be personal friends of council members or to have held some other city job. Finally, 80 percent of incumbents running for reelection are successful. Voluntary retirement is the most common exit from community politics. Political scientist Kenneth Prewitt observes that

> The election system provides advantages to those citizens who already have social and political resources; to those favorably located in the network of friendships which play such an important part in city politics; to those whose apprentice roles identify them as likely candidates for political office; to those who have natural organizational ties and support; and, finally, to those already in office if they choose to stand for reelection.[24]

COUNCIL MEMBERS: RESPONSIBLE POLICY MAKERS?

Mayor.
The elected chief executive officer of the city government.

The policy-making role of council members varies a great deal from city to city. Council members have more formal power in commission or weak-mayor forms of government, where the council itself sometimes appoints officials, prepares the budget, supervises departments, and performs other administrative tasks. However, in other cities—particularly strong mayor or manager cities—the council merely oversees city affairs. In these cities, the function of the council may be principally the representation of the interests of local constituents—forwarding complaints, making inquiries, pushing for new sidewalks or streetlights, and so forth.

Council members do *not* usually serve as either general policy innovators or general policy leaders. The role of the council is largely passive, granting or withholding approval in the name of the community when presented with proposals from a leadership outside of itself. The outside leadership is usually the manager, city departments, planning commission, citizen groups, or private enterprise.[25]

VOLUNTEERISM   Some council members have little interest in a political career and serve out of a sense of public service (frequently at considerable personal expense in time and energy). "Volunteerism" is probably most prevalent in suburban, small, and middle-class communities. Volunteers see their service as a sacrifice, and they are relatively immune from direct constituency pressure. Threats to oust them in the next election have little meaning. "I don't really give a damn whether I am reelected or not" is a common response. Moreover, the attitude of "volunteerism" results in councils that are "(a) more likely to vote against what they see as majority opinion; (b) less likely to feel under pressure from the public; (c) less likely to consider the upcoming election when choosing among policy alternatives; (d) less likely to facilitate group access to the council; and (e) less likely to perform services to constituents."[26]

ACCOUNTABILITY   The problem of political accountability in local politics is aggravated by several factors:

1. *The frequency of appointment to elected office.* It is probable that as many as one-quarter of the nation's council members initially come into office by appointment rather than election. They are appointed, usually by the mayor, to fill unexpired terms.

2. *The effective constituency is very small.* Given the low turnout in municipal elections, and the small constituencies served by a council member, only a very few votes may elect a person to office. A council member's personal friends, immediate neighbors, business associates, fellow church members, and acquaintances at the Rotary Club may be enough for election.

3. *Limited contact with citizens.* Few citizens know how to contact city officials, and even fewer citizens actually do so.[27] Moreover, citizen-initiated contacts are closely related to socioeconomic status, with higher-status individuals far more likely to contact city officials about a problem than middle- or lower-status persons.

4. *The infrequency of electoral defeat.* Incumbents running for reelection are hardly ever defeated. It is estimated that 80 percent of incumbent council members running for reelection are returned to office.[28] When they are defeated, it is frequently in groups, when several incumbents are turned out of office at once owing to a specific community controversy.

5. *The frequency of voluntary retirement from elected office.* The vast majority of council members voluntarily retire from office, over half of them after two

Council member.
In local government, an elected member of the governing body.

Volunteerism.
In local politics, serving in office out of a sense of public service with little or no interest in advancing one's political career.

Accountability.
In politics, the extent to which an elected official must answer to his or her constituents.

terms. Officeholders simply conclude that the obligations of office exceed the rewards.

All these factors, together with the attitude of volunteerism, tend to distance municipal government from direct citizen control.

REPRESENTATION   Despite this evidence of a lack of electoral accountability in local politics, some factors may compel council members to reflect the will of their constituents in policy making. First of all, volunteerism is becoming less prevalent over time, especially in large cities with competitive, partisan elections. We know that big-city council members are more likely to be attorneys and professional politicians, to aspire to higher office, and to spend more time on city affairs; we might infer from this that they would be more directly concerned with their constituents' views.

SHARED BELIEFS   Moreover, council members tend to reflect, in their own socioeconomic background, the characteristics of their constituents. This does not *ensure* that council members share the same attitudes as their constituents on all matters; indeed, the experience of being a public official itself can help to shape a council member's views and give a different perspective on public affairs than the constituents'. However, if council members have deep roots in their communities (many social contacts and group memberships; shared socioeconomic, ethnic, racial, and religious characteristics with their constituents), they may reflect these in their policy making, whether they are consciously aware of these "constituency influences" or not. The effects of shared community life may be very influential in shaping decision making in small, homogeneous communities where uniformity of outlook may amount to compulsion. In short, although "electoral accountability" may have little direct influence over council members, "belief sharing" may still assure some congruence between the views of community residents and the views of their representatives.[29]

CITY MANAGERS IN MUNICIPAL POLITICS

When council-manager government was first introduced as part of the municipal reform movement, managers were expressly admonished not to participate in community "politics." Early supporters of manager government believed in the separation of "politics" from "administration."[30] Politics, not only *party* politics but *policy* making as well, should be the exclusive domain of the elected city council. The manager was hired by the council to carry out its policy directives, and the manager could be removed by the council by majority vote at any time. This belief in the separation of policy making from administration was intended to produce "nonpolitical," efficient, and economical government, which middle-class supporters of the reform movement valued so highly. Popular control of government was to be guaranteed by making the manager's tenure completely dependent upon the will of the elected council.

However, after a few years of experience with manager government in America, it became increasingly apparent to the managers themselves that they could not escape responsibility for policy recommendations. It turned out to be very difficult in practice to separate policy making from administration. The first code of ethics of the Interna-

■

City manager.
The chief executive of a city government, who is appointed by the city council and responsible to it.

tional City Managers' Association (ICMA) stated flatly that "no manager should take an active part in politics." Managers agreed that they should stay out of partisan politics and election campaigns, but there was a great deal of debate about the role of managers in community policy making. In 1938, the ICMA revised its code of ethics to recognize the positive role of managers in policy leadership.[31]

MANAGERS AS POLICY LEADERS   Today, we are likely to find varying role orientations among city managers. Some see themselves as "policy managers," providing community leadership through their recommendations to their councils on a wide variety of matters. They believe they should innovate and lead on policy matters. Others see themselves as "administrative managers," restricting themselves to the supervision of the municipal bureaucracy and avoiding innovative policy recommendations, particularly in controversial areas. Ambivalent about innovation and leadership on policy matters, these managers avoid involvement in community issues.

Probably a majority of professionally trained city managers see themselves as "policy managers." Better-educated managers who have had experience in different cities and who aspire to move to larger cities and assume greater responsibilities are unlikely to settle for a restricted, administrative role. However, managers without professional training in city administration or those with engineering degrees, who have lived most of their lives in their own communities and who expect to remain there, may be more likely to accept a fairly narrow administrative role.[32]

MANAGERS AS ADMINISTRATORS   While most managers see themselves as policy leaders, most council members see managers in their traditional role of administrators. This means that prudent managers will not wish to *appear* to be policy makers even when they are. They seek to have others present their policy proposals to the community and avoid the brasher methods of policy promotion. Like any successful politician, city managers try to avoid taking public stands on the more controversial issues facing the community. Their dependence upon the council for their jobs prevents them from being too extreme in policy promotion. Managers can push their councils, but they can seldom fight them with any success. Open disputes between the manager and the council are usually resolved by the dismissal of the manager. Managers who assume strong policy-leadership roles have shorter tenures than those who do not.

Nevertheless, the manager is the most important policy initiator in most council-manager cities. Most managers determine the agenda for city council meetings. This permits them to determine the kinds of issues to be raised and the policy options to be considered. The council may not accept everything recommended by the manager, but the manager's recommendations will be given serious consideration. The city manager is the major source of information for most council members. The manager prepares the city budget; writes formal reports on city problems, defining the problems and proposing solutions; and advises and educates the council privately as well as publicly.

MANAGERS IN A DUAL ROLE   Thus, managers really have two important roles in community politics: administration and policy making. The administrative role involves the supervision of the municipal bureaucracy; this role requires administrative skills and technical expertise. Managers direct their personal staff, develop and control the city budget, and appoint and remove department heads. In most council-manager cities, managers try to guard these powers from direct council interference; these powers are the managers' most important formal resources.

HOW COUNCIL MEMBERS VIEW MANAGERS   What kind of managers do mayors and council members want? Doubtlessly, some mayors and council members want to retain a larger policy role for themselves and resent a manager who wants to run the show. These elected officials might try to recruit "administrative managers" by avoiding applicants with forceful personalities, high professional qualifications, and experience in other cities. However, we have already suggested that many council members are "volunteers" who prefer a passive role in policy making—approving or disapproving proposals brought before them by the manager and others. A weak manager can lengthen council meetings and significantly increase the council's workload. So we should not be surprised to find many council members welcoming policy leadership from the manager (as long as the manager avoids the appearance of dominating the council). Indeed, one study indicates that a majority of council members "expect the manager to take the lead" in budget decisions, hiring and firing personnel, reorganization of city departments, wage and salary negotiations, community improvements, and cooperative proposals with other communities.[33] Only in planning and zoning do council members say they want to retain leadership. Presumably these council members would try to recruit well-educated, professionally trained, experienced, and mobile managers to their community. However, past manager-council relations in a community may affect recruitment. Some communities may undergo cycles in council-manager relations: A council resentful of a strong manager replaces him or her with a weak one, only to find that their workload increases, decisions are postponed, complaints of inaction accumulate; and the council decides to find a new, stronger manager.

PROFESSIONALISM   Today, most city managers are professionals who have been trained in university graduate programs in public administration. They are familiar with budgeting and fiscal administration, public personnel management, municipal law, and planning. They tend to move from city to city as they advance in their professional careers. They may begin their careers as a staff assistant to a city official and then move to assistant city manager, then manager of a small town, and later perhaps of a larger city. About three-quarters of all city manager appointments are made from outside the city, and only about one-quarter are local residents, which indicates the professionalism of city management. The average tenure of managers who resigned or were removed from office has been about five years. One in ten managers reports having been fired at least once. Most of these found another job within six months but reported using up their savings or severance pay to survive between jobs. The three principal reasons given for having been fired were "poor working relationship with council," "politics," and "change in the council." All of these reasons might be termed *political.*

MAYORS IN CITY POLITICS

Today, more than ever before, the nation's cities need forceful, imaginative political leadership. The nation's major domestic problems—race relations, poverty, violence, congestion, poor schools, fiscal crisis—are concentrated in cities. Mayors are in the "hot seat" of American politics; they must deal directly with these pressing issues. No other elected official in the American federal system must deal face-to-face, eyeball-to-eyeball with these problems.

LIMITED POWERS   The challenges facing big-city mayors are enormous; however, their powers to deal with these challenges are restricted on every side. Executive power in major cities is often fragmented among a variety of elected officials—city treasurer, city clerk, city comptroller, district attorney, and so on. The mayor may also be required to share power over municipal affairs with county officials. Many city agencies and functions are outside the mayor's formal authority: Independent boards and commissions often govern important city departments—for example, the board of education, board of health, zoning appeals board, planning commission, civil service board, library board, park commission, sewage and water board, and so on. Even if the mayor is permitted to appoint the members of the boards and commissions, they are often appointed for a fixed term, and the mayor cannot remove them. The mayor's power over the affairs of the city may also be affected by the many special district governments and public authorities operating within the city, including public housing, urban renewal, sewage and water, mass transit, and port authority. Traditionally, school districts have been outside the authority of the mayor or city government. Mayors' powers over city finances may even be restricted—they may share budget-making powers with a board of estimate, and powers over expenditures with an elected comptroller or treasurer. Civil service regulations and independent civil service boards can greatly hamper mayors' control over their own bureaucrats. The activities of federal and state agencies in a city are largely beyond the mayor's control.

SELECTING MAYORS   The method of selecting mayors also influences their powers over city affairs. Some mayors are selected by their city councils or commissions and generally have little more power than other council members or commissioners. Their job is generally ceremonial: They crown beauty queens, dedicate parks, lay cornerstones, and lead parades. Larger cities and mayor-council cities generally elect their mayors. Mayors may be elected for anything from one to five years, but two-year and four-year terms are most common in American cities.

LEGISLATIVE POWERS   Mayors' legislative powers also vary widely. Of course, in all cities they have the right to submit messages to the council and to recommend policy. These recommendations will carry whatever prestige the mayor possesses in the community. Moreover, in council-manager and commission cities, mayors usually are themselves members of the council. In these cities where mayors are chosen by the council, they generally have voting power equal to that of other council members. In about one-third of mayor-council cities, the mayor also serves on the council; in about half of the mayor-council cities the mayor presides over meetings of the council and can cast a tie-breaking vote. In most cities where the mayor is *not* a member of the council, the mayor enjoys veto power over council-passed ordinances. The veto power helps distinguish between "strong-mayor" and "weak-mayor" cities.

ADMINISTRATIVE POWERS   Another distinction between "strong" and "weak" mayors is made on the basis of their powers of administration. Weak mayors have very limited appointing powers and even more limited removal powers. They have little control over separately elected boards and commissions or separately elected offices, such as clerk, treasurer, tax assessor, comptroller, and attorney. The council, rather than the mayor, often appoints the key administrative officers. No single individual has the complete responsibility for law enforcement or coordinating city administration.

POLITICAL POWERS   In summary, a mayor's ability to provide strong leadership in many cities is limited by fragmented authority, multiple elected officials, limited jurisdiction over important urban services, civil service, state or federal interference, and constraints placed upon that power by "reform" and "good-government" arrangements. Nevertheless, even though it is recognized that mayors have few formal powers to deal with the enormous tasks facing them, it is frequently argued that mayors can and should exercise strong leadership as "political brokers"—mediating disputes, serving as a channel of communications, bringing conflicting groups together for reasonable discussions of their differences, and suggesting solutions that diverse groups can accept in coping with the city's problems. In other words, the "ideal" mayor overcomes limited formal powers by skill in persuasion, negotiation, and public relations. Each "success" in resolving a particular problem "pyramids" the mayor's prestige and influence, and he or she eventually accumulates considerable informal power. The mayor can then direct energy and power toward accomplishing one or more of the numerous goals set for mayors: reducing racial tensions, providing effective law enforcement, speeding redevelopment and renewal of downtown areas and the relocation of persons living there, improving public schools, constructing low-cost housing, cleaning up the urban environment, finding ways to move people and things about the city speedily and efficiently, and, most of all, finding ways to finance these goals.

But this "ideal" city leadership requires that the mayor possess certain minimum resources.[34]

- Sufficient financial and staff resources in the mayor's office and in city government generally
- City jurisdiction over social-program areas—education, housing, urban renewal, etc.
- Mayor's jurisdiction within city government over these areas
- A salary that enables the mayor to spend full time on the job
- Friendly newspapers or television stations supportive of the mayor and his or her goals

- Political groups, including a political party, that the mayor can mobilize to attend meetings, parades, distribute literature, etc., on his or her behalf

Successful mayors must rely chiefly upon their own personal qualities of leadership: their powers to persuade, to sell, to compromise, to bargain, and to "get things done."[35] Mayors are not usually expected to initiate proposals for new programs or to create public issues. Nor is their primary concern the administration of existing programs, although they must always seek to avoid scandal and gross mismanagement, which would give their administrations a bad public "image." They must rely upon other public agencies, planners, citizens' groups, and private enterprise to propose new programs, and they can usually rely upon their department heads and other key subordinates to supervise the day-to-day administration of city government. Mayors are primarily promoters of public policy: Their role is to promote, publicize, organize, and finance the projects that others suggest.

MINORITIES AND WOMEN IN LOCAL POLITICS

Local politics is the entry level in the American political system for minorities as well as women. Currently about half of the one-hundred largest cities in the United States have minority or women mayors. All but a few of these cities have had minority or women mayors in the recent past.

MINORITY MAYORS   Black mayors have served in many cities with majority white populations, including New York, Chicago, Los Angeles, and Philadelphia, as well as cities with majority black populations, including Detroit; Washington, DC; and New Orleans.

The success of blacks and Hispanics in city politics, especially in majority white and Anglo cities, suggests that race is becoming less important as a criterion in voter choice for municipal leadership. However, voting patterns in city elections in which black and white candidates face each other indicate a continuing residue of racial politics. Black voters continue to cast their votes solidly for black candidates in these elections; white voters continue to give majority support to white candidates. The swing vote in these black–white election confrontations usually rests with 30 to 40 percent of white voters who are prepared to support qualified black candidates.

Successful black candidates in majority white cities have generally emphasized racial harmony and conciliation. They have stressed broad themes of concern to all voters— regardless of race. They have built coalitions that cut across racial, ethnic, and economic lines; many have worked their way up through the ranks of local organizations. They have avoided identification as "protest" candidates.

MINORITIES ON COUNCILS   Until recently, blacks were generally underrepresented on city councils across the country. That is to say, blacks held a smaller proportion of seats on city councils than the black percentages of city populations. But the steady rise in the number of black city council members and county commissioners over the last thirty years has brought black representation to rough proportionality in most Ameri-

**FIGURE 11–1
Minority
Population and
Representation on
City Councils**

Source: Data derived from "The Impact of At-Large Elections on the Representation of Blacks and Hispanics" by Susan Welch in *Journal of Politics* volume 52:4, pp. 1063, 1070; by permission of the author and the University of Texas Press.

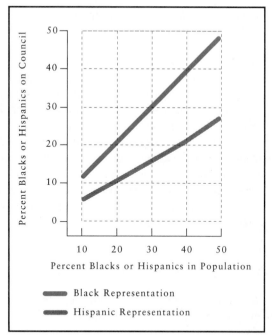

can cities. In cities in which blacks constitute 10 to 50 percent of the population, black representation on city councils generally reflects the black population percentage (see Figure 11–1). In cities in which the black population constitutes a majority (over 50 percent), black representation on city councils usually exceeds the black population percentage.[36]

In contrast, Hispanic representation on city councils is significantly below the Hispanic population percentages. Earlier we observed that Hispanic voter turnout was significantly lower than that for other social groups (see Chapter 4). Lower voter turnout among Hispanics is frequently attributed to cultural and language barriers and the resident alien status of many Hispanics. These factors, together with some structural features of reform government, including at-large elections, continue to create barriers to political mobilization of Hispanics.[37]

POLICY CONSEQUENCES   What are the policy consequences of increasing black representation on city councils? Perhaps the most obvious consequence is increased black *employment* in city jobs. Black employment at all levels of city administration—professional and managerial, police and fire, office and clerical, service and maintenance—tends to increase with increases in the black population of the city, as we might expect.[38] But the single most important determinant of black employment in administrative and professional positions is the proportion of blacks elected to city councils.[39] The employment of blacks in service and maintenance jobs does not require political representation. However, to get important city jobs, blacks must first win political power.[40]

Urban police departments have long been a focus of concern for minorities. Police policies have come under scrutiny for contributing to racial tensions, triggering riots, blocking minority aspirations, and shaping minority perceptions of justice. Many black mayors have campaigned on explicit pledges to reform police departments and adopt policies designed to make police responsive and sensitive to the concerns of minorities. The adoption of minority-oriented police policies, including increases in the number of minority police officers, has occurred with increases in black population percentages in cities, regardless of whether cities elect black mayors and council members. However, there is some evidence that the election of black mayors results in (1) accelerated recruitment of black police officers and (2) the adoption of citizen review boards to oversee police actions.[41]

Yet to date there is *no* evidence that cities with greater black representation on city councils, or even cities with black mayors, pursue significantly different taxing, spending, or service policies than do cities with little or no black representation. This is really not surprising; black city leaders face the same problems as white city leaders in raising revenue, fighting crime, improving housing, reducing congestion, removing garbage, and so on. It is possible, of course, that black neighborhoods receive better *delivery* of urban services under black leadership. However, the overall problems of cities may remain unaffected by substituting black leadership for white leadership.

The presence of blacks on city councils is important for city politics even if there is little impact on taxing and spending policies. Blacks in city government improve the image of that government among black residents; it helps to link minorities to city hall, to provide role models, and to sensitize white officials to minority concerns. "When minorities talk to the city council now, council members nod their heads rather than yawn."[42]

WOMEN IN LOCAL POLITICS   Women's participation in local politics has risen dramatically in recent years. Today, of the approximately 21,000 municipal council members serving in cities with populations over 10,000, over 4,500 or over 21 percent are women.[43] As late as 1975 this figure was estimated to be only about 4 percent. Women occupy about 16 percent of mayors' offices across the country.

The increase in women's political participation has taken place at all levels of government, with more women serving in Congress[44] and in state legislatures (see Chapter 6). The movement of women into politics generally is attributed to the movement of women into the work force and the changing cultural values redefining women's role in American society. At the local level, women may find fewer obstacles to political officeholding than at the state or national level. Local offices do not require women to move away from their home communities to the state capital or to Washington. Women candidates, unlike men, are seldom relieved of all of their home responsibilities when running for or occupying political office.[45] Moreover, campaigns for local office do not require as much money as state or congressional campaigns. Fund-raising has been a traditional obstacle to women candidates, although that barrier is diminishing relative to men over time. There is also a long tradition of women in volunteer community organizations, from hospitals and welfare agencies to cultural centers and neighborhood associations. Upon reexamining their traditional community roles, many women decided to use the knowledge and experience gained in volunteer work to move into elective politics:

> After devoting considerable time and energy to organizational life and civic activities, voluntary community service, or political party work, [a] woman sees it as only reasonable that she should be moving into elective or appointive positions of public responsibility.[46]

What are the policy consequences of increased women's representation on city councils? The best available evidence suggests that there are few significant policy differences between men and women council members, even on feminist issues.[47] For example, political scientist Susan Gluck Mezey found that both men and women on Connecticut councils supported abortions, day-care centers, and rape crisis centers. Typical liberal and conservative identifications were better predictors of how council members stood on issues than gender itself.[48]

INTEREST GROUPS IN COMMUNITY POLITICS

Interest group activity may be more influential in community politics than in state or national political affairs. Since the arena of local politics is smaller, the activities of organized interest groups may be more obvious at the local level.

THE CIVIC ASSOCIATIONS   At the local level, interest groups frequently assume the form of *civic associations*. Few communities are too small to have at least one or two associations devoted to civic well-being, and larger cities may have hundreds of these organizations. Council members usually name civic associations (service clubs, citizens' commissions, improvement associations) as the most influential groups or organizations that are active and appear before the council. This does not necessarily mean that economic interests or taxpayer associations are less active than civic associations, but probably that civic associations are the predominant style of organized interest group activity at the local level. Business people, reform groups, taxpayer associations, merchants, service clubs, developers, and so on organize themselves into civic associations for action at the local level. Civic associations generally make their appeals in terms of "the welfare of the community," "the public interest," "civic responsibility," "making Janesville a better place to live." In other words, civic associations claim to be community-serving rather than self-serving. Members belong to these groups as a hobby, because of the sense of prestige and civic participation they derive from membership. Occasionally, of course, participation in civic associations can be a stepping-stone to local office.

TAXPAYER GROUPS   Organized *taxpayer groups* generally stand for lower taxes and fewer governmental activities and services. Their most enthusiastic support comes from the community's larger taxpayers, generally business people with large investments in commercial or industrial property in the community.

ENVIRONMENTAL AND "GROWTH-MANAGEMENT" GROUPS   Environmental groups and opponents of residential and commercial development have become major

■
Civic association.
In local politics, an organization of citizens that works to further its own view of the best interest of the community.

forces in community politics throughout the nation. These groups are generally opposed to community growth, although they employ the term "growth management" to imply that they do not necessarily oppose all growth. But they are generally opposed to highway construction, street widening, tree cutting, increased traffic, noise and pollution, commercial or industrial development, or anything else that offends their aesthetic preferences. These groups generally reflect liberal reformist views of upper-middle-class residents who are secure in their own jobs and own their own homes. Indeed, restrictions on new housing construction directly benefit them by increasing the value of existing property. Municipal government offers many tools to restrict growth—planning regulations, zoning laws, building permits, environmental regulations, developmental charges and restrictions, street and utility access, and so on. (For further discussion, see Chapter 13.) Often, environmental "growth-management" groups combine with neighborhood associations to oppose specific developmental projects.

NEIGHBORHOOD GROUPS   *Neighborhood associations* frequently spring up when residents perceive a threat to their property values. They may be formed to oppose a rezoning that would allow new business and unwanted traffic in their neighborhood, or to oppose a new mobile home park, or to petition for stoplights or sidewalks or pothole repairs. Sometimes neighborhood associations will fight to keep out "undesirables," whose presence they feel will reduce property values. Neighborhood groups may protest the location of low-income housing, halfway houses for parolees, or mental health facilities. Neighborhood associations may also lead the fight *against* development, where residents will be displaced or their lifestyle threatened. They may oppose road building, urban renewal, or industrial and commercial development in or near their neighborhood. The NIMBY (not in my backyard) forces may be closely identified with "growth-management" efforts to slow or halt development. This posture places them in opposition to the local growth-oriented "power structure." (See Chapter 13.)

BUSINESS GROUPS   Traditionally, *business interests* were the most influential of all groups in community politics. Many business people or "economic notables" occupied an important role in the structure of community decision making or "the power structure." (See Chapter 13.) Business interests are also represented in local politics by organized groups: The chamber of commerce and the junior chamber of commerce, or "Jaycees," are found in nearly every community, representing the general views of business. The program of the chamber of commerce is likely to be more general than the interests of particular sectors of the business community—banks, utilities, contractors, real estate developers, downtown merchants, or bar and club owners. The chamber or the Jaycees can be expected to support lower taxes and more economy and efficiency in government operations. They are also active "promoters" of community growth and business activity. They can be expected to back civic improvements so long as it does not raise the tax rate too much. "Service to the community" creates a "favorable image," which the chamber and business people are anxious to cultivate.

Generally, the active members of the chamber of commerce or the Jaycees are younger business owners in the community who are still on their way "up" in business.

Growth-management.
In local government, efforts to limit or restrict population growth and commercial and industrial development.

Neighborhood association.
In local politics, an organization of the residents of a specific neighborhood that works to protect property values.

Owners of larger businesses, banks, utilities—the "big powers" in the community—are more likely to function informally in the community's power structure than to take an overt role in organized interest group activity.

The so-called service clubs—the Lions, Kiwanis, Rotarians, and others—are basically for business people. Their interests are likely to be more social than political, but their service projects often involve them in political activity and their meetings provide an excellent opportunity for speechmaking by political candidates.

The businesses most active in community affairs are those most directly affected by policies of local government, such as department stores, banks, utilities, contractors, real estate developers, bar and club owners, and television and newspaper interests.

BANKS   Banks often own, or hold the mortgages on, downtown business property. They have an interest in maintaining business, commercial, and industrial property values. Banks are also interested in the growth and prosperity of the city as a whole, particularly large business enterprises who are their primary customers. Banks are influential because they decide who is able to borrow money in a community and under what conditions. Banks are directly involved in local governments in financing municipal bond issues for public works, school buildings, and so on, and in pledging financial backing for urban renewal projects. Banks are also influential in land development, for they must provide the financial backing for real estate developers, contractors, businesses, and home buyers; hence they are interested in business regulation, taxation, zoning, and housing.

CONTRACTORS   Contractors are vitally interested in city government because the city has the power of inspection over all kinds of construction. Local governments enforce building, plumbing, electric, and other codes, which are of great interest to contractors. Some contractors, particularly road-grading and surfacing companies, depend on public contracts, and they are concerned with both city policy and the personnel who administer this policy. While municipal contracts are generally required by law to be given to the "low bidder" among "responsible" contractors, definitions about what is or is not a "low bid," and who is or who is not a "responsible" contractor, make it important for contractors to maintain close and friendly relationships with municipal officials. It is no accident that builders, contractors, and developers are a major source of campaign contributions for local office seekers.

REAL ESTATE DEVELOPERS   Real estate developers are particularly interested in planning, zoning, and subdivision control regulations and urban renewal programs. (These are discussed at length in Chapter 13.) Developers of residential, commercial, and industrial property must work closely with city government officials to coordinate the provision of public services—especially streets, sewage, water, and electricity. They must also satisfy city officials regarding planning and zoning regulations, building codes, fire and safety laws, and environmental regulations. Today, real estate developers must be highly skilled in governmental relations.

NEWSPAPERS   Newspapers are an important force in community politics. The influence of the press would be relatively minor if its opinions were limited to its editorial pages. The influence of the press arises from its power to decide what is "news," thereby focusing public attention on the events and issues that are of interest to the press. Newspaper writers must first decide what proportion of space in the paper will be devoted to local news in contrast to state, national, and international news. A big-city paper may give local news about the same amount of space that it gives to national or foreign news. Suburban or small-town papers, which operate within the circulation area of a large metropolitan daily, may give a greater proportion of the news space to local events than to national and international affairs. Crime and corruption in government are favorite targets for the press. Editors believe that civic crusades and the exposure of crime and corruption help sell newspapers. Moreover, many editors and writers believe they have a civic responsibility to use the power of the press to protect the public. In the absence of crime or corruption, newspapers may turn to crusades on behalf of civic improvements—like a city auditorium or cultural center.

The politics of newspapers can be understood in part by some insight into the economics of the newspaper business. Newspapers get two-thirds of their revenue from advertising. Over the years the newspapers' percentage of all advertising dollars has declined in the face of stiff competition from television. Many big-city newspapers have either merged or gone out of business because of a lack of sufficient advertising revenue to offset increasing costs; it was not a lack of readers that brought about their collapse. Moreover, it is important to know that downtown department stores provide the largest source of advertising revenue. Big-city newspapers have been hurt by the flight of the middle class to the suburbs and the declining role of downtown department stores in retail sales in the metropolitan areas. In metropolitan affairs, one can expect big-city newspapers to support the position of downtown interests. This means support for urban renewal, mass transit, downtown parking, and other pro–central-city policies in metropolitan affairs. On the other hand, suburban daily and weekly newspapers are supported by the advertising from suburban shopping centers, and they can be expected to take a pro-suburban position on metropolitan issues.

Newspapers are more influential in the absence of strong party organizations, which would compete with newspapers as channels of communication to the voters. Non-partisanship, lengthy ballots, and numerous referenda all contribute to the influence of newspapers. Any situation that tends to obscure candidates or issues to the voter contributes to the power of newspapers, since the voter is obliged to rely upon them for information. Newspapers doubtlessly have more influence in local than in state or national politics because of (1) the relative importance in local politics of middle-class groups who read newspapers, (2) the relative obscurity of local politics to voters in their reliance upon newspapers for information about local affairs, and (3) the relative weakening of party affiliations in local politics.

CHURCHES Any listing of influential interest groups in local politics should include the community's churches and church-related organizations. Ministers, priests, rabbis, and leaders of religious lay groups are frequently participants in community decision making. The Catholic Church and its many lay organizations are vitally concerned with the operation of parochial schools. Protestant ministerial associations in large cities may be concerned with public health, welfare, housing, and other social problems. Ministers and church congregations in small towns may be concerned with the enforcement of blue laws, limitations on liquor sales, prohibitions on gambling, and other public policies relative to "vice" and public morality.

MUNICIPAL EMPLOYEES   No one has a greater personal stake in municipal government than municipal employees—police, firefighters, street crews, transit employees, welfare workers, sanitation workers, clerks, secretaries. There are over 15 million state and local government employees in the nation (4.5 million state employees, and 10.7 million employees of cities, counties, school districts, and special districts). Their rate of voter turnout in municipal elections is very high, and they are politically influential in small towns and suburbs whether they are organized into unions or not.

DID YOU KNOW?

SALARIES OF PUBLIC OFFICIALS

	Mayors Median $8,400[b]	Managers Median $67,598
Cities over 1 million	133,004	120,000[c]
500,000–1 million	100,698	155,555
250,000–500,000	77,770	121,240
100,000–250,000	27,356	121,569
50,000–100,000	13,200	102,417
Under 50,000	8,699	88,543

Governors		Legislators[a]	
Median	$95,000	Median	$20,000
Highest		Highest	
New York	130,000	California	75,600
Illinois	126,590	New York	57,500
Michigan	124,195	Michigan	51,895
Washington	121,000	Illinois	47,039
Maryland	120,000	Massachusetts	46,410
Lowest			
Nebraska	65,000	New Hampshire	200
Arkansas	65,182		
Rhode Island	69,900		
Maine	70,000		
Colorado	70,000		

Highest-paid mayors		Un-paid mayors[d]
Chicago	175,000	Sacramento
Houston	133,552	Montgomery
New York	130,000	Columbus
San Francisco	129,356	Providence
Detroit	117,000	

[a]Annual salaries; does not include per diem, expenses, or other compensation
[b]Includes part-time mayors
[c]Mayor's chief administrative assistant
[d]Cities over 150,000 population

Sources: Council of State Governments, *Book of the States, 1998–99;* International City Managers' Association, *Municipal Yearbook, 1998.*

ON THE WEB

Most of the nation's city managers are members of the International City Managers' Association (ICMA). Each year the ICMA publishes the *Municipal Yearbook,* the most comprehensive collection of information on American cities. Unfortunately, the *Municipal Yearbook* is *not* on the ICMA Web Site, but the site does provide directions to sources of information important to city managers. These include a series of books on how to manage various aspects of city government, from planning, personnel, and budgeting to waste disposal, environmental protection, and mass transit. The ICMA Web site at

www.icma.org

does offer information on local government management issues.

The U.S. Conference of Mayors exercises considerable influence in Washington. Its annual meeting regularly attracts hundreds of mayors as well as presidential candidates and other national figures seeking to use this popular platform to express their views. The U.S. Conference of Mayors represents mayors of cities of 30,000 or more people. Its announced purpose is to "aid in the development of effective national urban policy." It lobbies heavily in Washington on behalf of federal grant-in-aid programs to cities. Its Web site at

> www.usmayors.org

includes the official policy positions of the organization on a wide variety of urban issues.

The National Civic League was formed more than a century ago to advance the municipal reform movement. Theodore Roosevelt was one of its founders. Today it continues to encourage city government reform. It is probably best known for its All American City Awards, which it presents annually to cities that it considers innovative and progressive, as well as "honest, efficient, and effective." Its Web site at

> www.ncl.org

includes stories of how particular cities dealt effectively with problems ranging from race relations to economic development and quality of life.

NOTES

1. Arguments over value of direct citizen participation are as old as democracy itself. See "Direct versus Representative Democracy" in Chapter 2. And see Samuel P. Huntington, *American Politics: The Promise of Disharmony* (Cambridge: Harvard University Press, 1981); and Jeffrey M. Berry, Kent E. Portney, and Ken Thompson, *The Rebirth of Urban Democracy* (Washington, DC: Brookings Institution, 1993).

2. Early arguments over public-regardingness are found in James Q. Wilson and Edward C. Banfield, "Public Regardingness as a Value Premise in Voting Behavior," *American Political Science Review,* 58 (December 1964), 876–87; and Roger Durand, "Ethnicity, Public-Regardingness and Referenda Voting," *Midwest Journal of Political Science,* 16 (May 1972), 259–68. More recent evidence that wealth and income lead citizens to be more supportive of public services is found in Evel Elliot, James Regens, and Barry Sheldon, "Exploring Variation in Public Support for Environmental Protection," *Social Science Quarterly,* 76 (March 1995), 41–52.

3. Herbert C. Alexander, *Reform and Reality: The Financing of State and Local Campaigns* (New York: Twentieth Century Fund Press, 1991).

4. Arnold Fleischmann and Lana Stein, "Campaign Contributions in Local Elections," *Political Research Quarterly,* vol. 51 (September 1998), 673–90.

5. See Raphael Sonenshein, "Bi-Racial Coalition Politics in Los Angeles," *P.S.,* 19 (September 1986), 582–90; "The Dynamics of Bi-Racial Coalitions," *Western Political Quarterly,* 42 (June 1989), 333–53; and Rufus Browning, Dale Rogers Marshall, and David Tabb, *Protest Is Not Enough* (Berkeley: University of California Press, 1984).

6. William L. Riordan, *Plunkitt of Tammany Hall* (New York: McClure, Phillips, 1905), p. 46.

7. Ibid., p. 52.

8. Edward C. Banfield and James Q. Wilson, *City Politics* (Cambridge, MA: Harvard-M.I.T. Press, 1963), chap. 9.

9. See Elmer E. Cornwell, Jr., "Bosses, Machines, and Ethnic Groups," *Annals of the American Academy of Political and Social Science* (May 1964), 27–39.

10. Lincoln Steffens, *Autobiography* (New York: Harcourt, Brace & World, 1931), p. 168.

11. See Richard J. Hofstadter, *The Age of Reform* (New York: Knopf, 1955); and Lorin Peterson, *The Day of the Mugwump* (New York: Random House, 1961).

12. Lincoln Steffens, *The Shame of the Cities* (New York: Sagamore Press, 1957), p. 10.

13. National Municipal League, *Model City Charter* (Chicago: National Municipal League, 1961).

14. Robert L. Lineberry and Edmund P. Fowler, "Reformism and Public Policy in American Cities," *American Political Science Review,* 61 (September 1967), 701–16. See also David R. Morgan and John P. Pelissero, "Urban Policy: Does Political

Structure Matter?" *American Political Science Review,* 74 (December 1980), 999–1005.

15. See also Susan Blackall Hansen, "Participation, Political Structure and Concurrence," *American Political Science Review,* 69 (December 1975), 1181–99.

16. Albert K. Karnig, "Private Regarding Policy, Civil Rights Groups, and the Mediating Impact of Municipal Returns," *American Journal of Political Science,* 19 (February 1975), 91–106.

17. See Alan D. Gaetano, "The Rise of the New Urban Political Machine." Paper presented at the Midwest Political Science Association Meeting, 1986.

18. John F. Persimos, "Ward Politics 21st-Century Style," *Governing* (October 1989), 46–50.

19. See also Raymond E. Wolfinger, "Why Political Machines Have Not Withered Away and Other Revisionists Thoughts," *Journal of Politics,* 34 (May 1972), 365–98.

20. Alan Ehrenhatt, *The United States of Ambition: Politicians, Power and the Pursuit of Office* (New York: Random House, 1991), p. 22.

21. Ibid., p. 14.

22. Timothy B. Krebs, "The Determinants of Candidate's Vote Share and the Advantage of Incumbency in City Council Elections," *American Journal of Political Science,* vol. 42 (July 1998), 921–35.

23. See Joel Lieske, "The Political Dynamics of Urban Voting Behavior," *American Journal of Political Science,* 33 (February 1989), 150–74.

24. Kenneth Prewitt, *The Recruitment of Political Leaders: A Study of Citizen-Politicians* (Indianapolis: Bobbs-Merrill, 1970), p. 148.

25. Of course, council members themselves are not likely to agree that their role is a passive one. They like to think of themselves as policy innovators—people of vision and leadership—who follow their own convictions in public affairs regardless of what others want them to do.

26. See Kenneth Prewitt, "Political Ambitions, Volunteerism, and Electoral Accountability," *American Political Science Review,* 64 (March 1970), 5–17.

27. Elaine B. Sharp, "Citizen-Initiated Contacting of Government Officials and Socio-Economic Status," *American Political Science Review,* 76 (March 1982), 109–15.

28. John J. Kirlin, "Electoral Conflict and Democracy in American Cities," *Journal of Politics,* 37 (February 1975), 262–69.

29. See David R. Morgan, "Political Linkage and Public Policy: Attitudinal Congruence Between Citizens and Officials," *Western Political Quarterly* (June 1973), 209–23.

30. Leonard D. White, *The City Manager* (Chicago: University of Chicago Press, 1927).

31. See Harold A. Stone, Don K. Price, and Kathryn H. Stone, *City Manager Government in the United States* (Chicago: Public Administration Service, 1940).

32. See Timothy A. Almy, "Local-Cosmopolitanism and U.S. City Managers," *Urban Affairs Quarterly,* 10 (March 1975), 243–77.

33. Alan L. Saltzstein, "City Managers and City Councils: Perceptions of the Division of Authority," *Western Political Quarterly,* 27 (June 1974), 275–87.

34. Jeffrey L. Pressman, "Preconditions of Mayoral Leadership," *American Political Science Review,* 66 (June 1972), 511–24.

35. See Melvin G. Holli, "American Mayors: The Best and the Worst Since 1960," *Social Science Quarterly,* vol. 78 (March 1997), 149–57. The five best: Richard J. Daley (Chicago, 1955–76); Henry Cisneros (San Antonio, 1981–89); Tom Bradley (Los Angeles, 1973–93); Dianne Feinstein (San Francisco, 1978–87); Andrew Young (Atlanta, 1982–90).

36. Susan Welch, "The Impact of At-Large Elections on the Representation of Blacks and Hispanics," *Journal of Politics,* 52 (November 1990), 1050–76.

37. See Rufus P. Browning, Dale Rodgers Marshall, and David H. Tabb, *Protest Is Not Enough* (Berkeley: University of California Press, 1984); Rodney E. Hero, "Hispanics in Urban Government," *Western Political Quarterly,* 43 (June 1990), 403–14; Jerry L. Polinard, Robert D. Wrinkle, and Thomas Longovia, "The Impact of District Elections on the Mexican American Community," *Social Science Quarterly,* 72 (September 1991), 609–14.

38. Peter K. Eisinger, "Black Employment in Municipal Jobs," *American Political Science Review,* 76 (June 1982), 380–92.

39. Thomas R. Dye and James Renick, "Political Power and City Jobs," *Social Science Quarterly,* 62 (September 1981), 475–86. See also Matthews

Hutchins and Lee Sigelman, "Black Employment in State and Local Government," *Social Science Quarterly,* 62 (March 1981), 79–87.

40. For an argument that black and Hispanic mayors do not increase minority city employment, but that black and Hispanic *council* members do so, see Brinck Kerr and Kenneth Mladenka, "Does Politics Matter?" *American Journal of Political Science,* 38 (November 1994), 918–43.

41. Grace Hall Saltzstein, "Black Mayors and Police Policies," *Journal of Politics,* 51 (August 1989), 525–44.

42. Browning, Marshall, and Tabb, *Protest Is Not Enough,* p. 41.

43. Center for the American Woman in Politics, Eagleton Institute of Politics, Rutgers University, 1998.

44. See Thomas R. Dye, *Politics in America,* 3rd ed. (Upper Saddle River, NJ: Prentice Hall, 1999), Chap. 10.

45. Ruth B. Mandel, *In the Running: The New Woman Candidate* (New Haven, CT: Ticknor and Fields, 1981), pp. 63–97.

46. Ibid., p. 13.

47. Susan Gluck Mezey, "Support for Women's Rights Policy," *American Politics Quarterly,* 6 (October 1978), 485–96. See also Albert K. Karnig and B. Oliver Walter, "Election of Women to City Councils," *Social Science Quarterly,* 56 (March 1976), 605–13.

48. However, assertions of "gender cleavage" in municipal politics, based on observations of a single city where men supported economic development projects and women opposed them, can be found in Paul Schumaker and Nancy Elizabeth Burns, "Gender Cleavages and the Resolution of Local Policy Issues," *American Journal of Political Science,* 32 (November 1988), 1070–95.

12

METROPOLITICS: CONFLICT IN THE METROPOLIS

QUESTIONS TO CONSIDER

Do you believe that suburban growth should be managed by government to prevent "sprawl"?

❏ Yes   ❏ No

Would a single metropolitanwide government provide better and cheaper public services than the multiple governments currently functioning in most metropolitan areas?

❏ Yes   ❏ No

Do multiple governmental units in large metropolitan areas provide people with better residential choices in terms of taxes and services?

❏ Yes   ❏ No

Are special district governments the best way to provide such services as water supply and sewerage, fire protection, and mass transit, on a metropolitanwide basis?

❏ Yes   ❏ No

THE METROPOLIS: SETTING FOR CONFLICT

Nearly four out of every five Americans live in population clusters called metropolitan areas. What is a metropolitan area? The U.S. Census Bureau calls a metropolitan area a "Metropolitan Statistical Area" (MSA) and defines it as a city of 50,000 or more people together with adjacent counties that have predominantly urban populations with close ties to the central city. (See Figure 12–1.)

Some metropolitan areas adjoin each other, creating a continuous urban environment over an extended area. One such "megalopolis" is the New York–Northern New Jersey–Long Island area, encompassing parts of three states, nine MSAs, and nearly 20 million people. The U.S. Census Bureau calls such an area a "Consolidated Metropolitan Statistical Area" (CMSA) and defines it as two or more adjoining MSAs with at least 1 million people in which a large number of workers commute between the MSAs. Half of the nation's population lives in the forty-five metropolitan areas with 1 million or more people. (See Table 12–1, p. 364.) While hundreds of local governments partition these metropolitan areas, people travel over these municipal boundaries often several times a day. Media markets—television, radio, newspapers—extend throughout these metropolitan areas. Most businesses depend on metropolitanwide markets for workers, suppliers, and customers. Cultural, restaurant, and entertainment centers serve people from throughout the metropolis.

The states have become "metropolitanized." Today thirty-five states have more than half of their populations concentrated in metropolitan areas. (See "Rankings of the States: Metropolitanization in the States.")

The very definition of metropolitan life involves *large numbers* of *different* types of people living *close together* who are socially and economically *dependent* upon one another.[1] *Numbers, density, heterogeneity,* and *interdependence* are said to be distinguishing characteristics of metropolitan life. It is not difficult to envision a metropolitan area as a large number of people living together; we can see these characteristics in metropolitan life from a map or an airplane window. However, it is more difficult to understand the heterogeneity and interdependence of people living in metropolitan areas.

HETEROGENEITY   The modern economic system of the metropolis is based upon a highly specialized and complex division of labor. Highly specialized jobs account for much of the heterogeneity in urban populations. Different jobs produce different levels of income, dress, and styles of living. People's jobs shape the way they look at the world and their evaluations of social and political events. In acquiring their jobs, people attain a certain level and type of education that also distinguish them from those in other jobs with different educational requirements. Metropolitan living concentrates people with all these different economic, educational, and occupational characteristics in a very few square miles.

ETHNIC AND RACIAL DIVERSITY   Ethnic and racial diversity are also present. In the nineteenth and early twentieth centuries, opportunities for human betterment in the cities attracted immigrants from Ireland, Germany, Italy, Poland, and Russia.

Metropolitan area. A city of 50,000 or more people together with adjacent counties with predominantly urban populations and with close ties to the central city.

Heterogeneity. In metropolitan areas, differences among people in occupation, education, income, race, and ethnicity.

FIGURE 12–1

Standard Metropolitan Statistical Areas

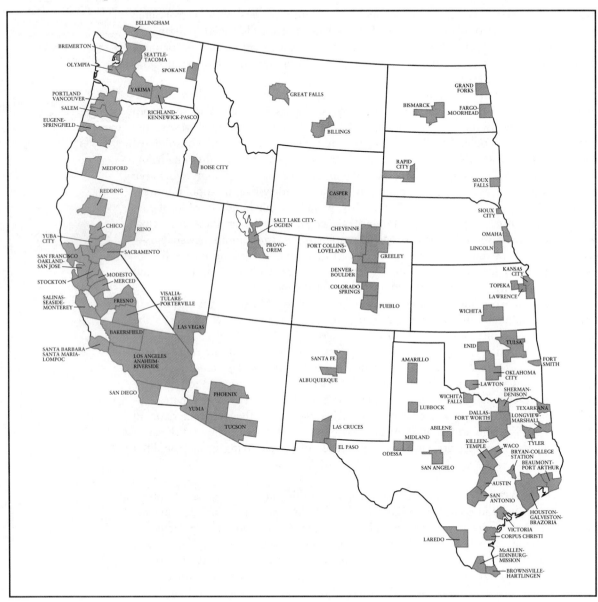

Source: U.S. Bureau of the Census.

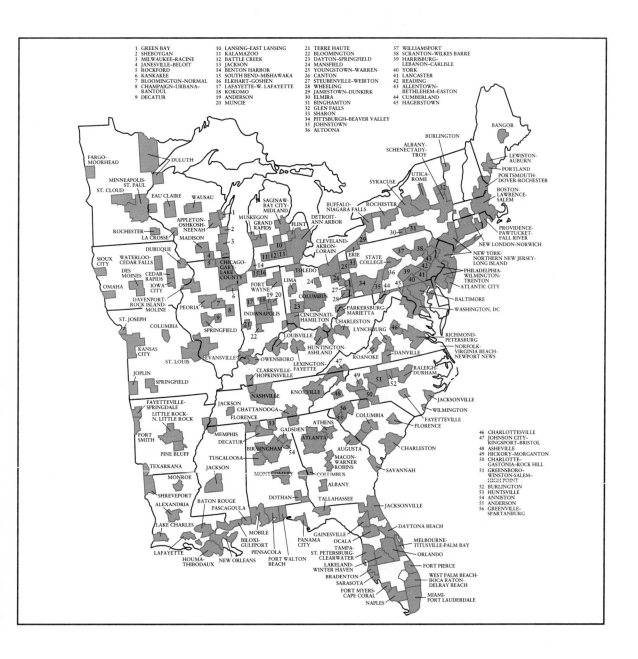

1 GREEN BAY
2 SHEBOYGAN
3 MILWAUKEE–RACINE
4 JANESVILLE–BELOIT
5 ROCKFORD
6 KANKAKEE
7 BLOOMINGTON–NORMAL
8 CHAMPAIGN–URBANA–
  RANTOUL
9 DECATUR

10 LANSING–EAST LANSING
11 KALAMAZOO
12 BATTLE CREEK
13 JACKSON
14 BENTON HARBOR
15 SOUTH BEND–MISHAWAKA
16 ELKHART–GOSHEN
17 LAFAYETTE–W. LAFAYETTE
18 KOKOMO
19 ANDERSON
20 MUNCIE

21 TERRE HAUTE
22 BLOOMINGTON
23 DAYTON–SPRINGFIELD
24 MANSFIELD
25 YOUNGSTOWN–WARREN
26 CANTON
27 STEUBENVILLE–WEIRTON
28 WHEELING
29 JAMESTOWN–DUNKIRK
30 ELMIRA
31 BINGHAMTON
32 GLEN FALLS
33 SHARON
34 PITTSBURGH–BEAVER VALLEY
35 JOHNSTOWN
36 ALTOONA

37 WILLIAMSPORT
38 SCRANTON–WILKES BARRE
39 HARRISBURG–
   LEBANON–CARLISLE
40 YORK
41 LANCASTER
42 READING
43 ALLENTOWN–
   BETHLEHEM–EASTON
44 CUMBERLAND
45 HAGERSTOWN

46 CHARLOTTESVILLE
47 JOHNSON CITY–
   KINGSPORT–BRISTOL
48 ASHEVILLE
49 HICKORY–MORGANTON
50 CHARLOTTE–
   GASTONIA–ROCK HILL
51 GREENSBORO–
   WINSTON-SALEM–
   HIGH POINT
52 BURLINGTON
53 HUNTSVILLE
54 ANNISTON
55 ANDERSON
56 GREENVILLE–
   SPARTANBURG

Table 12–1

METRO-AMERICA: METROPOLITAN AREAS WITH ONE MILLION OR MORE RESIDENTS					
New York	19.8	St. Louis	2.5	San Antonio	1.4
Los Angeles	15.3	Phoenix	2.5	New Orleans	1.3
Chicago	8.5	San Diego	2.5	Buffalo (NY)	1.2
Washington/Baltimore	6.9	Pittsburgh	2.4	Charlotte (NC)	1.2
San Francisco	6.5	Tampa	2.2	Hartford (CT)	1.2
Philadelphia	5.9	Denver	2.2	Salt Lake City	1.2
Boston	5.5	Cincinnati	1.9	Brownsville (TX)	1.2
Detroit	5.3	Portland (OR)	1.9	Providence (RI)	1.1
Dallas/Ft. Worth	4.4	Milwaukee	1.6	Greensboro (NC)	1.1
Houston	4.1	Kansas City	1.6	Rochester	1.1
Miami/Ft. Lauderdale	3.4	Sacramento	1.6	Las Vegas	1.1
Atlanta	3.3	Norfolk (VA)	1.5	Greensboro	1.0
Seattle/Tacoma	3.2	Indianapolis	1.5	Memphis	1.0
Cleveland	2.9	Columbus (OH)	1.4	Nashville	1.0
Minneapolis	2.7	Orlando	1.4	Oklahoma City	1.0

Source: U.S. Bureau of the Census, 1998.

African Americans in search of opportunities migrated to cities from the rural South. Today America's cities attract waves of immigrants from Mexico and other Latin American countries, Asia and the Philippines, and Haiti and other less developed nations of the world. Newcomers to the metropolis bring with them different needs, attitudes, and ways of life. The "melting pot" tends to reduce some of this diversity over time, but the pot does not "melt" people immediately, and there always seem to be new arrivals.

INTERDEPENDENCE   Yet despite social and economic differences, urban dwellers are highly dependent upon one another in their daily activities. Suburbanites, for example, rely upon the central city for newspapers, entertainment, hospitalization, and a host of other modern needs. Many also rely upon the central city for employment opportunities. Conversely, the central city relies upon the suburbs to supply both employees and customers. This interdependence involves an intricate web of economic and social relationships, a high degree of communication, and a great deal of daily physical interchange among residents, groups, and firms in a metropolitan area.

■

Fragmented government. Multiple governmental jurisdictions, including cities, townships, school districts, and special districts, all operating in a single metropolitan area.

FRAGMENTED GOVERNMENT   However, another characteristic of metropolitan areas is "fragmented" government. Suburban development, spreading out from central cities, generally ignored governmental boundaries and engulfed counties, townships, towns, and smaller cities. Some metropolitan areas even spread across state lines, and four metropolitan areas of the United States—Detroit, San Diego, El Paso, and Laredo—adjoin urban territory in Canada and Mexico. This suburbanization has meant that hundreds of governments may be operating in a single metropolitan area.

Thus, while metropolitan areas are characterized by social and economic interdependence, and consequently require coordinating mechanisms, metropolitan government is generally "fragmented" into many smaller jurisdictions, none of which is capable of governing the entire metropolitan area in a unified fashion.

POTENTIAL FOR CONFLICT   The metropolis presents a serious problem in *conflict* management. Because a metropolitan area consists of a large number of different kinds of people living closely together, the problem of regulating conflict and maintaining order assumes tremendous proportions. Persons with different occupations, incomes, and ethnic ties are known to have different views on public issues. People well equipped to compete for jobs and income in a free market view government housing and welfare programs differently than others not so well equipped. People at the bottom of the social ladder look at police—indeed, governmental authority in general—differently from the way those on higher rungs do. Homeowners and renters usually look at property taxation in a different light. Families with children and those without children have different ideas about school systems. And so it goes. Differences in the way people make their living, in their income levels, in the color of their skin, in the way they worship, in their style of living—all are at the roots of political life in the metropolis.

CITIES VERSUS SUBURBS

Suburbs account for most of the growth of America's metropolitan areas. Very few large *central cities* are growing in size; on the contrary, many are losing population. Metropolitan areas are growing because their *suburbs* are growing. New suburbs, most built since the 1970s on the outer fringes of metropolitan areas, are capturing increasing shares of both population and employment growth. Many central cities, especially in the Northeast and Midwest, as well as older inner-ring suburbs, are losing people and jobs (see Table 12–2).

SUBURBANIZATION   America's suburbanization was a product of technological advances in transportation—the automobile and the expressway.[2] In the nineteenth century an industrial worker had to live within walking distance of his or her place of employment. This meant that the nineteenth-century American city crowded large masses of people into relatively small central areas, often in tenement houses and other high-density neighborhoods. However, modern modes of transportation—first the streetcar, then the private automobile, and then the expressway—eliminated the necessity of workers living close to their jobs. The same technology that led to the suburbanization of residences also influenced commercial and industrial location. Originally industry was tied to waterways or railroads for access to suppliers and markets. This dependence was reduced by the development of motor truck transportation, the highway system, and the greater mobility of the labor force. Many industries located in the suburbs, particularly light industries, which did not require extremely heavy bulk shipments that could only be handled by rail or water. When industry and people moved

RANKINGS OF THE STATES

METROPOLITANIZATION IN THE STATES

Metropolitan Population Percentage

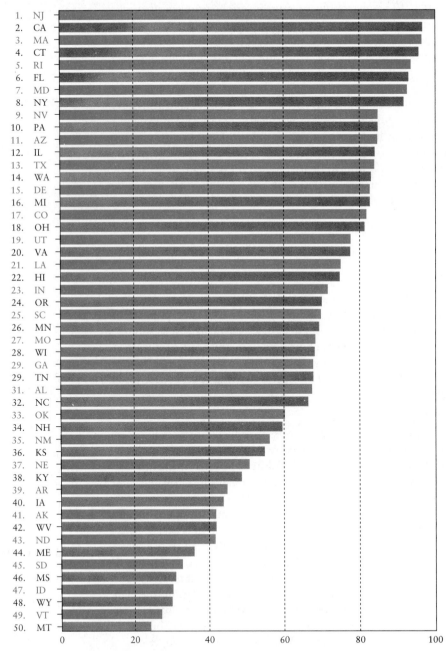

1.	NJ
2.	CA
3.	MA
4.	CT
5.	RI
6.	FL
7.	MD
8.	NY
9.	NV
10.	PA
11.	AZ
12.	IL
13.	TX
14.	WA
15.	DE
16.	MI
17.	CO
18.	OH
19.	UT
20.	VA
21.	LA
22.	HI
23.	IN
24.	OR
25.	SC
26.	MN
27.	MO
28.	WI
29.	GA
29.	TN
31.	AL
32.	NC
33.	OK
34.	NH
35.	NM
36.	KS
37.	NE
38.	KY
39.	AR
40.	IA
41.	AK
42.	WV
43.	ND
44.	ME
45.	SD
46.	MS
47.	ID
48.	WY
49.	VT
50.	MT

Source: U.S. Bureau of the Census.

Table 12–2

CITY DECLINE AND SUBURBAN GROWTH IN SELECTED METROPOLITAN AREAS		
	Central City Pop. Decline	*Suburban Pop. Growth*
Atlanta	-19%	396%
Baltimore	-25	87
Boston	-21	32
Chicago	-23	54
Cincinnati	-29	38
Cleveland	-44	29
Detroit	-41	30
Milwaukee	-17	41
Minneapolis	-27	110
New Orleans	-23	136
Philadelphia	-24	29
Pittsburgh	-41	3
St. Louis	-51	39
Washington, DC	-26	186

Note: Figures are percent change, 1960–95.

Source: U.S. Bureau of the Census.

to the suburbs, commerce followed. Giant suburban shopping centers sprang up to compete with downtown stores. Thus, metropolitan areas become decentralized over time as people, business, and industry spread themselves over the suburban landscape.

CITY–SUBURBAN DIFFERENCES   Social, economic, and racial conflict can be observed at all levels of government, but at the metropolitan level, it is most obvious in the conflict that occurs between central cities and their suburbs. At the heart of city–suburban conflict are the differences in the kinds of people who live in cities and suburbs. City–suburban conflict is at the heart of "the metropolitan problem"; that is, the failure to achieve metropolitanwide consensus on public policy questions affecting the entire metropolitan area and the failure to develop metropolitan government institutions. Social, economic, and racial differences between cities and suburbs are major obstacles to the development of metropolitanwide policies and government institutions.[3]

Of course, generalizing about cities and suburbs is a dangerous thing. Although we will talk about some common characteristics of cities and suburbs, students are cautioned that individual suburbs may be quite different from one another (just as there are wide differences between social and economic groups living in central cities). There are, for example, industrial suburbs, residential suburbs, black suburbs, wealthy suburbs, working-class suburbs, and so forth.[4] Nevertheless, a clear perception of the so-

■
"The metropolitan problem."
A reference to the frequent failure of governments to achieve metropolitanwide consensus or action on policy questions affecting the entire metropolitan area.

■

"Familism."
A reference to a child-centered lifestyle observed more frequently in suburbs than in central cities.

cial distance between cities and suburbs is important in understanding metropolitan politics.

SOCIAL CLASS   Cities and suburbs can be differentiated, first of all, on the basis of *social class*—the occupation, income, and educational levels of their population. The cultured class of an earlier era established "country" living as a symbol of affluence; widespread prosperity has made possible mass imitation of the aristocracy by an upwardly mobile middle-class population. The suburbs house greater proportions of white-collar employees, college graduates, and affluent families than any other sector in American life.

Status differentials in favor of suburbs are more pronounced in larger metropolitan areas; status differentials in smaller metropolitan areas are not as great as in larger areas, and sometimes even favor the city rather than the suburbs. However, on the whole, suburban living reflects middle-class values.

FAMILISM   Cities and suburbs can also be differentiated on the basis of "familism," or lifestyle. Perhaps the most frequently mentioned reason for a move to the suburbs is "the kids." Family after family list consideration of their young as the primary cause for their move to suburbia. A familistic, or child-centered, lifestyle can be identified in certain social statistics. A larger percentage of suburban families have children under eighteen than city families. In addition, the single-family, owner-occupied, free-standing home has become symbolic of familistic living in an affluent society. In central cities there are proportionately fewer children and more rental apartment living.

RACE   But perhaps the most important difference between cities and suburbs is their contrasting *racial composition*. The nonwhite percentage of all U.S. suburbs is about 7 percent, in contrast to a nonwhite percentage for all central cities of 22 percent. (See Table 12–3.)

POVERTY   Low-income, low-education, unskilled populations are concentrated in the central cities. Social problems are also concentrated in central cities—racial imbalance, crime, violence, inadequate education, poverty, slum housing, and so on. By moving to the suburbs, white middle-class families not only separate themselves from blacks and poor people but also place physical distance between themselves and the major social problems that confront metropolitan areas. This permits them, for the time being, to avoid the problems associated with poverty.

PARTIES   In general, large cities are much more Democratic than their suburban rings, which generally produce more Republican votes. While temporary shifts may occur from one election to another, this general pattern of Democratic cities and Republican suburbs is likely to prevail for the near future. As long as the national Democratic party represents central-city, low-income, ethnic, labor, and racial con-

Table 12–3

CHARACTERISTICS OF CITIES AND SUBURBS OF METROPOLITAN AREAS

	Metropolitan Areas			Outside Metropolitan Areas
	TOTAL	CITIES	SUBURBS	
Total population (000)	192,726	77,844	114,882	55,984
Percent of U.S. total	76.2	31.5	44.7	23.8
Growth: percent population increase 1980–1990	11.6	7.5	15.7	2.2
Age: percent under 18	25.3	24.7	25.7	26.6
Race: percent black	13.0	22.1	6.9	8.7
Home ownership: percent owning home	58.4	49.1	68.1	80.6
Percent families with children	33.2	30.0	35.6	34.8
Percent in Poverty	12.6	18.8	9.0	15.9

Source: U.S. Bureau of the Census.

stituencies, and the Republican party represents middle-class, educated, managerial, white, Anglo-Saxon Protestant constituencies, the political coloration of cities and suburbs is likely to be different.

COSTS OF GOVERNMENT   Large central cities show substantially higher operating expenditures per capita than their suburbs. The maintenance of a large physical plant for the entire metropolitan area requires city residents to make higher per capita operating expenditures than those required for suburbanites. In addition, many living costs in suburban communities are shifted from public to private spending (private septic tanks instead of public sewers, private instead of public recreation, and so on). Differences in the public services provided by city and suburban governments are greatest in the area of police protection, recreation, and health. This reflects a concentration in the city of people who are likely to require these public services, in contrast to the suburbs.

TAXES   The tax bill in suburbs is only slightly lower than in central cities. Taxes had much to do with the migration of the "pioneer" suburbanites, those who moved to the suburbs in the 1930s and 1940s. At that time, suburban living offered a significant savings in property taxation over what were thought to be heavy city taxes. However, the tax advantage of the suburbs turned out partly to be a "self-denying prophecy": The more people who fled to the suburbs to avoid heavy taxes, the greater the demand for public services in these new suburban communities, and the higher suburban taxes became to meet these new demands. Yet, the tax bill in most suburbs remains lower than in central cities. The difference in tax burden between city and suburb would be even greater if suburbanites did not choose to spend more per pupil in education than city residents, which produces higher school taxes in the suburbs. The suburbs also manage to limit their indebtedness more than cities, and most of the indebtedness incurred by the suburbs is for school rather than municipal purposes.

EXCEPTIONS   Finally, it should be noted that differences between cities and suburbs in smaller metropolitan areas do not appear to be as great as differences between cities and suburbs in larger metropolitan areas. In fact, all these generalizations about cities and suburbs are, indeed, generalizations. Individual cities and suburbs can be found that do not conform to these national patterns.

THE CONCENTRATION OF SOCIAL PROBLEMS IN THE INNER CITY

The nation's largest cities have become the principal location of virtually all of the social problems confronting our society—poverty, homelessness, racial tension, family instability, drug abuse, delinquency, and crime. (Some of these problems are discussed in other chapters—crime in Chapter 9, racial issues in Chapter 14, education in Chapter 15, and poverty and homelessness in Chapter 16.) But it is important to note here that these problems are all made worse by their concentration in the inner city. This concentration is a relatively recent occurrence; as late as 1970 there were higher rates of poverty in rural America than in the cities.

JOBLESSNESS   Why has the "inner city" become the locus of social problems? It has been argued that changes in the labor market from industrial goods-producing jobs to professional, financial, technical, and service jobs is increasingly polarizing the labor market into low-wage and high-wage sectors.[5] The decline in manufacturing jobs, together with a shift in remaining manufacturing jobs and commercial (sales) jobs to the suburbs, has left inner-city residents with fewer job opportunities. The rise in joblessness in the inner cities has in turn increased the concentration of poor people, added to the number of poor single-parent families, and increased welfare dependency.

MIDDLE-CLASS FLIGHT   At the same time, inner-city neighborhoods have experienced an out-migration of working-class and middle-class families. The number of inner-city neighborhoods in which the poverty rate exceeds 40 percent has risen sharply.[6] The loss of working- and middle-class families creates further social instability. In earlier decades most inner-city adults were employed, and they invested their income and time in their neighborhoods, patronizing churches, stores, schools, and community organizations. Their presence in the community provided "role models" for youth. But their out-migration has decreased contact between the classes, leaving the poorest members of the community isolated and "truly disadvantaged." Inner-city

■
Inner city.
The area of the central city in which poverty, joblessness, crime, and social dependency is most prevalent.

residents now lack not only nearby jobs, but also access to job information, social learning through working role models, and suitable (for example, employed) marriage partners.

THE TRULY DISADVANTAGED   It is argued that joblessness and poverty are much more demoralizing when concentrated in the inner city. Neighborhoods that have few legitimate employment opportunities, inadequate job information networks, and poor schools not only weaken the work ethic, but also give rise to illegal income-producing activities in the streets—drugs, crime, and prostitution. A jobless family living in a neighborhood where these ills are concentrated is influenced by the behaviors, beliefs, and perceptions of the people around them. These "concentration effects" make things worse. Moreover, the deterioration of inner-city neighborhoods saps the vitality of local businesses and public services, leading to fewer and shabbier movie theaters, restaurants, markets, parks, and playgrounds. Inner-city schools are particularly disadvantaged: As educational requirements for good jobs are rising, the quality of education available in the inner city is eroded by the concentration of children from poverty-impacted and disintegrating families. The fiscal burden on city governments increases: The cost of services to the inner city rises at the same time that the tax base is eroded by out-migrating businesses and working residents.

RACIAL TENSIONS AND RIOTING   The concentration of social problems in the inner city not only adds to their severity, but also removes them from direct observation by most Americans. Only when the inner city erupts in rioting and violence do many Americans turn their attention to the racial tensions, family breakdowns, joblessness, welfare dependency, crime and drugs, poor schools, and hopelessness that permeate so many core areas of our nation's large cities. And often the attention of policy makers, the media, and the general public is fleeting—it is "politics as usual" after the rioting has been quelled, with inner-city dwellers left to pick up the charred pieces.

Violence is not new to American cities. Three early riots—Watts in Los Angeles in 1965, and Newark and Detroit in 1967—were major civil disorders. Detroit was the worst of these outbreaks: A week of rioting left forty-three dead and more than 1,000 injured. Whole sections of the city were reduced to charred ruins and smoke. Over 1,300 buildings were totally demolished and 2,700 businesses sacked. President Lyndon Johnson appointed a National Commission on Civil Disorder to study the nature and causes of urban rioting. Among the commission's conclusions:

> Typically, rioting was a result of a complex relationship between underlying grievances and one or more "triggering" incidents. For example, grievances about allegedly abusive police practices . . . were often aggravated in the minds of many blacks by incidents involving the police, or the inaction of municipal authorities on complaints about police action.[7]

Many new "Great Society" social welfare programs were already under way at the time of these early riots. (We describe Head Start and other federal educational programs in Chapter 15; federal transportation and housing programs in Chapter 13; and

Medicare, Medicaid, and welfare programs in Chapter 16.) But despite the dramatic growth of federal social welfare programs and expenditures over the four decades, there was little noticeable improvement in conditions in the inner city. The Detroit experience was particularly disillusioning: Its inner city is a more depressed and dangerous place today than when the riots erupted in 1967. Its population plummeted from 1.6 million to 1 million as middle-class blacks and whites fled. It lost over one-third of its jobs. Efforts to stem the flight of the middle class and stabilize neighborhoods were largely ineffective. Thousands of abandoned apartments, stores, and business locations litter the inner city. If anything, the rioting accelerated the worsening of conditions.

The Los Angeles riots in 1992 were a bloody reminder that racial conflict and social misery in the nation's inner cities have not disappeared. The city's "Rodney King" riot was the nation's worst urban rioting of the twentieth century. It left over fifty people dead and many square miles of charred desolation in south-central Los Angeles. The triggering event was the not-guilty verdict rendered by a predominately white jury in suburban Simi Valley in the case of four white Los Angeles police officers accused of beating a black motorist, Rodney King. The case had attracted national attention owing to the fact that the beating had been videotaped and shown many times on national television. The verdict was regarded by both blacks and whites nationwide as a serious miscarriage of justice. Many blacks in the inner city regarded it as white support for continued police brutality and a signal to express their outrage.

Governments may be more effective in controlling riots than in ameliorating their underlying causes. Police reforms may have a more direct effect on the outbreak of rioting than anything else cities can do. Police departments that maintain close relationships with minority communities, train officers in benign conflict-resolution tactics, vigorously investigate and publish charges of police brutality, and endeavor to anticipate and respond quickly to events that might trigger riots may minimize unrest in their cities.

Despite a great deal of political rhetoric following urban rioting, neither Congress nor the president has responded with any clear solutions to the problems of the inner city. And it may be that these problems are largely beyond the reach of government policy: The breakdown of families, the drug culture, the loss of inner-city jobs, and racial and ethnic tensions have all proven to be highly resistant to anything government does. In later chapters we will examine government efforts in welfare, health, homelessness, housing, and education.

SUBURBAN "SPRAWL"

Suburban "sprawl" is often cited as the root cause of social, economic, and governmental problems in the nation's metropolitan areas. Sprawl—the outward extension of new low-density residential and commercial development from the core city—is seen as underlying many of the problems of inner-city life:

■

"Sprawl."
A negative reference to the outward extension of new low-density residential and commercial development from the central city.

> Central cities and older inter-ring suburbs have been left behind. They have lost millions of residents, particularly middle-class families who were the economic and social backbone of sustainable communities. Consequently these once-proud places now harbor higher and higher concentrations of the poor, particularly the minority poor, without the

fiscal capacity to grapple with the consequences: joblessness, family fragmentation, failing schools, and deteriorating commercial districts.[8]

But sprawl is also seen as increasingly problematic for suburban residents themselves:

> Suburban sprawl is eating our open spaces, creating mind-boggling traffic jams, bestowing on us endless strip malls and housing developments, and consuming an ever-increasing share of our resources.[9]

IDENTIFYING SUBURBAN "SPRAWL"   It is argued that *not* all suburbanization can be castigated as "sprawl." Rather, unwanted "sprawl" can be identified by the following characteristics:

- Unlimited outward extension of new development
- Low-density residential and commercial settlements
- Leapfrog development jumping out beyond established settlements
- Fragmentation of powers over land use among many small localities
- Dominance of transportation by private automobiles
- Widespread development of commercial strips
- Great fiscal disparities among localities
- Reliance mainly on trickle-down to provide housing to low-income households[10]

THE CAUSES OF SPRAWL   Suburban sprawl actually occurs because it is the preferred lifestyle of most Americans. Critics of sprawl—reformers, city planners, environmentalists—are reluctant to recognize the popular appeal of single-family homes on large lots with lawns, shrubs, and trees; open spaces for recreation; and quiet residential streets. Commercial businesses—supermarkets, shopping centers, malls—must follow their customers to the suburbs. And increasingly, industry, particularly financial, insurance, and other service companies, together with high-tech firms, want to be located nearer to the homes of their middle-class employees and to enjoy pleasant working surroundings. More commuting now takes place from suburb to suburb than from suburb to central city.

It is true, of course, that government policies have facilitated suburban sprawl. Suburbanization was accelerated after the federal Interstate and Defense Highway Act of 1955 provided the financial support for the interstate "I Highway" system (see "Transportation Policy" in Chapter 13). Federal housing insurance—FHA (Federal Housing Administration) and VA (Veterans Administration) mortgages—enabled millions of American families to fulfill their dream of owning their own suburban home. Even the deductibility of home mortgage interest payments from federal income taxation is cited as a contributor to suburbanization.

Open land is easier and cheaper to build upon than downtown areas that must first be cleared of older buildings. Federal aid has long been available to city governments to assist in the redevelopment of blighted areas (see "Housing and Community Development Policy" in Chapter 13). But city bureaucracies have been slow and cumbersome in

■
"Gentrification."
The movement of upper-class residents and trendy high-priced restaurants and boutiques to downtown locations.

the implementation of urban redevelopment. City regulatory agencies frequently make the costs of complying with building codes, zoning regulations, and planning and environmental controls so high that builders and developers cannot produce affordable homes for middle-class residents, let alone the poor, in downtown areas. Redevelopment plans for these areas often favor commercial or high-income residential projects that promise to both beautify the city and add to its taxable property value. Indeed, "gentrification" of downtown residential areas—attracting upper-class residents and trendy high-priced restaurants and boutiques—is often the deliberate design.

Finally, municipal governments in the suburbs contribute to sprawl when they themselves restrict growth, causing development to "leapfrog" to areas still farther from the central city. Suburban residents use the tools of municipal government to exclude low-income housing and other "undesirable" development (see "'No Growth' Politics" in Chapter 13).

CONFLICT OVER SPRAWL   Urban planners, environmentalists, and "growth management" proponents argue that governments in metropolitan areas must take a regional approach in fighting sprawl. They argue that sprawl increases the costs of highway building, water and sewer services, school busing, and other public infrastructure that must be extended over a wider area to accommodate low-density development. "Compactness" is said to equal "efficiency." But the evidence to support this argument is scanty; city governments actually tax and spend more per resident than suburban governments. Only public school costs are higher in suburbs, a fact that probably reflects residents' desire for better schools rather than inefficiency.

Environmentalists argue that sprawl devours green spaces, that increased automobile commuting fouls the air, that paving over land adds to global warming, and that precious farmland is being lost. Yet the automobile remains the near universal choice of Americans for transportation because of the freedom and flexibility it provides. Despite billions of dollars in federal, state, and local government taxpayer subsidies to mass transit (see "Transportation Policy" in Chapter 13), transit use remains at historical lows. And land is no longer the key factor in food production; each year American farmers grow more crops using less land.

THE CASE FOR METROPOLITAN CONSOLIDATION

"Fragmented" government—that is, the proliferation of governments in metropolitan areas and the lack of coordination of public programs—adds to the metropolitan problem. The objective of the metropolitan reform movement of the last forty years has been to reorganize, consolidate, and enlarge government jurisdictions. The goal is to rid metropolitan areas of "ineffective multiple local jurisdictions" and "governments that do not coincide with the boundaries of the metropolis."[11]

PUBLIC SERVICE   Many advantages are claimed for metropolitan governmental reorganization. First of all, the reorganization and consolidation of metropolitan governments is expected to bring about *improved public services* as a result of centralization. Consolidation of governments is expected to achieve many economies of large-scale operations and enable government to provide specialized public services, which "fragmented" units of government cannot provide. For example, larger water treatment plant facilities can deliver water at lower per gallon costs, and larger sewage disposal plants can handle sewage at a lower per gallon cost of disposal.

The problem with this argument is that most studies show that larger municipal governments are *un*economic and fail to produce improved services. Only in very small cities (with populations under 25,000) can economies of scale be achieved by enlarging the scope of government. In cities of over 250,000, further increases in size appear to produce *dis*economies of scale and lower levels of public service per person.

COORDINATION   Second, it is argued that metropolitan consolidation will provide the necessary *coordination of public services* for the metropolis. Study after study reported that crime, fire, traffic congestion, air pollution, water pollution, and so on do not respect municipal boundary lines. The transportation problem is the most common example of a coordination problem. Traffic experts have pleaded for the development of a balanced transportation system in which mass transit carries many of the passengers currently traveling in private automobiles. Yet mass transit requires decisive public action by the entire metropolitan area. Certainly, the city government is in a poor position to provide mass transit by itself without the support of the suburbanites.

EQUALITY   The third major argument for metropolitan consolidation stresses the need to eliminate *inequalities in financial burdens* throughout the metropolitan area. Suburbanites who escaped many city taxes continue to add to the cities' traffic and parking problems, use city streets and parks, find employment in the cities, use city hospitals and cultural facilities, and so on. By concentrating the poor, uneducated, unskilled minorities in central cities, we also saddle central cities with costly problems of public health and welfare, crime control, fire protection, slum clearance, and the like— all the social problems that are associated with poverty and discrimination. We concentrate these costly problems in cities at the same time that middle-class tax-paying individuals, tax-paying commercial enterprises, and tax-paying industries are moving into the suburbs. Thus, metropolitan-government fragmentation often succeeds in segregating financial needs from resources. The result is serious financial difficulty for many central cities.

RESPONSIBILITY   It is also argued that metropolitan government will *clearly establish responsibility for metropolitanwide policy.* One of the consequences of "fragmented" government is the scattering of public authority and the decentralization of policy making in the metropolis. This proliferation in the number of autonomous governmental units reduces the probability of developing a consensus on metropolitan policy. Each autonomous unit exercises a veto power over metropolitan policy within its jurisdiction; it is often impossible to secure the unanimity required to achieve metropolitan consensus on any metropolitanwide problem. An opponent of any particular solution need only find, among the countless independent governmental bodies whose consent is required, one that can be induced to withhold its consent in order to obstruct action. The dispersion of power among a large number of governmental units makes it possible for each of them to reach decisions without concern for the possible spillover effects, which may be harmful to other governments or residents of the metropolis.

THE CASE FOR "FRAGMENTED" GOVERNMENT

Suburb "bashing" is a common theme among central-city politicians, city newspaper columnists, and many reform-minded scholars who would prefer centralized metropolitan government.[12] But the suburbs house half of the nation's population, and it is important to try to understand why so many suburbanites prefer "fragmented" government. Many citizens do not look upon "the optimum development of the metropolitan region" as a particularly compelling goal. Rather, there are a variety of social, political, and psychological values at stake in maintaining the existing "fragmented" system of local government.

IDENTITY   First of all, the existence of separate and independent local governments for suburbs plays a vital role in developing and maintaining a sense of community *identity*. Suburbanites identify their residential community by reference to the local political unit. They do not think of themselves as residents of the "New York metropolitan region," but rather as residents of Scarsdale or Mineola. Even the existence of community problems, the existence of a governmental forum for their resolution, and the necessity to elect local officials heighten community involvement and identity. The suburban community, with a government small in scale and close to home, represents a partial escape from the anonymity of mass urban culture. The institutional apparatus of government helps the suburban community to differentiate itself from "the urban mass" by legislating differences in the size and design of buildings, neighborhood and subdivision plans, school policies, types and quality of public services, and tax expenditure levels.

ACCESS   The political advantages of a fragmented suburbia cannot easily be dismissed. The existence of many local governments provides *additional forums* for the airing of public grievances. People feel better when they can publicly voice their complaints against governments, regardless of the eventual outcome of their grievance. The additional points of access, pressure, and control provided by a decentralized system of local government give added assurance that political demands will be heard and perhaps even acted upon. Opportunities for individual participation in the making of public policy are expanded in a decentralized governmental system.

EFFECTIVENESS   Maintaining the suburb as an independent political community provides the individual with a sense of *personal effectiveness* in public affairs. The individual can feel a greater sense of manageability over the affairs of a small community. A smaller community helps relieve feelings of frustration and apathy which people often feel in their relations with larger bureaucracies. Suburbanites feel that their votes, their opinions, and their political activities count for more in a small community. They cling to the idea of grass-roots democracy in an organizational society.

INFLUENCE   Fragmented government clearly offers a larger number of groups the opportunity to *exercise influence* over government policy. Groups that would be minorities in the metropolitan area as a whole can avail themselves of government position and enact diverse public policies. This applies to blacks in the central city as well as to whites in the suburbs. Fragmented government creates within the metropolitan area a wide range of government policies. Communities that prefer, for example, higher standards in their school system at higher costs have the opportunity to implement this preference. Communities that prefer higher levels of public service or one set of services over another or stricter enforcement of particular standards can achieve their goals under a decentralized governmental system. Communities that wish to get along with reduced public services in order to maximize funds available for private spending may do so.

SCHOOLS   Racial imbalance and the plight of central-city schools are important forces in maintaining the political autonomy of suburban school systems in the nation's large metropolitan areas. Many suburbanites left the central city to find "a better place to raise the kids," and this means, among other things, better schools. As we have already observed, suburbs generally spend more on the education of each child than central cities. Moreover, the increasing concentration of blacks in central cities has resulted in racial imbalance in center-city schools. Efforts to end de facto segregation within the cities frequently involve busing school children into and out of ghetto schools in order to achieve racial balance. In Chapter 14 we will discuss de facto segregation in greater detail. However, it is important to note here that independent suburban school districts are viewed by many suburbanites as protection against the possibility that their children might be bused to inner-city schools. Autonomous suburban school districts lie outside the jurisdiction of city officials. While it is possible that federal courts may some day order suburban school districts to cooperate with cities in achieving racial balance in schools, the political independence of suburban schools helps to assure that their children will not be used to achieve racial balance in city schools.

METROPOLITAN GOVERNMENT AS MARKETPLACE

Fragmented metropolitan government means many different mixes of municipal services, public schools, and tax levels in the same metropolitan area. So why can't people "shop around" among local communities and move into the community where the mix of services, schools, and taxes best suits their individual preferences?

THE TIEBOUT MODEL   Economist Charles Tiebout argues that the existence of many local governments in the same area, all offering "public goods" (public schools, police and fire protection, water and sewer, refuse collection, streets and sidewalks) and various "prices" (taxes), provides a competitive and efficient government marketplace.[13] Families can choose for themselves what public goods they want at what price by simply moving to the community that best approximates their own preferences. Both families and businesses can "vote with their feet" for their preferred "bundle" of municipal services and taxes. Local governments must compete for residents and businesses by offering high-quality public services at the lowest possible tax rates. This encourages efficiency in local government.

MOBILITY?   The Tiebout model of efficient local government assumes that metropolitan residents have a high degree of *mobility*, that is, they can move anywhere in the

■

Tiebout model.
An economic theory that asserts that families and businesses in metropolitan areas can maximize their preferences for services and taxes by choosing locations among multiple local governments.

metropolitan area anytime they wish. The major criticism of this model is that many metropolitan residents do not enjoy unlimited mobility. The poor are limited by meager financial resources from "shopping" for the best governmental services. And minorities often confront barriers to residential mobility regardless of their economic resources.

EQUITY?   Moreover, the Tiebout model in its original formulation ignores the interdependence of the metropolis. Many public services are metropolitanwide in scope—urban expressways, mass transit, clean air and water, public health and hospitals, for example. These services cannot be provided by small local governments. Suburbanites use public facilities and services of cities when they work in the city or go to the city for entertainment. If they do not share in the costs of these services and facilities, they become "free riders," unfairly benefiting from services paid for by others. The major social problems of the city—poverty, racial tension, poor housing, crime and delinquency—are really problems of the entire metropolis.[14]

SATISFACTION?   Yet the Tiebout model is correct in asserting that there is a great variety of lifestyles, housing types, governmental services and costs *within* large metropolitan areas, and that most families take this into account when choosing a place of residence. And judging by the subjective evaluations of residents, many different types of neighborhoods are judged satisfactory by the people living in them. Quality-of-life studies usually ask respondents how "satisfied" they are with their neighborhoods. These studies reveal that people living in *all* types of neighborhoods express satisfaction with them. Indeed, even lower-income people living in substandard housing or areas considered slums by outsiders report being satisfied. (However, attachment to friends and relatives is a major source of their satisfaction, rather than governmental services.)[15] The fact that residents of many different kinds of communities express satisfaction with them lends implicit support to the Tiebout model. There is also evidence that business locational decisions within the metropolis are influenced by the "bundle" of governmental services and taxes offered by local governments.[16]

METROPOLITAN GOVERNMENT "SOLUTIONS"

Let us examine various strategies for metropolitan governmental consolidation in connection with the values of suburban independence and the need for coordinating governmental activity in metropolitan areas.

ANNEXATION   The most obvious method of achieving governmental consolidation in the metropolitan area would be for the central city to annex suburban areas. *Annexation* continues to be the most popular integrating device in the nation's metropolitan areas. Not all cities, however, have been equally successful in annexation efforts. Opposition to central-city annexation is generally more intense in the larger metropolitan areas. The bigger the metropolis, the more one can expect that suburbanites will defend themselves against being "swallowed up" or "submerged" by the central city. Central cities in smaller urbanized areas experience more success in annexing people than cities in large urbanized areas. Yet size does not appear to be the most influential

■
Annexation.
The extension of city boundaries over adjacent territory.

factor affecting annexation success. Actually, the "age" of a city seems more influential than its size in determining the success of annexation efforts. Over three-fourths of the area and population annexed to central cities in the nation in recent decades have been in newer cities of the West and South. City boundary lines in "older" metropolitan areas are relatively more fixed than in "newer" areas. Perhaps the immobility of boundaries is a product of sheer age. Over time, persons and organizations adjust themselves to circumstances as they find them. The longer these adjustments have been in existence, the greater the discomfort, expense, and fear of unanticipated consequences associated with change.[17]

CITY–COUNTY CONSOLIDATION   Three-quarters of the nation's metropolitan areas lie within single counties. From the standpoint of administration, there is much to be said for city–county consolidation. It would make sense administratively to endow county governments with the powers of cities and to organize them to exercise these powers effectively. Yet, important political problems—problems in the allocation of influence over public decision making—remain formidable barriers to strong county government. Suburbanites are likely to fear that consolidation will give city residents a dominant voice in county affairs. Suburbanites may also fear that city–county consolidation may force them to pay higher taxes to help support the higher municipal costs of running the city. (Actually, county governments usually do provide more benefits to city than suburban residents, while receiving more tax revenues from suburbanites than city residents.[18]) Suburbanites may not welcome uniform, countywide policies in taxation or zoning or any number of other policy areas. Suburbanites who had paid for their own wells and septic tanks will hardly welcome the opportunity to help pay for city water or sewer services. Suburbanites with well-established, high-quality public school systems may be unenthusiastic about integrating their schools with city schools in a countywide system, and so on. A variety of policy differences may exist between city and suburb, which will reflect themselves in any attempt to achieve city–county consolidation.

SPECIAL DISTRICTS   One of the more popular approaches to metropolitan integration is the creation of special districts or authorities charged with administering a particular function or service on a metropolitanwide or at least an intermunicipal level, such as a park, sewerage, water, parking, airport, planning, other district, or authority. (See Figure 12–2.) Because the special district or authority leaves the social and governmental status quo relatively undisturbed, important integrative demands are met with a minimum of resistance with this device. The autonomy of suburban communities is not really threatened, loyalties are not disturbed, political jobs are not lost, and the existing tax structure is left relatively intact. Special districts or authorities may be preferred by suburban political leaders when they believe it will lessen the pressure for annexation by the central city. Special districts or authorities may also be able to incur additional debt after existing units of government have already reached their tax and debt limits. Thus, special districts or authorities may be able to operate in an area wider than that of existing units of governments and at the same time enable governments to evade tax or debt limits in financing a desired public service. The nation's largest special districts—New York's Metropolitan Transportation Authority, Boston's Massachusetts Bay Transportation Authority, Washington's Metro Area Transit Au-

■

City–county consolidation.
The merger of a county and a city government into a single jurisdiction.

Special districts.
Local governmental units charged with performing a single function, often overlapping municipal boundaries.

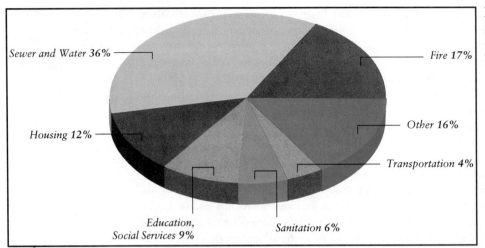

FIGURE 12–2
Special District
Governments
by Function

thority, Los Angeles County Transportation Commission, Port Authority of New York and New Jersey—collect and spend billions of dollars each year.

Yet, experience in the cities that have relied heavily upon special districts or authorities has suggested that these devices may create as many problems as they solve. Many special districts and authorities are governed by a quasi-independent board or commission, which, once established, becomes largely immune from popular pressures for change. These agencies may be quite independent of other governmental jurisdictions in the metropolis; their concerns might be water, air or water pollution control, city planning, and so on. Remoteness from popular control or close political responsibility often results in the professional administrators of these authorities exercising great power over their particular function. While authorities and special districts are supposed to be nonprofit governmental agencies, they often act very much like private enterprises, concentrating their resources on those activities that produce revenue and ignoring equally important non–revenue-producing responsibilities. Independent authorities often borrow money, collect tolls and service charges, and otherwise control their own finances in a manner very much like a private business. The structure of these districts and authorities usually confuses the voters and makes it difficult for the average citizen to hold officials of these agencies responsible for their decisions. Moreover, since these special districts and authorities are usually created for a single purpose, they often come to define the public interest in terms of the promotion of their own particular function—recreation, mass transit, water, parks, and so on—without regard for other metropolitan concerns. This "single-mindedness" can lead to competition and conflict between authorities and other governmental agencies in the region. Sooner or later, the problem of coordinating the activities of these independent authorities of special districts arises. Thus, even from the point of view of administrative efficiency, it is not clear whether the special district or authority, with its maze of divided responsibility, reduces or compounds the problem of governmental coordination in the metropolis in the long run.

INTERJURISDICTIONAL AGREEMENTS   Another approach to metropolitan integration is the interjurisdictional agreement. Voluntary cooperative agreements between governments in a metropolitan area are common. Agreements may take the form of informal verbal understandings that might involve, for example, the exchange between welfare departments of information on cases, or cooperation among police departments in the apprehension of a lawbreaker, or agreements among local fire departments to come to the assistance of each other in the event of a major fire. Agreements may also be *formal* interjurisdictional agreements among governments, perhaps to build and operate a major facility such as a garbage incinerator or a sewage treatment plant. Interjurisdictional agreements may provide for (1) one government performing a service or providing a facility for one or more other governments on a contractual basis, (2) two or more governments performing a function jointly or operating a facility on a joint basis, or (3) two or more local governments agreeing to assist and supply mutual aid to each other in emergency situations.

One of the attractions of interjurisdictional agreements is that they provide a means for dealing with metropolitan problems on a voluntary basis while retaining local determination and control. Interjurisdictional agreements do not threaten the existence of communities or governments. They do not threaten the jobs of incumbent public officials. Yet at the same time they enable governments to achieve the economies of scale and provide the specialized services that only a larger jurisdiction can make possible.

COUNCILS OF GOVERNMENT   Metropolitan councils of governments (COGs) are another form of integration in metropolitan areas. Metropolitan councils are associations of governments or government officials that provide an opportunity for study, discussion, and recommendations regarding common metropolitan problems. Not governments themselves, these COGs have no power to implement decisions but must rely instead upon compliance by member governments. Metropolitan councils provide an arena where officials of metropolitan governments can come together regularly, discuss problems, make recommendations, and, hopefully, coordinate their activities.[19]

Although COGs started slowly, the federal government provided the major stimulus to their acceptance by making federal planning funds available for metropolitanwide planning agencies. Today, most metropolitan areas have *some* organization functioning as a metropolitan council of government.

Generally, COGs strive for unity in their decisions because their recommendations must be acted upon by member governments who are unlikely to implement proposals they oppose. The result, for the most part, is that studies and recommendations of COGs are likely to be rather bland. It is very difficult for these councils to deal with the really divisive issues in the metropolis. Since councils have no authority to act upon metropolitan problems, they may be, in the words of Bollens and Schmandt, a "toothless tiger or—even worse—a protector of the inadequate status quo."[20]

Interjurisdictional agreements.
Voluntary contracts among local governments in a metropolitan area to perform services jointly or on behalf of each other.

Councils of government.
Associations of governments or government officials in metropolitan areas that study, discuss, and recommend solutions to metropolitanwide problems.

THE POLITICS OF METROPOLITAN CONSOLIDATION

City officials—mayors, managers, and council members—usually provide the public stimulus for annexation. Their immediate goal is to expand the tax base of the city; over the long run they seek growth and revenues. They do not want to see the city cut off from new residential, industrial, and commercial development on the rim of the

metropolis. Their primary strategy is to cultivate political support for various annexation efforts by offering city services—especially water and sewer, fire and police protection, street lighting and sidewalks—at reasonable prices to residents of areas
targeted for annexation. Sometimes builders and developers can be enticed to offer
land for annexation in exchange for city water, sewer, or streets. Cities with active
managers and planners are more likely to have continuous annexation programs.

City business interests, with capital already invested in downtown land, buildings,
and enterprises, are usually strong supporters of annexation. These city power structures are growth oriented (see Chapter 13). If the city government is cut off from new
sources of revenue, the costs of city government will increasingly fall on the shoulders
of downtown business. The downtown Chambers of Commerce, the city newspaper,
and the downtown civic (reform) organizations can all be expected to support the expansion of the city.

POLITICAL OPPOSITION   Political opposition to annexation and city expansion is
usually centered among suburban municipal officials and residents. They see continued
value in "fragmentation"—a sense of community identity, access to government, personal influence in a smaller governmental setting, insulation from city dwellers whose
lifestyles they do not share, and perhaps a desire to maintain racial isolation. They also
fear higher tax rates in the city, and they may not feel that the additional services offered by city government are worth the added cost. County or township officials may
take the lead in urging residents not to sign annexation petitions and to vote "no" if
an election is held; they may also challenge annexation petitions and votes in the
courts.

Political realities have frequently overwhelmed the "logic" of metropolitan consolidation. These political realities are deeply rooted in the social, economic, lifestyle, and
racial differences between cities and suburbs described earlier. The record of consolidation referenda shows more defeats than victories.[21] Yet reformers have not been in-
hibited by the dismal record thus far, and consolidation proposals of various kinds are
under discussion in a great many urban areas.

Consolidation involves considerable disruption for public officials—redesigning
governmental structure, reordering the authority of various offices, combining offices
and agencies, and enlarging the magnitude of government operations. Unless a *large*
majority of community influentials are *very* dissatisfied with the current state of affairs
and are motivated to actively support consolidation, there is little chance that consolidation efforts will be successful.[22]

CONSOLIDATION COMMISSIONS   Consolidation efforts usually begin with the formation of a charter commission to determine the form of the new consolidated government and write a charter for it. Usually the commission includes representatives of
both the city and county governments to be consolidated, together with some "citizen"
representatives. Sometimes the establishment of the commission itself is the subject of
a referendum; interestingly, referenda to establish a commission tend to pass more often than not, even though the final vote on consolidation is likely to be negative. Establishing a charter commission is more easily obtainable than consolidation itself.

CONSOLIDATION REFERENDA   The critical point of the consolidation battle is the referenda vote on the acceptance of the new consolidated-government charter. The form of the vote depends on state law: A "double majority" vote requirement means that a majority "yes" vote must be obtained within the city *and* within the area outside of the city. In contrast, a "double-count majority" vote requirement means that the vote of city residents is counted twice—once for the city and again for the county, because they are also county residents. It is much easier for consolidation to win under the "double-count" requirement. Consolidation campaigns are usually managed by reform groups especially selected for the purpose. They are typically mass-media-oriented campaigns rather than the grass-roots organizational, ward- and precinct-level campaigns of party organizations. Voter turnout is only slightly heavier than that of ordinary municipal elections—ranging from 30 percent to 60 percent. Contrary to the public pronouncements of reformers, a high turnout does *not* help passage; indeed, there is a slightly better chance of success if turnout is low.

Most consolidation proposals are defeated by *county* residents, that is, suburbanites. The average voter turnout level of suburbanites is much higher than city dwellers, and the percentage of "no" votes is much greater in the suburbs than in the city. Thus, overall voter response to consolidation proposals tends to support the notion that suburbanites prefer to maintain their identity and autonomy, their own governmental institutions, and their insulation from city people and problems. They do *not* want the improved public services, coordinated policies, or shared financial burdens that reformers urge upon them. While fear of higher taxes plays a role in suburban opposition, there appear to be many other social and psychological factors at work in helping to preserve suburban autonomy.

The fear of being "submerged" into a large, impersonal, unresponsive government is evidenced by the interesting fact that proposed consolidation charters that stipulate many elected representatives and separately elected administrators (sheriff, tax assessor, and so on) do better at the polls than the "streamlined," governmental charters preferred by reformers. In other words, a "Jacksonian" consolidation charter has a better chance of passage than one with a small legislative body and single strong executive.

RACE   Race is an increasingly important issue in consolidation campaigns. Most successful consolidation efforts have occurred in the South. A common appeal to suburbanites in the South is to vote to join the city in order to "save" it from black majority rule by "diluting" the black vote. However, the issue is complex and cuts both ways. Suburbanites may simply decide to stay out of a consolidated government precisely because it would include many central-city blacks. Blacks were traditionally expected to vote "yes" for economic reasons—to bring valuable suburban property into the tax base of the city. However, black support for consolidation will certainly turn to opposition if it appears that blacks will lose power in the outcome.[23]

REFORM   Political support for consolidation is usually greatest among civic and business organizations and newspapers. Their arguments for consolidation are familiar—improved services, better coordination, more equal financial burdens, and clearer lines of responsibility. Moreover, consolidation offers an opportunity to reorganize lo-

■
"Double majority" vote requirement.
In city–county consolidation referenda, the requirement that both city voters and voters living outside of the city must approve of the merger in order for it to take effect.

cal government: The new government may offer a manager form of government, a reduction in the number of elected officials, and a more orderly structure for the delivery
of municipal services.

THE TAX ISSUE   Does city–county consolidation save the taxpayers' money? Reformers have been *unable* to produce any convincing evidence that consolidation either improves governmental services or reduces governmental costs. Indeed, in careful
study of this important question, employing a before-and-after research design in similar "experimental" and "control" cities, researchers found "no measurable impact"
from consolidation on governmental costs of services.[24] This study focused on
Florida's Jacksonville/Duval County, which consolidated their governments, and
Tampa/Hillsborgh County, which did not. Both metropolitan areas are similar in socioeconomic composition, both operate under the same state laws, and both have the
same mayor-council form of government. Yet an examination of property taxes, total
expenditures, and policy protection in both cities from 1955 through 1981 (Jack-
sonville/Duval County consolidated in 1969) showed *no* significant short-term or
long-term differences between these two areas.

A RECORD OF FAILURE   Most consolidation efforts fail. Only about one-quarter of
the consolidation proposals that come to a vote are approved. These have all been single counties. Most have been in medium-size or smaller metropolitan areas. There have
been no adoptions in the Northeast or Midwest; all consolidations have taken place in
the South or West. Successful consolidations have always involved some unique political factors. Often it is necessary to allow some offices to remain separate in order to
secure political support for consolidation, for example, retaining a separate sheriff's
office and city police force, or retaining separate school districts.[25]

"METRO" GOVERNMENT   The American experience with federalism at the national
level has prompted consideration of federated governmental structures for metropolitan areas. A "metro" government with authority to make metropolitanwide policy in
selected fields might be combined with local control over functions that are "local" in
character. Metropolitan federation, in one form or another and at one time or another,
has been proposed for many major metropolitan regions in the nation. Yet, with the
exception of Toronto, Miami, and Nashville,[26] proposals for metropolitan federation
have been consistently rejected by both voters and political leaders. While metropolitan federation promises many of the advantages of governmental consolidation listed
earlier—administrative efficiency, economy of large-scale operation, elimination of financial inequalities, and public accountability for metropolitanwide policy—it seriously threatens many of the social, political, and psychological values in the existing
"fragmented" system of local government in the metropolis. Metropolitan federation
also poses a problem discussed earlier, that of deciding what is a "metropolitan" problem. In order to allocate functions to a "metro" government in a federation arrangement, one must first determine what is a metropolitan problem in which all the citizens
of the area have a responsibility (see *"People in Politics:* Alex Penelas, Metro Mayor").

■
"Metro" government.
A federated system of government for metropolitan areas in which powers are
divided between a compre-
hensive government encom-
passing the entire area and
multiple local governments
operating within the area.

PEOPLE IN POLITICS

ALEX PENELAS, METRO MAYOR

A youthful Alex Penelas was elected as Miami-Dade County's first executive mayor in 1996. He guides the largest metropolitanwide government in the United States, an area of more than 2 million residents.

The formation of Miami-Dade County in 1957 was the nation's first experiment in "Metro" government. It was approved by a bare majority of Dade County voters in a low-turnout referenda election that year. The Miami-Dade County Charter created a two-tiered system of government for the Miami metropolitan area. The Miami-Dade Metro government includes thirty municipalities as well as the unincorporated areas of Dade County. Each municipality has its own government and provides its own city services, including police and zoning. The City of Miami is the largest municipality, followed by Hialeah and Miami Beach.

The Miami-Dade Metro Charter gave the new government a number of functions previously performed by the local governments in the metropolitan area, including sewerage and water supply, transportation, traffic control, central planning, and "those municipal functions which are susceptible to area-wide control." This vagueness in the charter resulted in a great deal of court litigation over the powers of the Metro government. Miami Beach even attempted to secede from the metropolitan federation. Amendments to the charter that would have crippled the powers of the Metro government were defeated at the polls by very slim margins. Early opponents of Metro government included the Dade County League of Municipalities, municipal employee labor unions, many municipal officials, and local chambers of commerce. Metro supporters were concentrated among Miami's business and media leaders, including the Miami Chamber of Commerce and the powerful *Miami Herald* newspaper. The narrow victory of the Metro idea was attributed to the heavy influx of newcomers to the area in the absence of strong political parties.

Over the years the ethnic composition of Miami's metropolitan area population has changed radically. By the 1980s a Hispanic majority had emerged. Anglos as well as African Americans found themselves a minority in a county-manager governmental structure in which power was concentrated in a board of commissioners selected in countywide at-large elections. In response to a suit filed by African Americans claiming that at-large elections diluted their voting strength in violation of the federal Voting Rights Act, a federal court in 1992 ordered Miami-Dade to amend its charter to provide for the election of a thirteen-member governing commission, all to be elected from single-member districts. In the elections following this new plan, African Americans won four of the thirteen commission seats.

But at the same time, voters also chose to adopt a "Strong Mayor Charter Amendment," creating a new Metro mayor with many powers previously exercised by the commission, including the power to appoint and remove the county manager.

Alex Penelas was born in Miami of Cuban heritage. He attended local Biscayne College, now St. Thomas University, and later graduated from the University of Miami law school. Two years later he was elected councilman for the City of Hialeah, with its large Cuban American population. But while most Cuban Americans in the area affiliate themselves with the Republican party, Penelas became a Democrat. After one two-year term on the Hialeah council, the popular energetic Democrat won election to the metropolitan Miami-Dade Board of County Commissioners, becoming the youngest person ever elected to that body.

The charismatic Penelas became the first mayor of metropolitan Miami-Dade County in 1996, winning a stunning 61 percent of the vote. The only ethnic group he failed to win was the African Americans. Indeed, the campaign itself degenerated into an ethnic slugfest—Cuban Americans versus African Americans. Penelas spent almost $3 million on his campaign for the mayor's job. His critics claim he is too close to wealthy lobbyists, but Penelas has won high approval ratings in his role as a "strong" mayor. He was untarnished by corruption scandals and bankruptcy in the independent City of Miami. On the contrary, his handsome image and instinct for TV cameras have made him one of the state's leading Democratic hopefuls for higher office.

"I'm the classic example of why this is a great country," he says. "My parents came here thirty-five years ago. They did not even speak the language. Thirty-five years later, I'm able to run for what many people describe as the second most powerful job in Florida. Only in America!"

ON THE WEB

Governing magazine is the nation's leading monthly publication directed at state and local government officials. Its articles on politics, public affairs, and policy issues are timely and highly readable. Its Web site at

www.governing.com

offers "highlight" stories from current and past issues free to Web users. *Governing* also publishes an annual "State and Local Sourcebook," which contains comparative governmental information on states, counties, and cities.

Metropolitan Miami-Dade County is one of the nation's very few "metro" governments. It is a strong federation of thirty municipalities (the largest is the city of Miami), together with the unincorporated areas of Dade County. It has an elected mayor as well as an elected board of county commissioners. Its Web site at

www.miami-dade.fl.us

describes this unique two-tiered system of local governmnt. It contains the official charter of the metropolitan government as well as descriptions of all metro government services.

NOTES

1. See John Bollens and Henry Schmandt, *The Metropolis* (New York: Harper & Row, 1985).

2. Lewis Mumford, *The City in History* (New York: Harcourt, Brace, & World, 1961), p. 34.

3. Richard Child Hill, "Separate and Unequal: Government Inequality in the Metropolis," *American Political Science Review,* 68 (December 1974), 1557–68.

4. Kenneth Jackson, *Crabgrass Frontier: The Suburbanization of the United States* (New York: Oxford University Press, 1985).

5. See William Julius Wilson, *The Truly Disadvantaged* (Chicago: University of Chicago Press, 1987).

6. See Christopher Jencks and Paul E. Peterson, eds., *The Urban Underclass* (Washington, DC: Brookings Institution, 1991).

7. National Advisory Commission on Civil Disorders, *Report* (Washington, DC: Government Printing Office, 1968), p. 4.

8. Bruce Katz and Scott Bernstein, "The New Metropolitan Agenda," *Brookings Review,* vol. 16 (Fall 1998), p. 5.

9. Christine Todd Whitman, "The Metropolitan Challenge," *Brookings Review,* vol. 16 (Fall 1998), p. 3.

10. See Anthony Downs, "How America's Cities Are Growing," *Brookings Review,* vol. 16 (Fall 1998), p. 8.

11. John Harrigan, *Political Change in the Metropolis* (Boston: Little, Brown, 1985).

12. For an excellent analysis of the political values of scholars who study urban problems, see Brett W. Hawkins and Stephen L. Percy, "On Anti-Suburban Orthodoxy," *Social Science Quarterly,* 72 (September 1991), 478–90.

13. Charles Tiebout, "A Pure Theory of Local Expenditures," *Journal of Political Economy,* 64 (October 1956), 416–24.

14. Bollens and Schmandt, *The Metropolis.*

15. See Barrett A. Lee, "The Urban Unease Revisited: Perceptions of Local Satisfaction Among Metropolitan Residents," *Social Science Quarterly,* 62 (December 1987), 611–29; Craig St. John and Frieda Clark, "Race and Social Class Differences in the Characteristics Desired in Residential Neighborhoods," *Social Science Quarterly,* 65 (September 1984), 803–13.

16. See Mark Schneider, "Suburban Fiscal Disparities and the Location Decisions of Firms," *American Journal of Political Science,* 29 (August 1985), 587–605.

17. See Arnold Fleischmann, "The Politics of Annexation," *Social Science Quarterly,* 67 (March 1986), 128–41; Gary J. Miller, *Cities by Con-*

tract: *The Politics of Municipal Incorporation* (Cambridge, MA: MIT Press, 1981).

18. See Brett W. Hawkins and Rebecca M. Hendrick, "Do County Governments Reinforce City–Suburban Inequalities?" *Social Science Quarterly,* 25 (December 1994), 755–71.

19. The best-known councils of government include the Metropolitan Regional Council (New York), Southern California Association of Governments (Los Angeles), Northeast Illinois Planning Commission (Chicago), Southeast Michigan Council of Governments (Detroit), Associated Bay Area Governments (San Francisco), Metropolitan Washington Council of Governments (Washington), East-West Gateway Council (St. Louis), Northeast Ohio Areawide Coordinating Agency (Cleveland).

20. See Bollens and Schmandt, *The Metropolis,* pp. 379–80.

21. Vincent L. Marando and Carl Whitley, "City-County Consolidation: An Overview of Voter Response," *Urban Affairs Quarterly,* 8 (December 1972), 181–203.

22. For an interesting comparison of elite roles in successful (Jacksonville) and unsuccessful (Tampa) consolidation campaigns, see Thomas A. Henderson and Walter A. Rosenbaum, "Prospects for Consolidating Local Government: The Role of Elites in Electoral Outcomes," *American Journal of Political Science,* 17 (November 1973), 695–720.

23. See Richard L. Engstrom and W. E. Lyons, "Black Control or Consolidation: The Fringe Response," *Social Science Quarterly,* 53 (June 1972), 161–68.

24. J. Edwin Benten, "City-County Consolidation and Economies of Scale," *Social Science Quarterly,* 65 (March 1985), 190–98.

25. See Vincent L. Marando, "City-County Consolidation: Reform Regionalism Referenda and Requiem," *Western Political Quarterly,* 32 (December 1979), 409–21.

26. See Edward Sofen, *The Miami Metropolitan Experiment* (Bloomington: University of Indiana Press, 1963); Edward Sofen, "The Politics of Metropolitan Leadership: The Miami Experience," *Midwest Journal of Political Science,* 5 (February 1961), 18–38; Brett W. Hawkins, *Nashville Metro* (Nashville, TN: University of Vanderbilt Press, 1966); Brett W. Hawkins, "Public Opinion and Metropolitan Reorganization in Nashville," *Journal of Politics,* 28 (May 1966), 408–18.

13
COMMUNITY POWER AND LAND USE CONTROL

QUESTIONS TO CONSIDER
★ ★ ★ ★ ★ ★ ★ ★ ★ ★

Do your local elected public officials or a behind-the-scenes power structure make important decisions in your community?

- ☐ Elected public officials make important decisions
- ☐ Power structure runs things behind the scenes

Should economic growth in your community be limited in order to preserve the community's character and lifestyle?

☐ Yes ☐ No

Do you believe that property owners should be compensated by taxpayers when government regulations reduce the value of their land?

☐ Yes ☐ No

Do zoning laws, building codes, land use, and environmental regulations in your community add unnecessarily to the costs of housing?

☐ Yes ☐ No

MODELS OF COMMUNITY POWER

Who runs this town? Do the elected public officials actually make the important decisions? Or is there a "power structure" in this community that really runs things? If so, who is in the power structure? Are public officials "gofers" who carry out the orders of powerful individuals who operate "behind the scenes"? Or are community affairs decided by democratically elected officials acting openly in response to the wishes of many different individuals and groups? Is city government of the people, by the people, and for the people? Or is it a government run by a small "elite," with the "masses" of people largely apathetic and uninfluential in public affairs?

Social scientists have differed over the answers to these questions. Some social scientists posit an *elite model* of community power—that power in American communities is concentrated in the hands of relatively few people, usually top business and financial leaders. They believe that this "elite" is subject to relatively little influence from the "masses" of people. Other social scientists posit a *pluralist model* of community power—that power is widely shared in American communities among many leadership groups who represent segments of the community and who are held responsible by the people through elections and group participation. Interestingly, both elitist and pluralist models seem to agree that decisions are made by small minorities in the community. Direct, widespread, individual citizen participation in community decision making is more of an ideal than a reality. The *elite model describes a monolithic structure of power*, with a single leadership group making decisions on a variety of issues. The *pluralist model describes a polycentric structure of power*, with different leaders active in different issues and a great deal of competition, bargaining, and sharing of power among them.

Most "real" communities will probably fall somewhere in between—that is, along a continuum from the monolithic elite model of power to a diffused and polycentric pluralist model. Many social scientists are neither confirmed "elitists" nor "pluralists," but they are aware that different structures and power may exist in different communities. Yet these ideal models of community power may be helpful in understanding the different ways in which community power can be structured.

THE ELITE MODEL European social theory has long been at odds with democratic political writers about the existence and necessity of elites. The Italian political theorist, Gaetano Mosca, in his book *The Ruling Class*, wrote, "In all societies . . . two classes of people appear—a class that rules and a class that is ruled."[1] For Mosca, elitism is explained by the nature of social organization. Organization inevitably results in the concentration of political power in the hands of a few. Organized power cannot be resisted by an unorganized majority in which each individual ". . . stands alone before the totality of the organized minority. A hundred men acting uniformly in concert, with a common understanding, will triumph over a thousand men who are not in accord and can therefore be dealt with one by one."[2] Since organized power will prevail over individual effort in politics, sooner or later, organizations will come to be the

Elite model.
In community politics, the theory that power is concentrated in the hands of relatively few people, usually top business and financial leaders.

Pluralist model.
In community politics, the theory that power is widely dispersed with different leaders in different issue areas responding to the wishes of various interest groups as well as voters.

more important actors in political life. And organizations cannot function without leaders. In the words of European sociologist Robert Michels, "He who says organization, says oligarchy."[3]

POWER IN "MIDDLETOWN"   One of the earliest studies of American communities, the classic study of Middletown, conducted by sociologists Robert and Helen Lynd in the mid-1920s and again in the mid-1930s, confirmed a great deal of elitist thinking about community power.[4] The Lynds found in Muncie, Indiana, a monolithic power structure dominated by the owners of the town's largest industry. Community power was firmly entrenched in the hands of the business class, centering on, but not limited to, the "X family."[5] The power of this group was based upon its control over the economic life in the city, particularly its ability to control the extension of credit. The city was run by a "small top group" of "wealthy local manufacturers, bankers, the local head managers of . . . national corporations with units in Middletown, and . . . one or two outstanding lawyers." Democratic procedures and governmental institutions were so much window dressing for business control. The Lynds described the typical city official as a "man of meager calibre" and as "a man whom the inner business control group ignores economically and socially and uses politically." Perhaps the most famous quotation from the Lynds' study was a comment by a Middletown man made in 1935:

> If I'm out of work, I go to the X plant; if I need money I go to the X bank, and if they don't like me I don't get it; my children go to the X college; when I get sick I go to the X hospital; I buy a building lot or house in the X subdivision; my wife goes downtown to buy X milk; I drink X beer, vote for X political parties, and get help from X charities; my boy goes to the X YMCA and my girl to their YWCA; I listen to the word of God in X subsidized churches; if I'm a Mason, I go to the X Masonic temple; I read the news from the X morning paper; and, if I'm rich enough, I travel via the X airport.[6]

Perhaps the most influential elitist study of community politics was sociologist Floyd Hunter's *Community Power Structure,* a study of Atlanta, Georgia. According to Hunter, no one person or family or business dominated "Regional City" (a synonym for Atlanta), as might be true in a smaller town. Instead, Hunter described several tiers of community influentials, with business leaders dominating the top tier. (See "*Up Close:* Power in 'Regional City.'") The top decision makers were not formally organized but frequently met informally and passed down decisions to government leaders, city organizations, and other "figure heads."

THE PLURALIST MODEL   Modern pluralism does not mean a commitment to "pure democracy," where all citizens participate directly in decision making. The underlying value of individual dignity continues to motivate contemporary pluralist thought, but it is generally recognized that the town-meeting type of pure democracy is not really possible in an urban industrial society. To modern pluralists, individual participation has come to mean membership in *organized groups*. Interest groups become the means by which individuals gain access to the political system. Government is held responsi-

UP CLOSE

POWER IN "REGIONAL CITY"

Floyd Hunter's study of "Regional City" (Atlanta)[a] was very discomforting in suggesting that American communities were not really governed in a democratic fashion. Hunter's research challenged the notion of "grass-roots" democracy and raised doubts as to whether or not the cherished values of Jeffersonian democracy were being realized in civic life.

Hunter reported that a hierchially organized power structure in Atlanta made the major policy decisions for the city. Other substructures—governmental, religious, educational, professional, civic, and cultural—merely implemented these decisions. The substructures

> . . . are subordinate, however, to the interests of the policy makers who operate in the economic sphere of community life in Regional City. The institutions of the family, church, state, education, and the like draw sustenance from economic institutional sources and are thereby subordinate to this particular institution more than any other. . . . Within the policy forming groups the economic interests are dominant.[b]

Top power holders seldom operated openly. "Most of the top personnel in the power group are rarely seen in the meetings attended by the associational understructure personnel in Regional City."[c]

In Hunter's description of community decision making, decisions tended to flow *down* from top policy makers, composed primarily of business and financial leaders, to civic, professional, and cultural association leaders, religious and education leaders, and government officials, who implemented the program; and the masses of people had little direct or indirect participation in the whole process. Policy did not go *up* from associational groupings or from the people themselves.

Power in "Regional City"

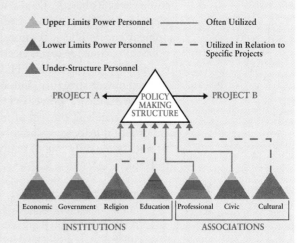

Source: Reprinted from *Community Power Structure: A Study of Decision Makers,* by Floyd Hunter. Copyright © 1953 by the University of North Carolina Press. Used by permission of the publisher.

According to Hunter, elected public officials are clearly part of the lower-level institutional substructure, which "executed" policy rather than formulated it. Finally, Hunter found that this whole structure was held together by "common interests, mutual obligations, money, habit, delegated responsibilities, and in some cases, by coercion and force."

[a]Floyd Hunter, *Community Power Structure* (Chapel Hill: University of North Carolina Press, 1953).
[b]Ibid., p. 94.
[c] Ibid., p. 90.

ble, not directly by individuals, but by organized interest groups and political parties. Pluralists believe that competition between parties and organized groups, representing the interests of their citizen members, can protect the dignity of the individual and offer a viable alternative to individual participation in decision making.

The pluralist model of community power stresses the fragmentation of authority, the influence of elected public officials, the importance of organized group activity, and the role of public opinion and elections in determining public policy. Who rules in the pluralist community? "Different small groups of interested and active citizens in different issue areas with some overlap, if any, by public officials, and occasional intervention by a large number of people at the polls."[7]

POWER IN NEW HAVEN   Perhaps the most influential of the pluralist community studies was Robert A. Dahl's *Who Governs?*, a detailed analysis of decision making in New Haven, Connecticut. Dahl chose to examine sixteen major decisions on redevelopment and public education in New Haven and on nominations for mayor in both political parties for seven elections. Dahl found a polycentric and dispersed system of community power in New Haven, in contrast to Hunter's highly monolithic and centralized power structure. Influence was exercised from time to time by many individuals, each exercising power over some issue but not over others. When the issue was one of urban renewal, one set of individuals was influential; in public education, a different group of leaders was involved. Business elites, who were said by Hunter to control Atlanta, were only one of many different influential groups in New Haven. According to Dahl,

> The economic notables, far from being a ruling group, are simply one of many groups out of which individuals sporadically emerge to influence the politics and acts of city officials. Almost anything one might say about the influence of the economic notables could be said with equal justice about a half dozen other groups in the New Haven community.[8]

The mayor of New Haven was the only decision maker who was influential in most of the issue areas studied, and his degree of influence varied from issue to issue:

> The mayor was not at the peak of a pyramid but at the center of intersecting circles. He rarely commanded. He negotiated, cajoled, exhorted, beguiled, charmed, pressed, appealed, reasoned, promised, insisted, demanded, even threatened; but he most needed support and acquiescence from other leaders who simply could not be commanded. Because he could not command them, he had to bargain.[9]

ELITISM IN AMERICAN COMMUNITIES

All known societies have some system of ranking their members. Sociologists use the term *stratification* to refer to the classification of individuals and the ranking of these classes along a superiority–inferiority scale. The United States Constitution guarantees legal and political equality of individuals, especially in its Equal Protection Clause; but in most other dimensions of society—income and wealth, occupation and institutional position, social status and lifestyle—we recognize differences among individuals and rank these differences according to their desirability.

■
Stratification.
The classification of individuals in society and their ranking along a superiority-inferiority scale.

POWER AND SOCIAL CLASS   The American system of stratification tends to be diamond shaped: a small upper class, a large middle class, and a somewhat smaller lower class. The advantage of numbers—an important source of power in the electoral system—accrues to the middle class, not the lower class. All other sources of power are distributed unequally from top to bottom:

- *Economic power.* The top stratum enjoys great wealth and income and control of corporations, banks, and other economic enterprises. The middle stratum has job skills, occupational positions, and moderate amounts of personal wealth and income. The lower stratum is largely economically dependent. Individuals in this stratum receive more governmental revenues than they produce.

- *Institutional position.* The top stratum occupies positions of authority in institutions that organize society's resources—corporations, banks, utilities, television networks and stations, newspapers, foundations, universities, law firms, civic and cultural organizations. The middle stratum occupies middle- and lower-level positions in these same organizations and may also occupy key positions in government, unions, recreational associations, and churches. The bottom stratum is seldom organized at all. Indeed, most organizations claiming to represent the poor are run by middle- and upper-class people.

- *Social status and lifestyle.* The top stratum enjoys education, travel, leisure, clubs, and a social and cultural life that is widely envied. The middle classes try to emulate the upper-class lifestyles and succeed to a limited degree. But lower-class lifestyle is restricted; goals are immediate and limited, and activities are protective or escapist.

Community decision making takes place within a stratified social system. It defies common sense to argue, as pluralists do,[10] that community decisions are *unaffected* by the stratification of economic power, institutional position, and lifestyle. Public officials—mayors, council members, commissioners, school board members, authority directors, and board members—as well as managers, administrators, and public employees, civic association officers, and interest group officers, all function within the larger stratified society. They must maintain and enhance their own income, position, and lifestyle; and their behavior will be patterned by the system of stratification.

Power is exercised in open public decisions *and* in the distribution of advantages and disadvantages among individuals and groups within society. Systemic power refers to influence that is attributed to the stratification system's distribution of advantages and disadvantages. It is the power that the top stratum enjoys because of its income and wealth, positional authority, and status and lifestyle.[11]

ANTICIPATED REACTIONS Systemic power may take many forms. Power is being exercised when public officials or administrators base their own behavior on the anticipated reactions of powerful people within the community. *A* has power over *B* if *B* modifies his or her conduct because of fear of *A*'s reaction or a need to stay in *A*'s good graces to obtain some future benefit. Note that *A* and *B* do not have to communicate directly. *A* may not even know what *B* is doing (or not doing) to win favor; there is no open public decision. The strength of this power relationship is determined by the distribution of wealth and income, position, and lifestyle in the larger society, and the desire of public officials and administrators to maintain and enhance their share of these benefits now or in the future.

AGENDA SETTING In agenda setting, power is being exercised in the selection of topics or problems to be addressed by government. Power is being exercised when someone suppresses an issue that might adversely affect their interests if it came up for

Systemic power. Influence attributable to the stratification system's distribution of advantages and disadvantages.

Anticipated reactions. In community politics, the tendency of public officials, without being told to do so, to make decisions that will win them favor among powerful people.

Agenda setting. In community politics, the power to decide what issues or problems will be addressed by government.

■

Non–decision making.
In community politics, limiting the scope of decision making to only those issues that are relatively unthreatening to power holders.

Opportunity costs.
In community politics, the resources required to call attention to issues and win favorable outcomes.

Public decision making.
Decisions affecting a community made by governmental bodies in open public meetings.

Private decision making.
Decisions affecting a community made by private individuals and businesses.

a public vote on the council. This is a direct yet covert exercise of power. But power is also being exercised by groups who regularly succeed in getting their issues placed on a crowded agenda when there is competition for the space. Power is also being exercised when other groups are unable to attract public attention to their problems or articulate their problems and present their case for public action.

NON–DECISION MAKING   Power is also exercised when social or political values or institutions limit public consideration to only those issues that are relatively unthreatening to the power holders.[12] *A* is exercising power over *B* when *A* succeeds in suppressing issues that might in their resolution be seriously detrimental to *A*'s preferences. In other words, elites exercise power when they prevent issues from becoming public controversies. This exercise of power is known as "non–decision making."[13] The pluralist researcher who concentrates his or her attention on open "concrete decisions" may overlook the possibility that public decision making has been deliberately limited to relatively noncontroversial matters, notwithstanding the fact that there are serious latent conflicts in a community.

OPPORTUNITY COSTS   With opportunity costs, power is being exercised when the costs of political success are higher for some groups than others. Persons in the top social stratum must expend a smaller proportion of their total resources than persons in the bottom social stratum to achieve a political goal. "The weak must struggle while the strong have only to ask."[14] Public officials and administrators frequently ask business and community leaders, "what things need doing?" The poor, by contrast, frequently need protests, marches, or direct action to call attention to their concerns. "The truly powerful are often able to achieve their aims with little effort, whereas those who are less powerful must make a much greater effort to achieve the same results."[15]

The disadvantaged in society often appear passive and quiescent. The pluralist researcher is obliged to conclude that they confront no serious problems or concerns. But quiescence may only signify that the poor are not well positioned to act on their grievances. With few resources, they cannot undertake costly battles that they are likely to lose. Indeed, when the poor *do* act politically, it is usually on behalf of some immediate and tangible benefit, rather than long-range or fundamental change. It is logical for the poor to spend their limited political resources for short-term goals with some likelihood of success.

DIFFERENT MODELS FOR PUBLIC AND PRIVATE DECISIONS   Perhaps elitist and pluralist models of community power can be reconciled by recognizing that some community decisions are public, that is, made by governmental bodies, while others are private, made by real estate developers, banks and mortgage companies, builders and land owners, investors and business people. Private decisions may have as much or even more impact on life in a community than decisions made by government. The pluralist model may be better suited for understanding public decision making, while the elite model may better describe private decision making. Indeed, many pluralists now acknowledge that economic elites have a "privileged position" regarding decisions that are vital to society.[16] If we are to understand the full range of decisions that shape the community—public and private—we will have to consider both public and private power. This requires an integration of studies of governmental decision making with studies of systemic forces—economic power, institutional position, social status, and lifestyle.

DIFFERENT MODELS PORTRAY DIFFERENT COMMUNITIES   Finally, power structures may vary across communities. Some communities may have more concentrated, pyramidal structures of power dominated by economic elites, while other communities may have diffused and multicentered power structures with competing citizens' groups, neighborhood associations, developers, environmentalists, and so forth. For example, large communities with a great deal of social and economic diversity, a competitive party system, and a variety of well-organized competing interest groups may tend to have *pluralist* decision-making systems. On the other hand, small communities with homogeneous populations, a single dominant industry, nonpartisan elections, and few competing organizations may have power structures resembling the *elite* model.

ECONOMIC POWER IN COMMUNITIES

Great power derives from control of economic resources. Most of the nation's economic resources are controlled by national institutions—industrial corporations, banks, utilities, insurance companies, investment firms, and the national government. Most of the forces shaping life in American communities arise outside of these communities; community leaders cannot make war or peace, or cause inflation or recession, or determine interest rates or the money supply.

CONTROL OF LAND USE   But there is one economic resource—land—which *is* controlled by communities. Land is a valuable resource: Capital investment, labor and management, and production must be placed somewhere. Traditionally, community power structures were composed primarily of economic elites whose goals were to maximize land values, real estate commissions, builders' profits, rent payments, and mortgage interest, as well as to increase revenues to commercial enterprises serving the community. Communities were traditionally dominated by mortgage-lending banks, real estate developers, builders, and landowners. They were joined by owners or managers of local utilities, department stores, attorneys and title companies, and others whose wealth was affected by land use. Local bankers who financed the real estate developers and builders were often at the center of the elite structure in communities. Unquestionably these community elites competed among themselves for wealth, profit, power, and preeminence. But they shared a consensus about intensifying the use of land. Corporate plants and offices, federal and state office buildings, and universities and colleges all contributed to the increased land values, not only on the parcels used by these facilities but also on neighboring parcels.

GROWTH AS SHARED ELITE VALUE   Growth was the shared elite value. The community elite was indeed a "growth machine."[17] Economic growth expands the work

■

"Growth machine."
In community politics, a reference to the consensus among elites that economic growth is in the common interest.

force and disposable income within the community. It stimulates housing development, retail stores, and other commercial activity. The economic elite understands that they all benefit, albeit to varying degrees, when economic growth occurs within the community. Not only must a community compete for new investments, but it must also endeavor to prevent relocation of investments it already has.

Attracting investors required the provision of good transportation facilities—highways, streets, rail access, and water and airport facilities. It required the provision of utilities—water, gas and electrical power, solid waste disposal, and sewage treatment. It required the provision of good municipal services, especially fire and police protection; the elimination of harassing business regulations and the reduction of taxes on new investments to the lowest feasible levels; the provision of a capable and cooperative labor force, educated for the needs of productive capital and motivated to work; and finally, the provision of sufficient amenities—cultural, recreational, aesthetic—to provide the corporate managers with a desirable lifestyle.

ELITE STRIVING FOR CONSENSUS   Community economic elites usually strive for consensus. They believe that community economic growth—increased capital investment, more jobs, and improved business conditions—benefit the entire community. According to Paul E. Peterson, community residents share a common interest in the economic well-being of the city:

> Policies and programs can be said to be in the interest of cities whenever the policies maintain or enhance the economic position, social prestige, or political power of the city as a whole.[18]

Community economic elites themselves would doubtlessly agree with Peterson. He adds that the interests of the city as a whole are closely bound to its export industries. These industries add net wealth to the community at large, while support and service industries merely transfer wealth within the community.

> Whatever helps them prosper redounds to the benefit of the community as a whole—perhaps four or five times over. It is just such an economic analysis (of the multiplier effect of export industries) that has influenced many local government policies. Especially the smaller towns and cities may provide free land, tax concessions, and favorable utility rates to incoming industries.[19]

The less economically developed a community, the more persuasive the argument on behalf of export industries.

GROWTH AS GOOD POLITICS   Economic elites expect local government officials to share in the growth consensus. Economic prosperity is necessary for protecting the fiscal base of local government. Growth in local budgets and public employment, as well as governmental services, depends upon growth in the local economy. Governmental growth expands the power, prestige, and status of government officials. Moreover, economic growth is usually good politics. Growth-oriented candidates for public office usually have larger campaign treasuries than antigrowth candidates. Growth-oriented candidates can solicit contributions from the community power structure. Finally, according to Peterson, most local politicians have "a sense of community responsibility." They know that if the economy of the community declines, "local business will suffer, workers will lose employment opportunities, cultural life will decline, and city land values will fall."[20]

POLITICAL POWER IN COMMUNITIES

Today, in many American communities, older economic elites have been replaced by newer political elites. Many of the old economic elites sold their businesses to national corporations and vacated their positions of community leadership. Locally owned stores and factories became manager-directed plants and chain stores. The result was a weakening of community loyalties in the business sector. The new corporate managers could easily decide, in response to national economic conditions, to close the local plant or store with minimal concern for the impact on the community. Local banks were merged into national banking corporations and local bankers were replaced by banking executives with few community ties. City newspapers that were once independently owned by families who lived in the communities were bought up by giant newspaper and publication chains. Instead of editors and reporters who expected to live the lives of their communities, city newspapers came to be staffed with people who hope to move up in the corporate hierarchy—people who strive primarily to advance their own careers, not the interests of the local community.

Professional politicians have moved into this vacuum in city after city, largely replacing the local bankers, real estate developers, chambers of commerce, and old-style newspaper editors who had dominated community politics for generations. The earlier economic elites were only part-time politicians who used local government to promote their economic interests. The new professional political elites work full time at local politics. They are drawn primarily by personal ambition, not so much for the wealth as for the power and celebrity that accompany running for and winning public office. They are not "screened" by economic elites or political parties, but rather they nominate themselves, raise their own funds, organize their own campaigns, and create their own publicity.

OPPOSITION TO GROWTH   Consensus on behalf of economic growth is sometimes challenged by political elites in communities. However much the economic elite may strive for consensus, some people do not like growth, and they are willing to use political power to stop it. Indeed, it has become fashionable in upper-middle-class circles today to complain loudly about the problems created by growth—congestion, pollution, noise, unsightly development, or the replacement of green spaces with concrete slabs. People who already own their houses and do not intend to sell them, people whose jobs are secure in government bureaucracies or tenured professorships, people who may be displaced from their homes and neighborhoods by new facilities, people who see no direct benefit to themselves from growth, and businesses or industries who fear the new competition that growth may bring to the community, all combine to form potentially powerful political alliances.[21]

■
**"No growth"
movement.**
In community politics, organized opposition to new residential, commercial, or
industrial development.

"Growth management."
In community politics, the
term preferred by opponents
of growth, suggesting that
growth should be limited to
that which does not change
the appearance or lifestyle of
the community.

City planning.
The original term for local
government's role in determining the location of streets
and other public facilities.

Not all of the opposition to growth is upper-middle-class in character. Students of community power have described the struggle of blacks and low-income neighborhood groups in opposing urban renewal and downtown city development. However, this literature suggests that traditional community elites are likely to be successful against this kind of opposition. We might speculate that the "growth machine" elites are more concerned about opposition from educated, affluent, upper-middle-class, "growth-management" homeowners than they are about opposition from minority, low-income neighborhood groups.

NO-GROWTH MOVEMENTS   No-growth movements (or, to use the current euphemism, "growth-management" movements) are *not* mass movements. They do *not* express the aspirations of workers for jobs or renters for their own homes. Instead, they reflect upper-middle-class lifestyle preferences of educated, affluent, articulate homeowners. Growth brings ugly factories, cheap commercial outlets, hamburger stands, fried chicken franchises, and "undesirable" residents. Even if new business or industry would help hold down local taxes, these affluent citizens would still oppose it. They would rather pay the higher taxes associated with no growth than change the appearance or lifestyle of their community. They have secure jobs themselves and own their homes; they are relatively unconcerned about creating jobs or building homes for less affluent citizens.

No-growth movements challenge traditional economic elites in many large and growing cities in the West and South. The no-growth leaders may themselves have been beneficiaries of community growth only five or ten years ago, but they quickly perceive their own interest in slowing or halting additional growth. Now that they have climbed the ladder to their own success, they are prepared to knock the ladder down to preserve their own style of living.

CONTROLLING THE USE OF LAND   The most significant and far-reaching powers of local governments in the United States center on their control of land use. Land is a scarce and valuable resource. Historically, its use was determined by private owners responding principally to free market economic forces—putting their land to its most productive use. But over time, land use decisions have been largely removed from private property owners and placed in the hands of local government agencies. Local governments respond to both economic and political forces in determining how land within their communities is to be used.

EARLY CITY PLANNING   City planning began in antiquity with the emergence of the first cities. Governing authorities have long determined the location of streets, squares, temples, walls, and fortresses. Most early American cities were planned as a gridiron of streets and squares in the fashion of William Penn's plan for Philadelphia in 1682. A notable exception to the gridiron pattern was Pierre L'Enfant's 1791 plan for Washington, DC, with radial streets slashing through the gridiron.[22] Until the early twentieth century, city planning was focused almost exclusively on the layout of streets and the location of public buildings and parks. A city's "master plan" was a map showing the location of present and future streets and public facilities. There was relatively little regulation of the use of private property.

COMPREHENSIVE PLANNING

But the reform movement of the early twentieth century (see "Reformers and Do-Gooders" in Chapter 11) brought with it a much broader definition of planning. "Comprehensive planning" involves not only the determination of the location of *public* facilities but also the control of *private* land uses.

Comprehensive planning involves the identification of community goals, the development of plans to implement these goals, and the use of governmental tools to influence and shape private and public decision making to serve these goals. Community goals are identified not only in land use and physical development policies, but also in those for population growth, health and safety, housing and welfare, education, transportation, economic development, culture, lifestyle and beautification, historic preservation, and environmental protection. According to the American Institute of Planners (AIP), planning is "a comprehensive, coordinated and continuing process, the purpose of which is to help public and private decision makers arrive at decisions which promote the common good of society."[23] Obviously this extended definition of planning plunges the planner deep into the political life of the community.

CONSTITUTIONAL CONCERNS—THE TAKINGS CLAUSE

How far can government go in regulating the use of property without depriving individuals of their property rights? The U.S. Constitution (Fifth Amendment) states clearly: "nor shall private property be taken for public use without just compensation." Taking land for highways, streets, and public buildings, even when the owners do not wish to sell, is known as eminent domain. A city or state must go to court and show that the land is needed for a legitimate public purpose; the court will then establish a fair price (just compensation) based on testimony from the owner, the city or state, and impartial appraisers. Eminent domain is a constitutional protection to American citizens against arbitrary government seizure of their land.

But what if a government does not "take" ownership of the property, but instead restricts the owner's use of it through regulation? Zoning ordinances, subdivision regulations, environmental regulations, or building and housing codes may reduce the value of the property to the owner. Should the owner be compensated for loss of use?

Courts have always recognized that governments can make laws to protect the health, safety, and general welfare of its citizens. Owners of property have never been entitled to any compensation for obeying laws or ordinances with a clear public purpose. But it was not clear that zoning restrictions were legitimate public purposes until 1926 when the U.S. Supreme Court upheld city zoning ordinances as "a proper exercise of police powers."[24] Cities are *not* required to compensate owners for lost value as a result of zoning regulations. Yet it was still argued that some planning and zoning provisions, especially those designed for beauty and aesthetics, had no relation to public health, safety, and welfare. They simply enacted somebody's taste over that of their neighbor. But in 1954 the U.S. Supreme Court upheld a very broad interpreta-

Comprehensive planning.
Local government involvement in determining community goals not only in land use and physical development, but also in population growth, health and safety, transportation, environment, and so forth.

Takings clause.
The clause in the U.S. Constitution's Fifth Amendment that prohibits government from taking private property without just compensation.

Eminent domain.
The judicial process by which government can take private property for public use by providing fair (just) compensation.

■
Regulatory devaluations.
Losses to property owners
resulting from government
regulations of land use.

tion of the police power: "It is within the power of the legislature to determine that the community should be beautiful as well as healthy, spacious as well as clean, well-balanced as well as carefully patrolled."[25] So it is difficult to challenge the constitutionality of planning and zoning as a "taking" of private property without compensation.

"TAKINGS"—WHEN CITIES GO TOO FAR   However, the U.S. Supreme Court has held that a regulation that denies a property owner *all* economically beneficial use of land (e.g., a state coastal zone management regulation preventing any construction on a beach lot) was a "taking" that required just compensation to the owner in order to be constitutional.[26] The Takings Clause of the Constitution's Fifth Amendment was designed to protect private property from unjust taking by government. Its purpose is "to bar Government from forcing some people alone to bear public burdens which, in all fairness and justice, should be borne by the public as a whole."[27] If a community wants open spaces, wildlife preserves, environmental havens, historic buildings, or other amenities, these should be paid for by all of the citizens of the community. Property should not be taken from private owners, even for public purposes, without compensation. All citizens should share in the costs of providing community amenities, not just the owners of particular properties.

The question remains, however, how far can government go in regulating land use without compensating property owners? Depriving land owners of *all* beneficial uses of their land without compensation is clearly unconstitutional. But what if their use of their land is devalued by 50 percent or 25 percent? Are governments constitutionally required to compensate them in proportion to their losses? In the past, federal courts have ruled that "mere diminution" in the value of property is not a "taking" within the meaning of the Fifth Amendment and hence does not require government to compensate landowners. However, in recent years both Congress and the federal courts, as well as some states, have undertaken to reconsider "how far" government can go in depriving property owners of valued uses of their land. Increasingly, regulatory devaluations of 50 percent or more are becoming highly suspect, and property owners have a reasonable chance of recovering compensation from governments.

PLANNING AND ZONING: INSTRUMENTS OF GOVERNMENT CONTROL

State laws authorize and often mandate that cities develop comprehensive plans. Traditionally the comprehensive plan was prepared by semi-independent *planning commissions* composed of private citizens appointed by the mayor and approved by the city council. These commissions rely heavily on *professional planners* to prepare the comprehensive plan. Professional planners are mostly university graduates in city planning. They are organized into the American Institute of Planners (AIP), which publishes its own journal and grants professional credentials to planners. Over time, however, independent, citizen planning commissions are gradually being replaced with planning departments within city government that are directly responsible to the mayor and council.

DEVELOPING POLITICAL SUPPORT FOR PLANNING   Citizen planning commissions are still retained in many communities to facilitate citizen input into the planning process and to develop political support for the comprehensive plan. Planning commissions often hold public hearings on the comprehensive plans and proposed changes to it.

The decisions of professional planners and planning commissions are officially considered advisory. That is, the comprehensive plan must be enacted by the city council to become law. The recommendations of the planning commission can be overturned by the city council. But the advice of a prudent planning staff, with the support of influential private citizens on the planning commission, cannot be easily ignored.

Planners, like reformers generally, claim to represent the welfare of the community as a whole. They are usually hostile to what they perceive to be narrow, self-serving interests in the community, especially business people, real estate developers, and property owners.

THE INFLUENCE OF PLANNERS   While the formal role of planners is advisory, they can have a substantial influence on community policy. In smaller cities, planners may be preoccupied with the day-to-day administration of the zoning and subdivision control ordinances. They may have insufficient time or staff to engage in genuine long-range comprehensive planning. In large cities, the planning staff may be the only agency that has a comprehensive view of community development. Although they may not have the power to "decide" about public policy, they can "initiate" policy discussions through their plans, proposals, and recommendations. The planners can project the image of the city of the future and thereby establish the agenda of community decision making. Their plans can initiate public discussion over the goals and values to be implemented in the community. The comprehensive plan can be a tool for mobilizing public interest in community development.

OPPOSITION TO PLANNING   There are, of course, some limitations on the influence of planners. First of all, many important decisions in community development are made by private enterprise rather than by government. Real estate interests, developers, builders, and property owners make many of the key decisions that shape the development of the community. Their actions are often determined by the economics of the marketplace. Property owners will try to find a way to make the most profitable use of their land, the ideas of the planners notwithstanding. Second, the planners can only advise policy makers; they are just one voice among many attempting to influence public decisions about land use and physical development.

The free market usually does a better job of allocating resources in a society than does government. Opponents of government planning and land use control argue that the decisions of thousands of individual property owners result in a better allocation of land than the decisions of government bureaucrats. Decentralized marketplace decisions allow more rapid adjustment to change and satisfy the preferences of more people than centralized bureaucratic decision making. Marketplace prices signal the most appropriate uses of land, just as they do the most appropriate uses of other resources.

Opponents also argue that requiring government permits for land uses—for new commercial, industrial, or residential developments and for new homes, buildings, or other structures—adds to the time and costs of development and the size of government bureaucracy (see Table 13-1). By adding to the costs of housing, planning places owning homes beyond the reach of many middle-class families. By adding to the costs of industry, or banning new industrial development altogether, planning limits the number of jobs created in a community. By empowering local officials to describe how land will be used, individual citizens are deprived of an important individual freedom.

Table 13–1

THE PRIVATE COSTS OF LOCAL PLANNING AND PERMITTING: SO YOU WANT TO BUILD AN OFFICE?

The following cost estimates for planning and permitting were compiled by a CPA firm for the construction of a small (10,000 sq. ft.) office building on a two-acre site in Tallahassee, Florida. The estimates assume complete *conformity* with all existing planning, zoning, building, environmental, and land use requirements. These are costs of *planning and permitting*, not construction!

Requirement	Time	Compliance Costs
Submit land use compliance inquiry to planning department	2 days	$530.00
Receive land use compliance certificate	10 days	—
Complete traffic and stormwater studies	30 days	$10,948.00
Receive water, sewer, and traffic certificates	10 days	$35,800.00
Prepare preliminary site plan	3 days	$1,500.00
Pre-application conference with planning department	15 days	—
Environmental Impact Part I review	7 days	$3,360.00
Approval from environmental management department	21 days	—
Prepare final site plan	14 days	$9,100.00
Approval of final site plan by planning review committee	45 days	—
Environmental Impact Part II review	2 days	$1,410.00
Receive environmental and building permits	60 days	$23,220.00
Total	206 days (6–7 months)	$85,868.00

Source: Based on a report in *Tallahassee Democrat*, April 28, 1993, p. 4D. Estimates by Moore, Bass & Bibler.

ZONING   Planning agencies usually prepare the zoning ordinance for the approval of the city council. The zoning ordinance divides the community into districts for the purpose of regulating the use and development of land and buildings. Zoning originated as an attempt to separate residential areas from commercial and industrial activity, thereby protecting residential property values. The zoning ordinance divides the community into residential, commercial, and industrial zones, and perhaps subdivisions within each zone, such as "light industrial" and "heavy industrial," or "single-family residential" and "multifamily residential." Owners of land in each zone must use their land in conformity with the zoning ordinance; however, exceptions are made for people who have used the land in a certain way before the adoption of the zoning ordinance. An ordinance cannot prevent a person from using the land as one has done in the past; thus, zoning laws can only influence land use if they are passed prior to the development of a community. Many new and rapidly expanding communities pass zoning ordinances too late—after commercial and industrial establishments are strung out along highways, ideal industrial land is covered with houses, good park and recreational land has been sold for other purposes, and so on.

Since the planning agency prepares the zoning ordinances as well as the comprehensive plan, the ordinance is expected to conform with the plan. In many communities, the role of the planning agency is strengthened by the requirement that a city council *must* submit all proposed changes in the zoning ordinance to the planning agency for its recommendation before any council action.

Changes in the zoning ordinance usually originate at the request of property owners. They may wish to change the zoning classification of their property to enhance its value—for example, to change it from single-family to multifamily residential, or from residential to commercial. Usually the planning agency will hold a public hearing on a proposed change before sending its findings and recommendation to the city council. The city council may also hold a public hearing before deciding on the change.

City councils can and sometimes do ignore the recommendations of their planning agencies when strong pressures are exerted by neighborhood groups or environmentalists opposed to rezoning, or by developers and property owners supporting it. However, the recommendations of planning agencies prevail in the vast majority of rezoning cases, indicating the power of the planners in community affairs.[28]

A zoning variance is a request for a limited and specific variation from the strict standards in a zoning ordinance as applied to a particular piece of property. Some cities create special boards to hear requests for zoning variances, and other cities allow their planning agency to grant zoning variances. The zoning variance may be the most abused of all zoning procedures. It is not intended to encourage "spot" zoning, grant special privileges, or circumvent the interest of the zoning ordinance, but this is frequently what happens.

SUBDIVISION CONTROL   Another means of implementing the master plan is subdivision regulations, which govern the way in which land is divided into smaller lots and made ready for improvements. Subdivision regulations, together with the zoning ordinance, may specify the minimum size of lots, the standards to be followed by real estate developers in laying out new streets, and the improvements developers must

Zoning.
Local government ordinances that divide communities into various residential, commercial, and industrial zones, and that require landowners to use their land in conformity with the regulations for the zone in which it is located.

Zoning variance.
An exception to the zoning ordinance applied to a particular piece of property.

Subdivision control.
Regulations governing the dividing of land areas into lots.

■
Building codes.
Local government regulations requiring building permits and inspections of new construction to ensure compliance with detailed specifications.

Capital improvements.
The planned schedule of new public projects by a local government.

provide, such as sewers, water mains, parks, playgrounds, and sidewalks. Often planning agencies are given direct responsibility for the enforcement of subdivision regulations. Builders and developers must submit their proposed "plats" for subdividing land and for improvements to the planning commission for approval before deeds can be recorded.

OFFICIAL MAP   The planning agency also prepares the *official map* of the city for enactment by the council. The official map shows proposed, as well as existing, streets, water mains, public utilities, and the like. Presumably, no one is permitted to build any structures on land that appears as a street or other public facility on the official map. Many cities require the council to submit to the planning agency for their recommendation any proposed action that affects the plan of streets or the subdivision plan and any proposed acquisition or sale of city real estate.

BUILDING AND CONSTRUCTION CODES   Most cities have building codes designed to ensure public health and safety. These codes are lengthy documents specifying everything from the thickness of building beams and the strength of trusses, to the type of furnaces, electric wiring, ventilation, fireproofing, and even earthquake resistance that must be incorporated into buildings. No construction may be undertaken without first obtaining a building permit, which must be prominently displayed at the building site. Building inspectors are then dispatched periodically to the site to see if work is progressing in conformance with the building codes. The planning agency does not usually administer the code (that is normally the function of a building or housing department), but the planners are usually consulted about proposed changes in the building code.

Housing codes are designed to bring existing structures up to minimum standards. They set forth minimum requirements for fire safety, ventilation, plumbing, sanitation, and building condition. As with building codes, enforcement is the responsibility of city government, but the planning commission is normally consulted about changes in the code.

CAPITAL IMPROVEMENTS   Comprehensive planning can also be implemented through a *capital improvement program*. This program is simply the planned schedule of public projects by the city—new public buildings, parks, streets, and so on. Many larger cities instruct their planning agencies to prepare a long-range capital improvement program for a five- or ten-year period. Of course, the council may choose to ignore the planning commission's long-range capital improvement program in its decisions about capital expenditures, but at least the planning commission will have expressed its opinions about major capital investments.

ENVIRONMENTAL REGULATIONS   Governments have increasingly turned to environmental laws and regulations to assert control over community development. State laws or local ordinances may designate "areas of critical concern" in an effort to halt development. Designation of such areas is usually very subjective; they may be swamps, forests, waterfront, or wildlife habitats, or even historic, scenic, or archeological sites. "Critical" may also refer to flood plains or steep hillsides or any other land on which governments wish to halt construction.

States and cities are increasingly requiring developers to prepare "environmental impact statements"—assessments of the environmental consequences of proposed construction or land use change. These statements are usually prepared by professional consultants at added cost to builders and developers.

In most cities and counties, enforcement of environmental regulations is the responsibility of separate environmental departments. This means that landowners and developers usually must deal with two separate bureaucracies. Planning departments are generally consulted in the preparation of environmental regulations.

PLANNING PRACTICES

The formal instruments of land use control are often considered too inflexible for optimum planning. Local governments and private property owners frequently seek ways to avoid the rigidities of zoning and subdivision ordinances and construction codes.[29] These regulations, when applied strictly and uniformly, often limit the freedom of architects and developers, produce a sterile environment through separation of land uses, and lead to excessive court litigation. So planners have increasingly turned to a variety of practices intended to minimize some of the worst consequences of land use regulation.

PUDs   One technique that has grown in popularity in recent years is planned urban development (PUD). PUD ordinances vary but typically they allow developers with a minimum number of acres (e.g., ten, twenty, or more) to have the option of abiding by conventional zoning, subdivision, and building codes, or alternatively submitting an overall site plan for the approval of the planning agency and council. PUD designs usually incorporate mixed residential and commercial uses, perhaps with single-family homes and apartments or condominiums, retail shops, hotels and restaurants, parks and open spaces, all included. Planners and councils often exercise considerable discretion in approving or rejecting or forcing modifications in PUDs, depending on their own preferences.

EXACTIONS AND IMPACT FEES   Many communities require developers to pay substantial fees or give over land to local government in exchange for approval of their land use plans. This practice, known as "exaction," is often defended as a charge to pay the local government's costs in connection with the new development, for example, additional roads or sewers needed or additional schools or parks required for new residents. A closely related practice is that of charging developers "impact fees" that are supposed to compensate the community for increased costs imposed by the development *beyond* the added tax revenues that the development will generate when completed. But it is virtually impossible to accurately calculate impact costs, if indeed a development actually does impose more costs on a community than the revenues it produces. So impact fees become just another cost to developers that are passed on to homebuyers and (through commercial tenants) to consumers.

DEVELOPER AGREEMENTS   Often conflict between local governments and developers are settled through developer agreements. Some states (e.g., California) specifically

■
PUD (planned urban development).
Special ordinances, usually negotiated among developers and city officials, that approve a mixed use—residential, commercial, and/or industrial—development plan.

Impact fees.
Fees required from developers by local governments in exchange for approval of plans, presumably compensating for the increased governmental costs created by the new development.

authorize municipalities to enter into such agreements, bypassing zoning, subdivision, and construction ordinances. In other states, often lawsuits, or the threat of lawsuits, by developers force municipalities into such agreements. The municipality benefits by being able to specify the details of a project. The developer benefits by obtaining a legally binding contract that cannot be changed later by the municipality as the project proceeds to completion.

No-Growth Politics

"No-growth" movements in communities are citizen efforts to halt or restrict population growth and economic development. Generally, no-growthers prefer the phrase "growth management" to "no-growth," implying that not all growth or development is undesirable. However, these movements generally support restrictive zoning laws, costly requirements placed on builders and developers, strong environmental regulations, high "impact fees" on new housing or commercial developments, protection of trees, green spaces, historic sites, and so on. Unrestricted growth threatens the aesthetic preferences of upper-middle-class homeowners. It brings congestion, noise, pollution, ugly factories, cheap commercial outlets, hamburger stands, fried chicken franchises, and "undesirable" residents.

WHO ARE THE NO-GROWTHERS?   Opposition to growth is generally concentrated among well-educated, upper-middle-class, white residents who own their own homes and whose income does not directly depend upon the economic health of the community. College and university faculty are fertile grounds for antigrowth movements. Home-owning, elderly persons on Social Security or retirement income often join in opposition to community change.[30] Restrictions on development help inflate the prices of existing homes. Hence it is in the economic interest of homeowners, once they have acquired their own homes, to oppose further development. While the rhetoric of "growth management" usually cites environmental, scenic, or historic rationales for limiting growth, the deliberate inflation of existing property values provides an economic interest in opposition to new development.

Generally, the traditional "community power structure" supports growth. Real estate developers, builders, mortgage bankers, and retail merchants generally seek to encourage economic development. However, occasionally larger, better-financed developers may support costly and cumbersome planning restrictions as a means of forcing smaller developers out of the local real estate market.

TACTICS OF NO-GROWTHERS   "No-growth" movements are influential in many large and growing cities—for example, Denver, Phoenix, San Francisco, San Jose, and Tucson. More importantly, *many upper-middle-class suburban communities* (even those in metropolitan areas with declining core cities) view growth restrictions as in their own interest. These cities may restrict growth through zoning laws, subdivision-control restrictions, utility regulations, building permits, environmental regulations, and even municipal land purchases. Zoning laws can rule out multifamily dwellings or specify only large expensive lot sizes for homes. Zoning laws can exclude heavy or "dirty" industrial development, or restrict "strip" commercial development along highways. Opposition to street widening, road building, or tree cutting can slow or halt development. Public utilities needed for development—water lines, sewage disposal, fire houses, and so on—can be postponed indefinitely. High development fees, utility hookup charges, or building permit costs can all be used to discourage growth. Unrealistic antipollution laws can also discourage growth. If all else fails, a community can buy up vacant land itself or make it a "wildlife refuge."

EFFECTS ON THE POOR Note that the burden of these policies falls not only on builders and developers (who are the most influential opponents of "no-growth" policies), but also on the poor, the working class, minorities, and non–property owners. These groups need the jobs that business and industry can bring to a community, and they need reasonably priced homes in which to live.

By restricting the supply of housing in a community, no-growth policies increase its costs. Higher housing costs restrict access for minorities and the poor. Indeed, many "growth-management" policies do not limit population growth but rather discourage the movement of minorities and the poor into a community.[31]

When suburban communities restrict growth, they are often distributing population to other parts of the metropolitan area.[32] The people kept out do not cease to exist; they find housing elsewhere in the metropolitan area. They usually end up imposing greater costs on other municipalities—central cities or larger, close-in suburbs—which are less able to absorb these costs than the wealthier upper-middle-class communities that succeeded in excluding them. What appears to be a local "growth" issue may be in reality a metropolitan "distribution" issue.

THE NIMBY SYNDROME Opponents of growth can usually count on help from community residents who will be directly inconvenienced by particular projects. Even people who would otherwise support new commercial or housing developments or new public facilities may voice the protest, "Not in my backyard!" earning them the NIMBY label. Many Americans want growth; they just do not want it near them.[33]

NIMBYs may be the noisiest of protest groups. They are the homeowners and voters who are most directly affected by a private or public project. They can organize, sue, petition, and demonstrate to block projects. And virtually every project inspires NIMBY opposition. NIMBYs are particularly active regarding waste disposal sites, incinerators, highways, prisons, mental health facilities, low-income public housing projects, power plants, pipelines, and factories.

NIMBYs are formidable opponents. While they may constitute only a small portion of the community, they have a very large stake in defeating a project. They have a strong motivation to become active participants—meeting, organizing, petitioning, parading, demonstrating. The majority of the community may benefit from the project, but because each person has only a small stake in its completion, no one has the same strong motivation to participate as the NIMBYs. Government agencies and private corporations seeking to locate projects in communities are well-advised to conduct professional public relations campaigns well in advance of ground breaking. When the power of the NIMBYs is added to that of "no-growth" forces, economic development can be stalemated.

■

NIMBY.
An acronym for "not in my backyard," referring to residents who oppose nearby public or private projects or developments.

■

Mortgage insurance.
Federal guarantees of home mortgages that allow lenders to offer homebuyers lower down payments and lower interest charges.

Public housing.
Federally aided housing programs carried out by local government agencies for low-income residents.

HOUSING AND COMMUNITY DEVELOPMENT POLICY

For over a half century, the federal government has pursued a national goal of "a decent home and suitable living environment for every American family." And the nation has made impressive strides toward achieving that goal. Today nearly two-thirds of all Americans own their own homes. Yet problems remain. Low-cost housing is in short supply. Homeownership is declining, especially among younger families. Indeed, liberals and conservatives alike agree that "affordability" is the principal problem facing American housing today.

The national effort in housing is centered in the U.S. Department of Housing and Urban Development (HUD). HUD is the federal department concerned primarily with mortgage insurance, public housing, community development, and related programs.

MORTGAGE INSURANCE   The federal government began as early as 1934 to guarantee private mortgages against default by the individual home buyer. The Federal Housing Administration (FHA), now a part of HUD, insures home mortgages and thereby helps banks, savings and loan associations, and other lending agencies to provide long-term, low down-payment mortgages for Americans wishing to buy their own homes. After checking the credit rating of the prospective buyer, FHA assures the private mortgage lender—bank, savings and loan company, or insurance company—of repayment of the loan in case the home buyer defaults. This reduces the risk and encourages mortgage lenders to offer more loans, lower down payments, and longer repayment periods. While these advantages in borrowing assist middle-class home buyers, note that the direct beneficiaries of mortgage insurance are the banks and mortgage-lending companies who are insured against losses. The Department of Veterans Affairs also provides VA insurance for veterans seeking mortgages.

FHA and VA mortgage insurance has been extremely successful in promoting homeownership among millions of middle-class Americans who have financed their homes through federally insured mortgages.

A great many of these mortgages financed suburban homes. In fact, the success of mortgage insurance programs may have contributed to the deterioration of the nation's central cities by enabling so many middle-class white families to acquire homes in the suburbs and leave the city behind. The FHA's mortgage insurance program is an entirely federal program, but its impact on city and suburban governments should not be underestimated.

HUD also subsidizes and insures apartment projects for low- and moderate-income families and housing projects for the elderly and handicapped. It also provides flood insurance and risk insurance in areas where private insurance is difficult to obtain.

THE TROUBLED HISTORY OF PUBLIC HOUSING   The Housing Act of 1937 initiated federal public housing programs to provide low-rent public housing for the poor who could not afford decent housing on the private market. The public housing program was designed for people without jobs or incomes sufficient to enable them to afford homeownership, even with the help of FHA mortgage insurance. HUD makes loans and grants to local public housing authorities established by local governments to build, own, and operate low-cost public housing. These housing authorities keep rents low in relation to their tenants' ability to pay. This means that local housing authorities operate at a loss and the federal government reimburses them. No community is required to have a public housing authority; it must apply to Washington and meet federal standards in order to receive federal financial support.

Public housing functioned fairly well in its early years. Its tenants were mostly working poor who sought temporary housing, could pay some rent, and moved on to the private housing market once their economic status improved. These were the people Congress intended to help when the program was originated during the Great Depression of the 1930s.

But by the 1950s, the occupants of most big-city public housing projects were the chronically unemployed, female-headed households whose only source of income was welfare payments. These occupants could not afford any rent, even for building maintenance costs, and public housing across the country deteriorated. Some public housing projects became uninhabitable.

Very often, the concentration of large numbers of poor persons with a great variety of social problems into a single, mass housing project compounded their problems. The cost of central-city land required many big cities to build high-rises of ten to twenty stories. These huge buildings frequently became unlivable—with crime in the hallways, elevators that seldom worked, drugs and human filth in halls and stairways, and families locking themselves in and alienating themselves from community life. Huge housing projects were impersonal and bureaucratic, and they often failed to provide many of the stabilizing neighborhood influences of the old slums. Children could be raised in public housing projects and never see a regularly employed male head of a household going to and from work. The behavior and value patterns of problem families were reinforced.

Moreover, removing thousands of people from neighborhood environments and placing them in the institution-like setting of large public housing developments very often increased their alienation or separation from society and removed what few social controls existed in the slum neighborhood. A family living in public housing that successfully found employment and raised its income level faced eviction to make room for more "deserving" families. Finally, black groups often complained that public housing was a new form of racial segregation, and, indeed, the concentration of blacks among public housing dwellers does lead to a great deal of de facto segregation in housing projects.

EFFORTS AT PUBLIC HOUSING REFORM Federal housing policy shifted somewhat under the "Great Society" banner of President Lyndon Johnson. The cabinet-level Department of Housing and Urban Development was created in 1965, and efforts began to move federal policy away from large publicly owned housing projects toward subsidies for private developers as well as local public housing agencies to build scatter-site low-income housing. Moreover, recognizing the fact that most public housing residents could not afford rents sufficient to maintain buildings adequately, HUD began subsidizing maintenance and operating costs, as well as capital expenditures, of local housing authorities. HUD limited rents to 25 percent (later raised to 30 percent) of tenants' income. To encourage the private market to provide low-income housing, a subsidy program known as "Section 8" paid rental vouchers to private apartment owners to house the poor. Some Section 8 money went directly to developers for new construction, but scandals eventually led to the elimination of construction subsidies, except for housing for the elderly and disabled.

During the Reagan and Bush presidencies, federal housing policy tilted toward "privatization"—greater efforts to encourage private developers to provide affordable low-income housing, as well as encouragement to tenants in public housing to manage their own developments and eventually purchase their own units. HUD Secretary Jack Kemp developed Home Ownership for People Everywhere (HOPE) to help public housing residents buy their units; but relatively few units were sold under HOPE, as residents confronted the problem of paying future maintenance costs of their purchased units.

PUBLIC HOUSING TODAY   Today there are about 3,400 local public housing authorities nationwide. They house about 3.4 million residents who pay no more than 30 percent of their income in rent. These residents are among the nation's poorest citizens; in 1992 the average *family* income in public housing was $7,394.[34] Most of this income is in the form of government welfare payments; only about one-quarter of public housing residents depend primarily on earned income. Over 1 million eligible families are on the waiting lists of public housing authorities for units to become available. Many "troubled" local housing authorities and projects have been taken over by HUD.[35] Some of the worst buildings have been demolished, and HUD now encourages local authorities to evict drug dealers.

COMMUNITY DEVELOPMENT   In the original Housing Act of 1937, the ideal of "urban renewal" was closely tied to public housing. Slums were to be torn down as public housing sites were constructed. Later in the Housing Act of 1949, the urban renewal program was separated from public housing, and the federal government undertook to support a broad program of urban redevelopment to help cities fight a loss in population and to reclaim the economic importance of the core cities. After World War II, the suburban exodus had progressed to the point where central cities faced slow decay and death if large public efforts were not undertaken. Urban renewal could not be undertaken by private enterprise because it was not profitable; suburban property was usually cheaper than downtown property, and it did not require large-scale clearance of obsolete buildings. Moreover, private enterprise did not possess the power of eminent domain, which enables the city to purchase the many separately owned small tracts of land needed to ensure an economically feasible new investment. For many years, the federal government provided financial support for specific renewal projects in cities.

■
Urban renewal.
The original term for federally aided programs carried out by local government agencies to rebuild blighted areas of central cities.

Community development block grants.
Consolidated federal grants to cities for planning, redevelopment, and public housing.

COMMUNITY DEVELOPMENT BLOCK GRANTS   In the Housing and Community Development Act of 1974, federal development grants to cities were consolidated into community development block grant (CDBG) programs. Cities and counties were authorized to receive these grants to assist them in eliminating slums; increasing the supply of low-income housing; conserving existing housing; improving health, safety, welfare, and public service; improving planning; and preserving property with special value. Community development block grants are based on a formula that includes population, housing overcrowding, and extent of poverty. No local "matching" funds are required. Communities are required to submit an annual application that describes their housing and redevelopment needs, and a comprehensive strategy for meeting those needs.

To ensure that the CDBG program remains targeted on the poor, the legislation requires localities and states to certify that not less than 60 percent of their CDBG funds are spent on activities that benefit low- and moderate-income persons. Low- and moderate-income persons are defined as those persons whose income does not exceed 80 percent of the median income for the area.

Community development block grants can be used by local authorities to acquire blighted land, clear off or modernize obsolete or dilapidated structures, and make downtown sites available for new uses. When the sites are physically cleared of the old structures, they can be resold to private developers for residential, commercial, or industrial use, and the difference between the costs of acquisition and clearance and the income from the private sale to the developers is paid for by the federal government. In other words, local authorities sustain a loss in their redevelopment activities, and this loss is made up by federal grants.

No city is required to engage in redevelopment, but if cities wish federal financial backing, they must show in their applications that they have developed a comprehensive program for redevelopment and the prevention of future blight. They must demonstrate that they have adequate building and health codes, good zoning and subdivision control regulations, sufficient local financing and public support, and a comprehensive plan of development with provisions for relocating displaced persons.

ECONOMICS OF DEVELOPMENT   Urban redevelopment is best understood from an economic standpoint. The key to success is to encourage private developers to purchase the land and make a heavy investment in middle- or high-income housing or in commercial or industrial use. In fact, before undertaking a project, local authorities frequently "find a developer first, and then see what interests that developer." The city cannot afford to purchase land, thereby taking it off the tax rolls, invest in its clearance, and then be stuck without a buyer. A private developer must be encouraged to invest in the property and thus enhance the value of the central city. Over time a city can more than pay off its investment by increased tax returns from redeveloped property and hence make a "profit." Thus, many people can come out of a project feeling successful—the city increases its tax base and annual revenues, the private developer makes a profit, and mayors can point to the physical improvements in the city that occurred during their administrations.

RELOCATION   Relocation is the most sensitive problem in redevelopment. Most people relocated by redevelopment are poor and black. They have no interest in moving simply to make room for middle- or higher-income housing, or business or industry, or universities, hospitals, and other public facilities. Even though relocated families are frequently given priority for public housing, there is not nearly enough space in public housing to contain them all. They are simply moved from one slum to another. The slum landowner is paid a just price for the land, but the renter receives only a small moving allowance. Redevelopment officials assist relocated families in finding new housing and generally claim success in moving families to better housing. However, frequently the result is higher rents, and redevelopment may actually help to create new slums in other sections of the city. Small business owners are especially vulnerable to relocation. They often depend on a small, well-known neighborhood clientele, and they cannot compete successfully when forced to move to other sections of the city.

POLITICS AND DEVELOPMENT   Political support for redevelopment has come from mayors who wish to make their reputation by engaging in large-scale renewal activities that produce impressive "before" and "after" pictures of the city. Business owners wishing to preserve downtown investments and developers wishing to acquire land in urban centers have provided a solid base of support for downtown renewal. Mayors, planners, the press, and the good-government forces have made urban redevelopment politically much more popular than public housing.

TRANSPORTATION POLICY

Few inventions have had such a far-reaching effect on the life of the American people as the automobile. Henry Ford built one of the first gasoline-driven carriages in America in 1893, and by 1900 there were 8,000 automobiles registered in the United States. The Model T was introduced in the autumn of 1908. By concentrating on a single unlovely but enduring model, and by introducing the assembly line processes, the Ford Motor Company began producing automobiles for the masses. Today, there are nearly 200 million registered motor vehicles in the nation and 3.9 million miles of roads. (See "*Rankings of the States:* Public Road and Street Mileage.")

HIGHWAY POLITICS   Highway politics are of interest not only to the automotive industry and the driving public, but also to the oil industry, the American Road Builders Association, the cement industry, the railroads, the trucking industry, the farmers, the outdoor advertising industry, and the county commissioners, taxpayer associations, ecologists and conservationists, and neighborhood improvement associations. These political interests are concerned with the allocation of money for highway purposes, the sources of funds for highway revenue, the extent of gasoline and motor vehicle taxation, the regulation of traffic on the highways, the location of highways, the determination of construction policies, the division of responsibility among federal, state, and local governments for highway financing and administration, the division of highway funds between rural and urban areas, and many other important outcomes in highway politics.

EARLY FEDERAL AID   It was in the Federal Aid Road Act of 1916 that the federal government first provided regular funds for highway construction under terms that gave the federal government considerable influence over state policy. For example, if states wanted to get federal money, they were required to have a highway department, and to have their plans for highway construction approved by federal authorities. In

PUBLIC ROAD AND STREET MILEAGE

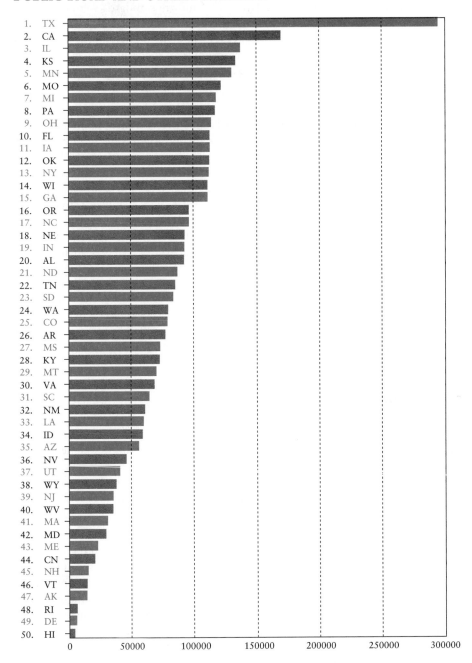

1. TX
2. CA
3. IL
4. KS
5. MN
6. MO
7. MI
8. PA
9. OH
10. FL
11. IA
12. OK
13. NY
14. WI
15. GA
16. OR
17. NC
18. NE
19. IN
20. AL
21. ND
22. TN
23. SD
24. WA
25. CO
26. AR
27. MS
28. KY
29. MT
30. VA
31. SC
32. NM
33. LA
34. ID
35. AZ
36. NV
37. UT
38. WY
39. NJ
40. WV
41. MA
42. MD
43. ME
44. CN
45. NH
46. VT
47. AK
48. RI
49. DE
50. HI

Source: U.S. Department of Transportation, Federal Highway Administration.

1921, federal aid was limited to a connected system of principal state highways, now called the "federal aid primary highway system." Uniform standards were prescribed and even a uniform numbering system was added, such as "US 1," or "US 30." The emphasis of the program was clearly rural. Later, the federal government also designated a federal aid "secondary" system of farm-to-market roads and provided for "urban extensions" of primary roads, in addition to the federal aid for the primary highway system.

THE INTERSTATE SYSTEM   Congress authorized a national system of interstate and defense highways in 1956 ("I" highways). The interstate system is the most important feature of the federal highway policy. Costs are allocated on the basis of 90 percent federal and 10 percent state. The Federal Highway Act of 1956, as amended, authorized 46,000 miles of highway, designed to connect principal metropolitan areas and industrial centers and thereby shifted the emphasis of federal highway activity from rural to urban needs. Although the system constitutes less than 2 percent of the total surfaced roads in the nation, it carries over 20 percent of all highway traffic. The U.S. Department of Transportation has been given strong supervisory powers, including the selection of routes, but administration and execution are still left to state highway departments. Federal monies are paid to the states, not to the contractors, as the work progresses.

The highways in the interstate system were originally designed to last twenty years. Currently the system is widely in need of repair, as are many highways throughout the states (see *"Rankings of the States:* Highway Conditions"). In 1998 Congress passed the largest transportation spending bill in history.

FEDERAL HIGHWAY MONEY   Revenue from the federal gasoline tax has long been "earmarked" for the Federal Highway Trust Fund. Since 1970, federal highway trust fund money has also been allocated to urban mass transit. Although the current federal gasoline tax is now nine cents per gallon, the revenue from this tax alone is insufficient to repair and maintain the nation's highway system.

Congress generally recognizes the need to rebuild the nation's highways. The real political fireworks center on requirements that Congress attaches to the receipt of federal highway funds.

SPEED LIMITS   An example of the controversies generated by federal highway policy was the long battle over speed limits. Prior to 1974 most states had speed limits of 70 miles per hour on interstate highways. A national speed limit of 55 was enacted by Congress during the Arab oil embargo as a means of saving gasoline. Congress mandated that a state be denied 10 percent of its federal highway aid if it failed to enact and enforce a 55-mph speed limit. But truckers and others who drive a great deal, particularly over long open stretches of interstate highway in the western United States, lobbied hard to eliminate the 55-mph national speed limit. They argued that the costs in billions of additional hours spent on the road were unreasonable, that the 55-mph speed limit was widely ignored anyway, and that it eroded respect for the law. The national speed limit was also seen as symbolic of federal intrusion in state affairs and a

HIGHWAY CONDITIONS

Percentage of roads in each state rated in poor, mediocre, or only fair condition, rather than good

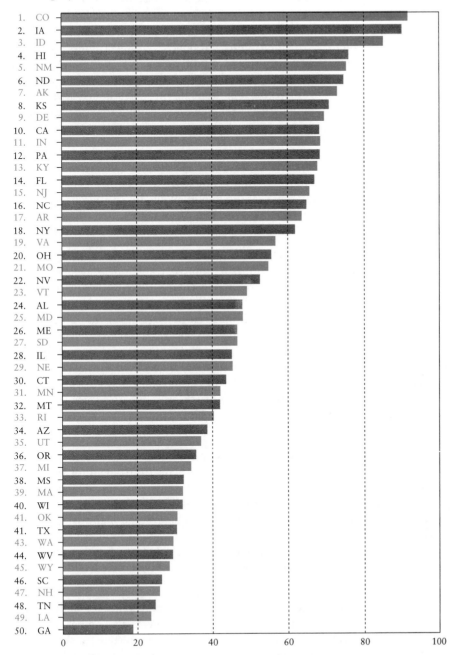

1.	CO	
2.	IA	
3.	ID	
4.	HI	
5.	NM	
6.	ND	
7.	AK	
8.	KS	
9.	DE	
10.	CA	
11.	IN	
12.	PA	
13.	KY	
14.	FL	
15.	NJ	
16.	NC	
17.	AR	
18.	NY	
19.	VA	
20.	OH	
21.	MO	
22.	NV	
23.	VT	
24.	AL	
25.	MD	
26.	ME	
27.	SD	
28.	IL	
29.	NE	
30.	CT	
31.	MN	
32.	MT	
33.	RI	
34.	AZ	
35.	UT	
36.	OR	
37.	MI	
38.	MS	
39.	MA	
40.	WI	
41.	OK	
41.	TX	
43.	WA	
44.	WV	
45.	WY	
46.	SC	
47.	NH	
48.	TN	
49.	LA	
50.	GA	

Source: American Society of Civil Engineers. Based on standards set by the Department of Transportation.

threat to American federalism. However, insurance companies and consumer safety groups lobbied hard to keep the 55-mph speed limit. In 1987 Congress relented; the speed limit on rural portions of interstate highways was raised to 65 mph.

Finally in 1995, twenty-one years after first imposing a national speed limit, Congress returned control of speed limits to the states. Arguments over speed and safety will be heard now in state capitals across the country. Proponents of lower limits argue that "speed kills" and that drivers will always exceed posted limits by 10 mph. Opponents contend that most drivers exceed speed limits only when they are set too low, and that safety is more closely related to enforcement of drunk driving and seat belt laws, as well as with improved auto safety, than with speed limits. Most eastern states have retained the 65-mph limit, but several western states have upped their limit to 70 or 75 mph.

THE TWENTY-ONE-YEAR-OLD DRINKING AGE   Currently, federal law also mandates that the Department of Transportation withhold 10 percent of a state's highway funds if it fails to enact a twenty-one-year-old minimum age for the purchase of alcoholic beverages. (See *"Up Close:* Federalism and the Drinking Age" in Chapter 3.)

TRAFFIC SAFETY   States have the responsibility for licensing drivers and vehicles and enforcing traffic laws. Prominent state efforts to improve traffic safety include mandatory seat belt laws, enforcement of laws prohibiting driving under the influence of alcohol (DWI), and the enforcement of maximum speed limit laws. Mandatory seat belt laws have been shown to more than double seat belt usage (from 20 to 50 percent or more); usage is higher in states where a violation is considered primary (where a driver can be ticketed for nonusage alone) rather than secondary (where a driver can be ticketed for seat belt violation only if stopped for another reason).[36] Studies have generally found that increased seat belt usage (as well as air bags) results in lower traffic fatality rates. Stepped-up enforcement of DWI laws has also been shown to reduce fatalities.[37]

AUTO SAFETY   Under pressure from consumer lobbies and the U.S. Department of Transportation, auto manufacturers gradually improved the safety of their products. The traffic death rate in the United States (the number of deaths from motor vehicle accidents per 100 million miles traveled) was 4.7 in 1970. This rate dropped significantly to 3.2 in 1975 following the federally mandated 55-mph speed limit. But the traffic death rate continued to drop during the 1980s even as average highway speeds returned to previous levels. The number of accidents, about 34 million per year, remained the same, but the death rate dropped to 1.8 by 1993. These figures suggest that auto safety improvements are allowing more people to survive accidents.

HIGHWAY POLITICS   The states retain the principal responsibility for building and maintaining the nation's highways. State and local governments also operate airports, port facilities, and mass transit. For many years, rural interests in state legislatures, together with representatives of the automobile, trucking, and oil industries, dominated transportation politics. Farmers wanted roads to move themselves and their products to cities; and auto, trucking, and oil interests wanted the states to build roads to subsidize their industries. The only opposition came from the railroads, which objected to the subsidization of their competitors, the truckers. But the railroads were an industry in decline, and the highway interests won most of the battles.

Highway interests in the states sought to separate highway departments from general state government and to separate gasoline tax revenues from general state revenues. Highway interests believed that their road-building programs would fare better when organization and funding were not in competition with other state programs. They succeeded in most states in obtaining (1) the creation of separate highway boards and commissions, and (2) the establishment of separate highway trust funds to receive gasoline tax revenues "earmarked" for highway construction and maintenance. Indeed, some states passed constitutional amendments preventing the "diversion" of gasoline taxes for nonhighway purposes. These policies guaranteed a continual flow of road-building funds and gave highways preferential treatment over other public programs. Today some southern and western states retain these special organizational and funding arrangements for highways.

INFRASTRUCTURE INVESTMENT AND ECONOMIC GROWTH   Highway construction, and infrastructure development generally, is widely recognized as a key component of economic development.[38] Nonetheless, while overall government spending has skyrocketed in recent decades, spending for public infrastructure (highways, bridges, ports, airports, sewers, etc.) has stagnated. Despite evidence that spending for highways is linked to economic development,[39] state and local government spending for highway construction and maintenance has declined from about 20 percent of total spending in 1962 to less than 6 percent in 1995.[40] This suggests not only that the nation is failing to invest in *new* public infrastructure, but also that older existing highways, bridges, sewers, and water mains are deteriorating over time.

Investment in public infrastructure—highways, bridges, sewage disposal and water treatment plants, airports, high-speed trains, communications, and even the electronic "superhighway"—is frequently praised by politicians in Washington. But it was very difficult to increase public works spending during the long period of horrendous federal budget deficits. Total federal spending for highways, mass transit, and air and water transportation remained stagnant for many years. Not until 1998 did Congress authorize major new transportation spending. Nonetheless, most public infrastructure spending—over 80 percent of the nation's total—is undertaken by state and local governments.

METROPOLITAN TRANSPORTATION   City planners and transportation specialists argue that the only way to relieve traffic congestion and preserve central cities is to get people out of private automobiles and onto public transit, that is, "to move people, not cars." Automobiles on expressways can move about 2,000 people per lane per hour; buses can move between 6,000 and 9,000; rail systems can carry up to 60,000 people per hour. In other words, one rail line is estimated to be equal to twenty or thirty expressway lanes of automobiles in terms of its ability to move people. Nationwide, many millions of hours are wasted by Americans sitting in traffic (see Table 13-2). The costs of this congestion exceed $100 billion a year, or $470 for every driver in the nation.[41]

Table 13–2

THE MOST CONGESTED BIG CITIES[a]	
Los Angeles, CA	1,921
New York, NY	1,702
San Francisco, CA	662
Washington, DC	631
Chicago, IL	631
Detroit, MI	538
Houston, TX	429
Boston, MA	349
Atlanta, GA	310
Philadelphia, PA	304

[a]Total vehicle hours (000) of delay.

Source: Statistical Abstract of the United States, 1997, p. 631.

However, the average citizen has a large investment in the automobile. Few Americans want to see their financial investment sit in a garage all day. Americans clearly prefer private automobile transportation and costly expressways to mass transit, regardless of the arguments of transportation experts. Only 5 percent of Americans use buses or trains to commute to work (see Table 13-3). The result is that mass transit facilities almost always lose money.

Almost all cities now experience heavy expressway congestion at rush hour and a resulting increase in time and cost to the average automobile commuter. But predictions about future expressway "gridlock" may prove inaccurate. The proportion of daily commuters who drive from the suburbs to work in central cities is gradually decreasing as more businesses move to the suburbs. Intersuburban commuting is increasing over time; circumferential expressways circling cities now carry more traffic than expressways leading into central cities.[42]

Rail-based mass transit facilities are usually designed for city–suburban commuting. As the central city fades as a center for employment and shopping, and more people travel from suburb to suburb, the ridership for mass transit decreases.[43]

Table 13–3

HOW AMERICANS GET TO WORK	
Drive alone	73.2%
Carpool	13.4%
Mass transit	5.3%
Walk	3.9%
Work at home	3.0%
Other	1.2%

Source: Federal Highway Administration, reported in USA Today, June 16, 1994.

THE CASE FOR SUBSIDIES   It is necessary to provide public subsidies to commuter-rail companies or to have governments operate these facilities at a loss if commuter service is to be maintained. Only a small portion of the costs of public transit come from the fares charged riders. However, it is argued that the cost of mass transit subsidies is very small in comparison with the cost of building and maintaining expressways. Thus, mass transit is considered cost-effective for many cities, even if fares do not meet operating expenses. Moreover, new, speedier, more comfortable, air-conditioned, high-capacity trains with fewer stops and more frequent trips may lure many riders back to public transportation.

Mass transit facilities are very costly, particularly for cities that do not already have commuter rail service. Proponents of greater federal aid for mass transit argue that cities and states do not have sufficient resources to build mass transit facilities. They argue that mass transit is cheaper than expressway construction and that expressways can never handle predicted traffic increases anyhow. They emphasize the costs of traffic jams in time and wages lost and their economic impact on central cities. Opponents of federal aid for mass transit object to the idea that the entire nation, including rural areas, should be asked to contribute to solving transportation problems of the nation's cities. Moreover, they are doubtful about the feasibility of convincing Americans that they should give up the convenience of their automobiles for mass transit.

FEDERAL MASS TRANSIT AID   For many years the federal government has subsidized the building of highways, particularly the interstate highways, where the federal government assumed 90 percent of the costs. It was not until the 1970s that the federal government showed any comparable interest in mass transit. (Indeed, the *interstate* highway system, despite its name, has carried a major share of *intra*metropolitan city–suburban traffic.) The energy crisis accelerated federal efforts in mass transit. In the Urban Mass Transit Act of 1974, the U.S. Department of Transportation was authorized to make grants to cities for both construction and operation of mass transit systems. In many cities, this simply meant the creation of a local mass transit authority and the purchase of buses. However, in some cities, massive new mass transit programs were developed with federal funds.

Among the most striking efforts in mass transit were San Francisco's BART (Bay Area Rapid Transit), Washington, DC's METRO, and Atlanta's MARTA (Metropolitan Atlanta Rapid Transit Authority). These are large projects into which the cities and the federal government pumped hundreds of million of dollars. They incorporated all of the latest features of modern, pleasant, rapid, convenient, and efficient mass transit. Nonetheless, ridership cannot pay for continuing operating costs, let alone the enormous costs of construction. Perhaps the worst example of federally subsidized mass transit is Miami's Metrorail. The costs were so great and the ridership so small that critics estimated it would have been cheaper for the federal government to buy every regular rider a Rolls-Royce.

DID YOU KNOW?

THE NATION'S BIGGEST LANDOWNER

Few people realize that the nation's largest landowner is the U.S. government. It owns nearly one-third of the total land area of the United States. Its land use policies are largely determined by the U.S. Department of the Interior. Federal land use policies are particularly important in those states where the U.S. government owns half or more of the total land area.

FEDERAL LAND OWNERSHIP

By % of State

1. Nevada	82.3	10. New Mexico	33.1	19. Michigan	9.8
2. Alaska	67.8	11. Washington	29.0	20. Florida	9.7
3. Utah	63.8	12. District of Columbia	28.2	21. Virginia	7.5
4. Idaho	62.6	13. Montana	27.7	22. Georgia	6.1
5. California	60.6	14. Louisiana	22.6	23. Vermont	6.0
6. Wyoming	48.8	15. Hawaii	16.5	24. South Dakota	5.6
7. Oregon	48.2	16. West Virginia	13.6	25. Mississippi	5.5
8. Arizona	43.3	17. New Hampshire	13.1	26. Kentucky	5.5
9. Colorado	34.1	18. Arkansas	10.2	27. Wisconsin	5.4

Less Than 5%

Tennessee	South Carolina	Illinois
Minnesota	Pennsylvania	Kansas
Missouri	Indiana	Ohio
North Dakota	Oklahoma	Maine
North Carolina	Texas	Rhode Island
Maryland	Alabama	New York
New Jersey	Massachusetts	Connecticut
Delaware	Nebraska	Iowa

Source: U.S. Department of Commerce, Bureau of the Census, *Statistical Abstract of the United States, 1992* (Washington, DC: Government Printing Office, 1992).

ON THE WEB

Community power structures are said to operate largely "behind the scenes." While many large city governments maintain Web sites (see "On the Web," chapter 10), informal yet influential structures of power within cities are unlikely to do so. However, one exception may be Greater Philadelphia First at

www.gpfirst.com

This organization closely parallels the power structure of Philadelphia. It was established in 1983 as an association of "business chief executives from 33 of the region's largest corporations committed to advancing the interests of the community. GPF works to improve the business climate, generate employment by attracting new investment, and market the region nationally and internationally." Its membership includes the chief executives of corporations such as Sun Oil Company, First Union Bank, Mellon Bank, Price Waterhouse, Bell Atlantic, Smith Kline Beacham, the *Philadelphia Inquirer,* and so on. Its published policy agenda includes economic development and educational reform.

The American Planning Association and its professional arm, the American Institute of Certified Planners, represents more than 30,000 planners, officials, and citizens involved in urban planning. It lobbies in

Washington to strengthen planning requirements as conditions for federal grants to states and cities. Its Web site at

www.planning.org

provides extensive information about planning and related subjects. It includes some articles from the organization's monthly publication, *Planning*. For students, it includes a catalog of books on planning, as well as information on how to become a certified planner.

The U.S. Department of Housing and Urban Development (HUD) maintains a Web site at

www.hud.gov

It contains information on all HUD programs including federal home loans, rental assistance, community development grants, and planning grants. A particularly interesting feature at this site is "HUD in Your Community," which allows users to click to their own state and their own city to learn what HUD programs are currently in operation there.

NOTES

1. Gaetano Mosca, *The Ruling Class* (New York: McGraw-Hill, 1939), p. 50.

2. Ibid., p. 51.

3. Robert Michels, *Political Parties* (Glencoe, IL: The Free Press, 1949).

4. Robert S. Lynd and Helen M. Lynd, *Middletown* (New York: Harcourt Brace & World, 1929); and *Middletown in Transition* (New York: Harcourt Brace & World, 1937). Other classic community studies include W. Lloyd Warner et al., *Democracy in Jonesville* (New York: Harper & Row, 1949); and August B. Hollingshead, *Elmtown's Youth* (New York: John Wiley, 1949).

5. The "X family," never identified in the Lynds' books, was actually the Ball family, glass manufacturers. As late as 1975 the Ball family exercised a controlling influence over the Ball Corporation, Ball Brothers Foundation, Ball Memorial Hospital, Muncie Aviation Corp., and Muncie Airport, Inc.; and E. F. Ball served as a director of American National Bank and Trust of Muncie, Borg-Warner Corp., Indiana Bell Telephone Co., Merchants National Bank of Muncie, and Wabash College. Ball State University in Muncie is named for the family.

6. Lynd and Lynd, *Middletown in Transition*, p. 74.

7. Aaron Wildavsky, *Leadership in a Small Town* (Totowa, NJ: Bedminster Press, 1964), p. 8.

8. Robert Dahl, *Who Governs?* (New Haven: Yale University Press, 1961), p. 72.

9. Ibid., p 204.

10. See Nelson W. Polsby, *Community Power and Political Theory*, 2d ed. (New Haven: Yale University Press, 1980).

11. See Clarence N. Stone, "Systemic Power in Community Decision-Making: A Restatement of Stratification Theory," *American Political Science Review*, 74 (December 1980), 978–90.

12. Bachrach and Baratz, "Two Faces of Power," pp. 947–53; Peter Bachrach and Morton S. Baratz, "Decisions and Nondecisions," *American Political Science Review*, 57 (September 1963), 632–42.

13. For an interesting debate over the concept of non–decision making, see Geoffrey Debnam, "Nondecisions and Power: The Two Faces of Bachrach and Baratz," and Peter Bachrach and Morton S. Baratz, "Power and Its Two Faces Revisited," *American Political Science Review*, 69 (September 1975), 889–904; see also Richard M. Merelman, "On the Neo-Elitist Critique of Community Power," *American Political Science Review*, 62 (June 1968), 451–60; Raymond Wolfinger, "Nondecisions and the Study of Local Politics," *American Political Science Review*, 65 (December 1971), 1063–80.

14. Ibid., p. 981.

15. Ibid.

16. Charles E. Lindbloom, *Politics and Markets* (New York: Basic Books, 1977), chap. 13.

17. See Harvey Molotch, "The City as Growth Machine," *American Journal of Sociology*, 82 (September 1976), 309–30; and "Capital and Neighborhood in the United States," *Urban Affairs Quarterly*, 14 (March 1979), 289–312.

18. Paul E. Peterson, *City Limits* (Chicago: University of Chicago Press, 1981), p. 20.

19. Ibid., p. 23.

20. Ibid., p. 29.

21. For a parallel argument, see Heywood T. Sanders and Clarence N. Stone, "Developmental Politics Reconsidered," *Urban Affairs Quarterly,* 22 (June 1987), 521–39; and Mark Schneider, "Undermining the Growth Machine," *Journal of Politics,* 54 (February 1992), 214–30.

22. See Anthony J. Catanese and James C. Snyder, *Urban Planning,* 2d ed. (New York: McGraw Hill, 1988).

23. American Institute of Planners, *AIP Planning Policies* (Washington, DC: Author, 1977).

24. *Village of Euclid, Ohio* v. *Amber Realty Company,* 272 U.S. 365 (1926).

25. *Berman* v. *Parker,* 348 U.S. 26 (1954).

26. *Lucas* v. *South Carolina Coastal Council,* 112 Sup.Ct. 2886 (1992).

27. *Dolan* v. *City of Tigard* (1994).

28. See Arnold Fleischmann and Carol A. Pierannunzi, "Citizens, Development Interests, and Local Land-Use Regulation," *Journal of Politics,* 52 (August 1990), 838–53.

29. See Alan Ehrenhalt, "The Trouble with Zoning," *Governing* (February 1998), 28–34.

30. See Charles E. Connerly and James E. Frank, "Predicting Support for Local Growth Controls," *Social Science Quarterly,* 67 (September 1986), 572–86.

31. See Todd Donovan and Max Neiman, "Local Growth Control Policy and Changes in Community Characteristics," *Social Science Quarterly,* 76 (December 1995), 780–93.

32. For discussions of why suburban communities adopt growth controls, see Mark Baldasarre, *Trouble in Paradise* (New York: Columbia University Press, 1986); John R. Logan and Min Zhou, "The Adoption of Growth Controls in Suburban Communities," *Social Science Quarterly,* 71 (March 1990), 118–29.

33. See Kent E. Portney, "Allaying the NIMBY Syndrome," *Hazardous Waste,* 1(1984), 411–21; and "Coping in the Age of NIMBY," *New York Times,* June 19, 1988.

34. *Congressional Quarterly Weekly Report,* April 10, 1993, p. 970.

35. See William Fulton, "Do Housing Authorities Have a Future?" *Governing* (February 1998), 40–43.

36. Jerome S. Legge, "Policy Alternatives and Traffic Safety," *Western Political Quarterly,* 43 (September 1990), 597–612.

37. For a summary of previous research on the effects of state traffic safety, as well as wellcrafted original research, see David J. Houston, Lilliard E. Richardson, and Grant W. Neeley, "Legislating Traffic Safety," *Social Science Quarterly,* 76 (June 1995), 328–45.

38. Governing's Special Report, "The Public's Capital: A Forum on Infrastructure Issues," *Governing* (July 1992).

39. See Thomas R. Dye, "Taxing, Spending, and Economic Growth in the States," *Journal of Politics,* 42 (November 1980), 1085–87.

40. *Statistical Abstract of the United States, 1997,* p. 300.

41. Ibid., p. 631.

42. U.S. Department of Transportation, *Demographic Change and Worktrip Travel Trends* (Washington, DC: Government Printing Office, 1985).

43. See Peter Gordon and Harry Richardson, "Notes from the Underground: The Failure of Mass Transit," *The Public Interest* (Winter 1989), 77–86.

14
POLITICS AND
CIVIL RIGHTS

QUESTIONS TO CONSIDER
★ ★ ★ ★ ★ ★ ★ ★ ★ ★

Do city government policies change significantly with the election of minority group members to the offices of mayor or city council?

❑ Yes ❑ No

If a city's schools are mostly black and the surrounding suburban schools are mostly white, should busing be used to achieve a better racial balance?

❑ Yes ❑ No

Should state and local governments be color blind with respect to the races in all of their laws and actions?

❑ Yes ❑ No

Do you generally favor affirmative action programs for women and minorities?

❑ Yes ❑ No

From Protest to Power

African Americans and Hispanics have made significant progress in urban politics in recent years. The progress of these minorities in city government has important implications for the future of the American political system, because these are the two largest minority groups in the country. Minorities were almost totally excluded from significant influence in city politics prior to the 1960s. We have already discussed increases in black representation in city councils (Chapter 11) and state legislatures (Chapter 6), and black political power in the nation's largest cities is a recognized fact of American politics. As former Atlanta Mayor Andrew Young said, "It's like the old preacher says: we ain't what we oughta be; we ain't what we gonna be; but thank God we ain't what we was."[1]

Variation in Responsiveness to Urban Minorities One important test of a democratic system is its responsiveness to the demands of newly mobilized groups. Comparative studies of city governments suggest that there are significant variations in their responsiveness to the demands of newly mobilized minority groups. In some cities, quite remarkable levels of responsiveness to minority interests have been achieved, and minority representatives have come to occupy positions of authority and respect. In other cities, white and minority leaders have been wary of each other, though significant concessions to minority interests have been made. And in still other cities, established interests have successfully resisted minority demands.

What determines the success or failure of minorities to gain influence in urban politics? The conditions associated with minority success appear to be:

- The absolute size of minority groups in the city.
- The size of supportive groups, especially white liberals.
- A strategy of combining protests with a willingness to form electoral coalitions.
- Protests by themselves produce only limited results. Extreme protests delay progress.[2]

Protest alone is insufficient to bring about lasting political change. Protest must be accompanied by political mobilization, the formation of electoral coalitions, and winning public office.

Policy Consequences of Minority Representation Do city government policies change as a result of minority incorporation into the political system? Black elected officials in cities perceive poverty and unemployment as more severe problems than do white officials in the same cities; and black officeholders are more likely to add race relations and racial balance in the distribution of city jobs and services to the policy agenda.[3] Another consequence of the election of blacks to public office, especially the mayor's office, is an increase in political participation among black citizens.[4]

But many city government policies, especially taxing and spending policies, are severely constrained by economic conditions and by limits and mandates set by the state and federal governments.[5] So it is unrealistic to expect major shifts in these policies to accompany the election of African Americans or Hispanics to city office. The policies that respond to minority representation in city government are those that deal directly with minority presence in government. Broad taxing and spending policies are largely *un*affected by minority influence in government. Examples of the kind of policy changes directly attributable to minority representation in government include the creation of police review boards, the appointment of more minorities to city boards and commissions, increasing use of minority contractors, and a general increase in the number of programs oriented toward minorities. Perhaps the most significant policy impact of minority representation on city councils is an increase in the number of minorities in city employment and their employment in higher-grade positions.[6]

THE STRUGGLE AGAINST SEGREGATION

The Fourteenth Amendment of the U.S. Constitution declares:

> All persons born or naturalized in the United States, and subject to the jurisdiction thereof, are citizens of the United States and of the State wherein they reside. No State shall make or enforce any law which shall abridge the privileges or immunities of citizens of the United States; nor shall any State deprive any person of life, liberty, or property, without due process of law; nor deny to any person within its jurisdiction the equal protection of the laws.

The language of the Fourteenth Amendment and its post–Civil War historical context leave little doubt that its original purpose was to achieve the full measure of citizenship and equality for African Americans. Some "radical" Republicans were prepared in 1867 to carry out the revolution in southern society that this amendment implied. Under military occupation, southern states adopted new constitutions that awarded the vote and full civil liberties to African Americans, and southern states were compelled to ratify the Thirteenth, Fourteenth, and Fifteenth Amendments to the U.S. Constitution. African American were elected to southern state legislatures and to the Congress; the first African American to serve in Congress, Hiram R. Revels, took over the U.S. Senate seat from Mississippi previously held by Confederate President Jefferson Davis.

However, by 1877 Reconstruction was abandoned. The national government was not willing to carry out the long and difficult task of really reconstructing society in the eleven states of the former Confederacy.[7] In what has been described as the "Compromise of 1877," the national government agreed to end military occupation of the South, give up its efforts to rearrange southern society, and lend tacit approval to white supremacy in that region. In return, the southern states pledged their support of the Union, accepted national supremacy, and agreed to permit the Republican candidate, Rutherford B. Hayes, to assume the presidency after the disputed election of 1876.

"SEPARATE BUT EQUAL"   The Supreme Court adhered to the terms of the compromise. The result was an inversion of the meaning of the Fourteenth Amendment so that by 1896 it had become a bulwark of segregation. State laws segregating the races were upheld so long as persons in each of the separated races were treated equally. The con-

■

Segregation.
Separation of people by
race; mandated by law in
schools and public facilities
in southern states prior to
the U.S. Supreme Court decision in *Brown v. Board of
Education of Topeka* in
1954, and prior to the Civil
Rights Act of 1964.

"Separate but equal."
The ruling by the U.S.
Supreme Court in 1896 that
segregated facilities were
lawful as long as the facilities were equal; a ruling reversed by the Court in
*Brown v. Board of Educa-
tion of Topeka* in 1954.

stitutional argument on behalf of segregation under the Fourteenth Amendment was
that the phrase "equal protection of the laws" did not prevent state-enforced separation of the races. Schools and other public facilities that were "separate but equal"
won constitutional approval.[8] This separate but equal doctrine remained the Supreme
Court's interpretation of the Equal Protection Clause of the Fourteenth Amendment
until 1954.

As a matter of fact, of course, segregated facilities, including public schools, were
seldom if ever equal, even with respect to physical conditions. In practice, the doctrine
of segregation was "separate and *un*equal." The Supreme Court began to take notice
of this after World War II. While it declined to overrule the segregationist interpretation of the Fourteenth Amendment, it began to order the admission of individual
blacks to white public universities, where evidence indicated that separate black institutions were inferior or nonexistent.[9]

NAACP   Leaders of the newly emerging civil rights movement in the 1940s and
1950s were not satisfied with court decisions that examined the circumstances in each
case to determine if separate school facilities were really equal. The National Association for the Advancement of Colored People (NAACP), led by Roy Wilkins, its executive director, and Thurgood Marshall, its chief counsel, pressed for a court decision
that segregation itself meant inequality within the meaning of the Fourteenth Amendment, whether or not facilities were equal in all tangible respects. In short, they wanted
a complete reversal of the "separate but equal" interpretation of the Fourteenth
Amendment, and a holding that laws *separating* the races were unconstitutional.

The civil rights groups chose to bring suit for desegregation in Topeka, Kansas,
where segregated black and white schools were equal with respect to buildings, curricula, qualifications and salaries of teachers, and other tangible factors. The legal strategy was to prevent the Court from ordering the admission of a black because *tangible*
facilities were not equal and to force the Court to review the doctrine of segregation itself.

BROWN V. BOARD OF EDUCATION OF TOPEKA   On May 17, 1954, the Court rendered
its decision in *Brown v. Board of Education of Topeka, Kansas:*

> Segregation of white and colored children in public schools has a detrimental effect upon
> the colored children. The impact is greater when it has the sanction of law, for the policy
> of separating the races is usually interpreted as denoting the inferiority of the Negro
> group. A sense of inferiority affects the motivation of a child to learn. Segregation with
> the sanction of law, therefore, has a tendency to retard the educational and mental devel-
> opment of Negro children and to deprive them of some of the benefits they would re-
> ceive in a racially integrated school system.[10]

The symbolic importance of the original *Brown v. Board of Education of Topeka* decision cannot be overestimated. While it would be many years before any significant
number of black children would attend formerly segregated white schools, the decision
by the nation's highest court undoubtedly stimulated black hopes and expectations.
African American sociologist Kenneth Clark writes:

This [civil rights] movement would probably not have existed at all were it not for the 1954 Supreme Court school desegregation decision which provided a tremendous boost to the morale of Negroes by its *clear* affirmation that color is irrelevant to the rights of American citizens. Until this time the Southern Negro generally had accommodated to the separatism of the black from the white society.[11]

STATE RESISTANCE TO DESEGREGATION

The Supreme Court had spoken forcefully in the *Brown* case in 1954 in declaring segregation unconstitutional. From a constituitional viewpoint, any state-supported segregation of the races after 1954 was prohibited. Article VI of the Constitution declares that the words of that document are "the supreme law of the land . . . anything in the constitution or laws of any state to the contrary notwithstanding." From a political viewpoint, however, the battle over segregation was just beginning.

SEGREGATION IN THE STATES   In 1954, the practice of segregation was widespread and deeply ingrained in American life. Seventeen states required the segregation of the races in public schools. These seventeen were:

Alabama	North Carolina	Kentucky
Arkansas	South Carolina	Maryland
Florida	Tennessee	Missouri
Georgia	Texas	Oklahoma
Louisiana	Virginia	West Virginia
Mississippi	Delaware	

The Congress of the United States required the segregation of the races in the public schools of the District of Columbia.[12] Four additional states—Arizona, Kansas, New Mexico, and Wyoming—authorized segregation upon the option of local school boards. (See Figure 14–1.)

Thus, in deciding *Brown* v. *Board of Education of Topeka,* the Supreme Court struck down the laws of twenty-one states and the District of Columbia in a single opinion. Such a far-reaching decision was bound to meet with difficulties in implementation. The Supreme Court did not order immediate nationwide desegregation, but instead it turned over the responsibility for desegregation to state and local authorities under the supervision of federal district courts.

The six border states with segregated school systems—Delaware, Kentucky, Maryland, Missouri, Oklahoma, and West Virginia—together with the school districts in Kansas, Arizona, and New Mexico that had operated segregated schools, chose not to resist desegregation. The District of Columbia also desegregated its public schools the year following the Supreme Court's decision.

RESISTANCE   Resistance to school integration was the policy of the eleven states of the Old Confederacy. Refusal of a school district to desegregate until it was faced with a federal court injunction was the most common form of delay. Other schemes included state payment of private school tuition in lieu of providing public schools,

FIGURE 14–1
Segregation Laws
in the United
States in 1954

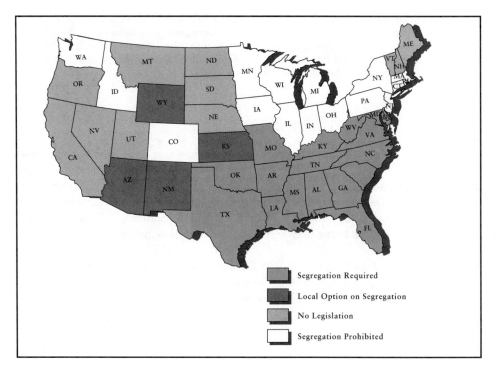

amending compulsory attendance laws to provide that no child shall be required to attend an integrated school, requiring schools faced with desegregation orders to cease operation, and the use of pupil-placement laws to avoid or minimize the extent of integration.[13] State officials also attempted to delay desegregation on the grounds that it would endanger public safety.[14] On the whole, those states that chose to resist desegregation were quite successful in doing so during the ten-year period from 1954 to 1964. Ten years after *Brown* v. *Board of Education of Topeka,* only about 2 percent of the black schoolchildren in the eleven southern states were attending integrated schools.

FEDERAL FUNDS   In the Civil Rights Act of 1964, Congress finally entered the civil rights field in support of court efforts to achieve desegregation. Among other things, the Civil Rights Act of 1964 provided that every federal department and agency must take action to end segregation in all programs and activities receiving federal financial assistance. It was specified that this action was to include termination of financial assistance if states and communities receiving federal funds refused to comply with federal desegregation orders. Acting under the authority of Title VI, the U.S. Office of Education (now the Department of Education) required all school districts in the seventeen formerly segregated states to submit desegregation plans as a condition of federal assistance. Progress toward desegregation was speeded up.

UNITARY SCHOOLS   The last vestige of legal justification for delay in implementing school desegregation collapsed in 1969 when the Supreme Court rejected a request by

Mississippi school officials for a delay in implementing school desegregation plans in that state. The Supreme Court declared that every school district was obligated to end dual school systems "at once" and "now and hereafter" to operate only unitary schools.[15] The effect of the decision—fifteen years after the original *Brown* case—was to eliminate any further legal justification for the continuation of segregation in public schools.

BUSING AND RACIAL BALANCING IN SCHOOLS

In *Brown* v. *Board of Education of Topeka, Kansas,* the Supreme Court found that segregation had "a tendency to retard the educational and mental development of Negro children and to deprive them of some of the benefits they would receive in a racially integrated school system." The U.S. Civil Rights Commission reported that even when segregation was "de facto," that is, a product of segregated housing patterns and neighborhood schools rather than direct discrimination, the adverse effects on African American students were still significant.[16] In northern urban school districts, the commission reported, predominantly black schools were less likely to have good libraries or advanced courses in sciences and languages than predominantly white schools and more likely to have overcrowded classrooms, poorly trained teachers, and teachers who were dissatisfied with their school assignments.

RACIAL BALANCE   Ending racial isolation in the public schools frequently involves busing schoolchildren into and out of segregated neighborhoods. The objective is to achieve a racial "balance" in public schools, so that each has roughly the same percentages of blacks and whites as are found in the total population of the entire school district. Indeed, in some large cities where blacks comprise the overwhelming majority of public school students, desegregation may require city students to be bused to the suburbs and suburban students to be bused to the core city.

FEDERAL COURT SUPERVISION   Federal district judges enjoy wide freedom in fashioning remedies for past or present discriminatory practices by governments. If a federal district court anywhere in the United States finds that any actions by governments or school officials have contributed to racial imbalances (e.g., in drawing school district attendance lines), the judge may order the adoption of a desegregation plan to overcome racial imbalances produced by official action. A large number of cities have come under federal district court orders to improve racial balances in their schools through busing.

In the important case of *Swan* v. *Charlotte-Mecklenburg Board of Education,* the Supreme Court upheld (1) the use of racial balance requirements in schools and the assignment of pupils to schools based on race, (2) "close scrutiny" by judges of schools that are predominantly of one race, (3) gerrymandering of school attendance zones as well as "clustering" or "grouping" of schools to achieve equal balance, and (4) court-ordered busing of pupils to achieve racial balance.

> Absent a constitutional violation there would be no basis for judicially ordering assignment of students on a racial basis. All things being equal, with no history of discrimina-

■
De facto segregation.
Racial imbalances not directly caused by official action but rather by neighborhood residential patterns.

Busing.
In public schools, the attempt to overcome racial imbalances by assigning pupils to schools by race rather than residence and therefore requiring the busing of students.

tion, it might well be desirable to assign pupils to schools nearest their homes. But all things are not equal in a system that has been deliberately constructed and maintained to enforce racial segregation. The remedy for such segregation may be administratively awkward, inconvenient, and even bizarre in some situations and may impose burdens on some; but all awkwardness and inconvenience cannot be avoided when remedial adjustments are being made to eliminate the dual school system.[17]

The Court was careful to note, however, that racial imbalance in schools is not itself grounds for ordering these remedies, unless it is also shown that some present or past governmental action contributed to the imbalance.

CROSS-DISTRICT BUSING   In the absence of any governmental actions contributing to racial imbalance, states and school districts are *not* required by the Fourteenth Amendment to integrate their schools. Thus, for example, where central-city schools are predominantly black, and suburban schools are predominantly white, owing to residential patterns, cross-district busing is not constitutionally required, unless it is shown that some official action brought about these racial imbalances. The Supreme Court threw out a lower federal court order for massive busing of students between Detroit and fifty-two suburban school districts. Although Detroit city schools were 70 percent black, none of the Detroit-area suburban school districts segregated students within their own boundaries. Chief Justice Burger, writing for the majority, said:

> The constitutional right for the Negro respondents residing in Detroit is to attend a unitary school system in that district. Unless petitioners drew the district lines in a discriminatory fashion, or arranged for the white student residing in the Detroit district to attend schools in Oakland or Macomb counties, they were under no constitutional duty to make provision for Negro students to do so.[18]

In a strong dissent, Justice Thurgood Marshall wrote:

> In the short run it may seem to be the easiest course to allow our great metropolitan areas to be divided up each into cities—one white, the other black—but it is a course, I predict, our people will ultimately regret.

This important decision means the largely black central cities, surrounded by largely white suburbs, will remain de facto segregated because there are not enough white students living within the city to achieve integration.

WHEN IS DESEGREGATION COMPLETE?   Many school districts in the South and elsewhere have operated under federal court supervision for many years. How long should court supervision continue, and what standards are to be used in determining when desegregation has been achieved once and for all? In recent years the Supreme Court under Chief Justice Rehnquist has undertaken to free some school districts from direct federal court supervision. Where the last vestiges of state-sanctioned discrimination have been removed "as far as practicable," the Supreme Court has allowed lower federal courts to dissolve racial balancing plans even though imbalances due to residential patterns continue to exist.[19]

CONTINUING RACIAL SEPARATION AND "WHITE FLIGHT"   Minority students now comprise the overwhelming majority of public school pupils in many large cities (including Detroit, Philadelphia, Boston, Atlanta, Chicago, Baltimore, Cleveland, Memphis, New Orleans, Newark, Richmond, St. Louis, and Washington, DC). In some cities, where extensive busing has been employed, "white flight" from the public schools is so widespread that the schools have ended up more segregated than before busing was imposed.[20] Currently *over two-thirds of all black public school pupils in the United States attend schools that have a majority of black students.*[21] The most racially segregated schools are found in Illinois, Michigan, New York, New Jersey, and Pennsylvania (in that order) with over half of their black pupils attending schools that are 90 to 100 percent black.

"White flight."
The movement of white residents away from central cities to suburbs in response to increasing numbers and percentages of minorities in neighborhoods and schools in the central cities.

QUALITY EDUCATION   The continuation of racial isolation in public schools has caused many educators to focus on the quality of education in predominately minority schools. According to the NAACP: "At the present time, we are more concerned with the quality of education. This has to take precedence over whether the schools are integrated. Having said that, we still support desegregation efforts and busing as a means to that end."[22]

THE CIVIL RIGHTS ACT OF 1964

The initial objective of the civil rights movement in America was to prevent discrimination and segregation as practiced by or supported by *governments,* particularly states, municipalities, and school districts. However, even while important victories for the civil rights movement were being recorded in the prevention of discrimination by governments, particularly in the *Brown* case, the movement began to broaden its objectives to include the elimination of discrimination in all segments of American life, private as well as public.

The Constitution does not govern the activities of private individuals. It is the laws of Congress and the states that govern the conduct of private individuals. When the civil rights movement turned to combating private discrimination, it had to carry its fight into the legislative branch of government. The federal courts could help restrict discrimination by state and local governments and school authorities, but only Congress, state legislatures, and city councils could restrict discrimination practiced by private owners of restaurants, hotels and motels, private employers, and other individuals who were not government officials.

The Civil Rights Act of 1964 passed both houses of Congress by better than a two-thirds favorable vote; it won the overwhelming support of both Republican and Democratic members of Congress. It was signed into law on July 4, 1964. It ranks with the Emancipation Proclamation, the Fourteenth Amendment, and *Brown* v. *Board of Education of Topeka* as one of the most important steps toward full equality for African Americans in America. (See "*People in Politics:* Martin Luther King, Jr.")

Among other things, the Civil Rights Act of 1964 provides:

* That it is unlawful to discriminate or segregate persons on the grounds of race, color, religion, or national origin in any place of public accom-

MARTIN LUTHER KING, JR.

The leadership in the struggle to eliminate discrimination and segregation from private life was provided by a young African American minister, Martin Luther King, Jr. King's father was the pastor of one of the South's largest and most influential congregations, the Ebenezer Baptist Church in Atlanta, Georgia. Martin Luther King, Jr., received his doctorate from Boston University and began his ministry in Montgomery, Alabama. In 1955 the black community of Montgomery began a year-long boycott with frequent demonstrations against the Montgomery city buses over segregated seating practices. The dramatic appeal and the eventual success of the boycott in Montgomery brought nationwide attention to its leader and led to the creation in 1957 of the Southern Christian Leadership Conference.

Nonviolent Direct Action

Under King's leadership the civil rights movement developed and refined political techniques for minorities in American politics, including *nonviolent direct action*. Nonviolent direct action is a form of protest that involves breaking "unjust" laws in an open, "loving," nonviolent fashion. The general notion of civil disobedience is not new; it played an important role in American

history from the Boston Tea Party to the abolitionists who illegally hid runaway slaves, to the suffragettes who demonstrated for women's voting rights, to the labor organizers who formed the nation's major industrial unions, to the civil rights workers of the early 1960s who deliberately violated segregation laws.

The purpose of nonviolent direct action is to call attention, or to "bear witness," to the existence of injustice. In the words of Martin Luther King, Jr., civil disobedience "seeks to dramatize the issue so that it can no longer be ignored." There should be no violence in true civil disobedience, and only "unjust" laws are broken. Moreover, the law is broken "openly, lovingly," with a willingness to accept the penalty. Martin Luther King, Jr., in his famous "Letter from Birmingham City Jail," explained:

> In no sense do I advocate evading or defying the law as the rabid segregationist would do. This would lead to anarchy. One who breaks an unjust law must do it *openly, lovingly* (not hatefully as the white mothers did in New Orleans when they were seen on television screaming, "nigger, nigger, nigger") and with a willingness to accept the penalty. I submit that an individual who breaks a law that conscience tells him is unjust, and willingly accepts the penalty by staying in jail to arouse the conscience of the community over its injustice, is in reality expressing the very highest respect for law.[a]

modation, including hotels, motels, restaurants, movies, theatres, sports areas, entertainment houses, and other places which offer to serve the public. This prohibition extends to all establishments whose operations affect interstate commerce or whose discriminatory practices are supported by state action. (Title II)

- That each federal department and agency shall take action to end discrimination in all programs or activities receiving federal financial assistance in any form. This action shall include termination of financial assistance. (Title VI)

- That it shall be unlawful for any employer or labor union with twenty-five or more persons after 1965 to discriminate against any individual in any fashion in employment, because of his race, color, religion, sex, or national origin, and that an Equal Employment Opportunity Commission shall be established to enforce this provision by investigation, conference, conciliation, persuasion, and, if need be, civil action in federal court. (Title VII)[23]

Marches in Birmingham and Washington

Perhaps the most dramatic confrontation between the civil rights movement and the southern segregationists occurred in Birmingham, Alabama, in the spring of 1963. In support of a request for desegregation of downtown eating places and the formation of a biracial committee to work out the integration of public schools, Martin Luther King, Jr., led several thousand Birmingham blacks in a series of orderly street marches. The demonstrators were met with strong police action, including fire hoses, police dogs, and electric cattle prods. Newspaper pictures of blacks being attacked by police and bitten by dogs were flashed all over the world. More than 25,000 demonstrators, including Dr. King, were jailed.

The Birmingham protest set off demonstrations in many parts of the country; the theme remained one of nonviolence, and it was usually whites rather than blacks who resorted to violence in these demonstrations. The culmination of the nonviolent philosophy was a giant, yet orderly, march on Washington, held on August 28, 1963. More than 200,000 blacks and whites participated in the march, which was endorsed by various labor leaders, religious groups, and political figures. The march ended at the Lincoln Memorial where Martin Luther King, Jr., delivered his most eloquent appeal, "I Have a Dream":

> I have a dream. It is a dream deeply rooted in the American dream. I have a dream that one day this nation will rise up and live up and live out the true meaning of its creed: "We hold these truths to be self-evident; that all men are created equal."

> I have a dream that one day on the red hills of Georgia the sons of former slaves and the sons of former slaveowners will be able to sit down together at the table of brotherhood.

> I have a dream that one day even the state of Mississippi, a desert state sweltering with the heat of injustice and oppression, will be transformed into an oasis of freedom and justice.

> I have a dream that my four little children will one day live in a nation where they will not be judged by the color of their skin but by the content of their character. . . .[b]

It was in response to this march that President John F. Kennedy sent a strong civil rights bill to Congress, which was passed after his death—the landmark Civil Rights Act of 1964. On the night of April 14, 1968, the world's leading voice of nonviolence was killed by an assassin's bullet.

[a]Martin Luther King, Jr., "Letter from Birmingham City Jail," April 16, 1963.
[b]Martin Luther King, Jr., August 28, 1963, at the Lincoln Memorial, Washington, DC.

FAIR HOUSING   For many years "fair housing" had been considered the most sensitive area of civil rights legislation. Discrimination in the sale and rental of housing was the last major civil rights problem on which Congress took action. Discrimination in housing had not been mentioned in any previous legislation; even the comprehensive Civil Rights Act of 1964 made no reference to housing. Prohibiting discrimination in the sale or rental of housing affected the constituencies of northern members of Congress more than any of the earlier, southern-oriented legislation. The prospects for a fair housing law were not very good at the beginning of 1968. When Martin Luther King, Jr., was assassinated, however, the mood of the nation and of Congress changed dramatically, and many felt that Congress should pass a fair housing law as a tribute to the slain civil rights leader. The Civil Rights Act of 1968 prohibited the following forms of discrimination:

- Refusal to sell or rent a dwelling to any person because of race, color, religion, or national origin.

- Discrimination against a person in the terms, conditions, or privileges of the sale or rental of a dwelling, or advertising the sale or rental of a dwelling indicating a preference or discrimination based on race, color, religion, or national origin.

The act applied to all apartments and houses, rented or sold by either real estate developers or by private individuals who used the services of real estate agents. It exempted private individuals who sold their own homes without the services of a real estate agent, provided they did not indicate any preference or discrimination in advertising in the sale or rental of a house.

AFFIRMATIVE ACTION BATTLES

Although the gains of the civil rights movement were immensely important, they were primarily gains in *opportunity,* rather than in *results.* The civil rights movement of the 1960s did not bring about major changes in the conditions under which most African Americans lived in America. Racial politics today center on the actual inequalities between blacks and whites in incomes, jobs, housing, health, education, and other conditions of life.

CONTINUING INEQUALITIES   The issue of inequality is often posed today as differences in the "life chances" of whites, blacks, and Hispanics. Figures can reveal only the bare outline of the life chances in American society (see Table 14–1). The average income of a black family is about 63 percent of the average white family's income. Over 25 percent of all black families are below the recognized poverty line, while only 11 percent of white families live in poverty. The unemployment rate for blacks is over twice as high as that for whites. Blacks are less likely to hold prestigious white-collar jobs in professional, managerial, clerical, or sales work. They do not hold many skilled craft jobs in industry but are concentrated in operative, service, and laboring positions. The civil rights movement opened up new opportunities for black Americans. But equality of *opportunity* is not the same as *absolute* equality.

POLICY CHOICES   What public policies should be pursued to achieve equality in America? Is it sufficient that government eliminate discrimination, guarantee "equality of opportunity," and apply "color-blind" standards to both blacks and whites? Or should government take "affirmative action" to overcome the results of past unequal treatment of minorities—that is, preferential or compensatory treatment to assist minority applicants for university admissions and scholarships, job hiring and promotion, and other opportunities for advancement in life?

The early emphasis of government policy, of course, was nondiscrimination. This approach began with President Harry Truman's decision to desegregate the armed forces in 1948 and was carried through to Title VI and Title VII of the Civil Rights Act of 1964 to eliminate discrimination in federally aided projects and private employment. Gradually, however, policy shifted from the traditional aim of *equality of opportunity* through nondiscrimination alone to affirmative action to establish "goals and timetables" to achieve greater *equality of results* between blacks and whites. While

■
Affirmative action.
Programs pursued by governments or private businesses to overcome the results of past discriminatory treatment of minorities and/or women by giving these groups special or preferential treatment in employment, promotion, admissions, and so forth.

Table 14–1

MINORITY LIFE CHANCES

Median Income of Families					
	1975	1980	1985	1995	1997
White	14,268	21,904	29,152	36,822	37,161
Black	8,779	12,674	16,786	23,054	23,482
Hispanic	9,551	14,716	19,027	23,535	24,906

Percentage of Persons Below Poverty Level					
	1975	1980	1985	1995	1997
White	9.7	10.2	11.4	11.2	11.0
Black	31.3	32.5	31.3	29.3	26.5
Hispanic	26.9	25.7	29.0	30.3	27.1

Percentage of Persons Over 25 Completing		
	HIGH SCHOOL	COLLEGE
White	83	24
Black	74	14
Hispanic	53	9

Unemployment Rate		
	1980	1985	1996
White	6.3	6.2	4.7
Black	14.3	15.1	10.5
Hispanic	10.1	10.5	8.9

Source: U.S. Bureau of the Census.

avoiding the term *quota,* the notion of affirmative action tests the success of equal opportunity by observing whether minorities achieve admissions, jobs, and promotions in proportion to their numbers in the population.

CONSTITUTIONAL ISSUES—THE BAKKE CASE The constitutional question posed by "affirmative action" programs is whether or not they discriminate against whites in violation of the Equal Protection Clause of the Fourteenth Amendment. The

U.S. Supreme Court first dealt directly with this question in *Regents of the University of California v. Bakke* (1978). The Court struck down a special admissions program for minorities at a state medical school on the grounds that it excluded a white applicant because of his race and violated his rights under the Equal Protection Clause.[24] Allan Bakke applied to the University of California Davis Medical School two consecutive years and was rejected; in both years black applicants with significantly lower grade point averages and medical aptitude test scores were accepted through a special admissions program that reserved sixteen minority places in a class of one hundred.[25] The University of California did not deny that its admission decisions were based on race. Instead, it argued that its racial classification was "benign," that is, designed to assist minorities, not to hinder them. The Supreme Court held that race and ethnic origin *may* be considered in reviewing applications to a state school without violating the Equal Protection Clause. However, the Court held that a *separate* admissions program for minorities with a specific quota of openings that were unavailable to white applicants violated the Equal Protection Clause. The Court ordered Bakke admitted to medical school and the elimination of the special admissions program. It recommended that California consider an admissions program developed at Harvard that considered disadvantaged racial or ethnic background as a "plus" in an overall evaluation of an application but did not set numerical quotas or exclude any persons from competing for all positions.[26]

AFFIRMATIVE ACTION AS A REMEDY FOR PAST DISCRIMINATION   The Supreme Court has generally approved of affirmative action programs when there was evidence of past discriminatory practices. In *United Steelworkers of America v. Weber* (1979), the Supreme Court approved a plan developed by a private employer and a union to reserve 50 percent of higher paying, skilled jobs for minorities.[27] In *United States v. Paradise* (1987), the Court upheld a rigid 50 percent black quota system for promotions in the Alabama Department of Safety, which had excluded blacks from the ranks of state troopers prior to 1972 and had not promoted any blacks higher than corporal prior to 1984. In a 5–4 decision, the majority stressed the long history of discrimination in the agency as a reason for upholding the quota system. Whatever burdens were imposed on innocent parties were outweighed by the need to correct the effects of past discrimination.[28]

CASES QUESTIONING AFFIRMATIVE ACTION   Yet the Supreme Court has continued to express concern about whites who are directly and adversely affected by government action solely because of their race. In *Firefighters Local Union v. Stotts* (1984), the Court ruled that a city could not lay off white firefighters in favor of black firefighters with less seniority.[29] In *Richmond v. Crosen* (1989), the Supreme Court held that a minority set-aside program in Richmond, Virginia, which mandated that 30 percent of all city construction contracts must go to "blacks, Spanish-speaking, Orientals, Indians, Eskimos, or Aleuts" violated the Equal Protection Clause of the Fourteenth Amendment.[30]

AFFIRMATIVE ACTION AND "STRICT SCRUTINY"   It is important to note that the Supreme Court has never adopted the color-blind doctrine first espoused by Justice

John Harlan in his *dissent* from *Plessy* v. *Ferguson*—that "our constitution is color-blind and neither knows nor tolerates classes among cities." If the Equal Protection Clause requires that the laws of the United States and the states be truly color-blind, then *no* racial preferences, goals, or quotas would be tolerated. This view has occasionally been expressed in minority dissents and concurring opinions.[31]

However, the Court has held that racial classifications in law must be subject to "strict scrutiny." This means that race-based actions by government—any disparate treatment of the races by federal, state, or local public agencies—must be found necessary to remedy past proven discrimination, or to further clearly identified, compelling, and legitimate government objectives. Moreover, it must be "narrowly tailored" so as not to adversely affect the rights of individuals. In striking down a federal construction contract "set-aside" program for small businesses owned by racial minorities, the Court expressed skepticism about governmental racial classifications: "There is simply no way of determining what classifications are 'benign' and 'remedial' and what classifications are in fact motivated by illegitimate notions of racial inferiority or simple racial politics."[32] The membership of the Supreme Court appears to be closely split over the meaning and use of "strict scrutiny" in affirmative action cases.[33]

The Court's cumulative decisions about affirmative action have not provided the nation with a clear or coherent interpretation of the Constitution. At least one Circuit Court of Appeals has held that *any* use of race as a university admission factor violates the Equal Protection Clause of the Fourteenth Amendment. This decision in *Hopwood* v. *Texas* requires the University of Texas system to end racial preferences in admission. The U.S. Supreme Court affirmed this Court of Appeals decision, yet warned that it may not fully agree with the Circuit Court opinion.[34] Generally, affirmative action programs are *more likely to be found constitutional* when (a) they are adopted as a remedy to past proven discrimination; (b) they serve a clearly identified, compelling, and legitimate government objective; (c) they are "narrowly tailored" to achieve this objective; and (d) they do not absolutely bar majority members from participation.

PUBLIC OPINION TOWARD AFFIRMATIVE ACTION   Most Americans, black and white, support "affirmative action" when it is defined as encouragement, training, and education for qualified minorities and women (see Table 14–2). However, black and white opinion differs sharply over "preferences" and "quotas" in hiring, promotions, and admissions. Whites oppose such measures, whereas blacks support them. Most whites believe that affirmative action programs should be phased out or ended now, while 80 percent of blacks believe they should be continued.

Aware of the popular opposition to "preferences" and "quotas," affirmative action programs are usually couched in more favorable terms—"goals," "ethnic representation," and "diversity." Yet, over time, increasing resentment among whites toward preferential treatment of minorities has weakened political support for affirmative action programs across the country.

OPPOSITION TO PREFERENCES   Opponents of affirmative action argue that government racial classifications violate the fundamental principle of equality under the law. "To pursue the concept of racial entitlement even for the most admirable and benign of purposes is to reinforce and preserve for future mischief the way of thinking

Table 14–2

PUBLIC OPINION ON AFFIRMATIVE ACTION: A CLOSER LOOK			
Do you favor or oppose the following?			
	All	*Whites*	*Blacks*
Providing job training programs for minorities and women to make them better qualified for jobs?			
Favor	69	64	95
Oppose	24	29	3
Providing special education classes for minorities and women to make them better qualified for college?			
Favor	63	59	82
Oppose	28	31	11
In order to make up for past discrimination, programs which impose quotas for racial minorities?			
Favor	19	15	48
Oppose	72	78	37
Do you believe that where there has been job discrimination against blacks in the past, preference in hiring or promotion should be given to blacks today?			
Yes, preference	35	31	62
No	52	57	23
Depends (vol.)	8	8	10
What do you think should happen to affirmative action programs—should they be ended now, or should they be phased out over the next few years, or should affirmative action programs be continued for the foreseeable future?			
Ended now	12	13	0
Phased out	40	45	17
Continued for future	41	35	80

Note: Excludes "Don't Knows."

Source: The Polling Report, December 22, 1997.

that produces race slavery, race privilege, and race hatred. In the eyes of the government, we are just one race here. It is American."[35] It is argued that America cannot "make up" for past discrimination by "discrimination in the opposite direction." It is "unfair" to discriminate against the current generation of white workers and students to compensate for a history of discrimination in which they did not participate. Some early supporters of affirmative action have come to believe that race-conscious programs are no longer necessary, that disadvantages in society today are more class-based than race-based, and that if preferences are to be granted at all they should be based on economic disadvantage, not race. Moreover, misgivings have been expressed by some African Americans about unfair stigmatizing of the supposed beneficiaries of affirmative action—a resulting negative stereotyping that "stamps minorities with a badge of inferiority and may cause them to develop dependencies or to adopt an attitude that they are 'entitled' to preferences."[36] White resentment against the perceived unfairness of affirmative action aggravates racial conflict, creating an "angry white male" backlash that erodes support for civil rights generally.

ARGUMENTS FOR CONTINUING AFFIRMATIVE ACTION   Yet most Americans agree that discrimination still exists in American society, even if they do not agree on what should be done about it. Many supporters of affirmative action would ideally prefer a society in which "our children will one day live in a nation where they will not be judged by the color of their skin but by the content of their character." Martin Luther King, Jr.'s dream remains the ultimate goal for the nation. But they see race-conscious policies as a continuing necessity to remedy current discrimination and the effects of past discrimination. America is not now nor has it ever been a "color-blind" society. "If we abandon affirmative action we return to the old white boy network."[37] They perceive affirmative action as a necessary tool in achieving equality of opportunity.

THE CALIFORNIA CIVIL RIGHTS INITIATIVE   A rethinking of affirmative action was inspired by a citizen's initiative placed on the ballot in California by popular petition and approved by 54 percent of the state's voters in 1996. The California Civil Rights Initiative added the following sentence to that state's constitution.

> Neither the state of California nor any of its political subdivisions or agents shall use race, sex, color, ethnicity or national origin as a criterion for either discriminating against, or granting preferential treatment to, any individual or group in the operation of the State's system of public employment, public education or public contracting.

The key words are "or granting preferential treatment to . . ."

Opponents argue that this initiative will set back the civil rights movement, that it will end the progress of minorities in education and employment, and that it will deny minorities the opportunity to seek assistance and protection from government. Supporters argue that it leaves all existing federal and state civil rights protections intact. It simply extends the rights of specially protected groups to all of the state's citizens. (See also *People in Politics:* "Ward Connerly and the Citizen's Initiative to Ban Affirmative Action" in Chapter 2.)

Following its adoption, opponents of the California Civil Rights Initiative filed suit in federal court arguing that it violated the Equal Protection Clause of the U.S. Constitution because it denied minorities and women an opportunity to seek preferential treatment by governments. But the U.S. Supreme Court upheld the constitutionality of the initiative: "Impediments to preferential treatment do not deny equal protection." The Court reasoned that the Constitution allows some race-based preferences to cor-

■
Hispanic.
A general reference to persons of Spanish-speaking ancestry and culture.

rect past discrimination, but it does not prevent states from banning racial preferences altogether.

THE EFFECTS OF ELIMINATING PREFERENCES   The California citizens' initiative barring racial and gender preferences has inspired similar mass movements in other states. But college and university officials and most government office-holders continue to oppose measures they regard as anti-affirmative-action. At the University of California–Berkeley and University of Texas–Austin law schools, minority admissions dropped following the elimination of racial preferences. It is not clear whether minority students unable to gain admission to prestigious institutions will enroll at other schools or be lost altogether as educated professionals and role models. An alternative to racial preferences in undergraduate admissions (adopted by Texas in 1998) may be the automatic admission of top academic students (perhaps the top 10 percent) at each high school in the state. Presumably this will allow students from schools with heavy minority enrollments to gain admission without reliance on standardized test scores. But opponents of this alternative argue that it "lets poor schools off the hook" and that the solution is to improve the performance of minority students in high schools everywhere.

HISPANIC POWER

The term *Hispanic* refers to persons of Spanish-speaking ancestry and culture, including Mexican Americans, as well as Puerto Ricans and Cubans. Today there are over 31 million Hispanics in the United States, comprising 11 percent of the U.S. population. There are over 35 million African Americans making up 12.9 percent of the population. (See Table 14–3).

The largest subgroup of Hispanics are Mexican Americans, some of whom are descendants of citizens living in the Mexican territory that was annexed to the United States in 1848. Most, however, have come to the United States in accelerating numbers in recent years. The largest Mexican American populations are found in Texas, Arizona, New Mexico, and California. (See Figure 14–2.) The second largest subgroup

Table 14–3

MINORITIES IN AMERICA—2000		
	Number	*Percentage of Population*
African Americans	35,456,000	12.9%
Hispanic Americans	31,366,000	11.4
Asian or Pacific Islander Americans	11,246,000	4.1
Native Americans, Eskimos, Aleuts	2,402,000	0.9
Total Population	274,634,000	100.0

Source: Statistical Abstract of the United States, 1997, p. 35.

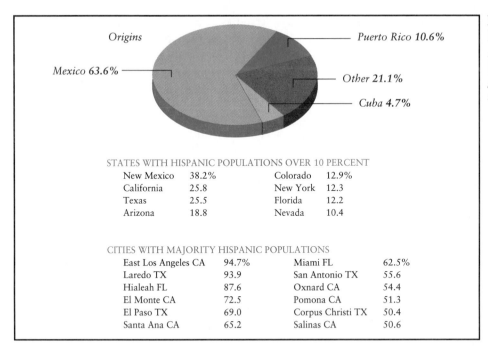

FIGURE 14–2
Hispanic
Americans in
States and Cities
*Source: Statistical Abstract of
the United States, 1994.*

Origins

Puerto Rico 10.6%

Mexico 63.6%

Other 21.1%

Cuba 4.7%

STATES WITH HISPANIC POPULATIONS OVER 10 PERCENT

New Mexico	38.2%	Colorado	12.9%
California	25.8	New York	12.3
Texas	25.5	Florida	12.2
Arizona	18.8	Nevada	10.4

CITIES WITH MAJORITY HISPANIC POPULATIONS

East Los Angeles CA	94.7%	Miami FL	62.5%
Laredo TX	93.9	San Antonio TX	55.6
Hialeah FL	87.6	Oxnard CA	54.4
El Monte CA	72.5	Pomona CA	51.3
El Paso TX	69.0	Corpus Christi TX	50.4
Santa Ana CA	65.2	Salinas CA	50.6

are Puerto Ricans, many of whom retain ties to the commonwealth and move back and forth from the island to the mainland, especially New York City. The third largest subgroup are Cubans, most of whom have fled from Castro's Cuba. They live mainly in the Miami metropolitan area. Each of these Hispanic groups has encountered a different experience in American life. Indeed, some evidence indicates that these groups identify themselves separately, rather than as Hispanics.[38]

If all Hispanics are grouped together for statistical comparisons, their median family income level is well below that of whites (see "Minority Life Chances," Table 14–1). Hispanic poverty and unemployment rates are also higher than those of whites. The percentage of Hispanics completing high school and college education is well below that of both whites and blacks, suggesting language or other cultural obstacles in education. Yet within these overall racial comparisons, there are wide disparities among subgroups as well as among individuals.

MEXICAN AMERICANS   For many years, agricultural business encouraged immigration of Mexican farm laborers willing to endure harsh conditions for low pay. Many others came to the United States as *indocumentados*—undocumented, or illegal, aliens. In the Immigration Reform Act of 1986 Congress offered amnesty to all undocumented workers who had entered the United States prior to 1982. But the act also required employers, under threat of penalties, to hire only people who can provide documentation of their legal status in the country. The result has been an increase in discrimination against Hispanics in hiring, as well as a booming business in counterfeit green (employment) and Social Security cards.

Although Mexican Americans have served as governors of Arizona and New Mexico and have won election to the U.S. Congress, their political power does not yet match their population percentages. Mexican American voter turnout is lower than other ethnic groups, perhaps because many are resident aliens or illegal immigrants not eligible to vote, or perhaps because of cultural factors that discourage political participation.

PUERTO RICANS   Puerto Rico is a commonwealth of the United States. Its commonwealth government resembles that of a state, with a constitution and elected governor and legislature, but the island has no voting members of the U.S. Congress and no electoral votes for president (see "The Commonwealth of Puerto Rico" in Chapter 1). As citizens, Puerto Ricans can move anywhere in the United States; many have immigrated to New York City.

Puerto Ricans have long debated whether to remain a commonwealth of the United States, apply for statehood, or seek complete independence from the United States. All of the participants in the debate agree that Puerto Ricans themselves should vote on the matter by referendum. In various referenda votes (1967, 1993, 1998), Puerto Ricans have voted to remain a commonwealth. Congress has considered holding its own referendum, but arguments over the conditions associated with various options, as well as who should be allowed to vote (Puerto Ricans currently living on the mainland or only those currently residing on the island) have slowed action.

CUBAN AMERICANS   Many Cuban Americans, especially those in the early waves of refugees from Castro's revolution in 1959, were skilled professionals and businesspeople, and they rapidly set about building Miami into a thriving economy. Although Cuban Americans are the smallest of the Hispanic subgroups, today they are better educated and enjoy higher incomes than the others. They are well organized politically, and they have succeeded in electing Cuban Americans to local office in Florida and to the U.S. Congress (see "*People in Politics:* Alex Penelas, Metro Mayor" in Chapter 12).

HISPANIC POLITICAL POWER   Hispanic power at the ballot box has not yet matched the Hispanic proportion of the population. To date, Hispanic voter turnout has been roughly half that of either whites or blacks. But Hispanic voter registration and election-day turnout are growing as more Hispanics become citizens and more become engaged in social and economic issues. The Hispanic vote is particularly important in the nation's largest states—California, Texas, New York, and Florida.

Mexican Americans in California and Texas and Puerto Ricans in New York have traditionally supported Democratic candidates, while a strong anticommunist heritage among Cubans has established a Republican voting trend in Florida. The Democratic party has generally appealed to the economic interests of Hispanics. The Republican party has tried to appeal to their strong, traditional family values, but the GOP's association with anti-immigration policies, especially in California, have alienated many Hispanics. In contrast, both governors George W. Bush in Texas and Jeb Bush in Florida have made effective appeals to Hispanic voters in their respective states. Both governors speak fluent Spanish and both have opposed anti-immigration policies. Hispanic voters may become an influential swing block if they respond positively to whichever party or candidate best addresses their concerns.

NATIVE AMERICANS AND TRIBAL GOVERNMENT

Christopher Columbus erred in his estimate of the circumference of the globe. He believed he had arrived in the Indian Ocean when he first came to the Caribbean. He mistook the Arawaks for people of the East Indies, calling them "Indios," and this Spanish word passed into English as Indians—a word that came to refer to all Native American peoples. But at the time of the first European contacts, these peoples had no common identity; there were hundreds of separate cultures and languages thriving in the Americas.

Although estimates vary, most historians believe that in the fifteenth century, 7 to 12 million people lived in the land that is now the United States and Canada; 25 million more lived in Mexico; and 60 to 70 million lived in the Western Hemisphere, a number comparable to Europe's population at the time. But in the centuries that followed, the native population of the Americas was devastated by warfare, famine, and, most of all, by epidemic diseases brought from Europe. Overall, the native population fell by 90 percent, the greatest human disaster in world history.

THE TRAIL OF BROKEN TREATIES   In the Northwest Ordinance of 1787, Congress, in organizing the western territories of the new nation, declared that:

> The utmost good faith shall always be observed toward the Indians. Their lands and property shall never be taken from them without their consent.

And later, in the Intercourse Act of 1790, Congress declared that public treaties between the United States government and the independent Indian "nations" would be the only legal means of obtaining Indian land. As president, George Washington forged a treaty with the Creeks: In exchange for land concessions, the United States pledged to protect the boundaries of the "Creek Nation" and allow the Creeks themselves to punish all violators of their laws within these boundaries. This semblance of legality was reflected in hundreds of treaties to follow. (And indeed, in recent years some Indian tribes have successfully sued in federal court for reparations and return of lands obtained in violation of the Intercourse Act of 1790 and subsequent treaties.) Yet, Indian lands were constantly invaded by whites. The resulting Indian resistance would typically lead to wars that would ultimately result in great loss of life among warriors and their families and the further loss of tribal land. The cycle of invasion, resistance, military defeat, and further land concessions, continued for a hundred years.

INDIAN WARS   The "Indian wars" were fought between the Plains Indian tribes and the U.S. Army between 1864 and 1890. Following the Civil War, the federal government began to assign boundaries to each tribe and created a Bureau of Indian Affairs (BIA) to "assist and protect" Indian peoples on their "reservations." But the reservations were repeatedly reduced in size until subsistence by hunting became impossible.

Malnutrition and demoralization of the native peoples were aided by the mass slaughter of the buffalo; vast herds, numbering perhaps as many as seventy million, were exterminated over the years. The most storied engagement of the long war occurred at the Little Big Horn River in South Dakota on June 25, 1876, where Civil War hero General George Armstrong Custer led elements of the U.S. Seventh Cavalry to destruction at the hands of Sioux and Cheyenne warriors led by Chief Crazy Horse, Sitting Bull, and Gall. But Custer's Last Stand inspired renewed army campaigns against the Plains tribes; the following year Crazy Horse was forced to surrender. In 1881, destitute Sioux under Chief Sitting Bull returned from exile in Canada to surrender themselves to reservation life. Among the last tribes to hold out were the Apaches, whose famous warrior, Geronimo, finally surrendered in 1886. Sporadic fighting continued until 1890, when a small, malnourished band of Lakota Sioux were wiped out at Wounded Knee Creek.

FEDERAL POLICY REVERSALS The Dawes Act of 1887 governed federal Indian policy for decades. The thrust of the policy was to break up tribal lands, allotting acreage for individual homesteads in order to assimilate Indians into the white agricultural society. Farming was to replace hunting, and tribal life and traditional customs were to be shed for English language and schooling. But this effort to destroy Indian culture never really succeeded. While Indian peoples lost over half of their 1877 reservation land, few lost their communal ties or accumulated much private property. The Dawes Act remained federal policy until 1934, when Congress finally reversed itself in the Indian Reorganization Act of 1934 and reaffirmed tribal ownership of land. Life on the reservations was often disparate. Indians suffered the worst poverty of any group in the nation, with high rates of infant mortality, alcoholism, and other diseases. The BIA, notoriously corrupt and mismanaged, encouraged dependency, and regularly interfered with Indian religious affairs and tribal customs.

NATIVE AMERICANS TODAY Today about 2.4 million people—less than 1 percent of the nation's population, identify themselves as American Indians. About 800,000 of these people live on tribal reservations and trust land, the largest of which is the Navaho and Hopi enclave in southwestern United States (see Figure 14–3). Yet these peoples remain the poorest and least healthy in America, with high incidences of infant mortality, suicide, and alcoholism. Approximately half of all Indians live below the poverty line.

Tribes.
Semisovereign Native American nations recognized by the U.S. government and exercising self-government on trust lands and reservations.

TRIBAL GOVERNMENT The U.S. Constitution (Article I, Section 8) grants Congress the full power "to regulate Commerce . . . with the Indian Tribes." States are prevented from regulating or taxing Indian tribes or extending their courts' jurisdiction over them, unless authorized by Congress. The Supreme Court recognizes Native Americans "as members of quasi-sovereign tribal entities"[39] with powers to regulate their own internal affairs, establish their own courts, and enforce their own laws, all subject to congressional supervision. Thus, for example, many Indian tribes chose to legalize gambling, including casino gambling, on reservations in states that otherwise prohibited the activity. As American citizens, Indians have the right to vote in state as well as national elections. Indians living off of reservations have the same rights and

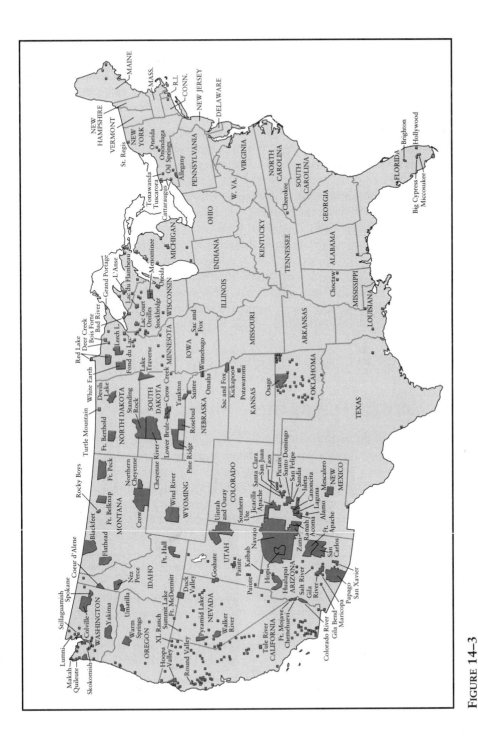

FIGURE 14–3

Native American Reservations and Trust Land

Source: U.S. Bureau of the Census, 1990 *Census of Population: American Indian and Alaska Native Areas; Indian Land Areas,* U.S. Dept. of the Interior, Bureau of Indian Affairs, 1993.

445

responsibilities as anyone else. Indians enrolled as members of tribes and living on reservations are entitled to certain benefits established by law and treaty. The Bureau of Indian Affairs (BIA) in the Department of Commerce continues to supervise reservation life.

TRIBES VERSUS STATES   In recent years, many tribal governments have reasserted their sovereignty and rights to self-government. The result has often led to strained relations with state and local governments. Disputes have arisen over casino gambling on reservations; state collection of taxes on gasoline, liquor, and cigarettes sold on reservations; and the enforcement of state environmental, natural resource, and wildlife protection laws within reservations. Some states have succeeded in negotiating compacts and agreements with tribal governments.

Under federal law, the Indian Gaming Regulatory Act of 1988, tribes must enter into compacts with states before they can open gambling casinos on tribal land. States must bargain "in good faith" in negotiating these compacts. States cannot tax the income from Indian casinos, but they may negotiate reimbursement for regulation and administration. About half of the states have negotiated such compacts. But in several states, including California, Texas, and Florida, tribes have opened casinos without state approval. State governments have been reluctant to enforce prohibitions on tribes: "I don't want another war with the Seminoles."[40]

AMERICANS WITH DISABILITIES

Throughout most of our nation's history, little thought was given to making public or private buildings or facilities accessible to blind, deaf, or mobility-impaired people.[41] But in 1990, Congress passed the sweeping Americans with Disabilities Act (ADA), which prohibits discrimination against the disabled in private employment, government programs, public accommodations, and telecommunications. The act is vaguely worded in many of its provisions, requiring "reasonable accommodations" for the disabled that do not involve "undue hardship." But the ADA mandates that:

1. The disabled cannot be denied employment or promotion if, with "reasonable accommodation," they can perform the duties of the job.
2. The disabled cannot be denied access to government programs or benefits. New buses, taxis, and trains must be accessible to disabled persons, including those in wheelchairs.
3. The disabled must enjoy "full and equal" access to hotels, restaurants, stores, schools, parks, museums, auditoriums, and the like. To achieve equal access, owners of existing facilities must alter them "to the maximum extent feasible"; builders of new facilities must ensure that they are readily accessible to disabled persons unless doing so is structurally impossible.

These federal mandates for accommodations of the disabled were not accompanied by any federal funds to employers or state and local governments to implement them (see "Coercive Federalism: Preemptions and Mandates" in Chapter 3).

GENDER EQUALITY

Until recently, gender issues had been determined largely by *state* laws, particularly laws governing marriage, divorce, employment, and abortion. State laws frequently differentiated between the rights and responsibilities of men and women. Women had many special protections in state laws, but often these protections limited opportunities for advancement and encouraged dependence upon men.

EMPLOYMENT   Traditionally, state laws governing employment considered women as frail creatures in need of special protections against long hours, heavy work, night work, and so on. Moreover, states did not guarantee equal pay and promotion opportunities for women or bar sexual discrimination in employment. However, Title VII of the federal Civil Rights Act of 1964 prevents sexual (as well as racial) discrimination in hiring, pay, and promotions. The Equal Employment Opportunity Commission, which is the federal agency charged with eliminating discrimination in employment, has established guidelines barring stereotyped classifications of "men's jobs" and "women's jobs." State laws and employer practices that differentiate between men and women in hours, pay, retirement age, and so on have been struck down.

GENDER CLASSIFICATIONS   Over the years, the Supreme Court ruled that states could no longer set different ages for men and women to become legal adults[42] or purchase alcoholic beverages;[43] women could not be barred from police or firefighting jobs by arbitrary height and weight requirements;[44] insurance and retirement plans for women must pay the same monthly benefits even though women on the average live longer;[45] and schools must pay coaches in girls' sports the same as coaches in boys' sports.[46] However, all-male and all-female schools are still permitted;[47] and Congress may draft men for military service without drafting women.[48] Gender protection under the Equal Protection Clause was also extended to men: The Supreme Court struck down a state law that allowed wives to obtain alimony from husbands but did not permit husbands to obtain alimony from wives.[49]

EDUCATION   Title IX of the Federal Education Act Amendment of 1972 dealt with sex discrimination in education. This federal law barred discrimination in admissions, housing, rules, financial aid, faculty and staff recruitment, pay, and—most troublesome of all—athletics. The latter problem has proven very difficult because men's football and basketball programs have traditionally brought in the money to finance all other sports and have received the largest share of school athletic budgets. (See also "*Up Close:* Sexual Harrassment.")

THE EARNINGS GAP   Yet women's earnings on average remain substantially below men's earnings. Today women earn only about 72 percent of what men earn. Despite federal laws barring direct gender discrimination in employment, the existence of a "dual" labor market, with male-dominated "blue-collar" jobs distinguishable from female-dominated "pink-collar" jobs, continues to be a major obstacle to economic equality between men and women. These occupational differences can be attributed to cultural stereotyping, social conditioning, and training and education that narrow the

UP CLOSE

SEXUAL HARASSMENT

The Civil Rights Act of 1964 (Title VII) makes it "an unlawful employment practice to discriminate against any individual with respect to . . . conditions or privileges of employment because of an individual's race, color, religion, *sex,* or national origin" [italics added]. The U.S. Supreme Court has declared that "sexual harassment" is a condition of employment that is outlawed by the Civil Rights Act. But what constitutes "sexual harassment"?

The Supreme Court has wrestled with the question of sexual harassment over the years. In 1986, the Court provided the following definition:

> Unwelcome sexual advances, requests for sexual favors, and other verbal or physical conduct of a sexual nature constitute sexual harassment when (1) submission to such conduct is made either explicitly or implicitly a term or condition of an individual's employment; (2) submission to or rejection of such conduct by an individual is used as the basis for employment decisions affecting such individual; or (3) such conduct has the purpose or effect of unreasonably interfering with an individual's work performance or creating an intimidating, hostile, or offensive working environment.[a]

There is no real difficulty in defining sexual harassment when jobs or promotions are conditioned on the granting of sexual favors. But problems arise in defining what is "an intimidating, hostile, or offensive working environment." This phrase may include dirty jokes, sexual innuendoes, the display of x-rated photos, or perhaps even unwanted proposals for dates. All of these definitions raise First Amendment questions regarding how far speech may be curtailed by law in the workplace. Moreover, some of these definitions about what is "offensive" or "unwanted" depend more on the subjective feelings of the individual employee than any objective standard of law.

Justice Sandra Day O'Conner tried to clarify some of these questions in 1993. Writing for the Court majority, she held that the particular words or actions objected to must be serious enough to make a "reasonable person," not just the plaintiff, perceive the work environment to be hostile. She indicated that a single incident is unlikely to constitute harassment; rather, courts should consider "the frequency of the discriminatory conduct, . . . its severity," and whether it "unreasonably interferes with an employee's work performance."[b]

What does a "reasonable person" believe to be sexual harassment? Some polls show that neither women nor men are likely to believe that sexual harassment includes repeated requests for a date, or the telling of dirty jokes, or comments on attractiveness—even though these behaviors often inspire formal complaints. Many college and university policies go well beyond the Supreme Court definition of sexual harassment, including the following:

- remarks about the person's clothing
- suggestive or insulting sounds
- leering or ogling a person's body
- remarks that degrade a person's gender

Overly broad and vague definitions of sexual harassment can undermine academic freedom and inhibit classroom discussions of important yet sensitive topics. Both faculty and students must feel free to express their views without fear of being labeled "insensitive" or charged with making others feel "uncomfortable." Students especially must feel free to express themselves on matters of gender, whether or not their ideas are immature or crudely expressed.

[a]*Meritor Savings Bank* v. *Vinson,* 477 U.S. 57 (1986).
[b]*Harris* v. *Forklift,* 126 L. Ed. 2d 295 (1993).

---

choices available to women. While significant progress has been made in recent years in reducing occupational sex segregation, nonetheless, many observers doubt that sexually differentiated occupations will be eliminated soon.

COMPARABLE WORTH   As a result of a growing recognition that the wage gap is more a result of occupational differentiation than direct discrimination, some feminist organizations have turned to another approach—the demand that pay levels in various occupations be determined by "comparable worth" rather than by the labor market. Comparable worth means more than paying men and women equally for the same work; it means paying the same wages for jobs of comparable value to the employer. It means that traditionally male and female jobs would be evaluated by governmental agencies or courts to determine their "worth" to the employer, perhaps by considering responsibilities, effort, knowledge, and skill requirements. Jobs adjudged to be comparable would have equal wages. Government agencies or the courts would replace the labor market in the determination of wage rates.

■
Comparable worth.
The argument that pay levels for traditionally male and traditionally female jobs should be equalized either by employers themselves or by government laws and regulations.

To date, the U.S. Equal Employment Opportunity Commission has rejected the notion of comparable worth and declined to recommend wages for traditionally male and female jobs. And so far the federal courts have refused to declare that different wages in traditionally male and female occupations are evidence of sexual discrimination in violation of federal law. However, some state governments and private employers have undertaken to review their own pay scales to determine if traditionally female occupations are underpaid.

BATTLES OVER ABORTION

Arguments over abortion touch on fundamental moral and religious principles. Proponents of legalized abortion, who often refer to themselves as "pro-choice," argue that a woman should be permitted to control her own body and should not be forced by law to have unwanted children. They cite the heavy toll in lives lost in criminal abortions and the psychological and emotional pain of an unwanted pregnancy. Opponents of abortion, who often refer to themselves as "pro-life," generally base their belief on the sanctity of life, including the life of the unborn child, which they believe deserves the protection of law—"the right to life." Many believe that the killing of an unborn child for any reason other than the preservation of the life of the mother is murder.

EARLY STATE LAWS   Historically, abortions for any purpose other than saving the life of the mother were criminal offenses under state law. About a dozen states acted in the late 1960s to permit abortions in cases of rape or incest, or to protect the physical health of the mother, and in some cases her mental health as well. Relatively few legal abortions were performed under these laws, however, because of the red tape involved—review of each case by several concurring physicians, approval of a hospital board, and so forth. Then, in 1970, New York, Alaska, Hawaii, and Washington enacted laws that in effect permitted abortion at the request of the woman involved with the concurrence of her physician.[50]

ROE V. WADE   The U.S. Supreme Court's decision in *Roe* v. *Wade* was one of the most important and far-reaching in the Court's history.[51] The Supreme Court ruled that the constitutional guarantee of "liberty" in the Fifth and Fourteenth Amendments included a woman's decision to bear or not to bear a child. The Supreme Court ruled that the word *person* in the Constitution did not include the unborn child. Therefore, the

Fifth and Fourteenth Amendments to the Constitution, guaranteeing "life, liberty and property," did not protect the "life" of the fetus. The Court also ruled that a state's power to protect the health and safety of the mother could not justify *any* restriction of abortion in the first three months of pregnancy. Between the third and sixth months of pregnancy, a state could set standards for abortion procedures in order to protect the health of women, but a state could not prohibit abortions. Only in the final three months could a state prohibit or regulate abortion to protect the unborn.

REACTIONS IN THE STATES   The Supreme Court's decision did not end the controversy over abortion. Congress declined to pass a constitutional amendment restricting abortion or declaring that the guarantee of life begins at conception. However, Congress banned the use of federal funds under Medicaid (medical care for the poor) for abortions (except to protect the life of a woman, and later, in cases of rape and incest). The Supreme Court upheld the constitutionality of federal and state laws *denying tax funds for abortions.*[52] While women retained the right to an abortion, the Court held that there was no constitutional obligation for governments to pay for abortions; the decision about whether to pay for abortions from tax revenues was left to Congress and the states.[53] However, efforts by the states to directly restrict abortion ran into Supreme Court opposition.[54]

ABORTIONS IN THE STATES   About 1.5 million abortions are performed each year in the United States. This is about 44 percent of the number of live births. About 85 percent of all abortions are performed at abortion clinics; others are performed in physicians' offices or in hospitals, where the cost is significantly higher. Most of these abortions are performed in the first three months; about 10 percent are performed after the third month. Abortion is more frequent in some states (New York, Nevada, New Jersey, California) than in other states (Utah, Idaho, West Virginia, Wyoming, South Dakota). (See *"Rankings of the States:* Abortion Rates.")

Why are abortions more frequent in some states than in others? A careful study of this question by political scientist Susan B. Hansen revealed that abortion rates were *not* related to unwanted pregnancies, that is, the "demand" for abortions.[55] Rather, abortion rates were related to state policies affecting the availability of abortion services, that is, to government policies affecting the "supply" of abortions. Among the reported findings were that abortion rates are higher in states that permitted abortion before *Roe* v. *Wade;* some states with low abortion rates (Utah and Idaho) have large Mormon populations; and greater state legislative support for abortion facilities and health services leads to higher abortion rates.

STATE RESTRICTIONS   Opponents of abortion won a victory in the *Webster* case in 1989 when the Supreme Court upheld a Missouri law sharply restricting abortions.[56] The right to abortion under *Roe* v. *Wade* was not overturned, but narrowed in application. The effect of the decision was to return the question of abortion restrictions to the states for decision.

The Court held that Missouri could deny public funds for abortions that were not necessary for the life of the woman and could deny the use of public facilities or public employees in performing or assisting in abortions. More important, the Court

ABORTION RATES

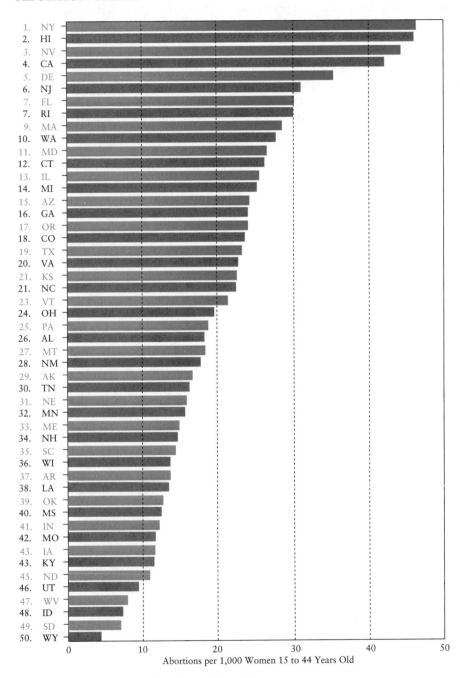

1.	NY
2.	HI
3.	NV
4.	CA
5.	DE
6.	NJ
7.	FL
7.	RI
9.	MA
10.	WA
11.	MD
12.	CT
13.	IL
14.	MI
15.	AZ
16.	GA
17.	OR
18.	CO
19.	TX
20.	VA
21.	KS
21.	NC
23.	VT
24.	OH
25.	PA
26.	AL
27.	MT
28.	NM
29.	AK
30.	TN
31.	NE
32.	MN
33.	ME
34.	NH
35.	SC
36.	WI
37.	AR
38.	LA
39.	OK
40.	MS
41.	IN
42.	MO
43.	IA
43.	KY
45.	ND
46.	UT
47.	WV
48.	ID
49.	SD
50.	WY

Abortions per 1,000 Women 15 to 44 Years Old

Source: Statistical Abstract of the United States, 1997, p. 87.

451

upheld the requirement for a test of "viability" after twenty weeks and a prohibition of an abortion of a viable fetus except to save a woman's life. The Court recognized the state's "interest in the protection of human life when viability is possible."

REAFFIRMING *ROE* V. *WADE*   Abortion has become such a polarizing issue that pro-choice and pro-life groups are generally unwilling to search out a middle ground. Yet the current Supreme Court appears to have chosen a policy of affirming a woman's right to abortion while upholding modest restrictions.

Pennsylvania is a state where pro-life forces won the support of the governor and legislature for a series of restrictions on abortion—physicians must inform women of risks and alternatives; a twenty-four-hour waiting period is required; minors must have consent of parents or a judge; spouses must be notified. These restrictions reached the Supreme Court in the case of *Planned Parenthood of Pennsylvania* v. *Casey* in 1992.[57]

Justice Sandra Day O'Connor took the lead in forming a moderate, swing bloc on the Court; her majority opinion strongly reaffirmed the fundamental right to abortion:

> Our law affords constitutional protection to personal decisions relating to marriage, pro-creation, contraception, family relationships, child rearing, and education. . . . These matters, involving the most intimate and personal choices a person may make in a life-time, choices central to personal dignity and autonomy, are central to the liberty pro-tected by the Fourteenth Amendment. . . . A woman's liberty is not so unlimited, however, that from the outset the State cannot show its concern for the life of the un-born, and at a later point in fetal development the State's interest in life has sufficient force so that the right of the woman to terminate the pregnancy can be restricted. We conclude the line should be drawn at viability, so that before that time the woman has a right to choose to terminate her pregnancy. . . .

Justice O'Connor went on to establish a new standard for constitutionally evaluating state restrictions: They must not impose an "undue burden" on women seeking abor-tion or place "substantial obstacles" in her path. All of Pennsylvania's restrictions were upheld except spousal notification.

The likelihood of states adopting restriction on abortion appears to be related to the size of their Catholic populations. It is in the states with large Catholic populations that pro-choice and pro-life forces are well organized and active in lobbying legisla-tures.[58]

ABORTION BATTLES IN THE STATES   Contentious debates over abortion continue in virtually all state capitals. Various legal restrictions on abortions have been passed in the states, including (1) *denial of public financing:* prohibitions on public financing of abortions; (2) *conscience laws:* laws granting permission to doctors and hospitals to refuse to perform abortions; (3) *fetal disposal:* laws requiring humane and sanitary dis-posal of fetal remains; (4) *informed consent:* laws requiring physicians to inform pa-tients about the development of the fetus and the availability of assistance in pregnancy; (5) *parental notification:* laws requiring that parents of minors seeking abortion be informed; (6) *spousal verification:* laws requiring spouses to be informed; (7) *hospitalization requirement:* laws requiring that late abortions be performed in hospitals; and (8) *clinic licensing:* laws setting standards of cleanliness and care in abortion clinics.

"PARTIAL-BIRTH" ABORTIONS   But perhaps the most inflamed arguments are inspired by efforts in the states to ban late-term "partial-birth" abortions of viable fetuses. The procedure is relatively rare. A physician induces a breech delivery with forceps, pulls out the fetus's legs and body, and then pierces the as-yet-undelivered skull and vacuums out the brain; the delivery is then completed. In 1996 and 1997, Congress enacted national bans on the procedure, only to have them vetoed by President Clinton.

The "partial-birth" abortion issue has energized antiabortion pro-life supporters in the states to seek bans on the procedure. By 1998, about twenty states had enacted such bans, although enforcement has sometimes been limited by court battles. The U.S. Supreme Court's language in its 1992 *Casey* decision (see previous discussion) appears to allow states to prohibit late-term abortions of viable fetuses. But state courts must wrestle with language in their own state constitutions.

ON THE WEB

A vast array of information on civil rights topics exists on the Internet. Many civil rights organizations have elaborate Web sites with sections on current topics, press releases, legislative affairs, programs, and publications. Among the more important sites is that of the National Association for the Advancement of Colored People (NAACP) at

www.naacp.org

The NAACP is the oldest and largest civil rights organization in the United States. It was founded in 1909 by black and white citizens committed to overcoming social injustices. It has a network of more than 2,200 local branches throughout the United States; its total membership exceeds 500,000. Its principal publication, *Crisis Magazine*, can be found at most libraries.

The National Organization of Women (NOW) is the most prominent feminist organization in the nation with 250,000 members in more than 500 chapters throughout the country. It was founded in 1966 "to take actions to bring about equality for all women." Its Web site at

www.now.org

contains a wealth of information on topics such as abortion and reproductive rights, affirmative action, sexual harassment, global feminism, lesbian rights, and violence against women.

The American Civil Liberties Union (ACLU) labels itself "the nation's foremost advocate of individual rights—litigating, legislating, and educating the public on a broad array of issues affecting individual freedom in the United States." It was founded in 1920 initially to assist people who were prosecuted for holding antiwar views during World War I. Today the ACLU focuses its attention on a wide variety of civil rights issues—arts censorship, capital punishment, lesbian and gay rights, immigrants' rights, privacy and technology, prisoners' rights, voting rights, and women's rights. Its Web site at

www.aclu.org

includes information and advocacy on these and related topics.

The American Civil Rights Institute (ACRI) is a relatively new organization created to oppose racial and gender preferences in affirmative action programs. The organization grew out of California's Proposition 209, the successful citizens' initiative that prohibits racial and gender preferences in that state's education, employment, and contracting. The institute's Web site at

www.acri.org

provides information on efforts in other states to pass legislation and/or generate citizens' initiatives to ban racial preferences.

NOTES

1. Quotation in Rufus P. Browning, Dale Rogers Marshall, and David H. Tabb, *Protest Is Not Enough: The Struggle of Blacks and Hispanics for Equality in Urban Politics* (Berkeley: University of California Press, 1984), p. 17.

2. Ibid., p. 8.

3. Carmine Scavo, "Racial Integration of Local Government Leadership in Small Southern Cities," *Social Science Quarterly,* 71 (June 1990), 362–72.

4. Lawrence Bobo and Franklin D. Gilliam, Jr., "Race, Sociopolitical Participation, and Black Empowerment," *American Political Science Review,* 84 (June 1990), 377–86.

5. See Paul Peterson, *City Limits* (Chicago: University of Chicago Press, 1981).

6. See Kenneth R. Mladenka, "Blacks and Hispanics in Urban Politics," *American Political Science Review,* 83 (March 1989), 165–91; Thomas R. Dye and James Renick, "Political Power and City Jobs: Determinants of Minority Employment," *Social Science Quarterly,* 62 (September 1981), 475–86.

7. C. Vann Woodward, *Reunion and Reaction: The End of Reconstruction* (Boston: Little, Brown, 1951).

8. *Plessy v. Ferguson,* 163 U.S. 537 (1896).

9. *Sweatt v. Painter,* 339 U.S. 629 (1950); *McLaurin v. Oklahoma State Regents,* 339 U.S. 637 (1950).

10. *Brown v. Board of Education of Topeka, Kansas,* 347 U.S. 483 (1954).

11. Kenneth B. Clark, *Dark Ghetto* (New York: Harper & Row, 1965), pp. 77–78.

12. The Supreme Court also ruled that Congress was bound to respect the equal protection doctrine imposed upon the states by the Fourteenth Amendment as part of the due process clause of the Fifth Amendment. *Bolling v. Sharpe,* 347 U.S. 497 (1954).

13. State laws that were obviously designed to evade constitutional responsibilities to end segregation were struck down in federal courts; but court litigation and delays slowed progress toward integration.

14. The Supreme Court declared that the threat of violence was not sufficient reason to deny constitutional rights to black children and again dismissed the ancient interposition arguments. *Cooper v. Aaron,* 358 U.S. 1 (1958).

15. *Alexander v. Holmes County Board of Education,* 396 U.S. 19 (1969).

16. United States Commission on Civil Rights, *Racial Isolation in the Public Schools,* 2 vols. (Washington, DC: Government Printing Office, 1967). See also James S. Coleman, *Equality of Educational Opportunity* (Washington, DC: Government Printing Office, 1966).

17. *Swan v. Charlotte-Mecklenburg County Board of Education,* 402 U.S. 1 (1971).

18. *Milliken v. Bradley,* 418 U.S. 717 (1974).

19. *Oklahoma City Board of Education v. Dowell,* 498 U.S. 237 (1991).

20. Michael W. Giles et al., "The Impact of Busing on White Flight," *Social Science Quarterly,* 55 (September 1974), 493–501. See also George M. Metcalf, *From Little Rock to Boston: The History of School Desegregation* (Westport, CT: Greenwood Press, 1985).

21. Howard W. Stanley and Richard G. Niemi, *Vital Statistics on American Politics, 1997–98* (Washington, DC: Congressional Quarterly Press, 1998), p. 373.

22. Statement by National Association for the Advancement of Colored People, reported in the *New York Times,* December 14, 1993, p. A11.

23. Opponents of the Civil Rights Act of 1964 argued that Congress unconstitutionally exceeded its delegated powers when it prohibited discrimination and segregation practiced by *privately owned* public accommodations and *private* employers. Nowhere among the delegated powers of Congress in Article I of the Constitution, or even in the Fourteenth or Fifteenth Amendments, is Congress specifically given the power to prohibit discrimination practiced by *private* individuals. In reply, supporters of the act argued that Congress has the power to regulate interstate commerce. Instead of relying upon the Fourteenth Amendment, which prohibits only *state-supported* discrimination, Congress was relying on its powers over interstate commerce. In unanimous opinions in *Heart of Atlanta Motel v. United States* and *Katzenbach v. McClung* in December 1964, the Supreme Court upheld the constitutionality of the Civil Rights Act. The Court held that Congress could, by virtue of its power over interstate commerce, prohibit discrimination in any establishment that serves or offers to serve interstate travelers or that sells food or goods previously moved in interstate commerce. This power over commerce included not only major establishments, like the Heart of Atlanta Motel, but also the family-owned Ollie's Barbecue serving a local clientele. *Heart of Atlanta Motel v. United States,* 379 U.S. 241 (1964); *Katzenbach v. McClung,* 379 U.S. 294 (1964).

24. *Regents of the University of California* v. *Bakke,* 438 U.S. 265 (1978).

25. Bakke's overall grade point average was 3.46, while the average for special admission students was 2.62. Bakke's MCAT scores were verbal–96, quantitative–94, science–97, general information–72; while the average MCAT scores for special admissions students were verbal–34, quantitative–30, science–37, general information–18.

26. The Bakke case did *not* affect overall minority enrollments in law schools and medical schools. Black and Hispanic enrollments continued to rise until the 1980s, when economic conditions appeared to have an adverse effect on minority enrollments. See John Gruhl and Susan Welch, "The Impact of the Bakke Decision on Black and Hispanic Enrollments in Medical and Law Schools," *Social Science Quarterly,* 71 (September 1990), 458–73.

27. *United Steelworkers* v. *Weber,* 443 U.S. 193 (1979).

28. *United States* v. *Paradise,* 480 U.S. 149 (1987).

29. *Firefighters Local Union* v. *Stotts,* 465 U.S. 561 (1981).

30. *Richmond* v. *Crosen,* 109 S. Ct. 706 (1989).

31. See Justice Antonin Scalia's dissent in *Johnson* v. *Transportation Agency of Santa Clara County,* 480 U.S. 616 (1987).

32. *Aderand Construction* v. *Pena* (1995).

33. Several major cases have split the Court 5 to 4, including *Aderand Construction* v. *Pena* (1995). At least two justices (Scalia and Thomas) believe that the Constitution requires a color-blind standard: "Under our Constitution, the Government may not make distinctions based on race." Three justices (O'Connor, Rehnquist, and Kennedy) apparently require "strict scrutiny" of racial distinctions by governments. And four justices (Stevens, Ginsburg, Souter, and Berger) appear willing to accept racial distinctions that are "benign" toward minorities even if these distinctions place an "incidental burden on some members of the majority."

34. *Hopwood* v. *Texas,* 78 F. 3d 932 5th U.S. Circuit, 1996.

35. Concurring opinion of Justice Antonin Scalia, *Aderand Construction* v. *Pena* (1995).

36. Concurring opinion of Justice Clarence Thomas, *Aderand Construction* v. *Pena* (1995).

37. Quote from Connie Rice of the NAACP, reported in *U.S. News and World Report,* February 13, 1995, p. 35.

38. See F. Chris Garcia, ed., *Latinos in the Political System* (Notre Dame, IN: Notre Dame University Press, 1988); Rudolpho O. dela Garza et al., *Latino Voices: Mexican, Puerto Rican, and Cuban Perspectives in American Politics* (Boulder: Westview Press, 1992).

39. *Morton* v. *Mancari,* 417 U.S. 535 (1974).

40. *Governing* (November 1998), p. 51.

41. See Joseph P. Shapiro, *No Pity: People with Disabilities Forging a New Civil Rights Movement* (New York: Times Books/Random House, 1993).

42. *Stanton* v. *Stanton,* 421 U.S. 7 (1975).

43. *Craig* v. *Boren,* 429 U.S. 191 (1976).

44. *Dothland* v. *Raulinson,* 433 U.S. 321 (1977).

45. *Arizona* v. *Norvis,* 103 S. Ct. 3492 (1983).

46. *E.E.O.C.* v. *Madison Community School District,* 55 U.S.L.W. 2644 (1987).

47. *Vorcheheimer* v. *Philadelphia School District,* 430 U.S. 703 (1977).

48. *Rostker* v. *Goldberg,* 453 U.S. 57 (1981).

49. *Orr* v. *Orr,* 440 U.S. 268 (1979).

50. See Christopher Z. Mooney and Mei-Hsien Lee, "Legislating Morality in the American States: Pre-*Roe* Abortion Reform," *American Journal of Political Science,* 39 (August 1995), 599–627.

51. *Roe* v. *Wade,* 410 U.S. 113 (1973).

52. *Harris* v. *McRae,* 448 U.S. 297 (1980).

53. For a review of state funding of abortions, see Kenneth J. Meier and Deborah R. McFarlane, "The Politics of Funding Abortion," *American Politics Quarterly,* 21 (January 1993), 81–101.

54. *Planned Parenthood of Missouri* v. *Danforth,* 428 U.S. 52 (1976); *Bellotti* v. *Baird,* 443 U.S. 622 (1979); *Akron* v. *Akron Center for Reproductive Health,* 103 S. Ct. 2481 (1983).

55. Susan B. Hansen, "State Implementation of Supreme Court Decisions: Abortion Rates Since *Roe* v. *Wade,*" *Journal of Politics,* 42 (1980), 372–95.

56. *Webster* v. *Reproductive Health Services,* 492 U.S. 490 (1989).

57. *Planned Parenthood* v. *Casey,* 112 S. Ct. 2791 (1992).

58. See Robert E. O'Conner and Michael B. Berkman, "Religious Determinants of State Abortion Policy," *Social Science Quarterly,* 76 (June 1995), 447–59.

15
THE POLITICS
OF EDUCATION

QUESTIONS TO CONSIDER
★ ★ ★ ★ ★ ★ ★ ★ ★ ★

Are SAT scores a good measure of the qualitative output of public schools?

☐ Yes ☐ No

Should private groups in a community be allowed to operate "charter" schools with public funds?

☐ Yes ☐ No

Do you favor the state providing tax-supported vouchers to parents to use at any public or private school of their choice?

☐ Yes ☐ No

Should school district superintendents be directly elected by the voters or appointed by school board members?

☐ Directly elected
☐ Appointed by school board

Should public schools be allowed to begin the day with voluntary prayer?

☐ Yes ☐ No

GOALS IN EDUCATIONAL POLICY

The primary responsibility for American public education rests with the fifty state governments and their local school districts. It is the largest and most costly of state functions. Today about 55 million pupils are in grade schools and high schools in America. About 48 million are in public schools and 7 million in private schools. About 15 million students are enrolled in institutions of higher education: community colleges, colleges, and universities.

EDUCATING CITIZENS   In 1647 the Massachusetts colonial legislature first required towns to provide for the education of children out of public funds. The rugged individualists of earlier eras thought it outrageous that one person should be taxed to pay for the education of another person's child. They were joined in their opposition to public education by those aristocrats who were opposed to arming the common people with the power that knowledge gives. However, the logic of democracy led inevitably to public education. The earliest democrats believed that the safest repository of the ultimate powers of society was the people themselves. If the people make mistakes, the remedy was not to remove power from their hands, but to help them in forming their judgment through education. Congress passed the Northwest Ordinance in 1787 offering land grants for public schools in the new territories and giving succeeding generations words to be forever etched on grammar school cornerstones: "Religion, morality, and knowledge being necessary to good government and the happiness of mankind, schools and the means for education shall ever be encouraged." When American democracy adopted universal suffrage, it affected every aspect of American life, and particularly education. If the people were to be granted the right of suffrage, they must be educated to the task. This meant that public education had to be universal, free, and compulsory.

ADVANCING SOCIAL GOALS   If there ever was a time when schools were only expected to combat ignorance and illiteracy, that time is far behind us. Today, schools are expected to do many things: resolve racial conflict and build an integrated society; improve the self-image of minority children; inspire patriotism and good citizenship; offer various forms of recreation and mass entertainment (football games, bands, choruses, cheerleaders, and the like); teach children to get along well with others and appreciate multiple cultures; reduce the highway accident toll by teaching students to be good drivers; eliminate unemployment and poverty by teaching job skills; end malnutrition and hunger through school lunch and milk programs; produce scientists and other technicians to continue America's progress in science and technology; fight drug abuse and educate children about sex and sexually transmitted diseases; and act as custodians for teenagers who have no interest in education but are not permitted to work or roam the streets unsupervised. In other words, nearly all the nation's problems are reflected in demands placed on schools. And, of course, these demands are frequently conflicting.

■

Northwest Ordinance. The first recognition by Congress in 1787 of the importance of education to democracy; provided grants of federal land to states for public schools.

EDUCATIONAL PERFORMANCE MEASUREMENT

Too often educational reports focus on "inputs"—measures of resources expended on education—rather than "outputs"—measures of an educational system's performance. Professional educators frequently resist performance measurement, especially comparisons between states or school districts. (The National Education Association's popular "Rankings of the States" focuses exclusively on enrollment, staff, and expenditure measures.) It is true that many performance measures, especially test scores, are controversial; many commentators argue that they do not measure the qualitative goals of education or that they are biased in one fashion or another. Certainly all interested citizens will welcome future refinements in educational performance measurement. But we cannot ignore performance simply because our measures are unrefined. We need to make reasoned use of the best available comparative measures of educational performance.

THE DROPOUT RATE   Certainly one measure of an educational system's performance is its ability to retain and graduate its students. National studies have consistently shown that high school dropouts tend to experience more unemployment and earn less over a lifetime than high school graduates. Yet often schools fail to convince young people that staying in school is a worthwhile endeavor.

The conflict over dropouts begins with arguments over how to measure the dropout rate. Three separate measures are regularly employed:

1. *School reported nonattendance:* Persons who are recorded by the schools as having stopped attending during the tenth, eleventh, and twelfth grades, as a percentage of total attendance.

This figure is preferred by professional educators because it is very low, about 5 percent.

2. *Dropout rate:* Persons age 18–24 who are not attending school and have not graduated from high school, as a percentage of all 18–24 year-olds.

The national dropout rate is about 14 percent.

3. *Graduation rate:* The number of public high school graduates as a percentage of ninth-graders four years earlier.

The national graduate rate is about 70 percent, indicating that about 30 percent of ninth-graders do not graduate four years later (see "*Rankings of the States:* Educational Performance").

The good news is that high school dropout rates are declining over time, however they are measured. Even so, dropout rates differ by race and ethnicity; the percentage of white 18–24-year-olds not attending or not graduated from school is about 14 percent; for blacks it is about 15 percent, and for Hispanics about 35 percent.[1] Dropout

EDUCATIONAL PERFORMANCE

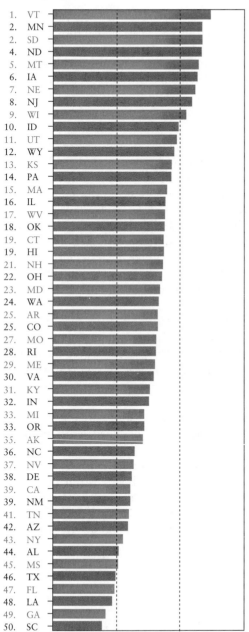

Percent of High School Graduates

1. VT
2. MN
2. SD
4. ND
5. MT
6. IA
7. NE
8. NJ
9. WI
10. ID
11. UT
12. WY
13. KS
14. PA
15. MA
16. IL
17. WV
18. OK
19. CT
19. HI
21. NH
22. OH
23. MD
24. WA
25. AR
25. CO
27. MO
28. RI
29. ME
30. VA
31. KY
32. IN
33. MI
33. OR
35. AK
36. NC
37. NV
38. DE
39. CA
39. NM
41. TN
42. AZ
43. NY
44. AL
45. MS
46. TX
47. FL
48. LA
49. GA
50. SC

40   60   80   100

Source: U.S. Department of Education; data for 1995.

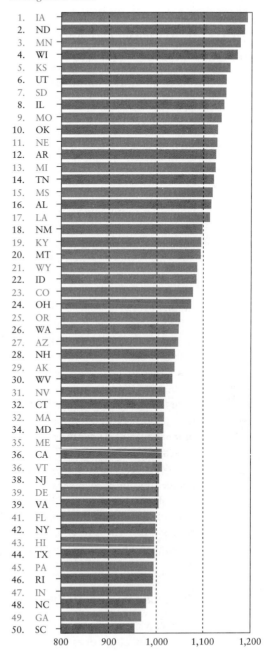

Average SAT Score

1. IA
2. ND
3. MN
4. WI
5. KS
6. UT
7. SD
8. IL
9. MO
10. OK
11. NE
12. AR
13. MI
14. TN
15. MS
16. AL
17. LA
18. NM
19. KY
20. MT
21. WY
22. ID
23. CO
24. OH
25. OR
26. WA
27. AZ
28. NH
29. AK
30. WV
31. NV
32. CT
32. MA
34. MD
35. ME
36. CA
36. VT
38. NJ
39. DE
39. VA
41. FL
42. NY
43. HI
44. TX
45. PA
46. RI
47. IN
48. NC
49. GA
50. SC

800   900   1,000   1,100   1,200

Source: College Board. Press release August 26, 1997.

■

SAT scores.
Verbal and math scores obtained on the national College Board Scholastic Assessment Test, required for admission to many colleges and universities.

rates are higher than the national average in southern states and states with large Hispanic populations.

CONTROVERSIES OVER TESTING   Performance testing of students is another controversial issue in educational circles. Professional educators argue that the acquisition of verbal and quantitative skills is not the only, or even perhaps the most important, product of public education. Educators often criticize the tests as culturally biased, unfair to minorities, or otherwise flawed. Nonetheless, public sentiment is strongly in favor of testing students' basic skills. Governors and state legislators have pressured educational administrators to engage in more testing.

SAT SCORES   For many years critics of modern public education cited declining scores on standardized tests, particularly the Scholastic Assessment Test (SAT), as evidence of the failure of the schools to teach basic reading and mathematics skills.[2] SAT scores declined dramatically during the 1960s and 1970s, ironically during a period in which per pupil educational spending was rising and the federal government initiated federal aid to education. (See Figure 15–1.) When the decline ended in 1982, it was attributed to increasing emphasis on basic skills and standardized testing. But changes in these test scores are also a function of how many students take the test. During the declining years, increasing numbers of students were taking the test—students who never aspired to college in the past and whose test scores did not match those of the earlier, smaller group of college-bound test takers.

The College Board, sponsors of the SAT, decided to "recenter" the scores in 1996 in recognition of the fact that national averages were unlikely to ever recover to the 500 mark. (Under the scoring system in effect since the 1940s, students over the past 30 years regularly averaged in the 420s on the verbal and in the 470s on the mathematical tests.) Critics charged that this artificial boost in scores was designed by educators to make American students appear better prepared and, thereby, to deflect criticism of the schools. Now it is possible to miss a few questions and still score a perfect 800; more than 500 students a year now register a perfect 1600 combined verbal and math scores.

Professional educators generally oppose efforts to assess state educational performance by comparing average SAT scores. Indeed, the College Board "strongly cautions against comparing states based upon SAT scores alone." (But see "*Rankings of the States:* Educational Performance.") In some states, more than 75 percent of graduating students take the test, while in other states fewer than 20 percent do so. Average scores are higher when only a small select group takes the test.

EDUCATIONAL REFORM

How can the quality of education be improved? Systematic research has made it clear that money alone does not guarantee good educational performance. The early landmark work of sociologist James Coleman, *Equality of Educational Opportunity* (popularly known as the Coleman report), demonstrated that pupil expenditures, teacher salaries, classroom size, facilities, and materials were *un*related to student achieve-

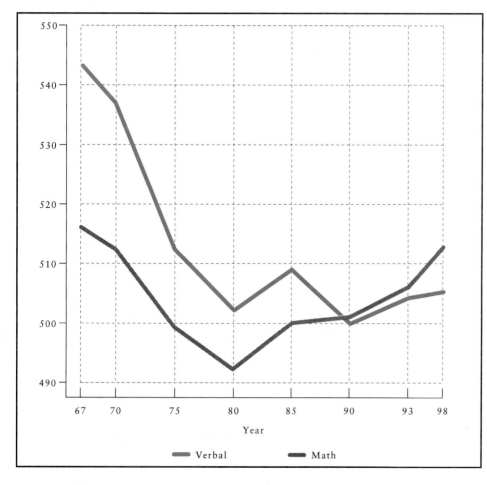

FIGURE 15–1
SAT Score Trends[a]

[a]Scores "recentered" in 1996; earlier scores revised and equated to current scale.

Source: College Board.

ment.[3] Student success is more closely related to characteristics of the home environment than to those of the schools. However, Coleman later demonstrated that student achievement levels are higher in schools in which there is a high expectation for achievement, an orderly and disciplined learning environment, an emphasis on basic skills, frequent monitoring of student progress, and teacher–parent interaction and agreement on values and norms.[4] These factors help explain why students from the same family backgrounds perform better in private and Catholic schools than in public schools.[5]

A NATION AT RISK   Educational reform was given impetus by an influential 1983 report by the National Commission on Excellence in Education entitled "A Nation At Risk."[6]

> Our nation is at risk. Our once unchallenged prominence in commerce, industry, science, and technological innovation is being overtaken by competitors throughout the world. . . .

■

**Minimum competence
testing.**
Tests of basic skills in reading, writing, and mathematics for elementary and high
school students.

> If an unfriendly foreign power had attempted to impose on America the mediocre ed-
> ucational performance that exists today, we might well have viewed it as an act of war.

The commission's recommendations set the agenda for educational policy debate in
the states. Among the many recommendations were these:

- A minimum high school curriculum of four years of English, three years
  of mathematics, three years of social science, and one-half year of computer science.
- Four to six years of foreign language study beginning in the elementary
  grades.
- Standardized tests for achievement for all of these subjects.
- More homework, a seven-hour school day, and a 200- to 220-day
  school year.
- Reliable grades and standardized tests for promotion and graduation.
- "Performance-based" salaries for teachers and rewards for "superior"
  teaching.

PERFORMANCE TESTING   Many state legislatures responded to the commission's
report and the demand for greater achievement in basic skills by requiring minimum
competence testing (MCT) in the schools. MCTs may be used as diagnostic tools to determine the need for remedial education, or minimum scores may be required for promotion or graduation. Currently, a number of states require students to pass a
minimum competence test to receive a high school diploma. (See "*Up Close:* The Texas
High-Stakes Test.") These tests usually require performance at an eighth- or ninth-
grade level.

Minimum competence tests force schools and teachers to place greater emphasis on
the "basics." Professional educators have been less enthusiastic about testing than citizen groups and state legislators. Educators contend that testing leads to narrow "test-
taking" education rather than broad preparation for life. Testing requires teachers to
devote more time to coaching students on how to pass an exam rather than preparing
them for productive lives after graduation.

But the most serious opposition to testing has come from minority group leaders
who charge that the tests are racially biased. Average black student scores are frequently lower than average white student scores, and a larger percentage of black students than white students are held back from promotion and graduation by testing.
Some black leaders charge that racial bias in the examination itself, as well as racial
isolation in the school, contribute to black–white differences in exam scores. Denying
a disproportionate number of black students a diploma because of the schools' failure
to teach basics may be viewed as a form of discrimination. However, to date, federal
courts have declined to rule that testing itself is discriminatory, as long as sufficient
time and opportunity have been provided to all students to prepare for the examination.

TESTING TEACHER COMPETENCY   Professional education groups have opposed
teacher competency tests on the grounds that standardized tests cannot really measure

UP CLOSE

THE TEXAS HIGH-STAKES TEST

Voters are increasingly demanding accountability in public education, and state legislators are under considerable pressure to impose performance testing on students. "Social promotion" is under severe attack. Indeed, a number of states have established "exit tests" requiring all high school students, even after passing their courses, to pass a standardized statewide test to receive their diplomas. Texas is a national leader in this high-stakes testing, having initiated it in 1985 at the urging of a committee chaired by Ross Perot.

Supporters argue that the test guarantees that high school graduates have at least mastered the basic skills. Moreover, they also argue that test scores can be used to gauge how well teachers and school administrators throughout the state are doing their jobs. The testing assures employers that the state's high school graduates can read and do math. Over time, scores have climbed in increasing percentages, and over two-thirds of the students now pass the test on the first try. (Students get eight tries over three years.)

Opponents contend that it is unfair to students who have already earned all of their high school credits to subject them to the added pressure of a single test in order to obtain their diplomas. They also argue that with so much riding on the test results for both teachers and students, there is a tendency to "teach to the test"—narrowly focusing on basic drills rather than broader and more useful knowledge. And finally it is pointed out that low-income and minority students fail the test at disproportionate rates.

The following is a sample question from the Texas Assessment of Academic Skills (TAAS).

The graph shows the percent of compact discs sold for each music category at Mike's Music Store last month.

Compact Disc Sales

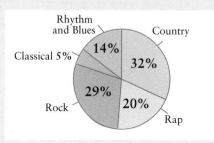

22. Which is a reasonable conclusion from the information on the graph?

   A Mike's Music Store doesn't sell cassette tapes.

   B Mike's customers don't like rhythm and blues music.

   C Classical compact discs are more popular than rap compact discs at Mike's.

   D Rap compact discs are less popular than rock compact discs at Mike's.

   E Fewer than 10 customers bought classical compact discs last month.

---

competency in the classroom. The National Education Association has opposed all testing of teachers; the American Federation of Teachers is willing to accept competency testing only for new teachers. The Educational Testing Service (which prepares the GRE, LSAT, and other standardized national examinations) offers a National Teacher Examination (NTE), which measures general knowledge, basic comprehension, and mathematical skills. Today, only a few states have adopted teacher competency tests, but the results have been disquieting. Large numbers of experienced teachers have failed the tests.

PAY AND RECRUITMENT   Another concern of the National Commission on Excellence in Education was the inability of the teaching profession to attract quality students. The average SAT scores of education majors are lower than the average scores of other students. It should not be surprising that education fails to attract many top

■

Merit pay.
In public education, pay increases designed to encourage and reward quality teaching.

students when average starting salaries for teachers nationwide are less than 75 percent of the average starting salaries for other graduates. Years ago, when women were excluded from many other professions, teaching attracted women of high ability even though salaries were low. But today, with expanded opportunities for women, the teaching profession cannot expect to attract quality graduates without offering competitive salaries.

MERIT PAY   Few state legislators are willing or able to raise all teachers' salaries to the level of other professionals. The adoption of "merit pay" provides a less costly option, yet one that promises to reward good teaching. Ideally, merit pay would help retain exceptional teachers and encourage quality teaching, without rewarding mediocrity through general (across-the-board) salary increases to all teachers. But the professional education groups fear that merit pay will become a substitute for adequate teachers' salaries. They also argue that there are no objective criteria for measuring "merit" in classroom teaching. Using student test scores would unfairly penalize teachers who taught disadvantaged students. And teacher scores on "pencil-and-paper" tests do not really measure classroom performance. And, of course, the subjective allocation of merit pay by principals and superintendents is potentially arbitrary. In short, merit pay plans often founder on an age-old question: What is good teaching?

EDUCATIONAL GOALS   The president and the nation's governors have generally agreed on the *goals* for American education. In 1991 President George Bush and the nation's governors, including Arkansas Governor Bill Clinton, agreed in *America 2000* to strive toward the following goals by the year 2000.[7]

* All children in America will start school ready to learn.
* The high school graduation rate is to increase to at least 90 percent.
* American students will leave grades four, eight, and twelve having demonstrated competency in challenging subject matter, including English, mathematics, science, history, and geography. (This recommendation endorses the National Assessment of Educational Progress, emphasizing standardized testing of basic skills.)
* U.S. students will be first in the world in science and mathematics achievement.
* Every adult American will become literate.
* Every school in America will be free of drugs and violence and will offer a disciplined environment conducive to learning.

"REINVENTING" EDUCATION

It is unlikely that the United States will reach its educational goals without a comprehensive restructuring of education. Simply spending more money on the current system of public education in the nation does not promise much in terms of improved performance. Nor do the imposition of tougher standards, more required courses, more hours in schools, and other top-down mandates from states to the schools.[8] Rather, good performance is associated with the sharing of high expectations among parents, teachers, and pupils; a mutual determination of goals, methods, and disciplinary standards among teachers, administrators, and parents; close monitoring of student progress by teachers and parents; and frequent interaction between parents and principals and teachers.[9] But the problem is how to bring about these conditions.

SCHOOL-BASED MANAGEMENT   The current fad in public education is "school-based management"—decentralized decision making in individual schools by principals, teachers, parents, and community members, rather than central offices of school districts. It is designed to give flexibility to people closest to the students and to foster within the community a sense of ownership and responsibility for the quality of education. Presumably principals, teachers, and parents at each school would decide about goals, curriculum, discipline, and perhaps even personnel. But it seldom works out that way. School-based councils often end up in conflict with central school district administrators, elected school boards, state and federal regulations, budgetary restrictions, and so on. Principals and teachers often feel that it takes time away from teaching, or requires additional efforts to reach community consensus.

MAGNET SCHOOLS   Another common reform proposal is the "magnet school." High schools might choose to specialize, some emphasizing math and science, others the fine arts, others business, and still others vocational training. Some schools might be "adopted" by business, professional organizations, or universities. Magnet schools, with reputations for quality, specialized instruction, are frequently recommended for inner-city areas in order to attract white pupils and reduce racial isolation.

CHARTER SCHOOLS   Yet another reform that has been advanced in a limited number of states is the "charter" school. Community educational groups, including public school teachers and parents, sign a "charter" with their school district or state education department to establish their own school. They receive waivers from most state and school district regulations to enable them to be more innovative; in exchange for this flexibility they promise to show specific student achievement. They usually receive tax money from the state and school district based on their enrollment. Minnesota was the first state, in 1991, to permit charter schools, and about a dozen states have followed suit; but relatively few charter schools have been established anywhere. (See *"Up Close:* Florida's Experiment with Charter Schools.")

PRIVATIZED PUBLIC SCHOOLS   A more radical version of the charter school is the privately contracted public school, where a private profit-making corporation contracts with the school district to provide schooling for its pupils, thus replacing the public schools. Private firms usually promise to provide pupil education at a lower cost to school districts than the districts regularly incur in providing schools themselves. The private firms make their profits from cost savings in instructional delivery and program management. And they usually promise to produce better results—higher test scores, fewer dropouts, more employable graduates. So far only limited experiments have taken place throughout the country.

But privatization is bitterly opposed by public school administrators, public school teachers, and especially teachers' unions. They argue that profit-making entrepreneurs

■
School-based management.
Reforms designed to decentralize educational decision making to individual schools rather than central school district administrations.

Magnet schools.
Schools emphasizing instruction in particular areas in an effort to improve quality and attract students.

Charter schools.
Schools operated with public funds by private community groups under a charter from public school districts.

UP CLOSE

FLORIDA'S EXPERIMENT WITH CHARTER SCHOOLS

In 1996 the Florida legislature first authorized the creation of charter schools in its school districts. Community groups may now petition their school boards for a charter to operate an independent school as an alternative to the district's public school system. Charter schools must meet local school district requirements, although appeals from district rejections may be taken to the commissioner of education. School districts must provide charter schools with a subsidy for each student enrolled equal to the amount spent for each pupil in its own schools.

Liberty City Charter School was among the first schools to be chartered in the state. It is located in a poor, predominantly black, old neighborhood of Miami. It had only a few months following passage of the authorizing legislation to find a building, recruit teachers, establish a curriculum, and enroll students. But it did so in the fall of 1996 on a shoestring budget.

Liberty City Charter School's principal backers were Republican gubernatorial candidate Jeb Bush and Democratic civil rights activist T. Willard Fair. Bush had played a major role in pushing the program through the state legislature against the opposition of the state educational bureaucracy and its teachers' union. Fair was instrumental in seeing to it

that the new law included a requirement that charter schools reflect the racial makeup of their neighborhoods.

At Liberty City Charter School, visitors see kindergarten, first-, and second-grade pupils dressed in sharp uniforms of red and blue, lining up in single file to enter classes with portraits of Martin Luther King, Jr., on the walls. Parents wishing to enroll their children must sign a "contract" committing themselves to volunteer to work at the school. The school's charter calls for its students to perform better than public school students in standard achievement tests, and it pledges the school to stress basic character development.

Testing at Liberty City and other charter schools has been intense. The success of the charter school movement probably rests on these schools demonstrating that they can teach children to read and write and add and subtract better than their peers in public schools. Character formation is much harder to measure. Critics warn that charter schools will segregate students; to date all of Liberty City's pupils are black. And they warn that charter school teachers will "teach to the test," artificially raising test scores while ignoring more basic problem-solving and social relations skills. But it may be several years before a sufficient number of charter schools can become well established and the achievement and character records of their students accurately assessed.

Source: Thomas R. Dye, *Politics in Florida* (Upper Saddle River, NJ: Prentice Hall, 1998).

do not have the community's best interest at heart, that private firms teach only test-taking skills at the expense of broader educational goals, and that there is no hard evidence so far that private firms can produce better educational results.

EDUCATIONAL VOUCHERS   An even more controversial version of parental choice involves educational vouchers that would be given to parents to spend at any school they choose, public or private. State governments would redeem the vouchers submitted by schools by paying specified amounts—perhaps the equivalent of the state's per pupil educational spending (the U.S. average was over $6,000 in 1998). All public and private schools would compete equally for students, and state education funds would flow to those schools that enrolled more students. Competition would encourage all schools to satisfy parental demands for excellence. Racial or religious or ethnic discrimination would be strictly prohibited in any private or public school receiving vouchers. Providing vouchers for private school education would be most effective for children from poor or disadvantaged homes. These children currently do not have the same option as children from more affluent homes of fleeing the public schools and enrolling in private academies.

■
Educational vouchers.
Vouchers given to parents to pay for their children's education at schools of their own choosing, redeemable by the schools in public funds from the state and school district.

OPPOSITION TO VOUCHERS Yet there is strong opposition to the voucher idea. The most vocal opposition comes from professional school administrators and state educational agencies. They argue that giving parents the right to move their children from school to school disrupts educational planning and threatens the viability of schools that are perceived as inferior. It may lead to a stratification of schools into popular magnet schools that would attract the best students, and less popular schools that would be left with the task of educating students whose parents were unaware of or uninterested in their children's education. Other opponents of choice plans fear that public education might be undermined if the choice available to parents includes the option of sending their children to private, church-related schools. Public education groups are fearful that vouchers will divert public money from public to private schools. As governor of Arkansas, Bill Clinton endorsed the notion of choice, but only *within* the public school system.[10]

CALIFORNIA VOTES TO REJECT VOUCHERS The educational choice movement was dealt a major setback in 1993 when California voters soundly defeated a citizens' initiative known as Proposition 174, Parental Choice in Education. Professional educators, teachers' unions, and liberal groups joined together to mount an expensive, highly publicized campaign to defeat the measure. Proposition 174 promised to "empower parents" by granting each schoolchild a "scholarship" (voucher) equal to about one-half of the average amount of state and local government aid per pupil in California (about $2,600). The money was to be paid directly to the schools in which parents chose to enroll their children. Either public or private schools could qualify as "scholarship-redeeming schools"; schools that discriminated on the basis of race, ethnicity, color, or national origin would not be eligible.

Opposition groups, including the powerful California Teachers Association, argued that the proposal would create "a two-tier system of schools, one for the haves, one for the have-nots." They portrayed vouchers as "an entitlement program offering wealthy families a private-school subsidy for their children, paid for by the taxpayers," noting that there was no means test for the vouchers. About 10 percent of California's schoolchildren were in private schools already; their parents would enjoy an immediate windfall benefit from the program. Opponents warned that public education would suffer grievously if both money and gifted students were removed from public schools. Although only half of the costs of educating a public school student would go into a voucher, it was argued that public schools would face financial difficulties from the implementation of the program. The initial costs of vouchers for pupils already attending private schools posed a major financial problem. No one could accurately estimate how many pupils would eventually transfer from public to private schools. Finally, opponents made inroads in the electorate by warning that taxpayers' money would go to religious schools and noting that the content of instruction and credentials of teachers were unregulated in the proposal.

THE LIMITED FEDERAL ROLE IN EDUCATION

Traditionally, education in America was a community responsibility. But today state governments have taken major responsibility for public education. The federal government remains largely an interested spectator in the area of educational policy. While it has taken the lead in guaranteeing racial equality in education, and separating religion from public schools, it has never assumed any significant share of the costs of education. The federal share of educational spending is usually under 10 percent. (See Table 15–1.)

EARLY FEDERAL AID   The federal government's role in education, however, is a longstanding one. In the famous Northwest Ordinance of 1787, Congress offered land grants for public schools in the new territories. Then in 1862 the Morrill Land Grant Act provided grants of federal land to each state for the establishment of colleges specializing in agricultural and mechanical arts. These became known as "land-grant colleges." In 1867, Congress established a U.S. Office of Education, which became the Department of Education in 1979. The Smith-Hughes Act of 1917 set up the first program of federal grants-in-aid to promote vocational education and enabled schools to provide training in agriculture, home economics, trades, and industries. In the National School Lunch and Milk programs, begun in 1946, federal grants and commodity donations are made for nonprofit lunches and milk served in public and private schools. In the Federal Impacted Areas Aid Program, begun in 1950, federal aid is authorized in "federally impacted" areas of the nation. These are areas where federal activities create a substantial increase in school enrollments or a reduction in taxable resources because of federally owned property. In response to the Soviet Union's success in launching "Sputnik," the first satellite into space in 1957, Congress became concerned that the American educational system might not be keeping abreast of advances made in other nations, particularly in science and technology. In the National Defense Education Act (NDEA) of 1958, Congress provided financial aid to states and public school districts to improve instruction in science, mathematics, and foreign languages.

ELEMENTARY AND SECONDARY EDUCATION ACT (TITLE I)   The Elementary and Secondary Education Act of 1965 marked the first large breakthrough in federal aid to education. Yet even ESEA was not a *general* aid-to-education program—one that would assist all public and private schools in school construction and teachers' salaries. The main thrust of ESEA is in "poverty-impacted" schools, instructional materials, and educational research and training. The Education Consolidation and Improvement Act of 1981 consolidated ESEA and related education programs into a single "Title I" block grant allowing the states greater discretion in how federal funds can be spent for compensatory education. This remains the largest federal aid-to-education program, accounting for over 60 percent of federal elementary and secondary education spending.

However, it is difficult to demonstrate that federal aid programs improve the quality of education in America.[11] Indeed, during the years in which federal aid was increasing, student achievement scores were *declining* (see Figure 15–1). Raising the educational achievement levels of America's youth depends less on the amount spent than on how it is spent.

Presidents and Congress are often tempted to direct state educational policies from Washington. To date, however, the goals set forth at national conferences have not

■

ESEA Title I.
The federal Elementary and Secondary Education Act, later amended into a federal block grant (Title I) to states to improve education.

Table 15–1

SOURCES OF FUNDS FOR PUBLIC EDUCATION IN THE UNITED STATES			
Percentage of Public Educational Expenditures by Source			
	1980	*1985*	*1990*	*1995*
Federal	10.7	7.9	7.4	8.3
State	46.7	47.6	45.5	42.3
Local	31.3	31.4	31.5	32.3
Other	11.3	13.1	15.5	17.1

Source: Statistical Abstract of the United States, 1997, p. 156.

been enacted into law, although Congress has considered proposals to make instruction in basic subjects and national testing a prerequisite to federal educational aid to the states.

ORGANIZING PUBLIC EDUCATION IN THE STATES

The fifty state governments, by means of enabling legislation, establish local school districts and endow them with the authority to operate public schools. There are over 14,000 local school boards, and 85,000 board members, who are chosen usually, but not always, by popular election. State laws authorize these boards to levy and collect taxes, borrow money, engage in school construction, hire instructional personnel, and make certain determinations about local school policy.

STATE SUPERVISION   Yet, in every state, the authority of local school districts is severely limited by state legislation. State law determines the types and rates of taxes to be levied, the maximum debt that can be incurred, the number of days schools shall remain open, the number of years of compulsory school attendance, the minimum salaries to be paid to teachers, the types of schools to be operated by the local boards, the number of grades to be taught, the qualifications of teachers, and the general content of curricula. In addition, many states choose the textbooks, establish course outlines, recommend teaching methods, establish statewide examinations, fix minimum teacher–pupil ratios, and stipulate course content in great detail. In short, the responsibility for public education is firmly in the hands of state governments.

State responsibility for public education is no mere paper arrangement. States ensure local compliance with state educational policy through (1) bureaucratic oversight, involving state boards of education, state commissioners or superintendents of education, and state departments of education, and (2) financial control through state allocation of funds to local school districts.

STATE BOARDS OF EDUCATION   Traditionally, state control over education was vested in state boards of education. In most states these boards are appointed by the governor; in some states they are composed of state officials; and in seven states (Colorado, Kansas, Louisiana, Michigan, Nebraska, New Mexico, and Texas) they are directly elected by the voters. These boards generally have the formal power to decide everything from teacher certification to textbook selection. However, in practice these boards rely heavily on the recommendations of the state commissioner of education and the state department of education.

STATE COMMISSIONERS OF EDUCATION   All states have chief education officers, variously entitled commissioner of education, state school superintendent, or superintendent of public instruction. In fourteen states this official is elected (Arizona, California, Florida, Georgia, Idaho, Louisiana, Montana, North Carolina, North Dakota, Oklahoma, South Carolina, Washington, Wisconsin, and Wyoming). In other states they are appointed by the governor or the state education board. The chief education officer may exercise the most important influence over education in the state, as public spokesperson for education, in testimony before the legislature, and as the head of the state department of education.

STATE DEPARTMENTS OF EDUCATION   State educational bureaucracies have greatly expanded in size and power over the years. They disburse state funds to local schools, prepare statewide curricula, select textbooks and materials, determine teacher qualifications, establish and enforce school building codes, and supervise statewide testing. Their principal tool in enforcing their control over local schools is the allocation of state educational money.

SCHOOL DISTRICT CONSOLIDATION   One of the most dramatic reorganization and centralization movements in American government in this century was the successful drive to reduce, through consolidation, the number of local school districts in the United States. In a thirty-year period (1950–1980), three out of every four school districts were eliminated through consolidation. Support for school district consolidation came from *state* school officials in every state. Opposition to consolidation was *local* in character.

STATE FINANCIAL CONTROL   States ensure the implementation of state educational policies through state grants of money to local school districts. Every state provides grants in one form or another to local school districts to supplement locally derived school revenue. This places the superior taxing powers of the state in the service of public schools operated at the local level. In every state, an equalization formula in the distribution of state grants to local districts operates to help equalize educational opportunities in all parts of the state. This enables the state to guarantee a minimum "foundation" program in education throughout the state. In addition, since state grants to local school districts are administered through state departments of education, state school officials are given an effective tool for implementing state policies, namely, withholding or threatening to withhold state funds from school districts that do not conform to state standards. The growth of state responsibility for school policy was accomplished largely by the use of money—state grants to local schools.

BATTLES OVER SCHOOL FINANCES

Public elementary and secondary schools enroll about 45 million students. Nationwide about $6,000 per year is spent on the public education of each child.[12] Yet national averages can obscure as much as they reveal about the record of the states in public education. Fifty state school systems establish policy for the nation, and this decentralization results in variations from state to state in educational policy. Only by examining public policy in all fifty states can the full dimension of American education be understood.

VARIATION AMONG STATES   In 1997, for example, public school expenditures for each pupil ranged from $3,837 in Utah to $9,455 in New Jersey. (See "*Rankings of the States:* Elementary and Secondary Education Spending Per Pupil.") Why is it that some states spend more than twice as much on the education of each child as other states? Economic resources are an important determinant of a state's willingness and ability to provide educational services. Education, and especially income, correlate significantly with variations among the states in per pupil expenditures for public education.

INEQUALITIES AMONG SCHOOL DISTRICTS   A central issue in the struggle over public education is that of distributing the benefits and costs of education equitably. Most school revenues are derived from *local* property taxes. In every state except Hawaii, local school boards must raise money from property taxes to finance their schools. This means that communities that do *not* have much taxable property cannot finance their schools as well as communities that are blessed with great wealth. Frequently, wealthy communities can provide better education for their children at *lower* tax rates than poor communities can provide at *higher* tax rates, simply because of disparities in the value of taxable property from one community to the next.

Disparities in educational funding among school districts *within* states can be quite large. A Congressional Research Service study reported disparities in excess of two to one (e.g., $8,000 versus $4,000) in per pupil spending among school districts in eleven states (New York, New Jersey, Ohio, Pennsylvania, Texas, Montana, Missouri, Michigan, Indiana, Illinois, and Georgia).[13]

SCHOOL INEQUALITIES AS A CONSTITUTIONAL ISSUE   Do disparities among school districts within a state deny "equal protection of laws" guaranteed by the Fourteenth Amendment of the U.S. Constitution and similar guarantees found in most state constitutions? The U.S. Supreme Court ruled that disparities in financial resources between school districts in a state, and resulting in inequalities in educational spending per pupil across a state, do *not* violate the Equal Protection Clause of the Fourteenth Amendment. There is no duty under the U.S. Constitution for a state to equalize educational resources within the state.[14]

However, in recent years *state courts* have increasingly intervened in school financing to ensure equality among school districts based on their own interpretation of *state* constitutional provisions (see "The New Judicial Federalism" in Chapter 9). Beginning with an early California state supreme court decision requiring that state funds be used

ELEMENTARY AND SECONDARY EDUCATION SPENDING PER PUPIL

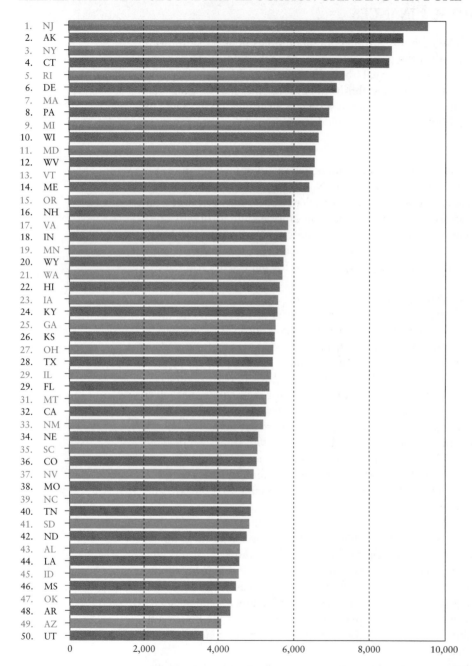

Source: National Education Association.

to help equalize resources among the state's school districts,[15] many state courts have pressured their legislatures to come up with equalization plans in state school grants to overcome disparities in property tax revenues among school districts. State court equalization orders are generally based upon *state* constitutional provisions guaranteeing equality.

STATE FUNDS VERSUS LOCAL PROPERTY TAXES   Local school district reliance on property taxation, combined with inequalities in property values among communities, creates an equity problem: Should less money be spent on children in poorer districts because of where their parents live? Heavy reliance on local property taxes to fund schools generally ensures that fiscal disparities among school districts will exist. But many school districts across the country have sued their respective state governments, claiming that heavy reliance on local property taxes to fund schools discriminates unfairly against poorer communities. A number of state supreme courts in recent years have agreed, and cases are currently pending in many other states. To achieve equity in school funding among communities, state courts are increasingly ordering their legislatures to substitute state general revenues for local property taxes. Michigan voters in 1993 approved a plan to abolish local school property taxes altogether and to replace their revenues by increasing the state's sales tax.

GOVERNING LOCAL SCHOOLS

Responsibility for many basic decisions in public education lies with the fourteen thousand separate school districts in America. In theory, these school districts are under local control. The people of the local school district are supposed to exercise that control through an elected *school board* and an elected or appointed *superintendent* who acts as the chief executive of the community schools. There is some variation to that pattern—in approximately a quarter of the nation's school districts, the boards are appointed rather than elected, usually by city councils, county commissions, mayors, or even judges. In theory, school boards exercise control over curriculum (that is, what should be taught in the schools), buildings and facilities, personnel (including both administrators and teachers), and perhaps most important of all, financing. In practice, however, as we have already seen, the concept of local control over education is heavily circumscribed by both state and federal laws.

WHO GOVERNS OUR SCHOOLS?   American schools face a dilemma in determining who should govern. Aside from the interference of federal and state administrative agencies, there is the recurring problem of "democracy" versus "professionalism." Is a democratically elected board, responsible to the citizens, an appropriate model of governance for the schools? Or should technical and policy issues be determined by professional educators who possess the necessary technical competence? Or should we continue to attempt to combine these two conflicting notions of governance?

Democratic theory assumes that schools are public institutions that should be governed by the local citizenry through their elected representatives. This was the original concept in American public education developed in the nineteenth century. However, as school issues became more complex, the knowledge of citizen school boards seemed insufficient to cope with the many problems confronting the schools—teaching innovations, curricular changes, federal and state mandates, multimillion-dollar building programs, special educational programs, and so forth. Over time, school superintendents and their administrative assistants came to exercise more and more control over day-to-day operations of the schools. Theoretically, superintendents only implement the policies of the board, but in practice they have assumed much of the policy making in local school districts. Superintendents keep in touch with the university schools of education; devote full time to their job; receive direct advice from attorneys, architects, accountants, and educational consultants; and generally set the agenda for school board meetings.

PROFESSIONALISM VERSUS DEMOCRACY   The resulting "professionalism" in education tangles directly with the "democratic" notion of control of schools. There are few meetings of local school boards that do not involve at least some tug-of-war between board members and the superintendent. (It is interesting to note that in European countries education has long been under the control of professionals, with little or no direct citizen participation in school governance.) Professional educators are frequently disdainful of the laypeople who compose the school board: The professionals must patiently explain matters of curriculum, faculties, personnel, and finance to citizen board members who are untrained in the matters about which they must decide. Professional educators often support the idea that "politics" should be kept out of education; to them, this means that nonprofessionals, even elected school board members, should not interfere in educational decisions.

THE SCHOOL DISTRICT SUPERINTENDENTS

The school district superintendents are usually professionally trained educators, either appointed by the local school board or separately elected on a nonpartisan ballot. The superintendent is responsible for the management of the public schools—hiring and supervising teachers and principals, planning and organizing the schools, preparing budgets and overseeing expenditures, and recommending policy to the board.

PROFESSIONAL DOMINANCE?   Superintendents are expected to bring professional expertise to the schools. But if citizen boards were once easily intimidated by professionally trained superintendents, such is seldom the case today:

> The American school superintendent, long the benevolent ruler whose word was law, has become a harried, embattled figure of authority. . . . Browbeaten by once subservient boards of education, teachers' associations and parents, the superintendent can hardly be blamed if he feels he has lost control of his destiny.[16]

■
School district superintendent.
The chief executive officer of a school district; may be directly elected or appointed by the school board.

School superintendents stress their professional expertise and rely heavily on their educational credentials to give weight to their policy recommendations. About three-quarters of school superintendents in large metropolitan areas hold doctoral degrees.[17]

Those without doctorates have at least a master's degree. Most superintendents earned their graduate degree *after* they had been employed several years as teachers.

RESPONSIBILITIES   School superintendents have three major responsibilities. First, the superintendents set the agenda for school board decisions. Second, the superintendent makes policy recommendations. Most agenda items will carry a recommendation. Third, the superintendent implements board decisions. In performing these responsibilities, superintendents, even more than city managers, provide strong leadership—advocating policy changes and selling programs to the community. Moreover, many superintendents, in contrast to city managers, involve themselves in school board elections, providing encouragement to candidates whom they respect.

LEADERSHIP   Professional superintendents do not expect to be overruled by their boards. Many of them have a "trust me or fire me" attitude that often makes compromise difficult. Nonetheless, the average tenure of appointed school superintendents is fairly long, about eight years. This is slightly longer than the average tenure of city managers (seven years).

A dominant role for school superintendents in educational policy, a role claimed on the basis of professional expertise and educational credentials, tends to minimize citizen participation in education decision making. But this role may be increasingly challenged. As one school superintendent acknowledged:

> The job of superintendent has changed radically over the past twenty years. . . . Now I have to deal with teacher militancy, closing schools, firing teachers, being more accountable for costs, and working with more active parents and citizens.[18]

However, school board members and interested citizens generally believe that popular control of education is a vital component of democracy. Schools should be "responsive" to community needs and desires. Frequently, citizen criticism has focused on the schools' failure to teach basic skills—reading, writing, and arithmetic. Another frequent source of citizen concern is the perceived retreat of the schools from traditional moral values. These issues have in turn raised the underlying question—who should govern our schools, professional educators or interested citizens?

SCHOOL BOARDS: RESPONSIBLE POLICY MAKERS?

Even if we accept the notion that schools should be governed by a democratically elected board, how can we know whether board members are accurately reflecting their constituents' desires and aspirations?

RECRUITMENT AND SELECTION   Like most decision makers, the nation's 85,000 school board members are unrepresentative of their constituents in socioeconomic background. Specifically, board members are more often male, white, middle-aged, better educated, more prestigiously employed, Republican, and Protestant and have lived in the county longer than their constituents.[19] They come disproportionately from "educational families"; many members have relatives in education, usually their

■
School board.
The elected governing body
of a school district.

spouse. Many school board members report that they were first prompted to run for the school board by friends already on the board; this suggests a perpetuation of similar kinds of people on school boards. Most school board elections are nonpartisan. Many members originally came to the board as appointees to replace individuals who left the board with unexpired terms. Seldom are incumbents defeated for reelection; two-thirds of the board members who leave office do so voluntarily. The average tenure of board members is about five years, compared to over eight years for superintendents. School board members do not ordinarily aspire to, or gain, higher political office. All of this suggests "volunteerism" among board members and difficulty in holding members accountable through the threat of electoral defeat.

BLACK REPRESENTATION   Black membership on the nation's large central-city school district boards reflects fairly accurately the black population in central cities.[20] Black representation on school boards has been linked to a variety of school policies: increased employment of black teachers; fewer black students disciplined, suspended, or dropping out; fewer black students assigned to special education classes; and more black students in gifted programs.

TEACHERS' UNIONS   The struggle for power over the schools between interested citizens, school board members, and professional educators has now been joined by still another powerful force—the nation's teachers' unions. Most of the nation's 2 million teachers are organized into either the older, larger National Education Association (NEA) or the smaller American Federation of Teachers (AFT), an affiliate of the AFL-CIO. Since its origin, the AFT has espoused the right to organize, bargain collectively, and strike, in the fashion of other labor unions. The AFT is small in numbers, but its membership is concentrated in the nation's largest cities, where it exercises considerable power. Traditionally, the NEA was considered a "professional" organization of both teachers and administrators. However, today state and district chapters of the NEA are organized as labor unions, demanding collective bargaining rights for their members and threatening to strike to achieve them. Both AFT and NEA chapters have shut down schools to force concessions by superintendents, board members, and taxpayers—not only in salaries and benefits, but also in pupil–teacher ratios, classroom conditions, school discipline, and other educational matters. As the teachers' unions grow stronger, the traditional question of whether citizens or professional administrators should run the schools will be made more complex: What role should teachers' unions have in determining educational policy?

FRUSTRATION ON THE BOARD   Yet, even school board members who try diligently to be responsive to their constituents are likely to face frustration in their job. Their friends, neighbors, and supporters in the community expect much more of them than they can deliver. As one frustrated board member lamented:

> America prides itself on local control of its schools; after four years on the board I have concluded that this notion of local control is a fallacy. . . . The state dictates graduation requirements and the minimum time to be spent on subjects . . . special education statutes require costly individualized educational plans for the mentally, physically and learning disabled. . . . In the critical matter of teacher performance, school boards are re-

stricted statutorily by the state and contractually by the teachers' union. . . . Antiquated state certification [of teachers] laws hamper boards further. . . .[21]

The result is that school board members can do little to improve educational outcome—to raise SAT scores, for example. Indeed, gifted student programs, computer education, and foreign language classes are routinely eliminated when budget shortfalls occur in order to preserve state-mandated programs.

THE POLITICS OF HIGHER EDUCATION

States have been involved in public higher education since the colonial era. State governments in the Northeast frequently made contributions to support private colleges in their states. The first university to be chartered by a state legislature was the University of Georgia in 1794. Before the Civil War, northeastern states relied exclusively on private colleges, and the southern states assumed the leadership in public higher education. The early curricula at southern state universities, however, resembled the rigid classical studies of the early private colleges—with heavy emphasis on Greek and Latin, history, philosophy, and literature.

EARLY FEDERAL SUPPORT It was not until the Morrill Land Grant Act of 1862 that public higher education began to make major strides in the American states. Interestingly, the eastern states were slow to respond to the opportunity afforded by the Morrill Act to develop public universities; eastern states continued to rely primarily on their private colleges and universities. The southern states were economically depressed in the post–Civil War period, and leadership in public higher education passed to the midwestern states. The philosophy of the Morrill Act emphasized agricultural and mechanical studies, rather than the classical curricula of eastern colleges, and the movement for "A and M" education spread rapidly in the agricultural states. The early groups of midwestern state universities were closely tied to agricultural education, including agricultural extension services. State universities also took over the responsibility for the training of public school teachers in colleges of education. The state universities introduced a broad range of modern subjects in the university curricula—business administration, agriculture, home economics, education, engineering. It was not until the 1960s that the eastern states began to develop public higher education (notably the State University of New York multicampus system).

PUBLIC HIGHER EDUCATION Today, public higher education enrolls three-quarters of the nation's college and university students. Perhaps more importantly, the nation's leading state universities can challenge the best private institutions in academic excellence. The University of California at Berkeley and the University of Michigan are deservedly ranked with Harvard, Yale, Princeton, Stanford, and Chicago.

Higher education in America is mass education. No other nation sends so large a proportion of its young people to college. Over 15 million Americans are enrolled in colleges and universities. Over half of all high school graduates enroll in college.

Table 15–2

HIGHER EDUCATION IN AMERICA			
	1970	*1980*	*1995*
Institutions			
Total	2,556	3,231	3,706
Four-year colleges and universities	1,665	1,957	2,244
Two-year colleges	891	1,274	1,462
Faculty (thousands)	474	686	910
Enrollment (thousands)			
Total	8,581	12,097	14,262
Four-year colleges and universities	6,290	7,571	8,769
Two-year colleges	1,630	4,526	5,493
Public	5,800	9,457	11,093
Private	2,120	2,640	3,169
Graduate	1,031	1,343	1,732
Undergraduate	7,376	10,495	12,232

Source: Statistical Abstract of the United States, 1997, p. 183.

ECONOMIC VALUE OF EDUCATION   An education may be its own reward, enhancing one's life regardless of economic circumstances. But there is also ample evidence that education improves one's earning potential. (See Figure 15–2.) At each level of advanced education, earnings are significantly enhanced.

COMMUNITY COLLEGES   In most states, community colleges are separate from state colleges and universities; the community colleges are really part of local government. They receive revenue from local property taxes as well as grants from the state and federal government. They are usually governed by a local board, whose members are elected or appointed from the communities served by the college.

Community colleges have been the fastest growing sector of American higher education. (See Table 15–2.) These colleges are designed to reflect the local area's requirements for higher education, and they usually offer both a general undergraduate curriculum that fulfills the first two years of a baccalaureate degree, and vocational and technical programs that fulfill community needs for skilled workers. Moreover, community colleges usually offer special programs and courses in adult higher education often in association with community groups.[22]

UNIVERSITY GOVERNANCE   The organization and governance of public higher education varies a great deal from state to state. Most states have established boards of trustees (or "regents") with authority to govern the state universities. One of the purposes of the boards is to insulate higher education from the vicissitudes of politics.

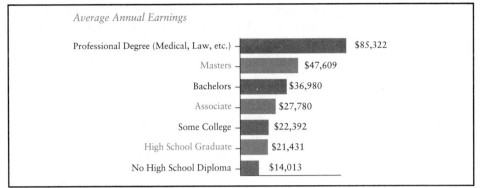

Average Annual Earnings

Professional Degree (Medical, Law, etc.)	$85,322
Masters	$47,609
Bachelors	$36,980
Associate	$27,780
Some College	$22,392
High School Graduate	$21,431
No High School Diploma	$14,013

FIGURE 15–2
The Economic Value of Education

Source: U.S. Bureau of the Census. Figures are from 1996.

Prominent citizens who are appointed to these boards are expected to champion higher education with the public and the legislature, as well as set overall policy guidelines for colleges and universities. In the past, there were separate boards for each institution and separate consideration by the governor's office and the legislature of each institution's budgetary request. However, the resulting competition caused state after state to create unified "university system" boards to coordinate higher education. These university system boards consolidate the budget requests of each institution, determine systemwide priorities, and present a single budget for higher education to the governor and the legislature. The stronger and more independent the university system board, the less likely that university and college funding will be distributed in a pork-barrel fashion by legislators seeking to enhance their local constituencies.

THE PRESIDENTS The key figures in university politics are the presidents. They are the chief spokespersons for higher education, and they must convince the public, the regents, the governor, and the legislature of the value of state universities. The presidents' crucial role is one of maintaining support for higher education in the state; they frequently delegate administrative responsibilities for the internal operation of the university to the vice-presidents and deans. Support for higher education among the public and its representatives can be affected by a broad spectrum of university activities, some of which are not directly related to the pursuit of knowledge. A winning football team can stimulate legislative enthusiasm and win appropriations for a new classroom building. University service-oriented research—developing new farm crops or feeds, assessing the state's mineral resources, advising state and local government agencies on administrative problems, analyzing the state economy, advising local school authorities, and so forth—may help to convince the public of the practical benefits of knowledge. University faculty may be interested in advanced research and the education of future Ph.D.s, but legislators and their constituents are more interested in the quality and effectiveness of undergraduate teaching.

THE FACULTY   The faculty traditionally identified themselves as professionals with strong attachments to their institutions. The historic pattern of college and university government included faculty participation in policy making—not only in determining academic requirements but also in budgeting, the hiring and firing of personnel, building programs, and so forth. However, government by faculty committee has proven cumbersome, unwieldy, and time-consuming in an era of large-scale enrollments, multimillion-dollar budgets, and increases in the size and complexity of academic administration. Increasingly, concepts of public "accountability," academic "management," cost control, centralized budgeting and purchasing have transferred power in colleges and universities from faculty to professional academic administrators.

THE UNIONS   The traditional organization for faculty was the American Association of University Professors (AAUP); historically, this group confined itself to publishing data on faculty salaries and officially "censoring" colleges or universities that violated longstanding notions of academic freedom or tenure. (*Tenure* ensures that faculty members who have demonstrated their competence by service in a college or university position for three to seven years cannot thereafter be dismissed except for "cause"—a serious infraction of established rules or dereliction of duty, provable in an open hearing.) In recent years, some faculty have become convinced that traditional patterns of *individual* bargaining over salaries, teaching load, and working conditions in colleges and universities should be replaced by *collective* bargaining in the style of unionized labor. The American Federation of Teachers of the AFL-CIO, as well as the National Education Association and the AAUP have sought to represent faculty in collective bargaining. Many states now authorize collective bargaining with the faculty of public colleges and universities if the faculty votes for such bargaining. Faculty collective bargaining is complicated by the fact that faculty continue to play some role in academic government—choosing deans and department heads, sitting on salary committees, and so forth.

STATE LEGISLATURES   The costs of public higher education are borne largely by taxpayers. Rarely does tuition at state colleges and universities pay for more than one-quarter of the costs of providing an education. Each year's higher education appropriations bill provides state legislatures with the opportunity to exercise their oversight of the state university system.

In recent years, public higher education has faced increased austerity as the demands for state spending on Medicaid, social services, and prison construction have risen dramatically. In most states, higher education is today receiving a *smaller* share of the state budget than in previous years. Moreover, state legislatures are increasingly interjecting themselves into college and university policy making, often intruding on the traditional powers of independent trustees and regents, as well as presidents and faculty.

The thrust of legislative interventions is to increase teaching loads and responsibilities of faculty. State legislators are rarely impressed with the research activities of faculty, even when these activities are funded by grants and contracts from federal agencies or private foundations. And legislators are more concerned with teaching *under*graduates than graduate students. Legislators often receive complaints from parents about closed or overcrowded classes encountered by the sons and daughters of their constituents, or the inability of a state university to admit qualified students. So many state legislators are demanding greater faculty "productivity," usually defined as teaching more classroom hours each week to more undergraduate students.[23]

FEDERAL ROLE   Federal aid to colleges and universities comes in a variety of forms. Historically, the Morrill Act of 1862 provided the groundwork for federal assistance in higher education. In 1890 Congress initiated several federal grants to support the operations of the land-grant colleges, and this aid, although very modest, continues to the present. Federal support for scientific research has also had an important impact on higher education. In 1950 Congress established the National Science Foundation (NSF) to promote scientific research and education through direct grants to university faculty and departments. (In 1965 Congress established a National Endowment for the Arts and Humanities, but these fields receive only a fraction of the amounts given to NSF.) In addition to NSF, many other federal agencies—the Department of Defense, the Department of Education, the U.S. Public Health Service, the Department of Health and Human Services, the Department of Housing and Urban Development, and so forth—grant research contracts to universities for specific projects. Thus, research has become a very big item in university life.

FEDERAL STUDENT AID   The federal government directly assists students through Basic Educational Opportunity Grants, commonly called "Pell Grants" for its sponsor, Senator Claiborne Pell (D.–Rhode Island). The program offers college students in good standing a money grant each year that is based on the amount their families could reasonably be expected to contribute to their educational expenses. The Stafford guaranteed student loan program encourages private banks to make low-interest loans to students. The federal government pays the interest charges while the student is in school and guarantees repayment in the event the student defaults on the payment after graduation. The Perkins national direct student loan program allows students to borrow from the financial aid offices of their own universities. Again, no interest is charged while the student is in college; repayment is delayed until after the student leaves school. Finally, a national work-study program uses federal funds to allow colleges and universities to employ students part time while they continue to go to school.

READING, WRITING, AND RELIGION

The First Amendment to the Constitution of the United States contains two important guarantees of religious freedom: (1) "Congress shall make no law respecting an establishment of religion, . . ." and (2) "Or prohibiting the free exercise thereof." The Due Process Clause of the Fourteenth Amendment made these guarantees of religious liberty applicable to the states and their subdivisions as well as to Congress.

"FREE EXERCISE" AND PRIVATE RELIGIOUS SCHOOLS   Most of the debate over religion in the public schools centers on the No Establishment Clause of the First Amendment rather than the Free Exercise Clause. However, it was respect for the Free Exercise Clause that caused the Supreme Court in 1925 to declare unconstitutional an

■

Free Exercise Clause.
The First Amendment clause of the U.S. Constitution, interpreted by the Supreme Court to prohibit states from closing religious schools or forcing all students to attend public schools.

No Establishment Clause.
The First Amendment clause of the U.S. Constitution, interpreted by the Supreme Court to prohibit government from aiding religious education or conducting religious ceremonies in public schools.

attempt on the part of a state to prohibit private religious schools and to force all children to attend public schools. In the words of the Supreme Court: "The fundamental theory of liberty upon which all governments in this Union repose excludes any general power of the state to standardize its children by forcing them to accept instruction from public teachers only. The child is not the mere creature of the state."[24] It is this decision that protects the entire structure of private religious schools in this nation.

THE MEANING OF "NO ESTABLISHMENT" A great deal of religious conflict in America has centered on the meaning of the No Establishment Clause, and the public schools have been the principal scene of this conflict. One interpretation of the clause holds that it does not prevent government from aiding religious schools or encouraging religious beliefs in the public schools, so long as it does not discriminate against any particular religion. Another interpretation of the No Establishment Clause is that it creates a "wall of separation" between church and state in America, which prevents government from directly aiding religious schools or encouraging religious beliefs in any way.

SUPPORT FOR PUBLIC AID TO RELIGIOUS SCHOOLS The Catholic Church in America enrolls over half of all private school students in the nation, and the Catholic Church has led the fight for an interpretation of the No Establishment Clause that would permit government to aid religious schools. As Catholic spokespeople see it, Catholic parents have a right to send their children to Catholic schools; and since they are taxpayers, they also expect that some tax monies should go to the aid of church schools. To do otherwise, they argue, would discriminate against parents who choose a religious education for their children. Those who favor government aid to religious schools frequently refer to the language found in several cases decided by the Supreme Court, which appears to support the idea that government can *in a limited fashion* support the activities of church-related schools. In *Cochran* v. *Board of Education* (1930), the Court upheld a state law providing free textbooks for children attending both public and parochial schools on the grounds that this aid benefited the *children* rather than the Catholic Church and hence did not constitute an "establishment" of religion within the meaning of the First Amendment.[25] In *Everson* v. *Board of Education* (1947), the Supreme Court upheld the provision of school bus service to parochial school children at public expense on the grounds that the "wall of separation between church and state" does not prohibit the state from adopting a general program which helps *all* children, regardless of religion, to proceed safely to and from schools.[26] These cases suggest that the Supreme Court is willing to permit some forms of aid to parochial school *children* that indirectly aids religion, so long as this is not directly used for the teaching of religion.

Proponents of public aid for church schools argue that these schools render a valuable public service by instructing millions of children who would have to be instructed by the state, at additional expense, if church schools were not available. Moreover, there are many precedents for public support of religious institutions: Church property has always been exempt from taxation; church contributions are deductible from federal income taxes; federal funds have been appropriated for the construction of religiously operated hospitals; chaplains are provided in the armed forces as well as in the

Congress of the United States; veterans' programs permit veterans to use their educational subsidies to finance college educations in Catholic universities; federal grants and loans for college construction are available to Catholic as well as to public colleges, and so on.

OPPOSITION TO PUBLIC AID TO RELIGIOUS SCHOOLS Opponents of aid to church schools argue that free public schools are available to the parents of all children regardless of religious denomination. If religious parents are not content with the type of school that the state provides, they should expect to pay for the establishment and operation of special schools. The state is under no obligation to finance the religious preferences in education of religious groups. In fact, they contend that it is unfair to compel taxpayers to support religion directly or indirectly; furthermore, the diversion of any substantial amount of public education funds to church schools would weaken the public school system.

The Supreme Court has also voiced the opinion that the No Establishment Clause of the First Amendment should constitute a "wall of separation" between church and state. In the words of the Court:

> Neither a state nor the federal government can set up a church. Neither can pass laws which aid one religion, aid all religions, or prefer one religion over another. Neither can force nor influence a person to go to or to remain away from church against his will, or force him to profess a belief or disbelief in any religion. No person can be punished for entertaining or professing religious beliefs or disbeliefs, for church attendance or nonattendance. No tax in any amount, large or small, can be levied to support any religious activities or institutions, whatever they may be called, or whatever form they may adopt to teach or practice religion. Neither a state nor the federal government can openly or secretly, participate in the affairs of any religious organizations or groups, and vice versa.[27]

The Supreme Court held in 1971 that it was unconstitutional for a state to pay the costs of teachers' salaries or instructional materials in parochial schools.[28] The Court acknowledged that it had previously approved the provision of state textbooks and bus transportation directly to parochial school children. Nevertheless, the Court held that state payments to parochial schools involved "excessive entanglement between government and religion" and violated both the establishment and free exercise clauses of the First Amendment. State payments to religious schools, the Court said, would require excessive government controls and surveillance to ensure that funds were used only for secular instruction. Moreover, the Court expressed the fear that state aid to parochial schools would create "political divisions along religious lines . . . one of the principal evils against which the First Amendment was intended to protect." However, in *Roemer* v. *Maryland* (1976) the Supreme Court upheld government grants of money to church-related *colleges and universities:* "Religious institutions need not be quarantined from public benefits which are neutrally available to all."[29]

PRAYER IN THE SCHOOLS Religious conflict in public schools also centers on the question of prayer and Bible-reading ceremonies conducted by public schools. The practice of opening the school day with prayer and Bible-reading ceremonies was once widespread in American public schools. Usually the prayer was a Protestant rendition of the Lord's Prayer, and Bible reading was from the King James version. To avoid the denominational aspects of these ceremonies, the New York State Board of Regents substituted a nondenominational prayer, which it required to be said aloud in each class in the presence of a teacher at the beginning of each school day:

> Almighty God, we acknowledge our dependence upon Thee, and we beg Thy blessings upon us, our parents, our teachers, and our country.

New York argued that this prayer ceremony did not violate the No Establishment Clause, because the prayer was denominationally neutral and because student participation in the prayer was voluntary. However, in *Engle* v. *Vitale* (1962), the Supreme Court stated that "the constitutional prohibition against laws respecting an establishment of a religion must at least mean in this country it is no part of the business of government to compose official prayers for any group of the American people to recite as part of a religious program carried on by government."[30] The Court pointed out that making prayer voluntary did not free it from the prohibitions of the No Establishment Clause; that clause prevented the *establishment* of a religious ceremony by a government agency, regardless of whether the ceremony was voluntary or not:

> Neither the fact that the prayer may be denominationally neutral, nor the fact that its observance on the part of the students is voluntary can serve to free it from the limitations of the establishment clause, as it might from the free exercise clause, of the First Amendment, both of which are operative against the states by virtue of the 14th Amendment. . . . The establishment clause, unlike the free exercise clause, does not depend on any showing of direct governmental compulsion and is violated by the enactment of laws which establish an official religion whether those laws operate directly to coerce nonobserving individuals or not.[31]

One year later, in the case of *Abbington Township* v. *Schempp,* the Court considered the constitutionality of Bible-reading ceremonies in the public schools.[32] Here again, even though the children were not required to participate, the Court found that Bible reading as an opening exercise in the schools was a religious ceremony. The Court went to some trouble in its opinion to point out that they were not "throwing the Bible out of the school," for they specifically stated that the study of the Bible or of religion, when presented objectively as part of a secular program of education, did not violate the First Amendment, but religious *ceremonies* involving Bible reading or prayer, established by a state or school, did so.

State efforts to encourage "voluntary prayer" in public schools have also been struck down by the Supreme Court as unconstitutional. When the state of Alabama authorized a period of silence for "meditation or voluntary prayer" in public schools, the Court ruled that this was an "establishment of religion." The Court said the law had no secular purpose, that it conveyed "a message of state endorsement and promotion of prayer," and that its real intent was to encourage prayer in public schools.[33] In a stinging dissenting opinion, Chief Justice Warren Burger noted that the Supreme Court itself opened its session with a prayer, that both houses of Congress opened every session with prayers led by official chaplains paid by the government: "To suggest that a moment of silence statute that includes the word *prayer* unconstitutionally endorses religion, manifests not neutrality but hostility toward religion."

DID YOU KNOW?

THE "BEST-EDUCATED" STATE POPULATIONS

Approximately 22 percent of the U.S. population over age twenty-five has completed a bachelor's degree or more. But the college-educated population spreads itself unevenly across the states. (Actually the District of Columbia, with its hordes of federal bureaucrats, can boast of the largest proportion of college-educated adults—37.6 percent.)

STATES RANKED BY COLLEGE-EDUCATED POPULATIONS

Top Ten (25% or more)		Average (20 to 25%)		Bottom Twenty (Below 20%)	
1 Colorado	30.2	11 New York	24.2	31 Florida	19.8
2 Massachusetts	30.0	12 Kansas	24.1	32 Ohio	19.5
3 Connecticut	28.4	13 Minnesota	23.3	33 South Dakota	19.4
4 New Jersey	27.9	14 Alaska	23.1	34 Idaho	19.1
4 Washington	27.9	14 Vermont	23.1	34 Michigan	19.1
6 New Hampshire	26.4	16 Oregon	22.9	36 Pennsylvania	18.7
7 Maryland	26.1	17 Utah	22.7	37 North Carolina	18.5
8 Virginia	25.8	18 Arizona	22.4	38 Iowa	18.4
9 Hawaii	25.1	19 New Mexico	22.2	38 Wyoming	18.4
10 California	25.0	20 Delaware	22.1	40 Nebraska	18.2
		20 Illinois	22.1	41 Nevada	17.6
		20 Texas	22.1	42 Mississippi	17.5
		23 Montana	21.9	43 Kentucky	17.2
		24 Georgia	21.1	44 South Carolina	16.7
		25 North Dakota	20.8	45 Louisiana	16.5
		26 Oklahoma	20.5	46 Arkansas	15.8
		26 Rhode Island	20.5	47 Tennessee	14.9
		28 Maine	20.4	48 Alabama	14.6
		29 Missouri	20.3	49 Indiana	14.1
		30 Wisconsin	20.0	50 West Virginia	12.2

However, if "best-educated" is defined as the highest percentage of adult *high school graduates,* then Utah (90.0%) must be ranked number one, and West Virginia (68.5%) ranked number fifty.

ON THE WEB

Most state education departments have their own Web sites that can be accessed through the state government homepages (see "On the Web" in Chapter 2). These sites usually provide extensive information on the organization and functioning of educational agencies of the state. Many larger school districts throughout the nation also maintain their own Web sites.

The largest and oldest independent organization in education is the National Education Association (NEA). It was founded in 1857 and today claims a membership of more than 2 million teachers, from preschool to the university level. Its Web site at

www.nea.org

describes the wide-ranging activities of the organization. The NEA combines professional activities (workshops, forums, publications, etc.) for teachers with union activities (organizing teachers' unions and negotiating contracts with school districts, colleges, and universities) and with lobbying activities in state capitals and in Washington.

School administrators are organized in the American Association of School Administrators. This organization's Web site at

> www.aasa.org

offers school officials current information on educational topics and reports on its lobbying activities, including its support for federal funding of schools and its strong opposition to private school vouchers. The organization also publishes a monthly magazine, *The School Administrator.*

The American Association of University Professors (AAUP) was founded in 1915 to defend academic freedom and tenure, advocate collegial governance, and support the due process rights of university professors. The AAUP regularly reports on faculty salaries at virtually every institution of higher education in the nation. It also investigates particularly egregious cases of infringement of academic freedom and due process and officially censures colleges and universities found to have violated the rights of professors. The AAUP Web site at

> www.aaup.org

reports on current issues of concern to professors, including the increasingly heavy use of low-paid adjunct and part-time faculty and graduate students to teach undergraduate courses.

The National Association of Scholars (NAS) was founded in 1989 to work toward "the restoration of intellectual substance, individual merit, and academic freedom in the university." The NAS Web site at

> www.nas.org

describes the organization's efforts to restore the classic works of Western civilization to the curriculum, to maintain the merit principle in faculty recruitment and promotion (rather than recruitment and promotion based on race or gender), and to defend faculty against "PC" (politically correct) infringements on academic freedom.

The U.S. Department of Education maintains a Web site at

> www.doe.gov

that describes all federal aid to education programs, including loans and financial aid programs for college students.

NOTES

1. *Statistical Abstract of the United States, 1997,* p. 175.

2. Administered nationally by the College Board, New York. The SAT was formerly named the Scholastic Aptitude Test.

3. James S. Coleman et al., *Equality of Educational Opportunity* (Washington, DC: Government Printing Office, 1966).

4. James S. Coleman et al., *High School Achievement* (New York: Basic Books, 1982).

5. James S. Coleman and Thomas Hoffer, *Public and Private High Schools* (New York: Basic Books, 1987).

6. National Commission on Excellence in Education, *A Nation At Risk* (Washington, DC: Government Printing Office, 1983).

7. U.S. Department of Education, *America 2000* (Washington, DC: Government Printing Office, 1991).

8. See John E. Chubb and Terry M. Moe, "Politics, Markets, and the Organization of Schools," *American Political Science Review,* 82 (December 1988), 1065–87; and their *Politics, Markets, and America's Schools* (Washington, DC: Brookings Institution, 1990).

9. James S. Coleman and Thomas Hoffer, *Public and Private High Schools* (New York: Basic Books, 1987).

10. Bill Clinton and Al Gore, *Putting People First* (New York: Times Books, 1992), p. 86.

11. See Brian Jendryka, "Failing Grade for Federal Aid," *Policy Review* (Fall 1993), 77–81.

12. *Statistical Abstract of the United States, 1997.*

13. *Congressional Quarterly Weekly Report,* March 27, 1993, p. 752.

14. *Rodriguez v. San Antonio Independent School District,* 411 U.S. 1 (1973).

15. *Serrano v. Priest,* 5 Cal. 594 (1971).

16. Harmon Zeigler, Ellen Kehoe, and Jane Reisman, *City Managers and School Superintendents* (New York: Praeger, 1985), p. 21.

17. Ibid., p. 40.

18. Ibid., p. 158.

19. See Trudy Haffron Bers, "Local Political Elites: Men and Women on Boards of Education," *Western Political Quarterly,* 31 (September 1978), 381–91.

20. Kenneth J. Meier and Robert E. England, "Black Representation and Educational Policy," *American Political Science Review,* 78 (June 1984), 393–403.

21. Quotations from a local school board member in Connecticut, in *Newsweek,* September 14, 1992.

22. Trudy Haffron Bers, "Politics Programs and Local Governments: The Case of Community Colleges," *Journal of Politics,* 40 (February 1980), 150–64.

23. See Charles Mathesian, "Higher Ed: The No-Longer-Sacred Cow," *Governing* (July 1995), 20–26.

24. *Pierce v. The Society of Sisters,* 268 U.S. 510 (1925).

25. *Cochran v. Board of Education,* 281 U.S. 370 (1930).

26. *Everson v. Board of Education,* 330 U.S. 1 (1947).

27. Hugo Black, majority opinion in *Everson v. Board of Education,* 330 U.S. 1 (1947).

28. *Lemon v. Kurtzman,* 403 U.S. 602 (1972).

29. *Roemer v. Maryland,* 415 U.S. 382 (1976).

30. *Engle v. Vitale,* 370 U.S. 421 (1962).

31. Ibid.

32. *Abbington Township v. Schempp,* 374 U.S. 203 (1963).

33. *Wallace v. Jaffree,* 105 S. Ct. 2479 (1986).

16

THE POLITICS OF POVERTY, WELFARE, AND HEALTH

POVERTY IN AMERICA

Political conflict over poverty in America begins with disagreement over its nature and extent, and then it proceeds to disputes over its causes and remedies.

HOW MANY POOR?   How much poverty really exists in America? According to the U.S. Bureau of the Census, there are between 35 and 40 million poor people in the United States. The official poverty rate (the number of people living in poverty as a percentage of the total population) has ranged between 13 and 15 percent in recent years (see Figure 16–1). This official definition of poverty includes all those Americans whose annual cash income falls below that which is required to maintain a decent standard of living. The dollar amounts of the poverty level change each year to take into account the effect of inflation.[1]

LIBERAL CRITICISM   This official definition of poverty has many critics. Some liberals believe poverty is underestimated because (1) the official definition does not take into account regional differences in the cost of living, climate, or accepted styles of living; (2) the official definition includes cash income from welfare and Social Security (without this government assistance, the number of poor would be much higher, perhaps 25 percent of the total population); and (3) the official definition does not count the many "near poor." There are nearly 50 million Americans or 19 percent of the population living below 125 percent of the poverty level.

CONSERVATIVE CRITICISM   Some conservatives also challenge the official definition of poverty: (1) It does not consider the value of family assets. People (usually older people) who own their own mortgage-free homes, furniture, and automobiles may have current incomes below the poverty line yet not suffer hardship; (2) there are many families and individuals who are officially counted as poor but who do not think of themselves as "poor people"—students, for example, who deliberately postpone income to secure an education; (3) more importantly, the official definition of poverty excludes "in kind" (noncash) benefits given to the poor by governments. These benefits include, for example, food stamps, free medical care, public housing, and school lunches. If these benefits were "costed out" (calculated as cash income), there may be only half as many poor people as shown in official statistics.

THREE DEFINITIONS OF POVERTY   Thus, in addition to the "official" government definition of poverty, we can also consider "latent poverty"—people who would be poor if there were no government welfare or Social Security programs—and "net poverty"—people who fall below the poverty line after costing out the value of in kind government benefits. The official poverty rate, the latent poverty rate, and the net poverty rate are shown in Figure 16–1.

VARIATIONS AMONG THE STATES   The official poverty rate varies considerably among the states (see "*Rankings of the States:* Poverty and Welfare"). Poverty in some states (notably New Mexico, Louisiana, and Mississippi) ranges up to 20 percent or

Poverty rate.
The percentage of the population whose annual cash income falls below that which is required, according to the federal government, to maintain a decent standard of living.

"Latent poverty."
People who would be poor if there were no government welfare or Social Security programs.

"Net poverty."
People who fall below the poverty line after costing out the value of in-kind government benefits.

more. Inasmuch as minority populations tend to experience poverty in greater proportions than others, it is not surprising that southern states with larger African American populations and southwestern states with larger Hispanic populations have higher poverty rates. And historically, the rural Appalachian Mountain populations, especially in West Virginia, have also experienced high poverty rates. As one might expect, the proportion of a state's population receiving cash welfare benefits tends to reflect a state's poverty rate. However, it should be noted that in all states the number and proportion of people receiving welfare benefits is well below the number and proportion of people living in poverty.

WHO ARE THE POOR?

Poverty occurs in many kinds of families and in all races and ethnic groups. However, some groups experience poverty in greater proportions than the national average.

FAMILY STRUCTURE   Poverty is most common among female-headed families. The incidence of poverty among these families in 1997 was over 30 percent, compared to only 5 percent for married couples (see Table 16–1). These women and their children comprise over two-thirds of all of the persons living in poverty in the United States. These figures describe "the feminization of poverty" in America. Clearly, poverty is closely related to the family structure. Today the disintegration of the traditional husband–wife family is the single most influential factor contributing to poverty.

FIGURE **16–1** Three Definitions of Poverty

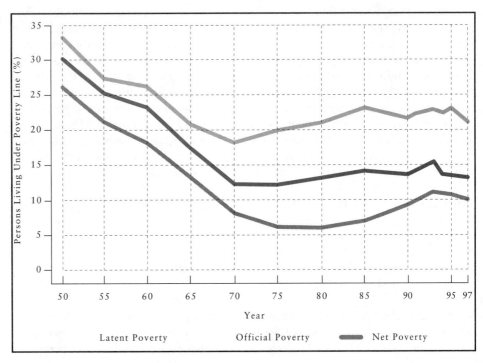

POVERTY AND WELFARE

Poverty Rate (in percents)[a]

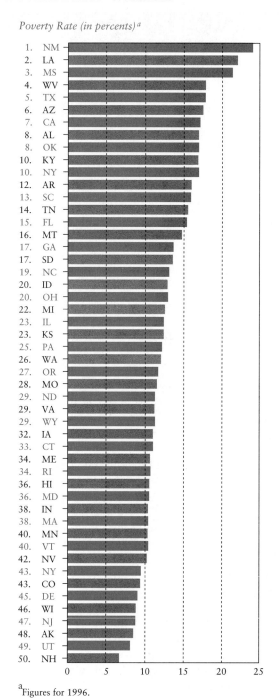

1.	NM
2.	LA
3.	MS
4.	WV
5.	TX
6.	AZ
7.	CA
8.	AL
8.	OK
10.	KY
10.	NY
12.	AR
13.	SC
14.	TN
15.	FL
16.	MT
17.	GA
17.	SD
19.	NC
20.	ID
20.	OH
22.	MI
23.	IL
23.	KS
25.	PA
26.	WA
27.	OR
28.	MO
29.	ND
29.	VA
29.	WY
32.	IA
33.	CT
34.	ME
34.	RI
36.	HI
36.	MD
38.	IN
38.	MA
40.	MN
40.	VT
42.	NV
43.	NY
43.	CO
45.	DE
46.	WI
47.	NJ
48.	AK
49.	UT
50.	NH

0   5   10   15   20   25

[a] Figures for 1996.

Recipients of Cash Assistance (in percents)[b]

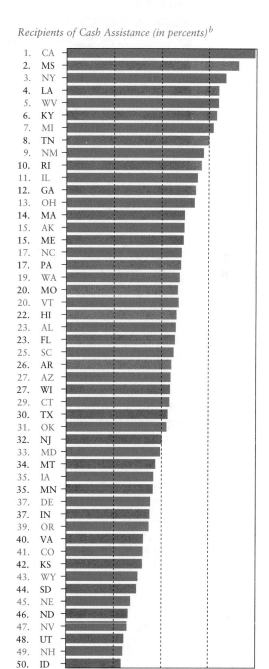

1.	CA
2.	MS
3.	NY
4.	LA
5.	WV
6.	KY
7.	MI
8.	TN
9.	NM
10.	RI
11.	IL
12.	GA
13.	OH
14.	MA
15.	AK
15.	ME
17.	NC
17.	PA
19.	WA
20.	MO
20.	VT
22.	HI
23.	AL
23.	FL
25.	SC
26.	AR
27.	AZ
27.	WI
29.	CT
30.	TX
31.	OK
32.	NJ
33.	MD
34.	MT
35.	IA
35.	MN
37.	DE
37.	IN
39.	OR
40.	VA
41.	CO
42.	KS
43.	WY
44.	SD
45.	NE
46.	ND
47.	NV
48.	UT
49.	NH
50.	ID

0   3   6   9   12

[b] Includes SSI and AFDC; figures for 1995 (before TANF reform).

Source: U.S. Bureau of the Census.

Table 16–1

POVERTY IN AMERICA	
Poverty definition 1997 (Nonfarm family of four)	$16,276
Number of poor	35.6 million
Poverty percentage of total population	13.3
Race (% poor)	
White	11.0
Black	26.5
Hispanic	27.1
Age (% poor)	
Under 18	19.9
Over 65	10.5
Family (% poor)	
Married couple	5.2
Single parent, mother only	31.6

Source: U.S. Bureau of the Census, Office of Statistics, 1998.

ETHNICITY   African Americans and Hispanics experience poverty in much greater proportions than whites. Over the years the poverty rate among blacks in the United States has been over twice the poverty rate among whites.

AGE   The aged in America experience *less* poverty than the nonaged. The aged are not poor, despite the popularity of the phrase "the poor and the aged." The poverty rate for persons over sixty-five years of age is *below* the national average. Moreover, the aged are much wealthier than the nonaged. They are more likely than younger people to own homes with paid mortgages. A large portion of their medical expenses is paid by Medicare. With fewer expenses, the aged, even with relatively smaller cash incomes, experience poverty in a different fashion than young mothers with children. Continuing increases in Social Security benefits over the years are largely responsible for this singular "victory" in the war against poverty.

WEALTH   Wealth is the net worth of all one's possessions—home value minus mortgage, auto value minus loan, business value minus debts, money in bank accounts, savings, stocks and bonds, and real estate. All calculations of poverty consider *income*, not *wealth*. It is theoretically possible for persons to have considerable wealth (e.g., to own a mortgage-free home and a loan-free automobile and have money in savings and investments), yet fall within the official definition of poverty because current cash income is low. Indeed, many of the *aged* who are counted as poor because their incomes are low have substantial accumulations of wealth. The U.S. Bureau of the Census esti-mates that in 1995 the net worth of the median family over age 65 was $104,100, compared to a net worth of only $11,400 for householders under age 35.[2] This sug-gests that the elderly are ten times wealthier than the young!

INEQUALITY IN AMERICA

Inequality in America has been increasing over the last thirty years. Income differences among American families decreased for most of the last century but have widened omi-nously in recent years. This reversal of historical trends has generated both political rhetoric and serious scholarly inquiry about its causes and consequences.

MEASURING INEQUALITY   Inequality is generally measured by income distribution among American families. Table 16–2 divides all families into five groups—from the lowest one-fifth of personal income to the highest one-fifth—and shows the percentage of total family personal income received by each of these groups over the years. (If per-fect income equality existed, each fifth of American families would receive 20 percent of all family personal income, and it would not be possible to rank fifths from highest to lowest.) The poorest one-fifth received 3.5 percent of all family personal income in 1929; by 1947, however, this group had increased its percentage of all family personal income to 5.0. (Most of this increase occurred during World War II.) The highest one-fifth received 54.5 percent of all family personal income in 1929; by 1947, however, this percentage had declined to 46.0. Another measure of income inequality is the per-centage of income received by the top 5 percent in America. The top 5 percent received 30.0 percent of all family personal income in 1929, but only about 21 percent in 1947.

But note that since 1968, the long-term trend toward greater equality in America has been reversed. The percentage of total family income received by the poorest one-fifth of families declined from 5.7 percent in 1968 to 4.4 percent in 1996. In contrast, the richest one-fifth of all families increased their share of total income from 40.6 to 45.8 percent; and the top 5 percent of families increased their share of all income from 14 to 20 percent.

■
Income distribution.
A measure of inequality; generally the percent of total family income received by each quintile (20 percent) of families from highest to low-est in terms of income.

Table 16–2

DISTRIBUTION OF FAMILY INCOME BY QUINTILES AND TOP 5 PERCENT, SELECTED YEARS								
Quintiles	*1929*	*1947*	*1954*	*1968*	*1974*	*1980*	*1990*	*1996*
Lowest	3.5	5.0	4.8	5.7	5.4	5.1	4.6	4.4
Second	9.0	11.0	11.1	12.4	12.0	11.6	10.8	10.1
Third	13.8	16.0	16.4	17.7	17.6	17.5	16.6	15.8
Fourth	19.3	22.0	22.5	23.7	24.1	24.1	23.8	23.2
Highest	54.4	46.0	45.2	40.6	41.0	41.6	44.3	45.8
Top 5 percent	30.0	20.9	20.3	14.0	15.3	15.3	17.4	20.0

Source: U.S. Bureau of the Census, *Current Population Reports.*

EXPLAINING INCREASES IN INEQUALITY   A variety of explanations have been put forth to explain this trend toward greater inequality: the decline of the manufacturing sector of the economy with its relatively high-paying blue-collar jobs; the rise in the number of two-wage families, making single-wage families relatively less affluent; and demographic trends, which include larger portions of female heads of households. But the globalization of trade is emerging as the principal cause of increasing inequality in America. America's unskilled and semiskilled workers are now competing with people around the world, including very low-wage workers in developing nations. In contrast, our high-tech workers, entrepreneurs, and investors benefit significantly from world trade. The result is that inequality has worsened among Americans even though the aggregate income of the nation has risen.[3]

AN OVERVIEW OF WELFARE POLICY

Public welfare has been a recognized responsibility of government in the United States since colonial days. As far back as the Poor Relief Act of 1601, the English Parliament provided workhouses for both the "able-bodied poor" (the unemployed) and poorhouses for widows and orphans, the aged, and the handicapped. Today, as many as half of all families in America receive some type of government payments (see Table 16–3).

Table 16–3

SOCIAL WELFARE FOR EVERYONE	
Percentage of U.S. Population Receiving Government Payments	
BENEFIT	%
Social Security	17
Medicare	15
Medicaid	14
Food stamps	11
Unemployment	4
School lunches	8
Government retirement	5
TANF (formerly AFDC)	4
SSI	4
Energy assistance	4
Educational assistance	3
Public housing	3
Veterans' benefits	2
Families receiving benefits	52%

Source: Data from *Statistical Abstract of the United States, 1997.*

SOCIAL SECURITY   The key feature of the Social Security Act is the Old-Age, Survivors, and Disability Insurance (OASDI) program; this is a compulsory social insurance program which gives individuals a legal right to benefits in the event of certain occurrences that cause a reduction in their income–old age, death of the head of the household, or permanent disability.[4] Both employees and employers must pay equal amounts toward employees' OASDI insurance. Upon retirement, an insured worker is entitled to monthly benefit payments based upon age at retirement and the amount earned during his or her working years. OASDI also ensures benefit payments to survivors of an insured worker, including the spouse if there are dependent children. However, if the spouse has no dependent children, benefits will not begin until he or she reaches retirement age. Finally, OASDI ensures benefit payments to people who suffer permanent and total disabilities that prevent them from working more than one year.

OASDI is a completely federal program, administered by the Social Security Administration in the Department of Health and Human Services. However, OASDI has an important indirect effect on state and local welfare programs, by removing people in whole or in part from welfare roles. Social Security has doubtlessly reduced the welfare problems that state and local governments would otherwise face.

UNEMPLOYMENT COMPENSATION   Another feature of the Social Security Act was that it induced states to enact unemployment compensation programs through the imposition of the payroll tax on all employers. A federal unemployment tax is levied on the payroll of employers of four or more workers, but employers paying into state insurance programs that meet federal standards may use these state payments to offset most of their federal unemployment tax. In other words, the federal government threatens to undertake an unemployment compensation program and tax if the states do not do so themselves. This federal program succeeded in inducing all fifty states to establish unemployment compensation programs. However, the federal standards are flexible, and the states have some freedom in shaping their own unemployment programs. In all cases, unemployed workers must report in person and show that they are willing and able to work in order to receive unemployment compensation benefits, and states cannot deny workers benefits for refusing to work as strikebreakers or refusing to work for rates lower than prevailing rates.

SUPPLEMENTAL SECURITY INCOME (SSI)   The federal government also directly aids certain categories of welfare recipients—the aged, the blind, and the disabled—under a program called Supplemental Security Income (SSI). A loose definition of "disabled"—including alcoholism and drug abuse among adults and attention deficiency among children—has led to rapid growth in the number of SSI recipients.

FAMILY ASSISTANCE   Family Assistance, officially Temporary Assistance to Needy Families, (formerly AFDC, or Aid to Families with Dependent Children), is a grant program to enable the *states* to assist needy families. States now operate the program and define "need"; they set their own benefit levels and establish (within federal guidelines) income and resource limits. Prior to welfare reform in 1996, AFDC was a *federal* entitlement program.

Social Security. The federal government's Old-Age, Survivors, and Disability Insurance program; for all employed Americans it is a compulsory program.

Supplemental Security Income (SSI). Direct federal cash assistance to the needy aged, blind, and disabled.

Temporary Assistance to Needy Families (TANF). Federal aid for state programs of cash assistance to poor families; replaced the AFDC federal entitlement program.

FOOD STAMPS   The federal food stamp program now distributes billions in federal monies to improve food and nutrition among the poor. Eligible persons may receive food stamps, generally from county welfare departments, which may be used to purchase food at supermarkets. This program has mushroomed very rapidly since its origins; eligibility for food stamps now extends to many people who are not poor enough to qualify for public assistance.

OTHER SOCIAL PROGRAMS   Public assistance recipients are generally eligible for participation in a variety of other social programs. These include school lunch and milk; housing assistance; job training; various educational and child-care programs and services; special food programs for women, infants, and children (WIC); home heating and weatherization assistance; free legal services; and more.

MOVING TOWARD WELFARE REFORM

Political conflict over welfare policy arises in part from a clash of values over individual responsibility and social compassion. As Harvard sociologist David Ellwood explains:

> Welfare brings some of our most precious values—involving autonomy, responsibility, work, family, community and compassion—into conflict. We want to help those who are not making it but in so doing, we seem to cheapen the efforts of those who are struggling hard just to get by. We want to offer financial support to those with low incomes, but if we do we reduce the pressure on them and their incentive to work. We want to help people who are not able to help themselves but then we worry that people will not bother to help themselves. We recognize the insecurity of single-parent families but, in helping them, we appear to be promoting or supporting their formation.[5]

A political consensus developed over the years that welfare policy in America was in need of reform. A variety of problems were commonly cited: the work disincentives created by the pyramiding of multiple forms of public assistance, the long-term social dependency that welfare programs seemed to encourage, and the adverse effects welfare assistance appeared to have on families.

WORK DISINCENTIVES   In most states, if a recipient of assistance took a full-time job, assistance checks were stopped. If the former recipient was then laid off, it took some time to get back on welfare. In other words, employment was uncertain, while assistance was not. Moreover, a family on the welfare rolls was generally entitled to participate in the food stamp program, to receive health care through Medicaid, to gain access to free or low-rent public housing, to receive free lunches in public schools, and to receive a variety of other social and educational benefits at little or no cost to themselves. If a family head on welfare took a job, he or she not only lost welfare assistance, but, more important perhaps, became ineligible for food stamps, Medicaid, public housing, and many other social services.

SOCIAL DEPENDENCY   About half of the people receiving welfare benefits at any one time were doing so temporarily; that is, they would leave the welfare rolls within two years. For these recipients, welfare payments were a relatively short-term aid that helped them over life's difficult times. But for others, welfare became a more permanent part of their lives. An "underclass" of persistently poor became dependent on welfare payments for much of their lives. About half of welfare recipients received aid for five years or more.

FAMILY EFFECTS   Traditional welfare policies also provided many disincentives to family life. Unwed parenthood has risen rapidly since 1970. Today nearly one-third of all births are to unmarried women (see Table 16–4). Many poor, young, unmarried women became dependent on welfare payments as teenagers when they first gave birth. It is argued that the availability of welfare cash payments, food stamps, Medicaid, and housing encouraged teenagers to have children, or at least removed the traditional hardships once associated with teenage pregnancy. Welfare benefits accompanying motherhood allowed these young women to live independently of the families in which they were raised, and to live independently of the child's father, thus encouraging these men to abandon their child support responsibilities.

THE FAILURE OF "WORKFARE"   In the federal Family Support Act of 1988, liberals and conservatives joined in an effort to reform the largest cash assistance program, Aid to Families with Dependent Children. The goal was to end long-term dependence on welfare. The act required that states develop a federal job training program (JOBS) for most adults receiving AFDC payments; provide child care for JOBS participants; furnish transitional child care and Medicaid for one year after a participant leaves AFDC to take a job; and strengthen child support enforcement programs.

But welfare rolls continued to rise in the 1990s despite the Family Support Act. Nationwide, welfare rolls increased from 10 million persons to nearly 15 million. No state "workfare" programs required all welfare recipients to take jobs, or even to en-

Table 16–4

RISING BIRTHS TO UNMARRIED WOMEN			
	All Races	*Whites*	*Blacks*
1950	5.0	4.0	17.0
1970	10.7	5.6	37.0
1975	14.3	7.3	46.8
1980	17.8	10.2	55.5
1985	22.0	14.5	60.1
1990	28.0	20.1	65.2
1995	32.6	25.4	70.4

Source: Statistical Abstract of the United States, 1997, p. 28.

■

Welfare reform.
Officially, the Temporary
Assistance to Needy Families
(TANF) program enacted in
1996, which included the
"devolution" of responsibility for cash assistance programs to the states.

roll in job training programs. Most programs allowed mothers with preschool children to opt out altogether. No state provided enough money to fund the necessary counseling and job training, child care, and health insurance, to permit any sizable number of people to move off of welfare rolls. Only about 10 percent of AFDC recipient parents participated in any education, job training, or job placement programs, and even fewer actually found jobs. Effective "workfare" reform—moving people off welfare rolls into jobs—proved to be more costly than simply providing welfare assistance.

WELFARE REFORM   After a great deal of controversy and two presidential vetoes, welfare reform finally became law in 1996. It was passed by a Republican Congress and signed by a Democratic president, but it was bitterly opposed by groups representing social workers, minorities, and the poor.

Welfare reform—officially Temporary Assistance to Needy Families (TANF)—ended the sixty-year-old federal cash entitlement program for low-income families with children—Aid to Families with Dependent Children (AFDC). TANF reflects the philosophy of "devolution" of responsibility to the states (see "Devolution: Can Federalism Be Revived?" in Chapter 3). TANF is essentially a federal block grant program that allocates lump sums to the states for cash welfare payments. Benefits and eligibility requirements for cash assistance are now largely decided by the states. However, conservatives in Congress imposed some tough-minded "strings" to this federal aid, including a two-year limit on continuing cash benefits and a five-year lifetime limit; a "family cap" that denies additional cash benefits to women already on welfare who bear more children; and the denial of cash welfare to unwed parents under eighteen years of age unless they live with an adult and attend school. Liberals in Congress obtained some modifications to the welfare reform act, including guarantees that states would not reduce their welfare funding below previous years' AFDC spending; exemptions from time limits and work requirements for some portion of welfare recipients; and community service alternatives to work requirements. (See "*Up Close:* Is Welfare Reform a Success?")

HEALTH CARE POLICY

Good health correlates best with factors over which doctors and hospitals have no direct control: heredity, lifestyle (smoking, eating, drinking, exercise, stress), and the physical environment. Historically, most of the reductions in death rates have resulted from public health and sanitation improvements, including immunization against smallpox, clean public water supplies, sanitary sewage disposal, improved diets, and increased standards of living. Many of the leading causes of death today, including heart disease, stroke, cirrhosis of the liver, AIDS, accidents, and suicides, are closely linked to personal habits and lifestyles and are beyond the reach of medicine. Thus, the greatest contribution to better health is likely to be found in altered personal habits and lifestyles, rather than in more medical care.

COMMUNITY PUBLIC HEALTH AND HOSPITALS   Public health and sanitation are among the oldest functions of local government. Keeping clean is still one of the major tasks of cities today, a task that includes street cleaning, sewage disposal, garbage col-

UP CLOSE

IS WELFARE REFORM A SUCCESS?

Supporters of welfare reform have declared it a success. Their claim is based primarily on the rapid exodus of over 2 million people from the nation's welfare rolls (see the figure following).

The number of welfare recipients in the nation has now dropped below 10 million—the lowest number in more than twenty-five years. Fewer than 4 percent of Americans are now

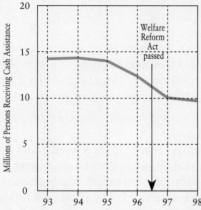

Source: As reported in *New York Times*, February 2, 1997, and January 21, 1998.

on welfare—the smallest proportion since 1970. No doubt some of this decline is attributable to strong growth of the economy: Declines in welfare rolls began *before* Congress passed its welfare reform law, and some decline may have occurred without reform. Many states have initiated their own reforms under "waivers" from the federal government even before Congress acted.

Virtually all states have now developed work programs for welfare recipients. Applicants for welfare benefits are now generally required to enter job-search programs, to undertake job training, and to accept jobs or community service positions.

Yet, although nearly everyone agrees that getting people off welfare rolls and onto payrolls is the main goal of reform, there are major obstacles to the achievement of this goal. First of all, a substantial portion (perhaps 25 to 40 percent) of long-term welfare recipients have handicaps—physical disabilities, chronic illnesses, learning disabilities, alcohol or drug abuse problems—that prevent them from holding a full-time job. Many long-term recipients have no work experience (perhaps 40 percent), and two-thirds of them did not graduate from high school. Almost half have three or more children, making day-care arrangements a major obstacle. It is unlikely that any counseling, education, job training, or job placement programs could ever succeed in getting these people into productive employment. Policy makers argue whether or not there are 5 million jobs available to unskilled mothers, but even if there were, most would be low paying and might not lift the women out of poverty.

lection, and the provision of a clean water supply. Very often these services are taken for granted in the United States, but in many underdeveloped countries of the world, health and sanitation are still major concerns.

Local public health departments are directly concerned with the *prevention* of disease. They engage in compulsory vaccination, immunization, and quarantine, as well as regulatory activity in the processing of milk and the safeguarding of water supplies.

In addition to the preventive activities of the public health departments, state and local governments also provide extensive, tax-supported hospital care. State and local governments provide both general and specialized hospitals, health centers, and nursing homes and very often subsidize private hospitals and medical facilities as well. New York City operates the nation's largest city hospital system, but almost every community subsidizes hospital facilities in some way. City and county hospitals and heavily subsidized private hospitals are expected to provide at least emergency care to indigent patients.

MEDICARE   The federal government added Medicare to the Social Security program in 1965. Medicare provides for prepaid hospital insurance for the aged, and low-cost voluntary medical insurance for the aged under federal administration. Medicare in-

■
Medicare.
Federal health insurance for
the aged.

■
Medicaid.
Federal aid to the states to provide health insurance for the poor.

cludes (1) a compulsory basic health insurance plan covering hospital costs for the aged, which is financed through payroll taxes collected under the Social Security system; and (2) a voluntary but supplemental medical program that will pay doctors' bills and additional medical expenses, financed in part by contributions from the aged and in part by the general tax revenues. Only aged persons are covered by Medicare.

MEDICAID   The federal government also provides federal funds under Medicaid to enable states to guarantee medical services to the poor. Each state operates its own Medicaid program. Unlike Medicare, Medicaid is a welfare program designed for needy persons; no prior contributions are required, and recipients of Medicaid services are generally welfare recipients. States can extend coverage to other medically needy persons if they choose to do so.

PAYING THE HEALTH CARE BILL   Government pays about 43 percent of all health care costs—through Medicare for the aged, Medicaid for the poor, and other government programs including military and veterans care. Private insurance pays for 38 percent of the nation's health costs; direct patient payments count for only 18 percent. (See Figure 16–2.)

HEALTH CARE INFLATION   The costs of health care in the United States have risen much faster than prices in general. Advances in medical technology have produced elaborate and expensive equipment. Hospitals that have made heavy financial investment in this equipment must use it as often as possible. Physicians trained in highly specialized techniques and procedures wish to use them. Physicians and hospitals are forced by the threat of malpractice litigation to use the most advanced tests and treatments.

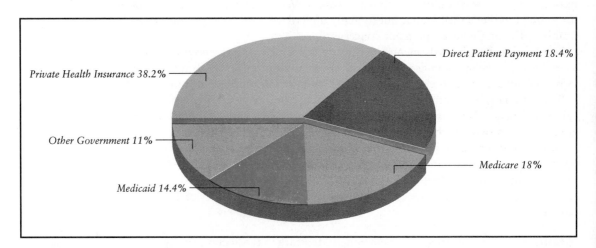

FIGURE 16–2 Who Pays the Health Bill
Source: Statistical Abstract of the United States, 1997.

COPING WITH COSTS   Various efforts have been made to counter rising costs. Private insurers have negotiated discounts with groups of physicians and with hospitals (so-called "preferred provider organizations") and have implemented rules to guide physicians about when patients should and should not receive costly diagnostic and therapeutic procedures (so-called "managed care"). The government has replaced payments to hospitals under Medicare based on costs incurred, with payment of fixed fees based on primary and secondary diagnoses at the time of admission (the diagnosis-related group, or DRG system). Government and private insurers have encouraged the expansion of health maintenance organizations (HMOs) that promise to provide a stipulated list of services to patients for a fixed fee and that are able to provide care at lower total costs than can other providers.

■

Health maintenance organizations (HMOs). Private health-care organizations that provide medical services for fixed fees.

However, many of the efforts by both private insurance companies and governments to control health care costs have created new problems. Cost-control regulations and restrictions add to administrative costs and create a mountain of paperwork for physicians and hospitals. Many insurance companies require preapproval of treatments. Patients and doctors complain that preapproval removes medical decision making from the physician and patient and places it in the hands of nonmedically trained insurance company employees. These problems are now reflected in many state legislative debates about HMO and medical insurance company practices. Among the more popular reforms are bills often referred to as "patient's bill of rights."

MEDICAID IN THE STATES   Medicaid is the costliest of all public assistance programs. States must pay about 45 percent of Medicaid's costs, with the federal government paying the remainder. Medicaid is the most rapidly growing item in the budget of most states.

Medicaid is increasingly becoming the last resort for people who have no medical insurance and for those whose insurance does not cover long-term illness or nursing home care. People confronted with serious or "catastrophic" illness who exhaust their private insurance or Medicare coverage are often forced to impoverish themselves in order to qualify for Medicaid. (Medicare pays for only 60 days of hospital care and 100 days of nursing home care.) Moreover, as the number and proportion of the very old in society rise (those 80 years and over comprise the nation's fastest-growing age group), the need for long-term nursing home care grows. Medicaid is the only program that covers nursing home care, but middle-class people must first "spend down" their savings or transfer their wealth to others in order to qualify for Medicaid. Nursing home care is now the single largest item in Medicaid spending. (See Figure 16–3.)

POLITICS AND HEALTH CARE REFORM

Health care reform centers on two central problems: controlling costs and expanding access. These problems are related: Expanding access to Americans who are currently uninsured and closing gaps in coverage require increases in costs, even while the central thrust of reform is to bring down overall health care costs.

Approximately 85 percent of the population of the United States is covered by either private health insurance, mostly through their employers, or government health insurance, including Medicare and Medicaid. However, about 15 percent of the population

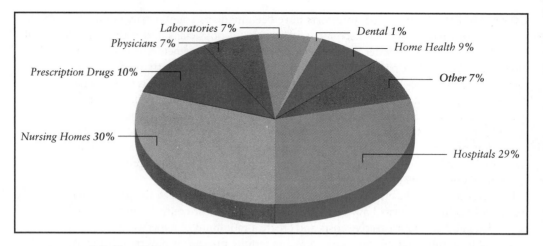

FIGURE 16–3 Medicaid Expenditures
Source: Statistical Abstract of the United States, 1997, p. 118.

has *no* medical insurance (see "*Rankings of the States:* Health Care). Most of the uninsured are working Americans and their families—people who are neither poor enough to qualify for Medicaid nor old enough to qualify for Medicare. These people may postpone or go without needed medical care or be denied medical care except in emergencies. Confronted with serious illnesses, they may be obliged to impoverish themselves in order to become eligible for Medicaid. Their unpaid medical bills must be absorbed by hospitals or shifted to paying patients and their insurance companies.

Yet expanding health care to the currently uninsured promises to add significantly to the already inflated costs of health care in the United States. The nation's total medical bill is now over 15 percent of the gross national product, the highest percentage in the world.

NATIONAL HEALTH CARE REFORM?   The Clinton administration and Congress battled many months over a massive health care reform program developed by a committee headed by First Lady Hillary Clinton. Yet despite Democratic majorities in both the House and Senate in 1993–94, the program failed. The battle itself engendered intense rivalries and much bitterness among parties, interest groups, and individual policy makers in Congress and the executive branch. It is not likely that the federal government will be able to undertake national health care reform very soon. Whatever advances are made in expanding health care coverage or reducing costs must come from the states or the private sector.

"PLAY OR PAY"   States have experimented with various methods of expanding health insurance coverage to those currently uninsured, including persons working for employers who do not provide insurance and persons who are unemployed. A "play or pay" approach requires all employers to either provide health insurance to all their workers and their dependents or alternatively pay into a state fund that would

HEALTH CARE

Lacking Health Insurance [a]

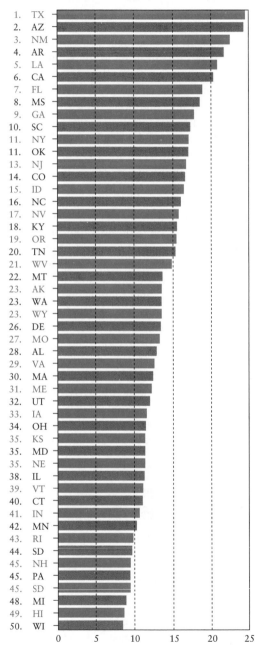

1.	TX	
2.	AZ	
3.	NM	
4.	AR	
5.	LA	
6.	CA	
7.	FL	
8.	MS	
9.	GA	
10.	SC	
11.	NY	
11.	OK	
13.	NJ	
14.	CO	
15.	ID	
16.	NC	
17.	NV	
18.	KY	
19.	OR	
20.	TN	
21.	WV	
22.	MT	
23.	AK	
23.	WA	
23.	WY	
26.	DE	
27.	MO	
28.	AL	
29.	VA	
30.	MA	
31.	ME	
32.	UT	
33.	IA	
34.	OH	
35.	KS	
35.	MD	
35.	NE	
38.	IL	
39.	VT	
40.	CT	
41.	IN	
42.	MN	
43.	RI	
44.	SD	
45.	NH	
45.	PA	
45.	SD	
48.	MI	
49.	HI	
50.	WI	

0 5 10 15 20 25

[a]Percent of population not covered by private government health insurance in 1996.

Infant Death Rate [b]

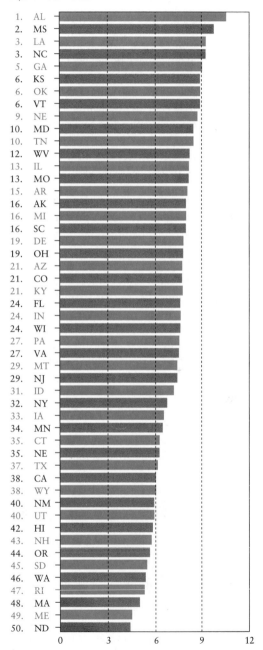

1.	AL	
2.	MS	
3.	LA	
3.	NC	
5.	GA	
6.	KS	
6.	OK	
6.	VT	
9.	NE	
10.	MD	
10.	TN	
12.	WV	
13.	IL	
13.	MO	
15.	AR	
16.	AK	
16.	MI	
16.	SC	
19.	DE	
19.	OH	
21.	AZ	
21.	CO	
21.	KY	
24.	FL	
24.	IN	
24.	WI	
27.	PA	
27.	VA	
29.	MT	
29.	NJ	
31.	ID	
32.	NY	
33.	IA	
34.	MN	
35.	CT	
35.	NE	
37.	TX	
38.	CA	
38.	WY	
40.	NM	
40.	UT	
42.	HI	
43.	NH	
44.	OR	
45.	SD	
46.	WA	
47.	RI	
48.	MA	
49.	ME	
50.	ND	

0 3 6 9 12

[b]Infant deaths per 1,000 live births, 1996.

purchase insurance for uncovered workers. Rules are usually established concerning the proportion of premium costs paid by employers and employees and the range of services covered. While this approach expands coverage, it does little to control costs.

MANAGED COMPETITION Some states have experimented with managed competition as an approach to health care cost containment. Management competition is an arrangement in which health insurance purchasing organizations (HIPOs) are organized to pool health insurance purchases (employers and individuals) in order to improve their bargaining power with insurers and providers. HIPOs are usually required to accept all applicants, including those with preexisting conditions. They receive government subsidies for members of groups expected to generate especially high costs. They negotiate costs either with insurance companies or directly with hospitals and physicians. Because of their size they are better able to collect information and identify providers that supply high-quality care at reasonable prices.

INTEREST GROUP BATTLES While there is widespread public support for the general goals of health care reform—expanding coverage and reducing costs—there is no agreement among the principal interest groups on health care politics about the details of reform. *Insurance companies* are unhappy with the notion of health insurance purchasing organizations that would bargain down insurance premiums or even bypass insurance companies altogether and deal directly with hospitals and physicians' groups. *Physicians* strongly oppose price controls and treatment guidelines; they also oppose any program that takes away patient choice of physicians. *Hospitals,* both public and private profit making, oppose government payment schedules. *Drug companies* want to see prescription drugs paid for by government-sponsored insurance, but they vigorously oppose price controls on drugs. Powerful *senior citizens'* lobbies want added benefits for the aged, including coverage for drugs, dental care, and nursing homes, but they oppose folding Medicare into other health care systems. *Opponents and supporters of abortion rights* battle over whether abortion services should be included in taxpayer-paid programs. All of these groups have strong lobbying organizations in state capitals and in Washington, DC, and all have PACs that contribute heavily to state and national political campaigns.

ON THE WEB

State government homepages generally provide direct links to state welfare agencies; these agencies frequently bear names such as "Children and Families," "Human Services," "Health Care," and so on.

The U.S. Department of Health and Human Services (HHS) maintains a Web site at

   www.dhhs.gov

It describes in detail all major federal health and welfare programs. Each of these programs has its own Web site linked to that of HHS. Among the more important program sites is that of the Administration for Children and Families (AFC); this is the agency that administers Temporary Assistance for Needy Families (TANF), the federal program that assists states in providing cash welfare aid. Another important site is the Health Care Finance Administration (HCFA), the agency that administers federal-state Medicaid programs.

The Social Security Administration maintains its own Web site at

www.ssa.gov

that not only describes the various benefits available under Social Security, but also provides information on "How to Apply" for old age and disability insurance benefits as well as Medicare. You can also submit a request for your own "Personal Earnings and Benefit Estimate Statement" over the Internet; this uses your personal Social Security account information.

The Children's Defense Fund is perhaps the most influential lobby group in Washington representing the poor. Its Web site at:

www.childrensdefense.org

presents arguments in support of increased funding for TANF, in opposition to welfare reform measures that limit benefits, and in support of the expansion of Medicaid to all children. The site also includes statistical information on "Children in the States" with each state separately listed.

NOTES

1. For example, the poverty level for an urban family of four in 1990 was $13,359; in 1993 it was $14,763. U.S. Bureau of the Census, *Statistical Abstract of the United States, 1995.*

2. *Statistical Abstract of the United States, 1997,* p. 480.

3. See Thomas R. Dye and Harmon Zeigler, *The Irony of Democracy,* Millennial Edition (Fort Worth, TX: Harcourt Brace, 2000).

4. The original act did not include disability insurance; this was added by amendment in 1950. Health insurance for the aged, "Medicare," was added by amendment in 1965.

5. David Ellwood, *Poor Support: Poverty in the American Family* (New York: Basic Books, 1988), p. 6.

17

THE POLITICS OF FINANCING AND TAXATION

QUESTIONS TO CONSIDER

★ ★ ★ ★ ★ ★ ★ ★ ★

What do you think is the fairest tax?

- ☐ Income tax
- ☐ Sales tax
- ☐ Property tax

Do you believe that state governments should operate lotteries?

- ☐ Yes
- ☐ No

Should state legislatures have constitu-

tional limits placed on their taxing authority?

- ☐ Yes
- ☐ No

If your city government is forced to reduce spending, do you think it should do so:

- ☐ Across the board on all services?
- ☐ Selectively on only certain services?

AN OVERVIEW OF GOVERNMENT FINANCES

Governments do many things that cannot be measured in dollars. Nonetheless, government expenditures are the best available measure of overall government activity. The expenditure side of a government's budget tells us what public funds are being spent for, and the revenue side tells us how these funds are being raised.

GOVERNMENT FINANCES AND THE GDP   Dollar figures in government budgets are often mind-boggling. The federal government spends over $1.7 *trillion* each year, and all state and local governments combined spend an additional $1 *trillion*. To better understand what these dollar figures mean, it is helpful to view them in relation to the nation's gross domestic product (GDP), the sum of all the goods and services produced in the United States in a year. (See Figure 17–1.)

In 1929 total governmental spending—federal, state, and local combined—amounted to only about 10 percent of the GDP. Today total governmental spending amounts to about 35 percent of the GDP. *Federal* spending accounts for about 20 percent of the GDP, and spending by all *state and local* governments adds another 15 percent.[1]

STATE AND LOCAL GOVERNMENT SPENDING   State and local governments direct most of their spending toward education, social services (welfare and health), public safety (police and fire), and transportation.

Education is the most costly of these functions; health costs are rising more rapidly than any other function. (See Figure 1–3, "How State and Local Governments Spend Their Money" in Chapter 1.)

STATE AND LOCAL GOVERNMENT REVENUES   State and local governments in the United States derive revenue from a variety of sources. Of course, taxes are the largest source of revenue, accounting for nearly 60 percent of all state and local revenue. Federal grants are another major source of state and local government revenue (see Chapter 3), accounting for about 20 percent of total revenues. User charges of various kinds, from water and sewer, liquor store and electric utility revenues, to transit fares and admission fees, account for about 15 percent of all state–local revenue. Lotteries now bring in about 2 percent of all state–local revenue, and the remainder is derived from insurance premiums, licenses, fines, and miscellaneous sources.

TYPES OF TAXES AND TAX POLITICS

The politics of taxation often center on the question of who actually bears the greatest burden of a tax, that is, which income groups must devote the largest proportion of their income to taxes. Taxes that require high-income groups to pay a larger percentage of their incomes in taxes than low-income groups are said to be progressive, while taxes that take a larger share of the income of low-income groups are said to be regressive. Taxation at equal percentage rates, regardless of income level, is said to be proportional.

Gross domestic product (GDP). The sum of all the goods and services produced in the United States in a year; a measure of the size of the U.S. economy.

Progressive taxes. Taxes that require high-income groups to pay a larger percentage of their income in taxes than low-income groups.

Regressive taxes. Taxes that take a larger share of the income of low-income groups than of high-income groups.

Proportional (flat-rate) taxes. Taxes that require all income groups to pay the same percentage of their income in taxes.

FIGURE **17–1**
Government
Spending
Expenditures as a
Percentage of GDP

Source: Advisory Commission
on Intergovernmental Relations, *Significant Features of
Fiscal Federalism 1994.*

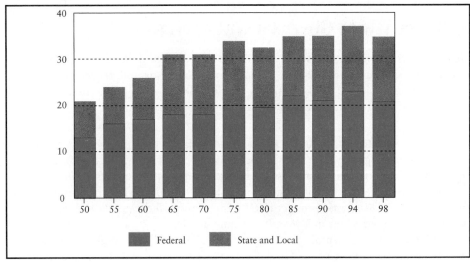

LOCAL PROPERTY TAXES   Property taxes are the largest source of revenue for *local* governments in the United States. (See Figure 17–2.) However, property taxes are usually regressive. This conclusion is based on the assumption that renters actually pay their property taxes through increased rentals levied by the landlord, and the further assumption that high-income groups have more wealth in untaxed forms of property (stocks, bonds, mutual funds, etc.). Since the property tax is the foundation of local tax structures in every state, it is reasonable to conclude that states that rely largely upon local governments for taxes and services are relying more upon regressive tax structures. Yet, in defense of property taxation, it is often argued that no other form of taxation is really feasible for local governments. Local sales and income taxes force individuals and businesses to leave the communities levying them; real estate, on the other hand, is less easy to move about and hide from local tax assessors. Real estate taxes are the only type of taxes that can be effectively collected by relatively untrained local tax officials.

Revenues from property taxation depend upon the property wealth of a community. Dependence upon property taxation means that wealthier communities will be able to raise more funds with less burden on taxpayers than communities without much property wealth. In other words, reliance on property taxation results in inequalities in burdens and benefits between wealthier and poorer communities.

The burden of property taxes depends on (1) the ratio of assessed value of property to the fair market value of the property; (2) the rate at which assessed property is taxed, which is usually expressed in mills, or tenths of a percent; and finally, (3) the nature and extent of tax exemptions and reductions for certain types of property. The ratio of assessed value to full market value may vary from one community to the next, even in states with laws requiring uniform assessment ratios throughout the state. The failure of communities to have periodic and professional tax evaluation means that taxes continue to be levied on old assessment figures, even while market values go up. The result, over time, is a considerable lowering of assessment ratios, and therefore

■
Assessed value.
The dollar value placed on a
property for tax purposes by
the local government assessor.

Market value.
The estimated value of a
property if sold on the open
market.

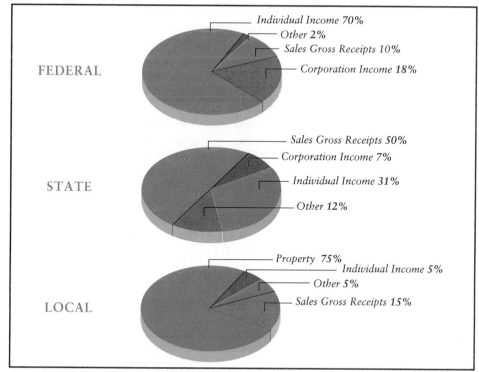

FIGURE 17–2
Sources of Tax
Revenue
Source: U.S. Bureau of the
Census, June 1998.

FEDERAL

- Individual Income 70%
- Other 2%
- Sales Gross Receipts 10%
- Corporation Income 18%

STATE

- Sales Gross Receipts 50%
- Corporation Income 7%
- Individual Income 31%
- Other 12%

LOCAL

- Property 75%
- Individual Income 5%
- Other 5%
- Sales Gross Receipts 15%

taxes, on older homes and businesses and industries. Tax assessors usually know the sale price of houses of newer residents, who must pay higher taxes than those paid by older residents. There are very few communities in which a suggestion of a reevaluation will not set off a heated debate between those who are enjoying a low assessment and those who are not. When a community tampers with reevaluation or a change in the ratio of assessed to market value, it threatens to change the incidence or distribution of tax burdens within a community. If new tax revenues are needed, it is much easier to simply increase the rate or millage to be applied against the assessed value of property. Many communities face state restrictions on maximum tax rates, or they are required to submit any proposed increase in tax rates to the voters in a referendum. These restrictions are usually favored by low-tax forces, which have succeeded in obtaining legislation at the state level that impairs the taxing abilities of local governments.

Some categories of property are exempt from taxation; these usually include properties that are used for nonprofit, charitable, religious, and educational, and other public purposes. Occasionally, such exemptions are attacked by those who feel that they are, in effect, subsidies to the exempted organizations; this is particularly true regarding exemptions for religious property. Exemptions for educational or public properties sometimes work a hardship on communities in which large public facilities or educational institutions are located. However, the exemptions that arouse the greatest controversy are usually those given by state and local governments to new business and industry, in an effort to induce them to locate in the state or community granting the exemption.

STATE SALES TAXES   While the property tax is the most important source of revenue for local communities, *the general sales tax is the most important source of tax revenue for state governments.* Consumers are a notoriously weak pressure group. It is difficult for them to count pennies dribbled away four or five at a time; the tax does not involve obvious payroll deductions, as in income taxation, or year-end bills, as in property taxation. As of 1998 only five states did *not* impose a general sales tax (Alaska, Delaware, Montana, New Hampshire, and Oregon).

State and local sales taxes are often considered regressive, that is, the poor are believed to devote a larger percentage of their income to paying these taxes than the wealthy. The regressivity of sales taxation is based upon the assumption that low-income groups must use most, if not all, of their income for purchases, while high-income groups devote larger shares of their income to savings. However, many states exclude some of the necessities of life from sales taxation, such as packaged food, rent, and medical expenses, in order to reduce the burden of sales taxation on the poor. Because of these exclusions, sales taxes in many states are not really regressive.

States generally rely more heavily on sales taxation than on income taxation. However, reliance upon one or the other type of tax varies from state to state. The decision to place primary reliance upon sales or income taxation is one of the most important policy choices facing state government. The yield from both types of taxation can be quite large.

There are several arguments on behalf of sales taxation in the states. The first is that sales taxation is the only major source of revenue left to the states—local governments must rely on property taxes, and the federal government has placed such a heavy tax burden on incomes that taxpayers will not countenance an additional state bite out of their paychecks. Moreover, sales taxes are not as visible as income or property taxes, since sales taxes are paid pennies at a time. Generally, the customer considers the sales tax as part of the price of an item. Taxpayers never add up the total they have paid in sales taxes, so sales taxation appears to be a relatively "painless" form of taxation. In addition, sales taxes ensure that low-income groups who benefit from public services will share in the costs of government. Actual hardships for the poor from sales taxes can be reduced by excluding food and other necessities from taxation, but the poor will pay taxes when purchasing luxury items. Finally, sales taxes are useful in reaching mobile populations, that is, tourists, commuters, and transients—people who derive benefits from a host state but who would not otherwise help pay for these benefits.

STATE INCOME TAXES   Today forty-one states tax all forms of individual income and two additional states tax nonwage income. But seven states eschew income taxation altogether, and two additional states do not tax wage income. (See Table 17–1.) Connecticut was the most recent state to enact an income tax in 1991. Fiscal pressures on state government continue to stir debate in the non–income tax states over the adoption of the tax.

Progressive state income taxes—income taxes with rates that rise with increases in income—are usually defended on the principle of "ability to pay"; that is, the theory that high-income groups can afford to pay a larger percentage of their income into taxation at no more of a sacrifice than that required of low-income groups who devote a smaller proportion of their income to taxation. The principle of a graduated income

Table 17–1

INCOME TAXATION IN THE STATES	

States Without Income Taxes	*States Taxing Interest, Dividends, and Capital Gains Only*
Alaska	New Hampshire
Florida	Tennessee
Nevada	
South Dakota	
Texas	
Washington	
Wyoming	

States Taxing Adjusted Gross Income (rate ranges in parentheses)

Alabama (2.0–5.0)	Kansas (3.5–7.7)	New York (4.0–7.1)
Arizona (2.9–5.2)	Kentucky (2.0–6.0)	North Carolina (6.0–7.7)
Arkansas (1.0–7.0)	Louisiana (2.0–6.0)	North Dakota (2.6–12.0)
California (1.0–9.3)	Maine (2.0–8.5)	Ohio (0.7–7.2)
Connecticut (3.0–4.5)	Maryland (2.0–5.0)	Oklahoma (0.5–7.0)
Colorado (5.0)	Massachusetts (5.9–12.0)	Oregon (5.0–9.0)
Delaware (3.1–6.9)	Michigan (4.4)	Pennsylvania (2.8)
Georgia (1.0–6.0)	Minnesota (6.0–8.5)	Rhode Island (27.5% federal)[a]
Hawaii (2.0–10.0)	Mississippi (3.0–5.0)	South Carolina (2.5–7.0)
Idaho (2.0–8.2)	Missouri (1.5–6.0)	Utah (2.3–7.0)
Illinois (3.0)	Montana (2.0–11.0)	Vermont (25% federal)[a]
Indiana (3.4)	Nebraska (2.5–6.7)	Virginia (2.0–5.8)
Iowa (0.4–9.0)	New Jersey (1.4–6.4)	West Virginia (3.0–6.5)
	New Mexico (1.7–8.5)	Wisconsin (4.9–6.9)

[a]State income taxes determined as a percentage of federal income tax liability.

Source: Data from Council of State Governments, *Book of the States, 1998–99* (Lexington: Council of State Governments, 1998), p. 270.

tax based on ability to pay, a principle accepted at the federal level in 1913 with the passage of the Sixteenth Amendment, together with the convenience, economy, and efficiency of income taxes, is generally cited by proponents of income taxation.

Personal income taxes in a few states are "flat rate" taxes of 3 percent (Illinois) or 5.0 percent (Colorado) of personal income. In other income tax states, the rates are "progressive"—rising from 1 or 2 percent, to 10 or 12 percent, with increases in income levels. Rhode Island and Vermont tie their *state* personal income tax to the *federal* income tax, by specifying that state taxes will be a specific percentage of federal taxes. Most states also have their own systems of exemptions.

CORPORATE TAXES In addition to property taxes paid to local governments, corporations in forty-six states pay a corporate income tax. (Nevada, Texas, Washington,

■

User charges.
As a form of government revenue, charges levied on specific users by a government agency for the services they use.

and Wyoming do not tax corporate income.) These taxes range from a 5 percent flat rate to sliding scales of 3 to 10 percent of net profits. Raising corporate taxes is popular with voters; individuals do not pay corporate taxes directly; but these taxes may be passed along to consumers in higher prices. The greatest barrier to higher state corporate taxes is the possibility that such taxes will cause corporations to locate in another state. It is difficult for a state to maintain a "good business climate" if its corporate taxes are high. Most studies find that industrial-location decisions are influenced by many factors other than taxes—for example, access to markets, raw materials, skilled labor, and energy. However, businesses expect their taxes to be kept in line with those of their competitors. In addition to corporate profits taxes, business looks at unemployment compensation and worker's compensation "premiums" (taxes) and the costs of environmental regulations.

LOTTERY AND GAMBLING REVENUE   Most states now have public lotteries as a means of raising money. However, lotteries bring in less than 2 percent of all state–local government revenue. The administrative costs, including prize money, run about 50 percent of the gross revenue. This compares very unfavorably with the estimated 5 percent cost of collecting income taxes, and with the only slightly higher cost of collecting sales taxes. Some states also receive income from horse racing, dog racing, and casino gambling. Nevada leads the way with nearly a quarter of its revenue coming directly from gambling taxes. Most states restrict gambling to parimutuel betting on the racetrack. The total revenues raised from such sources, however, make up less than 0.5 percent of all state–local revenues.

USER CHARGES   User charges are currently the fastest-growing source of state and local government revenue. Today, charges and miscellaneous revenues constitute nearly 25 percent of state–local revenue. (This figure is really a combination of user charges, utility and liquor store revenues, and miscellaneous revenues.) User charges directly link the benefits and costs of public goods in the fashion of the marketplace. Only those persons who actually use the government service pay for it. User charges include charges for water and sewerage, garbage collection, electricity supplied by municipalities, transit fares, toll roads, airport landing fees, space rentals, parking meters, stadium fees, admissions to parks, zoos, swimming pools, and so on.

EXPLAINING STATE TAX SYSTEMS

What accounts for differences in tax policy among the states? Total state–local tax revenues in 1995 varied from a high of over $7,000 per person in New York, to a low of $3,734 in Arkansas (see "*Rankings of the States:* Tax Burdens). This means that per capita tax levels of some states are twice as high as those of other states. (Alaska and Wyoming receive most of their tax revenues from *severance taxes* on oil, gas, and coal extracted from the land. The burden of these taxes falls on consumers throughout the nation rather than directly on these states' residents.)

Tax burdens, that is, taxes in relation to personal income, also vary considerably among the states. The concept of tax *burden* generally refers to taxes paid in relation

TAX BURDENS

State-Local Tax Revenue per Capita

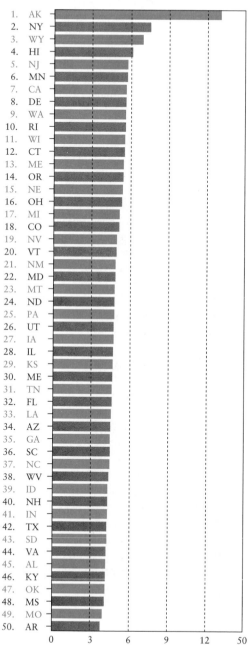

State-Local Tax Revenue
as Percent of Personal Income

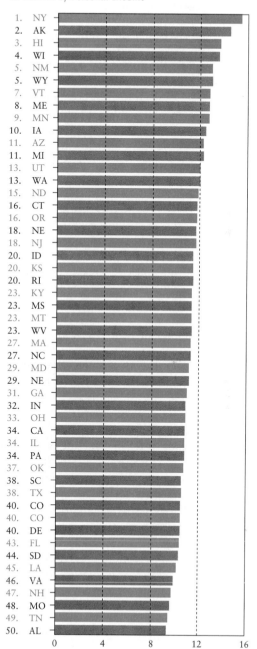

Source: Statistical Abstract of the United States, 1997.

■
Tax burden.
Taxes paid as a percentage
of personal income.

to personal income. Because of differences among the states in income levels, states with the highest per capita *levels of taxation* are not necessarily the same states with the highest *tax burdens*. The total tax burden in a state is measured by "state and local tax revenues as a percent of personal income." (See "*Rankings of the States:* Tax Burdens," right column.) The state–local tax burden averages about 11.4 percent of personal income in the United States.

TAX BURDENS   Among the fifty states, high levels of economic development usually reduce the burdens of taxation. Some wealthy states (for example, California) can collect a great deal of tax monies without taking a very large percentage of personal income. High tax burdens are not necessarily a product of high tax levels, although, of course, there is some relationship between these variables (for example, New York). It is possible to have low tax levels that, because of the lack of industry and low income levels, may be very burdensome—that is, quite high in relation to low incomes (for example, Mississippi).

RELIANCE ON LOCAL GOVERNMENT   Another important difference between richer and poorer states is in the degree of decentralization in state and local finance and administration. Local governments tend to play a greater role in the collection of taxes and the provision of public services in urban, high-income states, while state governments collect a greater portion of revenue and provide more services in rural, low-income states. Earlier, we observed that state governments in poorer rural states undertake more direct responsibilities in education, welfare, and highways. Low levels of economic development tend to force centralization upon these states. Wealthy urban states can afford to let local governments shoulder more responsibilities.

PROGRESSIVITY AND REGRESSIVITY   It is difficult to evaluate the overall progressivity or regressivity of state tax systems. It is generally believed that *overall* state and local government taxes are regressive; one estimate is that the lowest income group in America pays 12.6 percent of its income to state and local taxes, versus 8.4 percent for the highest income group.[2] This regressivity is largely attributed to state and local government reliance on sales and property taxation, rather than progressive income taxation. However, this estimate fails to consider the many types of exemptions to sales taxes found in various states (food, rent, medical care, etc.); these exemptions make sales taxes less regressive. They also fail to consider many property tax exemptions ("homestead" exemptions) found in many states that offer relief to owners of less expensive homes. Nevertheless, it is generally argued that states which rely more on income taxes (especially those states with progressive rate structures rather than flat rates) have more progressive tax systems.[3] Progressivity *increases* with higher levels of state income. It appears to be easier to make tax systems more progressive when the size of the economic pie is expanding.[4]

REVOLTING AGAINST TAXES

The United States is the land of tax revolts. The national tradition of revolting against taxes includes the Boston Tea Party in 1773, a leading event in the movement toward independence; Shay's Rebellion in 1786, an important stimulus to creating the Constitution of the United States; and the Whisky Rebellion of 1794, forcefully extinguished by President George Washington. The political culture of the nation has always reflected a distrust of government power. The total tax burden in the United States is less than most other advanced industrialized nations of the world. Yet opinion polls regularly show that most Americans believe their taxes are "too high."

POPULAR OPPOSITION TO RISING TAXES Voters appear to be very sensitive to levels of state and local taxation. That is to say, popular dislike of taxes rises with increases in real levels of taxation. (This is not as obvious a conclusion as it might seem; state and local taxes are not as visible to most people as federal taxes, and few people are informed or attentive to state and local matters.) Indeed, as state income taxes rise above 4 percent, levels of dislike begin to rise exponentially.[5] Likewise, when sales tax levels rise above 5 percent, opposition increases rapidly. Homeowners are much more likely to object to property taxation than renters, while renters are more likely to object to sales taxes than homeowners.

TAX LIMITATIONS Constitutional limits on taxes fall into several general categories. Of course, any specific plan may vary in details from the outlines described here:

Property-Tax Limits Some limitations are specifically directed at property taxes. These proposals may limit allowable tax rates to 10 or 15 mills of full value of property, limit annual assessment increases, and/or allow reassessments only when the property is sold. This form of limitation applies mainly to local goverments and school districts and may actually increase state taxes if state governments simply take over local services.

Personal-Income Limits A somewhat more complex scheme promises to limit state taxes to a certain percentage of the state's personal income. For example, if state taxes currently amount to 7 percent of a state's total personal income, a constitutional amendment could be offered to voters that limits all future state and local taxes to a total of no more than 7 percent of personal income. This prevents state government from growing at a faster rate than personal income, but it does allow tax revenues to rise.

Expenditure Limits Similar restrictions can be placed on total state *expenditures*— limiting spending to a certain percentage of a state's total personal income. Presumably expenditure limits would hold down taxes over the long run, and therefore expenditure limits can be considered as an indirect form of tax limitation.

Prohibitions on Specific Taxes State constitutions can be written or amended to prohibit certain types of taxes or require specific types of exemptions. For example, if the state constitution bars an income tax, this is a very effective tax limitation. States may also exempt specific items from sales taxes; some common exemptions include groceries, medicines, rents, and purchases by religious, educational, or charitable organizations.

Exemptions and Special Treatments The *homestead exemption* is an increasingly popular method of excluding some part of the value of owner-occupied homes from property taxes. Homestead exemptions go only to homeowners, not to businesses; these exemptions may be expressed in dollar amounts of assessed value (where the first $5,000 or $10,000 of assessed value of a home is nontaxable), or in terms of

■
Tax limits.
State constitutional limitations on taxing authority placed upon state and local governments.

percentages of assessed value (where the first 25 or 50 percent of assessed value of a home is nontaxable). *Personal property*-tax exemptions are common—exemptions of automobiles, boats, furniture, stocks and bonds, and the like—in part because of the difficulty in identifying and assessing the true value of these types of property. Some states have adopted *circuit-breaker* programs that exempt property from taxation for individuals who are poor, aged, disabled, and so forth.

IMPACT OF LIMITS   What impact have tax limits had on the state and local government operations? The consequences of tax limits have been greater for *local* than for state governments. Constitutional provisions limiting state government taxing or spending have generally failed to have any discernible effect on state taxing or spending levels.[6] However, local property tax limits have had the effect of increasing reliance of local governments on state aid as well as fees and charges.[7]

EXPLAINING TAX REVOLTS

Why do people support tax limitation measures? A variety of explanations have been offered and tested in opinion polls, but no single explanation seems to explain why people vote for or against tax limitations.[8]

THE SELF-INTEREST EXPLANATION   People who benefit most from government spending should oppose tax limitation measures, while people whose tax burdens are heaviest should support these measures. Despite the popularity of "rational" theory, this explanation finds only limited support in opinion surveys; high-income homeowners are only slightly more supportive of tax limits than beneficiaries of government services.

THE HIGH-TAX EXPLANATION   People who pay high taxes should support tax limitations, while people who pay modest taxes should show little interest in the tax revolt. Again, there is very little solid evidence to support this theory. Although people who say taxes are "high" tend to vote in favor of tax limitations, the states that have passed limitations are not necessarily the high-tax-burden states.

THE "WASTE-IN-GOVERNMENT" EXPLANATION   People who think government wastes a lot of money should support tax limitation proposals. Opinion polls do show a relationship between perceived waste and support for tax limits. This implies that tax limitation referenda can be defeated if people can be convinced that tax dollars are not wasted.

THE IDEOLOGICAL EXPLANATION   According to this explanation, conservatives should support tax limits, while liberals should oppose them. Indeed, according to this rationale, the tax revolt itself is a product of increasing conservatism of the electorate in the late 1970s and early 1980s. There is some support for this explanation in opinion polls: Conservatives and Republicans tend to support tax limitation measures more than liberals or Democrats.

THE FAIRNESS EXPLANATION   People who perceive the tax system as "unfair" should be more likely to vote for tax limitations than people who do not. Again, there is some limited evidence in opinion polls to support this explanation.

THE ALIENATION EXPLANATION   This explanation views the tax revolt as a reflection of declining confidence in government. Negative feelings about government go beyond perceptions of waste, or fairness, or burdensome taxation, and tap deeply felt resentment and alienation from the political system. Again, there is some limited support for this explanation in opinion polls.

It is not surprising that no single explanation of the tax revolt can be offered. Indeed, even a combination of all of the explanations mentioned here does not fully explain voting on tax proposals. Other explanations may be derived from *the specific characteristics of politics in the states* in which tax limitation referenda have been voted on. Still other explanations may focus on *the specific provisions of the tax limitation amendments* being voted upon.

CITY FISCAL STRESS AND CUTBACK MANAGEMENT

Fiscal stress does *not* refer to the annual struggle to balance the budget without raising taxes or cutting services. This struggle occurs in every city. Fiscal stress refers to a financial condition so unfavorable as to impair borrowing ability, require reduction of municipal services, pose a threat to public health and safety, and thus diminish the quality and satisfaction of urban life.[9] Fiscal stress occurs when cities have large municipal payrolls, large socially dependent populations, and heavy tax burdens, yet an eroding tax base, a weak or declining economy, and population loss.

Fiscal stress has widespread impact.[10] As a city tries to solve its budget problems, it raises taxes; imposes fees; reduces its work force; cuts back on maintenance of streets, bridges, buildings, and parks; and postpones capital construction projects. These measures further hurt the local economy. Businesses move away and cancel plans to expand. Unemployment increases as well as demands for help from government. As a city's deficits grow, its bonds become hard to sell to banks and investors. This forces up interest costs that further hurt the city's budget.

Fiscal stress imposes new administrative tasks for mayors and managers. These tasks have been labeled as "cutback management." Managing organizational decline—cutting back on spending and organizational activity, deciding who will be let go, what programs will be scaled down or terminated, and what citizens will be asked to make sacrifices—is not as much fun as managing an expanding organization.

DIFFICULT DECISIONS   Cutback management presents a host of problems for government officials. These include the following considerations:

> *Resist cutting or smooth the decline.* Should officials resist cutting by claiming it cannot be done without great injury to the city? Should they cut vital and popular programs first in order to stir opposition to the cut? By taking police and firefighters off the streets or closing the schools? By refusing to cut back until paydays are

Fiscal stress.
Unfavorable financial conditions that impair borrowing ability, require the reduction of services, and may threaten public health and safety.

Cutback management.
Deciding how to reduce spending and services in order to relieve fiscal stress.

Bob Englehart, *Dayton Journal Herald.*

missed and loans are defaulted? Or should officials try to smooth the cutback by cutting low-prestige programs, administrative personnel, social programs, and less vital services?

Take one deep gouge or a series of decrements. Should officials try to improve city finances with a single very difficult year by making one set of deep cuts in the budget? Or should they plan a series of smaller cuts over several years to minimize the impact of the cuts and hope that the financial condition of the city may turn around and the cutting can stop?

Share the pain or target the cuts. Should city officials cut all programs "across the board" in order to minimize pain, avoid conflict, maintain morale, and build team spirit in the organization? Or should they make hard decisions about what programs are not really necessary? Targeting cuts requires officials to identify and rank priorities; it generates intense political conflict and tends to be avoided until things get very bad and across-the-board cuts are no longer feasible.

Promote efficiency or equity. Should city officials favor the most efficient programs, usually police and fire protection, streets and sanitation, over the more costly social-service programs? Or should city officials act to protect the most dependent elements of the population?

CUTBACK STRATEGIES   What strategies can be employed by cities facing retrenchment? We have attempted to summarize some general strategies available to governments in confronting cutbacks:[11]

The no-change strategy: Across-the-board cuts, seniority retention, and hiring freezes. Across-the-board cuts appear to be popular. They distribute the pain of budget reductions equally across agencies and among services. However, eventually across-the-board strategies must be abandoned "as officials become aware that the reductions are permanent . . . that equal cuts are not fair, as some programs are more important than others."[12] A hiring freeze is also a convenient and popular short-run strategy to minimize the pain of cutbacks. Hiring freezes rely on "natural attrition" through resignations and retirements to cut down the size of the work force. It does not require politically difficult decisions about which employees are most essential. If natural attrition does not occur fast enough to meet budget deficits, the next strategy is seniority retention. A "last-in–first-out" rule in layoffs may be viewed by most employees as fair, although it may result in disproportionate harm to women and minorities if they were recruited to government more recently.

A hierarchy of community-needs strategy. An alternative strategy is for cities to set priorities for essential services. Decisions about what services are essential may differ from city to city, but in general we can expect a ranking (from most essential to least essential): public safety (police and fire), public works (streets, sewers, sanitation), administrative services, human services, leisure services.

A "privatizing" strategy. Some city services are "priceable"—users can be charged for them. Cities can charge users for garbage collection, water supply, ambulance service, special police services, transit, licensing, libraries, recreation, and so forth. So one retrenchment strategy is to increase the number and types of user charges for city services. A related strategy is to transfer these services to private enterprise, which can usually perform them cheaper than can the city government. User charges are politically popular because citizens can "see" what they are buying and they are not forced to buy anything they do not want.

A reduction in capital spending strategy. When tough times hit, one of the first responses is to cut back on capital spending—canceling or postponing new equipment purchases, new construction, major repairs. There are short-term advantages to this strategy; city employees can keep their jobs and service levels can be maintained. But over the longer term, this strategy can produce costly results, as streets, bridges, buildings, and equipment fail. Some capital investments can save money over the long run if they improve productivity and reduce labor costs.

A reduction in labor strategy. Cities may finally confront the necessity to reduce personnel costs—hiring freezes, layoffs, renegotiated labor contracts. The most labor-intensive city functions are police and fire protection, together with hospitals and schools in those cities that have these responsibilities. Cutbacks in police and fire personnel are politically unpopular. Indeed, city officials may threaten such cutbacks to force a reconsideration of the rollbacks.

WHEN ENDS DON'T MEET: STATE AND LOCAL DEBT

What happens when revenues fail to match expenditures in state and local government budgets? Most state constitutions require the operating budget of the state government, and those of local governments as well, to be balanced. In other words, most state constitutions prohibit deficits in *operating budgets*. Revenue estimates must match authorized expenditures in the appropriation act. If actual revenues fail to meet the estimates during the fiscal year, expenditures must be cut so that no deficit occurs at the end of the year.

CAPITAL FINANCING　However, state constitutions generally permit state and local governments to borrow funds for capital improvements, with provisions for repayment of the debt during the useful life of the project. State and local governments may sell bonds to finance traditional "essential functions"—roads, schools, parks, libraries, prisons, and government office buildings. These governments may also sell bonds to finance water and sewage systems, airports, ports, mass transportation facilities, solid waste disposal plants, hazardous waste disposal, single- and multifamily housing projects, and hospitals. In the world of municipal finance, these are referred to as "nonessential functions," even though we might argue that they are essential to a community. Finally, government may sell bonds to finance "private activities"—industrial development projects, trade and convention centers, sports arenas.

CONSTITUTIONAL RESTRICTIONS　State constitutions may place restrictions on these debts in the form of *debt ceilings*, limiting the total amount of money that a government can borrow (usually expressed as a percentage of the total assessed value of taxable property in the community); and *bond referenda* provisions, requiring that any bonded indebtedness (and the taxes imposed to pay off this indebtedness) be approved by the voters in a referendum. These restrictions usually apply only to general obligation bonds.

■
"Essential functions."
In local government finance, a reference to traditional services, such as road maintenance, schools, law-enforcement, prisons, parks, and the running of government offices.

"Nonessential functions."
In local government finance, a reference to services not necessarily undertaken by all local governments, such as mass transit, airports, housing, and hospitals.

GENERAL OBLIGATION VERSUS REVENUE BONDS   Bonds issued by state and local governments may be either general obligation bonds or revenue bonds. General obligation bonds are backed by "the full faith and credit" of the government that issues them. This pledges the full taxing powers of the government to pay both the principal and interest due on the bonds. Because these bonds are more secure, lenders are willing to accept lower interest rates on them. This saves the government (and the taxpayer) money in interest payments. Revenue bonds are not guaranteed by the issuing government but instead are backed by whatever revenues the project itself generates. Both the interest and principal of revenue bonds are paid from fees, and charges or rents ("revenues") generated by the project, rather than tax revenues of the government. Because these bonds are not backed by the full taxing powers of the government, lenders face greater risks and therefore require higher interest payments. Revenue bonds are not usually subject to constitutional debt ceilings or referendum requirements.

Government obligation (GO) bonds.
Bonds issued by governments that pledge their "full faith and credit," including tax revenues, to repayment.

Revenue bonds.
Bonds issued by governments for specific projects and backed only by whatever revenues the projects generate.

INDUSTRIAL DEVELOPMENT BONDS   Competition between municipalities for economic development has led to a vast expansion in industrial development bonds. These are revenue bonds issued by a municipality to obtain funds to purchase land and build facilities for private businesses. Pollution control revenue bonds are issued by municipalities to obtain funds to provide industries with air and water pollution control facilities. Municipalities sometimes issue single-family mortgage revenue bonds to assist home buyers, builders, and developers. Municipalities may issue hospital revenue bonds to assist private as well as public hospitals in the community. These types of revenue bonds blur the distinction between public and private business. At one time most state and local indebtedness was in the form of general obligation bonds. But industrial development, pollution control, mortgage revenue, and hospital bonds have become so popular that these nonguaranteed revenue bonds now constitute well over half of the outstanding municipal debt in the nation.

MUNICIPAL BOND INTEREST DEDUCTIBILITY   Traditionally, the federal government did not levy individual or corporate income taxes on the interest that lenders received from state and local government bonds. All municipal bond interest income was deductible from gross income for federal tax purposes. The original rationale for this deductibility was based on the federal ideal: The national government should not interfere with the operations of state governments and their subdivisions. "The power to tax is the power to destroy,"[13] and therefore neither level of government should tax the instrumentalities of the other. Later this rationale was replaced by more practical considerations: By not taxing municipal bond interest, the federal government was providing an incentive for investment in public infrastructure—schools, streets, hospitals, sewers, airports. Because the federal government forgoes taxing municipal bond income, we might consider these lost federal revenues as a subsidy to state and local governments and the people who lend money to them.

The deductibility of municipal bond interest from federal income taxation makes these bonds very attractive to high-income investors. This attraction allows state and local governments to pay out less interest on their tax-free bonds than corporations must pay out on comparable taxable corporate bonds. Thus, for example, if average *corporate* AAA-rated 30-year bonds are paying 7 percent interest (taxable), average *municipal* AAA-rated 30-year bonds might only pay 5 percent interest (tax free). Many investors would prefer the lower rate because it is tax free. In short, federal deductibility allows state and local governments to borrow money relatively cheaply.

PUBLIC BONDS FOR PRIVATE USES   But controversy arises when private businesses ask municipal governments to issue revenue bonds on their behalf—bonds that businesses use to finance everything from the purchase of single-family homes and the development of luxury apartments, to the building of industrial plants and commercial offices. Business prefers municipal revenue bond financing over its own direct financing because municipal bond interest rates are cheaper owing to federal deductibility. In other words, the issuance of municipal "private purpose" revenue bonds is really a device to obtain cheaper interest rates for business at the expense of lost revenues to the federal government.

FEDERAL TAX REFORM AND MUNICIPAL FINANCE   The Federal Tax Reform Act of 1986 distinguished between "essential function" bonds (bonds issued for roads, schools, parks, libraries, prisons, and government buildings), "nonessential function" bonds (bonds issued for water and sewer, transportation, multifamily housing, hazardous waste disposal, and health and education facilities), and "private activities" bonds (bonds for industrial development, pollution control, parking facilities, and sports and convention centers). Only essential function bond income is completely free of all federal income taxation. Nonessential bond income is subject to the federal alternate minimum tax (AMT), which means it may be taxable if the taxpayer has a large amount of tax-free income. And income from "private purpose" municipal bonds no longer enjoys tax-free status. These separate treatments complicate the municipal bond market for both governments and investors.

CITY DEBT PATTERNS   In examining total municipal indebtedness, we should consider both general obligation and revenue indebtedness. General obligation indebtedness of a city may range up to $1,000 per resident or more (New York City). Revenue indebtedness can range even higher, to over $3,000 per resident. Of course some cities avoid debt altogether. Indebtedness appears to be greater in cities in the Northeast, cities that undertake a wide variety of functions and services, and cities under fiscal strain.[14] (See "*Up Close:* Orange County Goes Bankrupt.")

WHEN A CITY GOES BUST

What happens when a city continually spends more than it receives in revenues, when its annual deficits pile up into a huge city debt, when banks and other lenders finally decide not to lend a city any more money? (See *Up Close:* Orange County Goes Bankrupt.) A number of large American cities have gone bust or come close to it, including New York City in 1975, Cleveland in 1979, Philadelphia in 1991, and Washington, DC, in 1995. But rather than officially declare bankruptcy and have federal bankruptcy courts take over fiscal control, these cities have been "rescued" by state and federal governments. Rescue, however, generally requires the city to turn over control of

UP CLOSE

ORANGE COUNTY GOES BANKRUPT

With a population of over 2.5 million, Orange County, California, is the fifth largest county in the United States. And as the home of Disneyland and aerospace giants like the McDonnell Douglas Corporation, it is one of America's wealthiest counties. Yet in 1994 it was forced to file for *bankruptcy*, unable to repay billions of dollars of loans that the county treasurer had borrowed from banks. How did it happen?

In addition to county funds, the Orange County treasurer managed a pool of short-term deposits by 185 municipalities, school districts, and local agencies in southern California. These were revenues that government bodies had collected but not yet spent; they were pooled in order to obtain higher interest rates, which would become an added source of revenue for these governments. The treasurer was expected to invest these pooled funds to obtain maximum returns with minimum risks.

For many years, the treasurer was praised for the high returns he produced from the investment pool; indeed, he was reelected to his post six times. But his investment strategy was, at the very least, "overly aggressive." He risked the $7.5 billion investment fund as collateral in order to borrow an additional $12.5 billion from banks in order to purchase bonds and other securities. His hope was that bond prices would rise, thus raising the value of the expanded $20 billion pool of bonds. But bond prices fell in 1994, shrinking the value of the pool. The county lost nearly $2 billion. The treasurer had guessed wrong about the direction of the bond market. When he was unable to repay bank loans that he had used to buy bonds, the county was forced to declare bankruptcy. The county, plus all of the governments that had deposited their revenues in the pool, were obliged to postpone projects and cut back on services while the federal bankruptcy court tried to sort out the county's debts.

The county's Board of Supervisors (the county commission) asked voters to approve a half-cent increase in the local sales tax to pay its debts, but the voters decisively (61 percent) turned down the proposal. The county's chief executive officer (manager) resigned in frustration.

The Board of Supervisors turned for help to Janice Mittermier, who was then serving as director of the county's John Wayne Airport, asking her to take over as chief executive officer. She was not thrilled with the offer but accepted it: "I did not think it was right to refuse to help." She knew that raising taxes was not an option, so she devised what she called a "Robin Hood" plan; she convinced the board and the state legislature to allow her to take funds appropriated for various government agencies in the county and to direct them to debt repayment. She convinced local governments to delay lawsuits for the repayment of funds they had invested in the county's pool. She cited the crisis as a reason to make many managerial changes and spending cutbacks. She eventually stabilized the county's finances and was named "Public Official of the Year" by *Governing* magazine.[a]

The lessons of the Orange County bankruptcy appear to be:

- Treasurers must resist political pressures to produce unreasonably high returns on invested public funds.
- Public funds must be managed conservatively, to preserve principal rather than maximize return.
- Governments must provide full disclosure of public fund investments and provide continuous oversight of investment strategies.

[a]*Governing* (November 1998).

its financial affairs to a control board. Control board members are appointed by the state or federal government. In exchange for an infusion of state or federal money, the control board imposes fiscal discipline on the city. The mayor and council are required to win board approval for their annual budgets.

A Municipal Assistance Corporation, or "Big MAC," was established in 1975 to rescue New York City and oversee its finances. It was successful over time in reestablishing the city's credit ratings. Big MAC's powers can be reactivated if New York City again develops large operating deficits. Somewhat weaker boards were imposed by Pennsylvania and Ohio on Philadelphia and Cleveland, but both cities responded by lowering deficits. In 1995 Congress was obliged to impose a five-member control board over Washington, DC. It can reject the city's budgets, impose its own spending plans on the city, and even order changes in the organization and staffing of the city's government and school system.

DID YOU KNOW?

HOW WALL STREET RATES YOUR CITY

Wall Street bond rating services, for example, Standard &
Poors, are designed to inform bond buyers about the financial
stability of borrowers. These major rating services report on
states and cities as well as private corporations. Standard &
Poors has developed a rating system that ranges from a high
of AAA (excellent), through AA (good), A (acceptable), BBB
(questionable), BB (poor), B (very poor), and CCC, CC, C,
(bankrupt). Most state governments are rated AAA or AA,
with only New York and Louisiana currently receiving a single A. But city finances vary across the nation:

New York, NY	BBB+
Los Angeles, CA	AA
Chicago, IL	A
Houston, TX	AA-
Philadelphia, PA	BBB
San Diego, CA	AA
Phoenix, AZ	AA+
Dallas, TX	AAA
San Antonio, TX	AA
Detroit, MI	BBB
San Francisco, CA	AA-
Baltimore, MD	A
Jacksonville, FL	AA
Columbus, OH	AAA
Milwaukee, WI	AA+
Memphis, TN	AA
El Paso, TX	AA
Washington, DC	B
Boston, MA	A+
Seattle, WA	AA+
Austin, TX	AA
Nashville-Davidson, TN	AA
Denver, CO	AA
Cleveland, OH	A
New Orleans, LA	BBB+
Oklahoma City, OK	AA

Fort Worth, TX	AA
Portland, OR	AA+
Kansas City, MO	AA
Charlotte, NC	AAA
Tucson, AZ	AA
Virginia Beach, VA	AA
Albuquerque, NM	AA
Atlanta, GA	AA
Honolulu, HI	AA
Tulsa, OK	AA
Sacramento, CA	AA
Miami, FL	B
St. Louis, MO	A-
Oakland, CA	AA-
Pittsburgh, PA	BBB
Cincinnati, OH	AA+
Minneapolis, MN	AAA
Omaha, NE	AAA
Toledo, OH	A
Colorado Springs, CO	AA-
Mesa, AZ	AA-
Buffalo, NY	BBB
Wichita, KS	AA
Arlington, TX	AA
Anaheim, CA	AA
Corpus Christi, TX	AA-
Louisville, KY	AA-
Birmingham, AL	AA
St. Paul, MN	AA+
Newark, NJ	A
Anchorage, AK	A
Aurora, CO	AA-
Norfolk, VA	AA
Lexington-Fayette, KY	AAA
Raleigh, NC	AAA
Rochester, NY	AA
Jersey City, NJ	BBB
Akron, OH	AA-
Richmond, VA	AA

ON THE WEB

Budget information for most states and large cities and counties can be accessed through their homepages. This information usually includes both sources of *revenue* and categories of *expenditures*.

The federal government's executive budget is prepared by the Office of Management and Budget (OMB).
Each year's federal budget can be accessed at

www.access.gpo.gov/su_docs/budget

While the federal budget may appear to be complex, dull, and dreary, it is really the heart of the federal policy-making process. And fortunately OMB provides summary pages of revenue sources and expenditure categories.

The National Taxpayers Union lobbies in Congress and state legislatures "to fight for the American taxpayer." This organization was founded in 1969 and claims to have more than 300,000 members scattered in all fifty states. Its Web site at

www.ntu.org

offers arguments in support of constitutional amendments to curtail spending, in support of lower taxes and taxpayer rights, and in opposition to wasteful government spending.

NOTES

1. See Edward T. Howe and Donald J. Reed, "The Historical Evolution of State and Local Tax Systems," *Social Science Quarterly,* vol. 78 (March 1997), 109–121.

2. Rober McIntyre, *A Far Cry from Fair* (Washington, DC: Citizens for Tax Justice, 1991.)

3. See David R. Morgan, "Tax Equity in the American States," *Social Science Quarterly,* 75 (September 1994).

4. Neil Berch, "Explaining Changes in Tax Incidence in the States," *Political Research Quarterly,* 48 (September 1995), 629–42.

5. Shawn Bowler and Todd Donovan, "Popular Responsiveness to Taxation," *Political Research Quarterly,* 48 (March 1995), 61–78.

6. James Cox and Davie Lowery, "The Impact of the Tax Revolt Era State Fiscal Caps," *Social Science Quarterly,* 71 (September 1990), 492–509.

7. Phillip G. Joyce and Daniel R. Mullins, "The Changing Fiscal Structure of State and Local Public Sector: The Impact of Tax and Expenditure Limits," *Public Administration Review,* 51 (May/June 1991), 240–53.

8. The following discussion relies on the theoretical concepts and reports of opinion surveys in David Lowery and Lee Sigelman, "Understanding the Tax Revolt: Eight Explanations," *American Political Science Review,* 75 (December 1981), 963–74; James M. Buchanan, "The Potential for Taxpayers Revolt in American Democracy," *Social Science Quarterly,* 59 (March 1979), 691–96; Paul Allen Beck and Thomas R. Dye, "Sources of Public Opinion on Taxes," *Journal of Politics,* 44 (February 1982), 172–82; Carl Ladd, "The Polls: Taxing and Spending,"

Public Opinion Quarterly, 43 (Spring 1979), 126–35; Susan Hansen, *The Politics of Taxation* (New York: Praeger, 1983).

9. David T. Stanley, "Cities in Trouble," in *Managing Fiscal Stress,* ed. Charles H. Levine (Chatham, NJ: Chatham, 1980).

10. Various measures of fiscal stress have been devised and applied to American cities. See Richard P. Nathan and Charles Adams, "Understanding Central City Hardship," *Political Science Quarterly,* 91 (Spring 1976), 51–61; David T. Stanley, "Cities in Trouble," in *Managing Fiscal Stress,* ed. Charles H. Levine (Chatham, NJ: Chatham, 1980); Terry N. Clark and Lorna Crowley Ferguson, *City Money* (New York: Columbia University Press, 1983).

11. See Stephen C. Brooks, "Urban Fiscal Stress: A Decade of Difference," Midwest Political Science Association Meeting, Chicago, 1993; Cal Clark and B. Oliver Walter, "Urban Political Cultures, Financial Stress, and City Fiscal Austerity Strategies," *Western Political Quarterly,* 44 (September 1991), 676–97; Terry N. Clark and Lorna Crowley Ferguson, *City Money* (New York: Columbia University Press, 1983).

12. Gregory B. Lewis, "Municipal Expenditures Through Thick and Thin," *Publius,* special issue (May 1984), 380–90.

13. *McCulloch* v. *Maryland,* 4 Wheaton 316 (1819).

14. See Elaine B. Sharp, "The Politics and Economics of the New City Debt," *American Political Science Review,* 80 (December 1986), 1241–58.

PHOTO CREDITS

Chapter Openings

CHAPTER 1   Damian Dovarganes/AP/Wide World Photos

CHAPTER 2   Judi Parks/AP/Wide World Photos

CHAPTER 3   The White House Photo Office

CHAPTER 4   Laima Druskis/Pearson Education/PH College

CHAPTER 5   L.M. Otero/AP/Wide World Photos

CHAPTER 6   Bob Daemmrich/Stock Boston

CHAPTER 7   Shayna Brennan/AP/Wide World Photos

CHAPTER 8   Louis Psihoyos/Matrix International, Inc.

CHAPTER 9   Laima Druskis/Pearson Education/PH College

CHAPTER 10   Michael Dwyer/Stock Boston

CHAPTER 11   Edward Reed/New York City Mayor's Office, Mayor's

                 Photo Unit

CHAPTER 12   A. Lichtenstein/Sygma Photo News

CHAPTER 13   David Zalubowski/AP/Wide World Photos

CHAPTER 14   Lionel Delevingne/Stock Boston

CHAPTER 15   Laima Druskis/Pearson Education/PH College

CHAPTER 16   Paul Conklin/Monkmeyer Press

CHAPTER 17   Gary A. Cameron/Corbis

People in Politics

Christine Whitman: Governor's Office, New Jersey

Ward Connerly: American Civil Rights Institute

Alfred Lawson, Jr.: Florida House of Representatives

Jesse Ventura: State of Minnesota

Tom Loftus: Wisconsin Legislative Reference Bureau

George W. Bush: Bob Daemmrich/Sygma

Rudolph Giuliani: Joel Page/AP Wide World Photos

Mary McCarty: West Palm Beach Commissioner's Office

Richard J. Daley: Mayor's Press Office, City of Chicago

Richard M. Daley: Mayor's Press Office, City of Chicago

Alex Penelas: Office of the Mayor

Martin Luther King, Jr.: J.P. Laffont/Sygma

INDEX

A

Abbington Township v. Schempp, 484, 487
abortion, 449–453
activists (party), 132–136
Aderand Construction v. Pena, 455
adjudication, 229
admission (states), 18–19
Advisory Commission on Intergovernmental
    Relations, 52
affirmative action, 42, 100–104, 240, 434–
    440
affirmative racial gerrymandering, 101–102
African Americans, 7, 9, 56–58, 100–104,
    161–165, 241, 321, 349–351, 423–
    440
Age Discrimination Act, 81
agenda setting, 393–394
alcohol, 71, 274–275
Alexander, Herbert C., 357
Alexander v. Holmes County, 454
Almy, Timothy A., 324, 358
Alt, James E., 257
amendments (state constitutions), 34–38
amendments (U.S. Constitution), 63–66
American Association of Retired Persons
    (AARP), 122
American Association of School Administrators,
    486
American Association of University Professors,
    480, 486
American Civil Liberties Union (ACLU), 453
American Civil Rights Institute (ACRI), 453
American Federation of Teachers, 476
American Planning Association, 420–421
American Security Council, 24
American Society for Public Administration,
    256
Americans with Disabilities Act, 81, 446
annexation, 378–379
apportionment, 170–175
appropriations, 250–251
Arizona v. Norvis, 455
Asbestos Hazard Emergency Act, 81
at-large elections, 320–321
Atkins, Burton M., 294
attorney general (state), 223–224
auditor (state), 224
auto safety, 416

B

Bachrach, Peter, 421
Baer, Michael A. 198
Baker v. Carr, 171, 197
Bakke Case, 435–436, 455
Baldasarre, Mark, 422
Banfield, Edward C., 333, 357
bankruptcy (municipal), 522–523
banks, 354
Baratz, Morton S., 421
Basehart, Harry, 198
Bates v. Jones, 52
Batton, James W., 123
Bauer, John R., 123
Beck, Paul Allen, 154
Bennett, Stephen Earl, 123
Benten, J. Edwin, 387
Berch, Neil, 525
Berkman, Michael B., 455
Berman v. Parker, 422
Berry, Jeffrey M., 357
Beyle, Thad, 226
bills of rights, state, 29
Black, Gordon S., 324
Bledsoe, Timothy, 324
Bobo, Lawrence, 454
Bollens, John, 386
Bolling v. Sharp, 454
bonds (state and local government), 520–523
Borrelli, Stephen A., 154, 226
Bowler, Shawn, 294, 525
Brace, Paul, 294
Brady Act, 82
Branti v. Finkel, 256
bribery, 112, 338
Brisbin, Richard A., Jr., 294
Brown, Robert D., 154
Brown v. Board of Education, 69, 426–431
Brown v. Thompson, 198
Browne, William P., 124
Browning, Rufus P., 357, 454
Bryant, Stephen N., 324
Buckley v. Valeo, 150, 155
budgetary process, 248–253
building codes, 404
Bullock, Charles, 154
bureaucracy (state), 227–257
Burns, Nancy Elizabeth, 359

Burris, Val, 87
Bush, George W., 208
busing, 429–431
Button, James, 197

C

cabinet (state), 213
Cain, Bruce E., 52
Caldeira, Gregory A., 123
California Civil Rights Initiative, 42, 439–440
California Teachers Association, 467
campaign finance, 147–153
campaigns (political), 94–95, 143–147,
    149–153
Cannon, Bradley, 294
capital punishment, 289–293
capitals, 121–122
Cassel, Carol A., 324
Cassie, William E., 115
Catanese, Anthony J., 422
Center for the American Woman and Politics,
    123, 196
centralized federalism, 76
charter, city, 308–310
charter schools, 465–466
Chase, Salmon P., 58
Children's Defense Fund, 505
Christian Coalition, 112
Chubb, John E., 225, 486
churches, 355–356
Cigler, Alan J., 124
cities, 300, 308–317
city commissions, 311–313
city-county consolidation, 379
civic associations, 352
civil disobedience, 118
civil rights, 17–18, 453–455
Civil Rights Act of 1964, 99, 431–432
Civil Rights Act of 1968, 433–434
civil war, 68–69
Clark, Kenneth B., 454
Clark, Terry N., 525
Clarke, Harold, 154
Clean Air Act, 81
Clinton, Bill, 487
coattails, 205
cocaine, 275
Cochran v. Board of Education, 482, 487
coercive federalism, 79–81
Coleman, James, 486
committees (legislative), 179–182
common cause, 112
"commonwealth," 20–21
community colleges, 478
community conflict, 297–299
community development, 410–412
Community Development Block Grants,
    410–411

community power, 388–422
comparable worth, 448–449
comparative studies, 2–3
comptroller (state), 224
Coner, John, 198
confederation, 54
conflict management, 297–299, 361–370
Conner v. Johnson, 198
Connerly, Ward, 42
conservatism, 12–15, 73–74
consolidation (metropolitan), 374–377,
    381–385
constitutions (state), 26–52
conventions (state constitutional), 34–38
conventions (party), 130, 132
Cooper v. Aaron, 454
cooperative federalism, 76
corporate taxes, 511–512
correctional policy, 285–289
corruption, 112, 339–340
council-manager government, 313–314
Council of State Governments, 73, 86
councils (city), 338–344
Councils of Government (COGs), 381
counties, 299–308
county administrators, 304, 306
county commissions, 302, 304
courts (state), 259
Cox, Daniel G., 226
Cox, James, 525
Craig v. Boren, 455
crime, 17, 271–285
crime rate, 271–274
Cronin, Thomas E., 52
culture (state), 14
cutback management, 517–520

D

Dahl, Robert A., 392, 421
Dahlkemper, Lesley, 197
Daley, Richard J., 332–333
Daley, Richard M., 332–333
Darcey, R., 197
Davis v. Bandemer, 198
Dawes, Act of 1887, 444
death penalty, 289–293
debt, 34, 520–523
"de facto" segregation, 429–431
democracy, 26–52, 38–50
Democratic Party, 127, 136–143, 153, 188–191,
    329–330
devolution, 81–83
Dillon, John F., 324
Dillon's rule, 309
district elections, 320–321
District of Columbia, 19–21, 65–66
districting, 170–175
Dolan v. City of Tigard, 422

Donovan, Todd, 422, 525
Dothland v. Raulinson, 455
Downs, Anthony, 386
dropout rate, 458–459
drugs, 274–278
dual federalism, 75–76
Durand, Roger, 357
Dye, Thomas R., 86, 141, 154, 358

E

E.E.O.C. v. Madison School District, 455
"earmarking," 252
education, 15, 426–431, 456–487
Ehrenhalt, Alan, 358, 422
Eisinger, Peter K., 358
Elazar, Daniel, 24, 86
Elementary and Secondary Education Act, 468–469
elitism, 389–390, 392–397
Elliot, Evel, 357
Ellis, Margaret E., 154
Ellwood, David, 496, 505
Elrod v. Burns, 256
employment (state), 234–240
Engle v. Vitale, 484, 487
Entman, Robert M., 198
environmental regulation, 18, 404
Equal Rights Amendment (ERA), 64–65
Erickson, Robert S., 24
Everson v. Board of Education, 482, 487
exaction, 405
extradition, 84

F

"familism," 368
family assistance, 495–498
Family Support Act of 1988, 497
Farnhorn, Paul G., 324
Fastnow, Christina, 225
Federal Tax Reform Act of 1986, 522
Federal Bureau of Investigation (FBI), 294
federalism, 54–87
Feigert, Frank B., 154
Ferejohn, J.A., 123
Fiorina, Morris, 123
fiscal stress, 517–520
Fleischmann, Arnold, 357, 386, 422
Fortson v. Dorsey, 198
Fowler, Edmund P., 357
Francis, Wayne L., 197
Freeman, Patricia K., 124, 196
Fulton, William, 422
fund-raising, 148–149
Furman v. Georgia, 290–291

G

Gaetano, Alan K., 358
Garcia, Chris F., 455
Garcia v. San Antonio Metropolitan Transit Authority, 78, 87
Garza, Rudolpho O. dela, 455
gender gap, 105
generation gap, 105–106
"gentrification," 374
Gerber, Elizabeth A., 52
gerrymandering, 101, 172–173
Gibson, James L., 154
Giles, Michael W., 454
Gilliam, Franklin D. 454
Giuliani, Rudolph, 282
Glick, Henry R., 294
Gore, Al, 247, 487
Gormley, William T., 226
Governing magazine, 386
governors, 29, 138, 199–226
grand jury, 284
grants-in-aid (federal), 66–75
Gray v. Sanders, 197
Greater Philadelphia First, 420
Gregory v. Ashcraft, 87
Grodzins, Morton, 87
Grofman, Bernard, 123
Gross Domestic Product (GDP), 507
"growth machine," 395–396
growth management, 352–353, 397–407
gun control, 32

H

Hadley, Charles D., 154
Hain, Paul Jr., 197
Hamilton, Alexander, 24
Handley, Lisa, 123
Hansen, Susan B., 52, 358, 525
Harper v. Virginia, 123
Harrigan, John, 386
Hawkins, Brett W., 386, 387
health, 15–16, 498–504
Heart of Atlanta Motel v. United States, 454
Hedge, David, 197
Henderson, Thomas A., 387
Hendrick, Rebecca M, 387
Herring, Mary, 197
higher education, 477–481
highways, 412–419
Hill, Kim Quaile, 123
Hill, Kevin, A., 123
Hill, Richard Child, 386
Hinton-Anderson, Angela, 123
Hispanics, 9, 100–104, 161–165, 241, 440–443
histories (state), 4–5, 27, 39–40
Hofstadter, Richard, 52
Holbrook, Thomas M. 340

Holli, Melvin G., 358
home rule, 310–311
Hopwood v. Texas, 437, 455
horizontal federalism, 83
housing, 408–412
Housing Act of 1937, 408–409
Housing and Urban Development (HUD),
    408–412, 421
Houston, David J., 422
Howard, Philip K., 256
Howe, Edward T., 525
Hrebenar, Ronald J., 116, 124
Huckshorn, Robert J., 154
Hunter, Floyd, 390–391
Huntington, Samuel P., 357

I

immigration, 10–12, 13
impact fees, 405
impeachment, 219–220
implementation, 228–229
income taxes (state), 510–511
incrementalism, 230, 251
incumbency, 167–168
Indians, 10, 443–446
inequality, 493–494
initiative, 38–50
"inner city," 370–372
interest groups, 28, 33, 106–117, 193–194,
    352–356
International City Managers Association, 356
interstate compacts, 84
item veto, 215–217

J

Jackson, Kenneth, 386
Jencks, Christopher, 386
Jewell, Malcolm E., 115, 198
Johnson, Lock K., 154
*Johnson v. Transportation Agency of Santa
    Clara County,* 455
Jones, Bryan D., 198
Joyce, Philip, 525
judicial decision making, 269–271
judicial selection, 266–269
judicial process, 259–264
judicial federalism, 262–263

K

Kane, Susan, L., 226
Karchev v. Daggett, 198
Karnig, Albert K., 324, 358

Kathlene, Lyn, 123
Katz, Bruce, 386
Katzenbach v. McClung, 454
Kenney, Patrick, 226
Key, V.O., Jr., 141, 154
Kilwein, John C., 294
King, Martin Luther, Jr., 432–433
Kirlin, John J., 358
Knack, Stephen, 123
Krebs, Timothy B., 358
Kuersten, Ashlyn, 294

L

Laghley, Jan E., 123
land use, 395–406
Lanoue, David J., 294
Lascher, Edward L., 52
Lawson, Al, 103
lawyers, 158–159, 260–262
leadership (legislative), 186–188
Lee, Barrett A., 386
legislatures, 29, 139, 156–198, 217–219
Lemon v. Kurtzman, 487
Leyden, Kevin M., 154, 226
liberalism, 12–15, 73–74
Lieske, Joel, 358
lieutenant governor, 223
limited government, 26
Lindbloom, Charles E., 421
Lineberry, Robert L., 357
Lipsky, Michael, 124
Little, Thomas H., 198
lobbying, 107–110, 193–194
Loftus, Tom, 187
logjams, 178–179
Loomis, Burdett A., 124
lotteries, 512
Lowry, Robert C., 257
Lucas v. South Carolina Coastal Council, 422
Lynd, Robert S., 421
Lynds, Robert and Helen, 390

M

Maass, Arthur, 340
machine, politics, 330–331
MacManus, Susan A., 123
Madison, James, 86
Maggiotto, Michael A., 197
magnet schools, 465
majority-minority districts, 101
Malbin, Michael, J., 154
managers (city), 344–346
mandates (federal) 79–81
Mandel, Ruth B., 359
Marando, Vincent L., 387

Marbury v. Madison, 68
marijuana, 275
Marshall, Dale Rodgers, 357, 454
Marshall, Thurgood, 430
mass transit, 417–419
Massachusetts v. Mellon, 87
Mathesian, Charles, 333, 487
mayor-council government, 314
mayors, 347–349
McCarty, Mary, 307
McCullough v. Maryland, 68, 525
McFarlane, Deborah R., 455
McIntyre, Robert, 525
McIver, John P., 24
Medicaid, 500–502
Medicare, 499–500
Meger v. Grant, 52
Meier, Kenneth J., 340, 455
Meinhold, Stephen S., 154
merit pay, 464
merit system, 235
"metro" government, 384–385
metropolitan areas, 360–387
Metropolitan Miami Dade County, 386
Mezey, Susan Gluck, 359
Michels, Robert, 421
"Middletown," 390
Milbraith, Lester, 124
militias, 32
Miller, Mark C., 197
Miller v. Johnson, 123
Milliken v. Bradley, 454
minimum competence testing, 462–463
Missouri plan, 268
Mladenka, Kenneth R., 359, 454
Mobile v. Bolden, 123, 320
Moe, Terry M., 486
Molotch, Harvey, 421
Mooney, Christopher A., 198, 455
Morehouse, Sarah M., 116, 124, 154
Morgan, David R., 357, 358, 525
Morrill Land Grant Act, 468, 477
mortgage insurance, 408
Morton v. Mancavi, 455
Mosca, Gaetano, 421
"motor voter" law, 96–97
Muller, Keith J., 226
Mumford, Lewis, 386
Municipal Assistance Corporation, 523

N

names (states), 22–23, 51
National Association for the Advancement of
   Colored People (NAACP), 426, 453
National Association of Counties, 73, 323
National Association of Scholars, 486
National Association of State Budget Officers,
   256

National Association of State Resource Execu-
   tives, 85
National Association of Towns and Townships,
   73
National Center for State Courts, 294
National Civil League, 357
National Commission on Excellence in Educa-
   tion, 461, 486
National Conference of State Legislatures, 73,
   196, 198
National Defense Education Act, 468
National Education Association, 476, 485
National Governors Association, 73, 225
*National Labor Relations Board v. Jones and
   Laughlin Steel,* 69
National League of Cities, 73, 323
National Organization of Women (NOW), 453
national supremacy, 59
National Taxpayers Union, 525
National Voter Registration Act, 81, 96–97
Native Americans, 10, 443–446
"necessary and proper" clause, 59
Neeley, Grant W., 422
neighborhood associations, 353
Neiman, Max, 422
New England towns, 308
new federalism, 77
newspapers, 354–355
NIMBYs, 407
non-decision-making, 394
nonpartisan elections, 317–320
Northwest Ordinance of 1787, 443
Nownes, Anthony, 124

O

O'Conner, Robert E., 455
O'Conner, Sandra Day, 452
Office of Management and Budget, 524
Oklahoma City Board of Education v. Dowell,
   454
Opheim, Cynthia, 198
Orange County, California, 523
organization (cities), 312
organization (counties), 305
organization (legislative), 175–188
organization (state), 230–234
organization (state education), 469–470
organizations (party), 131–136
Orr v. Orr, 455
Osborne, David, 86, 246–248, 256

P

parole, 289
participation (community politics) 325–359
participation (state politics) 89–124

parties, 125–155, 188–191, 329–330
Pataki, George E., 212
patronage, 235
Patterson, Samuel L., 123
Pelissero, John P., 357
"Pell Grants," 481
Penelas, Alex, 385
Peters, John G., 340
Peterson, Paul E., 386, 422, 454
Pierce v. Society of Sisters, 487
Pitkin, Hanna, 198
planned urban developments (PUDs), 405
Planned Parenthood of Missouri v. Danforth,
   455
Planned Parenthood of Pennsylvania v. Casey,
   452–455
planning, 398–406
plea bargaining, 284–285
Plessy v. Ferguson, 437, 454
pluralism, 390–392
police, 279–283
political action committees (PACs), 113,
   152
polling, 145
Pollock v. Farmers Loan, 87
Polsby, Nelson, 421
population growth, 3, 6–7
Portney, Kent E., 357, 422
poverty, 489–493
prayer (in schools), 483–484
preemptions (federal), 70–81
Press, Charles, 87
Pressman, Jeffrey, 358
Preston, Michael B., 333
Prewitt, Kenneth, 358
primary elections, 127–131
prisons, 285–289
privatization, 244–246
"privileges and immunities," 83–84
professionalism (city councils), 338, 341
professionalism (legislative) 117, 182–186
Project Vote Smart, 122
property taxes, 473, 508–509
prosecution, 283–285
protest, 117–120, 424
public housing, 408–412
Puerto Rico, 20–21

R

race, 7, 9, 56–58, 100–104, 161–165, 203, 241,
   292, 321, 370–372, 423–455
Radcliff, Benjamin, 123
real estate developers, 354
recall, 40–41
Reed, Donald J., 525
referenda, 40–50
reform, 28, 50, 243–248, 331–338
Regens, James, 357

Regents of the University of California v. Bakke,
   436, 455
Regional City, 390–391
registration, 96, 137
regulation, 229
"reinventing government," 246
religion (and schools), 481–484
Renick, James, 358
representational federalism, 77–78
Republican Party, 127, 136–143, 153, 188–191,
   329–330
reserved powers, 59–62
Resnick, David, 123
responsibilities (state), 15–18
"responsible party model," 125–126
Reynolds v. Sims, 197
Rhine, Staci L., 123
Richardson, Lillard E., 196, 422
Richmond v. Crosen, 436, 455
Riker, William, 123
Riordan, William L., 357
Rodriguez v. San Antonio, 487
Roe v. Wade, 449–453, 455
Roemer v. Maryland, 483, 487
Rosenbaum, Walter A., 123
Rosenthal, Alan, 52, 198, 226
Rostker v. Goldberg, 455
Royko, Mike, 333
Rule, Wilma, 197
Rundquist, Barry, 340
running for office, 94–95

S

Sabato, Larry 154
Safe Drinking Water Act, 81
Saint-Germain, Michelle A., 123
Saiz, Martin, 123
sales taxes, 510
Saltzstein, Alan L., 358
Saltzstein, Grace Hall, 359
SAT scores, 459–461
Savas, E.S., 256
Scalia, Antonin, 455
Schattschneider, E.E., 154
Schmandt, Henry, 386
Schneider, Mark, 386
school boards, 475–476
school districts, 300, 473–474
school superintendents, 474–475
schools, 15, 426–431
Schumaker, Paul, 359
secession, 68
secretary of state (state), 224–225
segregation, 56–58, 98–99, 425–434
senior citizens, 105–106
sexual harassment, 448
Sharp, Elaine B., 358, 525
Shaw v. Reno, 123

Sheffield, James E., 154
Sheldon, Barry, 357
sheriff, 280, 302
Shipiro, Joseph P., 455
Sigelman, Lee, 123
Simon, Dennis M., 225
slavery, 56–58, 98
Smith, A. Brock, 154
Smith v. Allright, 123
Social Security, 495
Sofen, Edward, 387
"soft money," 150–151
Sorauf, Frank J., 154
Souger, Donald R., 294
South Carolina v. Barker, 87
South Carolina v. Katzenbach, 123
South Dakota v. Debe, 71
Spear, Mary, 197
special districts, 300, 379–380
speed limits, 414, 415
"sprawl," 372–374
Squire, Peverill, 225
Standard Metropolitan Statistical Areas
     (SMSAs), 361–364
Stanley, David T., 525
Stanton v. Stanton, 455
Steffens, Lincoln, 357
Stein, Laura, 357
Stein, Robert M., 87, 225
Stevens, John Paul, 48–49
Stewart Joseph, 154
Stewart, Margaret C., 154
Stone, Clarence, 421, 422
stratification, 392
strikes, 241
Strikland, Ruth Ann, 87
Strom, Gerald, 340
subdivision control, 403–404
suburbs, 365–370, 372–374
sunset laws, 158
Supplemental Security Income, 495
Swan v. Charlotte-Mecklenburg, 429, 454

T

Tabb, David H., 357, 454
"takings," 399–400
Tarbels Case, 87
taxation, 18, 33–34, 43–46, 369–370, 506–525
Temporary Assistance to Needy Families,
     495–498
tenure, 209–211
term limits, 46–49, 168–170
Texas v. White, 69, 87
Thomas, Clarence, 49
Thomas, Clive, 116, 124
Thomas, Sue, 123
Thompson, Joel A., 115
Thornburg v. Gingles, 198, 123, 324

Tiebout, Charles M., 324
Tiebout Model, 377–378
Title IX, 447
tobacco, 57
town meeting government, 314–315
townships, 300, 307–308
transportation, 15 412–419
treasurer (state), 224
tribal government, 444–446
Tucker, Harvey J., 198

U

U.S. Census Bureau, 23
U.S. Conference of Mayors, 73, 357
U.S. v. Lopez, 82, 87
U.S. term limits, 52
U.S. Term Limits v. Thorton, 52
"uncontrollables," 252–253
unemployment compensation, 495
unions (public employee), 240–243
unitary system, 54
United States v. Paradise, 436, 455
United Steelworkers v. Weber 436, 455
universities (state), 477–481
urban renewal, 410–412
user charges, 512

V

Van Dunk, Emily, 197
Vandenbosch, Sue, 197
Ventura, Jesse "The Body," 203
veto, 215–217
victimization, 274
Village of Euclid v. Amber Reality, 422
violence, 118–117
"volunteerism," 343
voting, 89–100, 326–328
Voting Rights Act of 1965, 99
vouchers, 467–468

W

Wallace v. Jaffree, 487
Warner, W. Lloyd, 421
Webster v. Reproductive Health Services,
     455
Welch, Susan, 197, 324, 358
welfare, 15–17, 488–498
Wenzel, James T., 294
Werner, Emmy F., 197
Wesberry, v. Sanders, 197
Whicker, Marcia Lynn, 198
White Leonard D., 358

White v. Register, 198
"white flight," 431
"white primary," 98
Whitley, Carl, 387
Whitman, Christine, 386
Wiggins, Charles W., 124
Wildavsky, Aaron, 421
Wilson, James Q., 86
Wilson, William Julius, 386
Winters, Richard F., 226
Wolfinger, Raymond E., 358
women, 104–105, 161–165, 203–204, 241, 351–352, 447–453

Woodward, C. Vann, 454
"workfare," 497
Wright, Gerald C., 24

Z

Zeigler, Harmon, 198, 487
zoning, 403